Dictionary of
Leisure, Travel
and Tourism

third edition

Other titles you may find interesting:

Specialist dictionaries:

Dictionary of Accounting	0 7475 6991 6
Dictionary of Aviation	0 7475 7219 4
Dictionary of Banking and Finance	0 7475 6685 2
Dictionary of Business	0 7475 6980 0
Dictionary of Computing	0 7475 6622 4
Dictionary of Economics	0 7475 6632 1
Dictionary of Environment and Ecology	0 7475 7201 1
Dictionary of Human Resources and Personnel Management	0 7475 6623 2
Dictionary of ICT	0 7475 6990 8
Dictionary of Law	0 7475 6636 4
Dictionary of Marketing	0 7475 6621 6
Dictionary of Medical Terms	0 7475 6987 8

Easier English™ titles:

Easier English Basic Dictionary	0 7475 6644 5
Easier English Basic Synonyms	0 7475 6979 7
Easier English Dictionary: Handy Pocket Edition	0 7475 6625 9
Easier English Intermediate Dictionary	0 7475 6989 4
Easier English Student Dictionary	0 7475 6624 0
English Thesaurus for Students	1 9016 5931 3

Check Your English Vocabulary workbooks:

Academic English	0 7475 6691 7
Business	0 7475 6626 7
Computing	1 9016 5928 3
Human Resources	0 7475 6997 5
Law	1 9016 5921 6
Leisure, Travel and Tourism	0 7475 6996 7
IELTS	0 7475 6982 7
FCE +	0 7475 6981 9
TOEFL®	0 7475 6984 3

Visit our website for full details of all our books:
www.bloomsbury.com/reference

Dictionary of
Leisure, Travel and Tourism

third edition

BLOOMSBURY

Originally published by Peter Collin Publishing
as *Dictionary of Hotels, Tourism and Catering Management*

First published 1994, 1999
Second edition published 2003
This edition published 2005

Bloomsbury Publishing Plc
38 Soho Square, London W1D 3HB

Copyright © P. H. Collin 1994, 2003
This edition copyright © Bloomsbury Publishing Plc 2005

A CIP record for this book is available from the British Library

ISBN 0 7475 7222 4

1 3 5 7 9 10 8 6 4 2

Text Production and Proofreading
Katy McAdam, Heather Bateman, Emma Harris

All papers used by Bloomsbury Publishing are natural, recyclable
products made from wood grown in well-managed forests. The manufacturing
processes conform to the environmental regulations
of the country of origin.

Text processed and computer typeset by Bloomsbury
Printed and bound in Italy by Legoprint

Preface

This dictionary aims to provide the basic vocabulary of terms used in the leisure, travel and tourism industries; the fields covered include catering (restaurants and kitchens), hotels and guesthouses, travel, insurance and health and safety, together with terms relating to general business, such as accounts, personnel etc.

For this new edition of the dictionary we have expanded and edited the text to keep pace with changes in the industries. For example, readers will find terms related to food and drink (including different diets and types of coffee), ecotourism, extreme sports etc. At the same time, to make the dictionary more useful to students, we give phonetic transcriptions for all the headwords.

The main words and phrases are defined in simple English and in some cases the definitions have been expanded by explanatory comments. We also give quotations from specialist magazines and other publications relating to the subjects. The supplements at the back give additional information.

We are grateful to many people who have contributed to the work, in particular Joseph Armstrong and Hazel and David Curties who read the text and provided many valuable comments for the first edition. Also, many thanks to Marzena Przeczek for her invaluable contributions to the text.

Pronunciation Guide

The following symbols have been used to show the pronunciation of the main words in the dictionary.

Stress is indicated by a main stress mark (') and a secondary stress mark (,). Note that these are only guides, as the stress of the word changes according to its position in the sentence.

Vowels		*Consonants*	
æ	back	b	buck
ɑː	harm	d	dead
ɒ	stop	ð	other
aɪ	type	dʒ	jump
aʊ	how	f	fare
aɪə	hire	g	gold
aʊə	hour	h	head
ɔː	course	j	yellow
ɔɪ	annoy	k	cab
e	head	l	leave
eə	fair	m	mix
eɪ	make	n	nil
eʊ	go	ŋ	sing
ɜː	word	p	print
iː	keep	r	rest
i	happy	s	save
ə	about	ʃ	shop
ɪ	fit	t	take
ɪə	near	tʃ	change
u	annual	θ	theft
uː	pool	v	value
ʊ	book	w	work
ʊə	tour	x	loch
ʌ	shut	ʒ	measure
		z	zone

A

AA /ˌdʌb(ə)l 'eɪ/ *abbreviation* ROAD TRAVEL Automobile Association

AAA /ˌtrɪp(ə)l 'eɪ/ *abbreviation* ROAD TRAVEL American Automobile Association

AA rosette /ˌeɪ eɪ rəʊ'zet/ *noun* CATERING an award given by the AA to hotels and restaurants serving high-quality food. Abbr **AAR** (NOTE: The AA awards an establishment between one and five rosettes, depending on the quality of its food and service.)

abattoir /'æbətwɑː/ *noun* a place where animals are slaughtered for their meat

abbey /'æbi/ *noun* a Christian religious establishment for monks or nuns, consisting of living quarters and other buildings grouped round a church

COMMENT: In Great Britain, abbeys were abolished in the 16th century at the Reformation, but some abbey churches remain in use (such as Westminster Abbey); others are ruins (such as Fountains Abbey); others were converted into private houses (such as Lacock Abbey).

aboard /ə'bɔːd/ *adverb* on a ship ○ *The passengers went aboard at 10 p.m.* ○ *When the ship docked, customs officers came aboard to inspect the cargo.* □ **all aboard!** everyone come onto the ship, please!

above the line /ə,bʌv ðə 'laɪn/ *adjective* **1.** BUSINESS referring to income and expenditure before tax **2.** MARKETING advertising that has to be paid for and the cost of which includes a commission paid to an advertising agency. Compare **below-the-line advertising**

aboyeur /ˌæbɔɪ'ɜː/ *noun* CATERING the person in the kitchen at a restaurant who shouts the order from the waiter to the chefs, and pins the waiter's written order on a hook relating to a particular table. Also called **announcer**

abroad /ə'brɔːd/ *adverb* in or to another country ○ *The chairman is abroad on business.* ○ *We are going abroad on holiday.*

absenteeism /ˌæbs(ə)n'tiːɪz(ə)m/ *noun* BUSINESS the act of staying away from work for no good reason

'...absenteeism has since reduced and now stands at 1.8%' [*Caterer & Hotelkeeper*]

ABTA /'æbtə/ *abbreviation* Association of British Travel Agents

abv *abbreviation* BEVERAGES alcohol by volume

Academy of Culinary Arts /ə,kædəmi əv 'kʌlɪn(ə)ri ,ɑːts/ *noun* CATERING an association of chefs, restaurant managers and their suppliers, whose aim is to raise standards in food, cooking and service. Abbr **ACA**

accelerated freeze-drying /ək ,seləreɪtɪd 'friːz ,draɪɪŋ/ *noun* CATERING a method of preserving food by heating it for a short time, then freezing it rapidly and drying it in a vacuum. Abbr **AFD**

accept /ək'sept/ *verb* to take something which is being offered ○ *'All major credit cards accepted.'* ○ *Do you accept payment by cheque?*

access /'ækses/ *noun* a way of getting to a place ○ *The concert hall has access for wheelchairs.*

accessibility /ək,sesɪ'bɪlɪti/ *noun* the condition of a place or a facility, judged by whether it is easy for people, especially disabled people, to reach it or use it

accessible /ək'sesɪb(ə)l/ *adjective* **1.** easy to enter or to reach **2.** suitable or specially adapted for disabled people

accessible room /ək'sesɪb(ə)l ruːm/ *noun* a room with special facilities for disabled people

accident /'æksɪd(ə)nt/ *noun* an unpleasant event which happens suddenly and harms someone's health ○ *Accidents usually happen when people are tired or not concentrating on what they are doing.* □ **the airline has a good accident record** the airline has had few accidents, compared with other airlines □ **to have an accident** to crash, to hit something ○ *He had an accident as he was driving to the hotel.*

accident insurance /ˌæksɪd(ə)nt ɪn ˈʃʊərəns/ *noun* FINANCE insurance that will pay if an accident takes place

accolade /ˈækəleɪd/ *noun* an award given to someone as a sign of praise ○ *She received the highest accolade the association could give.* ◊ **Little Gem, ribbon**

'...there are 76 Blue Ribbon winners and 40 winners of the Little Gem – the highest accolade for guest accommodation' [*Caterer & Hotelkeeper*]

accommodate /əˈkɒmədeɪt/ *verb* to provide lodging for someone ○ *The hostel can accommodate groups of up to fifty hikers.*

'...the hall of residence accommodates 198 throughout the year with holiday visitors staying during vacation periods' [*Caterer & Hotelkeeper*]

accommodation /əˌkɒməˈdeɪʃ(ə)n/ *noun* a place to live ○ *Visitors have difficulty in finding hotel accommodation during the summer.* ○ *They are living in furnished accommodation.* ○ *The hotel has accommodation for fifty guests.* (NOTE: There is no plural form in British English, but US English also uses **accommodations**.)

'...an airline ruling requires airlines to provide a free night's hotel accommodation for full fare passengers in transit' [*Business Traveller*]

'...the airline providing roomy accommodations at below-average fares' [*Dun's Business Month*]

accommodation provider /əˌkɒmə ˈdeɪʃ(ə)n prəˌvaɪdə/ *noun* a place that offers rooms that can be used by tourists or other visitors, e.g. a hotel, guesthouse, B & B or hostel

accompanied /əˈkʌmp(ə)nid/ *adjective* TRAVEL travelling with an adult passenger

accompanied baggage /əˌkʌmp(ə)nid ˈbæɡɪdʒ/ *noun* AIR TRAVEL baggage belonging to a passenger who is travelling in the same plane

accompanied child /əˌkʌmp(ə)nid ˈtʃaɪld/ *noun* TRAVEL a child passenger travelling with an adult

accompaniment /əˈkʌmp(ə)nimənt/ *noun* CATERING a small helping of food which is served with a dish, e.g. croutons served with fish soup or grated Parmesan cheese served with minestrone

accompany /əˈkʌmp(ə)ni/ *verb* to go with somebody or something ○ *They travelled to Italy accompanied by their children.* ○ *They sent a formal letter of complaint, accompanied by an invoice for damage.* ○ *A white sauce is served to accompany the fish.*

accordance /əˈkɔːd(ə)ns/ *noun* □ **in accordance with** in agreement with or according to ○ *In accordance with your instructions we have deducted 10% to cover* breakages and deposited the balance in your current account. ○ *I am submitting the claim for damages in accordance with the advice of our solicitors.*

accordingly /əˈkɔːdɪŋli/ *adverb* in agreement with what has been decided ○ *We have received your letter and have altered the reservations accordingly.*

according to /əˈkɔːdɪŋ tuː/ *preposition* as somebody says or writes ○ *According to the leaflet, the tour should leave the central station at 10.30.* ○ *The air conditioning system was installed according to the manufacturer's instructions.*

account /əˈkaʊnt/ *noun* **1.** FINANCE a record of financial transactions over a period of time, such as money paid, received, borrowed or owed ○ *Please send me your account* or *a detailed* or *an itemised account.* **2.** BUSINESS (*in a shop*) an arrangement that a customer has to buy goods and pay for them at a later date, often the end of the month ○ *to have an account* or *a charge account* or *a credit account with Harrods* ○ *Put it on my account* or *Charge it to my account.* □ **to open an account** (*of a customer*) to ask a shop to supply goods that you will pay for at a later date □ **to open an account, to close an account** (*of a shop*) to start or to stop supplying a customer on credit □ **to stop an account** to stop supplying a customer until he or she has paid what is owed **3.** □ **on account** as part of the money owed ○ *He deposited £300 on account with the hotel.* **4.** BUSINESS a customer who does a large amount of business with a firm and has an account ○ *He is one of our largest accounts.* ○ *Our sales force call on their best accounts twice a month.* **5.** □ **the accounts of a business, a company's accounts** a detailed record of a company's financial affairs □ **to keep the accounts** to write each sum of money spent or received in the account book □ **annual accounts** accounts prepared at the end of a financial year □ **accounts payable** money owed by a company □ **accounts receivable** money owed to a company **6.** □ **to take account of sb** *or* **sth, to take sb** *or* **sth into account** to consider somebody or something when making a decision or calculation ○ *You have to take account of the traffic when working out how long it will take you to get to the airport.* ○ *We took into account the fact that you might want to stay an extra night.* ■ *verb* □ **to account for** to be responsible for something and able to explain what has happened to it or why it was done ○ *The cleaners have to account for all linen in guests' bedrooms.* ○

Reps have to account for all their expenses to the sales manager.

accountable /ə'kaʊntəb(ə)l/ *adjective* responsible for explaining to somebody what has happened to something or why it was done ○ *The bar steward is accountable to the beverage manager.* (NOTE: You are accountable **to** someone **for** something.)

accountancy /ə'kaʊntənsi/ *noun* FINANCE the work of an accountant ○ *He is studying accountancy* or *He is an accountancy student.* (NOTE: US English uses **accounting** in this meaning.)

accountant /ə'kaʊntənt/ *noun* **1.** BUSINESS somebody who keeps a company's accounts ○ *The books are kept by a freelance accountant.* **2.** BUSINESS somebody who advises a company on its finances ○ *We send all our tax queries to our accountant.* **3.** FINANCE somebody who examines accounts

account book /ə'kaʊnt bʊk/ *noun* BUSINESS a book which records sales and purchases

accounting /ə'kaʊntɪŋ/ *noun* FINANCE the work of recording money paid, received, borrowed or owed

'…applicants will be professionally qualified and have a degree in Commerce or Accounting' [*Australian Financial Review*]

accounting period /ə'kaʊntɪŋ ˌpɪəriəd/ *noun* BUSINESS the period usually covered by a company's accounts

accounts department /ə'kaʊnts dɪ ˌpɑːtmənt/ *noun* BUSINESS a section of a company which deals with money paid, received, borrowed or owed

accounts management /ə'kaʊnts ˌmænɪdʒmənt/ *noun* BUSINESS the management of a series of customers

accreditation /əˌkredɪ'teɪʃ(ə)n/ *noun* BUSINESS appointment as an agent by a company

accredited /ə'kredɪtɪd/ *adjective* TOURISM appointed by a company such as a hotel chain or a tour operator to act on its behalf

acetic acid /əˌsiːtɪk 'æsɪd/ *noun* CATERING an acid that turns wine into vinegar (NOTE: Acetic acid is also used as a preservative in food such as pickles.)

achieved /ə'tʃiːvd/ *adjective* done successfully

'…achieved room rates are in excess of $200 (£137) off a rack rate of $239–$339' [*Caterer & Hotelkeeper*]

acid /'æsɪd/ *noun* a chemical substance that is able to dissolve metals ○ *Hydrochloric acid is secreted in the stomach and forms part of the gastric juices.*

acidity /ə'sɪdɪti/ *noun* the level of acid in a solution ○ *The alkaline solution may help to reduce acidity.*

COMMENT: Acidity and alkalinity are measured according to the pH scale. pH7 is neutral; numbers above show alkalinity, while pH6 and below is acid.

acknowledge /ək'nɒlɪdʒ/ *verb* to tell a sender that a letter, package or shipment has arrived ○ *He has still not acknowledged my letter of the 24th.* ○ *We acknowledge receipt of your booking form and deposit.*

acknowledgment /ək'nɒlɪdʒmənt/, **acknowledgement** *noun* the act of acknowledging, or something, such as a letter, that tells the sender that something has been received ○ *She sent an acknowledgment of receipt.* ○ *They sent a letter of acknowledgment.*

action /'ækʃən/ *noun* **1.** the fact of doing something **2.** □ **out of action** out of order, not working ○ *The extractor fan is out of action.*

Action on Smoking and Health /ˌækʃən ɒn ˌsməʊkɪŋ ənd 'helθ/ *noun* an international organisation which promotes the rights of non-smokers. Abbr **ASH**

action-packed holiday /ˌækʃən pækt 'hɒlɪdeɪ/ *noun* TOURISM a holiday where you do a lot of exciting things

activity /æk'tɪvɪti/ *noun* something that someone does to pass time pleasantly

activity holiday /æk'tɪvɪti ˌhɒlɪdeɪ/ *noun* TOURISM a planned holiday during which you do interesting or exciting things such as painting, canoeing or rock-climbing

actual flying time /ˌæktʃuəl 'flaɪɪŋ ˌtaɪm/ *noun* the total time that an aircraft spends in the air during a flight, as opposed to its scheduled flight time or time spent waiting on the ground

acute /ə'kjuːt/ *adjective* MEDICAL referring to pain which is sharp and intense ○ *She had an acute attack of shingles.*

ad /æd/ *noun* MARKETING same as **advertisement** (*informal*) ○ *We put an ad in the shop window.* ○ *She found her job through an ad in the paper.*

adaptor /ə'dæptə/ *noun* something which holds a piece of equipment in a different way

adaptor plug /ə'dæptə plʌg/ *noun* TOURISM a plug which allows a piece of equipment to be plugged into a different-sized socket ○ *My hair-drier won't work here in France, because I haven't brought my adaptor plug.*

COMMENT: Adaptor plugs are necessary if you need to use electrical equipment in countries with different electrical systems

(British hair-driers in France; American computers in Germany, etc.) because the type of plug is different. Where Britain uses mainly three-pin plugs, in Europe most plugs have two round pins. In the USA, plugs have two flat pins. To change voltage (as in the USA, where the voltage is 110V), a transformer will also be necessary.

add /æd/ *verb* **1.** to put figures together to make a total ○ *The waiter forgot to add the wine when he made up our bill.* **2.** to put things together to make a large group ○ *We are adding to the restaurant staff.* ○ *By building the annexe, they have added thirty rooms to the hotel.* □ **this all adds to the company's costs** this makes the company's costs higher

added value /ˌædɪd ˈvæljuː/ *noun* BUSINESS an amount added to the value of a product or service, which is equal to the difference between its cost and the amount received when it is sold. Also called **value added**

addition /əˈdɪʃ(ə)n/ *noun* **1.** a person or thing which is added ○ *The management has stopped all additions to the hotel staff.* ○ *The Spanish-speaking receptionist is the latest addition to the personnel.* **2.** □ **in addition to** added to, as well as ○ *There are twelve registered letters to be sent in addition to this packet.* **3.** the act of adding figures to make a total ○ *You don't need a calculator to do simple addition.*

additional /əˈdɪʃ(ə)nəl/ *adjective* included as well as what there is already ○ *Additional charges can include telephone calls, room service, laundry, etc.* ○ *Apart from the tours listed in the brochure, we have arranged two additional visits to local vineyards.* ○ *Additional duty will have to be paid.*

additional premium /əˌdɪʃ(ə)nəl ˈpriːmiəm/ *noun* FINANCE a payment made to cover extra items in an existing insurance policy

additive /ˈædɪtɪv/ *noun* CATERING a chemical substance which is added to food to improve its appearance, smell or taste, or to prevent it from going bad ○ *The orange juice contains a number of additives.* ○ *Allergic reactions to additives are frequently found in employees in food processing factories.*

COMMENT: Colour additives are added to food to improve its appearance. Some are natural organic substances such as saffron, carrot juice or caramel, but other colour additives are synthetic. Other substances are added to food to prevent decay or to keep the food in the right form: these can be emulsifiers, which bind different foods together as mixtures in sauces, for example, and stabilisers, which can keep a sauce semi-liquid and prevent it from separating into solids and liquids. The European Union allows certain additives to be added to food and these are given E numbers.

add-on /ˈæd ɒn/ *noun* TOURISM an extra optional item, which is listed in the programme details of a conference or package tour, but for which an additional charge has to be paid

address /əˈdres/ *noun* the details giving the number, street and town where an office is or where a person lives □ **address list** a list of addresses ■ *verb* to write the details of an address on an envelope, etc. ○ *a letter addressed to the tourist information bureau* ○ *She addressed the letter* or *the parcel to the hotel manager.* ○ *Please address your enquiries to the information officer.*

add up /ˌæd ˈʌp/ *verb* to put several figures together to make a total ○ *to add up a column of figures* ○ *She made a mistake when adding up the bill.* □ **the figures do not add up** the total given is not correct

add up to /ˌæd ˈʌp tʊ/ *verb* to make a total of ○ *The total expenditure adds up to more than £1,000.*

adjoining /əˈdʒɔɪnɪŋ/ *adjective* next to something, or touching something ○ *There is an adjoining bathroom.* □ **adjoining rooms** rooms which are next to each other ○ *They asked to be put in adjoining rooms.* Compare **connecting rooms**

administration /ədˌmɪnɪˈstreɪʃ(ə)n/ *noun* BUSINESS the organisation, control or management of a company

administration costs /ədˌmɪnɪ ˈstreɪʃ(ə)n ˌkɒsts/, **administration expenses** /ədˌmɪnɪˈstreɪʃ(ə)n ɪkˌspensɪz/ *plural noun* BUSINESS the costs of management, not including production, marketing or distribution costs

administrative /ədˈmɪnɪstrətɪv/ *adjective* referring to administration ○ *administrative details* ○ *administrative expenses* ○ *administrative staff*

admission /ədˈmɪʃ(ə)n/ *noun* **1.** TOURISM same as **admittance** ○ *free admission on Sundays* ○ *There is a £1 admission charge.* ○ *Admission is free on presentation of this card.* **2.** ENTERTAINMENT somebody who has visited a museum ○ *We had 250 admissions last weekend.* **3.** the act of saying that something is correct or that something bad really happened ○ *The tour company refunded his deposit, with an admission that the brochure was incorrect.* **4.** the act of being registered as a hospital patient

admission charge /əd'mɪʃ(ə)n tʃɑːdʒ/ noun ENTERTAINMENT the price to be paid before going into a place, e.g. to see an exhibition or a sports event. Also called **entry charge**

admission fee /əd'mɪʃ(ə)n fiː/ noun ENTERTAINMENT same as **entrance fee**

admission ticket /əd'mɪʃ(ə)n ˌtɪkɪt/ noun ENTERTAINMENT same as **entrance ticket**

admit /əd'mɪt/ verb **1.** to allow someone to go in ○ *Children are not admitted to the bank.* ○ *Old age pensioners are admitted at half price.* **2.** to say that something is correct **3.** to say that something bad really happened ○ *The tour operator admitted that the courier had made a mistake.* (NOTE: **admitting – admitted**)

admittance /əd'mɪt(ə)ns/ noun the act of allowing someone to go in ○ *No admittance except on business.* ○ *Admittance restricted to ticket holders only.* Also called **admission 1**

adulterated /ə'dʌltəreɪtɪd/ adjective CATERING having had something added to it to increase its weight

ad valorem /ˌæd və'lɔːrəm/ phrase Latin BUSINESS showing that a tax is calculated according to the value of the goods taxed (*meaning 'according to value'*) ○ *ad valorem duty* ○ *ad valorem tax*

COMMENT: Most taxes are 'ad valorem'; VAT is calculated as a percentage of the charge made, income tax is a percentage of income earned, etc.

advance /əd'vɑːns/ noun **1.** FINANCE a sum of money paid as part of a payment to be made later ○ *Can I have an advance of $50 against next month's salary?* **2.** □ **in advance** early, before something happens ○ *To benefit from the low fare price you have to pay in advance.* ○ *Our prices are fixed in advance.* ○ *If you want to be sure of a seat, you need to book in advance.* ■ adjective done before something happens ○ *Advance bookings are 50% higher this year.* ○ *Most tour companies insist on advance payment when a booking is made.* ○ *You must give seven days' advance notice of changes in the itinerary.* ■ verb **1.** to arrange for something to happen earlier ○ *The flight departure has been advanced to 9.30 a.m.* **2.** to move a clock or watch to a later time ○ *When you cross from England to France, you should advance your watch by one hour.* ◊ **put forward**

Advance Purchase Excursion /əd ˌvɑːns ˌpɜːtʃɪs ɪk'skɜːʃ(ə)n/ noun AIR TRAVEL a specially cheap air fare that you must book a particular length of time before the flight and that you can only change or cancel by paying an extra charge. Abbr **APEX**

advance reservation /ədˌvɑːns ˌrezə 'veɪʃ(ə)n/ noun HOTELS a booking of a hotel room made in advance of the guest's arrival

adventure /əd'ventʃə/ noun a new, exciting and dangerous experience

adventure holiday /əd'ventʃə ˌhɒlɪdeɪ/ noun TOURISM a holiday where you do something exciting or dangerous

adventure tourism /əd'ventʃə ˌtʊərɪz(ə)m/ noun tourism or travel to places where you can have adventure holidays

adventure travel /əd'ventʃə ˌtræv(ə)l/ noun a holiday that involves strenuous and often risky outdoor activities in remote areas

advert /'ædvɜːt/ noun MARKETING same as **advertisement** (*informal*) ○ *classified adverts*

advertise /'ædvətaɪz/ verb MARKETING to announce that something is for sale, that a job is vacant or that a service is offered ○ *to advertise for a secretary* ○ *to advertise a new product*

advertised tour, advertised hotel noun TOURISM a tour or hotel which is detailed in a travel company's brochure

advertisement /əd'vɜːtɪsmənt/ noun MARKETING a notice which shows that something is offered or wanted, especially that something is for sale or that a job is vacant ○ *to put an advertisement in the paper* ○ *to answer an advertisement in the paper* Also called **ad**

advertiser /'ædvətaɪzə/ noun MARKETING a person or company that advertises ○ *The catalogue gives a list of advertisers.*

advertising /'ædvətaɪzɪŋ/ noun BUSINESS the business of using advertisements to try to persuade customers to buy a product or service

advisory /əd'vaɪz(ə)ri/ adjective that gives advice ○ *a hotel advisory service* ○ *He is acting in an advisory capacity.*

aerogramme /'eərəʊˌgræm/ noun same as **air letter**

aeroplane /'eərəpleɪn/ noun AIR TRAVEL a machine that flies in the air carrying passengers or cargo. Also called **plane**

aerosol /'eərəsɒl/ noun **1.** tiny particles of liquid that stay suspended in the atmosphere like a mist □ **aerosol dispenser** a container or device from which liquid can be sprayed in tiny particles **2.** a can that sprays out a liquid in the form of tiny drops

COMMENT: Commercial aerosols (that is, the metal containers) formerly used CFCs as propellants, but these are believed to be responsible for the destruction of ozone in the upper atmosphere and have been replaced by less destructive agents.

AFD *abbreviation* CATERING accelerated freeze-drying

affiliated /ə'fɪlieɪtɪd/ *adjective* BUSINESS connected with or owned by another company ○ *one of our affiliated hotels*

affinity charter /ə'fɪnɪti ˌtʃɑːtə/ *noun* a charter of an aircraft, ship or other means of transport arranged for an affinity group

affinity group /ə'fɪnɪti gruːp/ *noun* a group of people who have something in common, e.g. a special interest, or membership of an organisation or an ethnic community

aft /ɑːft/ *adjective, adverb* TRAVEL towards the back part of a ship or plane ○ *The game will be held on the aft recreation deck.* ○ *The dining saloon is aft of the passenger lounge.*

afternoon /ˌɑːftə'nuːn/ *noun* the part of the day between midday and evening

afternoon tea /ˌɑːftənuːn 'tiː/ *noun* CATERING a meal taken in the afternoon, usually between 4 and 5 o'clock. ◊ **cream tea, high tea, tea**

COMMENT: Afternoon tea is usually served in the hotel lounge (if open to non-residents), or in the residents' lounge if it is served only to residents. It will normally consist of sandwiches (traditionally with the crusts removed), small cakes or slices of cake, pastries and various types of tea. It can also include the cream, scones and jam associated with cream teas.

afters /'ɑːftəz/ *noun* CATERING the dessert course (*informal*) ○ *What do you want for afters?* ○ *What's on the menu for afters?* Compare **starter** (NOTE: Very informal, used often by children, but also humorously by adults.)

aftertaste /'ɑːftəteɪst/ *noun* a taste left in the mouth by food or drink after it has been swallowed

age /eɪdʒ/ *verb* FOOD to store food or a wine for a period of time to enable it to develop a desired flavour or become more tender

aged /'eɪdʒɪd/ *adjective* stored for a period of time in order to develop a desired flavour or become more tender

agency /'eɪdʒənsi/ *noun* BUSINESS **1.** an office or job of representing another company in an area ○ *They signed an agency agreement* or *an agency contract.* **2.** an office or business which arranges things for other companies (NOTE: The plural form is **agencies**.)

agency fare /'eɪdʒənsi feə/ *noun* TRAVEL a special fare offered by a travel agency to its customers ○ *American Express's agency fares, available to all customers, offer savings of 60 per cent plus.*

agency staff /'eɪdʒənsi stɑːf/ *noun* staff who are supplied by an agency and who are not members of the full-time staff

agent /'eɪdʒənt/ *noun* **1.** BUSINESS a person or company representing another person or another company in an area ○ *She is the local agent for the tour operator.* □ **agent's commission** money, often a percentage of sales, paid to an agent **2.** somebody in charge of an agency

AGM /ˌeɪ dʒiː 'em/ *abbreviation* annual general meeting

agreed price /əˌgriːd 'praɪs/ *noun* BUSINESS a price which has been accepted by both the buyer and seller

agreement /ə'griːmənt/ *noun* **1.** the state of having the same opinion as somebody else □ **they are in agreement with our plan** they agree with it **2.** a contract

agree with /ə'griː wɪð/ *verb* **1.** to say that you think the same way as somebody else or that what that person is saying is right ○ *I agree with James, we should take the earlier flight.* **2.** □ **not to agree with someone** to make someone ill □ **rich food does not agree with me** rich food makes me feel ill

agri-food /'ægri fuːd/ *adjective* referring to industries that are involved in the mass-production, processing and inspection of food made from agricultural products

AI *abbreviation* HOTELS all-inclusive

aid /eɪd/ *noun* **1.** help **2.** a machine, tool or drug which helps someone do something ○ *Food processors are useful aids in preparing food.*

AIDS /eɪdz/ *noun* a disease of the immune system, caused by the HIV virus, which is transmitted through blood or bodily secretions, destroys the body's ability to fight infections and is usually fatal. Full form **Acquired Immune Deficiency Syndrome**

ailment /'eɪlmənt/ *noun* MEDICAL an illness, though not generally a very serious one ○ *Many people with skin ailments come to the spa.*

aioli /eɪ'əʊli/ *noun* FOOD mayonnaise flavoured with garlic, used especially to garnish fish and vegetables

air /eə/ *noun* a method of travelling or sending goods using aircraft ○ *We went by air, rather than by boat.* ○ *Over long distances, air travel is quicker than taking the train.*

air ambulance /'eə ˌæmbjʊləns/ *noun* MEDICAL a plane or helicopter which acts as an ambulance

'...unless you are really in the backwoods and there is no modern equipment locally, the much-vaunted air-ambulance rescue is unlikely to materialise. You will only get flown home when the assistance company rules local care 'inadequate'' [*Wanderlust*]

airbridge /'eəbrɪdʒ/ *noun* AIR TRAVEL a covered walkway which connects an aircraft with the terminal building, so that passengers can walk onto or off the aircraft easily. Also called **finger 3**, **jetway**, **jetbridge**

Airbus /'eəbʌs/ *tdmk* a trademark for a large passenger jet aircraft manufactured by aerospace companies from different European countries working together

air carrier /'eə ˌkæriə/ *noun* AIR TRAVEL a company which sends cargo or passengers by air

air-conditioned /'eə kənˌdɪʃ(ə)nd/ *adjective* in which the temperature is controlled by an air-conditioner ○ *an air-conditioned restaurant*

air-conditioner /'eə kənˌdɪʃ(ə)nə/ *noun* a machine which controls the temperature in a room ○ *How can we turn the air-conditioner off?*

air-conditioning /'eə kənˌdɪʃ(ə)nɪŋ/ *noun* a system of controlling the temperature in a room, an office or a vehicle and stopping it becoming too hot ○ *If you hire a car in Texas, make sure it has air-conditioning.* □ **to turn the air-conditioning on** to start the cooling □ **to turn the air-conditioning off** to stop the cooling □ **to turn the air-conditioning down** to make a room warmer □ **to turn the air-conditioning up** to make a room cooler

air congestion /'eə kənˌdʒestʃ(ə)n/ *noun* AIR TRAVEL a situation where too many aircraft are using the air routes, leading to delays in flight times

aircraft /'eəkrɑːft/ *noun* AIR TRAVEL a machine which flies in the air, carrying passengers or cargo ○ *The airline has a fleet of ten commercial aircraft.* ○ *The company is one of the most important American aircraft manufacturers.* (NOTE: There is no plural form: *one aircraft, two aircraft.*) □ **to charter an aircraft** to hire an aircraft for a special purpose

aircrew /'eəkruː/ *noun* AIR TRAVEL all the people who help to fly an aircraft, e.g. the captain, copilot and navigator, considered as a group

air-dry /'eə draɪ/ *verb* CATERING to remove moisture from something by placing it in a current of air

air fares /'eə feəz/ *plural noun* AIR TRAVEL the amount of money charged for travel on aircraft

airfield /'eəfiːld/ *noun* AIR TRAVEL a field where small planes can land

air freight /'eə freɪt/ *noun* BUSINESS the shipping of goods in an aircraft ○ *to send a shipment by air freight*

air hostess /'eə ˌhəʊstɪs/ *noun* AIR TRAVEL same as **flight attendant**

air letter /'eə ˌletə/ *noun* a special sheet of thin blue paper, which when folded can be sent by air without an envelope. Also called **aerogramme**

airlift /'eəlɪft/ *verb* AIR TRAVEL to carry something or someone by air ○ *The climbers were airlifted to safety.*

airline /'eəlaɪn/ *noun* AIR TRAVEL a company which carries passengers or cargo by air ○ *Profits of major airlines have been affected by the rise in fuel prices.*

airline identification code /ˌeəlaɪn aɪ ˌdentɪfɪ'keɪʃ(ə)n ˌkəʊd/ *noun* AIR TRAVEL a set of letters which are given to all flights operated by an airline, e.g. BA for British Airways, LH for Lufthansa, AF for Air France

airline train /'eəlaɪn treɪn/ *noun* RAIL TRAVEL a train which takes passengers to and from an airport

airlink /'eəlɪŋk/ *noun* AIR TRAVEL a link between two places, using planes or helicopters

air mail /'eə meɪl/ *noun* a way of sending letters or parcels by air ○ *to send a package by air mail* ○ *Air-mail charges have risen by 15%.* □ **air-mail envelope** a very light envelope for sending air-mail letters □ **air-mail sticker** a blue sticker with the words 'by air mail', which can be stuck to an envelope or packet to show it is being sent by air

airmail /'eəmeɪl/ *verb* to send letters or parcels by air ○ *We airmailed the tickets to New York.*

air marshal /ˌeə 'mɑːʃ(ə)l/ *noun* AIR TRAVEL same as **sky marshal**

air miles /'eə maɪlz/ *plural noun* AIR TRAVEL a trademark for a system that gives people points when they purchase goods or services, which they can later use to get free air travel

air miss /'eə ˌmɪs/ *noun* AIR TRAVEL an incident where two aircraft come very close to each other when in the air, but without causing an accident

airpass /'eəpɑːs/ *noun* AIR TRAVEL a special ticket, paid for in advance, which allows unlimited travel by air in a country over a limited period of time

air passenger /'eə ˌpæsɪndʒə/ *noun* AIR TRAVEL a passenger travelling in an aircraft

airport /'eəpɔːt/ *noun* AIR TRAVEL a place where planes land and take off ○ *We leave from London Airport at 10.00.* ○ *O'Hare Airport is the main airport for Chicago.* □ **airport hotel** a hotel which is very near to an airport, and so is convenient for passengers who need to leave early in the morning, who arrive late at night, or who are in transit ○ *Stranded passengers were put up at the airport hotel at the airline's expense.*

airport bus /'eəpɔːt bʌs/ *noun* ROAD TRAVEL a bus which takes passengers to and from an airport

airport code /'eəpɔːt kəʊd/ *noun* AIR TRAVEL a set of letters which are used to identify a particular airport, e.g. LHR for London Heathrow or CDG for Charles de Gaulle

airport tax /'eəpɔːt tæks/ *noun* AIR TRAVEL a tax added to the price of an air ticket to cover the cost of running an airport

airport terminal /'eəpɔːt ˌtɜːmɪn(ə)l/ *noun* AIR TRAVEL the main building at an airport where passengers arrive and depart. Also called **terminal building**

airport transfer /'eəpɔːt ˌtrænsfɜː/ *noun* a transport service to take passengers from an airport to a hotel, conference centre or other point, or from there back to the airport

airsick /'eəsɪk/ *adjective* MEDICAL feeling sick because of the movement of an aircraft

airsickness /'eəsɪknəs/ *noun* MEDICAL sickness caused by the movement of an aircraft

airside /'eəsaɪd/ *adjective, adverb* AIR TRAVEL next to the part of an airport where aircraft stand □ **airside lounge** a departure lounge near the boarding gate

'Business class passengers have the use of a small and quiet airside lounge. There's an adequate supply of orange juice, coffee and newspapers' [*Business Traveller*]

'…airside, there is an Internet café, where passengers can make use of the Internet and/or see the latest business news on TV screens' [*Airliner World*]

airstrip /'eəstrɪp/ *noun* AIR TRAVEL a small rough landing place for aircraft ○ *The plane landed on a jungle airstrip.*

air taxi /'eə ˌtæksi/ *noun* a small commercial aircraft used for short flights between places not on a regular airline route

air terminal /'eə ˌtɜːmɪn(ə)l/ *noun* AIR TRAVEL a building in a town where passengers meet to be taken by bus or train to an airport outside the town

air ticket /'eə ˌtɪkɪt/ *noun* AIR TRAVEL a ticket to allow a passenger to travel by air

airtight /'eətaɪt/ *adjective* not allowing air to get in or out ○ *The goods are packed in airtight containers.*

air-traffic control /ˌeə ˌtræfɪk kən 'trəʊl/ *noun* AIR TRAVEL the organisation of the movement of aircraft in the air, especially when landing or taking off

air-traffic controller /ˌeə ˌtræfɪk kən 'trəʊlə/ *noun* AIR TRAVEL somebody who organises the movement of aircraft in the air

Air Travel Organisers' Licence /ˌeə ˌtræv(ə)l 'ɔːgənaɪzəz ˌlaɪs(ə)ns/ *noun* AIR TRAVEL a licence that has to be held by any company or person offering package holidays or charter flights and includes a bond to protect travellers if the company goes into liquidation. Abbr **ATOL**

airworthiness /'eəˌwɜːðɪnəs/ *noun* AIR TRAVEL the state of being able and safe to fly

aisle /aɪl/ *noun* TRAVEL (*in a train, aircraft, cinema, etc.*) a gap between rows of seats, where people may walk ○ *You're blocking the aisle and the stewardess can't get past with the drinks trolley.*

aisle seat /'aɪl siːt/ *noun* TRAVEL a seat in a train, plane, etc., next to an aisle

à la /'æ læ/ *phrase* CATERING a French phrase meaning 'in the style of' □ **à la russe** in the Russian style

à la carte /ˌæ læ 'kɑːt/ *adjective* CATERING made of several dishes ordered separately from a menu

à la carte menu /ˌæ læ ˌkɑːt 'menjuː/ *noun* CATERING a menu with many different dishes at different prices, from which a guest can choose what to eat ○ *They chose from the à la carte menu.*

à la mode /ˌæ læ 'mɒd/ *adverb* US CATERING served with ice cream ○ *apple pie à la mode*

alarm /ə'lɑːm/ *noun* a device which gives a loud warning ■ *verb* to frighten somebody ○ *We don't want to alarm the guests.*

alarm clock /ə'lɑːm klɒk/ *noun* a clock which rings a bell to wake you up

alcohol /'ælkəhɒl/ *noun* BEVERAGES **1.** a pure colourless liquid which is formed by the action of yeast on sugar solutions and forms part of drinks such as wine and whisky. Symbol C_2H_5OH **2.** a drink made from fermented or distilled liquid ○ *The restaurant will not serve alcohol to anyone under the age of 18.*

alcohol by volume /ˌælkəhɒl baɪ 'vɒljuːm/ *noun* BEVERAGES the amount of alcohol in a drink, shown on the label. Abbr **abv**

alcohol-free /ˌælkəhɒl 'friː/ *adjective* BEVERAGES containing no alcohol ○ *alcohol-free lager*

alcoholic /ˌælkə'hɒlɪk/ *adjective* BEVERAGES containing alcohol ○ *Alcoholic drinks are not allowed into some countries.*

alcoholism /'ælkəhɒlɪz(ə)m/ *noun* the excessive drinking of alcohol, which becomes addictive

alcopop /'ælkəʊpɒp/ *noun* a drink, manufactured and sold commercially, that is a mixture of a soft drink, e.g. lemonade, and alcohol

al dente /ˌæl denteɪ/ *adjective* referring especially to pasta that is cooked just long enough to be still firm and not too soft

ale /eɪl/ *noun* BEVERAGES British-type beer, especially bitter beer, but not lager

alfresco /æl'freskəʊ/ *adjective, adverb* in the open air ○ *We had an alfresco meal on the terrace overlooking the sea.*

algae /'ældʒiː/ *plural noun* tiny plants living in water or in moist conditions, which contain chlorophyll and have no stems or roots or leaves □ **blue-green algae** algae found mainly in fresh water □ **brown algae** brown seaweed

algaecide /'ældʒɪsaɪd/ *noun* a substance used to kill algae

alien /'eɪliən/ *noun* a person who is not a citizen of the country

alight /ə'laɪt/ *verb* to get off a vehicle (*formal*) ○ *Alight here for the Post Office.*

alimentary canal /ˌælɪˌment(ə)ri kə'næl/ *noun* a tube in the body going from the mouth to the anus and including the throat, stomach and intestines, through which food passes and is digested

alimentary system /ˌælɪ'ment(ə)ri ˌsɪstəm/ *noun* the arrangement of tubes and organs, including the alimentary canal, salivary glands, liver, etc., through which food passes and is digested

alimentation /ˌælɪmen'teɪʃ(ə)n/ *noun* the act of taking in food

alkali /'ælkəlaɪ/ *noun* a substance which neutralises acids and forms salts (NOTE: The British English plural is **alkalis**, but the US spelling is **alkalies**.)

alkaline /'ælkəlaɪn/ *adjective* containing more alkali than acid

alkalinity /ˌælkə'lɪnɪti/ *noun* the amount of alkali in something such as soil or water

COMMENT: Alkalinity and acidity are measured according to the pH scale. pH7 is neutral, and pH8 and upwards are alkaline. One of the commonest alkalis is caustic soda, used to clear blocked drains.

all /ɔːl/ *adjective, pronoun* everything or everyone ○ *All (of) the managers attended the meeting.* ○ *All the guests asked to go on the tour.* ○ *All the rooms are booked for the Christmas period.* ○ *The customs officials asked him to open all his cases.* ○ *All trains stop at Clapham Junction.*

allergen /'ælədʒən/ *noun* a substance which produces hypersensitivity

COMMENT: Allergens are usually proteins, and include foods, dust, animal hair, as well as pollen from flowers. Treatment of allergies depends on correctly identifying the allergen to which the patient is sensitive. This is done by patch tests, in which drops of different allergens are placed on scratches in the skin. Food allergens discovered in this way can be avoided, but it is hard to avoid other common allergens such as dust and pollen, and these have to be treated by a course of desensitising injections.

allergenic /ˌælə'dʒenɪk/ *adjective* producing or triggering an allergy ○ *the allergenic properties of fungal spores*

allergic /ə'lɜːdʒɪk/ *adjective* suffering from an allergy ○ *She is allergic to pollen.* □ **allergic agent** a substance that produces an allergic reaction

allergic reaction /əˌlɜːdʒɪk ri'ækʃən/ *noun* an effect produced by a substance to which a person has an allergy, such as sneezing or a skin rash ○ *He showed an allergic reaction to strawberries.*

allergy /'ælədʒi/ *noun* a sensitivity to particular substances such as pollen or dust, which cause a physical reaction ○ *She has an allergy to household dust.*

'…the parents of a boy with a life-threatening peanut allergy are moving to France to open holiday accommodation for people whose lives are affected by potentially fatal nut allergies' [*Caterer & Hotelkeeper*]

all-in /ˌɔːl 'ɪn/ *adjective* including everything

all-inclusive /ˌɔːl ɪnˈkluːsɪv/ *adjective* where the price paid includes everything and no further payments will be required ○ *tailor-made all-inclusive 16-day trips from £1,600 per person*

all-in price /ˌɔːl ɪn ˈpraɪs/, **all-in rate** /ˌɔːl ɪn ˈreɪt/ *noun* BUSINESS a price which covers all the items in a purchase, i.e. the goods, plus delivery, tax, insurance, etc., or all items in a tour such as travel, hotel accommodation and meals ○ *The hotel offers an all-in tariff of £550 a week.*

allocate /ˈæləkeɪt/ *verb* **1.** to share out things among various people ○ *The party were allocated rooms in the hotel annexe.* **2.** to divide something such as a sum of money in various ways, and share it out ○ *We allocate 10% of revenue to publicity.* ○ *$2,500 was allocated to furnishing the guests' lounge.*

allot /əˈlɒt/ *verb* TOURISM to allocate hotel rooms to a tour operator ○ *The group has been allotted 50 rooms in the hotel.* (NOTE: **allotting – allotted**)

allotment /əˈlɒtmənt/ *noun* TOURISM the act of allocating hotel rooms to tour operators

allow /əˈlaʊ/ *verb* **1.** to let someone do something ○ *Children are not allowed into the restaurant.* ○ *You are allowed six litres of duty-free wine.* ○ *The company allows all members of staff to take six days' holiday at Christmas.* **2.** to give someone something ○ *We will allow you a student discount.* ○ *The store allows a 5% discount to members of staff.* **3.** to accept something legally ○ *to allow a claim* or *an appeal*

allowable /əˈlaʊəb(ə)l/ *adjective* legally accepted

allowable expenses /əˌlaʊəb(ə)l ɪkˈspensɪz/ *plural noun* BUSINESS business expenses that can be claimed against tax

allowance /əˈlaʊəns/ *noun* **1.** money which is given for a special reason ○ *travel allowance* or *travelling allowance* ○ *foreign currency allowance* **2.** money removed in the form of a discount ○ *allowance for exchange loss*

'…most airlines give business class the same baggage allowance as first class' [*Business Traveller*]

allowed time /əˌlaʊd ˈtaɪm/ *noun* BUSINESS paid time that the management agrees an employee can spend on rest, cleaning or meals, but not working

allow for /əˈlaʊ fɔː/ *verb* **1.** to give a discount for something ○ *to allow for money paid in advance* ○ *to allow 10% for packing*

□ **gratuities are not allowed for** gratuities are not included **2.** to take something into account when calculating □ **allow 14 days for delivery of the visa** calculate that delivery of the visa will take at least 14 days

all-terrain boarding /ˌɔːl təˌreɪn ˈbɔːdɪŋ/ *noun* a form of skateboarding in which the rider travels over all types of terrain, especially down mountain slopes

almond /ˈɑːmənd/ *noun* NUTS a sweet nut from the almond tree ○ *trout with almonds* ○ *an almond cake*

almond paste /ˈɑːmənd peɪst/ *noun* FOOD same as **marzipan**

alongside /əˌlɒŋˈsaɪd/ *adverb, preposition* beside ○ *The ship berthed alongside the quay* or *came alongside the quay.*

alpine /ˈælpaɪn/ *adjective* referring to the Alps ○ *an alpine holiday resort*

'…it appears that rugby and soccer are far, far more dangerous than Alpine downhill skiing' [*Sunday Times*]

Alps /ælps/ *plural noun* TOURISM a mountainous area of Switzerland and North Italy, including parts of Austria, Slovenia and France ○ *The number of visitors to the Alps is increasing each year.* ○ *Climbers in the Alps are warned of the danger of avalanches.*

alternative /ɔːlˈtɜːnətɪv/ *noun* something which you do instead of something else ○ *What is the alternative to calling the trip off?* □ **we have no alternative** there is nothing else we can do ■ *adjective* able to take the place of something ○ *They were offered the choice of two alternative flights.* □ **to find someone alternative accommodation** to find someone another hotel room

altitude /ˈæltɪtjuːd/ *noun* height measured above the level of the sea

altitude sickness /ˈæltɪtjuːd ˌsɪknəs/ *noun* MEDICAL a condition caused by reduced oxygen in the air above altitudes of 7,000 to 8,000 feet (3,600 metres). Symptoms include headaches, breathlessness, fatigue, nausea and swelling of the face, hands and feet. Also called **mountain sickness**

a.m. /ˈeɪ ˈem/, **A.M.** US *abbreviation* referring to the morning period between midnight and midday ○ *The flight leaves at 9.20 a.m.* ○ *We will arrive at 10 a.m. local time.* ○ *If you phone before 8 a.m., calls are charged at a cheaper rate.*

amaretto /ˌæməˈretəʊ/ *noun* an almond-flavoured liqueur from Italy

ambassador /æmˈbæsədə/, **ambassadress** /æmˈbæsədres/ *noun* somebody who represents his or her country in another country. ◊ **consul, embassy**

ambience /'æmbiəns/ *noun* the character and atmosphere surrounding a place ○ *The new landlord has given the pub a friendly ambience.*

'…come and enjoy the ambience of a 16th Century Elizabethan Manor House' [*Sunday Times*]

ambient /'æmbiənt/ *adjective* surrounding a person or an object

ambient noise /ˌæmbiənt 'nɔɪz/ *noun* general noise which surrounds you, e.g. traffic noise, waterfalls, etc.

ambient quality standards /ˌæmbiənt 'kwɒlɪti ˌstændədz/ *plural noun* levels of acceptable clean air which a national body tries to enforce

ambient temperature /ˌæmbiənt 'temprɪtʃə/ *noun* the temperature of the air in which you live or work

amenity /ə'miːnɪti/ *noun* a facility for sports or entertainment ○ *The town offers amenities for children.* (NOTE: The plural form is **amenities**.)

'…rooms are stylish and uncluttered with every amenity, and service is generally good. Singles from DM310, doubles DM390' [*Business Traveller*]

amenity centre /əˌmiːnɪti 'sentə/ *noun* ENTERTAINMENT a building housing various entertainment facilities, such as a cinema, sports hall, gymnasium, auditorium and swimming pool

American /ə'merɪkən/ *adjective* relating to America or to the United States

American Automobile Association /əˌmerɪkən 'ɔːtəməbiːl əˌsəʊsieɪʃ(ə)n/ *noun* ROAD TRAVEL a major motoring organisation in the USA. Abbr **AAA**

American breakfast /əˌmerɪkən 'brekfəst/ *noun* CATERING a breakfast including coffee or tea, cereal, bacon or ham, and toast or waffles

American Express /əˌmerɪkən ɪk'spres/ *noun* TRAVEL a company offering a travel service, traveller's cheques, charge cards, and many other services worldwide ○ *Her American Express traveller's cheques were stolen.* Abbr **Amex**

americano /əˌmerɪ'kɑːnəʊ/ *noun* an espresso coffee diluted with hot water and containing no milk

Americanos /əˌmerɪ'kɑːnəʊz/ *noun* BEVERAGES a cocktail of campari and vermouth

American plan /ə'merɪkən plæn/ *noun* US HOTELS a hotel charge that includes all meals as well as the room charge. Compare **European plan**

American service /əˌmerɪkən 'sɜːvɪs/ *noun* CATERING **1.** a style of laying a table, in which each guest is given cutlery, a side plate, a napkin, glasses, and sometimes a coffee cup and saucer **2.** a way of serving food to guests, where the portions of food are placed on plates in the kitchen ready for service at table. Compare **French service**

Amex /'æmeks/ *abbreviation* American Express (*informal*) ○ *She paid by Amex or with his Amex card.*

amino acid /əˌmiːnəʊ 'æsɪd/ *noun* a chemical compound which is broken down from proteins in the digestive system and then used by the body to form its own protein ○ *Proteins are first broken down into amino acids.*

COMMENT: Amino acids all contain carbon, hydrogen, nitrogen and oxygen, as well as other elements. Some amino acids are produced in the body itself, but others have to be absorbed from food. The eight essential amino acids are: isoleucine, leucine, lysine, methionine, phenylalanine, threonine, tryptophan and valine.

ammonia /ə'məʊniə/ *noun* a gas with a strong smell, which is a compound of nitrogen and hydrogen and is used to make artificial fertilisers, or in liquid form as a refrigerant. Symbol **NH$_3$**

COMMENT: Ammonia is released into the atmosphere from animal dung. It has the effect of neutralising acid rain but in combination with sulphur dioxide it forms ammonium sulphate which damages the green leaves of plants.

amoeba /ə'miːbə/ *noun* a form of animal life, made up of a single cell (NOTE: The plural form is **amoebae**.The US spelling of amoeba is **ameba**.)

amoebic /ə'miːbɪk/ *adjective* referring to an amoeba

amoebic dysentery /əˌmiːbɪk 'dɪs(ə)ntri/ *noun* MEDICAL a mainly tropical form of dysentery that is caused by microbes that enter the body through contaminated water or unwashed food

amount /ə'maʊnt/ *noun* a quantity of something, especially money ○ *amount paid* ○ *amount deducted* ○ *a small amount of sugar* ○ *The amount owing is not enough to cover our costs.* ■ *verb* □ **to amount to** to make a total of ○ *Their debts amount to over £1m.*

amp /æmp/ *noun* the quantity of electricity flowing in a current ○ *a 3-amp plug*

amplifier /'æmplɪfaɪə/ *noun* a machine which makes a sound louder

Amtrak /'æmtræk/ *noun* RAIL TRAVEL the national system of railways in the US, which operates passenger services between main cities

amuse /ə'mjuːz/ *verb* **1.** to make someone laugh □ **to amuse yourself** to spend time happily ○ *On the final day of the tour there will be no organised visits, and members of the party will be left to amuse themselves in the town.* **2.** to make the time pass pleasantly for someone

amuse-bouche /ə,mjuːz 'buːʃ/, **amuse-gueule** /ə,mjuːz 'gɜːl/ *noun* CATERING a small appetiser served before a meal or while the customer is looking at the menu

amusement /ə'mjuːzmənt/ *noun* a feeling of pleasure caused by something that is funny or enjoyable

amusement arcade /ə'mjuːzmənt ɑː ,keɪd/ *noun* ENTERTAINMENT a hall with slot machines for playing games, etc.

amusement park /ə'mjuːzmənt pɑːk/ *noun* ENTERTAINMENT an open-air park with various types of entertainment such as roundabouts and shooting galleries

analyse /'ænəlaɪz/, **analyze** *verb* to examine in detail ○ *to analyse the accounts of a restaurant* ○ *to analyse the market potential for golfing holidays* ○ *When the food was analysed it was found to contain traces of bacteria.*

analysis /ə'næləsɪs/ *noun* a detailed examination and report ○ *job analysis* ○ *market analysis* ○ *sales analysis* ○ *to carry out an analysis of the market potential*

analyst /'ænəlɪst/ *noun* somebody who analyses ○ *market analyst* ○ *systems analyst*

anchor /'æŋkə/ *noun* SHIPS AND BOATS a heavy metal hook dropped to the bottom of the sea to hold a ship in one place ○ *The ship was at anchor.* □ **to drop anchor** to let an anchor fall to the bottom of the sea to hold a ship steady ■ *verb* SHIPS AND BOATS **1.** (*of a ship*) to drop anchor **2.** to hold with an anchor

anchorage /'æŋkərɪdʒ/ *noun* SHIPS AND BOATS a place where ships can anchor safely

anchovy /'æntʃəvi, æn'tʃəʊvi/ *noun* SEAFOOD a small fish with a strong, salty taste, used in dishes such as pizza and salade niçoise

ancient monument /,eɪnʃənt 'mɒnjʊmənt/ *noun* ENTERTAINMENT a very old building, especially one which belongs to the state and is open to visitors ○ *The chapel is an ancient monument and is protected.*

ancient site /,eɪnʃənt 'saɪt/ *noun* TOURISM a place where a town or buildings used to be, and where there are now only ruins or empty land

ancillary /æn'sɪləri/ *adjective* secondary

ancillary services /æn,sɪləri 'sɜːvɪsɪz/ *plural noun* HOTELS services such as cleaning and porterage in a hotel

angel hair /'eɪndʒəl heə/ *noun* pasta in the form of long, very fine strands

Angostura bitters /,æŋgəstjʊərə 'bɪtəz/ *trademark* BEVERAGES a trademark for a sharp-tasting liquid, added to gin and other drinks to make them bitter. Also called **bitters**

animator /'ænɪmeɪtə/ *noun* ENTERTAINMENT somebody employed to organise entertainments or other activities for guests in a hotel or holiday resort or for passengers on a ship

anise /æ'niːs/ *noun* SAUCES, ETC. a herb that produces a small aromatic fruit called aniseed, which is used for flavouring

aniseed /'ænɪsiːd/ *noun* FOOD the seed of the anise plant

COMMENT: Aniseed is much used in confectionery, especially in sweets. It is also the basis of several alcoholic drinks made in the Mediterranean area, such as pastis in France, ouzo in Greece, or raki in Turkey.

annexe /'æneks/ *noun* a less important building attached to a main building ○ *The party was put into the hotel annexe.*

announce /ə'naʊns/ *verb* to say something officially or in public ○ *The compere announced the results of the competition.* ○ *The pilot announced that there was some turbulence ahead.*

announcement /ə'naʊnsmənt/ *noun* the act of making something known in public ○ *the announcement of the appointment of a new hotel manager*

announcer /ə'naʊnsə/ *noun* CATERING same as **aboyeur**

annual general meeting /,ænjuəl ,dʒen(ə)rəl 'miːtɪŋ/ *noun* BUSINESS an annual meeting of all the shareholders of a company, when the company's financial situation is presented and discussed. Abbr **AGM** (NOTE: The US English is **annual meeting** or **annual stockholders' meeting.**)

annual pass /'ænjuəl pɑːs/ *noun* a pass that entitles a person to use facilities for a whole year

Annual Percentage Rate /ˌænjuəl pə 'sentɪdʒ ˌreɪt/ *noun* BUSINESS the rate of interest shown on an annual compound basis, including fees and charges. Abbr **APR**

answer /'ɑːnsə/ *noun* something that you say or write when someone has asked you a question ○ *I am writing in answer to your letter of October 6th.* ○ *My letter got no answer* or *There was no answer to my letter.* ○ *I tried to phone his office but there was no answer.* ■ *verb* to speak or write words to someone who has spoken to you or asked you a question □ **to answer a letter** to write a letter in reply to a letter which you have received

anteroom /'æntiruːm/ *noun* a room next to and adjoining a larger room ○ *The disco was held in the anteroom next to the bar.*

antibiotic /ˌæntibaɪ'ɒtɪk/ MEDICAL *adjective* stopping the spread of bacteria ■ *noun* a drug, e.g. penicillin, that is developed from living substances and stops the spread of microorganisms ○ *He was given a course of antibiotics.* ○ *Antibiotics have no use against virus diseases.*

COMMENT: Penicillin is one of the commonest antibiotics, together with streptomycin, tetracycline, erythromycin and many others. Although antibiotics are widely and successfully used, new forms of bacteria have developed which are resistant to them.

anticaking   additive /ˌæntɪ'keɪkɪŋ ˌædɪtɪv/ *noun* CATERING an additive added to food to prevent it becoming solid

antimalarial /ˌæntimə'leəriəl/ *noun, adjective* MEDICAL treating or preventing malaria (NOTE: Antimalarial drugs have names ending in **-oquine: chloroquine.**)

antioxidant /ˌænti'ɒksɪd(ə)nt/ *noun* CATERING a substance which makes oxygen less damaging, e.g. in the body or in foods or plastics

antipasto /'æntipæstəʊ/ *noun* a food served at the beginning of an Italian meal or as a snack

antiseptic /ˌæntɪ'septɪk/ MEDICAL *adjective* preventing harmful microorganisms from spreading ○ *She gargled with an antiseptic mouthwash.* ■ *noun* a substance which prevents germs growing or spreading ○ *The nurse painted the wound with antiseptic.*

antivenene /ˌæntivə'niːn/, **antivenom serum** *noun* MEDICAL serum which is used to counteract the poison from snake or insect bites

AOC *abbreviation* BEVERAGES appellation d'origine contrôlée

AONB *abbreviation* TOURISM Area of Outstanding Natural Beauty

aparthotel, apart'hotel *noun* HOTELS same as **apartment hotel** ○ *Amsterdam has a wide range of apartments and aparthotels.*

apartment /ə'pɑːtmənt/ *noun* a set of rooms in a large building, used as a separate living unit. Also called **flat** □ **apartment block** a block of flats

apartment hotel /ə'pɑːtmənt ˌhəʊtel/ *noun* HOTELS a hotel which is formed of a series of furnished rooms or suites and where all normal hotel services are provided, although each suite will have its own kitchenette

aperitif, apéritif *noun* BEVERAGES an alcoholic drink taken before a meal

COMMENT: The commonest apéritifs served in Britain are sherry, gin and tonic, whisky, or various martinis; outside Britain, port is drunk as an apéritif.

APEX /'eɪpeks/ *abbreviation* Advance Purchase Excursion

APEX fare /'eɪpeks feə/ *noun* AIR TRAVEL a specially cheap air fare that you must book a particular length of time before the flight and that you can only change or cancel by paying an extra charge

'…a cheap APEX fare has been introduced for a car and up to five passengers who book 28 days in advance and return within five days' [*Business Traveller*]

apologise /ə'pɒlədʒaɪz/ *verb* to say you are sorry ○ *We apologise for the delay in unloading baggage.* ○ *She apologised for being late.*

apology /ə'pɒlədʒi/ *noun* a statement in which you say you are sorry □ *to write a letter of apology* ○ *I enclose a cheque for £10 with apologies for the delay in answering your letter.* ○ *She was very annoyed and asked for an apology from the coach driver.* (NOTE: The plural form is **apologies.**)

appellation d'origine contrôlée /æpə ˌlæsiɒn ˌdɒrɪdʒin kɒn'trəʊleɪ/ *noun* BEVERAGES a French wine classification, indicating that the wine comes from a particular area and is of a particular quality. Compare **VDQS**

appetiser /'æpɪtaɪzə/, **appetizer** *noun* CATERING a snack taken with drinks before a meal

appetising /'æpɪtaɪzɪŋ/ *adjective* looking, smelling or tasting good

appetite /'æpɪtaɪt/ *noun* a need or wish to eat □ **good appetite** interest in eating food □ **poor appetite** lack of interest in eating food

apple /ˈæp(ə)l/ *noun* FRUIT the common hard, edible fruit of the apple tree *Malus domestica* □ **cider apple** an apple used for making cider

COMMENT: 6,000 apple varieties once grew in Britain, and all of them are recorded in the UK's National Apple Register. Recognised apple varieties include Cox's Orange Pippin, Granny Smith and Golden Delicious (dessert varieties) and Bramley's Seedling (cooking apple).

apple charlotte /ˌæp(ə)l ˈʃɑːlət/ *noun* DESSERTS a hot dessert made of stewed apples cooked in a case of soft sponge cake

apple crumble /ˌæp(ə)l ˈkrʌmb(ə)l/ *noun* DESSERTS a dessert made of cooked apples covered with a crumble top

apple dumplings /ˌæp(ə)l ˈdʌmplɪŋz/ *plural noun* DESSERTS pieces of apple cooked in dough

apple sauce /ˌæp(ə)l ˈsɔːs/ *noun* SAUCES, ETC. sauce made from cooked apples, served with meat, especially pork (NOTE: In US English, **apple sauce** can be eaten as a dessert, which in British English is called **stewed apples**.)

applicant /ˈæplɪkənt/ *noun* somebody who applies for something ○ *Visa applicants will have to wait at least two weeks.*

application /ˌæplɪˈkeɪʃ(ə)n/ *noun* an act of asking for something, usually in writing ○ *an application for a visa* or *a visa application* ○ *an application for a job* or *a job application*

application form /ˌæplɪˈkeɪʃ(ə)n ˌfɔːm/ *noun* a form which has to be filled in to apply for something ○ *to fill in an application (form) for a new passport* or *a passport application (form)*

apply /əˈplaɪ/ *verb* **1.** to ask for something, usually in writing ○ *to apply for a visa* or *for a passport* ○ *to apply in writing* ○ *to apply in person* □ **to apply for a job** to write offering your services to an employer ○ *Sixty people applied for jobs in the new restaurant.* **2.** to affect or be relevant to someone or something ○ *This clause applies only to travel in Africa.* (NOTE: **applying – applied**)

approved /əˈpruːvd/ *adjective* TOURISM formerly, the lowest grade in the English Tourist Board grading system

APR *abbreviation* BUSINESS Annual Percentage Rate

après-ski /ˈæpreɪ skiː/ *adjective* taking place in the evening after a day's skiing

apricot /ˈeɪprɪkɒt/ *noun* FRUIT the small yellow fruit from the deciduous tree *Prunus armeniaca*, similar to a small peach, but not as juicy ○ *You have a choice of marmalade or apricot jam for breakfast.*

apron /ˈeɪprən/ *noun* **1.** a piece of cloth worn over clothes to protect them when working ○ *The chef in the carvery wears a long white apron.* **2.** AIR TRAVEL (*in an airport*) a piece of tarmac on which planes can be parked for unloading, waiting, cleaning, etc.

'...the chances are you'll be decanted from the plane onto a hot and sticky apron for the further stifling bus ride to the cramped terminal' [*Business Traveller*]

'...much of the apron outside the hangars seems to be overflow parking area for aircraft awaiting departure slots' [*Airliner World*]

apron congestion /ˈeɪprən kənˌdʒestʃ(ə)n/ *noun* AIR TRAVEL a situation where too many planes try to use the apron at an airport, resulting in slower turnround times

aquatic /əˈkwætɪk/ *adjective* in water

aquatic sports /əˌkwætɪk ˈspɔːts/ *plural noun* SPORT activities which take place on or in water, e.g. swimming, water polo or scuba diving

arborio /ɑːˈbɔːriəʊ/ *noun* a short-grained rice used to make risotto and other Italian dishes

Arbroath smokie /ɑːˌbrəʊθ ˈsməʊki/ *noun* SEAFOOD a small whole haddock smoked to a brown colour (NOTE: **Arbroath smokies** are named after the town of Arbroath in Scotland.)

arctic /ˈɑːktɪk/ *adjective* referring to the area round the North Pole ○ *Polar bears hibernate during the long arctic winters.* ○ *Two arctic explorers have reached the North Pole.* ■ *noun* □ **the Arctic** the area round the North Pole ○ *The Arctic is home to polar bears.* □ **the High Arctic** the most northerly part of the Arctic

'...a whole range of pollutants are collected by the atmosphere over central Europe, and then carried by air currents to the High Arctic, where they fall back to earth in the weather' [*TGO – The Great Outdoors*]

area /ˈeəriə/ *noun* **1.** a measurement of the space taken up by something, calculated by multiplying the length by the width ○ *The area of this restaurant is 3,400 square feet.* ○ *We are looking for a shop with a sales area of about 100 square metres.* **2.** a region of the world ○ *The tour will visit one of the most inaccessible desert areas in the world.* **3.** a district or part of a town ○ *The office is in the commercial area of the town.* ○ *Their factory is in a very good area for getting to the motorways and airports.* **4.** part of a country, a division for commercial purposes ○ *Her sales area is the North-West.* ○ *He finds it difficult to cover all his area in a week.*

area code /ˈeəriə kəʊd/ *noun* a special telephone number which is given to a particular area ○ *The area code for central London is 020 7.*

area manager /ˌeəriə ˈmænɪdʒə/ *noun* a manager who is responsible for a part of the country

Area of Outstanding Natural Beauty /ˌeəriə əv aʊtˌstændɪŋ ˌnætʃ(ə)rəl ˈbjuːti/ *noun* TOURISM a region in England and Wales which is not a National Park but which is considered sufficiently attractive to be preserved from overdevelopment. Abbr **AONB**

arm /ɑːm/ *noun* **1.** the part of the body which goes from the shoulder to the hand □ **arm in arm** with their arms linked **2.** something shaped like an arm, or a piece at the side of a chair to rest your arms on ○ *The buttons for the music channels are in the arm of your seat.* ■ *verb* to equip with weapons

armband /ˈɑːmbænd/ *noun* a piece of cloth worn round your arm ○ *The tour leader will be wearing a red armband.*

armchair /ˈɑːmtʃeə/ *noun* a chair with arms ○ *Each bedroom is furnished with two armchairs and a TV.*

armed /ɑːmd/ *adjective* equipped with weapons ○ *Because of the dangerous situation, the party will travel with armed guards.*

armrest /ˈɑːmrest/ *noun* a part of a seat that you put your arm on ○ *The ashtray and sound buttons are in the armrest.* ○ *Please put your armrests into the horizontal position for landing.*

aroma /əˈrəʊmə/ *noun* a pleasant smell of something you can eat or drink (*formal*) ○ *the aroma of freshly ground coffee*

aromatic /ˌærəˈmætɪk/ *adjective* having a strong pleasant smell □ **aromatic herbs** herbs with a strong scent which are used to give a particular taste to food, e.g. rosemary or thyme

ARR *abbreviation* HOTELS average room rate

arr. *abbreviation* TRAVEL **1.** arrival **2.** arrived **3.** arrives

arrange /əˈreɪndʒ/ *verb* **1.** to put in order ○ *The hotel is arranged as a series of small bungalows with a central restaurant and swimming pool.* ○ *In the guide, the restaurants are arranged in alphabetical order.* ○ *Arrange the invoices in order of their dates.* **2.** to organise ○ *We arranged to have the meeting in their offices.* ○ *She arranged for a*

car to meet him at the airport. ○ *The courier will arrange transportation to the airport.* (NOTE: You arrange **for** someone to do something; you arrange **for** something to be done; or you arrange **to** do something.)

arrangement /əˈreɪndʒmənt/ *noun* the way in which something is organised ○ *She is making all the arrangements for her boss's visit to Spain.* ○ *The group complained that the arrangements for the trip to the ruins were not clear.*

arrival /əˈraɪv(ə)l/ *noun* **1.** the act of coming to a place ○ *We announce the arrival of flight AB 987 from Tangiers.* Abbr **arr. 2.** a person who arrives at a place ○ *The new arrivals were shown to the first-floor lounge.*

arrival date /əˈraɪv(ə)l deɪt/ *noun* TRAVEL the day on which a traveller or tour group arrives at a destination. Also called **date of arrival**

arrivals /əˈraɪv(ə)lz/ *noun* AIR TRAVEL a section of an airport where the passengers arrive

arrivals hall, arrivals lounge *noun* AIR TRAVEL a hall or lounge where passengers can be met or can sit and wait

arrival without notice /əˌraɪv(ə)l wɪð ʊt ˈnəʊtɪs/ *noun* HOTELS arrival at a hotel without having made an advance booking

arrive /əˈraɪv/ *verb* to reach a place ○ *The plane is due to arrive at 12.15.* ○ *They arrived at the hotel in the middle of the night.*

arrowroot /ˈærəʊruːt/ *noun* CATERING a thickening agent in the form of a white powder made from the root of a West Indian plant

art /ɑːt/ *noun* **1.** an activity in which people create beautiful or interesting objects or experiences, e.g. painting, drawing, sculpture, music, literature or dance **2.** beautiful or interesting objects, created e.g. by painting, drawing or sculpture ○ *When in Washington, you must not miss the Museum of Modern Art.*

art gallery /ˈɑːt ˌgæləri/ *noun* ENTERTAINMENT a museum of paintings, drawings or sculptures

artichoke /ˈɑːtɪtʃəʊk/ *noun* VEGETABLES **1.** □ **(globe) artichoke** a green vegetable like the flower of a thistle **2.** □ **(Jerusalem) artichoke** a root vegetable like a bumpy potato

COMMENT: Globe artichokes are in fact a type of thistle; the flower heads are cut before the flowers open and are boiled; the soft bottom parts of the outer leaves are eaten, often with vinaigrette, and then the prickly 'choke' in the centre has to be removed, and the base of the flower (called the 'heart') is cut up and eaten with vinaigrette. The 'heart' can also be served by itself as a salad. In a restaurant, the artichoke will be prepared in the kitchen before serving, so that the customer can eat it without too much difficulty. Jerusalem artichokes are quite different plants, but have a similar taste to globe artichokes. The roots are thick and oddly-shaped; they are peeled and boiled like potatoes, and eaten with butter or other sauces, or made into soup.

artificial sweetener /ˌɑːtɪfɪʃ(ə)l ˈswiːt(ə)nə/ noun a synthetic substance used in place of sugar to sweeten food

arts festival /ˈɑːtz ˌfestɪv(ə)l/ noun ENTERTAINMENT a large-scale event in which performances, exhibitions and competitions in music, drama, painting and handicrafts take place

asap /ˌeɪ es eɪ ˈpiː/, **ASAP** abbreviation as soon as possible (informal) ○ I want it done asap.

ascorbic acid /əˌskɔːbɪk ˈæsɪd/ noun CATERING Vitamin C, found in fresh fruit

ASH /æʃ/ abbreviation Action on Smoking and Health

ashore /əˈʃɔː/ adverb SHIPS AND BOATS on land, or onto the land from a ship ○ Passengers can go ashore for a couple of hours to visit the town.

ashtray /ˈæʃtreɪ/ noun a container for putting ash and unsmoked parts of cigarettes and cigars ○ The table was covered with dirty plates and the ashtray was full. ○ In the smoking compartments, ashtrays are provided in the armrests of the seats.

asparagus /əˈspærəgəs/ noun VEGETABLES a cultivated plant the new shoots of which you eat as a vegetable

COMMENT: Asparagus is a type of fern; the new shoots appear above the ground in late spring, and are cut off at ground level. They should be boiled, and then can be eaten hot with melted butter, or cold or warm with a vinaigrette dressing. Asparagus can also be made into soup. In England, asparagus can be eaten with the fingers, dipping the tip of the spear into the dressing, and nibbling them down to the point where they stop being tender. In other countries, asparagus is eaten with a knife and fork.

aspic /ˈæspɪk/ noun FOOD **1.** jelly made from the cooked juices of meat, poultry or fish **2.** a form of salad, with small pieces of cold meat, poultry, eggs or vegetables set in firm aspic jelly in a mould

assign /əˈsaɪn/ verb **1.** to give a place to someone ○ He was assigned a room on the ground floor. **2.** to give someone a job of work ○ She was assigned the job of checking the bathrooms.

assist /əˈsɪst/ verb to help somebody ○ The courier assisted the tourists at the customs checkpoint. (NOTE: You assist someone **in** doing something or **to do** something or **with** something.)

assistance /əˈsɪst(ə)ns/ noun help ○ Handicapped travellers may need assistance with their baggage.

'…all travel insurers have an international emergency helpline and in serious situations you will be put through to an assistance company which will have a doctor on duty at the end of the line, and normally a local agent to arrange the necessary medical treatment' [Wanderlust]

assistant /əˈsɪst(ə)nt/ noun a person who helps someone, usually as a job

assistant manager /əˌsɪst(ə)nt ˈmænɪdʒə/ noun somebody who helps a manager

assistant waiter /əˌsɪst(ə)nt ˈweɪtə/ noun CATERING same as **commis waiter**

assisted passage /əˌsɪstɪd ˈpæsɪdʒ/ noun a journey for an immigrant to a foreign country which is partly paid for by the government of that country to encourage immigration

assurance, assure, assurer ♦ insure

ATB abbreviation AIR TRAVEL automatic ticket and boarding pass

Atkins diet /ˈætkɪnz ˌdaɪət/ noun a plan to help people lose weight that suggests that they should eat a lot of protein and fat but little carbohydrate

ATM /ˌeɪ tiː ˈem/ abbreviation FINANCE automatic teller machine

atmosphere /ˈætməsfɪə/ noun the general feeling at a party or in a place, etc. ○ The hotel has a very romantic atmosphere, set on the banks of a beautiful mountain lake.

ATOL /ˈætɒl/ abbreviation Air Travel Organisers' Licence

attach /əˈtætʃ/ verb to fasten or link something to something else ○ I am attaching a copy of my previous letter. ○ Please find attached a copy of my letter of June 24th. ○ The tables are attached to the floor so they cannot move, even if the sea is rough. ○ The bank attaches great importance to the deal.

attaché /əˈtæʃeɪ/ noun a junior diplomat who does special work in an embassy □ **attaché case** a small case for carrying papers and documents

attend /əˈtend/ verb to be present at an event ○ They organised the protest meeting in the kitchen, but only a few of the kitchen *staff attended.* ○ *The chairman has asked all managers to attend the meeting.*

attendant /ə'tendənt/ *noun* **1.** somebody who is on duty in a public place such as a museum **2.** somebody who is on duty to help customers

attend to /ə'tend tuː/ *verb* to give careful thought to something and deal with it ○ *The managing director will attend to your complaint personally.* ○ *We have brought in experts to attend to the problem of installing the new computer.*

attention /ə'tenʃən/ *noun* the act of giving careful thought to something or dealing with it ○ *Your orders will have our best attention.*

attractive /ə'træktɪv/ *adjective* interesting and able to stimulate the senses or the mind ○ *There are some attractive bargains in weekend breaks.* ○ *The attractive scenery round the lake makes the hotel very popular with older guests.*

aubergine /'əʊbəʒiːn/ *noun* VEGETABLES the shiny purple-black fruit of the eggplant *Solanum melongena*, used as a vegetable. Also called **eggplant**

COMMENT: A native of tropical Asia, it is sometimes called by its Indian name 'brinjal'. Aubergines are used in Mediterranean cooking, especially stuffed with meat, or cooked with tomatoes in ratatouille and in moussaka.

audit /'ɔːdɪt/ BUSINESS *noun* an examination of the books and accounts of a company ○ *to carry out the annual audit* ■ *verb* to examine the books and accounts of a company ○ *to audit the accounts* ○ *The books have not yet been audited.*

auditing /'ɔːdɪtɪŋ/ *noun* BUSINESS the act of examining the books and accounts of a company

auditor /'ɔːdɪtə/ *noun* somebody who audits ○ *The AGM appoints the company's auditors.*

COMMENT: Auditors are appointed by the company's directors and voted by the AGM. In the USA, audited accounts are only required by corporations which are registered with the Stock Exchange Commission, but in the UK all limited companies must provide audited annual accounts.

auditorium /ˌɔːdɪ'tɔːriəm/ *noun* a large hall in which people can watch or listen to something, e.g. a show, concert or lecture (NOTE: The plural form is **auditoriums** or **auditoria**.)

auditors' report /'ɔːdɪtəz rɪˌpɔːt/ *noun* BUSINESS a report written by a company's auditors after they have examined the accounts of the company, certifying that, in the opinion of the auditors, the accounts give a 'true and fair' view of the company's financial position

au gratin /ˌəʊ 'grætæn/ CATERING ♦ **gratin**

au jus /ˌəʊ 'juː/ *adjective* referring to meat that is served in its own cooking juices

au naturel /ˌəʊ ˌnætrjʊ'rel/ *adv, adj* served simply and plainly, e.g. uncooked or without seasoning or salt

auto /'ɔːtəʊ/ *noun* ROAD TRAVEL same as **car**

autobahn /'ɔːtəʊbɑːn/ *noun* a motorway in Germany, Austria and other German-speaking countries

auto insurance /ˌɔːtəʊ ɪn'ʃʊərəns/ *noun* FINANCE insurance covering a car, its driver and others

automatic /ˌɔːtə'mætɪk/ *adjective* working or taking place without any person making it happen

'…using the new automatic ticket and boarding pass, travellers carrying hand baggage only will be allowed to check themselves in for a flight simply by swiping the card against a magnetic reader before boarding. Trials in Switzerland suggest the entire checking process for hand baggage carriers can be reduced to around 20 seconds' [*Business Travel*]

'…airlines and airports have been working towards automated ticket and boarding passes – called ATB2s – for several years, to avoid the problem of airport overcrowding which could become worse as European deregulation stimulates more air travel. As a result, airlines are accelerating the installation of ATB2 technology' [*Times*]

automatic landing equipment /ˌɔːtəmætɪk 'lændɪŋ ɪˌkwɪpmənt/ *noun* AIR TRAVEL computerised equipment in an aircraft, which allows it to land in bad weather or when visibility is bad

automatic pilot /ˌɔːtəmætɪk 'paɪlət/ *noun* AIR TRAVEL computerised equipment in an aircraft which allows it to fly without intervention from the captain

automatic teller machine /ˌɔːtəmætɪk 'telə məˌʃiːn/ *noun* FINANCE same as **cash dispenser**

automatic ticket and boarding pass /ˌɔːtəmætɪk ˌtɪkɪt ənd 'bɔːdɪŋ ˌpɑːs/ *noun* AIR TRAVEL an electronic ticket, which contains information about the passenger and the reservation on a magnetic strip. Abbr **ATB**

Automobile Association /'ɔːtəməbiːl əˌsəʊsieɪʃ(ə)n/ *noun* ROAD TRAVEL a major motoring association in the United Kingdom. ◊ **RAC**

autopilot /'ɔːtəʊpaɪlət/ *noun* TRAVEL same as **automatic pilot**

autumn /'ɔːtəm/ *noun* the season of the year between summer and winter ○ *The airline is offering autumn breaks of two- or three-night stays in the capital.* ○ *Fares tend to go down in the autumn and rise again at Christmas.* (NOTE: US English uses **fall** in this meaning.)

availability /ə,veɪlə'bɪlɪti/ *noun* **1.** the fact of being easy to obtain □ **offer subject to availability** the offer is valid only if the goods or services are available **2.** AIR TRAVEL the number of tickets available for a flight at a certain price

available /ə'veɪləb(ə)l/ *adjective* possible to obtain or buy ○ *available in all branches* ○ *item no longer available* ○ *items available to order only* ○ *funds which are made available for investment in small businesses* □ **available capital** capital which is ready to be used

avalanche /'ævəlɑːntʃ/ *noun* a heavy mass of snow sliding down a mountainside

avalanche season /'ævəlɑːntʃ ,siːz(ə)n/ *noun* late spring, when increasing temperatures make the snow melt on high mountains, and cause avalanches

average /'æv(ə)rɪdʒ/ *noun* a number calculated by adding together several figures and dividing by the number of figures added ○ *the average for the last three months* or *the last three months' average* ■ *adjective* in the middle ○ *average sales per restaurant* ○ *the average occupancy rates for the last three months* ○ *the average increase in prices*

average achieved room rate /,æv(ə)rɪdʒ ə,tʃiːvd 'ruːm ,reɪt/ *noun* HOTELS the average price received for room sales in a hotel, calculated by dividing the total amount charged for all rooms, each night, by the number of rooms occupied

avocado /,ævə'kɑːdəʊ/ *noun* VEGETABLES the pear-shaped green fruit of a tree originally growing in South and Central America, but now cultivated in Israel, Spain, the United States and elsewhere

COMMENT: The fruit has a high protein and fat content, making it very nutritious. It is normally served as an hors d'oeuvre. The fruit is cut in half and the stone removed. The hollow left by the stone can be filled with shrimps, etc., or the fruit can be served with vinaigrette which is poured into the hollow ('avocado vinaigrette'). Avocado made into a puree is called 'guacamole'.

avoid /ə'vɔɪd/ *verb* to try not to do something, or not to collide with or meet somebody or something ○ *You must avoid travelling on Friday evenings.* ○ *If you leave before 3 p.m. you will avoid the rush hour traffic.* ○ *He should try to avoid fatty food.* (NOTE: You avoid something or avoid **doing** something.)

award /ə'wɔːd/ *noun* a prize, medal, document or money that is given to somebody to show recognition of something good that he or she has done □ **award-winning** having won a prize ○ *an award-winning restaurant*

away /ə'weɪ/ *adverb* not here, somewhere else ○ *The managing director is away on business.* ○ *My assistant is away sick.*

azo dye /'eɪzəʊ daɪ/ *noun* CATERING a substance extracted from coal tar and added to food to give it colour

COMMENT: Many of the azo dyes (such as tartrazine) provoke allergic reactions; some are believed to be carcinogenic.

B

baby /'beɪbi/ *noun* a very young child who is not yet old enough to talk or walk

baby-listening service /'beɪbi ˌlɪs(ə)nɪŋ ˌsɜːvɪs/ *noun* HOTELS a service provided by a hotel, with a small microphone to put over a baby's cot, so that the parents can hear if the baby cries when they are not in the room

baby-sit /'beɪbi sɪt/ *verb* to look after children while their parents are out

baby-sitter /'beɪbi ˌsɪtə/ *noun* somebody who baby-sits

baby-sitting service /'beɪbi ˌsɪtɪŋ ˌsɜːvɪs/ *noun* HOTELS a service provided by a hotel, where a baby-sitter comes to the hotel room to look after a baby when the parents are out of the room

bacillary /bə'sɪləri/ *adjective* MEDICAL referring to bacilli □ **bacillary dysentery** dysentery caused by the bacillus *Shigella* in contaminated food

bacillus /bə'sɪləs/ *noun* MEDICAL a bacterium shaped like a rod (NOTE: The plural form is **bacilli**.) □ **Bacillus cereus** a microorganism found in cereals such as rice

back /bæk/ *noun* **1.** the opposite side to the front ○ *Write your address on the back of the envelope.* ○ *The conditions of sale are printed on the back of the invoice.* **2.** the opposite part to the front ○ *We want two seats at the back of the plane.* ○ *If you sit at the back of the bus, you may feel travel sick.* ○ *They complained that they couldn't see the stage from the back of the stalls.* ■ *adjective* referring to the past □ **back rent** rent owed ○ *The company owes £100,000 in back rent.* ■ *verb* **1.** ROAD TRAVEL to drive a car backwards ○ *He backed into the parking space.* ○ *She backed into the car behind.* **2.** □ **to back a bill** to sign a bill promising to pay it if the person it is addressed to is not able to do so

back cabin /ˌbæk 'kæbɪn/ *noun* AIR TRAVEL a section of seating in the back part of a plane, usually reserved for economy class

backcountry snowboarding /ˌbækkʌntri 'snəʊbɔːdɪŋ/ *noun* SPORT snowboard riding that is done away from resorts or in specially marked areas

backdate /bæk'deɪt/ *verb* BUSINESS to put an earlier date on a cheque or invoice ○ *Backdate your invoice to April 1st.* ○ *The pay increase is backdated to January 1st.*

back door /ˌbæk 'dɔː/ *noun* a door at the rear of a building

background /'bækgraʊnd/ *noun* **1.** the experiences, including education and family life, which someone has had ○ *What is his background* or *Do you know anything about his background?* ○ *His background is in the fast-food business.* ○ *The company is looking for someone with a background of success in the international hotel field.* **2.** information about a situation ○ *She explained the background of the claim for compensation.* ○ *I know the contractual situation as it stands now, but can you fill in the background details?*

backhander /'bækˌhændə/ *noun* a sum of money given secretly and illegally to somebody to persuade him or her to help you (*informal*)

backlog /'bæklɒg/ *noun* work which has piled up waiting to be done ○ *The airport is trying to cope with a backlog of flights held up by fog.* ○ *My assistant can't cope with the backlog of paperwork.*

back-of-house services /ˌbæk əv ˌhaʊs 'sɜːvɪsɪz/ *plural noun* HOTELS services that are based in the back part of a hotel, e.g. cleaning and providing supplies for the restaurant and bar. Also called **back-of-the-house services**

back-of-the-house staff /ˌbæk əv ˌhaʊs 'stɑːf/ *noun* HOTELS staff who work in the back of a hotel, e.g. kitchen staff and cleaners

back out /ˌbæk 'aʊt/ *verb* **1.** to stop being part of a deal or agreement ○ *The bank backed out of the contract.* ○ *We had to cancel the project when our German partners backed out.* **2.** ROAD TRAVEL to drive a car backwards out of a place ○ *He backed out of the garage.*

backpack /ˈbækpæk/ *noun* a large bag carried on the back when walking ○ *I'll have to take something out of my backpack – it's much too heavy.* Also called **rucksack** ■ *verb* to go walking, carrying your gear in a backpack ○ *If you backpack, you will become aware of how difficult the terrain is.*

backpacker /ˈbækpækə/ *noun* somebody who travels, or goes walking, carrying a backpack ○ *We picked up two backpackers who were hitching a lift into the Rockies.*

backpacking /ˈbækpækɪŋ/ *noun* TOUR-ISM the activity of going on long-distance trips or walks, carrying your clothes and equipment in a backpack ○ *We went backpacking round Greece.*

back pay /ˈbæk peɪ/ *noun* salary which has not been paid ○ *I am owed £500 in back pay.*

back payment /ˈbæk ˌpeɪmənt/ *noun* a payment that is due

back pocket /ˌbæk ˈpɒkɪt/ *noun* a pocket in the back of a pair of trousers ○ *His wallet was stolen from his back pocket.*

back tax /ˈbæk tæks/ *noun* BUSINESS a tax which is owed

back-to-back arrangement /ˌbæk tə ˈbæk əˌreɪndʒmənt/ *noun* HOTELS an arrangement covering travel and hotel accommodation, organised so that when one group arrives they occupy the same rooms as the previous group, who leave by the same plane

back up /ˌbæk ˈʌp/ *verb* **1.** to help or support someone or something ○ *He brought along a file of documents to back up his claim.* ○ *The waiter said the manager had refused to back him up in his argument with the customer.* **2.** to become jammed, because of not being able to go forwards ○ *Following the accident, traffic backed up along the motorway for several miles.* **3.** US ROAD TRAVEL to make a car go backwards ○ *Can you back up, please? I want to get out of the parking lot.* (NOTE: The British English for this is simply to **back.**)

backup /ˈbækʌp/ *adjective* supporting or helping ○ *We offer a free backup service to customers.* ○ *After a series of sales tours by representatives, the sales director sends backup letters to all the contacts.* □ **backup copy** a copy of a computer disk to be kept in case the original disk is damaged or lost ■ *noun* US AIR TRAVEL a delay in a flight caused by too much air traffic

bacon /ˈbeɪkən/ *noun* MEAT salt meat from a pig, which is sliced into thin strips and cooked before serving (NOTE: There is no

plural form: *some bacon*; *a pound of bacon*; for a single piece say **a rasher.**) □ **bacon and eggs** fried bacon and fried eggs, usually served at breakfast

COMMENT: There are various types of bacon: back bacon (which has more meat) and streaky bacon (which has more fat); bacon can be smoked (i.e. cured in smoke) or unsmoked (also called 'green' in British English). In the United States, bacon is sliced more thinly and cooked more than in the United Kingdom and is called 'crispy bacon'. Bacon is mainly eaten at breakfast, but it is often used in sandwiches (such as bacon, lettuce and tomato or BLT).

bacteria /bækˈtɪəriə/ *plural noun* MEDICAL submicroscopic organisms which help in the decomposition of organic matter, some of which are permanently present in the intestines of animals and can break down food tissue, and some of which cause disease (NOTE: The singular form is **bacterium.**)

COMMENT: Bacteria can be shaped like rods (bacilli), like balls (cocci) or have a spiral form (such as spirochaetes). Bacteria, especially bacilli and spirochaetes, can move and reproduce very rapidly.

bacterial /bækˈtɪəriəl/ *adjective* MEDICAL relating to bacteria or caused by bacteria □ **bacterial growth** the growth of bacteria in food

'…short-life products which support bacterial growth, such as meat, fish, poultry and egg dishes, rice, pasta, mousses and fresh cream products' [*Caterer & Hotelkeeper*]

bacterial contamination /bækˌtɪəriəl kənˌtæmɪˈneɪʃ(ə)n/ *noun* CATERING the state of something such as water or food that has been contaminated by bacteria

bactericidal /bækˌtɪərɪˈsaɪdəl/ *adjective* MEDICAL referring to a substance that destroys bacteria

bactericide /bækˈtɪərɪsaɪd/ *noun* MEDICAL a substance that destroys bacteria

Baedeker /ˈbaɪˌdekə/ *noun* a guidebook for travellers

bag /bæg/ *noun* **1.** a soft container made of plastic, cloth or paper, and used for carrying things ○ *She brought her lunch in a Harrods bag.* ○ *We gave away 5,000 plastic bags at the exhibition.* **2.** a soft case for carrying clothes when travelling ○ *He left his bag in the cabin.* ○ *The porter will carry your bags to the room.*

bagel /ˈbeɪg(ə)l/ *noun* BREAD, ETC. a ring-shaped bread roll with a slightly chewy texture

baggage /ˈbægɪdʒ/ *noun* TRAVEL suitcases or bags for carrying clothes when travelling

(NOTE: There is no plural form: to show one suitcase, etc., you can say **a piece of baggage**. Note also that British English uses **luggage** more often than **baggage**.)

COMMENT: Certain items are not allowed onto aircraft, and should not be packed in baggage. These include ammunition, explosives, radioactive substances, flammable liquids, and compressed gases. Battery-driven appliances such as clocks should be declared when checking in.

baggage allowance /ˌbæɡɪdʒ əˈlaʊəns/ *noun* AIR TRAVEL the weight of baggage which an air passenger is allowed to take free when travelling. Also called **free baggage allowance** (NOTE: The baggage allowance is usually 30kg for first-class or business class passengers and 20kg for tourist class passengers.)

baggage cart /ˈbæɡɪdʒ kɑːt/ *noun US* same as **luggage trolley**

baggage check /ˈbæɡɪdʒ tʃek/ *noun* AIR TRAVEL **1.** an examination of passengers' baggage to make sure it contains nothing dangerous or illegal **2.** a receipt given to a passenger for baggage which has been checked in, and which is usually stapled to the passenger's ticket counterfoil

baggage check-in /ˈbæɡɪdʒ ˌtʃek ɪn/ *noun* AIR TRAVEL a place where air passengers have their bags and suitcases weighed and hand them over to be put on the aircraft

baggage handler /ˈbæɡɪdʒ ˌhændlə/ *noun* AIR TRAVEL somebody who works at an airport, taking baggage off or putting it on planes

baggage label /ˈbæɡɪdʒ ˌleɪb(ə)l/ *noun* TRAVEL a label attached to a piece of baggage, with the owner's name and address on it

baggage lift /ˈbæɡɪdʒ lɪft/ *noun* HOTELS same as **luggage lift**

baggage lockers /ˈbæɡɪdʒ ˌlɒkəz/ *plural noun* TRAVEL a set of small cupboards, e.g. in an airport or railway station, where passengers can leave baggage locked away safely

baggage rack /ˈbæɡɪdʒ ræk/ *noun* HOTELS same as **luggage rack**

baggage reclaim /ˈbæɡɪdʒ ˌriːkleɪm/ *noun* TRAVEL same as **luggage claim**

baggage room /ˈbæɡɪdʒ ruːm/ *noun US* same as **left luggage office** (NOTE: The British English is **left luggage office**.)

baggage stand /ˈbæɡɪdʒ stænd/ *noun* HOTELS same as **luggage stand**

baggage ticket /ˈbæɡɪdʒ ˈtɪkɪt/ *noun* a piece of paper showing that you have left a piece of baggage with someone

baggage trolley /ˈbæɡɪdʒ ˌtrɒli/ *noun* same as **luggage trolley**

bagna cauda /ˌbænjə ˈkaʊdə/ *noun* SAUCES, ETC. a warm sauce of olive oil, garlic and anchovies, served as a dip for raw vegetables

baguette /bæˈɡet/ *noun* BREAD, ETC. a long loaf of French bread

bain-marie /ˌbæn məˈriː/ *noun* CATERING a pan holding hot water into which another vessel containing food to be cooked or heated is placed (NOTE: The plural form is **bains-marie**.)

COMMENT: In a large kitchen, bains-marie are used to keep food hot: items of cooked food are placed in trays over hot water.

baize /beɪz/ *noun* a soft felt cloth, usually green

COMMENT: Baize is used to cover restaurant tables to prevent the tablecloth from slipping off, to cover card tables or billiard tables, and to cover the door leading from a kitchen into a dining room to prevent the door from banging.

bake /beɪk/ *verb* CATERING to cook in an oven ○ *To cook the dish, bake in a hot oven for 30 minutes.* ○ *Pizzas are baked in a pizza oven.* □ **to bake blind** to cook a pastry case without a filling by covering it with paper and weighting it down with dried peas

baked /beɪkt/ *adjective* CATERING cooked in an oven

baked Alaska /ˌbeɪkt əˈlæskə/ *noun* DESSERTS a dessert made of ice cream covered with meringue, baked in an oven for a short time to cook the meringue, eaten before the ice cream melts

baked apple /ˌbeɪkt ˈæp(ə)l/ *noun* DESSERTS an apple which has been cored and filled with raisins and brown sugar, then baked in an oven

baked beans /ˌbeɪkt ˈbiːnz/ *plural noun* FOOD haricot beans, cooked in a tomato sauce, traditionally baked in the oven with pieces of pork and molasses, and called 'Boston baked beans', but now more generally available in cans

baked potato /ˌbeɪkt pəˈteɪtəʊ/ *noun* FOOD a potato cooked 'in its jacket', that is, baked in an oven without being peeled, then served cut open, with butter or various fillings such as cheese, chopped ham, baked beans, chilli, etc. Also called **jacket potato**

baker /ˈbeɪkə/ *noun* a person whose job is to make bread and cakes

bakery /'beɪkəri/, **baker's shop** noun a shop where bread is baked and sold

Bakewell tart /ˌbeɪkwel 'tɑːt/ noun DESSERTS a tart that has a pastry base covered with jam and topped with almond-flavoured sponge

baking /'beɪkɪŋ/ noun a method of cooking by placing something such as a bread or cake mixture in an oven

baking apple /'beɪkɪŋ ˌæp(ə)l/ noun FRUIT same as **cooking apple**

baking dish /'beɪkɪŋ dɪʃ/ noun CATERING a fireproof dish which can be put in the oven

baking powder /'beɪkɪŋ ˌpaʊdə/ noun a mixture containing sodium bicarbonate, starch and acids that is used to make cakes rise when they are cooked

baking sheet /'beɪkɪŋ ʃiːt/, **baking tray** /'beɪkɪŋ treɪ/ noun a flat sheet of metal for baking e.g. biscuits on

baking soda /'beɪkɪŋ ˌsəʊdə/ noun sodium bicarbonate, especially when used as a raising agent in cookery

baklava /bæk'lɑːvə/ noun DESSERTS a Turkish or Greek dessert made of thin pastry filled with chopped nuts and covered with honey

balance brought forward, **balance carried forward** noun FINANCE a balance which is entered in an account at the end of a period and is then taken to be the starting point of the next period

balanced diet /ˌbælənst 'daɪət/ noun a diet which contains the right quantities of basic nutrients

balance in hand /ˌbæləns ɪn 'hænd/ noun BUSINESS cash held to pay small debts and running costs. Also called **cash in hand**

balance sheet /'bæləns ʃiːt/ noun BUSINESS a statement of the financial position of a company at a particular time, such as the end of the financial year or the end of a quarter, showing the company's assets and liabilities ○ *The company balance sheet for 2001 shows a substantial loss.* ○ *The accountant has prepared the balance sheet for the first half-year.*

COMMENT: The balance sheet shows the state of a company's finances at a certain date; the profit and loss account shows the movements which have taken place since the end of the previous accounting period. A balance sheet must balance, with the basic equation that assets (i.e. what the company owns, including money owed to the company) must equal liabilities (i.e. what the company owes to its creditors) plus capital (i.e. what it owes to its shareholders). A balance sheet can be drawn up either in the horizontal form, with liabilities and capital on the left-hand side of the page (in the United States, it is the reverse) or in the vertical form, with assets at the top of the page, followed by liabilities, and capital at the bottom. Most are usually drawn up in the vertical format, as opposed to the more old-fashioned horizontal style.

balcony /'bælkəni/ noun **1.** a small terrace jutting out from the upper level of a building ○ *Each room has a balcony overlooking the sea.* ○ *Breakfast is served on the balcony.* **2.** ENTERTAINMENT an upstairs section of the auditorium of a theatre or cinema, above the stalls (NOTE: The plural form is **balconies**.)

ball /bɔːl/ noun ENTERTAINMENT a formal dance

balloon /bə'luːn/ noun **1.** a large round object which is inflated **2.** CATERING a brandy glass with a wide body tapering to a narrower mouth

ballooning /bə'luːnɪŋ/ noun the sport of racing large passenger-carrying balloons

ballroom /'bɔːlruːm/ noun a large room for formal dances

ball supper /'bɔːl ˌsʌpə/ noun CATERING a supper consisting of many light dishes, served as a continuous buffet during a ball

balsamic vinegar /bɒlˌsæmɪk 'vɪnɪgə/ noun SAUCES, ETC. thick rich Italian vinegar from unfermented grape juice, stored for years in wooden barrels

balti /'bælti/ noun a spicy dish originally from Pakistan that is traditionally served in the bowl-shaped pan it is cooked in

bamboo shoots /bæm'buː ʃuːt/ plural noun VEGETABLES young shoots from the bamboo plant, used in Chinese and Malaysian cooking

banana /bə'nɑːnə/ noun FRUIT the long yellow curved fruit of a large tropical plant

banana split /bəˌnɑːnə 'splɪt/ noun a dessert made of a banana cut lengthwise and filled with ice cream, cream and chocolate sauce

band /bænd/ noun ENTERTAINMENT a group of people who play music together

bandage /'bændɪdʒ/ MEDICAL noun a piece of cloth which is wrapped around a wound or an injured limb ○ *The waitress had a bandage round her hand.* ■ *verb* to wrap a piece of cloth around a wound or an injured limb ○ *She bandaged his leg* ○ *His arm is bandaged up.*

bandana /bæn'dænə/ noun a long scarf worn tied around your head to stop your hair from falling over your eyes or into food. ◊ **toque**

b. & b., **B & B** *abbreviation* HOTELS bed and breakfast

banger /'bæŋə/ *noun* MEAT a sausage (*informal*)

bangers and mash /ˌbæŋəz ənd 'mæʃ/ *noun* FOOD grilled sausages and mashed potatoes

bank /bæŋk/ *noun* **1.** the edge of a river, canal or lake **2.** FINANCE a business which holds money for its clients, which lends money at interest, and trades generally in money ◊ *He put all his earnings into his bank.* ◊ *I have had a letter from my bank telling me my account is overdrawn.* ◊ *Payment was made by a cheque drawn on a Swiss bank.* **3.** ENTERTAINMENT the money held by the organiser in a gambling game ■ *verb* FINANCE to deposit money into a bank or to have an account with a bank ◊ *He banked the cheque as soon as he received it.* □ **where do you bank?** where do you have a bank account? ◊ *I bank at* or *with Barclays.*

bank account /'bæŋk əˌkaʊnt/ *noun* FINANCE an account which a customer has with a bank, where the customer can deposit and withdraw money ◊ *to open a bank account* ◊ *to close a bank account* ◊ *How much money do you have in your bank account?* ◊ *If you let the balance in your bank account fall below £100, you have to pay bank charges.*

banker's order /'bæŋkəz ˌɔːdə/ *noun* FINANCE same as **standing order** ◊ *He pays his subscription by banker's order.*

bank holiday /ˌbæŋk 'hɒlɪdeɪ/ *noun* a public holiday when most people do not go to work and the banks are closed

COMMENT: Bank holidays in England and Wales are: New Year's Day, Good Friday, Easter Monday, the first Monday in May (May Day), the last Monday in May (Spring Bank Holiday), the last Monday in August (Summer Bank Holiday), Christmas Day and Boxing Day (December 26th). In Scotland, the first Monday in August and January 2nd are also Bank Holidays, but Easter Monday and the last Monday in August are not. In the United States, New Year's Day, 21st January (Martin Luther King Day), February 12th (Lincoln's birthday), the third Monday in February (Washington's birthday), the last Monday in May (Memorial Day), July 4th (Independence Day), the first Monday in September (Labor Day), the second Monday in October (Columbus Day), 11th November (Veterans' Day), the fourth Thursday in November (Thanksgiving) and Christmas Day are public holidays nationally, although there are other local holidays.

banking /'bæŋkɪŋ/ *noun* BUSINESS the business done by banks

banking account /'bæŋkɪŋ əˌkaʊnt/ *noun* FINANCE same as **bank account**

banking hours /'bæŋkɪŋ ˌaʊəz/ *plural noun* FINANCE the time when a bank is open for its customers ◊ *You cannot get money out of a bank outside banking hours.*

banking services /'bæŋkɪŋ ˌsɜːvɪsɪz/ *plural noun* FINANCE the services provided by a bank, e.g. withdrawal of money, cashing cheques and foreign currency exchange ◊ *Banking services are available in the departure lounge on the second floor.*

bank manager /'bæŋk ˌmænɪdʒə/ *noun* FINANCE somebody in charge of a branch of a bank ◊ *She asked her bank manager for a loan.*

bank note /'bæŋknəʊt/, **banknote** *noun* FINANCE a piece of printed paper money ◊ *He pulled out a pile of used bank notes.* (NOTE: The US English is **bill**.)

bank on /'bæŋk ɒn/ *verb* to be sure that something will happen ◊ *He is banking on getting a loan from his father to set up his restaurant.* ◊ *Do not bank on having fine weather in November.*

bank statement /'bæŋk ˌsteɪtmənt/ *noun* FINANCE a written statement from a bank showing how much money is in an account and what transactions have been made

banoffee /bæ'nɒfi/ *noun* a creamy filling made from bananas and soft toffee, in a pastry or biscuit base

banquet /'bæŋkwɪt/ *noun* CATERING a large formal dinner for many people

banqueting /'bæŋkwɪtɪŋ/ *noun* CATERING the work of arranging or giving large formal dinners

banqueting chef /'bæŋkwɪtɪŋ ʃef/ *noun* CATERING a chef who specialises in cooking for formal dinners ◊ *He worked as a banqueting chef in a large London hotel.*

banqueting manager, **banquets manager** *noun* HOTELS somebody in a hotel who is responsible for organising formal functions

banqueting room /'bæŋkwɪtɪŋ ruːm/ *noun* HOTELS a room in a hotel where banquets are organised

banqueting suite /'bæŋkwɪtɪŋ swiːt/ *noun* a series of rooms where banquets are organised

banquette /'bɒnkeɪt/ noun CATERING a seat along a wall in a restaurant ○ *Shall we sit on the banquette?*

'...banquette seating secures privacy' [*Evening Standard, Business Travel section*]

bap /bæp/ noun BREAD, ETC. a small round loaf of white bread

bar /bɑː/ noun 1. BARS a place where you can buy and drink alcohol ○ *The group met in the bar of the hotel.* 2. BARS a long counter in a pub from which drinks are served ○ *The bar only opens at 6 p.m.* ○ *He was sitting at the bar.* 3. CATERING a small shop, serving one special type of food

barback /'bɑːbæk/ noun a person whose job is to ensure that a bar is kept clean and supplied with drinks

barbecue /'bɑːbɪkjuː/ CATERING noun 1. food cooked in the open air, over a charcoal fire ○ *Here is a recipe for chicken barbecue.* 2. a meal or party, where the food is cooked on a barbecue ○ *We held a barbecue for twenty guests.* ○ *They were invited to a barbecue.* 3. a metal holder for charcoal over which food is cooked in the open air ○ *Light the barbecue at least half an hour before you start cooking.* ■ *verb* to cook food over a barbecue ○ *She was barbecuing sausages for lunch when it started to rain.* ○ *Barbecued spare ribs are on the menu.*

barbecue sauce /ˌbɑːbɪkjuː 'sɔːs/ noun a spicy sauce containing tomato, chilli and garlic, used on barbecued meat

barber /'bɑːbə/ noun somebody who cuts men's hair

COMMENT: Traditionally, a barber's shop has a red and white pole outside, as an advertisement.

barber's shop /'bɑːbəz ʃɒp/, **barber shop** /'bɑːbə ʃɒp/ noun a shop where men have their hair cut

bar chart /'bɑː tʃɑːt/ noun a diagram where quantities and values are shown as thick columns of different heights or lengths

bar code /'bɑː kəʊd/ noun BUSINESS a system of lines printed on a product which can be read by a computer to give a reference number or price. Also called **Universal Product Code**

COMMENT: Bar codes are found on most goods and their packages; the width and position of the stripes can be recognised by a bar-code reader and give information about the goods, such as price, stock quantities, etc. Many packaged foods, even fresh foods, are bar-coded to allow quicker data capture in the supermarket.

bard /bɑːd/ verb CATERING to put a strip of fat or fatty meat, such as a rasher of bacon, over meat to prevent it from drying out when cooking

bareboat charter /'beəbəʊt ˌtʃɑːtə/ noun SHIPS AND BOATS a system of chartering a ship where the owner provides only the ship, but not the crew, fuel or insurance

bargain /'bɑːɡɪn/ noun 1. an agreement on the price of something □ **to drive a hard bargain** to be a difficult negotiator □ **to strike a hard bargain** to agree a deal which is favourable to you □ **it is a bad bargain** it is not worth the price 2. something bought more cheaply than usual ○ *That car is a (real) bargain at £500.* ■ *verb* to discuss the terms of an agreement or sale ○ *You will have to bargain with the shopkeeper if you want a discount.* ○ *They spent two hours bargaining about* or *over the price.* (NOTE: You bargain **with** someone **over** or **about** or **for** something.)

bargain sale /ˌbɑːɡɪn 'seɪl/ noun MARKETING the sale of all goods in a store at cheap prices

barley /'bɑːli/ noun FOOD a common cereal crop *Hordeum sativum*, grown in temperate areas

COMMENT: Barley is grown in colder countries; it is used in the production of beer and whisky; it is also used to make Scotch broth.

barley sugar /'bɑːli ˌʃʊɡə/ noun FOOD a sweet made of boiled sugar, originally flavoured with barley

barley wine /'bɑːli waɪn/ noun BEVERAGES a very strong beer

barmaid /'bɑːmeɪd/ noun BARS a woman who serves in a bar ○ *She works as a barmaid in the local pub.*

barman /'bɑːmən/ noun BARS a man who serves in a bar ○ *The barman didn't know how to make cocktails.* (NOTE: The plural form is **barmen**.)

COMMENT: In the UK the terms 'barman' and 'barmaid' are not used in job advertisements to avoid sex discrimination; 'barperson' is used instead.

barometer /bə'rɒmɪtə/ noun an instrument for measuring atmospheric pressure, and therefore for forecasting the weather

barometric /bærə'metrɪk/ adjective referring to a barometer

barometric pressure /ˌbærəmetrɪk 'preʃə/ noun atmospheric pressure indicated by a barometer

barperson /'bɑːˌpɜːs(ə)n/ noun BARS a man or woman who serves in a bar

barrel /'bærəl/ *noun* a large round container for liquids ○ *beer served from the barrel* ○ *to sell wine by the barrel*

barrier cream /'bæriə kri:m/ *noun* a cream used to prevent damage to the skin from the sun

bar service /'bɑ: ˌsɜ:vɪs/ *noun* **1.** service in a bar **2.** a system where the customer orders, pays for and collects a drink or food from a bar

bar snacks /'bɑ: snæks/ *plural noun* CATERING small items of food available in a bar, e.g. pies or sandwiches

bar staff /'bɑ: stɑ:f/ *noun* BARS people who work in a bar in a hotel or behind a bar in a pub

bar stool /'bɑ: stu:l/ *noun* BARS a high seat used for sitting at a bar or counter

bartender /'bɑ:tendə/ *noun* BARS somebody who serves in a bar

bar trolley /'bɑ: ˌtrɒli/ *noun* AIR TRAVEL same as **drinks trolley**

base jumping /'beɪs ˌdʒʌmpɪŋ/ *noun* the extreme sport of parachuting from the tops of very tall natural objects or buildings

basement /'beɪsmənt/ *noun* an underground section of a building ○ *The central heating boiler is in the basement.*

basic discount /ˌbeɪsɪk 'dɪskaʊnt/ *noun* a normal discount without extra percentages ○ *We give 25% as a basic discount, but can add 5% for cash payment.*

basic pay /ˌbeɪsɪk 'peɪ/, **basic salary** /ˌbeɪsɪk 'sæləri/ *noun* BUSINESS a normal salary without extra payments

basic tax /'beɪsɪk tæks/ *noun* BUSINESS tax paid at the usual rate

basic wage /ˌbeɪsɪk 'weɪdʒ/ *noun* BUSINESS normal pay without any extra payments ○ *The basic wage is £110 a week, but you can expect to earn more than that with overtime.*

basil /'bæz(ə)l/ *noun* SAUCES, ETC. a herb *Ocimum basilicum* with strongly scented leaves, used especially in Italian cuisine

basin /'beɪs(ə)n/ *noun* a large bowl

basket /'bɑ:skɪt/ *noun* a container made of thin pieces of wood, wire or fibre woven together ○ *a basket of apples*

basket meal /'bɑ:skɪt mi:l/ *noun* CATERING a simple meal, usually of fried chicken, sausage or scampi, served in a basket with chips

basmati /bæz'mɑ:ti/ *noun* FOOD a type of long-grained rice with a special smell and flavour

bass /beɪs/ *noun* a type of fish that is found in rivers, lakes and seas and is caught for food

baste /beɪst/ *verb* CATERING to pour melted fat and juices over meat as it is cooking ○ *Don't forget to baste the chicken two or three times while it is roasting.*

bath /bɑ:θ/ *noun* **1.** the process of washing your whole body ○ *He has a cold bath every evening.* ○ *Baths are 200 francs extra.* ◊ **bubble bath, jacuzzi, Turkish bath** □ **to have a bath, to take a bath** to wash the whole body in a bath **2.** same as **bathtub** ○ *The chambermaid has not cleaned the bath.* (NOTE: The US English is **bathtub** or **tub**.) ■ *verb* to wash yourself or someone else in a bath ○ *She baths twice a day in hot weather.*

bathe /beɪð/ *noun* a swim, especially in the sea or in a river ○ *We went for a bathe before breakfast.* ■ *verb* **1.** to swim **2.** MEDICAL to wash something such as a wound carefully **3.** *US* to have a bath

bather /'beɪðə/ *noun* somebody who is swimming ○ *The beach was crowded with bathers when the shark was sighted.*

bathing /'beɪðɪŋ/ *noun* the activity of swimming in the sea, river or a pool ○ *The bathing is very safe here because the water is shallow.*

bathing cap /'beɪðɪŋ ˌkæp/ *noun* a rubber hat worn when swimming to prevent your hair getting wet

bathing costume /'beɪðɪŋ ˌkɒstju:m/ *noun* SPORT same as **swimming costume**

bath mat /'bɑ:θ mæt/ *noun* a small mat to step on as you get out of the bath

bath oil /'bɑ:θ ɔɪl/ *noun* scented oil to put in a bath

Bath Oliver /ˌbɑ:θ 'ɒlɪvə/ *noun* BREAD, ETC. a kind of round unsweetened biscuit, served with cheese

bathrobe /'bɑ:θrəʊb/ *noun* **1.** a loose coat of towelling worn before or after a bath **2.** *US* a man's dressing gown

bathroom /'bɑ:θru:m/ *noun* **1.** a room in a house or hotel with a bath, a washbasin and usually a toilet □ **room with private bathroom** *or* **with its own bathroom** hotel room with its own bathroom attached **2.** a room containing a toilet (*said instead of*) ○ *Where's the bathroom?* ○ *My daughter wants to go to the bathroom.*

bathroom fittings /'bɑ:θru:m ˌfɪtɪŋz/ *plural noun* fittings in a bathroom, such as a shower, wash basin, bidet, etc.

bathroom linen /'bɑ:θru:m ˌlɪnən/ *noun* towels and other cloth articles that are provided in a bathroom ○ *Guests complained that there was no fresh bathroom linen.*

bath salts /'bɑːθ sɔːlts/ *plural noun* scented crystals to put in a bath

bathtowel /'bɑːθtaʊəl/ *noun* a very large towel for drying yourself after a bath ○ *Remind me to give you a clean bathtowel.*

bathtub /'bɑːθtʌb/ *noun especially US* a large container filled with water to wash the whole body in. Also called **bath** *noun* 2, **tub** (NOTE: The British English term is **bath.**)

batter /'bætə/ *noun* FOOD a thin liquid mixture of flour, eggs and milk, used e.g. for making pancakes or toad-in-the-hole, or for coating fish before frying

battered /'bætəd/ *adjective* CATERING covered with batter and cooked ○ *battered prawns*

battery /'bæt(ə)ri/ *noun* **1.** an object that fits into a piece of electrical equipment to provide it with electric energy ○ *My calculator needs a new battery.* ○ *The battery has given out so I can't use my radio.* ○ *My mobile phone has a rechargeable battery.* **2.** a series of small cages in which thousands of chickens are kept

battery farming /'bæt(ə)ri ˌfɑːmɪŋ/ *noun* a system of keeping thousands of chickens in a series of small cages

COMMENT: Battery farming is a method of egg production which is very energy-efficient. It is criticised, however, because of the quality of the eggs, the possibility of disease and the polluting substances produced, and also on grounds of cruelty because of the stress caused to the birds.

battery hen /'bæt(ə)ri hen/ *noun* a chicken which spends its life confined in a small cage

battle site /'bæt(ə)l saɪt/ *noun* a place where a battle was fought

bay /beɪ/ *noun* **1.** SAUCES, ETC. a fragrant shrub whose leaves are used in cooking **2.** a large rounded inlet in a coast ○ *the Bay of Biscay* ◊ **Dublin Bay prawn**

BBQ *abbreviation* CATERING barbecue

beach /biːtʃ/ *noun* an area of sand or small stones by the edge of the sea ○ *They spent the afternoon on the beach.* ○ *You can hire parasols on the beach.* ○ *There are lifeguards on duty at the beach.*

beach chalet /'biːtʃ ˌʃæleɪ/ *noun* a small wooden holiday home, near or on a beach

beach hotel /'biːtʃ həʊˌtel/ *noun* a hotel that is on or near a beach

beach hut /'biːtʃ hʌt/ *noun* a small wooden building on a beach, where you can change, keep deckchairs, etc.

beach towel /'biːtʃ ˌtaʊəl/ *noun* a large towel usually used on the beach

beach umbrella /'biːtʃ ʌmˌbrelə/ *noun* a large coloured umbrella to use on a beach

bean /biːn/ *noun* VEGETABLES **1.** a seed or the long thin pod of various different plants, cooked and eaten ○ *runner beans* ○ *butter beans* **2.** a dried seed that is ground and is used in cooking or to make drinks ○ *coffee beans*

COMMENT: Kidney beans must be cooked thoroughly, as undercooked beans can contain a toxin which causes nausea.

bean curd /'biːn kɜːd/ *noun* same as **tofu**

bean sprouts /'biːn spraʊts/ *plural noun* VEGETABLES shoots of beans, eaten especially in Chinese cooking

bear /beə/ *noun* a large wild animal covered with fur ○ *There are bears near the campsite in the mountains.*

'…the danger Arctic explorers fear most is the polar bear' [*TGO – The Great Outdoors*]

béarnaise sauce /ˌbeəneɪz 'sɔːs/ *noun* a savoury sauce for meat, thickened with egg yolk and flavoured with tarragon

beat /biːt/ *verb* **1.** to win a game against another player or team ○ *They have beaten their rivals into second place in the package holiday market.* **2.** □ **to beat a ban** to do something which is forbidden by doing it rapidly before the ban is enforced **3.** to mix fast ○ *Beat the egg whites in a bowl.* (NOTE: **beating – beat – has beaten**)

Beaufort scale /'bəʊfət skeɪl/ *noun* a scale from 0 to 12 used to refer to the strength of wind

COMMENT: The Beaufort scale was devised in the 18th century by a British admiral. The descriptions of the winds and their speeds in knots are: 0: calm (0 knots); 1: light air (2 knots); 2: light breeze (5 knots); 3: gentle breeze (9 knots); 4: moderate breeze (13 knots); 5: fresh breeze (19 knots); 6: strong breeze (24 knots); 7: near gale (30 knots); 8: gale (37 knots); 9: strong gale (44 knots); 10: storm (52 knots); 11: violent storm (60 knots); 12: hurricane (above 60 knots).

Beaujolais /'bəʊʒəleɪ/ *noun* BEVERAGES a light French red wine from Burgundy which can be drunk cool

Beaujolais Nouveau /ˌbəʊʒəleɪ nuː 'vəʊ/ *noun* BEVERAGES Beaujolais wine which has just been made, sold from November onwards of the year in which the grapes are picked

beauty /'bjuːti/ *noun* the quality of being beautiful

beauty parlour /'bjuːti ˌpɑːlə/ *noun* a shop specialising in women's appearance. Also called **beauty salon**, **beauty shop**

beauty spot /'bjuːti spɒt/ *noun* a famous beautiful place ○ *The Lake District has some of the most famous beauty spots in England.*

béchamel sauce /ˌbeʃəmel 'sɔːs/ *noun* a rich sauce made from milk thickened with butter and flour and served hot

bed /bed/ *noun* a piece of furniture on which you sleep

bed, breakfast and evening meal /ˌbed ˌbrekfəst ənd ˌev(ə)nɪŋ 'miːl/ *noun* HOTELS a tariff in a hotel or guesthouse, covering a night's accommodation, breakfast and a meal taken in the evening

bed and board /ˌbed ən 'bɔːd/ *noun* a hotel charge that includes all meals as well as the room charge

bed and breakfast /ˌbed ən 'brekfəst/ *noun* HOTELS **1.** a tariff in a hotel or guesthouse, covering a night's lodging and breakfast ○ *bed and breakfast: £32.00* ○ *I only want to have bed and breakfast.* **2.** a guesthouse or private house, offering accommodation and breakfast ○ *We got a list of bed and breakfasts* or *B&Bs from the tourist office.* ▶ abbr **B & B**

bedclothes /'bedkləʊðz/ *plural noun* the coverings, e.g. sheets and blankets, on a bed

bedcover /'bedkʌvə/ *noun* a cloth which covers a bed during the daytime

bedding /'bedɪŋ/ *noun* the items, e.g. a mattress, sheets and pillows, that are put on a bed so that somebody can sleep in it ○ *Bedding is provided at extra cost.* ○ *Visitors are requested to bring their own bedding.*

bed linen /'bed ˌlɪnɪn/ *noun* sheets, pillowcases or duvet covers

bednight /'bednaɪt/ *noun* HOTELS one night's stay in a hotel, as considered for administrative purposes

'…the group is offering regional corporate deals, based on a minimum number of bednights: for example, 100 bednights would trigger a discount of a minimum of 10%, while over 1,000 bednights could mean up to a 45% discount' [*Business Traveller*]

bedroom /'bedruːm/ *noun* a room with a bed, in which someone sleeps ○ *a 42-bedroom hotel*

bedroomed /'bedruːmd/ *adjective* with a particular number of bedrooms ○ *a 42-bedroomed hotel*

bedside /'bedsaɪd/ *noun* a space at the side of a bed □ **bedside lamp** a lamp next to a bed □ **bedside table** a table next to a bed

bedside panel /ˌbedsaɪd 'pæn(ə)l/ *noun* HOTELS an electronic device placed on a guest's beside table, with controls for heating, lighting, air-conditioning, automatic curtain pulling, messaging, etc.

'…hanging the 'Do Not Disturb' sign on your door is so 20th century. Now bedside panels which allow you to adjust the room environment from the comfort of your bed may eradicate such hotel inconveniences. At home you have a bedtime routine, but in a strange hotel room you're constantly jumping out of bed to draw curtains or turn off lights. Now it's all in one place' [*National Geographic Traveler*]

bed-sitting room /bed'sɪtɪŋ ruːm/, **bed-sitter** /'bedsɪtə/, **bed-sit** /'bedsɪt/ *noun* a bedroom and living room combined

bedspread /'bedspred/ *noun* a decorative cloth to put over a bed

bedstead /'bedsted/ *noun* the solid frame of a bed

bed tax /'bed tæks/ *noun* a tax charged per occupant of a room in a hotel or other tourist accommodation

beef /biːf/ *noun* MEAT meat from a cow or a bull

beefburger /'biːfbɜːgə/ *noun* MEAT a round, flat cake of minced beef, grilled or fried and usually served in a toasted bread roll. Also called **burger**, **hamburger**

beef olives /ˌbiːf 'ɒlɪvz/ *plural noun* FOOD a dish made from thin slices of beef, stuffed and rolled

beefsteak /'biːfsteɪk/ *noun* MEAT same as **steak**

beefsteak tomato /ˌbiːfsteɪk tə'mɑːtəʊ/ *noun* VEGETABLES a large fleshy variety of tomato suitable for stuffing

beef stir-fry /ˌbiːf 'stɜː ˌfraɪ/ *noun* FOOD thin strips of beef cooked quickly with vegetables in hot oil

beef stroganoff /ˌbiːf 'strɒgənɒf/ *noun* a dish consisting of thin strips of beef cooked with onions and mushrooms in a sour cream sauce

beef suet /ˌbiːf 'suːɪt/ *noun* FOOD suet from cattle

beef Wellington /ˌbiːf 'welɪŋtən/ *noun* a dish consisting of a fillet of beef covered in pâté de foie gras, wrapped in pastry, and baked

beer /bɪə/ *noun* BEVERAGES **1.** an alcoholic drink made from grain and water ○ *She asked room service for a bottle of beer.* ○ *He drank a glass of beer.* **2.** a glass of beer ○ *Two beers, please.* ◊ **draught**, **real ale**

COMMENT: In Great Britain, the most popular beers are 'bitter' and 'lager'. 'Lager' is sold cold, but 'bitter' is served slightly cooler than room temperature. In Australia and the USA, all beers are served cold. Beer is either served from a bottle (or a can if you are buying it to drink away from the place where you bought it), but in pubs, can be served direct from the barrel. This is called 'draught beer'. In Great Britain, draught beer is sold in a glass mug (with a handle) or in a tall straight glass. Bottled beer is usually served in a goblet (i.e. a glass with a stem).

beer cellar /'bɪə ˌselə/ *noun* BARS a cellar where beer is kept or served

beer festival /'bɪə ˌfestɪv(ə)l/ *noun* **1.** a festival to celebrate the making of beer ○ *the Munich Beer Festival* **2.** an exhibition for advertising, sampling and selling different types of beer

beer garden /'bɪə ˌgɑːd(ə)n/ *noun* BARS a garden attached to a pub, in which people can sit to have their drinks

beermat /'bɪəmæt/ *noun* a small cardboard mat, usually with an advertisement for a brewery on it, placed under a glass to protect a surface in a pub or restaurant

beer pull, beer pump handle *noun* BARS one of a series of tall handles arranged on the bar of a pub, which draw beer up from casks in the cellar when pulled towards the bartender

beet /biːt/ *noun* US VEGETABLES same as **beetroot**

beetle /'biːt(ə)l/ *noun* an insect with hard covers that protect its folded wings

beetroot /'biːtruːt/ *noun* a vegetable with a dark red root, often eaten cooked as salad, or pickled with vinegar (NOTE: The US term is **beet**.)
  COMMENT: In Russian cuisine, beetroot is the main ingredient of borscht.

behave /bɪ'heɪv/ *verb* to act ○ *One of the group started to behave very strangely.*

behaviour /bɪ'heɪvjə/ *noun* a way of doing things ○ *Guests complained about the behaviour of young men in the bar on Saturday night.* (NOTE: The US spelling is **behavior**.)

bell /bel/ *noun* **1.** a metal cup-shaped object which makes a ringing sound when hit, or a mechanism to make a similar ringing sound **2.** □ **to give someone a bell** to phone someone (*informal*) ○ *I'll give you a bell when we've sorted out the details.*

bellboy /'belbɔɪ/, **bellhop** US /'belhɒp/ *noun* HOTELS a messenger boy employed in a hotel

bell captain /'bel ˌkæptɪn/ *noun* US HOTELS somebody in charge of the messengers in a hotel

bellpush /'belpʊʃ/ *noun* a button which rings a bell when pushed

below-the-line advertising /bɪˌləʊ ðə laɪn 'ædvətaɪzɪŋ/ *noun* MARKETING advertising that is not paid for, such as work by staff manning an exhibition, and for which no commission is paid to the advertising agency

benchmarking /'bentʃmɑːkɪŋ/ *noun* the process of comparing the performance of firms within an industry against a set of standards

Bermuda plan /bə'mjuːdə plæn/ *noun* a hotel tariff including accommodation and a full English or an American breakfast

berry /'beri/ *noun* FRUIT a small fleshy seed-bearing fruit of a bush, usually with many seeds in the same fruit, and the seeds enclosed in a pulp. ◊ **blackberry, blueberry, raspberry, strawberry** (NOTE: The plural form is **berries**.)
  COMMENT: Very many berries are used in cooking, or can be eaten raw.

berth /bɜːθ/ *noun* **1.** SHIPS AND BOATS a place in a harbour where a ship can tie up ○ *There are six ferry berths at Dover.* **2.** TRAVEL a bed on a ship or a train ■ *verb* TRAVEL to tie up at a berth ○ *The ship will berth at Rotterdam on Wednesday.*
  '…hire this new ship for the day when it is berthed alongside HMS Belfast in the Port of London from 23–28 June' [*Evening Standard*]

best-before date /ˌbest bɪ 'fɔː deɪt/ *noun* CATERING a date stamped on the label of a food product, which is the last date on which the product is guaranteed to be of good quality. Compare **sell-by date, use-by date**

best end /'best end/ *noun* MEAT a cut of meat, especially lamb, taken from the neck and formed of a series of chops joined together. ◊ **crown roast, rack of lamb**

best practice /ˌbest 'præktɪs/ *noun* the most effective and efficient method of achieving an aim or providing a service

Best Practice Forum /ˌbest 'præktɪs ˌfɔːrəm/ *noun* a system sponsored by the UK government to encourage high standards of professionalism in the hotel, catering and tourism industries

better /'betə/ *adjective* of higher quality than something else ○ *This year's results are better than last year's.* ○ *We will shop around to see if we can get a better price.*

beurre manié /ˌbɜː 'mænieɪ/ *noun* FOOD a mixture of butter and flour, added at the last minute to soups or stews to make them thicken (NOTE: **beurre manié** comes from the French and means 'kneaded butter'.)

beverage /'bev(ə)rɪdʒ/ *noun* a drink, either alcoholic or non-alcoholic

beverage cycle /'bev(ə)rɪdʒ ˌsaɪk(ə)l/ *noun* BUSINESS the cycle by which beverages pass from supplier to hotel or restaurant and then to the ultimate consumer

beverage manager /'bev(ə)rɪdʒ ˌmænɪdʒə/ *noun* BUSINESS somebody in charge of sales of drinks in a hotel

beverage sales /'bev(ə)rɪdʒ seɪlz/ *plural noun* BUSINESS the turnover from the sale of drinks

beware /bɪ'weə/ *verb* □ **beware of** watch out for ○ *'Beware of pickpockets!'*

BFL *abbreviation* business facilitated lease

BHA *abbreviation* HOTELS British Hospitality Association

bhaji /'bɑːʒi/ *noun* an Indian food, consisting of chopped vegetables in a spicy batter, deep-fried ○ *onion bhaji*

bhindi /'bɪndi/ *noun* VEGETABLES okra, as used in Indian cooking

B hotel /'biː ˌhəʊtel/, **B tariff hotel** /'biː ˌtærɪf ˌhəʊtel/ *noun* HOTELS same as **four-star hotel**

'...an increasing number of business travellers from the US and Europe are becoming budget conscious and are spending less on hotel accommodation and are staying in B tariff hotels. Such hotels usually have the same service and facilities as five-star hotels, except that the rooms may be slightly smaller and the decor may be different' [*South China Morning Post*]

BHT *abbreviation* butylated hydroxytoluene

bicarb /'baɪkɑːb/ *noun* FOOD same as **sodium bicarbonate** (*informal*)

bicarbonate of soda /baɪˌkɑːbənət əv 'səʊdə/ *noun* same as **sodium bicarbonate**

bicycle /'baɪsɪk(ə)l/ *noun* ROAD TRAVEL a vehicle with two wheels, which you ride on and pedal with your feet ○ *Bicycles can be hired by the hour or by the day.* Also called **pushbike**

bicycle path, **bike path** *noun* ROAD TRAVEL a special path for bicycles to ride on, either by the side of a road or as part of the pavement

bidet /'biːdeɪ/ *noun* a small low bath for washing your buttocks ○ *Each bathroom has a shower and a bidet.*

big game /ˌbɪg 'geɪm/ *noun* large wild animals which are hunted and killed for sport, e.g. elephants, tigers and lions

bike /baɪk/ *noun* ROAD TRAVEL same as **bicycle** (*informal*)

biker /'baɪkə/ *noun* ROAD TRAVEL somebody who rides a motorcycle ○ *A gang of bikers arrived in the village.*

biking /'baɪkɪŋ/ *noun* the activity of travelling on a bicycle ○ *They went for a biking holiday in Holland.*

bilberry /'bɪlb(ə)ri/ *noun* FRUIT a wild berry, which is blue when ripe, eaten raw with sugar and cream, or cooked in pies and jams ○ *The menu includes bilberry tarts.*

bi-level suite /ˌbaɪ ˌlev(ə)l 'swiːt/ *noun* a hotel suite that has rooms on two floors

Bilharzia /bɪl'hɑːtsiə/ *noun* MEDICAL a parasitic worm that enters the patient's bloodstream and causes bilharziasis

bilharziasis /ˌbɪlhɑː'saɪəsɪs/ *noun* MEDICAL a tropical disease caused by parasitic worms in the intestine or bladder (NOTE: Although, strictly speaking, **Bilharzia** is the name of the fluke, it is also generally used for the name of the disease.)

COMMENT: The disease is found in certain parts of Africa, Brazil and China and can be caught from bathing in rivers and lakes. The larvae of the fluke enter the skin through the feet and lodge in the walls of the intestine or bladder. They are passed out of the body in stools or urine and return to water, where they lodge and develop in the water snail, the secondary host, before going back into humans. Patients suffer from fever and anaemia.

bill /bɪl/ *noun* **1.** a written list of charges to be paid ○ *The receptionist printed out the bill.* ○ *Does the bill include VAT?* ○ *The bill is made out to Smith Ltd.* ○ *He left the hotel without paying his bill.* **2.** a list of charges in a restaurant ○ *Can I have the bill please?* ○ *The bill comes to £20 including service.* ○ *The waiter has added 10% to the bill for service.* ■ *verb* to present a bill to someone so that it can be paid ○ *The tour operators billed him for the extra items.*

billiards /'bɪliədz/ *noun* ENTERTAINMENT a game involving hitting balls with a long rod on a smooth table covered with green cloth, the object being to hit a white ball so that it sends a ball of another colour into one of the 'pockets' at the edge of the table. ◊ **pool**, **snooker** □ **billiard ball** a small hard ball used in the game of billiards □ **billiard room** a room in a hotel or pub with a billiard table □ **billiard table** a table on which billiards is played

billion /'bɪljən/ *noun* one thousand million (NOTE: In the US **billion** has always meant one thousand million, but in British English it formerly meant one million million, and is still sometimes used with this meaning.

With figures it is usually written **bn**: *$5bn* say 'five billion dollars'.)

bill of exchange /ˌbɪl əv ɪksˈtʃeɪndʒ/ *noun* FINANCE a document signed by the person authorising it, which tells, e.g. a bank to pay money unconditionally to a named person on a particular date

COMMENT: A bill of exchange is a document raised by a seller and signed by a purchaser, stating that the purchaser accepts that he owes the seller money, and promises to pay it at a later date. The person raising the bill is the 'drawer', the person who accepts it is the 'drawee'. The seller can then sell the bill at a discount to raise cash. This is called a 'trade bill'. A bill can also be accepted (i.e. guaranteed) by a bank, and in this case it is called a 'bank bill'.

bill of fare /ˌbɪl əv ˈfeə/ *noun* CATERING a menu

bin /bɪn/ *noun* **1.** a large container **2.** a section in a warehouse, store or wine cellar □ **a 32-bin wine list** a wine list with 32 sections □ **bin card** a card saying what is stored in the bin, e.g. the type and date of wine

binder /ˈbaɪndə/ *noun US* FINANCE same as **cover note**

binding /ˈbaɪndɪŋ/ *adjective* **1.** □ **this contract is binding on both parties** both parties have to do what the contract says **2.** the act of sticking things together ■ *noun* a small belt for attaching boots to skis

binding agent /ˌbaɪndɪŋ ˈeɪdʒ(ə)nt/ *noun* CATERING an additive which makes prepared food remain in its proper form and not disintegrate

biodegradability /ˌbaɪəʊdɪgreɪdəˈbɪlɪti/ *noun* the degree to which a material, e.g. packaging, can be decomposed by organisms such as bacteria or by the effect of sunlight or the sea

biodegradable /ˌbaɪəʊdɪˈgreɪdəb(ə)l/ *adjective* easily decomposed by organisms such as bacteria or by the effect of sunlight or the sea □ **biodegradable packaging** boxes, cartons, bottles, etc., which can be decomposed by organisms such as bacteria or by the effect of sunlight or the sea

'…human sewage is a totally biodegradable product, and sea and sunlight will break it down through the natural process of oxidation' [*Environment Now*]

COMMENT: Manufacturers are trying to produce more biodegradable products, as the effect of non-biodegradable substances (such as PVC) on the environment can be serious.

biodegradation /ˌbaɪəʊdegrəˈdeɪʃ(ə)n/ *noun* the breaking down of a substance by bacteria

biotechnology /ˌbaɪəʊtekˈnɒlədʒi/ *noun* the use of technology to manipulate and combine different genetic materials to produce living organisms with particular characteristics ○ *Artificial insemination of cattle was one of the first examples of biotechnology.* ○ *A biotechnology company is developing a range of new pesticides based on naturally occurring toxins.*

birdwatcher /ˈbɜːdwɒtʃə/ *noun* ENTERTAINMENT somebody who looks at birds for pleasure, or for scientific purposes ○ *Birdwatchers set up hides all round the lake.* (NOTE: A fanatical birdwatcher is called a **twitcher**.)

birdwatching /ˈbɜːdwɒtʃɪŋ/ *noun* ENTERTAINMENT the activity of looking at birds for pleasure, or for scientific purposes ○ *He goes birdwatching every weekend.* ○ *She belongs to a birdwatching club.*

birth certificate /ˈbɜːθ səˌtɪfɪkət/ *noun* a document which shows when and where someone was born

biryani /ˌbɪriˈjɑːni/ *noun* FOOD in South Asian cooking, a dish containing spicy coloured rice mixed with meat, fish or vegetables

biscotto /bɪsˈkɒtəʊ/ *noun* a hard oblong biscuit, often containing nuts

biscuit /ˈbɪskɪt/ *noun* FOOD a small hard cake, usually sweet

bisque /biːsk/ *noun* FOOD a cream soup made with shellfish ○ *lobster bisque*

bistro /ˈbiːstrəʊ/ *noun* a small restaurant or bar

bitter /ˈbɪtə/ *adjective* not sweet ○ *This aperitif is very bitter.* ○ *Marmalade is made from bitter oranges.* ■ *noun* BEVERAGES British beer, made bitter by adding hops ○ *She asked for a half of bitter.* ○ *Two pints of bitter, please.*

bitter lemon /ˌbɪtə ˈlemən/ *noun* a fizzy nonalcoholic drink flavoured with lemon

bitter orange /ˌbɪtə ˈɒrɪndʒ/ *noun* FRUIT same as **Seville orange**

bitters /ˈbɪtəz/ *noun* BEVERAGES same as **Angostura bitters**

black /blæk/ *adjective* of a very dark colour, the opposite of white ■ *verb* BUSINESS to forbid trading in particular goods or with particular suppliers ○ *Three firms were blacked by the government.* ○ *The union has blacked the hotel chain.*

black bean /ˈblæk biːn/ *noun* a black-seeded soya bean that is fermented for use in East Asian cookery

blackberry /ˈblækb(ə)ri/ *noun* FRUIT a small soft black berry, growing on plants with long spines, eaten in jams and pies. Also called **bramble**

blackboard /ˈblækbɔːd/ *noun* a board on a wall, which can be written on using white chalk ○ *Some dishes are not on the menu, but are written on a blackboard.*

black box /ˌblæk ˈbɒks/ *noun* AIR TRAVEL same as **flight recorder** ○ *After a crash, the first thing crash investigators do is to find the plane's black box.*

black bread /ˌblæk ˈbred/ *noun* a very dark rye bread that is particularly popular in Germany and Slavic countries

black coffee /ˌblæk ˈkɒfi/ *noun* BEVERAGES coffee without milk or cream

blackcurrant /ˌblækˈkʌrənt/ *noun* FRUIT a small round cultivated black berry, eaten cooked in jams and pies, used also in making soft drinks and liqueurs ○ *blackcurrant yoghurt* ○ *a pot of blackcurrant jam* ○ *a glass of blackcurrant juice* ◊ **kir**

black economy /ˌblæk ɪˈkɒnəmi/ *noun* BUSINESS work which is paid for in cash or goods, but not declared to the tax authorities

black-eyed bean /ˌblæk aɪd ˈbiːn/ *noun* a small beige bean with a black spot

Black Forest /ˌblæk ˈfɒrɪst/ *noun* an area of forest in south-west Germany

Black Forest gâteau /ˌblæk ˌfɒrɪst ˈgætəʊ/ *noun* DESSERTS a chocolate cake with cream and cherry filling covered with whipped cream and chocolate shavings

black market /ˌblæk ˈmɑːkɪt/ *noun* a system for buying and selling goods in a way which is not allowed by law, e.g. in a time of rationing ○ *There is a flourishing black market in secondhand jeans.* ○ *You can buy gold coins on the black market.* □ **to pay black-market prices** to pay high prices to get items which are not easily available

black olive /ˌblæk ˈɒlɪv/ *noun* VEGETABLES a ripe olive

blackout /ˈblækaʊt/ *noun* AIR TRAVEL a day, usually a public holiday, when cheaper fares are not available on flights

black pepper /ˌblæk ˈpepə/ *noun* dark brown seasoning made by grinding pepper seeds that have not had their black outer covering removed

black pudding /ˌblæk ˈpʊdɪŋ/ *noun* MEAT a dark sausage made with blood, usually fried in slices and eaten for breakfast

black tie /ˌblæk ˈtaɪ/ *adjective* referring to a formal evening banquet or reception at which men wear a bow tie and dinner jacket, both usually black ○ *The invitation to the gala performance was marked 'black tie'.* ◊ **white tie**

black treacle /ˌblæk ˈtriːk(ə)l/ *noun* FOOD same as **treacle**

blade /bleɪd/ *noun* **1.** the sharp cutting part of a knife **2.** SPORT a sharp metal strip attached to a boot to make an ice skate. ◊ **rollerblades**

blanch /blɑːntʃ/ *verb* CATERING to cook vegetables for a short time in boiling water

COMMENT: Vegetables should be blanched before being frozen. They can also be blanched before frying. Nuts and vegetables can also be blanched to remove their skins.

blancmange /bləˈmɒnʒ/ *noun* a cold dessert similar to jelly made with milk, sugar, flavourings and cornflour

bland /blænd/ *adjective* referring to food which is not spicy, irritating or acid □ **bland diet** a diet which contains mainly milk-based foods, boiled vegetables and white meat

blanket /ˈblæŋkɪt/ *noun* a thick cover which you put over you to keep warm ○ *Ask the reception for another blanket if you are cold.* ○ *Stewardesses bring round blankets and pillows on overnight flights.*

blanquette /blɒnˈket/ *noun* a dish consisting of white meat such as veal cooked in a white sauce

blast chiller /ˈblɑːst ˌtʃɪlə/ *noun* CATERING a machine for chilling food in a blast of freezing air ○ *It is best to use a blast chiller to cool hot food rapidly.*

blast freezing /ˈblɑːst ˌfriːzɪŋ/, **blast chilling** /ˈblɑːst ˌtʃɪlɪŋ/ *noun* CATERING a method of quick-freezing oddly shaped food, by subjecting it to a blast of freezing air

blend /blend/ *noun* a mixture, used especially of mixtures of different types of tea ■ *verb* to mix things together ○ *Blend together the melted butter and sugar.*

blender /ˈblendə/ *noun* CATERING a kitchen device for mixing different food items together thoroughly

blind /blaɪnd/ *noun* **1.** a covering over a window ○ *The maid closed the blinds to keep out the sun.* **2.** □ **the blind** people who cannot see ■ *adjective* not able to see ■ *adverb* without seeing □ **to taste blind** to taste a series of items, such as cheeses or wines, without being able to see their labels ○ *This evening we have 37 wines to taste blind.*

blind-tasting /'blaɪn ˌteɪstɪŋ/ *noun* ENTERTAINMENT a party where a series of items, such as cheeses or wines, are tasted without the tasters being able to see their labels ○ *a table with a series of bottles of sweet wine lined up for the blind-tasting*

blini /'bliːni/ *noun* BREAD, ETC. a small pancake made with yeast and buckwheat flour, traditional in Russia and other parts of Eastern Europe

blizzard /'blɪzəd/ *noun* a heavy snowstorm with strong winds

bloater /'bləʊtə/ *noun* SEAFOOD a dried whole salt herring

block /blɒk/ *noun* a group of things together ○ *They booked a block of seats in the middle of the plane.* ■ *verb* □ **to block a room** to keep a room reserved for someone who has booked it, so as to prevent double-booking

block booking /ˌblɒk 'bʊkɪŋ/ *noun* HOTELS a reservation in which a series of, e.g. seats or hotel rooms are all booked at the same time

blood poisoning /'blʌd ˌpɔɪz(ə)nɪŋ/ *noun* MEDICAL a condition in which bacteria are present in the blood and cause illness

Bloody Mary /ˌblʌdi 'meəri/, **bloody mary** *noun* BEVERAGES a cocktail of vodka and tomato juice with ice and Worcester sauce, lemon juice, salt and pepper

bloom /bluːm/ *noun* **1.** a powdery substance on the surface of a fruit such as grapes **2.** fine hair on the skin of some fruit such as peaches **3.** a flower □ **the apple trees are in full bloom** the apple trees are in flower

blowfly /'bləʊflaɪ/ *noun* the name for a number of species of fly, which deposit their eggs in flesh, especially meat

blow torch /'bləʊ tɔːtʃ/ *noun* CATERING a device which produces a gas flame used to heat the surface of dishes such as crème brûlée

BLT /ˌbiː el 'tiː/ *abbreviation* CATERING bacon, lettuce and tomato in a sandwich

blueberry /'bluːb(ə)ri/ *noun* FRUIT a wild berry, which is dark blue when ripe, eaten raw with sugar and cream, or cooked in pies and jams ○ *a portion of blueberry pie and whipped cream* ○ *Two blueberry muffins and coffee, please.*

bluebottle /'bluːˌbɒt(ə)l/ *noun* a two-winged fly, with a shining blue body, whose maggots live in decomposing meat

blue channel /'bluː ˌtʃæn(ə)l/ *noun* BUSINESS the exit from customs through which you pass if you are arriving from another EU country and are not importing goods which are liable to duty

blue cheese /ˌbluː 'tʃiːz/ *noun* DAIRY a type of cheese with blue fungus growth in it, e.g. Stilton or Roquefort

blue-cheese dressing /ˌbluː tʃiːz 'dresɪŋ/ *noun* SAUCES, ETC. a dressing for salad, made of mayonnaise or vinaigrette with blue cheese in it

blue flag beach /ˌbluː flæg 'biːtʃ/ *noun* a beach with sea water that meets the cleanliness requirements of the European Commission

Blue Ribbon Award /ˌbluː 'rɪbən əˌwɔːd/ *noun* HOTELS an award given by the RAC to hotels which are committed to high standards ○ *This year, there are 76 Blue Ribbon Award winners.*

BMC *abbreviation* SPORT British Mountaineering Council

board /bɔːd/ *noun* **1.** HOTELS meals at a hotel **2.** □ **to go on board** to go onto a ship, plane or train **3.** BUSINESS a group of people who run an organisation ○ *The bank has two representatives on the board.* ○ *Two directors were removed from the board at the AGM.* ◊ **board of directors, tourist board** □ **she was asked to join the board** she was asked to become a director □ **board meeting** a meeting of the directors of a company ■ *verb* AIR TRAVEL to go onto a ship, plane or train ○ *Customs officials boarded the ship in the harbour.* ○ *The party will board buses at the temple and proceed to the hotel for lunch.*

board and lodging /ˌbɔːd ən 'lɒdʒɪŋ/ *noun* room and food ○ *Board and lodging for three nights comes to £175.00.* Also called **room and board**

boarding /'bɔːdɪŋ/ *noun* TRAVEL the act of going onto a ship, plane or train ○ *Have your passport ready before boarding.*

boarding card /'bɔːdɪŋ kɑːd/, **boarding pass** US /'bɔːdɪŋ pɑːs/ *noun* AIR TRAVEL a card given to passengers who have checked in for a flight to allow them to board the plane, or a card given to passengers going on board a ship

boarding house /'bɔːdɪŋ haʊs/ *noun* TOURISM a small, privately run house where residents pay for accommodation and meals

board of directors /ˌbɔːd əv daɪ'rektəz/ *noun* BUSINESS a group of directors elected by the shareholders to run a company

COMMENT: Directors are elected by shareholders at the AGM, though they are usually chosen by the chairman or chief executive. A board will consist of a chairman (who may be non-executive), a chief executive or managing director, and a series of specialist directors in charge of various activities of the company (such as a finance director, production director or sales director). The company secretary will attend board meetings, but need not be a director. Apart from the executive directors, who are in fact employees of the company, there may be several non-executive directors, appointed either for their expertise and contacts, or as representatives of important shareholders such as banks.

boardroom /'bɔːdruːm/ *noun* a room where the directors of a company meet

boast /bəʊst/ *verb* to possess something, and be proud of it ○ *The hotel complex boasts an 18-hole golf course.*

boat /bəʊt/ *noun* a small vehicle that people use for moving on water ○ *rowing boat*

boatel /bəʊ'tel/ *noun* a waterside hotel where people travelling in boats can stay and moor them

boating /'bəʊtɪŋ/ *noun* SPORT the activity of going in small boats for pleasure, especially rowing or sailing ○ *a boating holiday on the Norfolk Broads*

-bodied /bɒdid/ *suffix* with a particular type of body

body /'bɒdi/ *noun* AIR TRAVEL the main part of an aircraft

boil /bɔɪl/ *verb* CATERING **1.** to heat water until it reaches 100°C ○ *You must boil the water* or *You must let the water boil before making tea.* ○ *They recommend you to boil the tap water before drinking it.* **2.** to cook something by putting it in boiling water ○ *Do you want boiled potatoes or chips with your steak?* ○ *The cabbage has been boiled too long.* ○ *I want my eggs boiled for three minutes.*

boil down /ˌbɔɪl 'daʊn/ *verb* to make a liquid mixture thicker by heating it rapidly until much of the liquid turns to steam

boiled egg /ˌbɔɪld 'eg/ *noun* FOOD an egg which has been cooked by boiling in water

boiled hock /ˌbɔɪld 'hɒk/ *noun* MEAT a joint of ham from the leg of a pig

boiler /'bɔɪlə/ *noun* CATERING a piece of kitchen equipment, which heats water for making hot drinks and also provides steam

boiling chicken, boiling fowl *noun* MEAT a chicken which is older and tougher and needs to be boiled to make it tender

boiling pan /'bɔɪlɪŋ pæn/ *noun* CATERING a large container used in a kitchen for boiling food and making soup

boil-in-the-bag /ˌbɔɪl ɪn ðə 'bæg/ *adjective* CATERING stored in a sealed plastic bag

and cooked by placing the bag in boiling water ○ *boil-in-the-bag frozen boeuf bourguignon*

boil off /ˌbɔɪl 'ɒf/ *verb* to remove liquid, e.g. alcohol, from a mixture by heating the mixture rapidly so that the liquid turns to steam

boil over /ˌbɔɪl 'əʊvə/ *verb* to reach boiling point and be so full of bubbles that some liquid spills from the container

bok choy /ˌbɒk 'tʃɔɪ/ *noun* VEGETABLES a Chinese cabbage with long white stalks and narrow green leaves

bolster /'bəʊlstə/ *noun* **1.** a long thick pillow, which is as wide as a double bed **2.** a thick round part of a knife, linking the blade to the handle

bombay mix /ˌbɒmbeɪ 'mɪks/ *noun* a spiced mixture of fried lentils and other dried foods, eaten as a snack or appetiser

bond /bɒnd/ *noun* FINANCE a piece of paper showing that money has been deposited □ **to post a bond** to deposit money with an organisation, as a form of surety ○ *The company was required to post a bond with ABTA.* ■ *verb* BUSINESS to deposit money with an organisation as surety against potential future loss ○ *The travel centre was bonded through the Association of British Travel Agents.*

'…the company is a fully bonded member of ABTA, which gives you that extra security and financial peace of mind. You know your money is secure.' [*Travel company brochure*]

bone /bəʊn/ *noun* one of the solid pieces in the body, which make up the skeleton ■ *verb* to take the bones out of something such as a chicken ○ *The rabbit is skinned, boned and then marinaded.* (NOTE: For fish, it is more usual to say 'to fillet' before the fish is cooked, or 'to debone' at table.)

boneless /'bəʊnləs/ *adjective* referring to meat or fish from which the bones have been removed in preparation for cooking or eating

boner /'bəʊnə/ *noun* CATERING a kitchen tool designed for boning meat or fish

boning /'bəʊnɪŋ/ *noun* the action of removing the bones from a chicken, rabbit, etc. ○ *the intricate boning of a quail*

book /bʊk/ *noun* a set of sheets of paper attached together ■ *verb* to reserve a place, a seat, a table in a restaurant or a room in a hotel ○ *to book a room in a hotel* or *a table at a restaurant* or *a ticket on a plane* ○ *I booked a table for 7.45.* ○ *He booked a ticket through to Cairo.* □ **to book someone into a hotel** *or* **onto a flight** to order a room or a plane ticket for someone ○ *He was booked* *onto the 09.00 flight to Zurich.* □ **the hotel** *or* **the flight** *or* **the restaurant is fully booked** *or* **is booked up** all the rooms or seats are reserved ○ *The restaurant is booked up over the Christmas period.* □ **to book someone in** to register somebody when he or she arrives at a hotel □ **to book someone out** to deal with the paperwork when somebody leaves a hotel, e.g. presenting the bill and getting it paid. ◊ **double-book**

booking /'bʊkɪŋ/ *noun* an arrangement to have something such as a seat, hotel room or a table in a restaurant kept for you ○ *Hotel bookings have fallen since the end of the tourist season.* □ **to make a booking** to reserve a room, a seat, a table, etc. ○ *We tried to make a booking for the week beginning May 1st, but the hotel was full.* □ **to confirm a booking** to say that a booking is certain

booking charge /'bʊkɪŋ tʃɑːdʒ/ *noun* ENTERTAINMENT money paid to an agency for their services in addition to the cost of the ticket when you buy a ticket through them. Also called **booking fee**

booking clerk /'bʊkɪŋ klɑːk/ *noun* ENTERTAINMENT somebody who sells tickets in a booking office

booking code /'bʊkɪŋ kəʊd/ *noun* AIR TRAVEL same as **fare code**

booking fee /'bʊkɪŋ fiː/ *noun* same as **booking charge**

booking form /'bʊkɪŋ fɔːm/ *noun* a form to be filled in when making a booking

booking office /'bʊkɪŋ ˌɒfɪs/ *noun* ENTERTAINMENT an office where you can book seats at a theatre or tickets for the railway

bookkeeping /'bʊkkiːpɪŋ/ *noun* BUSINESS the work of keeping the financial records of a company or an organisation

booklet /'bʊklət/ *noun* a small book with a paper cover

book sales /'bʊk seɪlz/ *plural noun* BUSINESS sales as recorded in the sales book

book up /ˌbʊk 'ʌp/ *verb* HOTELS to fill all the rooms in a hotel, all the tables in a restaurant or all the seats in a theatre

book value /'bʊk ˌvæljuː/ *noun* BUSINESS value as recorded in the company's books

booth /buːð/ *noun* a small place for one person, or a small group of people, to stand or sit

booze cruise /'buːz kruːz/ *noun* a trip across the English Channel to buy alcoholic drinks in a country where they cost less than they do in the United Kingdom (*informal*)

boracic acid /bəˌræsɪk 'æsɪd/, **boric acid** /ˌbɔːrɪk 'æsɪd/ *noun* a soluble white powder used as a general disinfectant. Symbol H_3BO_3

borax /'bɔːræks/ *noun* a white powder used as a household cleaner and disinfectant

Bordeaux /bɔː'dəʊ/ *noun* BEVERAGES wine from the west of France ○ *Some Bordeaux would be excellent with the venison.* ○ *I've ordered a bottle of Bordeaux.*

border /'bɔːdə/ *noun* a line that marks the point where one country or region ends and another begins

border crossing /'bɔːdə ˌkrɒsɪŋ/ *noun* TRAVEL a place on the border between two countries where people can cross and where there are passport controls and customs posts

borscht /bɔːʃt/ *noun* FOOD Russian soup, made with beetroot, other vegetables and small pieces of meat or sausage. It is eaten either cold or hot, with sour cream.

botanical gardens /bəˌtænɪk(ə)l 'ɡɑːd(ə)nz/ *noun* ENTERTAINMENT gardens which are set up for scientific study and the display of plants ○ *When you are in Hong Kong you must visit the botanical gardens.*

botel /bəʊ'tel/ *noun* SHIPS AND BOATS same as **boatel**

botrytised *adjective* CATERING made from grapes affected by Botrytis, which gives the wine a particularly sweet taste, or specially made to resemble this wine, possibly by adding sweeteners ○ *botrytised dessert wine*

bottle /'bɒt(ə)l/ *noun* a container for liquids, with a narrow neck, made of glass or plastic ○ *Can I have a bottle of mineral water, please.* ○ *She drank three bottles of lemonade.* ○ *He bought his wife a bottle of perfume in the duty-free shop.* ■ *verb* **1.** to put in bottles **2.** CATERING to preserve something by heating it inside a glass jar with a suction cap

COMMENT: Wine bottles have distinctive shapes. Burgundy, Beaujolais and Loire wines have bottles with tapered necks and wide bodies; Bordeaux wine bottles have shoulders and straight sides. German wine bottles have long tapering necks and taller, thinner bodies than French bottles.

bottled beer /ˌbɒt(ə)ld 'bɪə/ *noun* BEVERAGES beer in a bottle, as opposed to beer in a can, or draught beer

bottled water /ˌbɒt(ə)ld 'wɔːtə/ *noun* BEVERAGES water sold in bottles, as opposed to tap water

bottleneck /'bɒt(ə)lnek/ *noun* ROAD TRAVEL a narrow road where traffic often gets jammed

bottle opener /'bɒt(ə)l ˌəʊp(ə)nə/ *noun* BARS a device for opening bottles

bottom line /ˌbɒtəm 'laɪn/ *noun* FINANCE the last line in accounts, showing the net profit

botulism /'bɒtʃʊlɪz(ə)m/ *noun* MEDICAL a type of food poisoning caused by badly canned or preserved food

COMMENT: The symptoms include paralysis of the muscles, vomiting and hallucinations. Botulism is often fatal.

boudin /'buːdæn/ *noun* MEAT a French sausage similar to black pudding

bouillabaisse /ˌbuːjə'bes/ *noun* FOOD French fish soup, flavoured with olive oil and saffron

bouldering /'bəʊldərɪŋ/ *noun* SPORT rock climbing that involves undertaking short and extremely difficult slopes

bouncer /'baʊnsə/ *noun* somebody at the door of a club, whose job it is to prevent non-members or other unwanted guests from entering

bouncing cheque /ˌbaʊnsɪŋ 'tʃek/ *noun* FINANCE a cheque that cannot be cashed because the person writing it has not enough money in the account to pay it (*informal*) Also called **dud cheque**, **rubber cheque**

bound for /'baʊnd fɔː/ *adjective* going towards ○ *a ship bound for India*

bouquet garni /ˌbuːkeɪ gɑː'niː/ *noun* SAUCES, ETC. a bundle of herbs, used to flavour soups and stews, usually formed of thyme, parsley and bay leaves

bourbon /'bɜːbən/ *noun* US BEVERAGES corn whisky ○ *She drank a couple of bourbons* or *a couple of glasses of bourbon.*

bourguignonne /ˌbɔːgɪ'njɒn/ *adjective* cooked in a red wine sauce with mushrooms and small whole onions, in a style that originated in the Burgundy region of France

boutique /buː'tiːk/ *noun* a small specialised shop, especially for fashionable clothes, or a section of a department store selling fashionable clothes ○ *a jeans boutique* ○ *a ski boutique*

boutique hotel /buː'tiːk ˌhəʊtel/ *noun* HOTELS a usually small, up-market hotel, which has been designed by an interior decorator, and is considered very fashionable

'…having turned vintage properties into boutique hotels in the 1990s, smart contemporary designers now eye once-neglected motels, transforming them into stylish but affordable lodgings that stake out the middle ground between fashion and function' [*National Geographic Traveler*]

bovine /'bəʊvaɪn/ *adjective* referring to cattle

bovine spongiform encephalopathy /ˌbəʊvaɪn ˌspʌndʒɪfɔːm enˌkefə'lɒpəθi/ *noun* MEDICAL a fatal disease of cattle, affecting the nervous system. Abbr **BSE**

'BSE first appeared on English dairy farms in 1987. By December, 1988, 1,677 cattle had been slaughtered after contracting the infection. BSE is a new addition to a group of animal viruses known for about 200 years' [*Guardian*]

bow /baʊ/ *noun* SHIPS AND BOATS the front part of a ship

bowl /bəʊl/ *noun* a wide shallow container used for holding something such as food or liquids ○ *There was a bowl of fruit in the room with the compliments of the management.* ○ *She only had a bowl of muesli for breakfast.*

box /bɒks/ *noun* **1.** a cardboard, wood or plastic container ○ *The goods were sent in thin cardboard boxes.* ○ *The watches are prepacked in plastic display boxes.* **2.** ENTERTAINMENT a special section in a theatre, with chairs for two or three spectators

boxed /bɒkst/ *adjective* put in a box, or sold in a box

boxed set /ˌbɒkst 'set/ *noun* a set of items sold together in a box ○ *I bought him a boxed set of Beethoven's symphonies.*

box file /'bɒks faɪl/ *noun* a file for papers made like a box

box office /'bɒks ˌɒfɪs/ *noun* ENTERTAINMENT an office at a theatre or cinema where tickets can be bought

brace /breɪs/ *noun* (*of game birds*) a pair □ **a brace of pheasant(s)** a male and female bird sold together

brace position /'breɪs pəˌzɪʃ(ə)n/ *noun* AIR TRAVEL a position for an emergency landing, where the passenger sits bent forward with the hands behind the head

braise /breɪz/ *verb* CATERING to cook meat or vegetables in a covered pot with very little liquid ○ *I am going to braise the beef and onions.*

braised /breɪzd/ *adjective* CATERING cooked in a covered pot with very little liquid ○ *braised cabbage* ○ *braised beef and onions*

braising steak /'breɪzɪŋ steɪk/ *noun* MEAT good-quality beef suitable for braising

bramble /'bræmb(ə)l/ *noun* FRUIT a wild blackberry

bramble jelly /ˌbræmb(ə)l 'dʒeli/ *noun* FOOD jam made with blackberries

Bramley's seedling /ˌbræmliːz ˈsiːdlɪŋ/ noun FRUIT a common variety of cooking apple

bran /bræn/ noun FOOD the outside covering of the wheat seed, removed when making white flour, but an important source of roughage and some vitamin B ○ *Sprinkle a spoonful of bran onto the stew to increase the fibre content.*

branch /brɑːntʃ/ noun BUSINESS a local office of a bank or large business, or a local shop forming part of a large chain of shops ○ *The bank* or *The store has branches in most towns in the south of the country.* ○ *The insurance company has closed its branches in South America.* ○ *He is the manager of our local branch of Tesco.* ○ *We have decided to open a branch office in Chicago.* ■ verb □ **to branch out** to start a new, but usually related, type of business ○ *From selling train tickets, the company branched out into package holidays.*

branch manager /ˌbrɑːntʃ ˈmænɪdʒə/ noun BUSINESS somebody in charge of an office of a company

branch office /ˌbrɑːntʃ ˈɒfɪs/ noun a less important office, usually in a different town or country from the main office

brand /brænd/ noun BUSINESS a well-known make of product, which can be recognised by its name or by its design ○ *leading brands of drinks*

branded /ˈbrændɪd/ adjective displaying a brand name

branded pub /ˌbrændɪd ˈpʌb/ noun BARS a pub belonging to a chain, and known by the brand name of the chain

brand name /ˈbrænd neɪm/ noun BUSINESS the name of a particular make of product

brandy /ˈbrændi/ noun BEVERAGES **1.** a strong alcohol distilled from wine **2.** a glass of this alcohol ○ *He ordered three brandies and a port.*

COMMENT: Brandy is made in most wine-producing countries, such as Spain and Greece. Brandy from the Bordeaux region of France is called 'cognac'; that from south-west France is called 'Armagnac'. Brandy made in Burgundy is called 'marc de bourgogne'. In Germany, brandy is called 'Branntwein'.

brandy snap /ˈbrændi snæp/ noun BREAD, ETC. a thin rolled biscuit, flavoured with ginger

brandy sour /ˌbrændi ˈsaʊə/ noun BEVERAGES a cocktail of brandy, lemon juice and sugar

brass /brɑːs/ noun ENTERTAINMENT musical instruments made of brass ○ *a brass band*

brasserie /ˈbræsəri/ noun used as a name for a continental-style cafe ○ *Let's have lunch at the brasserie next door.* (NOTE: **Brasserie** comes from a French noun meaning 'brewery'.)

COMMENT: In France, brasseries belong to breweries and serve mainly beer, and also food. In England, they serve mainly wine.

brat pan /ˈbræt pæn/ noun CATERING a cooking pan for stewing, braising, poaching, etc., which can be tilted to drain off liquid

brawn /brɔːn/ noun MEAT chopped meat from the head of an animal, mixed with jelly to form a loaf

brazil nut /brəˈzɪl nʌt/ noun NUTS a hard nut with a rough crescent-shaped shell from a tropical tree

bread /bred/ noun food made from flour, water, a little fat or oil and usually a raising agent such as yeast or soda, then cooked in an oven

COMMENT: Most British bread is white (made from refined flour), but brown bread, or wholemeal bread, is becoming more and more popular.

bread and butter /ˌbred ən ˈbʌtə/ noun FOOD slices of bread spread with butter

bread and butter pudding /ˌbred ən ˌbʌtə ˈpʊdɪŋ/ noun DESSERTS a dessert made from slices of buttered bread with dried fruit and sugar, covered with a mixture of eggs and milk and baked in the oven

breadcrumb /ˈbredkrʌm/ noun a tiny piece of bread, either soft or hard

breadcrumbs /ˈbredkrʌmz/ plural noun FOOD dried bread, crushed into powder, used to cover fish or meat before frying

breaded /ˈbredɪd/ adjective CATERING covered with breadcrumbs before cooking ○ *breaded escalope of veal*

breadfruit /ˈbredfruːt/ noun VEGETABLES the starchy fruit of a tree grown in the Pacific Islands, which is used as a vegetable

bread knife /ˈbred naɪf/ noun **1.** a large knife with a serrated edge like a saw, used for cutting slices of bread from a loaf **2.** a small knife put on the bread plate, used for spreading butter on pieces of bread and cutting them

bread pudding /ˌbred ˈpʊdɪŋ/ noun BREAD, ETC. a rich cake made from bread soaked in milk, mixed with egg, sugar, spices and dried fruit, and baked

bread roll /ˌbred ˈrəʊl/ noun a small loaf of bread offered to the guests by the commis waiter while they are studying the menu

bread sauce /ˌbred 'sɔːs/ *noun* sauce made from white breadcrumbs, butter and milk, flavoured with onion, served hot as an accompaniment to roast chicken or turkey

bread stick /'bred 'stɪk/ *noun* BREAD, ETC. a long thin cylindrical biscuit, eaten as an appetiser

break /breɪk/ *noun* a short space of time, when you can rest ○ *She typed for two hours without a break.* ■ *verb* **1.** to fail to carry out the terms of a contract or a rule ○ *The company has broken the contract* or *the agreement.* ○ **to break an engagement to do something** not to do what has been agreed **2.** to stop doing something for a time ○ **to break one's journey** to stop travelling and pass some time in one place before going on ○ *They broke their journey in Bombay, before flying on to Hong Kong.*

breakages /'breɪkɪdʒɪz/ *plural noun* broken items ○ *Customers are expected to pay for breakages.*

breakbone fever /'breɪkbəʊn ˌfiːvə/ MEDICAL same as **dengue**

break down /ˌbreɪk 'daʊn/ *verb* **1.** to stop working because of mechanical failure ○ *The baggage carousel has broken down.* ○ *What do you do when your lift breaks down?* ○ *The visitors complained when the central air-conditioning system broke down.* **2.** BUSINESS to show all the items in a total list of costs, expenditure ○ *We broke the expenditure down into hotel, travel and entertainment costs.* ○ *Can you break down this invoice into travel costs and extras?*

breakdown /'breɪkdaʊn/ *noun* **1.** a situation in which a machine or vehicle stops working ○ *We cannot communicate with our Nigerian office because of the breakdown of the communications network.* ○ *They are trying to repair a breakdown in the refrigerating system.* **2.** a list that shows e.g. the cost of something item by item ○ *Give me a breakdown of the travel costs.*

break even /ˌbreɪk 'iːv(ə)n/ *verb* BUSINESS to balance costs and receipts, but not make a profit ○ *Last year the company only just broke even.* ○ *We broke even in our first two months of trading.*

breakeven point /ˌbreɪk 'iːv(ə)n pɔɪnt/ *noun* BUSINESS the point at which sales cover costs, but do not show a profit

breakfast /'brekfəst/ *noun* CATERING the first meal of the day

COMMENT: A traditional 'full English breakfast' may include cereals, porridge or stewed fruit (such as prunes), grilled fish (such as kippers), bacon and eggs, sausages, kidneys, fried or grilled tomatoes or mushrooms and fried bread, followed by toast and marmalade and tea or coffee.

breakfast bar /'brekfəst bɑː/ *noun* CATERING a variety of breakfast foods laid out on a table like a buffet in a hotel or restaurant

breakfast room /'brekfəst ruːm/ *noun* HOTELS a special room where breakfast is served

breast /brest/ *noun* meat from the chest part of a bird or animal ○ *breast of chicken* ○ *Do you want a wing or a slice of breast?*

breathe /briːð/ *verb* ○ **to let the wine breathe** to take the cork out of a bottle of red wine some time before it is to be drunk

brew /bruː/ *noun* BEVERAGES liquid which has been brewed ■ *verb* **1.** BARS to make beer **2.** to make tea (*also humorous*)

brewery /'bruːəri/ *noun* BARS a place where beer is made ○ *They have been making beer in that brewery for many, many years.* (NOTE: The plural form is **breweries**.)

brewpub /'bruːpʌb/ *noun* a restaurant or bar where the beer is made on the premises

bridge /brɪdʒ/ *noun* **1.** a road or path built over a road or river so that you can walk or drive from one side to the other **2.** SHIPS AND BOATS the top part of a ship where the captain stands **3.** ENTERTAINMENT a type of card game for four people

bridlepath /'braɪd(ə)lpɑːθ/, **bridleway** /'braɪd(ə)lweɪ/ *noun* a track in the country which can be used by walkers or by people on horseback

briefcase /'briːfkeɪs/ *noun* a flat case for carrying papers and documents ○ *He put all the files into his briefcase.*

brigade /brɪ'geɪd/ *noun* a group of people working together in a kitchen or restaurant

COMMENT: A kitchen brigade will be made up of the chef de cuisine, sous-chef, various specialised chefs and commis chefs. A restaurant brigade will be formed of the head waiter or maître d'hôtel, station waiters, wine waiters and assistant or commis waiters.

bright /braɪt/ *adjective* clear and sunny ○ *There will be bright intervals during the afternoon.*

brine /braɪn/ *noun* FOOD a solution of salt in water, used for preserving food

COMMENT: Some meat, such as bacon, is cured by soaking in brine; some types of pickles are preserved by cooking in brine; some foodstuffs are preserved in brine in jars.

brinjal /'brɪndʒəl/ *noun* VEGETABLES an Indian name for aubergine ○ *brinjal pickle*

brioche /'briɒʃ/ *noun* BREAD, ETC. a sweet French bread roll made from a dough enriched with eggs and butter

brisket /'brɪskɪt/ *noun* MEAT beef from the breast of an animal

brisling /'brɪzlɪŋ/ *noun* SEAFOOD a small sea fish, like a sardine

British Hospitality Association /,brɪtɪʃ ,hɒspɪ'tælɪti əsəʊsi,eɪʃ(ə)n/ *noun* HOTELS an association representing the British hotel, restaurant and catering industry. Abbr **BHA**

British Mountaineering Council /,brɪtɪʃ ,maʊntɪ'nɪərɪŋ ,kaʊns(ə)l/ *noun* SPORT a British organisation which protects the interests of climbers, hill walkers and mountaineers. Abbr **BMC**

British Summer Time /,brɪtɪʃ 'sʌmə ,taɪm/ *noun* the system of putting the clocks forward in Britain one hour in summer to provide extra daylight in the evening. Abbr **BST**

British Tourist Authority /,brɪtɪʃ 'tʊərɪst ɔː,θɒrɪti/ *noun* TOURISM a government organisation that is responsible for promoting tourism to Great Britain from foreign countries. Abbr **BTA**

broad bean /,brɔːd 'biːn/ *noun* VEGETABLES a large flat green seed cooked and eaten as a vegetable

broadcast /'brɔːdkɑːst/ ENTERTAINMENT *noun* a radio or television programme ■ *verb* to send out a message or programme by radio or television ○ *They broadcast an urgent storm warning.*

broccoli /'brɒkəli/ *noun* a vegetable that has a cluster of tight green, purple or white flower buds on the end of a broad stalk

brochette /brɒ'ʃet/ *noun* FOOD a small skewer on which chunks of food, especially meat or fish, are grilled and roasted, or food that has been cooked on a brochette

brochure /'brəʊʃə/ *noun* MARKETING a publicity booklet ○ *We sent off for a brochure about holidays in Greece or about ferry services.* ○ *Call now for our new summer brochure.*

broil /brɔɪl/ *verb especially US* CATERING to grill meat

broiler /'brɔɪlə/ *noun* **1.** MEAT a chicken which is young and tender and may be cooked by grilling **2.** *US* CATERING a pan or tray for grilling food on

broth /brɒθ/ *noun* FOOD a light soup

brown /braʊn/ *adjective* with a colour like earth or wood ■ *verb* to make something brown ○ *Brown the meat in hot fat.*

brown bread /,braʊn 'bred/ *noun* bread made from less refined brown flour

brownie /'braʊni/ *noun* BREAD, ETC. a small chocolate cake

brown rice /,braʊn 'raɪs/ *noun* FOOD rice which still has its outer covering

brown sugar /,braʊn 'ʃʊgə/ *noun* FOOD an unrefined or partly refined sugar in large brown crystals. Also called **Demerara sugar**

bruise /bruːz/ *verb* CATERING to crush food slightly to extract juice from it or bring out its flavour

brunch /brʌntʃ/ *noun* CATERING a meal served in the morning and early afternoon, between about 9.00 and 2.30, which is a combination of breakfast and lunch ○ *The hotel serves Sunday brunch in the main dining room.*

COMMENT: Brunch is especially popular on Sundays, when people tend to get up later than on other days of the week.

bruschetta /brʊ'sketə/ *noun* Italian bread toasted and drizzled with olive oil, usually served with added garlic and chopped tomatoes

Brussels sprout /,brʌs(ə)lz 'spraʊt/ *noun* VEGETABLES a small round green edible shoot from a type of cabbage. Also called **sprout**

COMMENT: Brussels sprouts are usually boiled or steamed and eaten served with butter.

brut /bruːt/ *adjective* BEVERAGES a French adjective meaning dry (*used only of champagne*) Compare **sec**

BSE *abbreviation* MEDICAL bovine spongiform encephalopathy

BST *abbreviation* British Summer Time

BTA *abbreviation* TOURISM British Tourist Authority

bubble and squeak /,bʌb(ə)l ən 'skwiːk/ *noun* FOOD a traditional dish of leftover cabbage, potatoes, meat, etc., fried together to make a crisp cake

bubble bath /'bʌb(ə)l bɑːθ/ *noun* **1.** a bath with liquid soap added to make a mass of foam **2.** the liquid soap used to put in a bath

bubbly /'bʌbli/ *noun* **1.** same as **champagne 2.** any cheap sparkling white wine

bucket /'bʌkɪt/ *noun* a round plastic or metal container with an open top and a handle □ **bucket-and-spade holiday** a traditional British holiday, where children play on the beach with buckets and spades

bucket shop /'bʌkɪt ʃɒp/ *noun* AIR TRAVEL an unbonded travel agent selling airline tickets at a discount (*informal*)

buck's fizz /ˌbʌks 'fɪz/ *noun* BEVERAGES a cold drink of champagne and fresh orange juice, typically served at breakfast

buckwheat /'bʌkwiːt/ *noun* FOOD a grain crop that is not a member of the grass family and can be grown on the poorest of soils. When buckwheat is ground into flour, it is used to make pancakes.

budget /'bʌdʒɪt/ *noun* **1.** FINANCE a plan of expected spending and income, usually for one year ○ *to draw up a budget* ○ *We have agreed the budgets for next year.* □ **advertising budget** money that it is planned to spend on advertising **2.** □ **budget price** a low price ■ *verb* FINANCE to plan probable income and expenditure ○ *We are budgeting for £10,000 of sales next year.*

budget fare /'bʌdʒɪt feə/ *noun* TRAVEL a fare that is cheaper than usual

budget hotel /'bʌdʒɪt ˌhəʊtel/ *noun* HOTELS a cheaper hotel ○ *Whatever happens, the group will retain its 199 budget hotels.*

budget travel /ˌbʌdʒɪt 'træv(ə)l/ *noun* cheap travel

buffalo mozzarella /ˌbʌfələʊ ˌmɒtsə'relə/ *noun* DAIRY a fresh mozzarella cheese made from a combination of water buffalo milk and cow's milk

buffalo wings /'bʌfələʊ wɪŋz/ *plural noun* fried chicken wings, usually served in barbecue sauce

buffet /'bʊfeɪ/ *noun* CATERING **1.** a meal where the food is laid out in dishes on a table, and each person helps himself or herself ○ *The hotel serves a buffet breakfast.* **2.** a snack bar in a place such as a railway station or airport

buffet car /'bʊfeɪ kɑː/ *noun* RAIL TRAVEL a railway coach which serves snacks and drinks which you may take back to your seat. Compare **restaurant car**

bug /bʌg/ *noun* a harmful organism, such as a virus, that causes a disease (*informal*)

built-in /ˌbɪlt 'ɪn/ *adjective* constructed as part of a building ○ *Each bedroom has a built-in wardrobe.*

bulb /bʌlb/ *noun* a glass ball which gives electric light ○ *There's a light bulb missing in the bedroom.*

bulgur /'bʊlgə/ *noun* FOOD wheat that has been parboiled, dried and cracked into small pieces. It is a common ingredient in south-western Asian and vegetarian cooking.

bulk /bʌlk/ *noun* □ **in bulk** in large amounts

'…by buying in bulk, companies can obtain hotel rooms at a fraction of the 'rack' rate, as well as airline tickets, often business class, below the quoted fare' [*Business Travel*]

bulk buying /ˌbʌlk 'baɪɪŋ/ *noun* BUSINESS the practice of buying large amounts of goods at a lower price. Also called **bulk purchase**

bulk discount /ˌbʌlk 'dɪskaʊnt/ *noun* a discount given to a purchaser who buys in bulk

bulkhead /'bʌlkhed/ *noun* TRAVEL an internal wall in a ship or aircraft

'…frequent flyers are able to identify their favourite place in the aircraft: seats next to cabin bulkheads or alongside exit doors usually offer extra legroom' [*Business Travel*]

bulk purchase /ˌbʌlk 'pɜːtʃɪs/ *noun* same as **bulk buying**

bulletin /'bʊlɪtɪn/ *noun* a piece of information, or a report on a situation ○ *the ship's daily news bulletin* □ **bulletin board** a board on which bulletins are pinned up

bullying /'bʊliɪŋ/ *noun* intimidation and harassment of someone by another member of staff in a more powerful position ○ *Bullying and harassment at work are major problems in the catering industry.*

bumping /'bʌmpɪŋ/ *noun* AIR TRAVEL a situation where someone takes the place of another less important person in a restaurant or on a plane (NOTE: If a plane is over-booked, cabin staff may ask passengers if they will volunteer to take a later flight in return for some financial reward. If no one volunteers, then non-fare-paying passengers will be asked to move, followed by passengers who have paid reduced fares.)

bun /bʌn/ *noun* BREAD, ETC. a small cake made of a bread-like dough, usually sweetened and flavoured

bunch /bʌntʃ/ *noun* **1.** a cluster of things tied together ○ *She bought a bunch of flowers in the market.* **2.** a cluster of fruit on the same stem ○ *a bunch of bananas* ○ *a bunch of grapes* (NOTE: The plural form is **bunches**.)

bungalow /'bʌŋgələʊ/ *noun* a house with only a ground floor ○ *They are staying in a bungalow by the sea.*

bungee /'bʌndʒiː/ *noun* TRAVEL an elastic strap with a hook at each end, used e.g. for attaching luggage onto a trolley or onto the back of a bicycle

bungee-jumping /'bʌndʒiː ˌdʒʌmpɪŋ/ *noun* SPORT a sport which consists of jumping from a high point such as a bridge, when attached by your ankles to a long elastic cable, so that instead of hitting the ground, you bounce up into the air ○ *I'd like to try* *bungee-jumping, but my girlfriend won't let me.*

bunk /bʌŋk/ *noun* TRAVEL a bed fixed to a wall in a boat, train or aircraft

bunk beds /ˈbʌŋk bedz/ *plural noun* two beds, one above the other, usually used for children in hotels

bunting /ˈbʌntɪŋ/ *noun* strings of little flags, used as decoration

bureau de change /ˌbjʊərəʊ də ˈʃɒnʒ/ *noun* FINANCE a French noun meaning an office where money can be changed into the currency of another country (NOTE: The plural form is **bureaus** or **bureaux de change**.)

burger /ˈbɜːgə/ *noun* MEAT same as **beefburger** ○ *The children want burgers and fries for lunch.*

burger bar /ˈbɜːgə bɑː/ *noun* CATERING a simple restaurant or stall serving burgers either to eat on the spot or to take away

Burgundy /ˈbɜːgəndi/ *noun* BEVERAGES wine from the Burgundy district in France

burn /bɜːn/ *verb* to cook something too much, so that it becomes brown or black ○ *He's burnt the sausages* ○ *I don't like burnt toast.* (NOTE: **burning – burnt** or **burned**) ■ *noun* MEDICAL an injury to skin and tissue caused by light, heat, radiation, electricity or chemicals ○ *You should hold that burn under cold water for a few minutes.*

burrito /bəˈriːtəʊ/ *noun* FOOD in Mexican cooking, a flour tortilla wrapped round a filling of meat, beans or cheese

bus /bʌs/ *noun* ROAD TRAVEL **1.** a large motor vehicle for carrying passengers ○ *He goes to work by bus.* ○ *She took the bus to go to her office.* **2.** same as **coach** ■ *verb* US CATERING to clear away dirty plates, cutlery, etc., from tables in a restaurant ○ *He spent the summer bussing tables in a downtown grill.* (NOTE: **bussing – bussed**)

busboy /ˈbʌsbɔɪ/, **busgirl, busser** *noun* US CATERING an assistant waiter who offers rolls, pours water, clears away dirty plates and cutlery, but does not take the order or serve the food ○ *I asked the busboy for some more water.*

business /ˈbɪznɪs/ *noun* **1.** the work of buying and selling things □ **business guest** a hotel guest who is on a business trip ○ *Business guests are spending more.* □ **business travel** travel for business purposes □ **on business** on commercial work ○ *She had to go abroad on business.* ○ *The chairman is in Holland on business.* **2.** a commercial company ○ *He owns a small travel business.* ○

She runs a mail-order business from her home. ○ *He set up in business as a tour guide.* □ **business correspondence** letters concerned with business **3.** types of business taken as a group □ **the travel business** all companies and services dealing with travel and tourism, such as trains, buses, planes, travel agents, hotels, etc. ○ *He's been in the travel business for 15 years.* □ **the hotel business** the business of running hotels

business address /ˈbɪznɪs əˌdres/ *noun* the details of number, street and town where a company is located

business card /ˈbɪznɪs kɑːd/ *noun* a card showing the name of a businessperson and the name and address of the company he or she works for

business centre /ˈbɪznɪs ˌsentə/ *noun* **1.** the part of a town where the main banks, shops and offices are located **2.** a large facility offering business services to businesspeople, especially at an airport, convention centre, railway station, etc., where they may need to use the facilities when travelling

business class /ˈbɪznɪs klɑːs/ *noun* AIR TRAVEL a type of airline travel that is less expensive than first class and more comfortable than tourist class, and that may offer better and wider seats, special meals, more free drinks, more choice of newspapers or special airport lounges

business cycle /ˈbɪznɪs ˌsaɪk(ə)l/ *noun* BUSINESS same as **trade cycle**

business district /ˈbɪznɪs ˌdɪstrɪkt/ *noun* the part of a town where the main banks, shops and offices are located

business expenses /ˈbɪznɪs ɪkˌspensɪz/ *plural noun* money spent on running a business, not on stock or assets

business facilitated lease /ˌbɪznɪs fəˌsɪləteɪtɪd ˈliːs/ *noun* a type of franchise, where a franchisee takes over an existing franchise on a short lease, buying the business with the cash which it generates. Abbr **BFL**

business fare /ˈbɪznɪs feə/ *noun* TRAVEL a tariff for business class passengers

business hours /ˈbɪznɪs ˌaʊəz/ *plural noun* the time, usually 9 a.m. to 5 p.m., when a business is open

business lounge /ˈbɪznɪs laʊndʒ/ *noun* AIR TRAVEL a special lounge for business class passengers, with comfortable chairs, coffee bar, etc., but also some business facilities such as Internet links, fax machines and secretarial help ○ *At the airport take refuge in a business lounge whatever class you're flying.*

businessman /'bɪznɪsmæn/ *noun* a man engaged in business

businessperson /'bɪznɪs,pɜːs(ə)n/ *noun* a man or woman engaged in business (NOTE: The plural form is **businesspeople**.)

business premises /'bɪznɪs ,premɪsɪz/ *plural noun* buildings in which the work of a business is done. Also called **commercial premises**

business services /'bɪznɪs ,sɜːvɪsɪz/ *plural noun* the various services needed to conduct business, e.g. Internet links, fax, answering service, and secretarial help, offered to businesspeople by a business centre in a hotel or at an airport

business tourism /,bɪznɪs 'tʊərɪz(ə)m/ *noun* travel by businesspeople to attend conferences and similar functions in foreign countries

business traveller /'bɪznɪs ,træv(ə)lə/ *noun* somebody who travels on business

business trip /'bɪznɪs trɪp/ *noun* a journey to discuss business matters with clients

businesswoman /'bɪznɪs,wʊmən/ *noun* a woman engaged in business

bus lane /'bʌs leɪn/ *noun* ROAD TRAVEL a part of a road where only buses may drive

busman's holiday /,bʌsmənz 'hɒlɪdeɪ/ *noun* a holiday or leisure activity that is similar to the work someone usually does for a living

bus stop /'bʌs stɒp/ *noun* ROAD TRAVEL a place where buses stop to pick up or drop passengers

busy /'bɪzi/ *adjective* occupied in doing something, e.g. in working ○ *She is busy preparing the annual accounts.* ○ *The manager is busy at the moment, but he will be free in about fifteen minutes.* ○ *The busiest time of year for stores is the week before Christmas.* ○ *Summer is the busy season for hotels.* □ **the line is busy** the telephone line is being used

busy season /'bɪzi ,siːz(ə)n/ *noun* HOTELS a period when a hotel or resort is busy

butcher /'bʊtʃə/ *noun* CATERING somebody who prepares and sells uncooked meat

butcher's /'bʊtʃəz/ *noun* CATERING a shop where uncooked meat is prepared and sold

butchery /'bʊtʃəri/ *noun* the work of using knives or other tools to remove meat from an animal's carcass

butler-style service /,bʌtlə staɪl 'sɜːvɪs/ *adjective, adverb* referring to a type of service in which guests help themselves to food and beverages which are brought round by waiters on trays

butter /'bʌtə/ *noun* DAIRY solid yellow fat made from cream

COMMENT: In a restaurant, butter is served either in a small individual dish or as separate portions (sometimes wrapped in metal foil) which are kept cold in a bed of ice.

butter bean /'bʌtə biːn/ *noun* VEGETABLES a large flat cream-coloured bean, dried before cooking

buttered /'bʌtəd/ *adjective* CATERING covered with butter ○ *hot buttered toast* ○ *buttered parsnips*

butterfly /'bʌtəflaɪ/ *verb* CATERING to split a piece of food such as meat or fish along its length, separating it into halves that remain joined

buttermilk /'bʌtəmɪlk/ *noun* DAIRY a thin milk left after butter has been churned

butternut squash /,bʌtənʌt 'skwɒʃ/ *noun* VEGETABLES a beige-coloured squash that is shaped like a club and has firm yellow-orange flesh

butterscotch /'bʌtəskɒtʃ/ *noun* DESSERTS a sweet made from butter and sugar

button /'bʌt(ə)n/ *noun* **1.** a small object stitched to clothes for attaching one part of clothing to another ○ *She asked room service if they could sew a button back on for him.* **2.** a small round object which you press to make a machine work ○ *a push-button phone* ○ *When you get into the lift, press the button for the floor you need.* ○ *She pressed the button to call the lift.*

button mushroom /'bʌt(ə)n ,mʌʃruːm/ *noun* VEGETABLES a small white mushroom with a round cap

butylated hydroxytoluene /,bjuːtɪleɪtɪd haɪ,drɒksi'tɒljuiːn/ *noun* FOOD a common additive used in processed foods containing fat to prevent the fat from oxidising. Abbr **BHT**

buyer /'baɪə/ *noun* a person who buys something, or whose job is to buy goods for a company

buyer's market /'baɪəz ,mɑːkɪt/ *noun* BUSINESS a market that is good for buyers because demand for a product is low and sellers have to charge low prices

buying forward /,baɪɪŋ 'fɔːwəd/ *noun* FINANCE same as **forward buying**

bylaw /baɪ lɔː/, **byelaw, by-law, bye-law** *noun* a rule or law made by a local authority or public body and not by central government ○ *The bylaws forbid playing ball in the public gardens.* ○ *According to the local* *bylaws, noise must be limited in the town centre.*

COMMENT: Bylaws must be made by bodies which have been authorised by Parliament, before they can become legally effective.

BYO *abbreviation* BARS bring your own

bypass /ˈbaɪpɑːs/ *noun* ROAD TRAVEL a road which goes round a town ■ *verb* to avoid a place, especially a busy or congested place, by taking a route around it

C

C *abbreviation* Celsius

CAA *abbreviation* AIR TRAVEL Civil Aviation Authority

cab /kæb/ *noun* **1.** ROAD TRAVEL same as **taxi** ○ *He took a cab to the airport.* ○ *The office is only a short cab ride from the railway station.* ○ *Cab fares are very high in New York.* □ **black cab** a London taxi. ◊ **minicab 2.** ROAD TRAVEL a separate compartment for a driver in a large vehicle such as a truck

cabaret /'kæbəreɪ/ *noun* ENTERTAINMENT entertainment given in a restaurant or club

cabbage /'kæbɪdʒ/ *noun* VEGETABLES a green leafy vegetable with a round heart or head

COMMENT: Green cabbage is usually eaten boiled; red cabbage may be eaten cooked or pickled in vinegar; white cabbage can be shredded to make coleslaw; in Germany and Eastern France, it is pickled in brine to make 'sauerkraut'.

cabin /'kæbɪn/ *noun* **1.** a wooden hut, used by hunters or skiers, also the sleeping area in a ski chalet **2.** SHIPS AND BOATS a separate room for a passenger on a ship ○ *She felt sick and went to lie down in her cabin.* **3.** AIR TRAVEL a separate area for passengers in a plane ○ *Passengers are requested to remain seated until the cabin doors are open.* ○ *The first-class cabin is in the front of the plane.* **4.** AIR TRAVEL a separate area for the pilot of a plane

'...cabin layouts, as with cabin service, good timekeeping, and flight frequency, are important influences on frequent travellers' choice of carrier' [*Business Travel*]

cabin attendant /'kæbɪn ə,tendənt/ *noun* AIR TRAVEL somebody who looks after passengers on a plane

cabin baggage /'kæbɪn ,bægɪdʒ/ *noun* AIR TRAVEL same as **carry-on baggage**

cabin class /'kæbɪn klɑːs/ *noun* TRAVEL a class of accommodation on some passenger ships that is lower than first class and higher than tourist class

cabin crew /'kæbɪn kruː/ *noun* AIR TRAVEL the members of airline staff who deal with the passengers on a plane

cabin lights /,kæbɪn 'laɪts/ *plural noun* AIR TRAVEL lights in the cabin of a plane ○ *Cabin lights will be dimmed for takeoff.*

cabin trunk /'kæbɪn trʌŋk/ *noun* SHIPS AND BOATS a trunk for taking on board a ship

cable /'keɪb(ə)l/ *noun* a thick rope or wire ○ *The ship was attached to the quay by cables.* ○ *The cable snapped and ten passengers died when their cable car fell to the floor of the valley.*

cable car /'keɪb(ə)l kɑː/ *noun* ENTERTAINMENT **1.** a vehicle which goes up a mountain, hanging on a wire cable **2.** *US* (*in San Francisco*) a type of tram which is pulled by a metal cable set in a channel in the road

cable television /,keɪb(ə)l ,telɪ'vɪʒ(ə)n/ *noun* ENTERTAINMENT a television system, where pictures are sent by cable

cab rank /'kæb ræŋk/ *noun* ROAD TRAVEL same as **taxi rank**

cacao /kə'kaʊ/ *noun* a dried fatty seed that is the source of cocoa, chocolate and other food products

caesar salad /,siːzə 'sæləd/ *noun* a salad made with lettuce, croutons, Parmesan cheese, and anchovies, with an egg-based dressing

cafe /'kæfeɪ/, **café** *noun* CATERING a small shop selling food and drink

café au lait /,kæfeɪ ːʊ 'leɪ/ *noun* BEVERAGES coffee with hot milk

café latte /,kæfeɪ 'læteɪ/ *noun* BEVERAGES same as **latte**

café noir /,kæfeɪ 'nwɑː/ *noun* BEVERAGES coffee without milk or cream

café set /'kæfeɪ set/ *noun* CATERING a piece of restaurant equipment which heats water and makes steam, for preparing hot drinks

cafeteria /,kæfə'tɪəriə/ *noun* CATERING a self-service restaurant, especially used by the staff in an office building or factory

cafeteria manager /ˌkæfəˈtɪəriə ˌmænɪdʒə/ *noun* CATERING somebody in charge of a cafeteria

cafeteria service /ˌkæfəˈtɪəriə ˌsɜːvɪs/ *noun* CATERING a style of serving food, where the customer takes a tray and helps himself or herself to hot or cold food from a buffet and pays for it at a till as he or she leaves the buffet

cafetière /ˌkæfəˈtjeə/ *noun* BEVERAGES a coffee pot with a plunger, which is pressed down to trap the coffee grounds at the bottom

'…cafetières are the most elegant method of serving coffee' [*Caterer & Hotelkeeper*]

caffeinated /ˈkæfiːneɪtɪd/ *adjective* containing caffeine

caffeine /ˈkæfiːn/ *noun* a stimulant found in coffee, tea and cola nuts

caffe latte /ˌkæfeɪ ˈlæteɪ/, **caffè latte** *noun* BEVERAGES same as **latte**

cake /keɪk/ *noun* BREAD, ETC. a sweet food made from flour, sugar, eggs, milk and other ingredients, baked in an oven ○ *Two pieces of cherry cake, please.* ○ *Have another slice of Christmas cake.* ○ *Would you like some chocolate cake?* □ **celebration cake** a special cake made to celebrate an event, such as a birthday

COMMENT: A cake can be quite large, and is cut into individual slices (as for a wedding cake, Christmas cake, birthday cake, etc.); alternatively, small cakes can be made, each for one person.

cake fork /ˈkeɪk fɔːk/ *noun* CATERING a small fork with two of the prongs joined together, used for eating cake or pastries. Also called **pastry fork**

cake knife /ˈkeɪk naɪf/ *noun* a thick wide knife used for cutting up cakes

cake shop /ˈkeɪk ʃɒp/ *noun* CATERING a shop which sells mainly cakes and pastries, and sometimes serves tea as well

cake tin /ˈkeɪk tɪn/ *noun* CATERING a tin for baking or keeping cakes in

calamari /ˌkæləˈmɑːri/ *plural noun* SEAFOOD squid served as food, especially in Mediterranean cookery

calamine lotion /ˈkæləmaɪn ˌləʊʃ(ə)n/ *noun* a lotion, based on zinc oxide, which helps relieve skin irritation such as that caused by sunburn

calculate /ˈkælkjʊleɪt/ *verb* **1.** to find the answer to a problem using numbers ○ *The bank clerk calculated the rate of exchange for the dollar.* **2.** to estimate something such as an amount or price ○ *I calculate that it will take us six hours to get to Madrid.*

calculation /ˌkælkjʊˈleɪʃ(ə)n/ *noun* the answer to a problem in mathematics ○ *According to my calculations, the hotel will cost us about £1,000.*

calculator /ˈkælkjʊleɪtə/ *noun* an electronic machine which works out the answers to problems in mathematics ○ *My pocket calculator needs a new battery.* ○ *He worked out the discount on his calculator.*

calendar /ˈkælɪndə/ *noun* a book or set of sheets of paper showing the days and months in a year, often illustrated with a series of pictures

calendar month /ˈkælɪndə mʌnθ/ *noun* a whole month as on a calendar, from the 1st to the 30th or 31st

calendar year /ˌkælɪndə ˈjɪə/ *noun* a whole year from the 1st January to 31st December

call /kɔːl/ *noun* **1.** a telephone conversation, or an attempt to get in touch with someone by telephone □ **to make a call** to dial and speak to someone on the telephone □ **to take a call** to answer the telephone □ **to log calls** to note all details of telephone calls made **2.** a visit to someone's home or place of work ■ *verb* **1.** to telephone someone ○ *I'll call you at your office tomorrow.* **2.** to phone someone to wake them up ○ *He asked to be called at 6.15.* **3.** □ **to call at a place** to visit a place ○ *The cruise liner calls at Palermo on June 14th.* □ **to call for someone** to come to find someone and take them away ○ *I'll call for you at 8.30, so wait for me in the lobby.*

call box /ˈkɔːl bɒks/ *noun* an outdoor telephone kiosk

calm /kɑːm/ *adjective* (*of the sea*) not rough ○ *The crossing was very calm, so no one was seasick.*

caloric /kəˈlɒrɪk/ *adjective* referring to calories

caloric energy /kəˌlɒrɪk ˈenədʒi/ *noun* an amount of energy shown as a number of calories

caloric requirement /kəˌlɒrɪk rɪˈkwaɪəmənt/ *noun* the amount of energy shown in calories that a person needs each day

calorie /ˈkæləri/ *noun* CATERING a unit of measurement of energy in food ○ *The tin of beans has 250 calories.* (NOTE: The **joule** is now more usual; also written **cal** after figures: *2,500 cal.*)

COMMENT: One calorie is the amount of heat needed to raise the temperature of one gram of water by one degree Celsius. The calorie is also used as a measurement of the energy content of food and to show the caloric requirement or amount of energy needed by an average person. The average adult in an office job requires about 3,000 calories per day, supplied by carbohydrates and fats to give energy and proteins to replace tissue. More strenuous physical work needs more calories. If a person eats more than the number of calories needed by his energy output or for his growth, the extra calories are stored in the body as fat.

calorific /ˌkælə'rɪfɪk/ *adjective* containing many calories, and so likely to be fattening

calorific value /ˌkælərɪfɪk 'vælju:/ *noun* CATERING the number of calories that a particular amount of a food contains ○ *The tin of beans has a calorific value of 250 calories.*

calzone /kæl'zəʊni/ *noun* a semicircular Italian turnover made from pizza dough with a savoury filling

camcorder /'kæmkɔːdə/ *noun* a portable cine-camera which records video pictures and sound

Camembert /'kæməmbeə/ *noun* DAIRY a small round soft French cheese that has an edible white rind and becomes stronger in flavour and softer in the centre as it ripens

camera /'kæm(ə)rə/ *noun* a piece of equipment for taking photographs ○ *They went on holiday and forgot to take their camera.* ○ *Did you remember to put a film in your camera?* ◊ **video camera**

camp /kæmp/ *noun* a place where people live in tents or cabins in the open ■ *verb* to spend a holiday in a tent ○ *We camped on the beach for two nights.* ○ *They spent two weeks camping in the Norwegian fiords.*

campaign /kæm'peɪn/ *noun* an organised attempt to achieve something

camp bed /'kæmp bed/ *noun* a folding bed

camper /'kæmpə/ *noun* somebody who goes camping ○ *A flash flood washed away the campsite and campers had to be rescued by the emergency services.*

camper van /'kæmpə væn/ *noun* ROAD TRAVEL a motor caravan equipped with bunks, kitchen equipment and furniture, in which people can drive around and park to stay overnight

camp fire /'kæmp faɪə/ *noun* a fire around which campers sit at night

campground /'kæmpgraʊnd/ *noun* US TOURISM same as **camping site**

camping /'kæmpɪŋ/ *noun* TOURISM the activity of going on holiday with a tent or caravan ○ *Camping holidays are cheaper than staying in hotels.* □ **to go camping** to

visit a place and stay in a tent ○ *We are going camping in Norway.*

camping site /'kæmpɪŋ saɪt/, **campsite** /'kæmpsaɪt/, **campingsite** *noun* TOURISM an area specially arranged for camping and caravans, with marked places for tents and communal toilets, washrooms and other facilities ○ *There are several well-equipped campsites near the lake.*

camping trailer /'kæmpɪŋ ˌtreɪlə/ *noun* ROAD TRAVEL a vehicle which is towed behind a car and which unfolds to form a tent

campus /'kæmpəs/ *noun* the area of land occupied by a university and the various buildings associated with it

campus holiday /'kæmpəs ˌhɒlɪdeɪ/ *noun* TOURISM a holiday spent in student accommodation on a campus, during the vacation when the students are not there

COMMENT: Campus holidays are cheaper than hotel-based holidays, and often are centred round an intellectual or artistic activity (study of drama, watercolour painting) or a sporting activity (rock-climbing, canoeing) which can be organised using the campus facilities.

Campylobacter /'kæmpɪləʊˌbæktə/ *noun* MEDICAL a bacterium which is a common cause of food poisoning in humans

COMMENT: Campylobacter exists in meat, offal, eggs, unpasteurised milk and shellfish. It cannot survive temperatures of over 65°C, so is destroyed by cooking.

CAMRA /'kæmrə/ *abbreviation* Campaign for Real Ale

can¹ /kæn/ *noun* a metal container for food or drink ○ *a can of orange juice* ■ *verb* CATERING to preserve food by sealing it in special metal containers

can² *abbreviation* 1. cancellation 2. cancelled

canal /kə'næl/ *noun* an artificial waterway ○ *You can take a boat trip round the canals of Amsterdam.* ○ *Holidays on canals are becoming very popular.* ○ *You can go canal cruising right across France.*

canal boat /kə'næl bəʊt/ *noun* SHIPS AND BOATS a long narrow boat made for going along British canals

canapé /'kænəpeɪ/ *noun* FOOD a small piece of bread or savoury biscuit with a topping, served as a snack, especially with drinks

canc. *abbreviation* 1. cancellation 2. cancelled

cancel /'kæns(ə)l/ *verb* 1. to stop something that has been agreed or planned ○ *to cancel an appointment* or *a meeting* ○ *He cancelled his booking at the last minute.* ○

There is no refund if you cancel less than three weeks before the date of departure. ○ *The flight was cancelled because the weather was too bad.* (NOTE: The British English is **cancelling – cancelled**, but the US English spelling is **canceling – canceled**.) **2.** □ **to cancel a cheque** to stop payment of a cheque that you have signed

cancellation /ˌkænsəˈleɪʃ(ə)n/ *noun* the act of stopping something that has been agreed or planned ○ *cancellation of a booking* or *a sailing* or *a flight* Abbr **can, canc.**

cancellation charge /ˌkænsəˈleɪʃ(ə)n ˌtʃɑːdʒ/ *noun* a charge which has to be paid by someone who cancels a booking

cancellation clause /ˌkænsəˈleɪʃ(ə)n klɔːz/ *noun* a clause in a contract which states the terms on which the contract may be cancelled

cancellation rate /ˌkænsəˈleɪʃ(ə)n ˌreɪt/ *noun* the number of people who cancel bookings, shown as a percentage of all bookings

c&b, C&B *abbreviation* conference & banqueting ○ *the C&B manager*

C & B manager /ˌsiː ənd ˈbiː ˌmænɪdʒə/ *abbreviation* HOTELS conference and banqueting manager

candle /ˈkænd(ə)l/ *noun* a stick of wax with a string in the centre, which you burn to give light ○ *a birthday cake with twenty-one candles*

candlelight /ˈkænd(ə)lˌlaɪt/ *noun* the light from candles ○ *The wedding guests want to dine by candlelight.*

candlelit /ˈkænd(ə)lˌlɪt/ *adjective* lit only by candles

candlelit supper /ˌkænd(ə)llɪt ˈsʌpə/ *noun* CATERING an evening meal lit by candles on the tables

candy /ˈkændi/ *noun* US FOOD **1.** a sweet food, made with sugar ○ *Eating candy is bad for your teeth.* (NOTE: There is no plural form in this meaning.) **2.** one piece of this food ○ *She bought a box of candies.* (NOTE: The plural in this meaning is **candies**; British English for this is **sweets**.)

candyfloss /ˈkændiflɒs/ *noun* FOOD melted sugar spun to make a fluffy pink mass, often sold at fairgrounds and open-air entertainments ○ *Stalls at the fair are selling cold drinks and candyfloss.* (NOTE: The US English is **cotton candy**.)

cane sugar /ˈkeɪn ˌʃʊgə/ *noun* sucrose obtained from sugar cane or sugar beet

canned /kænd/ *adjective* preserved in a metal container ○ *Canned soup is easy to prepare but it doesn't taste as nice as fresh.*

canned music /ˌkænd ˈmjuːzɪk/ *noun* recorded music, as played in hotels, restaurants, shopping malls and supermarkets

cannelloni /ˌkænəˈləʊni/ *plural noun* FOOD a type of wide tube-shaped pasta, stuffed with a meat, cheese or spinach filling

canoe /kəˈnuː/ SPORT *noun* a boat which is moved forward by one or more people using paddles ○ *She paddled her canoe across the lake.* ■ *verb* to travel in a canoe ○ *They canoed down the river.* ○ *We're going canoeing on Sunday.*

canoeing /kəˈnuːɪŋ/ *noun* SPORT the sport of going in a canoe ○ *Canoeing isn't my favourite sport – I don't like falling into cold water.* ○ *Canoeing down the rapids sounds a bit too dangerous for me.*

'…the course will include various outdoor activities such as climbing, trekking, canoeing and dry slope skiing' [*TGO – The Great Outdoors*]

canoeist /kəˈnuːɪst/ *noun* SPORT somebody who paddles a canoe ○ *We could see the helmets of the two canoeists in the distance.*

can opener /ˈkæn ˌəʊp(ə)nə/ *noun* US a tool for opening cans ○ *There's a can opener on the wall of the kitchen by the telephone.* (NOTE: The British English is **tin opener**.)

canopy /ˈkænəpi/ *noun* **1.** a small roof over a platform or balcony ○ *The balcony is protected by a glass canopy.* **2.** □ **(extraction) canopy** a wide ventilation system over a kitchen range

cantaloupe /ˈkæntəluːp/, **cantaloup** *noun* FRUIT a variety of melon with a green or yellow rough skin and scented orange-yellow flesh

canteen /kænˈtiːn/ *noun* **1.** CATERING a private self-service restaurant in an office block, factory or similar building **2.** a box containing knives, forks and spoons **3.** a portable flask for water

canyon /ˈkænjən/ *noun* a deep valley with steep sides, usually in North America ○ *If you go to the West of the USA, try to visit the Grand Canyon.*

canyoneering /ˌkænjəˈnɪərɪŋ/ *noun* SPORT the sport of travelling through canyons on foot, using skills such as abseiling, swimming, climbing and rafting

canyoning /ˈkænjənɪŋ/ *noun* SPORT the sport of climbing into and out of canyons

'…canyoning: in other words, jumping, scrambling and abseiling from misty peaks, down sheer rock faces and cascading falls' [*Wanderlust*]

capacity /kə'pæsɪti/ *noun* the amount which a container can hold □ **a capacity crowd** a crowd of people which fills all the seats in a stadium

caper /'keɪpə/ *noun* VEGETABLES the flowerbud of a Mediterranean bush, which is pickled and used in sauces or as a garnish for fish and meat

capital /'kæpɪt(ə)l/ *noun* **1.** same as **capital city 2.** BUSINESS money, property and assets used in a business ○ *a company with £10,000 capital* or *with a capital of £10,000*

capital assets /ˌkæpɪt(ə)l 'æsets/ *plural noun* BUSINESS property or machinery that a company owns and uses in its business, but that the company does not buy or sell as part of its regular trade. Also called **fixed assets**

capital break /'kæpɪt(ə)l breɪk/ *noun* TOURISM a short holiday in a capital such as Paris, Vienna or Rome

capital city /ˌkæpɪt(ə)l 'sɪti/ *noun* the main town in a country, usually where its government is located

capital expenditure /ˌkæpɪt(ə)l ɪk'spendɪtʃə/, **capital investment** /ˌkæpɪt(ə)l ɪn'vestmənt/, **capital outlay** /ˌkæpɪt(ə)l 'aʊtleɪ/ *noun* BUSINESS money spent on fixed assets such as property, machines or furniture

capitalise on /'kæpɪt(ə)laɪz ɒn/, **capitalize on** *verb* to take advantage of something ○ *Café owners capitalised on the good weather by putting tables and chairs out on the pavement.*

'English seaside resorts must capitalize on their architectural heritage if they are to find a niche in the holiday market of the future' [*Caterer & Hotelkeeper*]

capon /'keɪpɒn/ *noun* MEAT an edible cockerel which grows and increases in weight more rapidly than other birds because it has been castrated

cappuccino /ˌkæpə'tʃiːnəʊ/ *noun* BEVERAGES frothy Italian coffee, with whipped milk and a sprinkling of powdered chocolate

capsicum /'kæpsɪkəm/ *noun* VEGETABLES a group of plants grown for their pod-like fruits, some of which are extremely spicy and pungent. Others, including the red and green or sweet peppers, are less pungent and are used as vegetables. Also called **pepper**

capsule hotel /'kæpsjuːl həʊˌtel/ *noun* in Japan, a hotel in which the rooms are lockable cubicles

captain /'kæptɪn/ *noun* **1.** SHIPS AND BOATS somebody in charge of a ship or aircraft □ **the captain's table** a table in the dining room of a cruise liner, where the captain sits, with the most important passengers **2.** US CATERING a chief waiter who is in charge of a station, and takes the orders from customers

car /kɑː/ *noun* **1.** ROAD TRAVEL a small motor vehicle for carrying people **2.** US RAIL TRAVEL a railway carriage or wagon

carafe /kə'ræf/ *noun* CATERING a glass jar, for serving wine or water ○ *wines by the carafe* ○ *Can we have a carafe of ordinary water, please?*

COMMENT: Carafes are used for serving ordinary table wine or house wine. Wine sold in carafes is cheaper than wine in bottles; carafe sizes are quarter-litre, half-litre or litre. The carafes are measured and approved by the licensing authorities. In France, carafe wine is served in small jugs, called 'pichets'.

carafe wine /kə'ræf waɪn/ *noun* BEVERAGES the cheapest wine sold in a restaurant or bar

carambola /ˌkærəm'bəʊlə/ *noun* FRUIT the yellow fruit of an Indonesian tropical tree, which is used in preserves and drinks

caramel /'kærəməl/ *noun* **1.** DESSERTS a sweet made with sugar and butter **2.** FOOD burnt sugar

caramel custard /ˌkærə,mel 'kʌstəd/ *noun* DESSERTS same as **crème caramel**

caramelise /'kærəməlaɪz/ *verb* CATERING to heat sugar until it becomes brown

caramelised /'kærəməlaɪzd/ *adjective* CATERING referring to sugar that is heated until it is brown and melted ○ *cheese cake with caramelised orange and whisky sauce*

caramel oranges /ˌkærəmel 'ɒrɪndʒɪz/ *plural noun* DESSERTS slices of orange covered with a sauce of caramelised sugar

caravan /'kærəvæn/ *noun* ROAD TRAVEL **1.** a van with beds, table, washing facilities, etc., which can be towed by a car ○ *We got stuck behind a caravan on a narrow mountain road.* (NOTE: The US English for this is **trailer**.) **2.** a group of vehicles or animals travelling together, especially across a desert ○ *We joined a caravan of lorries going to Romania.*

caravanette /ˌkærəvæ'net/ *noun* a small camping van

caravanner /'kærəvænə/ *noun* TOURISM somebody who goes on holiday in a caravan

caravanning /'kærəvænɪŋ/ *noun* TOURISM the activity of going on holiday in a caravan ○ *We had a caravanning holiday in the South of France.*

caravan park /'kærəvæn pɑːk/ *noun* TOURISM a type of campground with permanently positioned caravans, which are rented to holidaymakers ○ *We rent a caravan in a caravan park.* Also called **trailer park**

caravanserai /ˌkærə'vænsəraɪ/ *noun* a large inn with a central courtyard, found in some eastern countries and used by caravans crossing the desert

caraway /'kærəweɪ/ *noun* SAUCES, ETC. a herb the seeds of which are used as a flavouring in bread and cakes

caraway seed /'kærəweɪ siːd/ *noun* the dried ripe fruit of the caraway plant. Use: spice.

carbohydrate /ˌkɑːbəʊ'haɪdreɪt/ *noun* CATERING an organic compound derived from sugar, which is the main ingredient of many types of food

   COMMENT: Carbohydrates are compounds of carbon, hydrogen and oxygen. They are found in particular in sugar and starch from plants, and provide the body with energy. Plants build up valuable organic substances from simple materials. The most important part of this process, which is called photosynthesis, is the production of carbohydrates such as sugars, starches and cellulose. They form the largest part of our food.

carbonade /ˌkɑːbə'nɑːd/ *noun* a stew made with beef and onions cooked in beer

carbonated /'kɑːbəneɪtɪd/ *adjective* referring to liquid which has had carbon dioxide put into it to make it fizzy ○ *a bottle of carbonated mineral water*

carbon dioxide /ˌkɑːbən daɪ'ɒksaɪd/ *noun* a colourless gas produced when carbon is burnt with oxygen. Symbol CO_2

   COMMENT: Carbon dioxide exists naturally in air and is produced by respiration and by burning or rotting organic matter. Carbon dioxide is used in solid form (called 'dry ice') as a means of keeping food cold. It is also used in fizzy drinks and has the E number 290.

carcinogen /kɑː'sɪnədʒən/ *noun* a substance which produces cancer

   COMMENT: Carcinogens are found in pesticides such as DDT, in asbestos, in aromatic compounds such as benzene, and in radioactive substances, etc.

carcinogenic /ˌkɑːsɪnə'dʒenɪk/ *adjective* causing cancer

card /kɑːd/ *noun* **1.** a small rectangle of stiff paper for writing on. ◊ **postcard 2.** ENTERTAINMENT a rectangle of stiff paper with a design on it used for playing games □ **they were playing cards** they were playing games of cards **3.** a small piece of stiff paper

with your name and address printed on it ○ *I asked the waiter for one of their cards.* **4.** FINANCE a piece of stiff plastic used for payment ○ *Do you want to pay cash or with a card?* ◊ **key card**

card game /'kɑːd geɪm/ *noun* ENTERTAINMENT a game played with cards

cardholder /'kɑːd,həʊldə/ *noun* FINANCE somebody who holds a credit card or bank cash card

card number /'kɑːd ,nʌmbə/ *noun* the number printed on a card, which has to be quoted when making a purchase by phone or when getting authorisation for a purchase

card phone /'kɑːd fəʊn/ *noun* a public telephone which works when you insert a phonecard

card reader /'kɑːd ,riːdə/ *noun* an electronic device which can read information on a magnetic card

card table /'kɑːd ,teɪb(ə)l/ *noun* ENTERTAINMENT a small table covered with green baize cloth, used for playing cards on

career /kə'rɪə/ *noun* a job that you are trained for, and that you expect to do all your life ○ *He made his career in the hotel trade.* ○ *She's hoping to start her career in tourism.*

career prospects /kə'rɪə ,prɒspekts/ *plural noun* the possibility of getting promoted in your work

car ferry /'kɑː ,feri/ *noun* SHIPS AND BOATS a boat which carries vehicles and passengers from one place to another across water

cargo /'kɑːgəʊ/ *noun* SHIPS AND BOATS goods carried, especially on a ship

cargo hold /'kɑːgəʊ həʊld/ *noun* the part of the hold in which cargo is carried

cargo ship /'kɑːgəʊ ʃɪp/ *noun* SHIPS AND BOATS a ship which carries only goods

car hire, car rental *noun* ROAD TRAVEL the business of lending cars to people for money

car hire firm /'kɑː haɪə ,fɜːm/ *noun* ROAD TRAVEL a company that owns cars and lends them to people for money. Also called **car rental firm**

car hirer /'kɑː ,haɪrə/ *noun* ROAD TRAVEL **1.** somebody who rents a car **2.** a company that owns cars and lends them to people for money

   '…the check-in counter at its Heathrow rental desk has full baggage facilities, so that car hirers handing in their keys can check in at the same time' [*Business Travel*]

Caribbean /ˌkærɪ'biːən/ *noun* the sea to the south of the United States and east of Mexico ○ *We went on a cruise round the*

Caribbean. ○ *Holidays in the Caribbean are very popular.* ■ *adjective* referring to the area and countries near the Caribbean Sea ○ *Caribbean holidays are very popular.* ○ *Goat is important in Caribbean food.*

car insurance /'kɑːr ɪnˌʃʊərəns/ *noun* FINANCE the business of insuring a car, the driver and passengers in case of an accident. Also called **motor insurance**

carnet /'kɑːneɪ/ *noun* BUSINESS an international document which allows dutiable goods to cross several European countries by road without paying duty until the goods reach their final destination

carnival /'kɑːnɪv(ə)l/ *noun* ENTERTAIN-MENT a festival, often with music, dancing and eating in the open air ○ *The carnival procession arrived in the main square.*

carob /'kærəb/ *noun* an edible powder with a taste similar to that of chocolate, made from the seeds and pods of an evergreen tree

carousel /ˌkærə'sel/, **carrousel** US *noun* AIR TRAVEL a device at an airport consisting of a turning platform or a large circular belt, where the baggage of arriving passengers is placed by baggage handlers so that the passengers can find it and take it away ○ *Baggage from flight AC 123 is on carousel number 4.*

carpaccio /kɑː'pætʃiəʊ/ *noun* MEAT a dish of raw beef sliced thinly, moistened with olive oil and lemon juice and seasoned

car park /'kɑː pɑːk/ *noun* a public place where you can leave a car when you are not using it (NOTE: In US English, this is a **parking lot**.)

carpet /'kɑːpɪt/ *noun* a woven or knotted covering for the floor ■ *verb* to cover with a carpet ○ *The corridors have been carpeted in beige.*

carpeting /'kɑːpɪtɪŋ/ *noun* a covering made of carpet, or a wide piece of carpet ○ *The carpeting for the entrance lobby needs to be renewed.*

car rental firm /ˌkɑː 'rent(ə)l ˌfɜːm/ *noun* ROAD TRAVEL same as **car hire firm**

carriage /'kærɪdʒ/ *noun* **1.** RAIL TRAVEL a coach for passengers on a train ○ *She was sitting in a first-class carriage, although she only had a second-class ticket.* **2.** BUSINESS the act of transporting goods from one place to another, or the cost of doing this ○ *Carriage is 15% of the total cost.*

carriageway /'kærɪdʒweɪ/ *noun* ROAD TRAVEL a road for vehicles, especially one of the two sides of a motorway ○ *The west-*

bound carriageway of the M4 is closed for repairs.

carrier /'kæriə/ *noun* **1.** TRAVEL a company that transports goods or passengers ○ *We only use reputable carriers.* ○ *The tour always uses Spanish carriers.* **2.** BUSINESS a vehicle or ship which transports goods □ **bulk carrier** a ship that carries large quantities of loose goods such as corn **3.** MEDICAL somebody who carries the bacteria of a disease in their body and who can transmit the disease to others without showing any sign of it themselves **4.** MEDICAL an insect which carries disease which may infect humans

'…cabin layouts, as with cabin service, good timekeeping, and flight frequency, are important influences on frequent travellers' choice of carrier' [*Business Travel*]

carrot /'kærət/ *noun* VEGETABLES a bright orange root vegetable (NOTE: Carrots are eaten boiled, steamed or braised; also shredded cold as a salad.)

carrot cake /'kærət keɪk/ *noun* a cake made with finely grated carrots that give it a moist texture and delicate flavour

carry /'kæri/ *verb* TRAVEL (*of a vehicle*) to be able to contain a particular number of passengers ○ *a ship carrying pilgrims to the Middle East* ○ *The plane was carrying twenty passengers and five crew.*

carrycot /'kærikɒt/ *noun* an open rectangular box with handles for carrying a baby in ○ *The baby was asleep in his carrycot.*

carry-on /'kæri ɒn/ *noun* a piece of luggage small enough to be carried in the cabin of an aircraft ■ *adjective* referring to luggage small enough to be carried and stowed in the cabin of an aircraft

carry-on baggage /ˌkæri ɒn 'bægɪdʒ/ *noun* AIR TRAVEL baggage which a passenger carries onto a plane. Also called **cabin baggage**, **hand luggage**

carsick /'kɑːsɪk/ *adjective* MEDICAL ill because of the movement of a car ○ *She gets carsick if she has to travel long distances.*

carsickness /'kɑːsɪknəs/ *noun* MEDICAL sickness caused by the movement of a car ○ *All our children are prone to carsickness, which makes long journeys impossible.*

carte /kɑːt/ *noun* CATERING a French noun meaning menu

carte du jour /ˌkɑːt du: 'ʒʊə/ *noun* CATERING 'menu of the day', a list of special dishes prepared for the day and not listed in the printed menu

carton /'kɑːt(ə)n/ *noun* **1.** a thick cardboard ○ *a folder made of carton* **2.** a box made of cardboard ○ *a carton of cigarettes*

cartouche /kɑːˈtuːʃ/ *noun* CATERING a round or oval piece of paper that is placed on top of food while it is being cooked in liquid, e.g. in a casserole, to keep the solid ingredients submerged

carve /kɑːv/ *verb* CATERING to cut up meat and poultry at the table or in the kitchen for service to the table ○ *The course teaches practical skills in carving a chicken, a duck, a smoked salmon, etc.*

carver /ˈkɑːvə/ *noun* **1.** CATERING somebody who carves meat, often a special waiter in a restaurant, who carves a joint brought to the side of a table on a trolley **2.** a chair with arms, placed at the head of a dinner table **3.** CATERING same as **carving knife**

carvery /ˈkɑːvəri/ *noun* CATERING a type of restaurant, where various hot roast meats are served at a buffet

carving knife /ˈkɑːvɪŋ naɪf/ *noun* CATERING a large sharp knife used for carving

carving station /ˈkɑːvɪŋ ˌsteɪʃ(ə)n/ *noun* US a large, often heated, platter on which a big joint of meat can be carved for serving to guests in a hotel or restaurant

carving trolley /ˈkɑːvɪŋ ˌtrɒli/ *noun* CATERING a special trolley with a joint of meat in a warming dish, and a flat surface for carving it, which can be wheeled from table to table in a restaurant

case /keɪs/ *noun* **1.** TRAVEL a box with a handle for carrying clothes and personal belongings when travelling ○ *The customs made him open his case.* ○ *She had a small case which she carried onto the plane.* **2.** a cardboard or wooden box for packing and carrying goods **3.** MEDICAL a single occurrence of a disease ○ *There were 12 cases of bird flu in Vietnam last year.* **4.** □ **a case of wine** a cardboard or wooden box containing twelve bottles

cash /kæʃ/ *noun* **1.** money in coins or notes □ **cash payment** payment in cash □ **cash purchase** purchase made in cash **2.** the act of using money in coins or notes □ **'cash', 'pay cash'** words written on a crossed cheque to show that it can be paid in cash if necessary □ **to pay cash** to pay the complete sum in cash □ **to pay cash down** to pay in cash immediately □ **cash price, cash terms** a lower price or terms which apply if the customer pays cash

cash bar /ˌkæʃ ˈbɑː/ *noun* BARS a bar where drinks have to be paid for in cash

cash book /ˈkæʃ bʊk/ *noun* a record of cash spent and received

cash box /ˈkæʃ bɒks/ *noun* a metal box for keeping cash in

cash budget /ˈkæʃ ˌbʌdʒɪt/ *noun* a plan of cash income and expenditure

cash card /ˈkæʃ kɑːd/ *noun* FINANCE a plastic card used to obtain money from a cash dispenser

cash desk /ˈkæʃ desk/ *noun* BUSINESS a place in a shop where you pay for the goods you wish to buy ○ *Please pay at the cash desk.*

cash discount /ˌkæʃ ˈdɪskaʊnt/ *noun* a discount given for payment in cash. Also called **discount for cash**

cash dispenser /ˈkæʃ dɪˌspensə/ *noun* FINANCE a machine which gives out money when a special card is inserted and instructions given

cashew nut /ˈkæʃuː nʌt/ *noun* a small sweetish nut with a curved shape, often eaten salted as a snack ○ *Bowls of cashew nuts and olives had been put out for the guests.*

cash flow /ˈkæʃ fləʊ/ *noun* BUSINESS cash which comes into a company from sales or the money which goes out in purchases or overhead expenditure □ **the company is suffering from cash flow problems** cash income is not coming in fast enough to pay the expenditure going out

cash flow forecast /ˈkæʃ fləʊ ˌfɔːkɑːst/ *noun* BUSINESS a forecast of when cash will be received or paid out

cash flow statement /ˈkæʃ fləʊ ˌsteɪtmənt/ *noun* BUSINESS a report which shows cash sales and purchases

cashier /kæˈʃɪə/ *noun* **1.** somebody who takes money from customers in a restaurant, hotel or shop ○ *Please pay the cashier.* **2.** FINANCE somebody who deals with customers' money in a bank

cashier's record /ˈkæʃɪəz ˌrekɔːð/ *noun* BUSINESS a record of transactions kept by a cashier

cash in hand /ˌkæʃ ɪn ˈhænd/ *noun* BUSINESS same as **balance in hand**

cash items /ˈkæʃ ˌaɪtəmz/ *plural noun* BUSINESS goods sold for cash

cashless payment /ˌkæʃləs ˈpeɪmənt/ *noun* FINANCE payment by credit card or cheque

cash on delivery /ˌkæʃ ɒn dɪˈlɪv(ə)ri/ *noun* BUSINESS a payment in cash when goods are delivered. Abbr **COD**

cash register /ˈkæʃ ˌredʒɪstə/ *noun* a machine which shows and adds up the prices of items bought, with a drawer for keeping the cash received

cash reserves /ˈkæʃ rɪˌzɜːvz/ *plural noun* BUSINESS money which a company keeps in cash deposits or bills in case of urgent need

cash sale /'kæʃ seɪl/ *noun* FINANCE a transaction paid for in cash. Also called **cash transaction**

cash settlement /ˌkæʃ 'set(ə)lmənt/ *noun* payment of a bill in cash

cash transaction /'kæʃ træn,zækʃən/ *noun* FINANCE same as **cash sale**

cash up /ˌkæʃ 'ʌp/ *verb* BUSINESS to count the money taken in, e.g. a shop or restaurant at the end of the day's business

cash voucher /'kæʃ ˌvaʊtʃə/ *noun* a piece of paper which can be exchanged for cash ○ *With every £20 of purchases, the customer gets a cash voucher to the value of £2.*

casino /kə'siːnəʊ/ *noun* a building where people can gamble

COMMENT: In Britain, casinos are strictly regulated and only a certain number are allowed to operate; the person running a casino has to be licensed to do so. Casinos often exist in European spa towns.

cask /kɑːsk/ *noun* BARS a large barrel

cask ale /'kɑːsk eɪl/ *noun* BEVERAGES beer served from wooden barrels

cassata /kə'sɑːtə/ *noun* DESSERTS an Italian ice cream with dried or candied fruit in it

casserole /'kæsərəʊl/ *noun* **1.** CATERING an ovenproof covered dish **2.** FOOD food cooked in a covered dish in the oven ○ *chicken casserole ○ casserole of lamb* ■ *verb* CATERING to cook something in a casserole ○ *casseroled hare*

cassette /kə'set/ *noun* a plastic case containing magnetic tape which can be used for listening to words or music, or recording sounds

cassoulet /'kæsəleɪ/ *noun* a French stew of haricot beans cooked in a casserole with meat

caster sugar /'kɑːstə ˌʃʊgə/ *noun* finely ground white sugar, often used in baking

castle /'kɑːs(ə)l/ *noun* a large fortified building ○ *The tour includes visits to Windsor Castle and Hampton Court Palace.*

COMMENT: Note that in Britain the word 'castle' is usually applied to medieval buildings, with towers, gatehouses, moats, etc. Windsor Castle is an example of this. In France, the word 'château', and in Germany, the word 'Schloss' can also be applied to buildings which in English would be called 'palaces' if large (compare 'Blenheim Palace'), or 'houses' if small (compare 'Ham House').

casual /'kæʒuəl/ *adjective* not permanent, not regular □ **on a casual basis** not as a per-

manent member of staff ○ *We have taken on some students for the summer period on a casual basis.*

casual labour /ˌkæʒuəl 'leɪbə/ *noun* workers who are hired for a short period

casual staff /'kæʒuəl stɑːf/ *noun* same as **casual labour**

casual work /'kæʒuəl wɜːk/ *noun* work for a short period

casual worker /ˌkæʒuəl 'wɜːkə/ *noun* an employee hired for a short period

catalogue price /'kæt(ə)lɒg praɪs/ *noun* BUSINESS same as **list price**

catch /kætʃ/ *verb* TRAVEL to be in time to get on a bus, train or plane before it leaves ○ *You'll have to run if you want to catch the 10.20 train.* ○ *They stayed overnight in Dover and caught the 5.30 ferry to Calais.* (NOTE: **catching – caught**)

category /'kætɪg(ə)ri/ *noun* a group of things or people with particular characteristics in common ○ *Customers will stay in the Hotel Select or in another of the same category.*

caterer /'keɪtərə/ *noun* a person or company supplying food and drink, especially for parties or similar events ○ *The wedding reception has been organised by outside caterers.*

cater for /'keɪtə fɔː/ *verb* to deal with, to provide for ○ *The store caters mainly for overseas customers.*

catering /'keɪtərɪŋ/ *noun* the business of supplying food and drink for parties or similar events □ **the catering industry, the catering trade** all the people and companies whose job is catering, considered as a group □ **the catering arm of the group** the part of the group which deals with catering

catering department /'keɪtərɪŋ dɪ ˌpɑːtmənt/ *noun* the department of a company which deals with catering

catering manager /'keɪtərɪŋ ˌmænɪdʒə/ *noun* the manager in charge of a catering service

catering operations /'keɪtərɪŋ ˌɒpəreɪʃ(ə)nz/ *plural noun* the organisation and work of catering as part of a large organisation

catering service /'keɪtərɪŋ ˌsɜːvɪs/ *noun* a service provided by a hotel or restaurant, offering to supply all the food and drink, etc., for a private party

catering staff /'keɪtərɪŋ stɑːf/ *noun* staff employed in the catering industry

'...basic grade A catering staff are paid IR£5.43 (£3.97) an hour' [*Caterer & Hotelkeeper*]

cathedral /kə'θiːdrəl/ *noun* a large church which is the seat of a bishop ○ *We went on a tour of cathedrals in the Midlands.* ○ *You can see the cathedral tower from miles away.* ○ *Canterbury Cathedral is one of the oldest in England.*

cathedral town /kə'θiːdrəl taʊn/ *noun* a city which has a cathedral

catsup /'kætsəp/ *noun US* SAUCES, ETC. tomato sauce, with special seasoning

cauliflower /'kɒliflaʊə/ *noun* VEGETA-BLES a cabbage-like vegetable with a large white flower head, which is eaten (NOTE: There is no plural form when referring to the food: *some cauliflower;They served cauliflower with the meat.*)

cauliflower cheese /ˌkɒliflaʊə 'tʃiːz/ *noun* FOOD a dish made of boiled cauliflower, covered with a cheese sauce and baked in the oven

cave /keɪv/ *noun* a large underground hole in rock or earth

caveat emptor /ˌkæviæt 'emptɔː/ *noun* BUSINESS the buyer is personally responsible for checking that what he or she buys is in good order (*meaning 'let the buyer beware'*)

'...the idea that buyers at a car boot sale should have any rights at all is laughable. Even those who do not understand Latin know that caveat emptor is the rule' [*The Times*]

cavern /'kævən/ *noun* a very large cave, formed by water that has dissolved limestone or other rock ○ *Under the castle, they discovered a cavern which had been used to hide smuggled goods.*

caviar /'kævɪɑː/, **caviare** *noun* FOOD the eggs of a sturgeon, an expensive delicacy ○ *There are several types of caviar, and all are very expensive.* ○ *Red caviar is popular and a little less expensive than black.*

COMMENT: Caviar is usually served in a small pot, on a bed of ice, with lemon; traditionally it is served as an hors d'oeuvre, with chilled vodka. Caviar is black, the eggs are very fine and from the Beluga sturgeon; there is a similar, but cheaper, form with larger red eggs.

cayenne pepper /ˌkeɪen 'pepə/ *noun* SAUCES, ETC. a very hot-tasting red powder made from ground seeds and pods of the *Capsicum*

CCTV /ˌsiː siː tiː 'viː/ *abbreviation* closed-circuit TV ○ *The shoplifters were filmed on CCTV cameras.*

ceiling fan /'siːlɪŋ fæn/ *noun* a fan attached to the ceiling

celebrated /'selɪbreɪtɪd/ *adjective* very famous ○ *Many celebrated chefs have worked in this hotel.* ○ *Bath is celebrated for its Roman buildings.* ○ *You must try some of our celebrated raisin cakes – they're a speciality of the town.*

celeriac /sɪ'lerɪæk/ *noun* VEGETABLES a vegetable with a thick root tasting like celery, often eaten grated as a salad or used to make a purée

celery /'seləri/ *noun* VEGETABLES a white- or green-stemmed plant, eaten cooked as a vegetable, or more frequently raw as a salad (NOTE: There is no plural form.) □ **a stick of celery** a piece of the stem of the celery plant, often served raw with cheese

cellar /'selə/ *noun* **1.** an underground room or rooms beneath a building ○ *A flight of stone steps leads down to the cellar.* ○ *We keep our wine in the cellar.* **2.** wine stored in a cellar ○ *The restaurant is well known for its cellar.*

COMMENT: A cellar should be kept at a steady temperature, to make sure that the wine or beer which is stored in it does not deteriorate. Wine should be stored at a temperature of about 10°C, and bitter beer at 13°C. Cellars are also converted to form bars or nightclubs.

cellar book /'selə bʊk/ *noun* a book which lists the details of the stock of wine kept in a cellar

cellarman /'seləmæn/ *noun* BARS somebody who looks after beer barrels in a pub or hotel

Celsius /'selsɪəs/ *adjective, noun* a scale of temperatures where the freezing and boiling points of water are 0° and 100° ○ *Do you use Celsius or Fahrenheit in the weather forecasts?* ○ *What is 75° Fahrenheit in Celsius?* Compare **Fahrenheit** (NOTE: **Celsius** is used in many countries, but not in the United States, where the Fahrenheit system is still preferred. It is usually written as a **C** after the degrees sign: **32°C** (say: 'thirty-two degrees Celsius'). Celsius used to be called **centigrade**.)

COMMENT: To convert Celsius temperatures to Fahrenheit, multiply by 1.8 and add 32. So 20°C is equal to 68°F. To convert Fahrenheit to Celsius, subtract 32 and divide by 1.8.

cent /sent/ *noun* **1.** FINANCE a small coin, one hundredth of a dollar or a euro ○ *The stores are only a 25-cent bus ride away.* ○ *They sell oranges at 10 cents each.* (NOTE: **Cent** is usually written **c** in prices: *25c*, but not when a dollar price is mentioned: *$1.25*.) **2. ♦ per cent**

centigrade /'sentɪgreɪd/ *noun* same as **Celsius** ○ *Do you use centigrade or Fahren-*

heit in the weather forecasts? ○ *What is 75° Fahrenheit in centigrade?*

centimetre /'sentɪmiːtə/ *noun* a measure of length equalling 0.39 inches, or one hundredth of a metre ○ *The paper is fifteen centimetres wide.* (NOTE: This is usually written **cm** after figures: *260cm*. The US spelling is **centimeter**.)

central /'sentrəl/ *adjective* **1.** organised from a centre **2.** conveniently placed for shops and other facilities ○ *The hotel is cheap but it's very central.*

central air conditioning /ˌsentrəl ˈeə kənˌdɪʃ(ə)nɪŋ/ *noun* an air-conditioning system in which cold air is pumped throughout a whole building

central booking system /ˌsentrəl ˈbʊkɪŋ ˌsɪstəm/ *noun* HOTELS a computerised system where bookings can be made at any hotel in a group through a central office

central heating /ˌsentrəl ˈhiːtɪŋ/ *noun* a heating system for a whole building from one single source

centralisation /ˌsentrəlaɪˈzeɪʃ(ə)n/, **centralization** *noun* BUSINESS the organisation of everything from a central point

centralise /'sentrəlaɪz/ *verb* to organise something from a central point ○ *All purchasing has been centralised in our main office.* ○ *The hotel group benefits from a highly centralised organisational structure.*

central post office /ˌsentrəl ˈpəʊst ˌɒfɪs/ *noun* same as **main post office**

central purchasing /ˌsentrəl ˈpɜːtʃɪsɪŋ/ *noun* purchasing organised by one main office for all departments or branches

central reservations bureau /ˌsentrəl ˌrezəˈveɪʃ(ə)n ˌbjʊərəʊ/ *noun* HOTELS a main office that organises reservations for hotels, etc., in many different places

centre /'sentə/ *noun* **1.** the middle part of something ○ *The waiter put the vase of flowers in the centre of the table.* ○ *There is a dance floor in the centre of the room.* **2.** a group of buildings for a special purpose **3.** an important town ○ *industrial centre* ○ *manufacturing centre* ○ *the centre for the shoe industry* **4.** a group of items in an account ○ *a cost centre* ○ *a profit centre* (NOTE: [all senses] The US spelling is **center**.)

centrepiece /'sentəpiːs/ *noun* the main item of a display on a table ○ *a decorative buffet centrepiece of fruit and flowers* ○ *A bowl of fruit will be fine as a centrepiece on the dining table.* (NOTE: The US spelling is **centerpiece**.)

cereal /'sɪəriəl/ *noun* **1.** FOOD a grain crop, e.g. wheat, barley or maize **2.** □ **(breakfast) cereal** a food made from the seeds of a cereal plant, which is usually eaten at breakfast ○ *He ate a bowl of cereal.* ○ *Put milk and sugar on your cereal.*

COMMENT: Buffet breakfasts may offer a variety of cereals in small individual packets.

certificate /sə'tɪfɪkeɪt/ *noun* an official document which proves or shows something

certificate of origin /sə,tɪfɪkət əv 'ɒrɪdʒɪn/ *noun* BUSINESS a document showing where goods were made

certificate of registration /sə,tɪfɪkət əv ,redʒɪ'streɪʃ(ə)n/ *noun* a document showing that an item has been registered

ceviche /se'viːʃ/ *noun* a Latin American dish of raw fish or shrimp marinated in lemon or lime juice and served as a type of salad with chopped onions and tomatoes

chafing dish /'tʃeɪfɪŋ dɪʃ/ *noun* CATERING a dish which keeps food hot at the table

chafing lamp /'tʃeɪfɪŋ læmp/ *noun* CATERING a small alcohol-burning lamp which is lit under a chafing dish. Also called **flambé lamp**

chain /tʃeɪn/ *noun* BUSINESS a group of hotels, restaurants or shops, all belonging to the same company ○ *a chain of hotels* or *a hotel chain* ○ *the chairman of a large restaurant chain* ○ *She runs a chain of pasta restaurants.*

'…the two small London catering chains are actively seeking to expand their operations in the capital' [*Caterer & Hotelkeeper*]

chair class /'tʃeə klɑːs/ *noun* a class of travel on railway trains in which passengers are provided with reclinable seats similar to those in aircraft

chairlift /'tʃeəlɪft/ *noun* SPORT an arrangement of simple seats attached to a moving cable, to allow skiers to be carried to the top of a mountain

chalet /'ʃæleɪ/ *noun* TOURISM a small holiday house, usually made of wood ○ *The company offers chalet holidays in Switzerland.*

chalet hotel /'ʃæleɪ həʊˌtel/ *noun* HOTELS a very large chalet, run as a hotel

chalet maid /'ʃæleɪ meɪd/ *noun* HOTELS a girl or older woman who does the cooking and cleaning for guests staying in a chalet in a ski resort

chambermaid /'tʃeɪmbəmeɪd/ *noun* HOTELS a girl or older woman who cleans hotel rooms and changes the linen ○ *Put a 'Do not disturb' sign outside your door if* *you don't want the chambermaid to wake you up.* Also called **maid 2**, **room maid**

chambré /'ʃɒmbreɪ/ *adjective* CATERING a French adjective meaning at room temperature

> COMMENT: Most red wines are best drunk at room temperature, around 20°C and should be brought up from the cellar well before serving, to allow them to warm up to the temperature of the restaurant. Lighter red wines (such as Beaujolais nouveau, Gamay, Sancerre rouge) can be served cool.

champ /tʃæmp/ *noun* VEGETABLES an Irish dish of mashed potatoes with milk and spring onions, eaten with melted butter

champagne /ʃæm'peɪn/ *noun* BEVERAGES a sparkling white wine from the northeast of France ○ *They opened a bottle of champagne to celebrate the birth of the baby.*

> COMMENT: Champagne comes from the north-eastern part of France, around the towns of Reims and Epernay. Many other countries produce sparkling white wine, and some of these are called 'champagne', although the use of the name by non-French producers is no longer allowed. Champagne is normally sweetish, but dry champagnes (called 'brut') are also popular. It should be served chilled, usually in tall narrow glasses called 'flutes'. It can also be served in a wide flat glass, called a 'champagne goblet'. It is served as an aperitif, and also at important functions, such as birthdays or weddings, where it is used to toast the bride and groom.

champers /'ʃæmpəz/ *noun* BEVERAGES same as **champagne** (*informal*)

champignon /'ʃɒmpiːnjɒn/ *noun* a mushroom, especially one cultivated for eating

chance sales /ˌtʃɑːns 'seɪlz/ *plural noun* CATERING (*in a hotel*) sales of food and drink to non-residents

change /tʃeɪndʒ/ *noun* **1.** money in coins or small notes □ **to give someone change for £10** to give someone coins or notes in exchange for a ten-pound note □ **change machine** a machine that gives small change for a larger coin or note **2.** money which you get back when you have given more than the correct price ○ *He gave me the wrong change.* ○ *You paid the £5.75 bill with a £10 note, so you should have £4.25 change.* □ **keep the change** keep it as a tip, said to waiters, etc. **3.** TRAVEL the act of getting off one train, aircraft or bus and getting onto another one to complete your journey ○ *Getting from Richmond to Islington on the Underground involves three changes.* ■ *verb* **1.** □ **to**

change a £10 note to give change in smaller notes or coins for a £10 note **2.** to give one type of currency for another ○ *to change £1,000 into dollars* ○ *We want to change some traveller's cheques.* **3.** TRAVEL to get off a train, aircraft or bus and get onto another one ○ *We changed trains in Newport.* ○ *You have to change twice during the journey.* □ **'all change'** an instruction to all the passengers on a train to get off and get onto another one **4.** to take off one set of clothes and put on another ○ *After the wedding reception, the bride and groom changed into their going-away clothes.*

changeable /'tʃeɪndʒəb(ə)l/ *adjective* changing often or likely to change soon ○ *The weather is changeable in July.*

changing of the guard /ˌtʃeɪndʒɪŋ əv ðə 'ɡɑːd/ *noun* ENTERTAINMENT a military ceremony, where one shift of soldiers on guard at an important building is replaced by another ○ *At 10.30, we're going to watch the changing of the guard at Buckingham Palace.*

changing room /'tʃeɪndʒɪŋ ruːm/ *noun* a special small room at e.g. a swimming pool, golf course or sauna, where you change from your everyday clothes into sports clothes

channel /'tʃæn(ə)l/ *noun* SHIPS AND BOATS a piece of water connecting two seas □ **the English Channel** the sea between England and France

Channel-hop /'tʃæn(ə)l hɒp/ *verb* to cross the English Channel to mainland Europe, usually for shopping or sightseeing, and return on the same day

Channel Tunnel /ˌtʃæn(ə)l 'tʌn(ə)l/ *noun* RAIL TRAVEL a tunnel for trains under the English Channel, linking England and France. Also called **Chunnel**

Chantilly /ʃæn'tɪli/ *noun* sweetened whipped cream that is often flavoured with vanilla

chapati /tʃə'pæti/ *noun* BREAD, ETC. a piece of flat unleavened Indian bread made from cereal flour and water

charcoal /'tʃɑːkəʊl/ *noun* CATERING a black fuel formed from wood which has been burnt slowly, used as fuel for barbecues and grills

charcoal grill /ˌtʃɑːkəʊl 'ɡrɪl/ *noun* CATERING burning charcoal over which a metal rack is placed on which food can be cooked

charcoal-grilled /'tʃɑːkəʊl ɡrɪld/ *adjective* CATERING grilled over hot charcoal ○ *a charcoal-grilled tuna steak*

charcuterie /ʃɑːˈkuːtəri/ *noun* cold cooked, cured, or processed meat and meat products

Chardonnay /ˈʃɑːdəneɪ/ *noun* a dry white wine made from Chardonnay grapes, which were originally grown in east-central France

charentais /ˈʃærənteɪ/ *noun* FRUIT a type of melon that is round and has a green striped skin and dark orange flesh

charge /tʃɑːdʒ/ *noun* **1.** □ **to be in charge of** to manage, to run something ○ *He's in charge of the booking office.* ○ *She's in charge of the children's crèche.* **2.** money which must be paid or the price of a service ○ *to make a small charge for rental* ○ *There is no charge for service* or *No charge is made for service.* □ **a token charge is made for heating** a small charge is made which does not cover the real costs at all **3.** an electric current ■ *verb* **1.** to ask someone to pay for services later □ **to charge a customer for packing, to charge the packing to the customer, to charge the customer with the packing** the customer has to pay for packing □ **to charge something to sth** to ask for payment to be put on an account ○ *Can I charge the restaurant bill to my room number?* ○ *He asked for the hotel bill to be charged to the company account.* **2.** to ask for money to be paid ○ *to charge £5 for delivery* ○ *How much does he charge?* □ **he charges £6 an hour** he asks to be paid £6 for an hour's work

'…traveller's cheques cost 1% of their face value – some banks charge more for small amounts' [*Sunday Times*]

chargeable /ˈtʃɑːdʒəb(ə)l/ *adjective* □ **repairs chargeable to the occupier** repairs which are to be paid for by the occupier

charge account /ˈtʃɑːdʒ əˌkaʊnt/ *noun* BUSINESS an arrangement that a customer has with a store or organisation to buy goods or services and to pay for them at a later date, usually when an invoice is sent at the end of the month

charge card /ˈtʃɑːdʒ kɑːd/ *noun* FINANCE a credit card for which a fee is payable, but which requires the user to pay off the total sum charged at the end of each month

chargrill /ˈtʃɑːgrɪl/ *verb* to grill food over charcoal on a barbecue or to roast it in a ridged pan that makes it look as if it has been barbecued

chargrilled, char-grilled *adjective* CATERING grilled under or over hot metal, so as to make the meat slightly black ○ *a chargrilled steak*

'…for fish lovers, there is chargrilled swordfish' [*Caterer & Hotelkeeper*]

charlotte /ˈʃɑːlət/ *noun* DESSERTS a dessert made with fruit or cream in a thin biscuit or pastry case

charlotte russe /ˌʃɑːlət ˈruːs/ *noun* DESSERTS a cold dessert of flavoured cream inside a case of thin sponge biscuits

chart /tʃɑːt/ *noun* **1.** SHIPS AND BOATS a map of a sea or river, showing the depth of water and where rocks and sandbanks are located **2.** a diagram showing information as a series of e.g. lines or blocks

charter /ˈtʃɑːtə/ *noun* the act of hiring transport for a special purpose. ◇ **bareboat charter** □ **boat on charter to Mr Smith** a boat which Mr Smith has hired for a voyage ■ *verb* to hire for a special purpose ○ *to charter a plane* or *a boat* or *a bus*

chartered /ˈtʃɑːtəd/ *adjective* hired for a special purpose

Chartered Institute of Environmental Health /ˌtʃɑːtəd ˌɪnstɪtjuːt əv ɪnˌvaɪrənmənt(ə)l ˈhelθ/ *noun* a British organisation founded in 1883 to promote public and environmental health. Abbr **CIEH**

'…the proposed European Food Authority (EFA) could be nothing but an expensive layer of bureaucracy if it is not given real enforcement powers, the Chartered Institute of Environmental Health (CIEH) has warned the MEPs. The CIEH believes the EFA, scheduled to be launched by 2002, should give priority to food-poisoning figures and improve the response to food-poisoning outbreaks, which it said was poor across the EU' [*Caterer & Hotelkeeper*]

charterer /ˈtʃɑːtərə/ *noun* SHIPS AND BOATS somebody who hires a boat or aircraft for a special purpose

charter flight /ˈtʃɑːtə flaɪt/ *noun* AIR TRAVEL a flight in an aircraft which has been hired to carry a particular group of people

chartering /ˈtʃɑːtərɪŋ/ *noun* the act of hiring for a special purpose

charter plane /ˈtʃɑːtə pleɪn/ *noun* AIR TRAVEL a plane that has been chartered

chateau, château *noun* **1.** TOURISM a country house, manor house or castle in France ○ *a tour of the Châteaux of the Loire* **2.** an estate where wine is made, usually referring to the wine-producing estates of the Bordeaux region (NOTE: **chateau** comes from the French noun meaning 'castle'. The plural form is **chateaus** or **châteaux**.) □ **chateau-bottled** bottled on the estate where it was produced

COMMENT: The word château does not necessarily imply a top quality wine, as many appellation contrôlée wines are called after the château where they are made. The major Bordeaux wines are all called after châteaux: Château Latour, Château Lafite, Château Mouton Rothschild, Château Lynch-Bages, Château Beychevelle, etc.

Chateaubriand /ˌʃætəʊ'briːɒn/ *noun* a thick beefsteak cut from the widest middle part of the fillet

chauffeur /'ʃəʊfə/ *noun* ROAD TRAVEL somebody who drives a car for someone □ **chauffeur-driven car** a large car that is driven by a chauffeur

chauffeuse /ʃəʊ'fɜːz/ *noun* ROAD TRAVEL a woman who drives a car for someone

cheap /tʃiːp/ *adjective, adverb* not costing a lot of money ○ *Are there any cheap hotels in London?* ○ *They always stay in the cheapest hotel possible.* □ **cheap rate** a rate which is not expensive ○ *cheap-rate phone calls* □ **to buy something cheap** to buy something at a low price □ **they work out cheaper by the box** these items are cheaper per unit if you buy a box of them

check /tʃek/ *noun* 1. an investigation or examination ○ *a routine check of the fire equipment* 2. US (*in a restaurant*) a bill 3. *US* same as **cheque** 4. *US* same as **tick** ■ *verb* to examine something to see if it is satisfactory ○ *Don't forget to check the bill to see if it is correct.* ■ *adjective* with a pattern of small squares ○ *The chef was wearing his traditional blue check trousers.* ○ *The French restaurant had red and white check tablecloths.*

checkbook /'tʃekbʊk/ *noun US* FINANCE same as **cheque book**

checked /tʃekt/ *adjective* with a pattern of small squares ○ *The chef was wearing his traditional blue checked trousers.* ○ *The French restaurant had red and white checked tablecloths.*

checked baggage /ˌtʃekt 'bægɪdʒ/ *noun* AIR TRAVEL baggage which has been weighed at the check-in and passed to the airline to be put onto the aircraft

check in /ˌtʃek 'ɪn/ *verb* 1. (*at a hotel*) to arrive at a hotel and write your name and address on a list ○ *He checked in at 12.15.* 2. AIR TRAVEL (*at an airport*) to give in your ticket to show you are ready to take the flight 3. □ **to check baggage in** to pass your baggage to the airline to have it weighed and put on the aircraft for you

check-in /'tʃek ɪn/ *noun* 1. HOTELS the act of arriving and registering 2. AIR TRAVEL same as **check-in desk**

check-in counter /'tʃek ɪn ˌkaʊntə/ *noun* AIR TRAVEL a counter where passengers check in

check-in desk /'tʃek ɪn ˌdesk/ *noun* AIR TRAVEL a place where passengers give in their tickets for a flight ○ *The check-in desk is on the first floor.*

checking /'tʃekɪŋ/ *noun* an examination or investigation ○ *The inspectors found some problems during their checking of the building.*

checking account /'tʃekɪŋ əˌkaʊnt/ *noun US* FINANCE a bank account on which you can write cheques

check-in procedure /'tʃek ɪn prəˌsiːdʒə/ *noun* HOTELS the formalities to be done when a guest checks in, e.g. allocating a room, taking the guest's name and asking the guest to sign the hotel register

check-in time /'tʃek ɪn ˌtaɪm/ *noun* TRAVEL the time at which passengers should check in

checklist /'tʃeklɪst/ *noun* HOTELS a list of things which have to be checked, such as doors that have to be locked or items of linen that should be ready in the bathroom

check out /ˌtʃek 'aʊt/ *verb* (*at a hotel*) to leave and pay for a room ○ *We will check out before breakfast.* ○ *Guests tend to check out on Thursdays.*

checkout /'tʃekaʊt/ *noun* 1. (*in a supermarket*) a place where you pay for the goods you have bought 2. (*in a hotel*) the act of leaving and paying the bill

checkout procedure /'tʃekaʊt prəˌsiːdʒə/ *noun* HOTELS the formalities to be done when a guest checks out, e.g. presenting the bill and making sure it is paid and taking the room key back

checkout time /'tʃekaʊt taɪm/ *noun* HOTELS the time by which you have to leave your room ○ *Checkout time is 12.00.*

checkpoint /'tʃekpɔɪnt/ *noun* a place where police or other officials stop and check people or vehicles

checkroom /'tʃekruːm/ *noun US* a place where you leave your coat or baggage

cheddar /'tʃedə/ *noun* a hard pale yellow or orange-red cheese with a flavour that ranges from mild to very strong, depending on its maturity

cheers! /'tʃɪəz/ *interjection* (*informal*) 1. thank you! 2. (*when drinking*) good health!

cheese /tʃiːz/ *noun* DAIRY a solid food made from cow's milk curds, also made from goat's milk and more rarely from ewe's milk and buffalo milk ○ *She ordered a cheese omelette.* □ **a cheese** a whole round cheese

COMMENT: There are many varieties of both hard and soft cheese: the British Caerphilly, Cheddar, Cheshire and Gloucester are all hard cheeses; the French Brie and Camembert are soft. Goat's cheese is almost always soft. In a British-style menu, cheese is served at the end of the meal, after the dessert, while in French-style menus, the cheese is served before the dessert. A selection of cheeses will be placed on a cheeseboard, with a knife: the waiter will help each guest to a small piece of various cheeses as the guest asks for them (see also 'plateau de fromages'). In Britain, cheese is served with water biscuits (or other dry crackers) and butter, and possibly celery; in France, cheese will be served with bread, but rarely with butter.

cheese and biscuits /ˌtʃiːz ənd ˈbɪskɪts/ *noun* CATERING a course in a meal, served after the main course, consisting of various types of cheese and dry or salt biscuits

cheeseboard /ˈtʃiːzbɔːd/ *noun* CATERING **1.** a flat piece of wood on which cheese is served **2.** a selection of cheeses served on a cheeseboard

cheeseburger /ˈtʃiːzbɜːɡə/ *noun* FOOD a hamburger with melted cheese on top

cheesecake /ˈtʃiːzkeɪk/ *noun* DESSERTS a tart with a sweet pastry base and a cooked cream cheese top, often covered with fruit

cheese fondue /ˌtʃiːz ˈfɒnduː/ *noun* FOOD a dish from Switzerland and Eastern France of melted cheese, wine and kirsch, into which cubes of bread are dipped. Also called **fondue bourguignonne**

cheese knife /ˈtʃiːz naɪf/ *noun* a knife with two points at the end of the blade, used for cutting and serving cheese

chef /ʃef/ *noun* CATERING **1.** somebody who is in charge of preparing food in a restaurant ○ *They've got a new chef at the King's Head, and the food is much better.* **2.** the name given to various specialised waiters

COMMENT: The executive chef organises the running of the kitchen, selecting menus, tasting dishes and supervising the specialist chefs working under him. A sous-chef is the assistant to an executive chef: in a large kitchen there might be several sous-chefs. Each chef de partie will have one or more commis chefs working under him. Each will have a title corresponding to the section of the kitchen in which he or she works: commis pâtissier, commis garde-manger, etc.

chef de cuisine /ˌʃef də kwɪˈziːn/ *noun* CATERING same as **chef**

chef de partie /ˌʃef də pɑːˈtiː/ *noun* CATERING the chef in charge of a particular section of a kitchen

chef de rang /ˌʃef də ˈrɒŋ/ *noun* CATERING same as **station waiter**

chef d'étage /ˌʃef deˈtɑʒ/ *noun* CATERING same as **floor attendant**

chef entremétier /ˌʃef ˌɒntrəˈmetieɪ/ *noun* CATERING same as **vegetable chef**

chef garde-manger /ˌʃef ɡɑːd ˈmɒŋʒeɪ/ *noun* CATERING same as **larder chef**

chef pâtissier /ˌʃef pəˈtiːsieɪ/ *noun* CATERING same as **pastry chef**

chef poissonnier /ˌʃef pwæˈsɒnieɪ/ *noun* CATERING same as **fish chef**

chef potager /ˌʃef pɒˈtɑʒeɪ/ *noun* CATERING same as **soup chef**

chef restaurateur /ˌʃef ˌrest(ə)rəˈtɜː/ *noun* CATERING the chef in charge of the à la carte menu

chef rôtisseur /ˌʃef ˌrəɪtiˈsɜː/ *noun* CATERING same as **roast chef**

chef saucier /ˌʃef ˈsɔːsieɪ/ *noun* CATERING same as **sauce chef**

chef's hat /ˈʃefs hæt/ *noun* CATERING a tall white hat, traditionally worn by chefs, which indicates who is the main chef, and which is also useful in keeping the hair out of sight. Also called **toque**

chef's salad /ˌʃfes ˈsæləd/ *noun* a tossed green salad with added tomatoes, sliced hard-boiled eggs and thin strips of meat and cheese

chef's special /ˌʃefs ˈspeʃ(ə)l/ *noun* CATERING a special dish, sometimes one which the chef is famous for, which is listed separately on the menu

chef tournant /ˌʃef ˈtɔːnɒnt/ *noun* CATERING a chef who is available to work in any of the sections of a kitchen, helping out when other chefs are ill or on holiday

chef traiteur /ˌʃef treɪˈtɜː/ *noun* CATERING the chef in charge of outside functions, such as buffets or meals which are prepared in the kitchen, but served in a different venue

chemical toilet /ˌkemɪk(ə)l ˈtɔɪlət/ *noun* a toilet where the waste matter is decomposed by chemicals

cheque /tʃek/ *noun* FINANCE **1.** a note to a bank asking them to pay money from your account to the account of the person whose name is written on the note ○ *He wrote out a cheque for £10* or *a £10 cheque.* ○ *You can pay by cash, cheque or credit card.* (NOTE: The US spelling is **check.**) **2.** □ **to cash a cheque** to exchange a cheque for cash □ **to**

endorse a cheque to sign a cheque on the back to show that you accept it □ **to make out a cheque to someone** to write someone's name on a cheque ○ *Who shall I make the cheque out to?* □ **to pay by cheque** to pay by giving a cheque, and not by using cash or a credit card □ **to pay a cheque into your account** to deposit a cheque □ **to sign a cheque** to sign on the front of a cheque to show that you authorise the bank to pay the money from your account □ **to stop a cheque** to ask a bank not to pay a cheque you have written

cheque account /'tʃek ə,kaʊnt/ *noun* FINANCE same as **current account**

cheque book /'tʃek bʊk/ *noun* FINANCE a booklet of new cheques (NOTE: The US spelling is **checkbook**.)

cheque card /'tʃek kɑːd/, **cheque guarantee card** /,tʃek ,gærən'tiː kɑːd/ *noun* FINANCE a plastic card from a bank which guarantees payment of a cheque up to a particular amount, even if the user has no money in his or her account

cherry /'tʃeri/ *noun* FRUIT a small summer fruit, usually dark red, but also light red or almost white, growing on a long stalk (NOTE: The plural form is **cherries**.)

cherry pie /,tʃeri 'paɪ/ *noun* DESSERTS a pie filled with cherries

cherry tomato /'tʃeri tə,mɑːtəʊ/ *noun* VEGETABLES a variety of very small tomato

chervil /'tʃɜːvɪl/ *noun* SAUCES, ETC. a herb used to flavour soups

chestnut /'tʃesnʌt/ *noun* a bright red-brown nut

COMMENT: The sweet chestnut, *Castanea sativa*, is eaten in sauces with roast meat, is made into sweet purée or eaten hot roasted over charcoal in the street. There is another chestnut tree which is common in Britain, the horse chestnut, *Aesculus hippocastanum*, which has similar brown nuts which are not edible.

chestnut purée /,tʃesnʌt 'pjʊəreɪ/ *noun* SAUCES, ETC. a purée made of cooked sweet chestnuts, usually with added sugar and vanilla

chest of drawers /,tʃest əv 'drɔːz/ *noun* a piece of bedroom furniture made of several sliding compartments

chez /ʃeɪ/ *noun* meaning 'at the home or business of', frequently used in the names of French restaurants, as in 'Chez Victor'

chianti /ki'ænti/ *noun* BEVERAGES a dry red wine from Tuscany, Italy

chicken /'tʃɪkɪn/ *noun* MEAT a common farm bird that is eaten as food and produces

the eggs that are most commonly used in cooking ○ *chicken soup* ○ *chicken salad* ○ *chicken sandwich* ○ *We had roast chicken for lunch.*

COMMENT: Chicken is the most widely used meat in Britain, and also one of the cheapest.

chicken Kiev /,tʃɪkɪn 'kiːev/ *noun* FOOD a boned piece of chicken, filled with garlic and butter, which is covered in breadcrumbs and deep-fried

chickpea /'tʃɪkpiː/ *noun* VEGETABLES a pale yellow seed about the size of a large pea, cooked as a vegetable

chicory /'tʃɪkəri/ *noun* VEGETABLES a vegetable with a conical white head of crisp leaves, eaten raw as a salad or cooked and served with a sauce. ◊ **endive**

chief steward /,tʃiːf 'stjuːəd/ *noun* TRAVEL the most important or most experienced steward on a ship or plane. Also called **senior steward**

chiffon /'ʃɪfɒn/ *adjective* CATERING referring to food with a light fluffy texture, usually created by adding whipped egg whites or gelatin

chiffonade /'ʃɪfənɑːd/ *noun* VEGETABLES vegetables that have been shredded or finely chopped, often used as a garnish for other foods

child /tʃaɪld/ *noun* a young person ○ *A group of children were playing on the beach.* (NOTE: The plural form is **children**.)

child-friendly /,tʃaɪld 'frendli/ *adjective* liking and understanding children and their special needs ○ *It is a child-friendly hotel with baby-sitting facilities and a children's pool.*

children's menu /'tʃɪldr(ə)nz ,menjuː/ *noun* CATERING a special menu for children (NOTE: Children's menus usually contain fast food items, such as hamburgers or hot dogs.)

children's play area, children's playground *noun* ENTERTAINMENT an area outside a pub, hotel or restaurant, or in a town garden, or inside a ferry, where children can play

children's room /'tʃɪldr(ə)nz ruːm/ *noun* BARS a room in a pub, usually away from the bar, where children can eat

child's portion, children's portion *noun* a small portion of food served in a restaurant for a child

chill /tʃɪl/ *verb* to make food cold ○ *chilled orange juice*

COMMENT: Low temperature retards the rate at which food spoils. Pre-cooked foods should be cooled rapidly down to – 3°C and eaten within five days of production. Certain high-risk chilled foods should be kept below 5°C; these foods include soft cheese and various pre-cooked products. Eggs in shells can be chilled for short-term storage (i.e. up to one month) at temperatures between –10°C and – 16°C. Bread goes stale quickly at chill temperatures. Potatoes, lettuces and strawberries must not be chilled at all.

chilled food /ˌtʃɪld ˈfuːd/ *noun* food which has been prepared, then made cold

chilled storage /ˌtʃɪld ˈstɔːrɪdʒ/ *noun* CATERING a place where food can be stored at low temperatures ○ *You can re-use the food if it has been returned to, and kept in, chilled storage at or below 5° C.*

chiller /ˈtʃɪlə/ *noun* CATERING a machine for chilling food. ◊ **blast chiller**

chilli /ˈtʃɪli/ *noun* SAUCES, ETC. a very hot-tasting pod with seeds in it, available fresh as green or red chillis, dried or preserved in cans or bottles. Also called **chilli pepper** (NOTE: The US spelling is **chili**.)

　COMMENT: Chilli is available fresh as green or red chillis, dried or preserved in cans or bottles. The dried pods are ground to make Cayenne pepper.

chilli con carne /ˌtʃɪli kɒn ˈkɑːni/ *noun* FOOD a Mexican dish of beans, minced beef and chilli sauce

chilli pepper /ˈtʃɪli ˌpepə/ *noun* SAUCES, ETC. same as **chilli**

chilli sauce /ˌtʃɪli ˈsɔːs/ *noun* tomato sauce flavoured with chilli

chilly /ˈtʃɪli/ *adjective* quite cold ○ *You should pack a warm pullover, as even the summer evenings can be chilly in the mountains.*

china /ˈtʃaɪnə/, **chinaware** *noun* CATERING cups, saucers and other dishes made from fine white clay

　'…at his newly opened restaurant, he said that he chose white Italian bone china because 'plain food needed a plain backdrop'' [*Caterer & Hotelkeeper*]

Chinese gooseberry /ˌtʃaɪniːz ˈɡʊzb(ə)ri/ *noun* FRUIT same as **kiwi fruit**

Chinese restaurant syndrome /ˌtʃaɪniːz ˈrest(ə)rɒnt ˌsɪndrəʊm/ *noun* MEDICAL an allergic condition that gives people violent headaches after eating food flavoured with monosodium glutamate, which is used in Chinese cooking. ◊ **monosodium glutamate**

chip /tʃɪp/ *noun* 1. FOOD a small stick-shaped piece of potato, fried in oil or fat ○ *fried eggs and chips* ○ *She had a hamburger and a portion of chips.* 2. US FOOD a thin slice of potato, fried till crisp and eaten cold as a snack (NOTE: In British English, this is called a **crisp**.) 3. a small piece of something

chip & PIN /ˌtʃɪp ən ˈpɪn/ *adjective* referring to a system in which customers prove their identity with a four-digit personal identity number rather than a signature when paying with a card

chipolata /ˌtʃɪpəˈlɑːtə/ *noun* MEAT a small thin sausage, usually made of finely ground pork

chip shop /ˈtʃɪp ʃɒp/ *noun* CATERING same as **fish-and-chip shop**

chit /tʃɪt/ *noun* a bill for food or drink in a club

chitterlings /ˈtʃɪtəlɪŋz/ *plural noun* MEAT the small intestines of pigs, used for food

chive /tʃaɪv/ *noun* SAUCES, ETC. an onion-like herb, of which the leaves are used as a garnish or in soups and salads

chlorinate /ˈklɔːrɪneɪt/ *verb* to disinfect or sterilise something with chlorine

chlorination /ˌklɔːrɪˈneɪʃ(ə)n/ *noun* sterilisation by adding chlorine ○ *Chlorination tablets can be added to water to make it safe to drink.*

　COMMENT: Chlorination is used to kill bacteria in drinking water, in swimming pools and sewage farms, and has many industrial applications such as sterilisation in food processing.

chlorinator /ˈklɔːrɪneɪtə/ *noun* an apparatus for adding chlorine to water

chlorine /ˈklɔːriːn/ *noun* a powerful greenish gas, used to sterilise water

choc /tʃɒk/ *noun* FOOD a chocolate (*informal*)

choc-ice /ˈtʃɒk aɪs/ *noun* DESSERTS a hard block of ice cream covered with chocolate

chocolate /ˈtʃɒklət/ *noun* 1. DESSERTS a popular sweet food made from the cocoa bean □ **chocolate biscuit, chocolate cake, chocolate ice cream** biscuit, cake, or ice cream flavoured with chocolate 2. DESSERTS a small sweet made from chocolate ○ *A box of chocolates was left with the compliments of the management.* ○ *The coffee is served with a small plate of chocolate mints.* 3. □ **a chocolate-box cottage** a typical English cottage, with thatched roof and flowers growing all round, as often formerly shown on the lids of chocolate boxes

　COMMENT: Good quality dark chocolate contains a minimum of about 70% cocoa solids, while good quality milk chocolate contains about 34% cocoa solids.

chocolate box /'tʃɒklət bɒks/ *noun* CATERING a decorated box in which chocolates are packed

chocolate chip /ˌtʃɒklət 'tʃɪp/ *noun* FOOD a small piece of hard chocolate, used in ice cream, biscuits or cakes ○ *mint chocolate chip ice cream*

chocolate chip cookie /ˌtʃɒklət tʃɪp 'kʊki/ *noun* BREAD, ETC. a sweet biscuit made with little pieces of hard chocolate inside

chocolatier /ˌtʃɒklə'tɪə/ *noun* a maker or seller of chocolates

choke /tʃəʊk/ *noun* **1.** ROAD TRAVEL (*in a car engine*) a valve which reduces the flow of air to the engine, or a knob on the dashboard of a car which activates this valve ○ *You need to pull out the choke to start the car.* ○ *This model has an automatic choke.* **2.** VEGETABLES the central inedible part of a globe artichoke ■ *verb* **1.** to block something such as a pipe ○ *The canal was choked with weeds.* **2.** to stop breathing properly because something such as a piece of food is blocking the throat □ **to choke on something** to take something into the windpipe instead of the gullet, so that the breathing is interrupted ○ *He choked on a piece of bread* or *A piece of bread made him choke.*

cholera /'kɒlərə/ *noun* MEDICAL a serious bacterial disease spread through food or water that has been infected by *Vibrio cholerae* ○ *A cholera epidemic broke out after the flood.*

COMMENT: The infected person suffers diarrhoea, cramp in the intestines and dehydration. The disease may be fatal and vaccination is only effective for a relatively short period (no more than six months).

cholera vaccine /'kɒlərə ˌvæksiːn/ *noun* MEDICAL a vaccine which protects to some degree against cholera

chop /tʃɒp/ *noun* MEAT same as **rib** ○ *pork chop* ○ *lamb chop* ■ *verb* to cut something roughly into small pieces with a knife or other sharp tool

chopped livers /ˌtʃɒpt 'lɪvəz/ *plural noun* FOOD a Jewish dish, made of cooked chicken livers chopped up into small pieces

chopping board /'tʃɒpɪŋ bɔːd/ *noun* CATERING a piece of thick wood, used in a kitchen to cut up food on. Also called **cutting board**

chopsticks /'tʃɒpstɪks/ *plural noun* CATERING a pair of small sticks used in the Far East to eat food or to stir food when cooking ○ *He said he didn't know how to use chopsticks and asked for a knife and fork instead.*

chorizo /tʃə'riːzəʊ/ *noun* MEAT a very spicy Spanish or Mexican pork sausage

choux pastry /ˌʃuː 'peɪstri/ *noun* BREAD, ETC. a soft glossy egg-rich pastry that puffs up into a hollow case when baked

chowder /'tʃaʊdə/ *noun* US FOOD fish soup ○ *clam chowder*

COMMENT: Chowders are made from ordinary white fish or from shellfish such as lobsters or clams. The fish is cooked with vegetables and milk or cream is added to make a thick soup.

Christian name /'krɪstʃən neɪm/ *noun* the first name or given name, as opposed to a surname or family name ○ *I know his surname's Smith, but what's his Christian name?*

Christmas /'krɪsməs/ *noun* a Christian festival on December 25th, celebrated as the birthday of Jesus Christ, when presents are given ○ *Have you opened your Christmas presents yet?* ○ *The hotel has special rates for Christmas Day.*

COMMENT: Special food eaten at Christmas time includes Christmas pudding and mince pies (eaten at Christmas lunch or dinner), and Christmas cake, eaten at tea time. Typical decorations for Christmas include a Christmas tree with small lights, holly with red berries, and mistletoe.

Christmas cake /'krɪsməs keɪk/ *noun* FOOD a specially rich fruit cake, decorated with icing

Christmas Day /ˌkrɪsməs 'deɪ/ *noun* December 25th

Christmas decorations /'krɪsməs dekəˌreɪʃ(ə)nz/ *plural noun* coloured papers, bunting, holly, mistletoe, etc., used to decorate a restaurant or hotel for Christmas

Christmas holidays /ˌkrɪsməs 'hɒlɪdeɪz/ *plural noun* the holiday period from at least December 24th to after January 1st

Christmas lunch /ˌkrɪsməs 'lʌntʃ/ *noun* CATERING a special lunch menu with turkey and cranberry sauce, Christmas pudding and mince pies

Christmas party /ˌkrɪsməs 'pɑːti/ *noun* **1.** a party held to celebrate Christmas ○ *A number of Christmas parties are already booked.* **2.** a group of people who are celebrating Christmas

Christmas pudding /ˌkrɪsməs 'pʊdɪŋ/ *noun* DESSERTS a rich fruit pudding, cooked by steaming, served with brandy butter sauce

chronological order /ˌkrɒnəlɒdʒɪk(ə)l ˈɔːdə/ *noun* arrangement by the order of the dates

Chunnel /ˈtʃʌn(ə)l/ *noun* RAIL TRAVEL same as **Channel Tunnel**

church /tʃɜːtʃ/ *noun* a large building for Christian religious ceremonies ○ *The oldest building in the village is St Mary's Church.* ○ *The times of the church services are given on the board outside.* (NOTE: The plural form is **churches**.)

chute /ʃuːt/ *noun* **1.** a slide into water in a swimming pool ○ *The kids screamed as they slid down the chute into the pool.* **2.** a slide to send things down to a lower level ○ *A chute from the first floor will speed up the laundering process.*

chutney /ˈtʃʌtni/ *noun* SAUCES, ETC. a sweet and spicy relish made from fruit, spices, sugar and vinegar

ciabatta /tʃəˈbætə/ *noun* a flat white Italian bread made with olive oil

cider /ˈsaɪdə/ *noun* BEVERAGES an alcoholic drink made from apple juice ○ *Somerset and Devon are famous for their cider.* ○ *In Brittany, cider is served with pancakes.*

COMMENT: Cider is usually naturally fizzy; it can be sweet or dry. Strong traditional cider is known as 'scrumpy', especially in south-western England.

CIEH *abbreviation* Chartered Institute of Environmental Health

cigar /sɪˈɡɑː/ *noun* a tight roll of dried tobacco leaves which you can light and smoke ○ *He smoked a large cigar after his meal.* ○ *The restaurant offers a wide choice of Cuban cigars.*

cinema /ˈsɪnɪmə/ *noun* ENTERTAINMENT a theatre where films are shown

cinemagoer /ˈsɪnɪməˌɡəʊə/ *noun* ENTERTAINMENT somebody who goes to the cinema

cinema ticket /ˈsɪnɪmə ˌtɪkɪt/ *noun* ENTERTAINMENT a ticket which allows you a seat in a cinema

cinnamon /ˈsɪnəmən/ *noun* SAUCES, ETC. a spice made from the bark of a tropical tree ○ *Add a pinch of ground cinnamon to the apple pie.* ○ *Add a cinnamon stick to the hot wine.* ○ *Cinnamon toast is a favourite of American children.*

COMMENT: Cinnamon is used to flavour sweet dishes, cakes and drinks.

circle /ˈsɜːk(ə)l/ *noun* ENTERTAINMENT a row of seats above the stalls in a theatre ○ *We got tickets for the upper circle.*

circus /ˈsɜːkəs/ *noun* **1.** ENTERTAINMENT a travelling show, often given under a large tent, with animals, clowns, acrobats, etc. ○ *We went to the circus last night.* ○ *The circus is coming to town for the bank holiday weekend.* **2.** ROAD TRAVEL a busy roundabout or road junction in a large town ○ *Oxford Circus is where Oxford Street crosses Regent Street.* (NOTE: The plural form is **circuses**.)

citizen /ˈsɪtɪz(ə)n/ *noun* **1.** a person who comes from a particular country or has the same right to live there as someone who was born there ○ *She became an Irish citizen in 1991.* ○ *He was born in Germany, but is now a British citizen.* **2.** somebody with full rights as an inhabitant of a country ○ *She became an Irish citizen in 1991.* ○ *He was born in Germany, but is now a British citizen.*

citric acid /ˌsɪtrɪk ˈæsɪd/ *noun* CATERING an acid found in citrus fruit such as oranges, lemons and grapefruit

citrus fruit /ˈsɪtrəs fruːt/ *noun* FRUIT the edible fruits of evergreen citrus trees, grown throughout the tropics and subtropics. The most important are oranges, lemons, grapefruit and limes. Citrus fruit have thick skins, are very acidic and are an important source of Vitamin C.

city /ˈsɪti/ *noun* **1.** a large town ○ *The largest cities in Europe are linked by hourly flights.* **2.** □ **the City** the old centre of London, where banks and large companies have their main offices

city break /ˈsɪti breɪk/ *noun* TOURISM a short holiday in a large city usually over a weekend, at a specially low tariff □ **city break operator** a travel agent who organises city breaks

city centre /ˌsɪti ˈsentə/ *noun* the centre of a city ○ *It's more convenient to stay in city-centre hotels, but they can be noisy.*

city hall /ˌsɪti ˈhɔːl/ *noun* a building where the administration of a city is

city terminal /ˌsɪti ˈtɜːmɪn(ə)l/ *noun* AIR TRAVEL an air terminal in the centre of a large town

Civil Aviation Authority /ˌsɪvɪl ˌeɪvi ˈeɪʃ(ə)n ɔːˌθɒrəti/ *noun* AIR TRAVEL a British government agency that regulates the operation of civilian airlines. Abbr **CAA**

civil law /ˌsɪv(ə)l ˈlɔː/ *noun* the laws relating to arguments between individuals and the rights of individuals

claim /kleɪm/ *noun* an official request for something, e.g. for money owed to you by an insurance company ■ *verb* to say you own something that has been left behind or lost ○ *No one has claimed the umbrella left in the reception.*

claim check /ˈkleɪm tʃek/ *noun* a token used when leaving luggage, one half of which is attached to the luggage and the other half of which the owner keeps and presents to collect it

claim form /ˈkleɪm fɔːm/ *noun* FINANCE a form which has to be filled in when making an insurance claim

claret /ˈklærət/ *noun* BEVERAGES red wine from Bordeaux ○ *We had a good bottle of claret with our meal.*

clarify /ˈklærɪfaɪ/ *verb* **1.** to make butter or fat clear by gently heating it and removing any impurities **2.** to make a liquid clear and pure, usually by filtering it

class /klɑːs/ *noun* **1.** a category or group into which things are classified according to quality or price **2.** a group of children or adults who go to school or college together

classification /ˌklæsɪfɪˈkeɪʃ(ə)n/ *noun* a way of putting into classes according to quality

COMMENT: The English Tourism Council uses the following classification symbols: for hotels there are five grades of stars (one star to five stars). For facilities offered by inns, farmhouses, bed and breakfast accommodation, boarding houses, etc., there are five grades, shown by diamonds (one diamond to five diamonds). For facilities offered by self-catering accommodation there are five grades, also shown by one to five stars.

classified ads /ˌklæsɪfaɪd ˈædz/ *plural noun* MARKETING advertisements listed in a newspaper under special headings, such as 'property to let' or 'job vacancies' ○ *Look in the classified ads to see if there are any cottages to let in Wales.* Also called **small ads**, **want ads**

classified directory /ˌklæsɪfaɪd daɪˈrekt(ə)ri/ *noun* BUSINESS a book which lists businesses grouped under various headings, such as 'computer shops' or 'newsagents'

classify /ˈklæsɪfaɪ/ *verb* to put something into classes or categories

classy /ˈklɑːsi/ *adjective* of good quality (*informal*) ○ *It's a really classy joint.* ○ *This isn't a very classy restaurant but the food is good.*

clean /kliːn/ *adjective* free from dirt, waste products or unwanted substances ○ *The maid forgot to put clean towels in the bathroom.* ■ *verb* to remove dirt ○ *When we got into the room, we found that the bath had not been cleaned properly.*

cleaner /ˈkliːnə/ *noun* **1.** a machine which removes dirt **2.** a person who cleans a build-

ing such as a house or an office ○ *The cleaners didn't empty my wastepaper basket.*

cleaning /ˈkliːnɪŋ/ *noun* **1.** the act of making something clean ○ *The cleaning of the house after the party took hours.* ○ *The cleaning staff come on shift at 5.30.* **2.** clothes which are going to be sent for dry-cleaning or which have been returned after dry-cleaning ○ *She ran through the rain to her car with an armful of cleaning.*

cleanliness /ˈklenlinəs/ *noun* the state or degree of being clean ○ *The inspectors criticised the cleanliness of the kitchens.* ○ *A person of rather doubtful cleanliness applied for a job as a waiter.*

'…one member of staff has the job of constantly checking cleanliness of the serving area' [*Caterer & Hotelkeeper*]

clear /klɪə/ *verb* to remove dirty plates, cutlery and glasses from a surface such as a table

clearance /ˈklɪərəns/ *noun* **1.** the act of removing dirty plates, cutlery and glasses from a surface such as a table **2.** AIR TRAVEL permission to take off

clearance certificate /ˈklɪərəns səˌtɪfɪkət/ *noun* BUSINESS a document showing that goods have been passed by customs

clear profit /ˌklɪə ˈprɒfɪt/ *noun* FINANCE profit after all expenses have been paid ○ *We made $6,000 clear profit on the deal.*

clementine /ˈkleməntiːn/ *noun* an orange-coloured citrus fruit that is a cross between a tangerine and a Seville orange

clerical staff /ˈklerɪk(ə)l stɑːf/ *noun* same as **office staff**

clerk US /klɑːk/ *noun* somebody who works in an office

client /ˈklaɪənt/ *noun* BUSINESS somebody with whom business is done, or somebody who pays for a service

clientele /ˌkliːɒnˈtel/ *noun* BUSINESS all the clients of a business, or all the customers of a shop

cliff /klɪf/ *noun* a high rock face, usually by the sea ○ *He went for a walk along the top of the cliffs.* ○ *Their first view of England was the white cliffs of Dover.*

cliff jumping /ˈklɪf ˌdʒʌmpɪŋ/ *noun* the sport of jumping from a high point such as a cliff into water

climate /ˈklaɪmət/ *noun* the general weather conditions in a particular place ○ *The South Coast has a very mild climate.* ○ *The climate in Central Europe is hot in the summer and cold and dry in the winter.*

climb /klaɪm/ *noun* the act of going up ○ *It's a stiff climb to the top of the hill.* ■ *verb* **1.** to go up, over or down something using arms and legs ○ *to climb a tree* **2.** SPORT to climb mountains ○ *She plans to climb the highest mountains in Scotland.* ○ *They went climbing in the Alps.*

climber /'klaɪmə/ *noun* SPORT somebody who climbs mountains ○ *The climbers roped themselves together and set off up the slope.*

'Machapuchhre, 22,960ft, the Nepalese peak that has been closed to climbers for nearly half a century, could be opened up to mountaineers later this year' [*TGO – The Great Outdoors*]

climbing /'klaɪmɪŋ/ *noun* SPORT same as **mountaineering** ○ *popular activities such as mountaineering, climbing, hill walking* ○ *Climbing is not a sport for young children.* ○ *We had a climbing holiday last Easter.* ○ *She brought her climbing equipment with her.*

clingstone /'klɪŋstəʊn/ FRUIT ♦ **peach**

clip joint /'klɪp dʒɔɪnt/ *noun* ENTERTAINMENT a low-class club or bar, where guests are charged too much for their drinks

cloakroom /'kləʊkruːm/ *noun* **1.** a room where people can leave coats and hats when going into e.g. a restaurant, theatre or museum **2.** a public toilet (*informal*)

cloakroom attendant /'kləʊkruːm ə ˌtendənt/ *noun* somebody in charge of a cloakroom

cloakroom ticket /'kləʊkruːm ˌtɪkɪt/ *noun* a ticket to show that you have left your coat, hat or bag in a cloakroom

cloaks /kləʊks/ *noun* same as **toilet** (*informal*)

clock /klɒk/ *noun* a machine for telling the time □ **bedside clock** a clock placed next to a bed □ **to work right round the clock** to work all day long

clock golf /'klɒk gɒlf/ *noun* ENTERTAINMENT a game like golf where you hit the ball into a central hole from points round a circle

clock in /ˌklɒk 'ɪn/, **clock on** /ˌklɒk 'ɒn/ *verb* (*of a worker*) to record the time of arriving for work by putting a card into a special timing machine

clocking in /ˌklɒkɪŋ 'ɪn/, **clocking on** /ˌklɒkɪŋ 'ɒn/ *noun* the act of arriving for work and recording the time on a time-card

clocking out /ˌklɒkɪŋ 'aʊt/, **clocking off** /ˌklɒkɪŋ 'ɒf/ *noun* the act of leaving work and recording the time on a time-card

clock out /ˌklɒk 'aʊt/, **clock off** /ˌklɒk 'ɒf/ *verb* (*of a worker*) to record the time of leaving work by putting a card into a special timing machine

clock radio /ˌklɒk 'reɪdiəʊ/ *noun* a radio and clock combined

close *adjective* /kləʊs/ □ **close to** very near, almost ○ *The hotel is close to the railway station.* ■ *verb* /kləʊz/ **1.** to stop doing business for the day ○ *The office closes at 5.30.* ○ *We close early on Saturdays.* **2.** to stop doing business altogether ○ *If this summer is as bad as the last one, the hotel may be forced to close.* □ **he closed his building society account** he took all the money out and stopped using the account ◇ **to close an account 1.** to stop supplying a customer on credit **2.** to take all the money out of a bank account and ask the bank to remove it

closed /kləʊzd/ *adjective* not open, not doing business ○ *Most shops in Germany are closed on Saturday afternoons.* ○ *All the banks are closed on the National Day.*

closed-circuit TV /ˌkləʊzd ˌsɜːkɪt tiː 'viː/ *noun* a system where a TV picture is transmitted from a camera to receivers within a closed circuit. It is used e.g. for surveillance in factories, shops and banks, and for showing pictures of events to people who are not able to attend the event themselves. ○ *The conference was relayed to the lobby on closed-circuit TV.* ○ *The shoplifters were filmed on closed-circuit TV cameras.* Abbr **CCTV**

closing /'kləʊzɪŋ/ *adjective* final, coming at the end □ **closing date** last date ■ *noun* the act of shutting a shop, or the fact of being shut

closing time /'kləʊzɪŋ taɪm/ *noun* the time when a shop or office stops work or when a pub stops selling alcohol

clotted cream /ˌklɒtɪd 'kriːm/ *noun* DAIRY thick solid cream made from milk which has been heated to boiling point, produced especially in the south-west of England

cloud /klaʊd/ *noun* a mass of vapour or smoke in the air ○ *Do you think it's going to rain? – Yes, look at those grey clouds.* ○ *The plane was flying above the clouds.*

cloud-capped /'klaʊd kæpt/ *adjective* topped with clouds

cloudy /'klaʊdi/ *adjective* **1.** covered with clouds ○ *a cloudy sky* ○ *The north coast is often cloudy.* **2.** not clear, not transparent ○ *My beer looks cloudy.*

club /klʌb/ *noun* **1.** a group of people who have the same interest, or a place where these people meet ○ *The members of the old people's club went to the seaside for the day.* ○ *She has applied to join the sports club.* **2.** a place where people can dance to recorded music and that usually has bars and other facilities

clubbing /ˈklʌbɪŋ/ *noun* the activity of going to clubs or nightclubs

club class /ˈklʌb klɑːs/ *noun* AIR TRAVEL a specially comfortable class of seating on a plane, though not as luxurious as first class

clubs /klʌbz/ *plural noun* one of the black suits in a pack of cards, which has a symbol shaped like a leaf with three parts ○ *She had the five of clubs in her hand.* (NOTE: The other black suit is **spades**; **hearts** and **diamonds** are the red suits.)

club sandwich /ˌklʌb ˈsændwɪdʒ/ *noun* FOOD a sandwich made of three slices of bread, with a filling of meat, salad, fish, etc., between them. Also called **double-decker 2**

cm *abbreviation* centimetre

coach /kəʊtʃ/ *noun* **1.** ROAD TRAVEL a large comfortable bus, operated for long-distance travellers on a regular route ○ *They took a coach tour of southern Spain.* **2.** ROAD TRAVEL a large comfortable bus, used by a group of tourists to travel long distances, not on a regular scheduled route, and often abroad ○ *The coach driver fell asleep while driving.* ○ *Coach travel is considerably cheaper than travelling by train.* **3.** RAIL TRAVEL a carriage for passengers on a train ○ *Passengers for Donniford should board the last two coaches of the train.* **4.** SPORT somebody who trains someone in a sport ○ *The hotel has a professional tennis coach available for lessons.*

coach class /ˈkəʊtʃ klɑːs/ *noun* US AIR TRAVEL same as **economy class**

coach party /ˈkəʊtʃ ˌpɑːti/ *noun* TOURISM a group of tourists, travelling by coach

coach station /ˈkəʊtʃ ˌsteɪʃ(ə)n/ *noun* ROAD TRAVEL the central terminus from which coaches leave, and where coach journeys terminate, which usually has a ticket office, waiting rooms, refreshments and other facilities

coach tour /ˈkəʊtʃ ˌtʊə/ *noun* TOURISM a tour of various places, in a coach

coach trip /ˈkəʊtʃ trɪp/ *noun* TOURISM an excursion by coach

coast /kəʊst/ *noun* the parts of a country that are by the sea ○ *The south coast is the warmest part of the country.* ○ *Let's drive down to the coast this weekend.* □ **from coast to coast** from the sea on one side of a country to the sea on the other side ○ *He crossed the USA from coast to coast.* ■ *verb* **1.** ROAD TRAVEL to ride in or on a vehicle without

using the engine or the pedals **2.** SHIPS AND BOATS (*of a boat*) to sail along a coast

coastal /ˈkəʊst(ə)l/ *adjective* referring to the coast ○ *coastal navigation* ○ *the coastal resorts of southern England*

coastal resort /ˈkəʊst(ə)l rɪˌzɔːt/ *noun* TOURISM a holiday town on the coast ○ *Brighton is a popular coastal resort.*

coasteering /kəʊˈstɪərɪŋ/ *noun* SPORT a sport that takes place along a coast and combines scrambling, rock climbing, traversing, swimming and cliff jumping

coaster /ˈkəʊstə/ *noun* **1.** SHIPS AND BOATS a ship which sails from port to port along the coast ○ *We sailed round Africa on a small coaster.* **2.** CATERING a flat dish or small mat for standing a bottle or glass on ○ *Here's a coaster to put your glass on.*

coastguard /ˈkəʊstgɑːd/ *noun* somebody who watches over a stretch of coast, looking out for accidents at sea or illegal activities such as smuggling ○ *Coastguards stopped a fishing boat suspected of carrying drugs.*

coastline /ˈkəʊstlaɪn/ *noun* the edge of the coast ○ *the rocky Cornish coastline*

coat /kəʊt/ *noun* a piece of outdoor clothing which covers the top part of the body ○ *You'll need to put your winter coat on – it's just started to snow.* ○ *She was wearing a black fur coat.*

coat-hanger /ˈkəʊt ˌhæŋə/ *noun* a piece of wood, wire or plastic on which you hang clothes in a wardrobe ○ *There were no coat-hangers in the hotel wardrobe.*

coat-hook /ˈkəʊt hʊk/ *noun* a hook on a wall or door for hanging clothes on

cob /kɒb/ *noun* BREAD, ETC. a round loaf of bread ○ *Could you stop at the bakery and buy a wholemeal cob?*

cob nut /ˈkɒb nʌt/ *noun* NUTS a large hazelnut ○ *This bag of mixed nuts includes cob nuts and walnuts.*

cockle /ˈkɒk(ə)l/ *noun* SEAFOOD a small edible shellfish with a double shell ○ *We bought some cockles from a stall by the seafront.*

cockpit /ˈkɒkpɪt/ *noun* AIR TRAVEL the forward area in an aircraft from where the aircraft is controlled by the pilot

cockroach /ˈkɒkrəʊtʃ/ *noun* a large brown or black beetle ○ *In hot damp climates, cockroaches are commonly found in houses.* (NOTE: The plural form is **cockroaches.**)

COMMENT: Two types of cockroach are common: the oriental cockroach, *Blatta orientalis,* and the German cockroach,

Blatta germanica. Both live in dirty areas of buildings, such as badly cleaned kitchens. They can carry Salmonella and Staphylococcus.

cocktail /ˈkɒkteɪl/ *noun* **1.** BEVERAGES a mixture of alcoholic drinks, containing at least one spirit, usually served before a meal ○ *A Bloody Mary is a cocktail of vodka and tomato juice.* **2.** FOOD a mixture of food

COMMENT: Cocktails are mixes of various alcohols and juices, as opposed to long drinks (whisky and soda, gin and tonic), where the alcohol is diluted. Most alcohols can be used as a basis for cocktails: the commonest are gin (gin and French, gin and Italian), vodka (screwdriver, Bloody Mary) and whisky (whisky sour, Manhattan).

cocktail bar /ˈkɒkteɪl bɑː/ *noun* BARS a bar where cocktails are served

cocktail lounge /ˈkɒkˌteɪl laʊndʒ/ *noun* BARS a smart lounge bar in a hotel

cocktail party /ˈkɒkteɪl ˌpɑːti/ *noun* CATERING an evening party where you drink cocktails or other drinks and eat snacks, before going on to a proper meal

cocktail shaker /ˈkɒkteɪl ˌʃeɪkə/ *noun* BARS a metal container into which the barperson puts the various ingredients of a cocktail, which are then shaken vigorously

cocktail snacks /ˈkɒkˌteɪl snæks/ *plural noun* CATERING small items of food such as olives or peanuts, served with drinks before a meal

cocktail stick /ˈkɒkteɪl stɪk/ *noun* CATERING a little piece of wood used to stick in food such as small sausages to make it easier to serve

cocoa /ˈkəʊkəʊ/ *noun* **1.** FOOD a powder made from chocolate beans ○ *There's a tin of cocoa on the shelf next to the cooker.* ○ *Add cocoa powder to icing sugar to make chocolate icing.* **2.** BEVERAGES a drink made from this powder ○ *I'll warm up some milk to make some cocoa.* ○ *He always has a cup of cocoa before going to bed.*

COMMENT: Cocoa is obtained from beans which are the seeds of the *Theobroma cacao* tree and which are contained in a red or green fleshy fruit. The beans contain a fat (cocoa butter), which is removed in preparing cocoa for drinking. Cocoa beans are the raw material of chocolate, and extra fat and sugar are added in its preparation.

cocoa bean /ˈkəʊkəʊ biːn/ *noun* the bean-shaped seed of the cacao tree, which is used for making cocoa powder and chocolate

cocoa butter /ˈkəʊkəʊ ˌbʌtə/ *noun* a thick oily solid obtained from cocoa beans,

used in making chocolate, cosmetics and suntan oils

coconut /ˈkəʊkənʌt/ *noun* NUTS a large nut from a tropical palm tree containing a white edible pulp ○ *I don't like biscuits with coconut in them.*

coconut milk /ˈkəʊkənʌt mɪlk/ *noun* **1.** liquid inside a coconut **2.** a white creamy liquid made from coconut pulp, used in Malaysian and Thai cooking

cod /kɒd/ *noun* SEAFOOD a large white sea fish, *Gadus morhua* ○ *He ordered a plate of fried cod and chips.* (NOTE: The plural form is **cod**.) □ **cod liver oil** oil from the livers of cod, taken as a source of vitamins A and D

COD, c.o.d. *abbreviation* cash on delivery

code /kəʊd/ *noun* **1.** a system of numbers, letters or symbols used to represent language or information □ **machine-readable codes** sets of signs or letters, such as bar codes or postcodes, which can be read by computers **2.** a set of rules

code of practice /ˌkəʊd əv ˈpræktɪs/, **code of ethics** /ˌkəʊd əv ˈeθɪks/ *noun* BUSINESS rules drawn up by an association which the members must follow when doing business

code-sharing /ˈkəʊd ˌʃeərɪŋ/ *noun* AIR TRAVEL a system where two or more airlines sell seats for a flight, and identify the flight using their own two-letter codes, but only one of them actually operates the aircraft

coffee /ˈkɒfi/ *noun* BEVERAGES **1.** the crushed beans of the coffee plant *Coffea*, used to make a hot drink **2.** a drink made from ground coffee beans or powder, mixed with hot water ○ *Would you like a cup of coffee?* ○ *I always take sugar with my coffee.* ○ *The doctor told me to avoid tea and coffee.*

COMMENT: The two main varieties of coffee are Arabica and Robusta. The Arabica shrub *(Coffea arabica)* was originally grown in the southern parts of the highlands of Ethiopia, and was later introduced into south-western Arabia. It represents 75% of the world's total coffee production. Arabica coffee beans are generally considered to produce a higher quality drink than those obtained from the Robusta coffee plant *(Coffea canephora)* which originated in West Africa. Robusta coffee has a stronger and more bitter taste than Arabica. The most important area for growing coffee is South America, especially Bolivia, Brazil and Colombia, though it is also grown in Kenya and Indonesia.

coffee bar /ˈkɒfi bɑː/ *noun* CATERING a small bar serving mainly coffee, non-alcoholic drinks and snacks

coffee beans /'kɒfi biːnz/ *plural noun* FOOD small fruit from the coffee tree, which are dried and roasted to make coffee

coffee break /'kɒfi breɪk/ *noun* a short rest time during work when the employees can drink coffee

coffee cake /'kɒfi keɪk/ *noun* BREAD, ETC. a cake made with coffee flavouring

coffee cup /'kɒfi kʌp/ *noun* a cup for coffee

COMMENT: Coffee is served in large cups at breakfast (when it is usually taken with milk or cream) and in small cups after a meal. The small coffee cup is called a 'demi-tasse'.

coffee grinder /'kɒfi ˌɡraɪndə/ *noun* a machine for grinding coffee beans into powder for making coffee

coffee grounds /'kɒfi ɡraʊndz/ *plural noun* crushed coffee beans left at the bottom of a cup or coffee jug after the coffee has been served

coffeehouse /'kɒfihaʊs/ *noun* a place where coffee and other refreshments are served

coffee ice cream /ˌkɒfi aɪs 'kriːm/ *noun* DESSERTS ice cream flavoured with coffee

coffee lounge /'kɒfi laʊndʒ/ *noun* CATERING a restaurant which serves coffee and cakes

coffee machine /'kɒfi məˌʃiːn/ *noun* CATERING a machine which provides coffee and other drinks when a coin is inserted

coffeemaker /'kɒfiˌmeɪkə/ *noun* a small pot for making coffee, e.g. a percolator or espresso machine

coffee pot /'kɒfi pɒt/ *noun* CATERING a pot in which coffee is made or served

coffee shop /'kɒfi ʃɒp/ *noun* HOTELS a less formal restaurant in a hotel, where light meals and snacks are served ○ *It will be quicker to have lunch in the coffee shop than in the main restaurant.*

coffee spoon /'kɒfi spuːn/ *noun* a very small spoon, used with a small coffee cup

coffee table /'kɒfi ˌteɪb(ə)l/ *noun* a low table on which coffee cups are put

cognac /'kɒnjæk/ *noun* BEVERAGES brandy made in western France ○ *We were served an excellent cognac after dinner.*

coin /kɔɪn/ *noun* a piece of metal money ○ *He gave me two 50p coins in my change.* ○ *I need some 10p coins for the telephone.*

cola /'kəʊlə/ *noun* **1.** FOOD a tree that comes originally from West Africa, but which is also grown in the West Indies and South America. Its nut-like fruit contains caffeine, and can be chewed or used to make cola drinks. **2.** BEVERAGES a fizzy sweet drink ○ *The kids would like two colas please.*

cold /kəʊld/ *adjective* not warm or hot ○ *The machines work badly in cold weather.* ○ *The reception area was so cold that the staff started complaining.* ○ *The coffee machine also sells cold drinks.*

cold buffet /ˌkəʊld 'bʊfeɪ/ *noun* CATERING a buffet with cold dishes to choose from

cold consommé /ˌkəʊld kɒn'sɒmeɪ/ *noun* FOOD a jelly-like soup, which is served cold

cold cuts /'kəʊld kʌts/ *plural noun* US MEAT a plate of slices of cold cooked meat such as ham or salami

cold pack /'kəʊld pæk/ *noun* the packing and sterilisation of uncooked food in jars or tins

cold-pressed /'kəʊld prest/ *adjective* referring to high-grade olive oil produced from the first pressing of the raw olives

cold room /'kəʊld stɔː/, **cold store** *noun* CATERING a room where stores of food are kept cool, so as to prevent the food from going bad

cold storage /ˌkəʊld 'stɔːrɪdʒ/ *noun* CATERING the keeping of food in a cold place to prevent it from going bad ○ *Return the food to cold storage.*

coleslaw /'kəʊlslɔː/ *noun* FOOD a salad of shredded white cabbage mixed with mayonnaise

coley /'kəʊli/ *noun* SEAFOOD a type of sea fish

collar /'kɒlə/ *noun* MEAT a cut of meat, especially bacon, taken from an animal's neck ■ *verb* CATERING to pickle meat by soaking it in salt or brine with seasonings and flavouring ingredients, then rolling, boiling and pressing it

collect /kə'lekt/ *verb* **1.** to make someone pay money which is owed □ **to collect a debt** to go and make someone pay a debt **2.** to take someone or something away from a place ○ *A car will come to collect you from the hotel at 8.30.* ■ *adjective, adverb* US referring to a phone call where the person receiving the call agrees to pay for it ○ *He called his office collect.*

collect call /kə'lekt kɔːl/ *noun* US same as **reverse-charge call**

college /'kɒlɪdʒ/ *noun* a teaching institution for adults and young people ○ *She is taking a course at the catering college.* □ **college of further education** a college for study after secondary school

colour /'kʌlə/ *noun* the appearance which an object has in light, e.g. red, blue or yellow (NOTE: The US spelling is **color**.) □ **colour film**, **colour TV** a film or TV which is not black and white

colour coding /'kʌlə ˌkəʊdɪŋ/ *noun* indicating different usages by colour
COMMENT: Electric wires are colour coded as red (= live), blue (= neutral) and yellow-green (=earth). It has been suggested that kitchen knives should be colour-coded to identify knives used to cut raw meat, fish, vegetables, etc., so as to avoid possible contamination.

colouring /'kʌlərɪŋ/ *noun* CATERING a substance which colours a processed food
COMMENT: Colouring additives have E numbers 100 to 180. Some are natural pigments, such as riboflavine (E101), carrot juice (E160) or chlorophyll (E140) and are safe. Others, such as tartrazine (E102) and other azo dyes are suspected of being carcinogenic. Also suspect is caramel (E150), which is the most widely used colouring substance.

come to /'kʌm tuː, ˌkʌm 'tuː/ *verb* to add up to a particular amount ○ *The bill comes to £125.*

comfort /'kʌmfət/ *noun* conditions that make it easy for the body to rest and feel relaxed

comfortable /'kʌmf(ə)təb(ə)l/ *adjective* soft and relaxing ○ *There are more comfortable chairs in the lounge, if you find the dining room chairs too hard.*

comfortably /'kʌmf(ə)təbli/ *adverb* in a soft, relaxed or relaxing way ○ *If you're sitting comfortably, I'll explain to you what the work involves.*

comfort food /'kʌmfət fuːd/ *noun* CATERING simple food, like the food you had as a child, which makes you feel happy and contented

comfort station /'kʌmfət ˌsteɪʃ(ə)n/ *noun US* a public toilet

commend /kə'mend/ *verb* to say that something or someone is good (*formal*) ○ *She was highly commended by the judges for her cake decorations.* □ **highly commended**, **commended** former grades in the English Tourism Council's grading system for hotels, bed and breakfasts, and guesthouse accommodation

commercial /kə'mɜːʃ(ə)l/ *adjective* referring to business ■ *noun* MARKETING an advertisement on TV or radio

commercial attaché /kə'mɜːʃ(ə)l ə ˌtæʃeɪ/ *noun* BUSINESS a diplomat whose job is to promote the commercial interests of his or her country

commercial directory /kə'mɜːʃ(ə)l daɪ ˌrekt(ə)ri/ *noun* BUSINESS a book which lists all the businesses and businesspeople in a town. Also called **trade directory**

commercial district /kə'mɜːʃ(ə)l ˌdɪstrɪkt/ *noun* the part of a town where offices and shops are situated

commercial hotel /kə,mɜːʃ(ə)l həʊ'tel/ *noun* BUSINESS a hotel which specialises in business travellers

commercial load /kə,mɜːʃ(ə)l 'ləʊd/ *noun* TRAVEL the amount of goods or number of passengers which a bus, train or plane has to carry to make a profit

commercial port /kə,mɜːʃ(ə)l 'pɔːt/ *noun* BUSINESS a port which has only goods traffic

commercial premises /kə,mɜːʃ(ə)l 'premɪsɪz/ *plural noun* BUSINESS same as **business premises**

commercial property /kə,mɜːʃ(ə)l 'prɒpəti/ *noun* buildings used as offices or shops

commercial traveller /kə,mɜːʃ(ə)l 'træv(ə)lə/ *noun* BUSINESS a salesperson who travels round an area visiting customers on behalf of his or her company

commis /'kɒmiː/ *noun* an assistant in a restaurant or kitchen

commis chef /ˌkɒmi: 'ʃef/ *noun* CATERING an assistant chef to a chef de partie

commis de salle /ˌkɒmi: də 'sæl/ *noun* CATERING an assistant to a chef de rang, helping him or her to organise a restaurant

commis saucier /ˌkɒmi: 'sɔːsieɪ/ *noun* CATERING an assistant to the chef saucier, helping him or her prepare sauces

commission /kə'mɪʃ(ə)n/ *noun* BUSINESS money paid to a salesperson or an agent, usually a percentage of the sales made ○ *She gets 10% commission on everything she sells.* □ **he charges 10% commission** he asks for 10% of sales as his payment

commissionable /kə'mɪʃ(ə)nəb(ə)l/ *adjective* on which commission will be paid to the agent

commission agent /kə'mɪʃ(ə)n ˌeɪdʒənt/ *noun* an agent who is paid by commission, not by fee

commissionaire /kə,mɪʃə'neə/ *noun* somebody, usually in uniform, who stands at the entrance to a hotel, restaurant or club, and welcomes guests

commis waiter /ˌkɒmi: 'weɪtə/ *noun*
CATERING a waiter who helps a station
waiter. Also called **assistant waiter**

common carrier /ˌkɒmən 'kæriə/ *noun*
TRAVEL a firm which carries goods or passengers, and which anyone can use

common ownership /ˌkɒmən
'əʊnəʃɪp/ *noun* BUSINESS a situation where
a business is owned by the employees who
work in it

common salt /ˌkɒmən 'sɔːlt/ *noun*
SAUCES, ETC. a white powder used to make
food, especially meat, fish and vegetables,
taste better

common thyme /'kɒmən taɪm/ *noun*
SAUCES, ETC. a herb used to flavour various
dishes. Also called **French thyme**

communicable disease /kə
ˌmjuːnɪkəb(ə)l dɪ'ziːz/ *noun* MEDICAL a disease which can be passed from one person to
another or from an animal to a person

communicate /kə'mjuːnɪkeɪt/ *verb* to
pass information to someone ○ *He finds it
impossible to communicate with his staff.* ○
*Communicating with head office has been
quicker since we started e-mailing them.*

communication /kəˌmjuːnɪ'keɪʃ(ə)n/
noun the act of passing information on to
other people ○ *Communication with the head
office has been made easier by e-mail.* □ **to
enter into communication with someone**
to start discussing something with someone,
usually in writing ○ *We have entered into
communication with the relevant government department.*

communication cord /kəˌmjuːnɪ
'keɪʃ(ə)n ˌkɔːd/ *noun* RAIL TRAVEL a wire in
a train carriage, which you pull to stop the
train in an emergency

communications /kəˌmjuːnɪ
'keɪʃ(ə)nz/ *plural noun* a means of contacting people or passing messages, e.g. telephone and radio ○ *After the flood, all communications with the outside world were
broken.*

commute /kə'mjuːt/ *verb* to travel to
work in town every day ○ *She commutes 70
miles a day.*

commuter /kə'mjuːtə/ *noun* somebody
who travels to work every day

commuter flight /kə'mjuːtə flaɪt/ *noun*
AIR TRAVEL a flight between towns used regularly by commuters

commuter train /kə'mjuːtə treɪn/ *noun*
RAIL TRAVEL a train used regularly by commuters

compactor /kəm'pæktə/ *noun* same as
waste compactor

companion /kəm'pænjən/ *noun* TRAVEL
somebody travelling with a passenger

COMMENT: Some airlines offer special promotional fares for a second person travelling with a full-fare-paying passenger.

company /'kʌmp(ə)ni/ *noun* BUSINESS a
business or group of people organised to buy,
sell or provide a service

**company booking, company reserva-
tion** *noun* BUSINESS a booking made on
behalf of a company, usually at a discount to
the usual rate

company discount /ˌkʌmp(ə)ni
'dɪskaʊnt/ *noun* BUSINESS a discount given
to people working for a particular company

company policy /ˌkʌmp(ə)ni 'pɒlɪsi/
noun BUSINESS the company's agreed way of
doing things ○ *It is against company policy
to give more than thirty days' credit.* ○ *Company policy is to submit all contracts to the
legal department.*

compartment /kəm'pɑːtmənt/ *noun*
TRAVEL a section of a train carriage or of a
plane, separated from other sections ○ *I had
to go through the business compartment to
get to the buffet car.*

compensate /'kɒmpənseɪt/ *verb* to pay
someone for damage or a loss ○ *The airline
refused to compensate him when his baggage
was lost.* (NOTE: You compensate someone
for something.)

compensation /ˌkɒmpən'seɪʃ(ə)n/
noun □ **compensation for damage** payment
for damage done □ **compensation for loss of
property** payment to someone whose property has been stolen or lost

competitive price /kəm'petɪtɪv praɪs/
noun MARKETING a low price aimed to compete with a rival product

complain /kəm'pleɪn/ *verb* to say that you
are not satisfied ○ *He complained about the
price of meals in the restaurant.* ○ *She complained that no one spoke English in the
hotel.* (NOTE: You complain **to** someone
about something or **that** something is no
good.)

complaint /kəm'pleɪnt/ *noun* **1.** an
expression of dissatisfaction about something or someone **2.** MEDICAL an illness

complaints department /kəm'pleɪnts
dɪˌpɑːtmənt/ *noun* BUSINESS a section of a
store or office which deals with complaints
from customers

complaints procedure /kəm'pleɪnts
prəˌsiːdʒə/ *noun* BUSINESS a way of pre-

senting complaints formally from a customer to management

compliment /'kɒmplɪmənt/ *noun* a nice thing that you say to someone about their appearance or about something good they have done ■ *verb* to tell someone that they have done well or look nice ○ *The manager complimented the staff on their efficient service.* ○ *I would like to compliment the chef on an excellent meal.*

complimentary /ˌkɒmplɪ'ment(ə)ri/ *adjective* given free ○ *Each guest receives a complimentary box of chocolates.*

complimentary **room** /ˌkɒmplɪment(ə)ri 'ruːm/ *noun* a hotel room that a person can stay in without paying, e.g. as a prize in a marketing campaign or as compensation for a complaint

complimentary **ticket** /ˌkɒmplɪment(ə)ri 'tɪkɪt/ *noun* a free ticket, given as a present

compliments slip /'kɒmplɪmənts slɪp/ *noun* BUSINESS a piece of paper with the name and address of the company printed on it, which may be sent with documents or gifts instead of a letter

comply /kəm'plaɪ/ *verb* □ **to comply with** to observe a rule or obey an order

compote /'kɒmpɒt/ *noun* fruit cooked in sugar or syrup, served as a hot or cold dessert

comprehension /ˌkɒmprɪ'henʃən/ *noun* an understanding of how something works

'…the starter involved a lot of elements in one dish, including the intricate boning of a quail, comprehension of a classical farce, the preparation of a good quality aspic and the neat reconstruction of the quail' [*Caterer & Hotelkeeper*]

comprehensive /ˌkɒmprɪ'hensɪv/ *adjective* including everything

comprehensive **insurance** /ˌkɒmprɪhensɪv ɪn'ʃʊərəns/ *noun* FINANCE an insurance policy that covers you against all risks which are likely to happen

comptroller /kən'trəʊlə/ *noun* HOTELS somebody who controls the finances in a hotel

compulsory /kəm'pʌlsəri/ *adjective* that must be done, taken or complied with ○ *a compulsory injection against cholera*

computer /kəm'pjuːtə/ *noun* an electronic machine that processes and keeps information automatically, and that can be used for connecting to the Internet and sending e-mails ○ *computer system consisting of a microprocessor and six terminals*

computerise /kəm'pjuːtəraɪz/, **computerize** *verb* to change something from a manual system to one using computers ○ *Our booking system has been completely computerised.*

computerised /kəm'pjuːtəraɪzd/, **computerized** *adjective* worked by computers ○ *a computerised reservation system*

'…independent hotels wishing to attract international business will be at a disadvantage if they are not linked to a global computerized booking system' [*Caterer & Hotelkeeper*]

computer-linked /kəm'pjuːtə lɪŋkt/ *adjective* linked by computer ○ *All the hotels in the group use a computer-linked booking system.*

computer **printout** /kəm,pjuːtə 'prɪntaʊt/ *noun* a printed copy of information from a computer ○ *Our travel agents provided each member of the tour with a printout of flight details and hotel reservations.*

computer reservation system /kəm ,pjuːtə ,rezə'veɪʃ(ə)n ,sɪstəm/ *noun* TRAVEL a system by which e.g. flights or rooms in hotels can be booked from the terminal in the travel agent's office or from an in-flight terminal system direct to a central booking computer. Abbr **CRS**

'…direct satellite links into ground-based computer reservations systems will let you book or change tickets and hotel rooms from your seat, thanks to today's ever more sophisticated computer reservations systems – known in the industry as CRS networks – which put travel agents and, increasingly, their customers directly on line to most of the available airline seats and business hotel rooms in the world' [*Business Travel*]

computer **terminal** /kəm'pjuːtə ,tɜːmɪn(ə)l/ *noun* a keyboard and screen, by which information can be put into a computer or can be called up from a database

concentrate /'kɒnsəntreɪt/ CATERING *verb* to remove water from a liquid or substance so that it becomes thicker and has a stronger flavour ■ *noun* a food substance or liquid that has been concentrated to make it thicker or stronger in flavour

concern /kən'sɜːn/ *noun* **1.** BUSINESS a business or company □ **his business is a going concern** his company is working and making a profit □ **sold as a going concern** sold as an actively trading company **2.** a worried feeling about a problem ○ *The management showed no concern at all for the safety of the guests.* ■ *verb* to be connected with or to affect somebody or something ○ *The problem does not concern you directly as you are not involved in running the restaurant.*

concession /kən'seʃ(ə)n/ *noun* **1.** MARKETING the right to be the only seller of a product in a place ○ *She runs a jewellery* *concession in the hotel lobby.* **2.** TOURISM a reduced fare or entrance charge given to particular people such as employees or retired employees of the transport company ○ *full price: £6.00, concessions: £4.00* **3.** an allowance

concessionaire /kən,seʃə'neə/ *noun* MARKETING somebody who has the right to be the only seller of a product in a place

concessionary /kən'seʃ(ə)nəri/ *adjective* given as a concession

concessionary fare /kən,seʃ(ə)nəri 'feə/ *noun* TRAVEL a reduced fare for particular types of passenger such as employees or retired employees of the transport company ○ *Concessionary rates are offered to OAPs and students.*

concierge /,kɒnsi'eəʒ/ *noun* **1.** a French noun meaning a person who guards the door of a block of flats or offices, and decides who can come in **2.** (*in a hotel*) a member of staff who provides special services for guests, such as getting theatre or tour tickets for them

'I sometimes think that many of our guests stay at the hotel as much for the concierge service as for the rooms' [*The Sunday Times*]

condense /kən'dens/ *verb* CATERING to make something, especially a food, denser by removing water

condensed milk /kən,denst 'mɪlk/ *noun* DAIRY milk that is thickened by evaporating most of the water content and then sweetened

condiment /'kɒndɪmənt/ *noun* CATERING a seasoning used to give taste to food and put directly onto food at the table by the eater, e.g. salt, pepper or mustard (*formal*) ○ *Could you pass the condiments, please.* Compare **cruet**

COMMENT: The commonest condiments are salt, pepper, mustard, vinegar, pickles, mayonnaise and tomato sauce. In some restaurants, they are in pots on the table, and in self-service restaurants they may be provided in small sachets.

condition /kən'dɪʃ(ə)n/ *noun* **1.** a state that something or someone is in ○ *Snow conditions are good.* ○ *The meteorological office forecast poor weather conditions.* **2.** something that has to be done, especially duties which have to be carried out as part of a contract □ **on condition that** provided that ○ *They were granted the lease on condition that they paid the legal costs.* **3.** MEDICAL a particular illness, injury or disorder ○ *I have to use strong sunblock because of my skin condition.*

conditioning /kən'dɪʃ(ə)nɪŋ/ *noun* CATERING the process of making meat more tender by keeping it for some time at a low temperature. ◊ **air-conditioning**

conditions of employment /kən,dɪʃ(ə)nz əv ɪm'plɔɪmənt/, **conditions of service** *noun* the terms of a contract of employment

conditions of sale /kən,dɪʃ(ə)nz əv 'seɪl/ *noun* the agreed terms under which a sale takes place

condominium /,kɒndə'mɪniəm/ *noun* an individually owned flat or house within a building or an area of land that is owned jointly by all the residents

conducted tour /kən,dʌktɪd 'tʊə/ *noun* TOURISM same as **guided tour**

conductor /kən'dʌktə/ *noun* **1.** TRAVEL somebody who takes money and gives out tickets on a bus or tram **2.** US RAIL TRAVEL somebody in charge of a train (NOTE: The British English is **railway guard**.)

cone /kəʊn/ *noun* FOOD a round tube of biscuit, tapering to a point, used for serving ice cream ○ *Children like to suck the ice cream out of the bottom of a cone.* Also called **cornet**

confectionery /kən'fekʃən(ə)ri/ *noun* **1.** a shop selling sweets and chocolates **2.** FOOD sweets and chocolates ○ *The bread shop also sells confectionery.*

conference /'kɒnf(ə)rəns/ *noun* **1.** a meeting of people to discuss problems □ **to be in conference** to be in a meeting **2.** a large meeting where people who are interested in the same thing come together ○ *the annual conference of the Electricians' Union* ○ *2,000 people attended the conference on genetic engineering.* **3.** AIR TRAVEL an informal agreement between airlines or shipping lines to restrict competition on particular routes

'…two thirds of the UK's 100 or so universities take conference business in vacation time and 30 have year-round management centres' [*Caterer & Hotelkeeper*]

conference and banqueting manager /,kɒnf(ə)rəns ənd 'bæŋkwɪtɪŋ ,mænɪdʒə/ *noun* HOTELS the manager of the department in a hotel which organises conferences and banquets. Abbr **C & B manager**

conference centre /'kɒnf(ə)rəns ,sentə/ *noun* a series of meeting rooms, with bedrooms, restaurants, etc., built specially for holding large meetings. Also called **convention centre**

conference facilities /ˈkɒnf(ə)rəns fə
ˌsɪlɪtiz/ *plural noun* facilities for conferences, e.g. large halls, loudspeakers and
video systems, as well as catering and
accommodation for large numbers of delegates

conference organiser /ˈkɒnf(ə)rəns
ˌɔːgənaɪzə/ *noun* somebody whose job is to
organise conferences

conference phone /ˈkɒnf(ə)rəns fəʊn/
noun a telephone so arranged that several
people can speak into it from around a table

conference room /ˈkɒnf(ə)rəns ruːm/
noun a room where small meetings can take
place. Also called **meeting room**

conference sales manager
/ˌkɒnf(ə)rəns ˈseɪlz ˌmænɪdʒə/ *noun*
HOTELS somebody in charge of organising
conferences held in a hotel

conference timetable /ˌkɒnf(ə)rəns
ˈtaɪmteɪb(ə)l/ *noun* a list of speakers or
events at a conference

conference venue /ˈkɒnf(ə)rəns
ˌvenjuː/ *noun* a place where a conference is
being held

configuration /kənˌfɪgjəˈreɪʃ(ə)n/ *noun*
AIR TRAVEL the layout of the seats in an aircraft

configure /kənˈfɪgə/ *verb* AIR TRAVEL to
plan the layout of seats in an aircraft

'...the economy class was configured 3–4–3 and
both seat pitch and legroom were comfortable'
[*Business Traveller*]

confirm /kənˈfɜːm/ *noun* to make something definite or to tell someone that something is certain to happen ○ *I am writing to
confirm the booking made by telephone.* ○
*The dates of the concerts have been con-
firmed by the pop group's tour manager.*

confirmation /ˌkɒnfəˈmeɪʃən/ *noun* the
act of making something definite □ **confirmation of a booking** the act of telling someone that you definitely intend to take a flight
or hotel room that you have previously
booked □ **he received confirmation from
the hotel that the deposit had been
received** he was told by letter or by phone
that the hotel had definitely received the
deposit

confit /ˈkɒnfi/ *noun* meat such as goose,
duck or pork that has been cooked and preserved in its own fat

congestion /kənˈdʒestʃən/ *noun* a state
in which there are too many people or vehicles in the space available and movement is
difficult ○ *Flights have been delayed
because of congestion at London Airport.*

congestion charge /kənˈdʒestʃən
tʃɑːdʒ/ *noun* a charge that has to be paid by
motorists who wish to drive into an area
where there is a lot of traffic, e.g. the centre
of London

congress /ˈkɒŋgres/ *noun* a meeting of a
group of people ○ *the annual congress of the
society* ○ *This year's party congress will be
held in Blackpool.*

connect /kəˈnekt/ *verb* to link one person
or thing with another ○ *The hotel is connected to a major European hotel chain.* □
**the flight from New York connects with a
flight to Athens** the plane from New York
arrives in time for passengers to catch the
plane to Athens

connecting /kəˈnektɪŋ/ *adjective* **1.** □
connecting rooms rooms which are next
door to each other and have a door which
connects them **2.** □ **connecting flight** *or*
train a plane or train that passengers will be
on time to catch and that will take them to
their next destination ○ *Check at the helicopter desk for connecting flights to the city centre.* ○ *There are no connecting trains to Hal-
ifax after 10.00 p.m.*

connection /kəˈnekʃən/ *noun* **1.** TRAVEL
a plane or train that passengers will be on
time to catch and that will take them to their
next destination **2.** something that joins two
things together or associates one thing with
another **3.** □ **in connection with** referring to
○ *I want to speak to the restaurant manager
in connection with the service.*

connections /kəˈnekʃ(ə)nz/ *plural noun*
people you know □ **he has connections in
the theatre** he has friends or knows people
who work in the theatre

conserve /ˈkɒnsɜːv/ *noun* a food consisting of fruit in a thick sugar syrup, like jam
but less firmly set and usually containing
larger pieces of fruit

consolidate /kənˈsɒlɪdeɪt/ *verb* **1.**
TRAVEL to group bookings made in different
travel agencies together **2.** BUSINESS to
group several items from different suppliers
together to make one shipment ○ *The shipment to India is being consolidated, and will
leave Southampton Docks on Tuesday.*

consolidation /kənˌsɒlɪˈdeɪʃ(ə)n/ *noun*
1. TRAVEL the grouping together of ticket
bookings from different travel agencies **2.**
BUSINESS the grouping together of items
from different suppliers into one large shipment

consolidator /kənˈsɒlɪdeɪtə/ *noun* AIR
TRAVEL a company which groups together
bookings made by various agencies so as to

get cheaper group fares on ordinary scheduled flights

'...airline consolidators which sell scheduled airline tickets at greatly reduced prices are basically seen by many as the acceptable face of bucket shops' [*The Sunday Times*]

consommé /kɒn'sɒmeɪ/ *noun* FOOD a clear soup made from meat, poultry, fish or vegetables ○ *Many of the passengers were ill, and could only eat a little chicken consommé.* ○ *For a change, add some sherry to your beef consommé.*

consortium /kən'sɔːtiəm/ *noun* HOTELS a group of companies such as independent hotels which work together (NOTE: The plural form is **consortia**.)

constructive dismissal /kən,strʌktɪv dɪs'mɪs(ə)l/ *noun* a situation where an employee does not leave his or her job voluntarily but because of pressure from the management

consul /'kɒnsəl/ *noun* a representative of a country in another country, dealing with questions relating to nationals of his or her own country and issuing visas for foreigners who wish to enter it ○ *the British Consul in Lisbon* ◊ **ambassador**

consular /'kɒnsjʊlə/ *adjective* referring to a consul ○ *The consular offices are open every weekday.* □ **consular agent** a person with the duties of a consul in a small foreign town

consulate /'kɒnsjʊlət/ *noun* the house or office of a consul ○ *There will be a party at the consulate on National Day.* ○ *The consulate is closed on Sundays.* ○ *Members of the consulate staff visited the accident victims in hospital.* ◊ **embassy**

COMMENT: Consulates deal with administrative details, such as passports and visas, but also look after their own nationals when they are in trouble, for instance when they lose their money, get arrested, etc.

consul-general /,kɒnsəl 'dʒen(ə)rəl/ *noun* the main consul, who supervises several staff, or several consuls, in different parts of the country

consumables /kən'sjuːməb(ə)lz/ *plural noun* things which are bought and used, such as stationery, food and drink

consume /kən'sjuːm/ *verb* to use something, especially to eat food ○ *The guests consumed over 100 hamburgers.*

consumer protection /kən,sjuːmə prə'tekʃən/ *noun* BUSINESS actions that are intended to make sure that people are not cheated by unfair or illegal manufacturers or traders

consumption /kən'sʌmpʃ(ə)n/ *noun* **1.** the act of consuming ○ *The consumption of alcohol on the premises is not allowed.* □ **not for human consumption** not to be eaten by people ○ *The meat was condemned as unfit for human consumption.* **2.** the quantity consumed ○ *a car with low petrol consumption* ○ *The hotel has a heavy consumption of gas.*

contact /'kɒntækt/ *noun* **1.** somebody whom you know and whom you can ask for help or advice ○ *He has many contacts in the city.* ○ *Who is your contact in the Ministry of Tourism?* **2.** the act of communicating with someone □ **I have lost contact with them** I do not communicate with them any longer □ **he put me in contact with a good lawyer** he introduced me to a good lawyer ■ *verb* to write to someone or talk to them on the telephone ○ *He tried to contact his office by phone.* ○ *Can you contact the courier at the airport?*

container terminal /kən'teɪnə ,tɜːmɪn(ə)l/ *noun* SHIPS AND BOATS an area of a harbour where container ships are loaded or unloaded

contaminant /kən'tæmɪnənt/ *noun* a substance that contaminates ○ *This is one of the contaminants of our drinking water.*

contaminate /kən'tæmɪneɪt/ *verb* to make something impure by touching it or by adding something to it ○ *Supplies of drinking water were contaminated by refuse from the factories.* ○ *A whole group of tourists fell ill after eating contaminated food.*

contamination /kən,tæmɪ'neɪʃ(ə)n/ *noun* **1.** the act of making something impure by touching it or by adding something to it **2.** CATERING a state of impurity caused by the presence of substances that are harmful to living organisms ○ *We examine items of food for damage and possible signs of contamination.*

content /'kɒntent/ *noun* the amount of something which is contained in a substance ○ *These foods have a high starch content.* ○ *Dried fruit has a higher sugar content than fresh fruit.*

contents insurance /'kɒntents ɪn ,ʃʊərəns/ *noun* FINANCE an insurance policy which covers damage to or theft of items kept in a building

continent /'kɒntɪnənt/ *noun* **1.** one of the seven large land areas in the world, e.g. Africa or Europe **2.** □ **the Continent** (*in Britain*) the rest of Europe from the point of view of Great Britain itself, which is an island □ **on the Continent** in Europe ○ *When you drive on the Continent remember to drive on* *the right.* □ **to the Continent** to Europe ○ *They go to the Continent on holiday each year, sometimes to France, sometimes to Switzerland.*

continental /ˌkɒntɪ'nent(ə)l/ *adjective* **1.** referring to a continent **2.** referring to or typical of Europe excluding the United Kingdom ○ *We've decided to take a continental holiday this year.*

continental breakfast /ˌkɒntɪnent(ə)l 'brekfəst/ *noun* CATERING a light breakfast of coffee, chocolate or tea, with rolls, croissants or bread

continental climate /ˌkɒntɪnent(ə)l 'klaɪmət/ *noun* a climate of hot dry summers and very cold winters ○ *Germany has a continental climate which is quite different from ours in Britain.*

continental plan /ˌkɒntɪ'nent(ə)l plæn/ *noun* US HOTELS a hotel tariff including accommodation and a continental breakfast

continental quilt /ˌkɒntɪ'nent(ə)l kwɪlt/ *noun* same as **duvet**

contingency plan /kən'tɪndʒənsi plæn/ *noun* a plan which will be put into action if something happens that no one expects to happen. Also called **emergency plan**

contingency reserve /kən'tɪndʒənsi rɪ ˌzɜːv/ *noun* money set aside in case it is needed urgently. Also called **emergency plan**

contraband /'kɒntrəbænd/ *noun* □ **contraband (goods)** goods brought into a country illegally, without paying customs duty

contract /'kɒntrækt/ *noun* a legal agreement between two parties ○ *I asked the operations manager to draw up a contract.* ○ *We signed the contract last week.* □ **the contract is binding on both parties** both parties signing the contract must do what is agreed □ **under contract** bound by the terms of a contract ○ *The firm is under contract to deliver the goods by November.*

contract caterer /ˌkɒntrækt 'keɪtərə/ *noun* CATERING a company that provides food and drink under the terms of a contract

contract catering /ˌkɒntrækt 'keɪtərɪŋ/ *noun* CATERING the work of providing food and drink under the terms of a contract

contract cleaner /ˌkɒntrækt 'kliːnə/ *noun* BUSINESS a company that cleans e.g. offices or public buildings under the terms of a contract

contract cleaning /ˌkɒntrækt 'kliːnɪŋ/ *noun* the work of cleaning offices, public buildings etc., under the terms of a contract

contract law /'kɒntrækt lɔː/ *noun* the laws relating to private agreements

contract of employment /ˌkɒntrækt əv ɪm'plɔɪmənt/ *noun* a contract between employer and employee showing what rights and duties each of them has

contractor /kən'træktə/ *noun* somebody who carries out a particular job in accordance with a signed agreement

contract rate /'kɒntrækt reɪt/ *noun* a special rate received by large companies which regularly use a particular hotel chain

contract rooms /'kɒntrækt ruːmz/ *plural noun* rooms which are used regularly by a company and so are available at a discounted rate

contracts manager /'kɒntrækts ˌmænɪdʒə/ *noun* the manager who deals with the contracts for such things as catering and cleaning

control /kən'trəʊl/ *noun* the power to keep somebody or something in order or to be able to direct them □ **under control** kept in check ○ *Expenses are kept under tight control.* ○ *The police tried to keep the soccer fans under control.* □ **out of control** not kept in check ○ *The fans have got out of control.* ○ *Planning authorities have allowed the hotel building boom to get out of control.* ■ *verb* **1.** □ **to control a business** to have the power to decide what a business will do ○ *The business is controlled by a company based in Luxembourg.* ○ *The tour company is controlled by its majority shareholder which is a hotel group.* **2.** to keep something or somebody in order or to limit what they are allowed to do ○ *Police tried to control the tourists.*

control button /kən'trəʊl ˌbʌt(ə)n/ *noun* a button that switches on a machine or a radio or TV set, or allows you to control how the machine operates

controlled atmosphere packaging /kənˌtrəʊld ˌætməsfɪə 'pækɪdʒɪŋ/ *noun* CATERING the packaging of foods in sealed containers filled with a mixture of air and other gases, which allows a longer shelf-life

controlled temperature storage /kən ˌtrəʊld ˌtemprɪtʃə 'stɔːrɪdʒ/ *noun* CATERING the storage of food at temperatures between –1°C and +4°C

controller /kən'trəʊlə/ *noun* BUSINESS somebody who controls something, especially the finances of a company

control tower /kən'trəʊl ˌtaʊə/ *noun* AIR TRAVEL a high building at an airport, which houses the radio operators who direct planes on landing or takeoff

convenience /kən'viːniəns/ *noun* □ **at your earliest convenience** as soon as you find it possible

convenience food /kən'viːniəns fuːd/ *noun* CATERING food which is prepared and cooked before it is sold, so that it needs only heating to be made ready to eat

convenience store /kən'viːniəns stɔː/ *noun* a small store selling food or household goods that is open until late at night or even 24 hours a day

convenient /kən'viːniənt/ *adjective* suitable, handy ○ *A bank draft is a convenient way of sending money abroad.* ○ *Is 9.30 a convenient time for the meeting?*

conveniently /kən'viːniəntli/ *adverb* handily ○ *The hotel is conveniently situated next to the railway station.*

convention /kən'venʃən/ *noun* **1.** a general meeting of an association or political party ○ *They are holding their annual convention in Chicago.* **2.** a formal agreement between several countries ○ *an international convention on human rights*

convention centre /kən'venʃ(ə)n ˌsentə/ *noun* same as **conference centre**

conversion /kən'vɜːʃ(ə)n/ *noun* the act of changing something into something else

conversion price /kən'vɜːʃ(ə)n praɪs/, **conversion rate** /kən'vɜːʃ(ə)n reɪt/ *noun* FINANCE the rate at which a currency is changed into a foreign currency

convert /kən'vɜːt/ *verb* FINANCE to change money of one country for money of another ○ *We converted our pounds into Swiss francs.*

convertibility /kənˌvɜːtə'bɪləti/ *noun* FINANCE the ability to exchange one currency for another easily

convertible /kən'vɜːtəb(ə)l/ *noun* ROAD TRAVEL a car with a roof that can be folded back or removed ○ *You can hire a small convertible for $100 a day.*

convertible currency /kənˌvɜːtəb(ə)l 'kʌrənsi/ *noun* FINANCE a currency which can easily be exchanged for another

cook /kʊk/ CATERING *noun* somebody who prepares food in a restaurant ○ *He worked as a cook in a pub during the summer.* ■ *verb* to heat food in order to prepare it for eating ○ *The meat is cooked for six hours in a clay oven.*

cookbook /'kʊkbʊk/ *noun* same as **cookery book** ○ *I gave her an Indian cookbook for her birthday.* ○ *If you're not sure how long to cook turkey, look it up in the cookbook.*

cook chill, cook freeze *noun* CATERING methods of preparing food for preserving, where the food is cooked to a particular temperature and then chilled or frozen

cook-chill /'kʊk tʃɪl/ *adjective* CATERING referring to food that is cooked, packaged and refrigerated, and then reheated before serving

cooked /kʊkt/ *adjective* CATERING heated to prepare it for eating ○ *The children seem to prefer raw carrots to cooked ones.* ○ *The meat isn't cooked enough – it's tough.*

cooked breakfast /ˌkʊkt 'brekfəst/ *noun* FOOD a breakfast that includes cooked food, e.g. bacon, eggs and sausages

cooker /'kʊkə/ *noun* CATERING a device for cooking food, which runs on gas, electricity, charcoal, etc. ○ *Each suite has a kitchen with a fridge, a dishwasher and a small gas cooker.* Also called **stove**

cookery /'kʊk(ə)ri/ *noun* the act of preparing food or a style of preparing food ○ *French provincial cookery* ○ *He's decided to go to cookery classes.*

cookery book /'kʊk(ə)ri bʊk/ *noun* a book of recipes, showing how dishes should be prepared ○ *The restaurant sells a cookery book, written by the chef.*

cookie /'kʊki/ *noun* US BREAD, ETC. a small hard sweet biscuit, made of flour, water, sugar and other flavourings

cooking /'kʊkɪŋ/ *noun* CATERING **1.** the act of preparing food, usually by heating ○ *The cooking in this restaurant is first-class.* ○ *He does the cooking, while his wife serves in the restaurant.* **2.** a particular style of preparing food ○ *The restaurant specialises in French provincial cooking.* ○ *A wok is used for stir-fry cooking.*

cooking apple /'kʊkɪŋ ˌæp(ə)l/ *noun* FRUIT a sour apple which is used for cooking, with sugar. Also called **baking apple**

cooking fat /'kʊkɪŋ fæt/, **cooking oil** *noun* CATERING refined oil used in frying, roasting, baking, etc.

cooking pot /'kʊkɪŋ pɒt/ *noun* CATERING a pot used for cooking

cool /kuːl/ *adjective* quite cold ○ *Wines should be stored in a cool cellar.* ○ *It gets cool in the evenings in September.* ■ *noun* a colder area which is pleasant ○ *After the heat of the square, it is nice to sit in the cool of the monastery garden.* ■ *verb* to make something cool, or to become cool ○ *It is best to use a blast chiller to cool hot food rapidly.*

cool box /'kuːl bɒks/, **cool bag** *noun* CATERING an insulated container for keeping food and drink cool, e.g. on a picnic. Also called **esky** (NOTE: The Australian English is **esky**.)

cooler /ˈkuːlə/ *noun* a device or machine which cools ○ *It's going to be a hot day, so you had better put the food for the picnic in the cooler.* ○ *A wine cooler will keep white wine at the right temperature.* ○ *The pantry has a 3-door cooler.*

copilot /ˈkəʊpaɪlət/ *noun* AIR TRAVEL a second pilot in an aircraft, who helps the captain ○ *When the pilot felt ill, his copilot took over the controls.*

coq au vin /ˌkɒk əʊ ˈvæn/ *noun* a dish of chicken cooked in red wine with other ingredients

cordial /ˈkɔːdiəl/ *noun* a fruit drink, especially one that is sold in concentrated form and diluted with water

cordon bleu /ˌkɔːdɒn ˈblɜː/ *adjective* CATERING top-quality, done or working to a very high standard ○ *a cordon bleu chef*

core /kɔː/ *noun* the central part of a fruit such as an apple or pear ■ *verb* CATERING to remove the core from something such as an apple or pear ○ *Peel and core the apples before putting them in the oven.*

corer /ˈkɔːrə/ *noun* a special knife for removing the core from an apple or other fruit

coriander /ˌkɒriˈændə/ *noun* SAUCES, ETC. an aromatic plant whose seeds, green leaves and roots are used in cookery (NOTE: The US term is **cilantro**.)

cork /kɔːk/ *noun* BARS a piece of soft bark from a cork oak tree, used to close a bottle ○ *She pulled the cork out of the bottle.*

corkage /ˈkɔːkɪdʒ/ *noun* CATERING a payment made by a customer to a restaurant, for permission to bring his or her own wine and have it opened by the wine waiter (NOTE: The US English is **cork charge**.)

corked /kɔːkt/ *adjective* **1.** with a cork in it **2.** BEVERAGES tasting of vinegar, because of a dirty or faulty cork

corkscrew /ˈkɔːkskruː/ *noun* BARS a device for taking corks out of bottles ○ *I've forgotten the corkscrew – how can we open the bottle?*

corky /ˈkɔːki/ *adjective* BEVERAGES same as **corked 2**

corn /kɔːn/ *noun* FOOD maize, a cereal which is used to make flour and of which the seeds are also eaten

corn cob /ˈkɔːn kɒb/ *noun* VEGETABLES a woody stem of maize, to which the seeds are attached

corned beef /ˌkɔːnd ˈbiːf/ *noun* MEAT beef that has been salted and usually canned

corned beef hash /ˌkɔːnd biːf ˈhæʃ/ *noun* US FOOD a dish made of corned beef, onions and mashed potatoes, cooked in the oven

corner /ˈkɔːnə/ *noun* a place where two streets or two walls join ○ *The Post Office is on the corner of the High Street and London Road.*

corner room /ˈkɔːnə ruːm/ *noun* a room situated at the corner of a building

corner seat /ˈkɔːnə siːt/ *noun* a seat in the corner

corner shop /ˈkɔːnə ʃɒp/ *noun* a small, privately owned, general store in a town, often on a street corner

corner table /ˈkɔːnə ˌteɪb(ə)l/ *noun* CATERING a table in a corner of a restaurant, popular because it is more intimate

cornet /ˈkɔːnɪt/ *noun* FOOD same as **cone**

cornflakes /ˈkɔːnfleɪks/ *plural noun* FOOD a breakfast cereal, made of flat crisp pieces of corn, eaten with milk and sugar

cornflour /ˈkɔːnflaʊə/, **cornstarch** US /ˈkɔːnstɑːtʃ/ *noun* FOOD a powdery flour made from maize, used to thicken sauces

Cornish pasty /ˌkɔːnɪʃ ˈpæsti/ *noun* FOOD a pie of meat and potatoes wrapped in pastry, a common food in pubs

corn oil /ˈkɔːn ɔɪl/ *noun* FOOD an edible oil made from corn

corn on the cob /ˌkɔːn ɒn ðə ˈkɒb/ *noun* VEGETABLES a piece of maize, with seeds on it, served hot, with butter and salt

corn syrup /ˈkɔːn ˌsɪrəp/ *noun* FOOD a sweet liquid made from corn

corporate /ˈkɔːp(ə)rət/ *adjective* relating to a company

corporate card /ˈkɔːp(ə)rət kɑːd/ *noun* FINANCE a credit card which belongs to a company, and is used by an individual employee

corporate catering /ˌkɔːp(ə)rət ˈkeɪtərɪŋ/ *noun* BUSINESS catering for business guests, organised by a catering company for a large corporation

corporate client /ˌkɔːp(ə)rət ˈklaɪənt/ *noun* a company that is a client of a hotel, restaurant or airline

corporate entertaining /ˌkɔːp(ə)rət ˌentəˈteɪnɪŋ/ *noun* BUSINESS arrangements made by a company to entertain its business guests

corporate guests /ˌkɔːp(ə)rət ˈgests/ *plural noun* businesspeople visiting e.g. a hotel

corporate hospitality /ˌkɔːp(ə)rət ˌhɒspɪˈtælɪti/ *noun* free entertainment offered by a company to important customers or trading partners, e.g. at major sporting events ○ *Corporate hospitality is a fast growing sector.*

corporate rate /ˈkɔːp(ə)rət reɪt/ *noun* a special rate for people travelling on business

corporate travel /ˌkɔːp(ə)rət ˈtræv(ə)l/ *noun* TRAVEL travel on business by executives of a large company, paid for and organised by the company

COMMENT: Very large companies may employ the services of a single travel agency, and that agency may have an office in the company headquarters.

corporation tax /ˌkɔːpəˈreɪʃ(ə)n tæks/ *noun* BUSINESS a tax on profits made by companies

corridor /ˈkɒrɪdɔː/ *noun* a long, narrow passage ○ *The toilets are the second door on the left at the end of the corridor.*

cos /kəz/ *noun* VEGETABLES a type of lettuce with long stiff dark green leaves. Also called **romaine**

cost /kɒst/ *noun* the amount of money which has to be paid for something ○ *What is the cost of a first-class ticket to New York?* ○ *Travel costs are falling each year.* ○ *We cannot afford the cost of two separate rooms.* ■ *verb* to have a price ○ *How much does the camera cost?* ○ *This cloth costs £10 a metre.*

cost analysis /ˈkɒst əˌnæləsɪs/ *noun* BUSINESS an examination in advance of how much it will cost to make a new product

cost-benefit analysis /ˌkɒst ˈbenɪfɪt əˌnæləsɪs/ *noun* BUSINESS analysis that compares the costs and benefits of different ways of using available resources

cost centre /ˈkɒst ˌsentə/ *noun* BUSINESS a group or machine whose costs can be itemised and to which fixed costs can be allocated

costing /ˈkɒstɪŋ/ *noun* BUSINESS the calculation of a selling price, based on the costs of making a product ○ *I can't do the costing for the banquet until I have all the details of what the client wants.*

cost plus /ˌkɒst ˈplʌs/ *noun* BUSINESS a system of calculating a price, by taking the cost of production of goods or services and adding a percentage to cover the supplier's overheads and margin ○ *We are charging for the work on a cost plus basis.*

cost price /ˈkɒst praɪs/ *noun* BUSINESS a selling price that is the same as the price which the seller paid for the item

cot /kɒt/ *noun* a child's bed with sides. ◊ **carrycot**

cottage /ˈkɒtɪdʒ/ *noun* a little house in the country

cottage cheese /ˌkɒtɪdʒ ˈtʃiːz/ *noun* DAIRY mild white cheese formed into soft grains, which is made from skimmed milk and so has a very low fat content

cottage holiday /ˈkɒtɪdʒ ˌhɒlɪdeɪ/ *noun* TOURISM a holiday spent in a small cottage in the country

cottage pie /ˈkɒtɪdʒ paɪ/ *noun* FOOD minced beef cooked in a dish with a layer of mashed potatoes on top. Compare **shepherd's pie**

cottager /ˈkɒtədʒə/ *noun* a holidaymaker who stays at a small holiday home in the country or beside the sea

cotton candy /ˌkɒtən ˈkændi/ *noun* US FOOD thin threads of melted sugar which are spun in a drum and sold as a mass attached to a stick ○ *stalls at the fair selling cold drinks and cotton candy* (NOTE: The British English is **candyfloss**.)

couchette /kuːˈʃet/ *noun* RAIL TRAVEL a sleeping berth on a train, usually separated from others by a curtain or light partition

cough /kɒf/ *noun* a sound made when somebody has an irritation in the throat and air is sent out of the lungs suddenly ○ *He gave a little cough to attract the waitress's attention.* ○ *She has a bad cough and cannot make the speech.* ■ *verb* to send air out of the lungs suddenly because the throat is irritated ○ *The smoke made him cough.* ○ *He has a cold and keeps on coughing and sneezing.*

coulis /ˈkuːli/ *noun* a thin purée of fruit or vegetables used as a garnish

counter /ˈkaʊntə/ *noun* **1.** BUSINESS a long flat surface in a shop for displaying and selling goods **2.** BARS a similar long flat surface in a bar ○ *She sat at the counter to eat her breakfast.*

counter service /ˈkaʊntə ˌsɜːvɪs/ *noun* **1.** the serving of food to people sitting at a counter **2.** CATERING same as **cafeteria service**

counter staff /ˈkaʊntə stɑːf/ *noun* staff who work behind a counter

country /ˈkʌntri/ *noun* **1.** an area of land which has borders and governs itself ○ *The insurance covers drivers driving in the countries of the EU.* ○ *Some African countries have tourist offices in London.* (NOTE: The plural form is **countries**.) **2.** land which is not near a town ○ *The tour is mainly in the country, but with two nights in the town.* ○

Road travel is difficult in country areas. □ **up country** in the interior of a country, usually away from large towns □ **'country style'** words attached to various food products, which imply that the food is traditionally made when in fact it is mass-produced

country club /ˌkʌntri 'klʌb/ *noun* ENTERTAINMENT a club in the country, usually offering special sports facilities such as golf, horse riding, etc.

country code /ˈkʌntri kəʊd/ *noun* a number dialled after the international access code and before the area code when making a call to another country

country house hotel /ˌkʌntri haʊs həʊ 'tel/ *noun* HOTELS a hotel which is in a large house in the country

country inn, country pub *noun* BARS a pub in the country

country of origin /ˌkʌntri əv 'ɒrɪdʒɪn/ *noun* BUSINESS the country where a product is manufactured

country park /ˈkʌntri pɑːk/ *noun* ENTERTAINMENT an area in the countryside set aside for the public to visit and enjoy

countryside /ˈkʌntrisaɪd/ *noun* the land away from towns, with fields, woods and farms ○ *the beautiful English countryside in spring* ○ *The countryside is in danger of being covered in new houses.* (NOTE: There is no plural form.)

Countryside and Rights of Way Act /ˌkʌntrisaɪd ənd raɪts əv 'weɪ ˌækt/ *noun* an Act of Parliament passed in 2000, which regulates access to open countryside, rights of way on footpaths and bridleways, and the supervision of Areas of Outstanding Natural Beauty

coupe /kuːp/ *noun* 1. CATERING a wide flat glass on a stem, used for serving ice cream and other sweets 2. FOOD ice cream or sorbet, served in a wide flat dish with a stem, sometimes with cream and sauces 3. CATERING a wide flat glass for serving champagne (NOTE: Champagne is more often served in tall slim glasses, called 'flutes'.)

coupon ad /ˈkuːpɒn æd/ *noun* MARKETING an advertisement with a form attached, which is to be cut out and returned to the advertiser with your name and address for further information

courgette /kɔːˈʒet/ *noun* VEGETABLES the fruit of the marrow at a very immature stage in its development, cut when green or yellow in colour and between 10 and 20 cm long

courier /ˈkʊriə/ *noun* 1. BUSINESS a person or company taking messages or packages

from one place to another by car, motorcycle or aircraft 2. TOURISM somebody who goes with a party of tourists to guide them on a package tour ○ *The courier met us at the airport.*

courier service /ˈkʊriə ˌsɜːvɪs/ *noun* 1. a service provided by a person or company taking messages and packages from one place to another by car, motorcycle or aircraft 2. a service which provides a guide to go with a party of tourists to guide them on a package tour

course /kɔːs/ *noun* 1. CATERING one part of a meal ○ *a five-course meal* ◊ **main course** 2. a series of lessons ○ *She attended a course for junior hotel managers.* ○ *The hotel offers weekend courses in watercolour painting.*

COMMENT: A meal may have several courses: the **first course** (or starter), which can be soup or pâté or other savoury food; the **main course**, with meat or fish, served with vegetables; and the **sweet course** (or dessert) with puddings, pies, ice cream, etc. Sometimes a meal can have four courses, with a separate **fish course** as well as a meat course. More elaborate meals, such as banquets or gastronomic meals, can have five or more courses, with cheese being served as a separate course.

court /kɔːt/ *noun* SPORT an area where a game of tennis or squash, etc., is played ○ *The tennis courts are behind the hotel.*

court bouillon /ˌkɔːt 'buːjɒn/ *noun* FOOD a liquid used for poaching fish, made with water flavoured with vegetables, herbs and wine or vinegar

courteous /ˈkɜːtiəs/ *adjective* very polite ○ *I found the hotel staff particularly courteous.*

courtesy /ˈkɜːtəsi/ *noun* politeness ○ *The hotel staff showed us every courtesy.* □ **by courtesy of** with the kind permission of □ **courtesy bus, car, coach** a bus, car or coach that transports guests from the airport to a hotel, a car park, etc., free of charge

courtesy phone /ˈkɜːtəsi fəʊn/ *noun* HOTELS a free telephone service, usually for calling rooms within a hotel, for contacting a special service such as a central hotel reservation system or for calling a taxi

courtyard /ˈkɔːtjɑːd/ *noun* a small yard surrounded by buildings ○ *The hotel is built round a courtyard with fountains and palm trees.* ○ *There is a paved courtyard behind the restaurant.*

couscous /ˈkuːskuːs/ *noun* FOOD 1. wheat flour in the form of granules which are cooked by steaming **2.** a North African dish of meat and vegetables stewed in a spicy sauce, served with steamed semolina

cover /ˈkʌvə/ *noun* **1.** □ **under cover** under a roof, not in the open air ○ *If it rains the buffet will be served under cover.* **2.** □ **to ask for additional cover** to ask an insurance company to increase the amount for which you are insured □ **to operate without adequate cover** to operate without being protected by insurance **3.** CATERING (*in a restaurant*) a place for a customer at a restaurant table, with the cutlery and glasses already set out ○ *a dinner for sixty covers* ○ *He bought a fifty-cover restaurant.* ■ *verb* **1.** □ **to cover a risk** to insure against a risk ○ *The insurance covers fire, theft and loss of work.* □ **to be fully covered** to have insurance against all risks □ **the damage was covered by the insurance** the insurance company paid for the damage **2.** BUSINESS to have enough money to pay, or to ask for security against a loan which you are making **3.** BUSINESS to earn enough money to pay for costs, expenses etc. ○ *We do not make enough sales to cover the expense of running the shop.* ○ *Breakeven point is reached when sales cover all costs.*

'…we're doing 700–800 covers a week' [*Caterer & Hotelkeeper*]

cover charge /ˈkʌvə tʃɑːdʒ/ *noun* CATERING a charge in addition to the charge for food

covered market /ˌkʌvəd ˈmɑːkɪt/ *noun* ENTERTAINMENT a market which is not in the open air, but with stalls or small shops in a special building

covering letter /ˌkʌvərɪŋ ˈletə/ *noun* a letter sent with documents to say why they are being sent

cover note /ˈkʌvə nəʊt/ *noun* a letter from an insurance company giving details of an insurance policy and confirming that the policy exists (NOTE: The US English for this is **binder**.)

crab /kræb/ *noun* **1.** SEAFOOD an edible ten-footed crustacean with large pincers, which walks sideways ○ *She ordered a crab sandwich.* **2.** same as **crabmeat**

crab apple /ˈkræb ˌæp(ə)l/ *noun* FRUIT a bitter wild apple used to make crab apple jelly

crabmeat /ˈkræbmiːt/ *noun* the flesh of a crab used as food

crab stick /ˈkræb stɪk/ *noun* a stick-shaped piece of processed fish that has been flavoured and coloured to resemble crabmeat

cracker /ˈkrækə/ *noun* **1.** BREAD, ETC. a dry unsweetened biscuit ○ *After the main course they served cheese and crackers.* **2.** □ **(Christmas) cracker** a colourful paper tube which makes a little bang when it is pulled, given at Christmas parties ○ *We had mince pies and pulled crackers.* ○ *What did you get in your cracker? – A paper hat and a puzzle.*

COMMENT: Christmas crackers have little presents inside them; usually folded paper hats, small plastic toys and 'mottoes' (pieces of paper with bad jokes written on them).

cradle /ˈkreɪd(ə)l/ *noun* CATERING a type of basket with handles for holding a bottle of vintage red wine, so that the wine can be served without holding the bottle upright and the sediment is not disturbed

craft food /ˈkrɑːft fuːd/ *noun* food that is carefully prepared from high-quality ingredients, as opposed to fast food

cramped /kræmpt/ *adjective* too small or too close together ○ *On some aircraft, the seating in tourist class can be very cramped.*

cranberry /ˈkrænb(ə)ri/ *noun* FRUIT a wild red berry, used to make a sharp sweet sauce ○ *She drank a glass of cranberry juice.*

cranberry sauce /ˈkrænb(ə)ri sɔːs/ *noun* SAUCES, ETC. a sharp sweet red sauce, eaten with meat, in particular turkey

crash /kræʃ/ *noun* **1.** TRAVEL an accident in a car, bus, coach, plane or train ○ *The car was damaged in the crash.* ○ *The plane crash killed all the passengers* or *All the passengers were killed in the plane crash.* **2.** a financial collapse ○ *250 travellers lost all their money in the crash of the tour company.* ■ *verb* **1.** to hit something and be damaged ○ *The plane crashed into the mountain.* ○ *The truck crashed into the post office.* **2.** to collapse financially ○ *The tour company crashed with debts of over £1 million.* ○ *Two groups of tourists were stranded when the travel group crashed.*

crayfish /ˈkreɪfɪʃ/ *noun* SEAFOOD a kind of freshwater crustacean like a small lobster (NOTE: The plural form is **crayfish**. The US English spelling is **crawfish**.)

cream /kriːm/ *noun* **1.** DAIRY the rich fat part of milk **2.** MEDICAL a medicinal oily substance, used to rub on the skin ■ *verb* CATERING to mix ingredients together until they form a smooth mixture

cream cake /ˈkriːm ˌkeɪk/ *noun* BREAD, ETC. any cake or pastry filled with whipped cream

cream cheese /ˌkriːm ˈtʃiːz/ *noun* DAIRY a soft smooth cheese which can be spread easily

cream cheese and chives /ˌkriːm tʃiːz ən ˈtʃaɪvz/ *noun* FOOD chives, chopped and mixed with cream cheese to form a spread

cream cracker /ˌkriːm ˈkrækə/ *noun* a crisp savoury biscuit usually eaten with cheese

creamed potatoes /ˌkriːms pəˈteɪtəʊ/ *plural noun* FOOD same as **mashed potatoes**

creamer /ˈkriːmə/ *noun* a cream substitute, used especially in coffee or tea

cream horn /ˌkriːm ˈhɔːn/ *noun* BREAD, ETC. a cone of puff pastry filled with whipped cream

cream of asparagus soup /ˌkriːm əv ə ˌspærəgəs ˈsuːp/ *noun* FOOD asparagus soup with milk or cream added

cream of mushroom soup /ˌkriːm əv ˌmʌʃruːm ˈsuːp/ *noun* FOOD mushroom soup with milk or cream added

cream tea /ˌkriːm ˈtiː/ *noun* CATERING afternoon tea, served with scones, thick cream and jam

crèche /kreʃ/ *noun* a place where small children can be left by their parents, to be looked after by qualified staff ○ *The ship has a crèche for children over two years old.*

credit /ˈkredɪt/ *noun* **1.** BUSINESS the time given to a customer before he or she has to pay ○ *to give someone six months' credit* ○ *to sell on good credit terms* □ **he has exceeded his credit limit** he has borrowed more money than he is allowed to □ **to open a line of credit** *or* **a credit line** to make credit available to someone □ **on credit** without paying immediately ○ *We buy everything on sixty days' credit.* ○ *The company exists on credit from its suppliers.* **2.** FINANCE money received by a person or company and recorded in the accounts □ **account in credit** an account where more money has been received than is owed

credit account /ˈkredɪt əˌkaʊnt/ *noun* FINANCE an account that a customer has with a shop which allows him or her to buy goods and pay for them later ○ *to open a credit account*

credit agency /ˈkredɪt ˌeɪdʒənsi/, **credit bureau** /ˈkredɪt ˌbjʊərəʊ/ *noun* FINANCE a company which reports on the creditworthiness of customers to show whether they should be allowed credit

credit balance /ˈkredɪt ˌbæləns/ *noun* FINANCE a balance in an account, showing that more money has been received than is owed by a person or company ○ *The account has a credit balance of £1,000.*

credit card /ˈkredɪt kɑːd/ *noun* FINANCE a plastic card which allows you to borrow money and to buy goods without paying for them immediately

credit card sale /ˈkredɪt kɑːd ˌseɪl/ *noun* FINANCE a transaction paid for by credit card

credit entry /ˈkredɪt ˌentri/ *noun* FINANCE an entry on the credit side of an account

credit facilities /ˈkredɪt fəˌsɪlɪtiz/ *plural noun* BUSINESS an arrangement with a bank or supplier to have credit so as to buy goods

credit freeze /ˈkredɪt friːz/, **credit squeeze** /ˈkredɪt skwiːz/ *noun* FINANCE a period when lending by banks is restricted by the government

credit limit /ˈkredɪt ˌlɪmɪt/ *noun* FINANCE a fixed amount which is the most a customer can owe on credit

credit note /ˈkredɪt nəʊt/ *noun* FINANCE a note showing that money is owed to a customer ○ *The company sent the wrong order and so had to issue a credit note.*

credit rating /ˈkredɪt ˌreɪtɪŋ/ *noun* FINANCE the amount which a credit agency feels a customer should be allowed to borrow

crème /krem/ *noun* DAIRY a French noun meaning cream

crème brûlée /ˌkrem ˈbruːleɪ/ *noun* DESSERTS a dessert of egg custard with a topping of caramelised sugar

crème caramel /ˌkrem ˌkærəˈmel/ *noun* DESSERTS a dessert of egg custard topped with a thin sauce of browned sugar. It is usually served turned upside down onto the serving plate, though sometimes served in the bowl in which it is cooked. Also called **caramel custard**

crème fraîche /ˌkrem ˈfreʃ/ *noun* DAIRY a form of slightly sour cream which keeps well

creole /ˈkriːɒl/ *adjective* FOOD referring to food cooked in the spicy highly flavoured way associated with the French Creole people of New Orleans, usually with tomatoes, hot peppers, onions and rice

crêpe /krep/ *noun* FOOD a thin pancake usually served rolled up or folded with a filling

crêpe suzette /ˌkrep suːˈzet/ *noun* a pancake prepared with orange sauce and flambéed with an orange-flavoured liqueur or brandy

cress /kres/ *noun* VEGETABLES a plant whose seedlings are used for salads, especially together with seedlings of mustard ○ *The sandwiches were served with a garnish of mustard and cress.* ○ *We had egg and cress sandwiches.* ◊ **mustard and cress**, **watercress**

crew /kruː/ *noun* TRAVEL a group of people who work on a plane, ship, etc. ○ *The ship carries a crew of 250.* ■ *verb* to form the crew for a boat, plane, etc. ○ *Fully-crewed yacht charters are also available.*

crew rest seat /ˌkruː 'rest ˌsiːt/ *noun* AIR TRAVEL a seat on an aircraft for the use of a member of the crew during a long flight

crime prevention /'kraɪm prɪˌvenʃ(ə)n/ *noun* actions to stop crime being committed, e.g. fitting burglar alarms and window locks

crisp /krɪsp/ *adjective* hard, able to be broken into pieces and making a noise when you bite it ○ *These biscuits are not crisp any more, they have gone soft.* ■ *noun* FOOD a thin slice of potato, fried till crisp and eaten cold as a snack ○ *We always take packets of crisps with us on picnics.* (NOTE: The US English is **potato chip.**)

crispy bacon /ˌkrɪspi 'beɪkən/ *noun* MEAT thin slices of bacon, fried or grilled until they are hard and crisp

critic /'krɪtɪk/ *noun* ENTERTAINMENT somebody who examines something and comments on it, especially somebody who writes comments on new plays, films or restaurants for a newspaper ○ *The restaurant was praised by all the critics.* ○ *She has been the restaurant critic of the 'Standard' for the last twenty years.*

criticise /'krɪtɪsaɪz/, **criticize** *verb* to make an unfavourable comment about someone or something, or to say that something or someone is wrong or is working badly, etc. ○ *The manager criticised the receptionist for not being polite to the guests.* ○ *The design of the new restaurant has been criticised.*

criticism /'krɪtɪsɪz(ə)m/ *noun* an unfavourable comment

crockery /'krɒkəri/ *noun* plates, cups and saucers, etc.

croissant /'kwæsɒŋ/ *noun* BREAD, ETC. a rolled pastry, made in the shape of a crescent moon, often served at breakfast

croissanterie /'kwæsɒntəri/ *noun* CATERING a snack bar serving hot croissants with various fillings

croquet /'krəʊki/ *noun* ENTERTAINMENT a lawn game played with hoops, balls and mallets ○ *Let's have a game of croquet while the weather is fine.* ○ *The hotel has a swimming pool, and offers croquet and tennis.*

COMMENT: Croquet is a game for two to four players who try to hit a ball through a series of small metal hoops using a long mallet, and finish by hitting a stake; shots are taken in turn, but bonus shots are earned by hitting the ball through the hoop or by hitting an opponent's ball with your own.

croquet lawn /'krəʊki lɔːn/ *noun* ENTERTAINMENT a special lawn set out with hoops for playing croquet

croquette /krɒ'ket/ *noun* FOOD a small ball or cake of mashed potato, minced meat, vegetables or fish, covered with breadcrumbs and fried ○ *Steak is served with croquette potatoes.*

cross /krɒs/ *verb* to go across ○ *Concorde took only three hours to cross the Atlantic.* ○ *To get to the bank, you turn left and cross the street at the post office.*

cross- /krɒs/ *prefix* across ○ *cross-harbour ferry services*

cross-channel /ˌkrɒs 'tʃæn(ə)l/ *adjective* across the English Channel

cross-channel ferry /ˌkrɒs ˌtʃæn(ə)l 'feri/ *noun* SHIPS AND BOATS a ferry which takes passengers or vehicles between England and France

cross-channel services /ˌkrɒs ˌtʃæn(ə)l 'sɜːvɪsɪz/ *plural noun* SHIPS AND BOATS ferry, hovercraft or hydrofoil services across the English Channel

cross-contamination /ˌkrɒs kənˌtæmɪ'neɪʃ(ə)n/ *noun* CATERING contamination from one type of food to another and back again ○ *Cover and store fresh and raw foods separately to avoid the risk of cross-contamination.*

cross-country /ˌkrɒs 'kʌntri/ *adjective* across the country, not necessarily following paths

cross-country skiing /ˌkrɒs ˌkʌntri 'skiːɪŋ/ *noun* SPORT skiing for long distances following marked tracks across country, as opposed to downhill skiing. Also called **XC skiing**

crossed cheque /ˌkrɒst 'tʃek/ *noun* FINANCE a cheque with two lines across it showing that it can only be deposited at a bank and not exchanged for cash

crossed line /ˌkrɒst 'laɪn/ *noun* a situation when two telephone conversations get mixed

crossing /'krɒsɪŋ/ *noun* the act of going across water ○ *The crossing was rough because of the storm.* ○ *We had a good crossing, and sat on the deck most of the time.*

cross-training /'krɒs ˌtreɪnɪŋ/ *noun* training in the work of several different departments of an organisation

crouton /'kruːtɒn/, **croûton** *noun* BREAD, ETC. a small piece of fried or toasted bread, served with soup or as part of a salad

crowd /kraʊd/ *noun* a mass of people ○ *Crowds of people were queuing to get into the exhibition.* ○ *If you travel early, you will avoid the crowds of Christmas shoppers.*

crowded /'kraʊdɪd/ *adjective* **1.** with many people ○ *The Oxford Street shops are always crowded in the week before Christmas.* ○ *The airport was crowded with holidaymakers.* **2.** busy ○ *We have a crowded itinerary.*

'...recent snow shortages have meant that areas which have had good snow have become especially crowded' [*Sunday Times*]

crown /kraʊn/ *noun* **1.** a gold and jewelled headdress for a king, queen, emperor, etc. ○ *The crown of St Wenceslas is in Prague cathedral.* **2.** (*rating system*) an indicator of quality ○ *The hotel rates three crowns in the guide.* **3.** the monarchy □ **the Crown Jewels** jewels belonging to the British monarch, which are on display in the Tower of London

COMMENT: The rating system formerly used by the English Tourism Council for the facilities offered by hotels, bed and breakfasts and boarding houses was shown by crowns.

crown cap /'kraʊn kæp/ *noun* BARS a metal bottle cap with a soft lining

crown roast /'kraʊn rəʊst/ *noun* MEAT a dish of lamb, formed of two pieces of best end of neck, tied together to form a shape like a crown

CRS *abbreviation* TRAVEL computer reservation system

cru /kruː/ *noun* BEVERAGES used to refer to a classified or named vineyard, or an appellation contrôlée wine from that vineyard (NOTE: **cru** comes from the French noun meaning 'growth'.)

crudités /'kruːdɪteɪ/ *plural noun* small pieces of raw vegetables e.g. carrots and cucumber, eaten as an appetiser or snack, often with a dip

cruet /'kruːɪt/ *noun* CATERING a set of containers for salt, pepper, mustard, etc., which is put on the table, or kept on a special stand ○ *Can you pass me the cruet, please?* Compare **condiment**

cruise /kruːz/ *noun* TOURISM a holiday consisting of a long journey in a ship, stopping at different places ○ *They went on a winter cruise to the Caribbean.* ○ *The cruise takes us round the Mediterranean.* ■ *verb* **1.** SHIPS AND BOATS to sail from place to place for pleasure ○ *They spent May cruising in the Aegean.* ○ *The ship cruised from island to island.* **2.** to go along at a regular speed

cruise holiday /'kruːz ˌhɒlɪdeɪ/ *noun* a holiday that is spent taking a cruise

cruise line /'kruːz laɪn/ *noun* a company offering cruises in large luxurious liners

cruise liner /'kruːz 'laɪnə/, **cruise ship** /'kruːz 'ʃɪp/ *noun* SHIPS AND BOATS a ship which takes holidaymakers on cruises

cruiser /'kruːzə/ *noun* SHIPS AND BOATS a small motorboat, with cabins, which goes on rivers or lakes

cruising altitude /'kruːzɪŋ ˌæltɪtjuːd/ *noun* AIR TRAVEL the usual height at which a plane is flying

crumb /krʌm/ *noun* a small piece that has broken off some dry food such as bread, cake or biscuits ○ *After the meal, the waiters brushed the crumbs from the table.* ○ *The table was covered with crumbs.* (NOTE: To show different types of crumbs, you can say **breadcrumbs, cake crumbs,** etc.)

crumb down /'krʌm daʊn/ *verb* to remove crumbs from the tablecloth between courses

COMMENT: Crumbing down can be done with a special brush, but is often done by flicking or wiping the table with the service cloth.

crumble /'krʌmbəl/ *noun* DESSERTS a dessert made of fruit covered with a cake mixture of flour, fat and sugar

crumpet /'krʌmpɪt/ *noun* a flat bun with small holes in its surface that is eaten toasted with butter

crush /krʌʃ/ *verb* to reduce fruit or vegetables to juice and pulp by pressing ■ *noun* BEVERAGES a drink containing the juice from crushed fruit

crushed ice /ˌkrʌʃt 'aɪs/ *noun* CATERING ice which has been broken into very small pieces, used to cool dishes set out on a serving table

crust /krʌst/ *noun* **1.** BREAD, ETC. the hard outer part of a loaf of bread or of a roll or of a slice of bread ○ *a plate of cucumber sandwiches with the crusts cut off* **2.** FOOD the pastry top of a pie ○ *The crust of the pie had sagged in the middle.*

Crustacea /krʌs'teɪʃə/ *noun* a class of animals which have hard shells which are shed periodically as the animals grow, e.g. crabs or lobsters

crustacean /krʌ'steɪʃ(ə)n/ *noun* SEAFOOD an animal with a hard shell, usually living in the sea, e.g. a lobster, crab or shrimp ○ *The crayfish is a freshwater crustacean.*

crusty loaf /ˌkrʌsti 'ləʊf/ *noun* BREAD, ETC. a loaf with a particularly hard crust

cryogenic freezing /ˌkraɪədʒenɪk 'friːzɪŋ/ *noun* freezing to very low temperatures

crystallised fruit /ˌkrɪstəlaɪzd 'fruːt/ *noun* FOOD fruit that has been preserved by soaking in a strong sugar solution

CSQ *abbreviation* customer service questionnaire

cubic measure /ˌkjuːbɪk 'meʒə/ *noun* volume in cubic feet or metres, calculated by multiplying height, width and length

cucumber /'kjuːkʌmbə/ *noun* VEGETABLES a long cylindrical green vegetable used in salads or for pickling

COMMENT: Cucumber is usually sliced thinly, and can be used to make sandwiches. It is also used with mint and yoghurt to make tsatsiki.

cuisine /kwɪ'ziːn/ *noun* a style of cooking ○ *Chinese cuisine is very different from European.* ○ *The hotel restaurant serves Lebanese cuisine.* (NOTE: **cuisine** comes from the French noun meaning 'kitchen'.)

culinary /'kʌlɪn(ə)ri/ *adjective* referring to cooking ○ *I'm no culinary expert but I love good food.* ◊ **Master of Culinary Arts**

'…the college wishes to appoint a chef/manager to lead its small catering team in providing a high quality service to students and staff. Good culinary skills and a financially aware approach to business are essential' [*Caterer & Hotelkeeper*]

cultural /'kʌltʃər(ə)l/ *adjective* relating to the works of art produced by a particular nation or group of people or to their customs and traditional way of life

cultural travel /ˌkʌltʃər(ə)l 'træv(ə)l/ *noun* travel for the purpose of seeing works of art or learning about the traditions and way of life of other nations

culture /'kʌltʃə/ *noun* **1.** the traditional customs and way of life of a people or group **2.** artistic and intellectual activities

cumin /'kjuːmɪn/ *noun* the seeds of a plant of the carrot family used as a spice

cup /kʌp/ *noun* a container for drinking hot liquids, always with a saucer ○ *I would like a cup of tea, please.* ○ *She drank two cups of coffee.* ○ *Tea is 50p a cup.*

cupboard /'kʌbəd/ *noun* a large piece of furniture with shelves and doors, or an alcove in a wall with shelves and doors

cup cakes /'kʌp keɪks/ *plural noun* BREAD, ETC. little individual cakes baked in special paper cups

curd /kɜːd/ *noun* DAIRY the solid substance formed when milk coagulates, which is used for making cheese. Compare **whey**

curd cheese /'kɜːd tʃiːz/ *noun* US DAIRY same as **cottage cheese**

curdle /'kɜːd(ə)l/ *verb* CATERING to make food, especially milk products, go sour

curds /kɜːdz/ *plural noun* DAIRY same as **curd**

cure /kjʊə/ *verb* CATERING to preserve fish or meat by salting or smoking ■ *noun* MEDICAL a particular way of making someone well or of stopping an illness ○ *Some doctors believe that acupuncture is a good cure for arthritis.*

COMMENT: Meat is cured by keeping it in brine or dry salt for some time; both salting and smoking have a dehydrating effect on the meat, preventing the reproduction and growth of microorganisms harmful to humans.

cured ham /ˌkjʊəd 'hæm/ *noun* MEAT ham which has been soaked in salt water and then smoked

currant /'kʌrənt/ *noun* FRUIT a small dried black grape ○ *fruit cake with currants, sultanas and raisins in it* ◊ **blackcurrant, redcurrant**

COMMENT: Currants are smaller and blacker than raisins or sultanas; they are all forms of dried grapes.

currant bun /'kʌrənt bʌn/ *noun* BREAD, ETC. a bun with currants in it

currency /'kʌrənsi/ *noun* FINANCE money in coins and notes which is used in a particular country (NOTE: **Currency** has no plural when it refers to the money of one country: *He was arrested trying to take currency out of the country.*)

'…the strong dollar's inflationary impact on European economies, as national governments struggle to support their sinking currencies and push up interest rates' [*Duns Business Month*]

'…today's wide daily variations in exchange rates show the instability of a system based on a single currency, namely the dollar' [*Economist*]

currency converter /'kʌrənsi kən ˌvɜːtə/ a table or computer program that enables you to calculate what the value of a sum of money in one currency would be in another currency

currency note /'kʌrənsi nəʊt/ *noun* FINANCE a bank note

current /'kʌrənt/ *noun* a flow of water or electricity ∎ *adjective* relating to the present time □ **current rate of exchange** today's rate of exchange

current account /'kʌrənt ə,kaʊnt/ *noun* FINANCE an account in a bank from which the customer can withdraw money when he or she wants by writing cheques ○ *to pay money into a current account* Also called **cheque account**

current assets /,kʌrənt 'æsets/ *plural noun* BUSINESS assets used by a company in its ordinary work, such as materials, finished goods, cash, monies due etc., and which are held for a short time only

current liabilities /,kʌrənt laɪə'bɪlɪtiz/ *plural noun* BUSINESS debts that a company has to pay within the next accounting period

current price /,kʌrənt 'praɪs/ *noun* the price that is being charged now

curriculum vitae /kə,rɪkjʊləm 'viːtaɪ/ *noun* BUSINESS a summary of a person's career showing details of education and work experience ○ *Candidates should send a letter of application with a curriculum vitae to the human resources manager.* Abbr **CV** (NOTE: The plural form is **curriculums vitae** or **curricula vitae**. The US English is **résumé**.)

curried /'kʌrɪd/ *adjective* CATERING served with a curry sauce ○ *a plate of curried lamb and rice* ○ *curried prawns*

curry /'kʌri/ *noun* FOOD an Indian food prepared with spices ○ *We ordered a lamb curry.* ○ *I want chicken curry and rice.*

curry paste /'kʌri peɪst/, **curry powder** /'kʌri 'paʊdə/ *noun* SAUCES, ETC. a hot spicy paste or powder, used to make Indian dishes

curtain /'kɜːtən/ *noun* a long piece of material hanging by hooks from a pole, covering a window or door ○ *Can you close the curtains, please?* ∎ *verb* □ **to curtain off** to separate with a curtain ○ *The end of the dining room is curtained off to form a private meeting room.* ◇ **to draw the curtains 1.** to open the curtains **2.** to close the curtains ○ *Draw the curtains – it's getting cold.*

custard /'kʌstəd/ *noun* SAUCES, ETC. a sweet yellow sauce made with milk and powder of cornflour and vanilla

custard apple /'kʌstəd ,æp(ə)l/ *noun* FRUIT the sweet pulpy fruit of a tree grown in the West Indies

custody /'kʌstədi/ *noun* the state of being looked after, kept or detained by somebody ○ *The jewels were in the custody of the man-*

ager, and he had placed them in the hotel safe. ○ *The hijacker was taken into police custody on landing.*

custom /'kʌstəm/ *noun* **1.** BUSINESS the use of a restaurant, hotel, bar or shop by regular customers □ **to lose someone's custom** to do something which makes a regular customer go to another restaurant, shop, etc. **2.** something that people usually do, or have done for a long time ○ *It's an old Greek custom to smash plates at the end of a meal.*

custom-built /'kʌstəm bɪlt/, **custom-made** /,kʌstəm 'meɪd/ *adjective* made specially for one customer ○ *He drives a custom-built Rolls Royce.*

customer /'kʌstəmə/ *noun* BUSINESS a person or company that buys goods or services ○ *The shop was full of customers.* ○ *Can you serve this customer first, please?* ○ *He is a regular customer of ours.*

customer appeal /'kʌstəmər ə,piːl/ *noun* BUSINESS something which attracts customers to a product

customer care agent /,kʌstəmə 'keə ,eɪdʒənt/ *noun* a person whose job is to look after customers and ensure that they receive satisfactory service

customer service department /,kʌstəmə 'sɜːvɪs dɪ,pɑːtmənt/ *noun* BUSINESS a department which deals with customers and their complaints and orders

customised /'kʌstəmaɪzd/ *adjective* specifically designed to meet the special requirements of a person or group

customs /'kʌstəmz/ *noun* BUSINESS a government department which organises the collection of taxes on imports ∎ *plural noun* an office of this department at a port, airport or national border ○ *He was stopped by customs.* ○ *Her car was searched by customs.* □ **to go through customs** to pass through the area of a port or airport where customs officials examine goods □ **to take something through customs** to carry something illegal through the customs area without declaring it □ **the crates had to go through a customs examination** the crates had to be examined by customs officials

Customs and Excise /,kʌstəmz ən 'eksaɪz/ *noun* BUSINESS a government department which deals with taxes on imports, with taxes on products such as alcohol produced in the country, and also with Value Added Tax

customs barrier /'kʌstəmz ,bæriə/ *noun* customs duty intended to prevent imports

customs duty /'kʌstəmz ˌdjuːti/ *noun* BUSINESS a tax paid on goods brought into or taken out of a country. Also called **import duty**

customs entry point /ˌkʌstəmz 'entri pɔɪnt/ *noun* BUSINESS a place at a border between two countries or at an airport or port, where goods are declared to customs

customs examination /'kʌstəmz ɪg ˌzæmɪneɪʃ(ə)n/ *noun* BUSINESS an examination of goods or baggage by customs officials

customs officer /'kʌstəmz ˌɒfɪsə/, **customs official** /'kʌstəmz əˌfɪʃ(ə)l/ *noun* somebody who works for the customs

customs union /'kʌstəmz ˌjuːnjən/ *noun* BUSINESS an agreement between several countries that goods can travel between them without paying duty, while goods from other countries have to pay special duties

cut /kʌt/ *verb* **1.** to remove pieces from something, or divide it into pieces, with a knife ○ *He cut off two slices of ham.* **2.** to damage the skin with something sharp ○ *She cut her hand opening the can.* **3.** to make lower ○ *They have cut the prices of tours.* □ **to cut down on cigarettes** *or* **on expenses** to reduce the number of cigarettes you smoke or the amount of money you spend

cut in /ˌkʌt 'ɪn/ *verb* CATERING to mix fat into flour using a metal blade

cutlery /'kʌtləri/ *noun* knives, forks and spoons ○ *Can you put the cutlery out on the tables, please.* ○ *Airlines say that passengers often steal pieces of cutlery.*

cutlet /'kʌtlət/ *noun* FOOD a flat cake of minced meat or fish, covered with breadcrumbs and fried ○ *a veal cutlet*

cut of meat /ˌkʌt əv 'miːt/ *noun* MEAT a piece of meat cut in a special way from a larger piece

cut-price /ˌkʌt 'praɪs/ *adjective* MARKETING sold at a cheaper price than usual ○ *cut-price goods* ○ *cut-price petrol*

cutting board /'kʌtɪŋ bɔːd/ *noun* CATERING same as **chopping board**

cvs *abbreviation* CATERING covers

cyclamate /'saɪkləmeɪt/ *noun* CATERING a sweetening substance used instead of sugar, believed to be carcinogenic and banned in the USA, UK and elsewhere as a food additive

cycle /'saɪk(ə)l/ *noun* **1.** ROAD TRAVEL same as **bicycle 2.** a period during which something works or develops and then returns to its starting point ■ *verb* to travel on a bicycle

cycle hire /'saɪk(ə)l ˌhaɪə/ *noun* the rental of a bicycle for a period, paid for at a particular rate per hour, per half-day, per day or per week

cycle path /'saɪk(ə)l pɑːθ/ *noun* a special path for cyclists ○ *There are thousands of cycle paths in Holland.*

cycling /'saɪklɪŋ/ *noun* the activity of riding on a bicycle ○ *to go on a cycling holiday*

cyclist /'saɪklɪst/ *noun* somebody who rides a bicycle ○ *The police told the crowds to stand back as the cyclists were passing.*

D

d *abbreviation* TRAVEL departs

daily /'deɪli/ *adjective* happening every day □ **a daily flight to Washington** a flight which goes to Washington every day at the same time □ **a daily newspaper, a daily** a newspaper that is produced every day

daily room rate /ˌdeɪli 'ruːm ˌreɪt/ *noun* HOTELS the rate that is charged for staying in a hotel room for one day or night

daiquiri /'daɪk(ə)ri/ *noun* an iced cocktail made from rum, lemon or lime juice, and sugar or syrup

dairy /'deəri/ *noun* a room or building where butter and cheese are made ■ *adjective* **1.** relating to or containing milk or milk products **2.** relating to those foods, including milk products, eggs, fish and vegetables, that Jewish dietary law allows on occasions when milk is consumed

dairy produce /'deəri ˌprɒdjuːs/, **dairy products** *noun* DAIRY foods prepared from milk, including milk itself, cream, yoghurt, butter, cheese, etc.

damage /'dæmɪdʒ/ *noun* **1.** the breaking or physical spoiling of something □ **to suffer damage** to be harmed □ **to cause damage** to harm something ○ *The fire caused damage estimated at £100,000.* **2.** □ **to bring an action for damages against someone** to take someone to court and claim damages ■ *verb* to break or partially destroy something ○ *stock which has been damaged by water* ○ *The storm damaged the telephone lines.*

damages /'dæmɪdʒɪz/ *plural noun* money claimed as compensation for harm done ○ *to claim £1,000 in damages* ○ *to be liable for damages* ○ *to pay £25,000 in damages*

damage survey /'dæmɪdʒ ˌsɜːveɪ/ *noun* a report on damage done

damson /'dæmzən/ *noun* FRUIT a small purple plum, or the tree which bears this fruit

dance /dɑːns/ *noun* ENTERTAINMENT an evening entertainment where people dance to music ○ *There is a 21st birthday dance at the hotel this evening.* ■ *verb* ENTERTAINMENT to move in time to music □ **restaurant licensed for music and dancing** a restaurant that has a special permit allowing music to be played for customers to dance to

dance band /'dɑːns bænd/ *noun* ENTERTAINMENT a band which plays music for dances

dance floor /'dɑːns flɔː/ *noun* ENTERTAINMENT a specially polished floor for dancing on

dangerous /'deɪndʒərəs/ *adjective* likely to cause injury or damage ○ *Tourists are warned that it is dangerous to go out alone at night.*

Danish pastry /ˌdeɪnɪʃ 'peɪstri/, **Danish** /'deɪnɪʃ/ *noun* BREAD, ETC. a sweet pastry cake with jam or fruit folded in it

dark chocolate /dɑːk 'tʃɒklət/ *noun* chocolate that has no added milk and is darker and less sweet than milk chocolate

dash /dæʃ/ *noun* a small quantity of something added to something else, so as to improve its flavour

date /deɪt/ *noun* **1.** numbers indicating the day, month and year ○ *I have received your letter of yesterday's date.* ○ *The dates of the exhibition have been changed.* **2.** FRUIT the small sweet brown fruit of the date palm, a staple food of many people in the Middle East ■ *verb* to put a date on a document ○ *The cheque was dated March 24th.* ○ *You forgot to date the cheque.* □ **to date a cheque forward** to put a future date on a cheque

date code /'deɪt kəʊd/ *noun* signs or numbers which indicate a sell-by date

date coding /'deɪt ˌkəʊdɪŋ/ *noun* the act of putting a sell-by date on a product

date of arrival /ˌdeɪt əv ə'raɪv(ə)l/ *noun* TRAVEL same as **arrival date**

date of birth /ˌdeɪt əv 'bɜːθ/ *noun* the date on which someone was born ○ *Please write your date and place of birth on the registration form.*

date stamp /'deɪt stæmp/ *noun* a device with rubber figures which can be moved, used for marking the date on documents or for marking the sell-by date on goods

dauphinois /ˌdəʊfɪnˈwɒl/ *adjective* CATERING thinly sliced and baked in milk or cream, sometimes with garlic or cheese

dawn /dɔːn/ *noun* the beginning of a day, when the sun rises ○ *We set off for the pyramids at dawn, so you'll have to get up very early.*

day /deɪ/ *noun* **1.** a period of 24 hours ○ *a ten-day tour of southern Spain* ○ *There are thirty days in June.* ○ *The first day of the month is a public holiday.* □ **three clear days** three whole working days ○ *You will get a refund only if you give ten clear days' notice of cancelling.* ○ *Allow four clear days for the cheque to be paid into the bank.* **2.** the period from morning to night **3.** the work period from morning to night □ **she took two days off** she did not come to work for two days □ **he works three days on, two days off** he works for three days, then has two days' holiday □ **to work an eight-hour day** to spend eight hours at work each day

daylight /ˈdeɪlaɪt/ *noun* the light of day

Daylight Saving Time /ˌdeɪlaɪt ˈseɪvɪŋ taɪm/ *noun* a system of putting the clocks forward one hour in summer to provide extra daylight in the evening. Abbr **DST**. Also called **Summer Time**

daypack /ˈdeɪpæk/ *noun* a small rucksack or bag for carrying things needed during the day

day rate /ˈdeɪ reɪt/ *noun* HOTELS a tariff for using a hotel room during the day

day release /ˌdeɪ rɪˈliːs/ *noun* BUSINESS an arrangement where a company allows an employee to go to college to study for one or two days each week ○ *She is attending a day release course for hotel managers.*

day return ticket /ˌdeɪ rɪˈtɜːn ˌtɪkɪt/ *noun* TRAVEL a ticket available at a lower price if you go and come back on the same day

day room /ˈdeɪ ruːm/ *noun* a communal room for use during the day rather than the evening

day shift /ˈdeɪ ʃɪft/ *noun* a shift worked from early morning to late afternoon ○ *There are 150 men on the day shift.*

day trip /ˈdeɪ trɪp/ *noun* TOURISM a tour or excursion which leaves in the morning and returns the same evening

day tripper /ˈdeɪ ˌtrɪpə/ *noun* TOURISM somebody who goes on a day trip

dB *abbreviation* decibel

DB & B, DBB *abbreviation* HOTELS dinner, bed and breakfast

dead /ded/ *adjective* **1.** not alive any more ○ *Six people were dead as a result of the accident.* **2.** not working □ **the line went dead** the telephone line suddenly stopped working □ **dead loss** total loss ○ *The car was written off as a dead loss.*

dead season /ˈded ˌsiːz(ə)n/ *noun* TOURISM the time of year when there are few tourists about

dear /dɪə/ *adjective* **1.** costing a lot of money ○ *Clothes are very dear in the market, but carpets are cheap.* **2.** a word used when starting a letter □ **Dear Sir, Dear Madam** addressing a man or woman whom you do not know, or addressing a company □ **Dear Sirs** addressing a company □ **Dear Mr Smith, Dear Mrs Smith, Dear Miss Smith** addressing a man or woman whom you know □ **Dear James, Dear Julia** addressing a friend or a person you do business with

debit /ˈdebɪt/ *noun* BUSINESS an entry in accounts showing a debt or an expense. Compare **credit** ■ *verb* □ **to debit an account** to charge an account with a cost ○ *Her account was debited with the sum of £25.*

debit balance /ˈdebɪt ˌbæləns/ *noun* BUSINESS a balance in an account, showing that the company owes more money than it has received

debit card /ˈdebɪt kɑːd/ *noun* FINANCE a plastic card, similar to a credit card, but which debits the holder's account immediately through an EPOS system

debone /diːˈbəʊn/ *verb* CATERING to take the bones out of meat or fish ○ *The waiter should be able to debone a grilled sole at the table.*

decaf, decaff (*informal*) *noun* a decaffeinated drink, especially coffee ■ *adjective* BEVERAGES same as **decaffeinated**

decaffeinated /diːˈkæfɪneɪtɪd/ *adjective* BEVERAGES from which the caffeine has been removed ○ *decaffeinated coffee* ○ *decaffeinated tea*

decant /dɪˈkænt/ *verb* CATERING **1.** to pour vintage wine from a bottle into another container, so as to remove the sediment ○ *The sommelier has practical skill in decanting port or a Bordeaux.* **2.** to put jam, marmalade, pickle, etc., from large jars into small serving dishes for each table

decanter /dɪˈkæntə/ *noun* CATERING **1.** an open glass bottle into which wine is decanted, and from which the wine is served **2.** a glass bottle with a glass stopper, in which drinks such as whisky, port or sherry may be stored for a time

decibel /'desɪbel/ *noun* a unit used to measure the intensity of sound ○ *People living near the airport complained that the noise of aircraft overhead was well over the decibel limit.* ○ *The noise readings of 90–95 decibels are considered excessive.* Abbr **dB**

COMMENT: Any sound above the 85 dB level can affect your hearing, especially if it continues for a time. An average conversation is about 60 dB, a motorcycle is 88 dB and a jet plane flying overhead is 130 dB.

decimal /'desɪm(ə)l/ *noun* a number in a system based on ten ○ *Three-quarters is 0.75 in decimals.*

decimal point /,desɪm(ə)l 'pɔɪnt/ *noun* a dot which indicates the division between a whole unit and its smaller parts, as in 4.25

deck /dek/ *noun* **1.** SHIPS AND BOATS a flat floor in a ship □ **lower decks** the decks below the main deck **2.** ROAD TRAVEL a floor on a bus

deckchair /'dektʃeə/ *noun* a long folding chair, made of canvas and wood, used to sit on out of doors ○ *She spent the afternoon sitting in a deckchair trying to do a crossword.*

deckchair attendant /'dektʃeə ə,tendənt/ *noun* somebody who is in charge of deckchairs for hire in a park or on a beach, making sure that the chairs are kept clean and dry, and collecting money from people who hire them

deck plan /'dek plæn/ *noun* SHIPS AND BOATS a plan displayed in a ship, showing the various decks and what can be found on them ○ *Look on the deck plan to find where the coffee lounge is.*

deck quoits /'dek kɔɪts/ *noun* ENTERTAINMENT a game played on the deck of a ship, in which players throw rings, trying to hook them over posts set in the deck

declaration /,deklə'reɪʃ(ə)n/ *noun* an official statement

declare /dɪ'kleə/ *verb* to make an official statement □ **to declare goods to customs** to state that you are importing goods which are liable to customs duty ○ *The customs officials asked him if he had anything to declare.* ○ *Go through the green channel if you have nothing to declare.*

decline /dɪ'klaɪn/ *noun* the fact of going downwards or becoming less ○ *a welcome decline in the number of cases of pollution* ○ *Tourist visits have gone into a sharp decline.* ■ *verb* **1.** to refuse something such as an invitation ○ *He declined to come to lunch.* **2.** to become less in numbers or amount ○ *Visitor figures declined sharply over the last year.*

'…half-way through the two-week tour he said that an American hotel had declined his card although he had not breached the limit' [*Caterer & Hotelkeeper*]

decorate /'dekəreɪt/ *verb* **1.** to paint a room or a building or to put new wallpaper in a room **2.** to cover something with pretty or colourful things to make it look attractive or to celebrate an occasion ○ *The streets were decorated with bunting for the music festival.* **3.** CATERING to put coloured icing on a cake ○ *Christmas cakes are decorated with holly leaves and berries.*

decorations /,dekə'reɪʃ(ə)nz/ *plural noun* flags, lights and other ornaments used to make a place look prettier to celebrate an occasion ○ *The restaurant staff came in early to put up Christmas decorations.*

dedicated /'dedɪkeɪtɪd/ *adjective* set aside for a special purpose □ **dedicated Business class lounge** a lounge set aside for Business class passengers only

'…the best conference hotels provide a dedicated member of staff for each conference to liaise with the organizer and ensure the event proceeds smoothly' [*Caterer & Hotelkeeper*]

dedicated line /,dedɪkeɪtɪd 'laɪn/ *noun* a telephone line used only for a particular purpose

deduct /dɪ'dʌkt/ *verb* to remove money from a total ○ *The hotel deducted £3 from the room price.* ○ *She deducted a sum to cover breakages.* ○ *After deducting costs the gross margin is only 23%.*

deductible /dɪ'dʌktɪb(ə)l/ *adjective* possible to deduct □ **some travelling expenses are not tax-deductible** tax has to be paid on those expenses

deduction /dɪ'dʌkʃən/ *noun* the act of removing money from a total, or the money removed ○ *Net salary is salary after deduction of tax and social security payments.*

deep-fat fryer /,diːp fæt 'fraɪə/ *noun* CATERING same as **deep fryer**

deep-freeze /'diːp friːz/ CATERING *noun* a powerful refrigerator for freezing food and keeping it frozen ○ *I'll put the chicken in the deep-freeze until next week.* ■ *verb* to freeze food and keep it frozen ○ *We deep-freeze a lot of the vegetables from our garden.* ○ *He bought some deep-frozen shrimps.*

deep-fried /,diːp 'fraɪd/ *adjective* CATERING cooked in deep oil or fat

deep-fry /'diːp fraɪ/ *verb* CATERING to cook food in a deep pan of boiling oil or fat

deep fryer /,diːp 'fraɪə/ *noun* an electrical appliance for deep-frying food. Also called **deep-fat fryer**

deep pan pizza /ˌdiːp pæn ˈpiːtsə/ *noun* FOOD an American-style pizza with a thicker base and more ingredients than usual

deep-vein thrombosis /ˌdiːp veɪn θrɒmˈbəʊsɪs/ *noun* MEDICAL coagulated blood in the deep veins of a leg or the pelvis. Abbr **DVT**. Also called **economy class syndrome**

COMMENT: Deep-vein thrombosis can affect air travellers who have not enough leg room in economy class during long-haul flights because airlines have reduced the space between seats. Passengers are recommended to walk up and down the aisle at least once every hour during a long flight.

defreeze /diːˈfriːz/ *verb* CATERING to thaw frozen food

defrost /diːˈfrɒst/ *verb* **1.** to remove ice which has formed inside a refrigerator or freezer **2.** CATERING to thaw frozen food ○ *A large turkey will take 24 hours to defrost.*

deglaze /diːˈɡleɪz/ *verb* CATERING to dissolve fragments remaining in a frying or roasting pan by heating them and adding a liquid so as to make a sauce

dehydrate /ˌdiːhaɪˈdreɪt/ *verb* **1.** CATERING to remove water from something in order to preserve it ○ *If you want to use dehydrated mushrooms, you must soak them in water for some time.* **2.** to lose water ○ *After two days without food or drink, he became severely dehydrated.*

COMMENT: Food can be dehydrated by drying in the sun (as in the case of dried fruit), or by passing through various industrial processes, such as freeze-drying. Water is more essential than food for a human being's survival. During the day, if a person drinks less liquid than is passed out of the body in urine and sweat, he or she will begin to dehydrate.

dehydrated milk /ˌdiːhaɪdreɪtɪd ˈmɪlk/ *noun* DAIRY milk that has been dried and reduced to a powder. Also called **dried milk**

dehydration /ˌdiːhaɪˈdreɪʃ(ə)n/ *noun* **1.** CATERING the removal of water from something in order to preserve it **2.** loss of water ○ *After a long tennis match in blistering heat both players were suffering from dehydration.*

delay /dɪˈleɪ/ *noun* the interval between the time at which something was planned to happen and the later time at which it actually happens ○ *There was a delay of thirty minutes before the flight left* or *The flight left after a thirty-minute delay.* ○ *We are sorry for the delay in replying to your letter.* ■ *verb* **1.** to make someone late ○ *She was delayed because her taxi had an accident.* **2.** to put

something off until later ○ *The company has delayed payment of all invoices.*

delegate *noun* /ˈdelɪɡət/ somebody who is attending a conference or meeting as a representative of an organisation ○ *The delegates all wear name badges.* □ **conference delegate** a person attending a conference ○ *We are expecting the first of the conference delegates to arrive this evening.* ■ *verb* /ˈdelɪɡeɪt/ to pass authority or responsibility to someone else ○ *The manager finds it difficult to delegate.* ○ *She delegated the job of checking the keys to the junior reception clerk.*

Delhi belly /ˌdeli ˈbeli/ *noun* MEDICAL diarrhoea which affects people travelling in foreign countries as a result of eating unwashed fruit or drinking water which has not been boiled (*humorous*)

deli /ˈdeli/ *noun* same as **delicatessen** (*informal*) ○ *We got some bagels from the deli opposite the hotel.*

delicacy /ˈdelɪkəsi/ *noun* a delicious but rare thing to eat ○ *They served all sorts of delicacies at the Chinese banquet.*

delicatessen /ˌdelɪkəˈtes(ə)n/ *noun* a shop selling cold meats and imported or specialised food products, and usually also sandwiches and snacks ○ *We bought some salad and pies at the delicatessen.*

delicious /dɪˈlɪʃəs/ *adjective* tasting very good ○ *Italian ice cream is delicious.* ○ *Can I have another piece of that delicious cake?*

delivery time /dɪˈlɪv(ə)ri taɪm/ *noun* the number of days before something will be delivered

de luxe /ˌdɪ ˈlʌks/ *adjective* very expensive or of very high quality ○ *a de luxe tour of India* ○ *The airline offers first-class passengers a bag of de luxe toiletries.* (NOTE: **de luxe** was formerly the highest grade in the English Tourism Council grading system for accommodation.)

demand /dɪˈmɑːnd/ *noun* **1.** the act of asking for something **2.** BUSINESS the need for goods or services at a particular price ○ *There was an active demand for interpreters during the trade fair.* □ **to meet a demand, to fill a demand, to keep up with demand** to supply what is needed ○ *The factory had to increase production to meet the extra demand.* ○ *The office cleaning company cannot keep up with the demand for its services.* □ **there is not much demand for this item** not many people want to buy it □ **this book is in great demand, there is a great demand for this book** many people want to buy it ■ *verb* to ask firmly for something ○

She demanded a refund. ○ *The suppliers are demanding immediate payment of their outstanding invoices.*

Demerara sugar /ˌdeməreərə ˈʃugə/ *noun* FOOD same as **brown sugar**

demi chef de rang /ˌdemi ʃef də ˈrɒŋ/ *noun* CATERING the deputy to a chef de rang

demi-pension /ˌdemi ˈpenʃən/ *noun* HOTELS same as **half board**

demi-tasse /ˈdemi tæs/ *noun* a small coffee cup

dengue /ˈdeŋgi/ *noun* MEDICAL a tropical disease caused by an arbovirus, transmitted by mosquitoes, where the patient develops a high fever, pains in the joints, headache and rash. Also called **breakbone fever**

denomination /dɪˌnɒmɪˈneɪʃ(ə)n/ *noun* FINANCE a unit of money on a coin, bank note or stamp ○ *coins of all denominations* ○ *small denomination notes* ○ *The bank refused to accept low denomination coins.*

density /ˈdensɪti/ *noun* the number of people per unit of area

dep. *abbreviation* TRAVEL departs

depart /dɪˈpɑːt/ *verb* to leave ○ *The plane departs from Paris at 11.15.*

department /dɪˈpɑːtmənt/ *noun* **1.** a specialised section of a large company ○ *Write to the complaints department about the service in the hotels on the tour.* **2.** a section of a large store selling one type of product ○ *You will find beds in the furniture department.* **3.** one of the sections of the government. Abbr **dept**

department store /dɪˈpɑːtmənt stɔː/ *noun* BUSINESS a large shop with sections for different types of goods

departure /dɪˈpɑːtʃə/ *noun* the act of going away ○ *Your departure time is 3 o'clock.* ○ *The plane's departure was delayed by two hours.* ○ *Flight departures are delayed because of the discussions over air traffic controllers' pay.*

departure date /dɪˈpɑːtʃə deɪt/ *noun* TRAVEL the day on which a traveller or tour group leaves

departure lounge /dɪˈpɑːtʃə laʊndʒ/ *noun* AIR TRAVEL a room in an airport where passengers wait to get on their planes after going through passport control and baggage check

departures /dɪˈpɑːtʃəz/ *noun* AIR TRAVEL the part of an airport terminal that deals with passengers who are leaving

departure tax /dɪˈpɑːtʃə tæks/ *noun* TRAVEL a tax payable by passengers leaving a country

deplane /diːˈpleɪn/ *verb* AIR TRAVEL to get off a plane ○ *The party will deplane at Delhi.* Opposite **enplane**

deposit /dɪˈpɒzɪt/ *noun* FINANCE money given in advance so that the thing which you want to buy will not be sold to someone else ○ *to pay a deposit on a room* ○ *You will need to pay a 10% deposit to secure the booking.*

deposit account /dɪˈpɒzɪt əˌkaʊnt/ *noun* BUSINESS an account which pays interest but on which notice usually has to be given to withdraw money

depot /ˈdepəʊ/ *noun* TRAVEL a building where the vehicles used by a transport service are kept ○ *Buses leave the central bus depot every hour.*

dept *abbreviation* department

deregulate /diːˈregjʊleɪt/ *verb* BUSINESS to remove government restrictions from an industry

deregulation /diːˌregjʊˈleɪʃ(ə)n/ *noun* the removal of official restrictions ○ *Deregulation of US airlines resulted in fierce competition and price-cutting.*

descent /dɪˈsent/ *noun* **1.** the act of going down ○ *The descent into the mine takes just under three minutes.* **2.** (*of aircraft*) the period during which an aircraft comes down to land ○ *Passengers must fasten their seatbelts prior to descent.*

'…if you must travel with a cold, use a decongestant 10 minutes before take-off and descent' [*Evening Standard Business Travel*]

desiccated /ˈdesɪkeɪtɪd/ *adjective* dried

desiccated coconut /ˌdesɪkeɪtɪd ˈkəʊkənʌt/ *noun* FOOD the white flesh of a coconut, which has been dried ○ *She used desiccated coconut to make the cakes.*

designated carrier /ˌdezɪgneɪtɪd ˈkæriə/ *noun* AIR TRAVEL an airline that is licensed to operate a service between two countries

designator /ˈdezɪgneɪtə/ *noun* AIR TRAVEL a two-letter code by which an airline is identified

desk /desk/ *noun* a table, often with drawers, used for writing on ○ *desk diary* ○ *desk drawer* ○ *desk light*

desk clerk /ˈdesk klɑːk/ *noun* a hotel receptionist

desk pad /ˈdesk pæd/ *noun* a pad of paper kept on a desk for writing notes

desk research /ˈdesk rɪˌsɜːtʃ/ *noun* the work of looking for information which has already been published, e.g. in a directory

dessert /dɪˈzɜːt/ *noun* CATERING a sweet dish eaten at the end of a meal ○ *What do you* *want for dessert?* ○ *I have eaten so much, I don't want any dessert.* □ **dessert fork**, **dessert knife** a smaller fork and knife used to eat dessert

COMMENT: On formal menus, a dessert is a course of fruit or nuts taken after the cheese and before coffee is served. On an ordinary menu, a dessert can take the form of a pudding, pastry, ice or fresh fruit.

dessert grapes /dɪˈzɜːt ɡreɪps/ *plural noun* FRUIT grapes which are eaten raw, and not used to make wine

dessert menu /dɪˈzɜːt ˌmenjuː/ *noun* CATERING a special separate menu for desserts in a restaurant

dessertspoon /dɪˈzɜːtspuːn/ *noun* CATERING a spoon for eating desserts, which is smaller than a soup spoon, but larger than a teaspoon

dessert trolley /dɪˈzɜːt ˌtrɒli/ *noun* CATERING a table on wheels on which desserts are taken to each table in a restaurant. Also called **sweet trolley**

dessert wine /dɪˈzɜːt waɪn/ *noun* BEVERAGES a sweet wine that is served with a dessert, e.g. muscat (NOTE: There is usually no plural form: **desserts** means types of dessert.)

destination /ˌdestɪˈneɪʃ(ə)n/ *noun* a place to which something is sent, or to which someone is going ○ *The ship will take ten weeks to reach its destination.* ■ *adjective* done or happening at a place that a person has to travel to reach ○ *destination dining*

destination wedding /ˌdestɪˈneɪʃ(ə)n ˌwedɪŋ/ *noun* a wedding that takes place in a far-off location that the couple and their guests have to travel to

detect /dɪˈtekt/ *verb* to notice something that could be difficult to see, hear or smell ○ *A smoke detector detects the presence of smoke.*

detector /dɪˈtektə/ *noun* an apparatus that notices something that is difficult to see, hear or smell

detergent /dɪˈtɜːdʒənt/ *noun* a cleaning substance which removes grease and bacteria from clothes, dishes, etc. ○ *This detergent will not harm your skin.*

detour /ˈdiːtʊə/ *noun* a journey away from the usual or planned route ○ *We made a detour to visit the caves.* ○ *We had to make a detour because of the roadworks.*

detrain /diːˈtreɪn/ *verb* RAIL TRAVEL to get off a train

develop /dɪˈveləp/ *verb* **1.** to grow and change, or to change something so that it becomes larger or more complicated ○ *We*

are developing the harbour facilities to allow larger ferries to berth. ○ *The company is developing a chain of motorway self-service restaurants.* **2.** to produce and fix a photograph from film ○ *We can develop your film in an hour.*

developed country /dɪˌveləpt ˈkʌntri/ *noun* a country which has an advanced manufacturing system

developer /dɪˈveləpə/ *noun* **1.** a liquid for developing photographs **2.** somebody who builds property

developing country /dɪˌveləpɪŋ ˈkʌntri/, **developing nation** /dɪˌveləpɪŋ ˈneɪʃ(ə)n/ *noun* a country which is not fully industrialised

development /dɪˈveləpmənt/ *noun* the construction of new buildings, or new buildings constructed on an area of land ○ *Unrestricted hotel development has ruined the coastline.* ○ *Proposals for a £70m leisure development have been abandoned in favour of a shopping centre.*

development zone /dɪˈveləpmənt zəʊn/ *noun* BUSINESS an area that has been given special help by a government to encourage businesses and factories to set up there. Also called **enterprise zone**

dextrose /ˈdekstrəʊz/ *noun* a simple sugar found in fruit and also extracted from corn starch

dhal, dal *noun* FOOD an Indian term for pulses such as lentils and pigeon peas, or a curry or soup prepared from these pulses

diabetes /ˌdaɪəˈbiːtiːz/ *noun* MEDICAL one of a group of diseases, but most commonly used to refer to diabetes mellitus, a disease where the body cannot control sugar absorption because the pancreas does not secrete enough insulin

diabetic /ˌdaɪəˈbetɪk/ *adjective* MEDICAL referring to diabetes □ **diabetic food** food with a low sugar content which can be eaten by people suffering from diabetes ■ *noun* MEDICAL a person who has diabetes

dial /ˈdaɪəl/ *verb* to call a telephone number on a telephone ○ *to dial a number* ○ *to dial the operator* ○ *Dial 9 to get an outside line.*

dialling /ˈdaɪəlɪŋ/ *noun* the act of calling a telephone number

dialling code /ˈdaɪəlɪŋ kəʊd/ *noun* a special series of numbers used to make a call to another town

dialling tone /ˈdaɪəlɪŋ təʊn/ *noun* a noise made by a telephone to show that it is ready for you to dial a number

diamond /'daɪəmənd/ *noun* a very hard, clear, precious stone

diamond rating /'daɪəmənd ˌreɪtɪŋ/ *noun* TOURISM a method of rating inns, farmhouses and bed and breakfasts, used by the English Tourism Council ○ *an award-winning 5 diamond bed and breakfast* ○ *Diamond rating is intended for B & Bs and guesthouses.*

'...because neither rating is appropriate, some of my competitors are diamond-rated (often three and four diamonds), while others are star-rated (two stars). After all, many small hotels are opting for a diamond rating because they get more diamonds than they would stars. Whatever the ETC's intentions about educating the public on the difference between the scales, it cannot be denied that more diamonds look better than fewer stars' [*Caterer & Hotelkeeper*]

diarrhoea /ˌdaɪə'riːə/, **diarrhea** *US noun* MEDICAL a condition in which a patient frequently passes liquid faeces ○ *He had an attack of diarrhoea after going to the restaurant.* ○ *She complained of mild diarrhoea.*

COMMENT: Diarrhoea can have many causes: types of food or allergy to food; contaminated or poisoned food; infectious diseases, such as dysentery; sometimes worry or other emotions.

diary /'daɪəri/ *noun* a book in which you can write notes or appointments for each day of the week □ **to keep a diary** to write down what you have felt or done each day ○ *The children on the study tour have to keep a diary of the places they visit.*

dice /daɪs/ *verb* CATERING to cut food into small cubes ○ *diced potato*

diet /'daɪət/ *noun* **1.** the amount and type of food eaten ○ *The average western diet is too full of carbohydrates.* □ **low-calorie diet** a diet with few calories, which can help a person to lose weight **2.** the act of eating only particular types of food, either to become thinner, to cure an illness or improve a condition □ **to be on a diet** to eat only particular types of food, especially in order to become thin or to deal with an illness ○ *Two of the passengers are on diets.* ■ *verb* to reduce the quantity of food you eat, or to change the type of food you eat, in order to become thinner or healthier

dietary /'daɪət(ə)ri/ *adjective* referring to a diet

dietary fibre /'daɪət(ə)ri ˌfaɪbə/ *noun* CATERING fibrous substances in food, which cannot be digested. Also called **roughage**

COMMENT: Dietary fibre is found in cereals, nuts, fruit and some green vegetables. It is believed to be necessary to help digestion and avoid developing constipation, obesity, appendicitis and other digestive problems.

Dietary Reference Values /ˌdaɪət(ə)ri 'ref(ə)rəns ˌvæljuːz/ *plural noun* a list published by the British government of nutrients that are essential for health. Abbr **DRV**

dieter /'daɪətə/ *noun* somebody who is on a diet ○ *Dieters should try the new low-fat yoghurt.*

dietetics /ˌdaɪə'tetɪks/ *noun* FOOD the study of food and its nutritional value

dietician /ˌdaɪə'tɪʃ(ə)n/, **dietitian** *noun* somebody who specialises in the study of nutrition and advises on diets ○ *The dietician warned me not to eat too much red meat.*

difference /'dɪf(ə)rəns/ *noun* the way in which two things are not the same □ **to split the difference** to share the payment of the difference between two prices

differential /ˌdɪfə'renʃəl/ *adjective* showing a difference

digest /daɪ'dʒest/ *verb* MEDICAL to break down food in the stomach and intestine and convert it into elements which can be absorbed by the body □ **I cannot digest my dinner** I am feeling unwell after my dinner

digestible /daɪ'dʒestɪb(ə)l/ *adjective* possible to digest ○ *I don't find raw garlic very digestible.*

digestif /ˌdiːʒes'tiːf/ *noun* BEVERAGES an alcoholic drink taken after a meal to help the digestion, e.g. brandy or a liqueur

digestion /daɪ'dʒestʃən/ *noun* MEDICAL the act of breaking down food in the stomach and intestine and converting it into elements which can be absorbed by the body ○ *Brown bread helps the digestion.*

digestive /daɪ'dʒestɪv/ *adjective* helping you to digest something

digestive biscuit /daɪˌdʒestɪv 'bɪskɪt/ *noun* BREAD, ETC. a sweet wholemeal biscuit

digit /'dɪdʒɪt/ *noun* a single number ○ *a seven-digit phone number*

digital clock /ˌdɪdʒɪt(ə)l 'klɒk/ *noun* a clock which shows the time as a series of figures, e.g. 12:05:23, rather than on a circular dial

dignitary /'dɪgnɪt(ə)ri/ *noun* someone with a high rank or position

dill /dɪl/ *noun* a herb of the parsley family used as flavouring or a garnish

dim /dɪm/ *verb* to make a light less bright ○ *The captain dimmed the cabin lights before takeoff.*

dime /daɪm/ *noun US* FINANCE a ten-cent coin

dimmer switch /'dɪmə swɪtʃ/ *noun* a light switch which makes a light less bright

dim sum /'dɪm sʌm/ *noun* FOOD a southern Chinese style lunch, where many different small dishes are served

dine /daɪn/ *verb* to have dinner or to eat an evening meal □ **to dine out** to have dinner away from home or in a restaurant outside the hotel where you are staying □ **to dine in** to have dinner at home or in the restaurant of the hotel where you are staying

diner /'daɪnə/ *noun* 1. somebody who is eating an evening meal □ *When the restaurant caught fire, the diners ran into the street.* 2. RAIL TRAVEL a dining car on a train 3. *US* CATERING a small restaurant selling simple hot food (NOTE: Originally, these were made from old dining cars from railway trains.)

dinghy /'dɪŋi/ *noun* SHIPS AND BOATS a small boat ○ *We spent the day in a dinghy, pottering around the harbour.* (NOTE: The plural form is **dinghies**.)

dining car /'daɪnɪŋ kɑː/ *noun* RAIL TRAVEL a railway carriage where meals are served ○ *The dining car joins the train at Lyon.*

dining room /'daɪnɪŋ ruːm/ *noun* HOTELS a room in a hotel where people eat ○ *We were sitting in the dining room having supper when my husband was called to the phone.*

dining table /'daɪnɪŋ ˌteɪb(ə)l/ *noun* CATERING a table on which meals are served and eaten (NOTE: **Dining table** refers to the piece of furniture; however, when you are eating at it, it is called the **dinner table**.)

dinner /'dɪnə/ *noun* CATERING an evening meal ○ *Dinner is served at 7.30.* ○ *The restaurant is open for dinner or serves dinner from 7.30 to 11.30.* ○ *Half-board includes breakfast and dinner, but not lunch.*

dinner-dance /'dɪnə dɑːns/ *noun* ENTERTAINMENT a formal dinner followed by dancing to music played by a live band ○ *The company is having a Christmas dinner-dance at the Imperial Hotel.*

dinner jacket /'dɪnə ˌdʒækɪt/ *noun* a formal jacket worn with a bow tie, both usually black. Abbr **DJ**

dinner party /'dɪnə ˌpɑːti/ ENTERTAINMENT 1. a private dinner to which guests are invited 2. (*in a restaurant*) a group of people having dinner together

dinner plate /'dɪnə pleɪt/ *noun* a wide flat plate for serving the main course on

dinner service /'dɪnə ˌsɜːvɪs/ *noun* CATERING a set of matching plates and bowls for serving a main meal

dinner table /'dɪnə ˌteɪb(ə)l/ *noun* CATERING a table where people eat

dip /dɪp/ *noun* 1. a sudden drop in an area of land ○ *Watch out – there's a dip in the road which makes it difficult to see oncoming cars.* 2. SAUCES, ETC. a purée into which vegetables or pieces of bread can be dipped as cocktail snacks ○ *small pieces of pitta bread with a bowl of avocado dip* ○ *They served fried prawns with bowls of chilli dip.* 3. a short bathe or swim ○ *We went for a quick dip before breakfast.* ○ *Are you coming for a dip in the pool?* ■ *verb* 1. □ **to dip something into sth** to put something quickly into a liquid ○ *She dipped the biscuit into her coffee.* ○ *She dipped her hand into the stream.* 2. □ **to dip your headlights** to lower the beam of the headlights of your car ○ *Please dip your headlights in the tunnel.*

dip card /'dɪp kɑːd/ *noun* HOTELS a type of magnetic key card which is pushed down into a slot and then pulled out again when the door unlocks

direct /daɪ'rekt/ *verb* to tell or show someone how to go to a place ■ *adjective* going straight from one place to another ○ *They took the most direct route to Paris.* ■ *adverb* straight, without any changes of direction or stops □ **to fly direct** to fly from one place to another with no changes ○ *British Airways now flies direct to Nassau four times a week.* □ **to dial direct** to contact a phone number yourself without asking the operator to do it for you ○ *You can dial New York direct from London if you want.*

'…remember, a direct flight is not the same as a nonstop flight – several connections may be cheaper than the nonstop option' [*Sunday Times Travel Section*]

direct debit /daɪˌrekt 'debɪt/ *noun* BUSINESS a system where a customer allows a company to charge costs to his or her bank account automatically and where the amount charged can be increased or decreased with the agreement of the customer

direct flight /ˌdaɪrekt 'flaɪt/ *noun* AIR TRAVEL a flight which goes from one place to another, though with stops in between, as opposed to a nonstop flight

directions /daɪ'rekʃənz/ *plural noun* instructions telling somebody how to go somewhere ○ *He gave her directions to get to the Post Office.*

direct mail /daɪˌrekt 'meɪl/ *noun* MARKETING a method of selling a product by sending publicity material to possible buyers through the post

direct-mail advertising /daɪˌrekt meɪl ˈædvətaɪzɪŋ/ *noun* MARKETING advertising by sending leaflets to people through the post even though they have not asked for them

director /daɪˈrektə/ *noun* BUSINESS somebody appointed by the shareholders to help run a company

directory /daɪˈrekt(ə)ri/ *noun* BUSINESS a list of people or businesses with information about their addresses and telephone numbers

direct service organisation /ˌdaɪrekt ˈsɜːvɪs/ *noun* part of the permanent staff of a local authority, which runs a section of the authority's services such as staff catering. Abbr **DSO**

direct tax /daɪˌrekt ˈtæks/ *noun* BUSINESS a tax paid directly to the government, e.g. income tax

disability /ˌdɪsəˈbɪlɪti/ *noun* a condition in which part of the body does not function in the usual way and makes some activities difficult or impossible ○ *Some hotels cater specifically for people with severe disabilities.*

Disability Discrimination Act /ˌdɪsəbɪləti dɪˌskrɪmɪˈneɪʃ(ə)n ˌækt/ a law in the UK that requires businesses to make their premises as accessible as possible to disabled people

disabled /dɪsˈeɪb(ə)ld/ *adjective* suffering from a physical or mental condition which makes some activities difficult or impossible (NOTE: More polite or formal terms for the **disabled** are **people with disabilities** or **people with special needs**.) ■ *noun* □ **the disabled** people with physical disabilities, taken as a group ○ *The library has facilities for the disabled.*

disabled access /dɪsˈeɪb(ə)ld ˌækses/ *noun* entrances with sloping ramps instead of steps, which are easier for people in wheelchairs to use

disabled toilets /dɪsˌeɪb(ə)ld ˈtɔɪlətz/ *plural noun* a public toilet with a larger room and wider doors than usual to make it easier for people in wheelchairs to use

disagree /ˌdɪsəˈɡriː/ *verb* **1.** to say that you do not think the same way as someone ○ *They all disagreed about what to do next.* **2.** □ **cabbage disagrees with me** cabbage makes me feel ill

disc jockey /ˈdɪsk ˌdʒɒki/ *noun* ENTERTAINMENT somebody who announces and plays recorded music at a nightclub or on the radio ○ *He's the most popular disc jockey at the hotel nightclub.* Abbr **DJ**

disco /ˈdɪskəʊ/ *noun* ENTERTAINMENT a place or party where people dance to recorded music

discoloration /dɪsˌkʌləˈreɪʃ(ə)n/ *noun* a change of colour, especially a change of colour of fruit

discolour /dɪsˈkʌlə/ *verb* to change the colour of something ○ *Fruit can be discoloured by the use of sprays.* (NOTE: The US spelling is **discolor**.)

discontinue /ˌdɪskənˈtɪnjuː/ *verb* not to continue to do something ○ *The ferry service to the island has been discontinued.*

discotheque /ˈdɪskətek/ *noun* ENTERTAINMENT same as **disco**

discount *noun* /ˈdɪskaʊnt/ a percentage by which a full price is reduced to a buyer by the seller ○ *to give a discount on summer holidays booked before Christmas* □ **10% discount for quantity purchases** you pay 10% less if you buy a large amount of goods □ **10% discount for cash, 10% cash discount** you pay 10% less if you pay in cash ■ *verb* /dɪsˈkaʊnt/ BUSINESS to reduce prices in order to increase sales ○ *Tour operators are discounting prices on package holidays.*

discount fare /ˈdɪskaʊnt feə/ *noun* TRAVEL a reduced fare, though with restrictions on travel

    '…unofficially discounted fares are fares sold at a discount to the officially approved full or promotional rates. Discounting is now commonplace in most countries.' [*Business Traveller*]

discount for cash /ˌdɪskaʊnt fə ˈkæʃ/ *noun* same as **cash discount**

discount holiday /ˈdɪskaʊnt ˌhɒlɪdeɪ/ *noun* a package holiday where the price is reduced

discount store /ˈdɪskaʊnt stɔː/ *noun* a shop which specialises in cheap goods bought at a high discount

discretionary /dɪˈskreʃ(ə)n(ə)ri/ *adjective* possible to carry out if someone wants to

discretionary income /dɪˌskreʃ(ə)n(ə)ri ˈɪnkʌm/ *noun* FINANCE income that a person has left after spending on basic necessities and that is therefore available for spending on leisure activities

discrimination /dɪˌskrɪmɪˈneɪʃ(ə)n/ *noun* the act of treating people in different ways because of class, religion, race, language, colour or sex

disease /dɪˈziːz/ *noun* MEDICAL a serious illness of animals, plants or humans

disembark /ˌdɪsɪmˈbɑːk/ *verb* TRAVEL to get off a vehicle, especially a ship or plane ○ *The passengers disembarked at the ocean terminal.*

disembarkation /ˌdɪsɪmbɑːˈkeɪʃ(ə)n/ noun TRAVEL the act of getting off a ship or plane

disembarkation card /ˌdɪsembɑːˈkeɪʃ(ə)n kɑːd/ noun TRAVEL a card that allows you to get off a plane or boat, and return after a short time

dish /dɪʃ/ noun **1.** CATERING a large plate for serving food □ **to wash the dishes, to do the dishes** to wash the plates, glasses, cutlery and cooking utensils that have been used for a meal **2.** CATERING part of a meal, or a plate of prepared food ○ *Ratatouille is a Provençal dish of stewed vegetables.* ■ *verb* □ **he is dishing up the food** he is serving the meal

dishcloth /ˈdɪʃklɒθ/ noun a cloth for washing dishes ○ *She mopped up the red wine with a dishcloth.*

dishwasher /ˈdɪʃwɒʃə/ noun a machine for washing dishes

dishwasher-proof /ˈdɪʃwɒʃə pruːf/ adjective that can be washed in a dishwasher without suffering harm

dish-washing /ˈdɪʃ ˌwɒʃɪŋ/ noun CATERING the washing of dirty plates, glasses, etc.

disinfectant /ˌdɪsɪnˈfektənt/ noun a substance designed to kill germs

dismiss /dɪsˈmɪs/ verb □ **to dismiss an employee** to remove an employee from a job ○ *He was dismissed for being consistently late.*

dismissal /dɪsˈmɪs(ə)l/ noun the removal of an employee from a job

COMMENT: An employee can complain of unfair dismissal to an industrial tribunal, or of wrongful dismissal to the County Court.

dismissal procedure /dɪsˌmɪs(ə)l prə ˈsiːdʒə/ noun BUSINESS the correct way of dismissing an employee, following the rules in the contract of employment

dispense bar /dɪˈspens bɑː/ noun CATERING a bar for serving drinks other than bottles of wine for guests in a restaurant

dispense cellar /dɪˈspens ˌselə/ noun a cellar in which wine is kept for immediate serving

dispenser /dɪˈspensə/ noun a machine which automatically provides something such as an object, a drink or some food, often when money is put in ○ *automatic dispenser* ○ *towel dispenser*

'…five-litre milk dispensers are made from stainless steel. A separate base takes an ice or freezer bag to keep the milk cool. Fruit juice dispensers have the same base, but there is a choice of four-, five- or six-litre cylinders' [*Caterer & Hotelkeeper*]

display /dɪˈspleɪ/ noun a show or exhibition ○ *The hotel lobby has a display of local crafts.*

display ad /dɪˈspleɪ æd/ noun MARKETING an advertisement which is well designed to attract attention

display case /dɪˈspleɪ keɪs/ noun MARKETING a table or counter with a glass top, used for showing items for sale

display pack /dɪˈspleɪ pæk/ noun MARKETING a specially attractive box for showing goods for sale

disposable /dɪˈspəʊzəb(ə)l/ adjective designed to be used and then thrown away ○ *disposable cups*

disposable income /dɪˌspəʊzəb(ə)l ˈɪnkʌm/ noun BUSINESS income left after tax and national insurance have been deducted

dispute /dɪˈspjuːt, ˈdɪspjuːt/ noun □ **to adjudicate** *or* **mediate in a dispute** to try to settle a dispute between other parties

distil /dɪˈstɪl/ verb **1.** CATERING to make strong alcohol by heating wine or other alcoholic liquid and condensing it **2.** to make pure water by heating impure water and collecting the vapour (NOTE: [all senses] The US spelling is **distill**.)

distillation /ˌdɪstɪˈleɪʃ(ə)n/ noun the act of distilling water or alcohol

distilled water /dɪˌstɪld ˈwɔːtə/ noun BEVERAGES pure water

distiller /dɪˈstɪlə/ noun BEVERAGES somebody who distils alcohol ○ *He is an important distiller of Scotch whisky.*

distillery /dɪˈstɪləri/ noun BEVERAGES a factory for distilling alcohol ○ *On our tour of the islands we visited several whisky distilleries.* (NOTE: The plural form is **distilleries**.)

district /ˈdɪstrɪkt/ noun a section of a country or of a town □ **the commercial district, the business district** the part of a town where offices and shops are located ○ *The hotel is well placed in the main business district of the town.*

disturb /dɪˈstɜːb/ verb to bother or worry someone, or to interrupt someone □ **'do not disturb'** a notice placed on a hotel room door, to ask the hotel staff not to come into the room

disturbance /dɪˈstɜːbəns/ noun an occasion on which someone is disturbed ○ *The fans caused a disturbance in the hotel bar.*

dive /daɪv/ noun **1.** a jump downwards into water head first **2.** BARS a disreputable bar (*informal*) ■ *verb* to jump into water head first

diver /'daɪvə/ *noun* somebody who jumps into water head first, or who swims under water

diversion /daɪ'vɜːʃ(ə)n/ *noun* ROAD TRAVEL a change to a planned or normal route in order to avoid e.g. roadworks or flooding ○ *All traffic has to take a diversion and rejoin the motorway 10km further on.*

divert /daɪ'vɜːt/ *verb* to send somebody or something to another place or in another direction ○ *Because of fog in London, flights have been diverted to Manchester.* ○ *Traffic has been diverted to avoid the town centre.*

diving /'daɪvɪŋ/ *noun* **1.** the sport of jumping into water head first **2.** SPORT the activity of swimming under water to explore or as a sport ○ *diving holidays on the Barrier Reef* ○ *We went diving in the Red Sea.* ○ *The resort offers swimming, surfing and diving.*

diving board /'daɪvɪŋ bɔːd/ *noun* ENTERTAINMENT a plank at a swimming pool from which people plunge into the water

DJ *abbreviation* **1.** dinner jacket **2.** disc jockey

docent /'dəʊs(ə)nt/ *noun* a tourist guide working in some museums or cathedrals

dock /dɒk/ *noun* SHIPS AND BOATS a harbour, a place where ships can load or unload □ **the docks** the part of a town where the harbour is ○ *Cars should arrive at the docks 45 minutes before sailing time.* ■ *verb* to go into dock ○ *The ship docked at 17.00.*

docker /'dɒkə/ *noun* somebody who works in the docks

dockside /'dɒksaɪd/ *noun* SHIPS AND BOATS the edge of a dock where ships load or unload ○ *Customs officers were waiting at the dockside to board the ship.*

dockyard /'dɒkjɑːd/ *noun* SHIPS AND BOATS a place where ships are built or repaired ○ *The damaged liner was towed into the dockyard for repair.*

doctor /'dɒktə/ *noun* a person whose job is to look after people who are ill (NOTE: **Doctor** is shortened in names to **Dr**: *Dr Thorne is the hotel doctor.*) □ **the hotel doctor** the doctor who is on call to treat guests who become ill in the hotel

document /'dɒkjʊmənt/ *noun* a piece of paper with writing on it ○ *Customs will ask to see the relevant documents concerning the shipment.*

documentation /ˌdɒkjʊmen'teɪʃ(ə)n/ *noun* all the papers referring to something ○ *Please send me the complete documentation concerning the sale.*

dogfish /'dɒgfɪʃ/ *noun* SEAFOOD same as **huss**

doggy bag /'dɒgi bæg/ *noun* a bag that a customer at a restaurant can use to take home any leftover food from a meal

dollar /'dɒlə/ *noun* FINANCE a unit of money used in the United States and other countries ○ *fifty Canadian dollars* ○ *The US dollar rose 2%.* ○ *It costs six Australian dollars.* (NOTE: This is usually written **$** before a figure: *$250*. The currencies used in different countries can be shown by the initial letter of the country: *Can$* (Canadian dollar), *Aus$* (Australian dollar), etc.)

dollar area /'dɒlər ˌeəriə/ *noun* FINANCE an area of the world where the dollar is the main trading currency

domestic /də'mestɪk/ *adjective* BUSINESS referring to the home market or to the market of the country where the business is situated

domestic consumption /dəˌmestɪk kən'sʌmpʃən/ *noun* the use of something in the home. Also called **home consumption**

domestic flight /də'mestɪk flaɪt/ *noun* AIR TRAVEL a flight inside a country. Also called **internal flight**

domestic terminal /də'mestɪk ˌtɜːmɪn(ə)l/ *noun* AIR TRAVEL an airport terminal for flights to destinations inside the country only ○ *Passengers arriving on international flights transfer to the domestic terminal for onward flights to destinations inside the country.*

domestic tourist /də'mestɪk ˌtʊərɪst/ *noun* TOURISM a tourist who is visiting another area of the same country where he or she lives

don /dɒn/ *verb* to put on clothes ○ *Instructions for donning the life jacket are given on the card in the pocket in front of your seat.* ○ *Visitors to the factory have to don protective clothing.* (NOTE: **donning – donned**)

done /dʌn/ *adjective* cooked as thoroughly as required

doner kebab /ˌdɒnə kə'bæb/ *noun* FOOD a Turkish meat dish, where a large piece of meat is cooked on a spit in front of a grill, and slices are cut off and served with pitta bread and salad, usually as a takeaway

door /dɔː/ *noun* a barrier of wood, glass or metal, which closes an entrance

doorkeeper /'dɔːkiːpə/ *noun* somebody who is on duty at a main door

doorkey /'dɔːkiː/ *noun* the key to a door ○ *Do not forget to give back your doorkey when you leave the hotel.*

doorknob /'dɔːnɒb/ *noun* a handle for opening and shutting a door ○ *She hung a 'do not disturb' sign on the doorknob.*

doorman /'dɔːmən/ *noun* a man who stands at the door of a restaurant, hotel, club, etc. ○ *The doorman would not let us in because we were wearing jeans.* (NOTE: The plural form is **doormen**.)

dorm /dɔːm/ *noun* TRAVEL same as **dormitory** (*informal*)

dormitory /'dɔːmɪtri/ *noun* a large room in which many people sleep, e.g. at a boarding school or in a hostel

dormobile /'dɔːməˌbiːl/ *tdmk* ROAD TRAVEL a trademark for a small motor caravan, now no longer manufactured

double /'dʌb(ə)l/ *adjective* **1.** twice as large ○ *double quantity* **2.** with two parts, or for two people ○ *double garage*

double bed /ˌdʌb(ə)l 'bed/ *noun* a bed for two people

double-bedded room /ˌdʌb(ə)l ˌbedɪd 'ruːm/ *noun* HOTELS a room with two beds, usually two twin beds

double boiler /ˌdʌb(ə)l 'bɔɪlə/ *noun* CATERING a cooking utensil made up of two saucepans, one of which fits on top of the other, the lower pan containing hot water and the top pan containing the food to be cooked. Also called **double saucepan**

double-book /ˌdʌb(ə)l 'bʊk/ *verb* HOTELS to reserve the same hotel room or plane seat for two people at the same time, usually by mistake ○ *We had to change our flight as we were double-booked.*

double-booking /ˌdʌb(ə)l 'bʊkɪŋ/ *noun* HOTELS the act of booking two people into the same hotel room or the same seat on a plane at the same time by mistake

double cream /ˌdʌb(ə)l 'kriːm/ *noun* DAIRY thick cream with a high fat content

double-decker /ˌdʌb(ə)l 'dekə/ *noun* **1.** ROAD TRAVEL a bus with two decks ○ *Double-decker buses are common in London.* Compare **singledecker** **2.** FOOD same as **club sandwich**

double-decker sandwich /ˌdʌb(ə)l ˌdekə 'sændwɪtʃ/ *noun* FOOD same as **club sandwich**

double glazing /ˌdʌb(ə)l 'gleɪzɪŋ/ *noun* two panes of glass in windows, to keep out cold air and noise ○ *All the rooms in the hotel have double glazing to reduce noise from the airport.*

double occupancy /ˌdʌb(ə)l 'ɒkjʊpənsi/ *noun* HOTELS the occupancy of a room by two people

double-park /ˌdʌb(ə)l 'pɑːk/ *verb* ROAD TRAVEL to park alongside a car which is already parked at the side of the street

double-parking /ˌdʌb(ə)l 'pɑːkɪŋ/ *noun* ROAD TRAVEL the act of parking alongside a car which is already parked at the side of the street

double room /ˌdʌb(ə)l 'ruːm/ *noun* a room for two people

double saucepan /ˌdʌb(ə)l 'sɔːspən/ *noun* CATERING same as **double boiler**

double whisky /ˌdʌb(ə)l 'wɪski/ *noun* BEVERAGES a portion of whisky, twice the amount of a usual measure

dough /dəʊ/ *noun* FOOD an uncooked mixture of water and flour for making bread or pizza ○ *The chef was kneading the dough for the pizza.*

doughnut /'dəʊnʌt/ *noun* BREAD, ETC. a small round or ring-shaped cake cooked by frying in oil ○ *You dip freshly made doughnuts in sugar.*

downgrade /'daʊngreɪd/ *verb* to reduce something to a less important level ○ *He was downgraded from first class to business class.* ○ *Her job was downgraded in the company reorganisation.*

'…according to a recent poll of more than 400 leading companies, 49 per cent said they had downgraded the class of travel and hotel of their executives' [*Business Travel*]

downhill *adverb* /daʊn'hɪl/ towards the bottom of a hill ■ *noun* /'daʊnhɪl/ SPORT same as **downhill skiing**

downhill skiing /ˌdaʊnhɪl 'skiːɪŋ/ *noun* SPORT the activity of skiing fast down slopes, as opposed to cross-country skiing

down-market /'daʊn ˌmɑːkɪt/ *adjective* cheaper and appealing to a less sophisticated section of the population. Compare **up-market**

down payment /ˌdaʊn 'peɪmənt/ *noun* BUSINESS part of a total cost paid in advance

downpour /'daʊnpɔː/ *noun* a heavy fall of rain

downstairs /daʊn'steəz/ *adverb* towards or in the lower part of a building or vehicle ○ *All the guests ran downstairs when the alarm rang.* ■ *adjective* in the lower part of a building or vehicle ○ *There is a downstairs bar for guests.* ■ *noun* the lower part of a building or vehicle ○ *If the downstairs is full, there are spare tables upstairs.* Compare **upstairs**

downtown /'daʊntaʊn/ *noun, adjective, adverb* US BUSINESS in or to the central area or business district of a town ○ *Her office is in downtown New York.* ○ *We want to stay in* *a quiet downtown hotel.* ○ *They established a restaurant downtown.*

draft /drɑːft/ *noun US* same as **draught**

draft beer /ˈdrɑːft bɪə/ *noun US* BEVERAGES same as **draught beer**

drain /dreɪn/ *verb* to remove a liquid from something ○ *Boil the potatoes for ten minutes, drain and leave to cool.*

drain cycle /ˈdreɪn ˌsaɪk(ə)l/ *noun* CATERING the last of a series of operations in a dishwasher, when the water is drained and the dishes left to dry

drapes /dreɪps/ *plural noun US* curtains

draught /drɑːft/ *noun* **1.** a current of cold air which blows into a room, train, bus, etc. ○ *She sat in a draught and caught a cold.* **2.** SHIPS AND BOATS the depth of water in which a ship can float (NOTE: [all senses] The US spelling is **draft**.)

draught beer /ˈdrɑːft bɪə/ *noun* BEVERAGES beer which is served from a barrel, and not in a bottle or can

draw /drɔː/ *verb* **1.** BEVERAGES to leave tea to stand so that the flavour is fully extracted from the tea leaves **2.** CATERING to remove the innards from a carcass before cooking it

drawer /ˈdrɔːə/ *noun* a sliding compartment in a desk or cupboard which you open by pulling on a handle

drawing room /ˈdrɔːɪŋ ruːm/ *noun* a room for sitting and talking in, but not eating ○ *The guests' drawing room is on the right of the main entrance.*

dredge /dredʒ/ *verb* CATERING to sprinkle or cover food with a coating of icing sugar, flour or sugar

dregs /dregz/ *plural noun* cold remnants of a drink, left in a cup or glass

dress /dres/ *noun* **1.** a piece of woman's or girl's clothing, covering more or less the whole body **2.** special clothes ■ *verb* **1.** to put on clothes, especially formal clothes ○ *We're expected to dress for dinner when we're sitting at the captain's table.* **2.** CATERING to prepare something such as a chicken for cooking **3.** MEDICAL to clean a wound and put a covering over it

dress circle /ˈdres ˌsɜːk(ə)l/ *noun* ENTERTAINMENT the first balcony of seats above the stalls in a theatre

dress coat /ˈdres kəʊt/ *noun* a man's formal long black coat

dressed crab /drest kræb/, **dressed lobster** *noun* FOOD cooked crab or lobster, with the legs removed and the flesh broken up and put back into the shell

dressing /ˈdresɪŋ/ *noun* **1.** the act of putting on clothes **2.** SAUCES, ETC. a sauce for salad ○ *a bottle of Italian dressing* ○ *Would you like French dressing or Thousand Island dressing?* **3.** MEDICAL a covering or bandage applied to a wound to protect it

dressing table /ˈdresɪŋ ˌteɪb(ə)l/ *noun* a bedroom table with mirrors

dried /draɪd/ *adjective* preserved by dehydration, which removes water and so slows down deterioration ○ *dried mushrooms* ○ *sun-dried tomatoes*

dried fruit /ˈdraɪd ˈfruːt/ *noun* fruit that has been dehydrated to preserve it for later use

dried milk /ˌdraɪd ˈmɪlk/ *noun* DAIRY same as **dehydrated milk**

drier /ˈdraɪə/ *noun* same as **dryer**

drill /drɪl/ *noun* □ **boat drill**, **fire drill** a procedure to be carried out to help people to escape from a sinking boat or from a burning building

drink /drɪŋk/ *noun* **1.** liquid which someone swallows ○ *Would you like a drink?* ○ *Drinks are served before the meal on transatlantic flights.* **2.** BEVERAGES an alcoholic drink ○ *Drinks are being served on the terrace.* □ **he has a drink problem** he is an alcoholic □ **he was much the worse for drink** he was drunk ■ *verb* to swallow liquid ○ *She was so thirsty she drank four glasses of lemonade.* ○ *Do you want something to drink with your meal?* □ **she doesn't drink** she never drinks alcohol □ **let's drink to the success of the tour** let us raise our glasses and wish it success

COMMENT: The word 'drink' is often used to refer to alcoholic drinks.

drinkable /ˈdrɪŋkəb(ə)l/ *adjective* able to be drunk, or quite nice to drink ○ *This wine is hardly drinkable.*

drinking chocolate /ˈdrɪŋkɪŋ ˌtʃɒklət/ *noun* FOOD sweet chocolate powder, used to make a hot drink ○ *I have a cup of drinking chocolate before I go to bed.*

drinking-up time /ˌdrɪŋkɪŋ ˈʌp ˌtaɪm/ *noun* a period allowed in a public house after official closing time, when drinks already bought may be finished

drinking water /ˈdrɪŋkɪŋ ˌwɔːtə/ *noun* BEVERAGES water which is safe to drink, as opposed to water for washing ○ *Don't use that tap, it's not drinking water.*

drinks trolley /ˈdrɪŋks ˌtrɒli/ *noun* AIR TRAVEL a trolley on an aircraft, with various drinks that are served by stewards or stewardesses. Also called **bar trolley**

drip /drɪp/ *noun* a small drop of liquid, falling regularly from a tap or container

dripping /'drɪpɪŋ/ *noun* FOOD the fat that melts off meat when it is being cooked and hardens when cold, used for frying, basting and making pastry

drip tray /'drɪp treɪ/ *noun* BARS a tray placed under a tap to catch drips, e.g. under a beer tap

drive /draɪv/ *noun* **1.** ROAD TRAVEL a ride in a motor vehicle **2.** ROAD TRAVEL the way in which a car is propelled or guided □ **car with front-wheel drive** a car where the engine is connected directly to the front wheels □ **car with left-hand drive** a car where the driver sits on the left-hand side **3.** a path leading to a house wide enough for a car to drive along it ■ *verb* ROAD TRAVEL to make a car, lorry, etc., go in a particular direction ○ *He was driving to work when he heard the news on the car radio.* ○ *She drives a tour bus.* (NOTE: **driving – drove – has driven**)

drive along /ˌdraɪv ə'lɒŋ/ *verb* ROAD TRAVEL to ride along a road in a motor vehicle

drive away /ˌdraɪv ə'weɪ/ *verb* ROAD TRAVEL to go away in a motor vehicle

drive back /ˌdraɪv 'bæk/ *verb* ROAD TRAVEL to go or come back in a motor vehicle

drive in /ˌdraɪv 'ɪn/ *verb* to go in by car ○ *Each car that drives in is issued with a ticket.*

drive-in /'draɪv ɪn/ *adjective, noun* ENTERTAINMENT a bank, cinema or restaurant, where customers are served as they sit in their cars ○ *We went to see the movie at the local drive-in.* □ **drive-in cinema** *or* **restaurant** a cinema or restaurant where you can drive in in a car and watch a film or eat while still sitting in the car

drive on /ˌdraɪv 'ɒn/ *verb* to continue one's journey ○ *The policeman signalled us to drive on.*

driver /'draɪvə/ *noun* ROAD TRAVEL somebody who drives ○ *You pay the driver as you get on the bus.* ○ *Don't talk to the driver when the bus is in motion.*

driving licence /'draɪvɪŋ ˌlaɪs(ə)ns/, **driver's license** *US* /'draɪvəz ˌlaɪs(ə)ns/ *noun* ROAD TRAVEL a permit that allows you to drive

drizzle /'drɪz(ə)l/ *noun* a thin mist of rain ○ *A thin drizzle was falling so we took our umbrellas.* ■ *verb* to rain lightly ○ *It's drizzling outside, so you'd better wear a raincoat.*

drizzly /'drɪzli/ *adjective* raining lightly ○ *We get a lot of drizzly weather in September.*

drop /drɒp/ *verb* to fall, to go to a lower level ○ *Take a warm sweater, because at night the temperature can drop quite sharply.* □ **the wind dropped** the wind stopped blowing hard

drop off /ˌdrɒp 'ɒf/ *verb* □ **to drop someone off** to let someone who is a passenger in a car get out somewhere ○ *Can you drop me off at the post office?*

drop-off charge /'drɒp ɒf ˌtʃɑːdʒ/ *noun* TRAVEL an extra charge for leaving a hired car at a different place from where it was hired

DRV *abbreviation* Dietary Reference Values

dry /draɪ/ *adjective* **1.** not wet **2.** with no rain **3.** BEVERAGES not sweet, used especially of wine ○ *A dry white wine is served with fish.* ○ *Some German wines are quite dry.* ○ *I prefer dry champagne to sweet champagne.* **4.** forbidding alcohol ○ *The whole state is dry.* ■ *verb* to remove water from something ○ *Guests are asked not to hang clothes to dry on the balcony.*

dry-clean /ˌdraɪ 'kliːn/ *verb* to clean something with chemicals ○ *We have sent the curtains away to be dry-cleaned.*

dry-cleaner's /ˌdraɪ 'kliːnəz/ *noun* a shop where clothes are dry-cleaned ○ *When I got my suit back from the dry-cleaner's there was a button missing.*

dry-cleaning /ˌdraɪ 'kliːnɪŋ/ *noun* clothes which are ready to be sent to be dry-cleaned or which have been returned after having been dry-cleaned ○ *She ran through the rain to her car with an armful of dry-cleaning.*

dry-cure /ˌdraɪ 'kjʊə/ *verb* CATERING to preserve fish or meat in salt crystals as opposed to brine

dry-cured bacon /ˌdraɪ kjʊəd 'hæm/ *noun* MEAT bacon which has been cured in salt

dry dock /ˌdraɪ 'dɒk/ *noun* SHIPS AND BOATS a dock where the water is pumped out to allow repairs to be done to a ship

dryer /'draɪə/ *noun* a machine which dries, especially a machine to dry clothes

dry ginger /ˌdraɪ 'dʒɪndʒə/ *noun* BEVERAGES same as **ginger ale**

dry ice /ˌdraɪ 'aɪs/ *noun* carbon dioxide in solid form

COMMENT: Dry ice is extremely cold, with a temperature of −78°C, and is used for keeping food such as ice cream cold when being transported.

drying /'draɪɪŋ/ *noun* CATERING a method of preserving food by removing moisture, either by leaving it in the sun, as for dried fruit, or by passing it through an industrial process

dry martini /ˌdraɪ mɑːˈtiːni/ *noun* BEVERAGES a cocktail of gin and French vermouth, served with an olive

dry season /ˈdraɪ ˌsiːz(ə)n/ *noun* a period of the year when it does not rain much

dry slope /ˈdraɪ sləʊp/ *noun* SPORT a ski slope made of artificial snow

dry slope skiing /ˌdraɪ sləʊp ˈskiːɪŋ/ *noun* SPORT the activity of skiing on artificial snow slopes

dry stores /ˈdraɪ stɔːz/ *noun* BUSINESS a storeroom where dry goods such as tins and packets of food are kept

dry wine /ˌdraɪ ˈwaɪn/ *noun* BEVERAGES wine which is not sweet

DSO /ˈdiːsəʊ/ *abbreviation* BUSINESS direct service organisation

DST *abbreviation* Daylight Saving Time

dual carriageway /ˌdjuːəl ˈkærɪdʒweɪ/ *noun* ROAD TRAVEL a road with two lanes in each direction, with a barrier between the pairs of lanes ○ *There's a dual carriageway ahead, so we'll soon be able to overtake that tractor.* (NOTE: The US English for this is **two-lane highway**.)

Dublin Bay prawn /ˌdʌblɪn beɪ ˈprɔːn/ *noun* SEAFOOD a large prawn, often served as scampi

duchesse potatoes /ˌdʌtʃes pə ˈteɪtəʊz/ *plural noun* FOOD creamed potatoes with beaten egg added, piped into small mounds and baked in an oven

duck /dʌk/ *noun* **1.** a common water bird **2.** MEAT the meat of this bird used as food
   COMMENT: Roast duck is traditionally eaten with orange sauce.

duckling /ˈdʌklɪŋ/ *noun* a small duck ○ *We had roast duckling and orange sauce.*

dud cheque /ˌdʌd ˈtʃek/ *noun* FINANCE same as **bouncing cheque** (*informal*)

dude /djuːd/ *noun* US a visitor to a dude ranch

dude ranch /ˈduːd rɑːntʃ/ *noun* TOURISM a ranch that people visit as a tourist attraction and where they can stay and spend a holiday

due diligence /ˌdjuː ˈdɪlɪdʒəns/ *noun* CATERING a requirement of the food safety legislation that food producers must take all reasonable care that the food they produce is safe, and is produced and packed in a way which prevents contamination

dumb waiter /ˌdʌm ˈweɪtə/ *noun* CATERING **1.** a sideboard in a restaurant, on which cutlery and condiments are kept ready for use **2.** a device for raising and lowering trays of food or dirty dishes between floors of a building, e.g. when the kitchen is in the basement

dummy pack /ˈdʌmi pæk/ *noun* an empty pack for display in a shop

dumping /ˈdʌmpɪŋ/ *noun* BUSINESS the act of getting rid of excess goods cheaply in an overseas market

dumpling /ˈdʌmplɪŋ/ *noun* FOOD a small ball of paste, often with a filling, which is boiled or steamed

dune /djuːn/ *noun* a mound or hill of sand, either on a beach or in the desert

dupe /djuːp/ *noun* a duplicate reservation (*informal*)

durian /ˈdjʊəriən/ *noun* FRUIT a tropical fruit from a tree that grows in south-east Asia
   COMMENT: The fruit has an extremely unpleasant smell, but is highly regarded as a dessert fruit in south-east Asia.

durum wheat /ˈdjʊərəm wiːt/ *noun* FOOD a hard type of wheat grown in southern Europe and used to make pasta
   COMMENT: The best pasta is made with 100% durum wheat and should be labelled to this effect.

dusk /dʌsk/ *noun* twilight, the period in the evening just before it gets dark ○ *The gardens close at dusk.*

dust /dʌst/ *noun* a thin layer of dry dirt ■ *verb* **1.** to remove dust from something ○ *The chambermaid has not dusted the room.* **2.** CATERING to sprinkle sugar onto a cake

dustbin /ˈdʌstbɪn/ *noun* a large container for collecting rubbish ○ *She put the rest of the dinner in the dustbin.* ○ *He threw the letter into the dustbin.* Also called **trashcan**, **garbage can**

duster /ˈdʌstə/ *noun* a cloth for removing dust ○ *Rub the surface down with a duster.*

dustpan /ˈdʌstpæn/ *noun* a small wide shovel for scooping up dirt

dustproof cover /ˌdʌstpruːf ˈkʌvə/ *noun* a cover that prevents dust from getting into something

Dutch /dʌtʃ/ *adjective* coming from or made in the Netherlands □ **to go Dutch** to share the cost of a meal equally between everyone

Dutch treat /ˌdʌtʃ ˈtriːt/ *noun* a party where each person pays his or her share

dutiable goods /ˌdjuːtiəb(ə)l ˈɡʊdz/, **dutiable items** *plural noun* BUSINESS goods on which a customs duty has to be paid

duty /ˈdjuːti/ *noun* **1.** a piece of work that a person has to do ○ *One of her duties is to*

see that the main doors are locked at night.
2. something that you are legally or morally expected to do **3.** BUSINESS a tax that has to be paid ○ *to take the duty off alcohol* ○ *to put a duty on cigarettes* □ **goods which are liable to duty** goods on which customs or excise tax has to be paid

'Canadian and European negotiators agreed to a deal under which Canada could lower its import duties on $150 million worth of European goods' [*Globe and Mail (Toronto)*]

'...the Department of Customs and Excise collected a total of N79m under the new advance duty payment scheme' [*Business Times (Lagos)*]

duty-free /ˌdjuːti 'friː/ *adjective, adverb* sold with no tax to be paid ○ *He bought a duty-free watch at the airport* or *He bought the watch duty-free at the airport.*

'...despite the abolition of duty-free in the European Union, BAA is able to offer EU passengers a wide range of duty-paid alcohol and tobacco' [*Heathrow International Traveller*]

duty-free alcohol /ˌdjuːti friː 'ælkəhɒl/ *noun* BEVERAGES an alcoholic drink which can be bought in a duty-free shop

duty-free allowance /ˌdjuːti 'friː ə ˌlaʊəns/ *noun* BUSINESS the amount of dutiable goods which a person can take into a country without paying tax ○ *She had several bottles more than the duty-free allowance and so was charged duty.*

duty-free shop /ˌdjuːti 'friː ʃɒp/ *noun* a shop at an airport or on a ship where goods can be bought without paying duty

duty manager /ˌdjuːti 'mænɪdʒə/ *noun* the manager who is on duty at the present time

duty of care /ˌdjuːti əv 'keə/ *noun* a duty which every citizen has not to act negligently

duty of care code /ˌdjuːti əv 'keə ˌkəʊd/ *noun* a list of guidelines which staff must follow, e.g. regarding the safe disposal of waste

COMMENT: The duty of care code requires businesses which produce waste to ensure that it is carefully stored until it is disposed of, that it is disposed of by a registered waste disposal contractor and that a written record is kept each time the waste is removed.

duty-paid goods /ˌdjuːti 'peɪd ɡʊdz/ *plural noun* BUSINESS goods on which tax has been paid

duty roster /'djuːti ˌrɒstə/ *noun* a list of times showing when each person is on duty ○ *Have a look on the duty roster to see when you're next on duty.*

duvet /'duːveɪ/ *noun* a large bag filled with feathers, used to cover a bed ○ *I prefer a duvet to blankets, because it is lighter.*

duvet cover /ˌduːveɪ 'kʌvə/ *noun* a decorative bag used to cover a duvet

DVT *abbreviation* MEDICAL deep-vein thrombosis

dysenteric /ˌdɪsən'terɪk/ *adjective* MEDICAL referring to dysentery

dysentery /'dɪs(ə)ntri/ *noun* MEDICAL an infection and inflammation of the colon causing bleeding and diarrhoea

COMMENT: Dysentery occurs mainly in tropical countries. The symptoms include diarrhoea, discharge of blood and pain in the intestines. There are two main types of dysentery: bacillary dysentery, caused by the bacterium *Shigella* in contaminated food; and amoebic dysentery or amoebiasis, caused by a parasitic amoeba *Entamoeba histolytica* spread through contaminated drinking water.

E

E111 *noun* MEDICAL a form used in the EU, which entitles a resident of one EU country to free medical treatment in another EU country

e. & o.e. *abbreviation* errors and omissions excepted

early /'ɜːlɪ/ *adjective, adverb* **1.** before the usual time ○ *Let's have an early lunch.* ○ *You should leave the hotel early to miss the rush-hour traffic.* □ **at an early date** very soon **2.** at the beginning of a period of time ○ *He took an early flight to Paris.* □ **we hope for an early resumption of services** we hope services will start again soon

early arrival /ˌɜːlɪ əˈraɪv(ə)l/ *noun* HOTELS a guest who arrives at a hotel earlier than expected

early bird special /ˌɜːlɪ bɜːd ˈspeʃ(ə)l/ *noun* **1.** a specially reduced fare for travel very early in the morning **2.** a specially cheap meal if the meal is taken early in the morning

early closing day /ˌɜːli ˈkləʊzɪŋ deɪ/ *noun* a weekday, usually Wednesday or Thursday, when many shops close in the afternoon

early morning call /ˌɜːlɪ ˌmɔːnɪŋ ˈkɔːl/ *noun* same as **morning call**

early morning tea /ˌɜːlɪ ˌmɔːnɪŋ ˈtiː/ *noun* BEVERAGES tea brought to a guest's bedroom early in the morning, often with the day's newspaper and sometimes with letters

earplug /'ɪəplʌg/ *noun* a ball of wax or cotton, which is pushed into the ear so that you cannot hear anything ○ *Luckily we took earplugs with us, as the traffic outside our room was very noisy.*

east /iːst/ *noun* one of the points of the compass, the direction of the rising sun ○ *The sun rises in the east.* ○ *The pilgrims turned towards the east.* □ the **Far East** countries to the east of India □ the **Middle East** countries to the east of Egypt and west of Pakistan ■ *adjective* referring to the east ■ *adverb* towards the east ○ *Drive east along the motorway for ten miles.*

eastbound /'iːstbaʊnd/ *adjective* going towards the east ○ *All eastbound trains have been cancelled.* ○ *The eastbound carriageway of the motorway is closed.*

East End /ˌiːst ˈend/ *noun* the part of London to the east of the City of London, regarded as having a very distinctive traditional culture

Easter /'iːstə/ *noun* a Christian festival in March or April

Easter Day /'iːstə deɪ/, **Easter Sunday** /'iːstə ˈsʌndeɪ/ *noun* a Sunday holiday celebrating Christ's rising from the dead

Easter egg /'iːstər eg/ *noun* FOOD a chocolate or sugar egg eaten at Easter

easterly /'iːstəli/ *adjective* towards the east □ **in an easterly direction** towards the east

eastern /'iːst(ə)n/ *adjective* referring to the east ○ *Bulgaria is part of Eastern Europe.* ○ *The best snow is in the eastern part of the mountains.*

easternmost /'iːst(ə)nməʊst/ *adjective* furthest east

eastward /'iːstwəd/ *adjective, adverb* towards the east

eastwards /'iːstwədz/ *adverb* towards the east

east wind /ˌiːst ˈwɪnd/ *noun* a wind that blows from the east

easy terms /ˌiːzi ˈtɜːmz/ *plural noun* BUSINESS a price that is easy to pay because it is spread in instalments over a period of time ○ *The shop is let on very easy terms.*

eat /iːt/ *verb* **1.** to put food into your mouth and swallow it **2.** to have a meal ○ *Eat as much as you like for £5.95!* (NOTE: **ate – eaten**) □ **to eat in** to have a meal at home or in the restaurant of the hotel where you are staying □ **to eat out** to have dinner away from home or in a restaurant outside the hotel where you are staying

eatable /'iːtəb(ə)l/ *adjective* good enough to eat ○ *This meat is hardly eatable.*

eatables /'iːtəb(ə)lz/ *plural noun* things to eat

eater /'i:tə/ *noun* somebody who eats ○ *She's a light eater – she just picks at her food.*

eatery /'i:təri/ *noun US* a restaurant, or a place where you can eat (*informal*) ○ *a well-known eatery on 5th Avenue* (NOTE: The plural form is **eateries**.)

eating apple /'i:tɪŋ ˌæp(ə)l/ *noun* FRUIT a sweet apple which may be eaten raw

eating place /'i:tɪŋ pleɪs/ *noun* a place where you can eat, e.g. a restaurant, cafeteria or canteen

EC *abbreviation* European Community (NOTE: This is now called the **European Union (EU)**.)

éclair /eɪ'kleə/ *noun* a long thin cylinder of choux pastry filled with whipped cream and topped with chocolate or coffee icing

ecolabelling /'i:kəʊˌleɪb(ə)lɪŋ/ *noun* a system by which products or services that are considered not to be harmful to the environment, or to be less harmful than others, are given a special label

E. coli /ˌi: 'kəʊlaɪ/ *noun* MEDICAL a Gram-negative bacillus associated with acute gastroenteritis and traveller's diarrhoea. Full form **Escherichia coli**

economic cycle /ˌi:kənɒmɪk 'saɪk(ə)l/ *noun* BUSINESS same as **trade cycle**

economy /ɪ'kɒnəmi/ *noun* **1.** actions intended to save money or resources **2.** the way in which a country makes and uses money, or the financial state of a country

economy car /ɪ'kɒnəmi kɑː/ *noun* ROAD TRAVEL a car which does not use much petrol

economy class /ɪ'kɒnəmi klɑːs/ *noun* AIR TRAVEL the cheapest category of seat on a plane ○ *to travel economy class* Also called **tourist class**

'...let no one pretend that taking a long-haul Economy class flight is a pleasurable experience' [*Business Traveller*]

economy class syndrome /ɪ'kɒnəmi klɑːs ˌsɪndrəʊm/ *noun* MEDICAL same as **deep-vein thrombosis** (*informal*)

'...the term 'Economy Class Syndrome' was coined in 1988 but it is only over the last few years that any serious attempt has been made to study the causes of this health hazard' [*Wanderlust*]

economy flight fare /ɪ'kɒnəmi flaɪt ˌfeə/ *noun* AIR TRAVEL the lowest fare available

economy passenger /ɪ'kɒnəmi ˌpæsɪndʒə/ *noun* AIR TRAVEL somebody who travels in economy class ○ *The airline provides more leg-room for full-fare economy passengers.*

economy size pack /ɪ'kɒnəmi saɪz ˌpæk/ *noun* BUSINESS a packet of goods that works out cheaper to buy, usually because it contains more. Also called **family pack**

ecotourism /'i:kəʊˌtʊərɪz(ə)m/ *noun* TOURISM tourism that is responsible and respects the culture and lifestyle of the local people, and in general does nothing to damage the local environment

ecotourist /'i:kəʊˌtʊərɪst/ *noun* TOURISM a responsible tourist who eats local food, uses local transport, lives the lifestyle of local people and respects their culture, and in general does nothing to damage the local environment

Edam /'i:dæm/ *noun* a mild Dutch cheese with a slightly rubbery texture, typically formed into balls covered with red wax

edible /'edɪb(ə)l/ *adjective* referring to something that can be safely eaten ○ *How can you tell which mushrooms are edible and which are poisonous?*

EDP /ˌi: di: 'pi:/ *abbreviation* electronic data processing

eel /iːl/ *noun* SEAFOOD a long thin fish which looks like a snake ○ *She ordered some smoked eel.* ○ *He had a plate of jellied eels.*

COMMENT: Eels may be eaten smoked (usually with horseradish sauce) or stewed in the traditional London fashion – 'jellied eels'.

EFA *abbreviation* CATERING European Food Authority

effect /ɪ'fekt/ *noun* a change that happens as the result of an action done by somebody

efficiency /ɪ'fɪʃ(ə)nsi/ *noun* the ability to work well and to produce the right result or the right work quickly

efficient /ɪ'fɪʃ(ə)nt/ *adjective* able to work well and do what is necessary without wasting time, money or effort

efficiently /ɪ'fɪʃ(ə)ntli/ *adverb* in an efficient way ○ *The waitresses served the 250 diners very efficiently.*

EFT /ˌi: ef 'ti:/ *abbreviation* FINANCE electronic funds transfer

e.g. *abbreviation* for example, such as ○ *The contract is valid in some countries (e.g. France and Belgium) but not in others.*

egg /eg/ *noun* FOOD **1.** an oval object with a hard shell, produced by a female bird from which a baby bird comes ○ *a duck's egg* ○ *quail eggs* **2.** an egg produced by a domestic hen, the type of egg most commonly used as food for humans ○ *You need three eggs to make this cake.*

egg cosy /ˈeg ˌkəʊzi/ noun CATERING a little cover put over a boiled egg to keep it hot (NOTE: The plural form is **egg cosies**.)

eggcup /ˈegkʌp/ noun a holder for a boiled egg ○ *They served boiled eggs in eggcups shaped like chickens.*

egg custard /ˌeg ˈkʌstəd/ noun DESSERTS a sweet sauce, made with eggs and milk, flavoured with vanilla, baked until set and eaten warm or cold

egg noodles /ˌeg ˈnuːd(ə)lz/ plural noun FOOD noodles made with flour, water and egg

eggplant /ˈegplɑːnt/ noun US VEGETABLES a plant with shiny purple-black fruit, used as a vegetable. Also called **aubergine**

eggs Benedict /ˌegz ˈbenədɪkt/ noun ham and a poached egg in hollandaise sauce on a slice of toast or a split toasted muffin

eggshell /ˈegʃel/ noun the shell around an egg ○ *I found a big piece of eggshell in my omelette.*

egg timer /ˈeg ˌtaɪmə/ noun a device for timing how long an egg is boiled for

egg white /ˈeg waɪt/ noun FOOD the part of the egg which is not yellow. Also called **white**

EHO abbreviation Environmental Health Officer

elastic /ɪˈlæstɪk/ adjective not rigid, able to stretch and contract

elastic demand /ɪˌlæstɪk dɪˈmɑːnd/ noun BUSINESS a demand which can expand or contract easily because of small changes in price

electric /ɪˈlektrɪk/ adjective worked by electricity ○ *The flat is equipped with an electric cooker.*

electrical /ɪˈlektrɪk(ə)l/ adjective referring to electricity ○ *The engineers are trying to repair an electrical fault.*

electricity /ɪˌlekˈtrɪsɪti/ noun a current used to make light, heat or power ○ *The electricity was cut off this morning, so the air-conditioning could not work.* ○ *Our electricity bill has increased considerably this quarter.* ○ *Electricity costs are an important factor in our overheads.*

electronic /ˌelekˈtrɒnɪk/ adjective referring to machines that use transistors or integrated circuits to operate, or to systems that rely on computers and computer networks

electronic billing /ˌelektrɒnɪk ˈbɪlɪŋ/ noun a system for charging customers and paying bills by credit or debit card online

electronic data processing /ˌelektrɒnɪk ˈdeɪtə ˌprəʊsesɪŋ/ noun the act of selecting and examining data stored in a computer to produce information. Abbr **EDP**

electronic funds transfer /ˌelektrɒnɪk ˈfʌndz ˌtrænsfɜː/ noun FINANCE a system for transferring money from one account to another electronically, as when using a smart card. Abbr **EFT**

electronic organiser /ˌelektrɒnɪk ˈɔːgənaɪzə/ noun same as **personal organiser**

electronic point of sale /ˌelektrɒnɪk ˌpɔɪnt əv ˈseɪl/ noun BUSINESS a system where sales are charged automatically to a customer's credit card or debit card and stock is controlled by the shop's computer. Abbr **EPOS**

electronic ticketing /ˌelektrɒnɪk ˈtɪkɪtɪŋ/ noun a computerised system used by airlines which gives passengers a special code number instead of a physical ticket

electroplated nickel silver /ɪˌlektrəpleɪtɪd ˌnɪk(ə)l ˈsɪlvə/ noun CATERING same as **silver plate**

elevator /ˈelɪveɪtə/ noun US a machine which carries people or goods from one floor to another in a building ○ *Take the elevator to the 26th floor.* Compare **escalator**, **travelator** (NOTE: The British English is **lift**.)

elevenses /ɪˈlev(ə)nzɪz/ noun CATERING a snack served in the middle of the morning (informal)

e-mail /ˈiː meɪl/ noun 1. electronic mail, a system of sending messages from one computer to another, using telephone lines ○ *You can make your booking by e-mail if you want.* ○ *I'll give you the e-mail address of the hotel.* 2. a message sent by e-mail ○ *I had two e-mails from him this morning.* ■ verb to send a message using electronic mail ○ *I e-mailed the hotel about the change of plan.*

embark /ɪmˈbɑːk/ verb TRAVEL to go onto a ship or aircraft ○ *The passengers embarked at Southampton.*

embarkation /ˌembɑːˈkeɪʃ(ə)n/ noun TRAVEL the action of going onto a ship or plane

embarkation card /ˌembɑːˈkeɪʃ(ə)n kɑːd/ noun SHIPS AND BOATS a card given to passengers getting onto a ship

embassy /ˈembəsi/ noun a building where an ambassador has his or her office ○ *The British Embassy is holding a party for exhibitors at the trade fair.*

embus /ɪmˈbʌs/ verb ROAD TRAVEL to get on a bus or put people on a bus

emergency /ɪˈmɜːdʒənsi/ *noun* a dangerous situation such as a fire or an accident, where decisions have to be taken quickly □ **the government declared a state of emergency** the government decided that the situation was so dangerous that the police or army had to run the country □ **in case of emergency, in an emergency** if a dangerous situation develops ○ *In an emergency, press the red button.*

'…the problem with emergency evacuation systems is that they do not adequately satisfy safety needs during emergencies. Many systems use emergency powered signs placed high on walls or above doors. These work well when you can see them, but smoke rises, decreasing visibility and increasing the risk of confusion' [*Hotel Security Worldwide*]

emergency exit /ɪˌmɜːdʒənsi ˈeɡzɪt/ *noun* a special way out of a building, used if there is a fire or other emergency. Also called **fire exit**

emergency plan /ɪˈmɜːdʒənsi plæn/ *noun* same as **contingency plan**

emergency reserves /ɪˌmɜːdʒ(ə)nsi rɪˈzɜːvz/ *plural noun* same as **contingency plan**

emigrant /ˈemɪɡrənt/ *noun* somebody who leaves one country to settle in another. Compare **immigrant**

emigrate /ˈemɪɡreɪt/ *verb* to leave your country to live in another ○ *My daughter and her family have emigrated to Australia.* Compare **immigrate**

emigration /ˌemɪˈɡreɪʃ(ə)n/ *noun* the act of leaving your country to live in another ○ *19th-century governments encouraged emigration to the colonies.* Compare **immigration**

Emmental /ˈeməntɑːl/ *noun* DAIRY a type of hard cheese from Switzerland with large holes and a mild nutty flavour

employ /ɪmˈplɔɪ/ *verb* to give someone regular paid work □ **to employ twenty staff** to have twenty people working for you □ **to employ twenty new staff** to give work to twenty new people

employee /ɪmˈplɔɪiː/ *noun* a person employed by a company ○ *Employees of the firm are eligible to join a profit-sharing scheme.* ○ *Relations between management and employees have improved.* ○ *The company has decided to take on new employees.*

employee conduct report /ɪmˌplɔɪiː ˈkɒndʌkt rɪˌpɔːt/ *noun* BUSINESS a report on how an employee has performed over a given period of time

employee turnover /ɪmˌplɔɪiː ˈtɜːnəʊvə/ *noun* BUSINESS same as **labour turnover** ○ *Under the new management, employee turnover has dropped.*

emporium /ɪmˈpɔːriəm/ *noun* a large shop (NOTE: The plural form is **emporia**.)

emptor /ˈemptə/ BUSINESS ♦ **caveat emptor**

empty /ˈempti/ *adjective* with nothing inside, or with no people present ○ *The restaurant was half-empty.* ○ *The ski resorts are empty because there is no snow.* ■ *noun* an empty bottle or case

emulsifier /ɪˈmʌlsɪfaɪə/, **emulsifying agent** /ɪˈmʌlsɪfaɪɪŋ ˈeɪdʒənt/ *noun* CATERING a substance added to mixtures of food such as water and oil to hold them together, and also added to meat to increase the water content so that the meat is heavier. ◊ **stabiliser**

COMMENT: In the EU, emulsifiers and stabilisers have E numbers E322 to E495.

emulsify /ɪˈmʌlsɪfaɪ/ *verb* CATERING to mix two liquids so thoroughly that they will not separate

enclose /ɪnˈkləʊz/ *verb* to put something inside an envelope with a letter ○ *to enclose a leaflet about the hotel* ○ *a letter enclosing a cheque* ○ *I am enclosing a copy of our current room rates.* ○ *Please find the cheque enclosed herewith.*

enclosure /ɪnˈkləʊʒə/ *noun* a document enclosed with a letter ○ *letter with enclosures* (NOTE: Usually shortened to **encl.** when written at the end of a letter.)

en croute /ˌɒn ˈkruːt/ *adjective*, *adverb* enclosed in a pastry crust

endemic /enˈdemɪk/ *adjective* MEDICAL referring to any disease which is very common in specific places ○ *Yellow fever is endemic to parts of Central Africa.*

endive /ˈendɪv/ *noun* **1.** FRUIT a green salad plant similar to a lettuce, with curly bitter-tasting leaves **2.** VEGETABLES a vegetable with a conical head of white crisp leaves packed firmly together, eaten raw in salads or cooked with a sauce. ◊ **chicory**

energy value /ˈenədʒi ˌvæljuː/ *noun* CATERING the amount of energy produced by a given amount of a particular food

engaged /ɪnˈɡeɪdʒd/ *adjective* busy, e.g. of a telephone line ○ *You cannot speak to the manager – his line is engaged.*

engaged tone /ɪnˈɡeɪdʒd təʊn/ *noun* a sound made by a telephone when the line dialled is busy ○ *I tried to phone the complaints department but I just got the engaged tone.*

English /'ɪŋglɪʃ/ *adjective* referring to England ∎ *noun* the language spoken in the UK, the USA and many other countries ○ *Do you speak English?* ○ *The hotel has an English-speaking manager.*

English breakfast /ˌɪŋglɪʃ 'brekfəst/ *noun* FOOD a meal of cereals, bacon, eggs, toast and marmalade, served with tea or coffee, often served as a buffet in motels and hotel chains

COMMENT: A traditional 'full English breakfast' may include cereals, porridge, or stewed fruit (such as prunes), grilled fish (such as kippers), bacon and eggs, sausages, kidneys, fried or grilled tomatoes or mushrooms and fried bread, followed by toast and marmalade and tea or coffee.

English Heritage /ˌɪŋglɪʃ 'herɪtɪdʒ/ *noun* an official organisation responsible for preserving historic buildings such as ancient monuments, and landscapes in England

English service /ˌɪŋglɪʃ 'sɜːvɪs/ *noun* CATERING a way of serving at a meal, where the waiter or waitress serves each guest from a large dish, serving from the guest's left

English Tourism Awards /ˌɪŋglɪʃ 'tʊərɪz(ə)m əˌwɔːdz/ *plural noun* TOURISM prizes given annually by the regional tourist boards, with a finalist chosen each year for the whole country

English Tourism Council /ˌɪŋglɪʃ 'tʊərɪz(ə)m ˌkaʊns(ə)l/ *noun* TOURISM an organisation which promotes tourism in England and promotes tourism to England from other parts of the United Kingdom. It is formed of several regional tourist boards. Abbr **ETC**

COMMENT: The council grades hotels, bed and breakfasts, self-catering cottages and campsites according to various grading systems: hotels are rated according to a star system (one star to five stars); guest accommodation (bed and breakfasts, farmhouses, inns, guesthouses, etc.) are rated according to a diamond system (one to five diamonds); self-catering accommodation is also rated according to a star system (one to five stars).

English Tourist Board /ˌɪŋglɪʃ 'tʊərɪst ˌbɔːd/ *noun* TOURISM one of twelve regional organisations forming part of the English Tourism Council. Also called **Tourist Board**

enhance /ɪn'hɑːns/ *verb* to make something better or stronger

enhancement /ɪn'hɑːnsmənt/ *noun* something which makes a service better

enhancer /ɪn'hɑːnsə/ *noun* CATERING an artificial substance which increases the fla-

vour of food, or even the flavour of artificial flavouring that has been added to food

COMMENT: In the EU, flavour enhancers added to food have the E numbers E620 to 637.

en pension /ˌen 'penʃən/ *adjective* □ **en pension terms**, **en pension rate** a special price for guests staying in a hotel who take all their meals in the hotel (the same as 'full board'); normally in Britain this will include breakfast, lunch and dinner, and in some traditional hotels morning coffee and afternoon tea; there will probably be a reduced menu for 'en pension' guests, which will not include special dishes found on the 'à la carte' menu

en pension rate /ˌen 'penʃən ˌreɪt/ *noun* HOTELS same as **full board**

enplane /en'pleɪn/ *verb* AIR TRAVEL to get onto an aircraft

enquire /ɪŋ'kwaɪə/, **enquiry** same as **inquire, inquiry**

en route /ˌɒn 'ruːt/ *adverb* on the way ○ *We stopped for lunch en route to the coast.* ○ *The ship ran into a storm en route to the Far East.*

en suite /ˌen 'swiːt/ *adverb*, *adjective* □ **bedroom with bathroom en suite**, **bedroom with en suite bathroom** a bedroom with a bathroom leading off it ○ *The hotel has 25 bedrooms, all en suite.* □ **the hotel has 25 bedrooms, all en suite** all the bedrooms have en suite bathrooms ○ *The new motel has 20 en suite bedrooms.*

enter /'entə/ *verb* **1.** to go into or to come into a place ○ *The group entered France by road.* ○ *Several immigrants enter the country illegally every day.* ◊ **entrance, entry 2.** to write information on a book or a form, or to type information into a computer system ○ *to enter a name on a list* **3.** □ **to enter into** to begin ○ *to enter into relations with someone* ○ *to enter into negotiations with a foreign government* ○ *to enter into a partnership with a legal friend* ○ *to enter into an agreement* or *a contract*

entering /'entərɪŋ/ *noun* the act of writing something in a record

enterprise zone /'entəpraɪz zəʊn/ *noun* BUSINESS same as **development zone**

entertain /ˌentə'teɪn/ *verb* to give guests a meal and sometimes accommodation

entertainer /ˌentə'teɪnə/ *noun* a person who sings, dances, tells jokes or performs tricks to entertain people

entertainment /ˌentə'teɪnmənt/ *noun* **1.** the act of offering meals or accommodation to visitors **2.** TRAVEL games, films, etc., offered to amuse passengers

entertainment allowance /ˌentə'teɪnmənt əˌlaʊəns/ *noun* BUSINESS money which a manager is allowed by his or her company to spend on meals with visitors

entertainment expenses /ˌentə'teɪnmənt ɪkˌspensɪz/ *plural noun* money spent on giving meals, theatre tickets, etc., to business visitors

entertainment officer /ˌentə'teɪnmənt ˌɒfɪsə/ *noun* somebody who is responsible for organising sports competitions, shows, dances or cabarets for passengers on a ship

entitle /ɪn'taɪt(ə)l/ *verb* to give somebody the right to do something ○ *The token entitles you to two free admissions to the museum.* ○ *He is entitled to ten days' holiday a year.*

'…membership of the club, free to business travellers and conference delegates, entitles guests to 10% discounts on their room bill and the hotel's business centre facilities' [*Business Traveller*]

entrain /ɪn'treɪn/ *verb* to get on a train or put people on a train

entrance /'entrəns/ *noun* a way in, or the act of going in ○ *The taxi will drop you at the main entrance.* ○ *The group will meet at the London Road entrance of the hotel.*

entrance fee /'entrəns fiː/ *noun* ENTERTAINMENT money which you have to pay to go into something such as an exhibition. Also called **admission fee**

entrance hall /'entrəns hɑːl/ *noun* same as **front hall**

entrance ticket /'entrəns ˌtɪkɪt/ *noun* ENTERTAINMENT a ticket which allows you to go into something such as an exhibition. Also called **admission ticket**

entrée /'ɒntreɪ/ *noun* CATERING **1.** the main course in a meal, e.g. fish or meat, or a vegetarian dish ○ *You have the choice of three starters and four entrées.* **2.** formerly, a dish of meat served after the fish course and before the main course in a formal meal

entremets /'ɒntrəmeɪ/ *noun* CATERING the sweet course, consisting of e.g. puddings, pastries or ices

entry /'entri/ *noun* **1.** the act of going in ○ *to pass a customs entry point* ○ *entry of goods under bond* **2.** the door or opening where you go into a place **3.** a piece of written information in a ledger or register ○ *The police looked at the entries in the hotel's register.* □ **to make an entry in a ledger** to write down information referring to receipts or expenditure in a ledger

entry charge /'entri tʃɑːdʒ/ *noun* ENTERTAINMENT same as **admission charge**

entry clearance /'entri ˌklɪərəns/ *noun* an official document that entitles the holder of a student or work permit to enter the UK for a period of six months or longer

entry visa /'entri ˌviːzə/ *noun* a visa allowing someone to go into a country

E number /'iː ˌnʌmbə/ *noun* FOOD a classification number given to a food additive by the European Union

COMMENT: Additives are classified as follows: colouring substances: E100 – E180; preservatives: E200 – E297; antioxidants: E300 – E321; emulsifiers and stabilisers: E322 – E495; acids and bases: E500 – E529; anti-caking additives: E530 – E578; flavour enhancers and sweeteners: E620 – E637.

environmental /ɪnˌvaɪrən'ment(ə)l/ *adjective* referring to the environment

environmental annoyance /ɪnˌvaɪrənment(ə)l ə'nɔɪəns/ *noun* a nuisance caused by such environmental factors as traffic noise

Environmental Health Officer /ɪnˌvaɪrənment(ə)l 'helθ ˌɒfɪsə/ *noun* an official of a local authority who examines the environment and tests for air pollution, bad sanitation, noise pollution, etc. Abbr **EHO**. Also called **Public Health Inspector**

environmental hygiene /ɪnˌvaɪrənment(ə)l 'haɪdʒiːn/ *noun* the study of health and how it is affected by the environment

environmental quality standards /ɪnˌvaɪrənment(ə)l 'kwɒləti/ *plural noun* the amount of an effluent or pollutant which is accepted in an environment, e.g. the amount of trace elements in drinking water or the amount of additives in food

EPNS *abbreviation* CATERING electroplated nickel silver

epos /'iːpɒs/, **EPOS** *abbreviation* BUSINESS electronic point of sale

equator /ɪ'kweɪtə/ *noun* an imaginary line running round the surface of the earth, at an equal distance from the North and South Poles

COMMENT: Crossing the equator (or 'crossing the line') is the subject of elaborate rituals on ships. Passengers who are crossing the equator for the first time are shaved, thrown into the swimming pool, etc., and finally presented with a certificate from the captain.

equip /ɪ'kwɪp/ *verb* to provide something with machinery ○ *a holiday flat equipped with washing machine and dishwasher* ○ *The ship has a fully-equipped gymnasium.* ○ *All* *rooms in the hotel are equipped with hair dryers and coffeemakers.*

equipment /ɪ'kwɪpmənt/ *noun* machinery and furniture required to make a factory or office work ○ *kitchen equipment* ○ *kitchen equipment supplier* ○ *kitchen equipment catalogue*

ergot /'ɜːgət/ *noun* a fungus which grows on rye

error /'erə/ *noun* a mistake ○ *She made an error in calculating the total.* □ **errors and omissions excepted (e. & o.e.)** a note on an invoice to show that the seller has no responsibility for mistakes on the invoice

escalator /'eskəleɪtə/ *noun* a moving staircase, with metal steps that move upwards or downwards. Compare **elevator, lift, travelator**

escalope /'eskælɒp/ *noun* MEAT a thin slice of meat, especially veal, pork, chicken or turkey. ◊ **Wiener schnitzel**

escape /ɪ'skeɪp/ *verb* the act of getting away from prison or from a difficult situation ○ *Escape with us to the tropical island of Barbados.*

escapism /ɪ'skeɪpɪz(ə)m/ *noun* activities that stop you from thinking about real life

escargot /'eskɑːgəʊ/ *noun* a snail that is cooked and served as food, especially presented in its shell with melted garlic butter

escort *noun* /'eskɔːt/ somebody who accompanies another person ○ *She wore red silk and her escort wore a kilt.* ■ *verb* /ɪ'skɔːt/ to accompany someone ○ *The courier escorted the group into the hotel.* ○ *I was escorted around by our local MP.* ○ *The liner entered harbour escorted by a flotilla of yachts.*

escorted /ɪ'skɔːtɪd/ *adjective* accompanied by a guide or courier ○ *two operators with escorted tours of Italy* ○ *We offer several escorted touring holidays in South America.*

esky /'eski/ *noun* Aus CATERING same as **cool box**

espresso /e'spresəʊ/ *noun* BEVERAGES **1.** a type of strong Italian coffee, made in a special machine, where steam or boiling water is forced through ground coffee under pressure ○ *an espresso machine* **2.** a cup of this coffee ○ *Two cups of espresso* or *two espressos, please.*

essence /'es(ə)ns/ *noun* CATERING a concentrated plant extract containing its unique flavour and fragrance

essential amino acids /ɪˌsenʃəl ə ˌmiːnəʊ 'æsɪdz/ *plural noun* the eight amino acids which are essential for growth, but which cannot be synthesised and so must be obtained from food or medicinal substances

essential fatty acid /ɪˌsenʃəl ˌfæti 'æsɪd/ *noun* an unsaturated fatty acid which is essential for growth, but which cannot be synthesised and so must be obtained from food or medicinal substances

essential foodstuffs /ɪˌsenʃəl 'fuːd ˌstʌfs/ *plural noun* very important, staple foods such as bread and rice

establishment /ɪ'stæblɪʃmənt/ *noun* **1.** a business or organisation ○ *He runs an important catering establishment.* **2.** the number of people working in a company □ **to be on the establishment** to be a full-time employee □ **kitchen with an establishment of fifteen** a kitchen with a budgeted staff of fifteen

estimate *noun* /'estɪmət/ **1.** a calculation of the probable cost, size or time of something **2.** a calculation of how much something is likely to cost in the future, given to a client so as to get him to make an order ○ *to ask a builder for an estimate for building the annexe* ○ *Before we can give the grant we must have an estimate of the total costs involved.* □ **to put in an estimate** to state in writing the probable costs of carrying out a job ○ *Three firms put in estimates for the job.* ■ *verb* /'estɪmeɪt/ **1.** to calculate the probable cost, size or time of something ○ *to estimate that it will cost £1m* or *to estimate costs at £1m* ○ *We estimate current sales at only 60% of last year's.* **2.** □ **to estimate for a job** to state in writing the probable costs of carrying out a job ○ *Three firms estimated for the refitting of the bar.*

estimated /'estɪmeɪtɪd/ *adjective* calculated approximately ○ *Costs were slightly more than the estimated figure.*

estimated time of arrival /ˌestɪmeɪtɪd ˌtaɪm əv ə'raɪv(ə)l/ *noun* TRAVEL the time when an aircraft, a coach or a group of tourists is expected to arrive. Abbr **ETA**

estimated time of departure /ˌestɪmətɪd ˌtaɪm əv dɪ'pɑːtʃə/ *noun* TRAVEL the time when an aircraft, a coach or a group of tourists is expected to leave. Abbr **ETD**

ETA *abbreviation* TRAVEL estimated time of arrival

ETC *abbreviation* TOURISM English Tourism Council

ETD *abbreviation* estimated time of departure

ethnic /'eθnɪk/ *adjective* referring to a particular race or country

ethnic food /'eθnɪk fuːd/ *noun* CATERING food from a particular country which is not European, e.g. Chinese or Indian food

ethnic restaurant /ˌeθnɪk 'rest(ə)rɒnt/ *noun* CATERING a restaurant serving ethnic food

e-ticket /'iː ˌtɪkɪt/ *noun* AIR TRAVEL an electronic ticket, which does not exist on paper, but is stored in the airline's booking system, and can be referred to using a reference number

e-ticketing /'iː ˌtɪkɪtɪŋ/ *noun* AIR TRAVEL the process of issuing e-tickets

etiquette /'etɪket/ *noun* the correct way of behaving in public ○ *Banqueting staff must learn the correct etiquette involved in wedding receptions.*

EU *abbreviation* European Union ○ *EU ministers met today in Brussels.* ○ *The USA is increasing its trade with the EU.*

EUFIC *abbreviation* European Food Information Council

euro /'jʊərəʊ/ *noun* FINANCE a currency adopted as legal tender in several European countries from January 1st, 2002 ○ *Many articles are priced in euros.* ○ *What's the exchange rate for the euro?* (NOTE: This is written € before numbers: *€250:* say: 'two hundred and fifty euros'.)

'...cross-border mergers in the European Union have shot up since the introduction of the euro' [*Investors Chronicle*]

COMMENT: The countries which are joined together in the European Monetary Union and have adopted the euro as their common currency are: Austria, Belgium, Finland, France, Germany, Greece, Ireland, Italy, Luxembourg, the Netherlands, Portugal and Spain.

Euro- /jʊərəʊ/ *prefix* referring to Europe or the European Union

euro account /'jʊərəʊ əˌkaʊnt/ *noun* FINANCE a bank account in euros

Europe /'jʊərəp/ *noun* 1. the continent of Europe, the part of the world to the west of Asia, extending from Russia to Ireland ○ *Most of the countries of Western Europe are members of the EU.* ○ *Poland is in eastern Europe, and Greece, Spain and Portugal are in southern Europe.* ○ *Canadian visitors to Europe have risen by 25%.* **2.** the same area, but not including the UK ○ *Holidays in Europe are less popular than last year.* **3.** the European Union including the UK ○ *Canadian exports to Europe have risen by 25%.* **4.** other EU countries but not including the UK ○ *British sales to Europe have increased this year.*

European /ˌjʊərə'piːən/ *adjective* referring to Europe ○ *They do business with several European countries.*

European food /ˌjʊərəpiːən 'fuːd/ *noun* CATERING food from a country in Europe, e.g. French, Spanish or Greek food

European Food Authority /ˌjʊərəpiːən 'fuːd ɔːˌθɒrəti/ *noun* CATERING a European organisation formed in 2002, which provides scientific advice on food safety, collects data on diets and exposure to risks, and keeps the public informed about food safety. Abbr **EFA**

'...the proposed European Food Authority (EFA) could be nothing but an expensive layer of bureaucracy if it is not given real enforcement powers, the Chartered Institute of Environmental Health (CIEH) has warned MEPs. The CIEH believes the EFA, scheduled to be launched by 2002, should give priority to food-poisoning figures and improve the response to food-poisoning outbreaks, which it said was poor across the EU.' [*Caterer & Hotelkeeper*]

European plan /ˌjʊərə'piːən plæn/ *noun* HOTELS **1.** a hotel tariff which covers the room charges and service charges, including a simple continental breakfast **2.** *US* a hotel tariff which covers the room charges and service charges but no meals. Compare **American plan**

European Union /ˌjʊərəpiːən 'juːniən/ *noun* a group of European countries linked together by the Treaty of Rome, basing their cooperation on the four fundamental freedoms of movement: of goods, capital, people and services. Abbr **EU**

COMMENT: The European Community was set up in 1957 and changed its name to the European Union when it adopted the Single Market. It has now grown to include fifteen member states. These are: Austria, Belgium, Denmark, Finland, France, Germany, Greece, Ireland, Italy, Luxembourg, the Netherlands, Portugal, Spain, Sweden and the United Kingdom; other countries are negotiating to join. The member states of the EU are linked together by the Treaty of Rome in such a way that trade is more free, that money can be moved from one country to another freely, that people can move from one country to another more freely, and that people can work more freely in other countries of the group.

Eurostar /'jʊərəʊstɑː/ *tdmk* RAIL TRAVEL **1.** a train service from England to France and Belgium, through the Channel Tunnel ○ *Eurostar is often used by businesspeople who want to go to the centre of Brussels.* **2.** a train on the Eurostar service ○ *We took the 8.25 Eurostar to Paris.*

evacuate /ɪ'vækjueɪt/ *verb* to get people to leave a place such as a dangerous building, an aircraft on fire, etc. ○ *The hotel guests were evacuated by the fire service.*

evacuation /ɪˌvækjuˈeɪʃ(ə)n/ *noun* the act of getting people out of a dangerous building, aircraft, etc. ○ *Complete evacuation of the aircraft took 12 minutes.* ○ *We have to practise evacuation drill every week.*

'…evacuation of a building in darkness or smoke is always difficult and hazardous. Whether it is a fire, or a storm, an explosion or any major or minor emergency, nothing makes it more frightening than darkness' [*Hotel Security Worldwide*]

evacuation plan /ɪˌvækjuˈeɪʃ(ə)n plæn/ *noun* HOTELS a diagram pinned up in a hotel room, showing guests how to escape if there is a fire

evacuation route /ɪˌvækjuˈeɪʃ(ə)n ruːt/ *noun* a way, clearly indicated by signs and diagrams, which people must follow to escape from a dangerous building

evaporated milk /ɪˌvæpəreɪtɪd ˈmɪlk/ *noun* milk that has been thickened by removing some of the water by evaporation

evening /ˈiːvnɪŋ/ *noun* the part of the day between the afternoon and night ○ *They took an evening flight to Madrid.* ○ *The evening meal is served from 7.30 to 10.30.*

evening dress /ˈiːvnɪŋ dres/ *noun* formal clothes worn to an evening banquet or reception, consisting of long dresses for women and dinner jacket and bow tie for men

event /ɪˈvent/ *noun* ENTERTAINMENT a party or other special occasion, e.g. a wedding reception, birthday party, etc.

event manager /ɪˈvent ˌmænɪdʒə/ *noun* a person who is in charge of organising events that take place at a particular venue

event marketing /ɪˈvent ˌmɑːkɪtɪŋ/ *noun* the work of advertising a venue as a good place in which to hold events

event operations manager /ɪˌvent ˌɒpəˈreɪʃ(ə)nz ˌmænɪdʒə/ *noun* HOTELS a manager in a hotel who organises special events

exact /ɪɡˈzækt/ *adjective* very correct ○ *The exact time is 10.27.* ○ *The salesgirl asked me if I had the exact sum, since the shop had no change.*

exactly /ɪɡˈzæktli/ *adverb* not more, not less ○ *The total cost was exactly £6,504.* ○ *The train arrived exactly on time at 10.03.*

examination /ɪɡˌzæmɪˈneɪʃ(ə)n/ *noun* **1.** the act of looking at something or somebody very carefully to see what they are like or whether anything is wrong with them **2.** a written or spoken test ○ *He passed his management examinations.* ○ *She came first in*

the final examination for the course. ○ *He failed his proficiency examination and so had to leave his job.*

examine /ɪɡˈzæmɪn/ *verb* to look at someone or something very carefully to see what they are like or whether anything is wrong with them ○ *The customs officials asked to examine the inside of the car.*

exceed /ɪkˈsiːd/ *verb* to go beyond something ○ *He was exceeding the speed limit.*

excess /ˈekses/ *adjective* more than what is allowed □ **in excess of** above, more than ○ *Quantities in excess of twenty-five kilos are charged at a higher rate.*

'…most airlines give business class the same baggage allowance as first class, which can save large sums in excess baggage' [*Business Traveller*]

excess baggage /ˌekses ˈbæɡɪdʒ/ *noun* **1.** baggage which is heavier than the weight allowed as free baggage for a certain category of ticket **2.** an extra payment at an airport for taking baggage which is heavier than the usual passenger's allowance

excess fare /ˌekses ˈfeə/ *noun* TRAVEL an extra fare to be paid, such as for travelling first-class with a second-class ticket or for travelling further than originally intended

excessive /ɪkˈsesɪv/ *adjective* too large ○ *excessive costs*

exchange /ɪksˈtʃeɪndʒ/ *noun* **1.** the act of giving one thing for another **2.** the act of giving someone an amount of foreign currency that is equal in value to an amount in his or her own currency. ◊ **foreign exchange** ■ *verb* **1.** □ **to exchange one article for another** to give one thing in place of something else ○ *He exchanged his ticket for a flight on Monday 22nd for a ticket on the same flight on the following Wednesday.* ○ *If the trousers are too small you can take them back and exchange them for a larger pair.* ○ *Goods can be exchanged only on production of the sales slip.* **2.** FINANCE to change money of one country for money of another ○ *to exchange euros for pounds*

exchangeable /ɪksˈtʃeɪndʒəb(ə)l/ *adjective* possible to exchange

exchange control /ɪksˈtʃeɪndʒ kənˌtrəʊl/ *noun* FINANCE control by a government of the way in which its currency may be exchanged for foreign currencies ○ *The government had to impose exchange controls to stop the rush to buy dollars.*

exchange premium /ɪksˈtʃeɪndʒ ˌpriːmiəm/ *noun* FINANCE an extra cost above the usual rate for buying a foreign currency

exchange rate /ɪks'tʃeɪndʒ reɪt/ *noun* FINANCE the price at which one currency is exchanged for another ○ *What is today's exchange rate* or *the current exchange rate for the dollar?* ○ *There is a surcharge of 10% because of the fall in the exchange rate.* Also called **rate of exchange**

excise duty /'eksaɪz ˌdjuːti/ *noun* BUSINESS a tax on particular goods produced in a country, e.g. alcohol and petrol

exciseman /'eksaɪzmæn/ *noun* somebody who works in the Excise Department

Excise officer /'eksaɪz ˌɒfɪsə/ *noun* an official of the Excise Department

exclude /ɪk'skluːd/ *verb* to shut out something from somewhere ○ *Damage by fire is excluded from the policy.*

excluding /ɪk'skluːdɪŋ/ *preposition* not including ○ *The total cost, excluding gratuities, is £1,520.00 per person for the 6-night trip.*

exclusive /ɪk'skluːsɪv/ *adjective* **1.** not including something or somebody □ **exclusive of tax** not including tax **2.** expensive and only available for use by a few people, not open to everyone ○ *an exclusive Caribbean holiday resort* ○ *The new health club is very exclusive.* ○ *They stay in an exclusive Swiss ski resort.*

excursion /ɪk'skɜːʃ(ə)n/ *noun* ENTERTAINMENT a short visit, often no longer than one day, returning to the place from which you left ○ *We're planning an excursion to Brighton.* ○ *The whole school went on an excursion to the zoo.*

excursion fare /ɪk'skɜːʃ(ə)n feə/ *noun* AIR TRAVEL a special cheap fare offered on particular journeys, or the lowest air fare on a domestic route

excursionist /ɪk'skɜːʃ(ə)nɪst/ *noun* someone who goes on an excursion, especially for pleasure

excursion rate /ɪk'skɜːʃ(ə)n reɪt/ *noun* AIR TRAVEL same as **excursion fare**

executive /ɪg'zekjʊtɪv/ *noun* BUSINESS an important businessman who makes decisions

executive chef /ɪgˌzekjʊtɪv 'ʃef/ *noun* CATERING the main chef in charge of a large restaurant, with many other chefs reporting to him

executive class /ɪg'zekjʊtɪv klɑːs/ *noun* AIR TRAVEL a better and more expensive type of air travel, especially for businesspeople

executive jet /ɪgˌzekjʊtɪv 'dʒet/ *noun* AIR TRAVEL a small jet aircraft for use by a few passengers, usually important businesspeople

executive lounge /ɪg'zekjʊtɪv laʊndʒ/ *noun* a lounge in an airport or hotel for the use of people who are travelling first-class

executive room /ɪg'zekjʊtɪv ruːm/ *noun* a high-quality room in a hotel for use especially by businesspeople

executive suite /ɪg'zekjʊtɪv swiːt/ *noun* a special suite of rooms in a hotel for businesspeople

executive travel /ɪgˌzekjʊtɪv 'træv(ə)l/ *noun* TRAVEL business travel by important businesspeople

exempt /ɪg'zempt/ *adjective* not covered by a rule or law, or not forced to obey a law □ **exempt from tax**, **tax-exempt** not required to pay tax ○ *As a non-profit-making organisation we are exempt from tax.* ■ *verb* BUSINESS to free something from having tax paid on it or someone from having to pay tax ○ *Non-profit-making organisations are exempted from tax.* ○ *Food is exempted from sales tax.*

exemption /ɪg'zempʃ(ə)n/ *noun* BUSINESS the act of freeing something from a contract, from having tax paid on it, or the act of freeing someone from having to pay tax

exhibit /ɪg'zɪbɪt/ *noun* **1.** something which is shown ○ *The buyers admired the exhibits on our stand.* **2.** a collection of objects or goods shown, or a single section of an exhibition ○ *the British Trade Exhibit at the International Computer Fair* ■ *verb* □ **to exhibit at the Motor Show** to display new models of cars or new products at the Motor Show

exhibition /ˌeksɪ'bɪʃ(ə)n/ *noun* **1.** ENTERTAINMENT a show of works of art ○ *There is a Goya exhibition on at the Prado.* ○ *Have you visited the Turner exhibition at the Tate Gallery?* **2.** BUSINESS a show of goods so that buyers can look at them and decide what to buy ○ *The government has sponsored an exhibition of good design.* ○ *We have a stand at the Ideal Home Exhibition.*

exhibition hall /ˌeksɪ'bɪʃ(ə)n hɔːl/ *noun* BUSINESS a place where goods are shown so that buyers can look at them and decide what to buy

exhibition stand /ˌeksɪ'bɪʃ(ə)n stænd/ *noun* BUSINESS a separate area or structure at an exhibition or a commercial fair where a company exhibits its products or services. Also called **fair booth**

exhibitor /ɪgˈzɪbɪtə/ *noun* BUSINESS a company that shows products at an exhibition

exit /ˈegzɪt/ *noun* a way out of a building or area ○ *The customers all rushed towards the exits.*

expatriate /eksˈpætriət/ *noun* somebody who lives and works in another country

expedition /ˌekspɪˈdɪʃ(ə)n/ *noun* a trip made by a group of people for a particular purpose, such as to discover unknown territory

expedition pole /ˌekspɪˈdɪʃ(ə)n ˌpəʊl/ *noun* SPORT a type of strong ski pole, used when mountain climbing

expenditure /ɪkˈspendɪtʃə/ *noun* the amount of money spent. Also called **spend** (NOTE: There is no plural form in British English, but American English often uses **expenditures**.) □ **below-the-line expenditure** exceptional payments which are separated from a company's normal accounts □ **the company's current expenditure programme** the company's spending according to the current plan □ **heavy expenditure on equipment** spending large sums of money on equipment

expense account /ɪkˈspens əˌkaʊnt/ *noun* BUSINESS money which a businessperson is allowed by his or her company to spend on travelling and entertaining clients in connection with his or her business ○ *He charged his hotel bill to his expense account.* ○ *I'll put this lunch on my expense account.*

expenses /ɪkˈspensɪz/ *plural noun* money that somebody has to spend in order to be able to do his or her job and that can be claimed back from his or her employer □ **the salary offered is £30,000 plus expenses** the company offers a salary of £30,000 and will repay any expenses incurred by the employee in the course of his or her work □ **all expenses paid** with all costs paid by the company ○ *The company sent him to San Francisco all expenses paid* or *He went on an all-expenses-paid trip to San Francisco.* □ **to cut down on expenses** to reduce spending

expensive /ɪkˈspensɪv/ *adjective* costing a lot of money ○ *First-class air travel is becoming more and more expensive.*

expire /ɪkˈspaɪə/ *verb* to come to an end ○ *The lease of the hotel expires in 2010.* □ **his passport has expired** his passport is no longer valid

expiry /ɪkˈspaɪəri/ *noun* the fact of coming to an end ○ *You need to renew your car insurance before the expiry of the previous policy.*

expiry date /ɪkˈspaɪəri deɪt/ *noun* the last date on which something can be used ○ *What is the expiry date on your credit card?*

explore /ɪkˈsplɔː/ *verb* to make a journey or trip to find out about a place or to see something that you have never seen before ○ *These trips offer plenty of opportunities to get out and explore.* ○ *Explore the sights or relax by the pool.*

export *noun* /ˈekspɔːt/ **1.** a product made in one country and sold to another **2.** the business of selling goods to other countries ■ *verb* /ɪkˈspɔːt/ BUSINESS to send goods to buyers in other countries. Compare **import**

export licence /ˈekspɔːt ˌlaɪs(ə)ns/, **export permit** /ˈekspɔːt ˌpɜːmɪt/ *noun* BUSINESS a document which allows goods to be exported

express /ɪkˈspres/ *adjective* rapid, very fast ○ *express letter* ○ *express delivery* ■ *noun* a very fast train or coach ○ *We're taking the 10.25 express to Edinburgh.* ■ *verb* **1.** to show something ○ *This chart shows visitors from Europe expressed as a percentage of the total number of tourists coming to the UK each year.* **2.** to send very fast ○ *We expressed the order to the customer's warehouse.*

expressly /ɪkˈspresli/ *adverb* clearly in words ○ *The contract expressly forbids sales to the United States.*

express service /ɪkˌspres ˈsɜːvɪs/ *noun* a very fast train, coach, delivery of parcels, etc.

expressway /ɪkˈspresw eɪ/ *noun* US ROAD TRAVEL a fast road with few junctions ○ *Take the expressway south to junction 20.* (NOTE: The British English is **motorway**.)

ext *abbreviation* extension

extender /ɪkˈstendə/ *noun* CATERING a food additive which makes the food bigger or heavier without adding to its food value

extension /ɪkˈstenʃən/ *noun* (*in a hotel or office*) an individual telephone linked to the main switchboard ○ *Can you get me extension 21?* ○ *The restaurant manager is on extension 53.*

external /ɪkˈstɜːn(ə)l/ *adjective* outside a country

external account /ɪkˌstɜːn(ə)l əˈkaʊnt/ *noun* FINANCE an account in a British bank held by somebody who is living in another country

external audit /ɪkˌstɜːn(ə)l ˈɔːdɪt/ *noun* BUSINESS an audit carried out by an independent auditor who is not employed by the company. Also called **independent audit**

external auditor /ɪkˌstɜːn(ə)l ˈɔːdɪtə/ *noun* BUSINESS an independent person who audits a company's accounts and who is not a member of the staff of the company

external phone /ɪkˌstɜːn(ə)l ˈfəʊn/ *noun* a phone directly linked to an outside line

external trade /ɪkˌstɜːn(ə)l ˈtreɪd/ *noun* BUSINESS same as **overseas trade**

extinguish /ɪkˈstɪŋgwɪʃ/ *verb* to put out a fire

extinguisher /ɪkˈstɪŋgwɪʃə/ *noun* an apparatus, usually in the form of a cylinder containing liquid, foam or powder, that is used to put out fires

COMMENT: Foam extinguishers cover a fire with a mixture of water, air and foam-producing chemicals; carbon dioxide extinguishers send out liquid carbon dioxide which turns to solid white 'snow' on contact with air and then turns back to gas again under the effect of heat; this has the effect of smothering the fire. Water-based extinguishers should not be used for fires in electrical equipment or involving burning oils.

extra /ˈekstrə/ *adjective* added, more than usual ○ *to charge 10% extra for postage* ○ *There is an extra charge for a single room.* ○ *The staff are paid extra pay for working on Sundays.*

extra bed /ˌekstrə ˈbed/ *noun* HOTELS an additional bed brought into a room for a guest ○ *The hotel is very full but we can put an extra bed in the room if you want.*

extra charge /ˌekstrə ˈtʃɑːdʒ/ *noun* an additional charge on top of what is already paid ○ *There is no extra charge for heating.*

extract /ˈekstrækt/ *noun* a concentrated product obtained by first dissolving a substance and then evaporating the liquid in which it is dissolved

extractor /ɪkˈstræktə/ *noun* a machine which removes something from somewhere

extractor fan /ɪkˈstræktə fæn/ *noun* a fan which sucks air out of a place ○ *When you switch on the light in the bathroom, the extractor fan switches on.*

extras /ˈekstrəz/ *plural noun* something added to what is usual or expected, or something not included in the original price ○ *Packing and postage are extras.*

extra virgin olive oil /ˌekstrə ˌvɜːdʒɪn ˈɒlɪv ˌɔɪl/ *noun* FOOD olive oil produced from the first pressing, which has a low acidity

extremely /ɪkˈstriːmli/ *adverb* very, to a very great degree ○ *It is extremely difficult to spend less than $50.00 a day on meals.* ○ *The restaurant service is extremely efficient.*

extreme sport /ɪkˌstriːm ˈspɔːt/ *noun* a sport in which participants deliberately seek out dangerous or even life-threatening experiences

F

FAA *abbreviation* US AIR TRAVEL Federal Aviation Administration

face /feɪs/ *noun* the front part of the head ■ *verb* to turn towards somebody or something □ **the room faces east** the room looks towards the east

facecloth /'feɪsklɒθ/, **face flannel** /'feɪs 'flænəl/ *noun* a small square of towelling for washing the face or body ○ *The hotel provides you with a bath towel, a small towel and a facecloth in your bathroom.*

face towel /'feɪs ˌtaʊəl/ *noun* a small towel for drying the hands and face

facilities /fə'sɪlɪtiz/ *plural noun* equipment or buildings which make it easy to do something ○ *storage facilities*

facility /fə'sɪlɪti/ *noun* **1.** □ **there are no facilities for unloading**, **there are no unloading facilities** there is no way in which cargo can be unloaded here □ **the museum has facilities for the disabled** the museum has special ramps, special lifts, etc., to allow people with disabilities to visit it **2.** a single large building ○ *We have opened our new warehouse facility.*

'...the airport currently handles around 1.3 million passengers a year, with the new facility making it able to cope with over 2 million' [*Airliner World*]

facsimile copy /fæk,sɪmɪli 'kɒpi/ *noun* an exact copy of a document

faecal /'fiːk(ə)l/ *adjective* referring to faeces (NOTE: The US spelling is **fecal.**)

faecal matter /'fiːk(ə)l ˌmætə/ *noun* solid waste matter from the bowels ○ *Faecal matter was found in the drinking supplies.*

faeces /'fiːsiːz/ *plural noun* solid waste matter passed from the bowels through the anus (*formal*) (NOTE: The US spelling is **feces.**)

Fahrenheit /'færənhaɪt/ *noun* a scale of temperatures where the freezing and boiling points of water are 32° and 212°. Compare **Celsius** (NOTE: **Fahrenheit** is used in the United States, but is less common in the United Kingdom. It is normally written as an

F after the degree sign: **32°F**. Say: 'thirty-two degrees Fahrenheit'.)

COMMENT: To convert Fahrenheit to Celsius, subtract 32 and divide by 1.8. To convert Celsius temperatures to Fahrenheit, multiply by 1.8 and add 32. So 68°F is equal to 20°C.

fair /feə/ *noun* **1.** ENTERTAINMENT a group of sideshows, amusements, food stalls, etc., set up in one place for a short time **2.** same as **trade fair** ■ *adjective* honest or correct

fair booth /'feə buːð/ *noun* US BUSINESS same as **exhibition stand**

fair copy /ˌfeə 'kɒpi/ *noun* a document which is written or typed with no changes or mistakes

fair deal /ˌfeə 'diːl/ *noun* an arrangement where both parties are treated equally ○ *The group feel they did not get a fair deal from the holiday company.*

fairly /'feəli/ *adverb* **1.** quite, relatively ○ *The hotel is fairly close to the centre of town.* **2.** in a way that is right, giving people what they deserve ○ *to treat somebody fairly*

fair price /ˌfeə 'praɪs/ *noun* a good price for both buyer and seller

Fair Trade /ˌfeə 'treɪd/ *noun* a system that ensures that producers in developing countries are paid a proper price for the goods they supply

faites marcher /ˌfet 'mɑːʃeɪ/ *phrase* CATERING used by waiters to ask the kitchen to get a dish ready (NOTE: **faites marcher** comes from the French phrase meaning 'get something started'.)

fajitas /fə'hiːtəz/ *plural noun* FOOD a dish consisting of beef or other meat, especially chicken, that has been marinated, grilled, cut into strips and served in a soft tortilla

fall /fɔːl/ *noun* **1.** a drop ○ *a fall in temperature* **2.** US autumn ○ *You should go to New England for the fall.* ○ *The fall colours are at their best in the first week of October.* ■ *verb* **1.** to drop down to the ground **2.** to become less in amount or value ○ *The temperature fell to –30°.*

falls /fɔːlz/ *plural noun* a large waterfall ○ *Victoria Falls* ○ *Niagara Falls*

false alarm /ˌfɔːls əˈlɑːm/ *noun* a warning signal which is false

famed /feɪmd/ *adjective* well known ○ *The town is famed for its cheese festival.*

familiarisation /fəˌmɪliəraɪˈzeɪʃ(ə)n/, **familiarization** *noun* the process of getting to know something well

familiarisation trip /fəˌmɪliəraɪ ˈzeɪʃ(ə)n ˌtrɪp/ *noun* TOURISM a visit organised by an airline, tourist resort, etc., so that journalists and tour operators can get to know the facilities offered

familiarise /fəˈmɪliəraɪz/ *verb* □ **to familiarise yourself with** to get to know something well ○ *The booking clerks were sent on a course to familiarise themselves with the new computer system.*

family /ˈfæm(ə)li/ *noun* a group of people who are related to each other, especially mother, father and children ○ *The Jones family are going on holiday to Spain.* □ **a family-owned and run hotel** a hotel which belongs to the family who run it and is not part of a chain

family name /ˈfæm(ə)li neɪm/ *noun* the name of a family such as Smith, Jones, etc. as opposed to the first name or Christian name. Also called **surname**

family pack /ˈfæm(ə)li pæk/, **family size** /ˈfæm(ə)li saɪz/ *noun* BUSINESS same as **economy size pack**

family plan /ˈfæm(ə)li plæn/ *noun* HOTELS a room charge which allows members of a family to enjoy reduced rates

family room /ˈfæm(ə)li ruːm/ *noun* **1.** a room in a pub for parents and children, with comfortable chairs for the adults, and toys for the children **2.** a bedroom for a family, with a main bed for the parents and a small bed or beds or bunk beds for children

family-style service /ˌfæm(ə)li staɪl ˈsɜːvɪs/ *noun* a type of service in which food is brought to the table in dishes and the guests help themselves

family suite /ˈfæm(ə)li swiːt/ *noun* HOTELS a series of rooms in a hotel, suitable for a family, typically, two bedrooms, a sitting room and a bathroom

famous /ˈfeɪməs/ *adjective* very well known ○ *The company owns a famous department store in the centre of London.*

fan /fæn/ *noun* **1.** a piece of equipment for moving air to make people or things cooler ○ *We put electric fans in the reception to try to keep cool.* **2.** an enthusiastic supporter of something or someone, such as a team or a pop group ○ *There was a crowd of fans waiting for him outside the theatre.* □ **a Liverpool fan** a supporter of Liverpool football team

fancy /ˈfænsi/ *adjective* □ **fancy prices** high prices ○ *I don't want to pay the fancy prices they ask in London shops.*

fancy goods /ˈfænsi gʊdz/ *plural noun* small attractive items

F & B *abbreviation* HOTELS food and beverage

farce /fɑːs/ *noun* FOOD a French noun meaning stuffing

fare /feə/ *noun* **1.** TRAVEL the price that you have to pay for a journey ○ *Train fares have gone up by 5%.* ○ *The government is asking the airlines to keep air fares down.* **2.** ROAD TRAVEL a passenger in a taxi ○ *He picked up a fare in Oxford Street and took him to Kensington.* **3.** (*especially in publicity*) food ○ *good country fare*

fare code /ˈfeə kəʊd/ *noun* AIR TRAVEL a code on an airline ticket that indicates which class the passenger will be travelling in ○ *The fare code F stands for first class.* Also called **booking code**

farinaceous /ˌfærɪˈneɪʃəs/ *adjective* CATERING referring to flour, containing starch

farinaceous foods /ˌfærɪˈneɪʃəs fuːdz/ *plural noun* CATERING foods such as bread which are made of flour and have a high starch content

farinose /ˈfærɪnəʊz/ *adjective* consisting of or producing food starch

farm /fɑːm/ *noun* an area of land used for growing crops and raising animals ○ *We went to spend the week on a farm in Devon.* ■ *verb* to grow crops or raise animals on a farm

farmed /fɑːmd/ *adjective* raised on a farm

'…when farmed cod reaches price compatibility with wild cod, demand will leap' [*Caterer & Hotelkeeper*]

farmhouse /ˈfɑːmhaʊs/ *noun* a house where a farmer and his or her family live ■ *adjective* referring to something as you might find in a farm

'…a description such as 'farmhouse vegetables' should be banned because it is meaningless' [*Food Standards Agency*]

farmhouse holiday /ˈfɑːmhaʊs ˌhɒlideɪ/ *noun* TOURISM a holiday in the country, living on a farm

farming /ˈfɑːmɪŋ/ *noun* the work of managing a farm, of growing crops or of raising animals or fish for sale

'...farming fish is cheaper and provides better consistency of quality than wild fish' [*Caterer & Hotelkeeper*]

farmstay /ˈfɑːmsteɪ/ *noun* a stay on a farm as a paying guest, providing some experience of rural life

farm tourism /ˌfɑːm ˈtʊərɪz(ə)m/ *noun* TOURISM holidays spent on farms

fascia /ˈfeɪʃə/ *noun* a board over a shop on which the name of the shop is written

fast food /ˈfɑːst fʊd/ *noun* cooked food which can be prepared, bought and eaten quickly, e.g. hamburgers, hot dogs or pizzas ○ *She decided to invest in a fast-food franchise.*

fast-food outlet /ˌfɑːst ˈfuːd ˌaʊtlət/ *noun* a snack bar or restaurant offering fast food, often part of a franchise operation

fast lane /ˈfɑːst leɪn/ *noun* same as **outside lane**

fat /fæt/ *adjective* **1.** (*of a person*) big and round, overweight ○ *Two fat men got out of the little white car.* ○ *I'm getting too fat – I need to slim.* **2.** thick ○ *a fat file of complaints on the manager's desk* **3.** CATERING containing a lot of fat ○ *fat bacon* ■ *noun* FOOD a white oily substance in the body, which stores energy and protects the body against cold ○ *She asked for a slice of lamb without too much fat.* ○ *If you don't like the fat on the meat, cut it off.*

fathom /ˈfæðəm/ *noun* a measure of the depth of water equalling 6 feet or 1.8 metres ○ *The ship sank in fifty fathoms of water.*

fattening /ˈfæt(ə)nɪŋ/ *adjective* CATERING that makes you fat ○ *Low-fat yoghurt isn't fattening.*

fatty acid /ˌfæti ˈæsɪd/ *noun* CATERING an acid which is an important substance in the body, e.g. stearic acid

COMMENT: Fat is a necessary part of the diet because of the vitamins and energy-giving calories that it contains. Fat in the diet comes from either animal fats or vegetable fats. Animal fats such as butter, fat meat or cream, are saturated fatty acids. It is believed that the intake of unsaturated and polyunsaturated fats (mainly vegetable fats and oils and fish oil) in the diet, rather than animal fats, helps keep down the level of cholesterol in the blood and so lessens the risk of atherosclerosis. A low-fat diet does not always help to reduce weight.

faucet /ˈfɔːsɪt/ *noun US* same as **tap** ○ *The faucet in the bathroom is leaking.*

fauna /ˈfɔːnə/ *noun* the wild animals of an area ○ *The flora and fauna of South America.* Compare **flora** (NOTE: The plural form is **faunae**.)

favourite /ˈfeɪv(ə)rət/ *adjective* very popular or that you like most ○ *a favourite tourist spot* ○ *my favourite method of relaxing*

fax /fæks/ *noun* **1.** a system for sending an exact copy of a document via the telephone ○ *We received a fax of the order this morning.* **2.** a document sent by this method ○ *Can you confirm the booking by fax?* ○ *Most hotels will accept confirmation of a booking by fax.* ■ *verb* to send a message by fax ○ *The details of the offer were faxed to the brokers this morning.* ○ *I've faxed the documents to our New York office.*

fax paper /ˈfæks ˌpeɪpə/ *noun* a special paper which is used in fax machines

FDF *abbreviation* Food and Drink Federation

feasibility /ˌfiːzəˈbɪlɪti/ *noun* the ability to be done ○ *to report on the feasibility of a project*

feasibility study /ˌfiːzəˈbɪlɪti ˌstʌdi/ *noun* a study to see if something can be done

feast /fiːst/ *noun* **1.** a special religious day when a saint is remembered or a special event is celebrated ○ *Today is the Feast of St Nicholas.* **2.** a very large meal ■ *verb* to eat a very large meal

feather duster /ˌfeðə ˈdʌstə/ *noun* a brush made of feathers for removing dust

feature /ˈfiːtʃə/ *noun* an important part or aspect of something ○ *The gastronomic restaurant is a feature of the hotel.* ○ *Long fjords are a feature of the coastline of Norway.* ■ *verb* to show as an important item ○ *The tour features a visit to the Valley of the Kings.*

Federal Aviation Administration /ˌfed(ə)rəl ˌeɪviˈeɪʃ(ə)n ˌædmɪnɪstreɪʃ(ə)n/ *noun* AIR TRAVEL a US government agency which regulates the operation of civilian airlines. Abbr **FAA**

fee /fiː/ *noun* **1.** a sum of money that has to be paid for something **2.** the money paid for work carried out by a professional person such as an accountant, a doctor or a lawyer ○ *director's fees* ○ *consultant's fee* ○ *We charge a small fee for our services.*

feed /fiːd/ *noun* a meal, especially given to babies ■ *verb* **1.** to give food to a person or an animal ○ *The student cafeteria feeds two thousand people a day.* **2.** AIR TRAVEL to pass aircraft from an international route into domestic services (NOTE: **feeds – fed**)

feeder /ˈfiːdə/ *noun* TRAVEL a road, railway or airline that carries traffic from a relatively small place to a city in order to connect with the main routes

feeder airline /ˈfiːdə ˌeəlaɪn/ *noun* AIR TRAVEL an airline that connects with a hub and enables passengers to catch long-distance flights

fell /fel/ *noun* an area of high moorland, with few trees, especially in the north of England ○ *The popularity of the Lake District fells is well known.*

fennel /ˈfen(ə)l/ *noun* a herb with seeds and feathery leaves that have a light aniseed flavour

ferment /fəˈment/ *verb* to change something into alcohol by the effect of yeast on sugar ○ *Cider has to ferment for at least ten weeks before it is ready to drink.*

fermentation /ˌfɜːmenˈteɪʃ(ə)n/ *noun* a chemical change brought about in liquids usually leading to the production of alcohol ○ *They added sugar to encourage fermentation.*

Ferris wheel /ˈferɪs wiːl/ *noun* ENTERTAINMENT a large vertical wheel in a funfair, with seats hanging from it ○ *You get a marvellous view of the town from the top of the Ferris wheel.*

ferry /ˈferi/, **ferryboat** /ˈferibəʊt/ *noun* SHIPS AND BOATS a boat which takes passengers or goods across water ○ *We are going to take the night ferry to Belgium.*

festival /ˈfestɪv(ə)l/ *noun* **1.** a religious celebration which comes at the same time each year ○ *The party will be in Hong Kong for the Lantern Festival.* **2.** ENTERTAINMENT an event, often lasting several days, where entertainment is provided ○ *We saw some excellent plays at the Edinburgh Festival this year.*

FET /ˌef iː ˈtiː/ *abbreviation* foreign escorted tour

feta /ˈfetə/ *noun* a firm crumbly salty cheese made from sheep's or goat's milk and preserved in brine, originally from Greece

fête /feɪt/ *noun* ENTERTAINMENT a small public event, usually in the open air, with stalls, sideshows and competitions ○ *I hope it doesn't rain for the village fête.* ○ *The school summer fête will be held next Saturday.*

fettuccine /ˌfetəˈtʃiːni/ *noun* pasta made in narrow flat strips, slightly narrower and thicker than tagliatelle

feuilleté /ˈfɜːɪəteɪ/ *noun* FOOD a French noun meaning an open or covered pie of flaky pastry ○ *a feuilleté of langoustines*

FFP *abbreviation* frequent flyer programme

FICC *abbreviation* International Federation of Camping and Caravanning

field /fiːld/ *noun* □ **in the field** outside the office, among the customers ○ *We have sixteen reps in the field.*

field research /ˈfiːld rɪˌsɜːtʃ/, **field work** /ˈfiːld wɜːk/ *noun* an examination of the situation among possible customers, as opposed to desk research ○ *They did a lot of field work to find the right market for their new service.*

fifth freedom /ˌfɪfθ ˈfriːdəm/ *noun* AIR TRAVEL the right to use a carrier of one country to take passengers between two other countries

fig /fɪg/ *noun* FRUIT the juicy sweet fruit of a semi-tropical tree grown mainly in Mediterranean countries and eaten either as fresh figs or dried figs ○ *We sat under the tree and ate figs and goat's cheese.*

fill /fɪl/ *verb* **1.** to make something full ○ *The waiter filled her glass again.* **2.** □ **to fill a gap** to provide a product or service which is needed, but which no one has provided before ○ *The new series of golfing holidays fills a gap in the market.* **3.** □ **to fill a post, a vacancy** to find someone to do a job ○ *Your application arrived too late – the post has already been filled.*

filled baguette /ˌfɪld bæˈget/ *noun* FOOD a sandwich made of a piece of French bread sliced in two, and filled with salad, tuna, ham, etc.

filled bap /ˌfɪld ˈbæp/ *noun* FOOD a sandwich made of a bap sliced in two, and filled with salad, tuna, ham, etc.

fillet /ˈfɪlɪt/ *noun* **1.** MEAT a piece of good-quality meat, with no bones ○ *fillet of beef* ○ *fillet of pork* **2.** CATERING a piece of fish which the bones have been taken out of ○ *We ordered fried fillet of sole.* ■ *verb* CATERING to take the bones out of a fish ○ *Ask the waiter to fillet the fish for you.*

filleter /ˈfɪlɪtə/ *noun* CATERING somebody who fillets fish

fillet steak /ˌfɪlɪt ˈsteɪk/ *noun* MEAT a thick slice of beef from the best-quality and most expensive cut

fill in /ˌfɪl ˈɪn/ *verb* to write the necessary information in the blank spaces in a form ○ *Fill in your name and address in block capitals.*

filling /ˈfɪlɪŋ/ *noun* CATERING food used to put inside some other food, e.g. in a sandwich, pie, cake, chocolates, etc.

fill out /ˌfɪl ˈaʊt/ *verb* to write the required information in the blank spaces in a form ○ *To get customs clearance you must fill out three forms.*

fill up /ˌfɪl ˈʌp/ *verb* **1.** to make something completely full, or to become completely full ○ *He filled up the car with petrol.* **2.** to finish writing the necessary information on a form ○ *He filled up the form and sent it to the bank.*

filo /ˈfaɪləʊ/ *noun* BREAD, ETC. very thin sheets of pastry dough used to make papery crisp small pastries or large dishes, used especially in Greek cooking

filter /ˈfɪltə/ *noun* **1.** a piece of cloth, plastic or paper or a mass of crystals through which water or air passes and which holds back solid particles such as dirt ○ *The filter in the swimming pool has become clogged.* ○ *The inspector asked the restaurant to replace the filter on the air extractor.* **2.** a piece of paper through which coffee passes in a coffee machine ■ *verb* to pass liquid through a paper or cloth filter, or through crystals, to remove impurities ○ *The water is filtered through a cloth before being used.*

filter coffee /ˌfɪltə ˈkɒfi/ *noun* BEVERAGES coffee which is made by passing boiling water through coffee grounds, often in a paper cone

final destination /ˌfaɪn(ə)l ˌdestɪˈneɪʃ(ə)n/ *noun* TRAVEL a place reached at the end of a journey after stopping at several places en route. Also called **ultimate destination**

finance /ˈfaɪnæns/ *noun* **1.** BUSINESS money used by a company, provided by the shareholders or by loans **2.** the work of managing the money used by a business or organisation ■ *verb* to provide money to pay for something ○ *The development of the marina was financed by the local council.*

finances /ˈfaɪnænsɪz/ *plural noun* the money or cash that a person or business has available ○ *the bad state of the company's finances*

financial /faɪˈnænʃəl/ *adjective* concerning money

financial adviser /faɪˌnænʃəl ədˈvaɪzə/ *noun* BUSINESS a person or company giving advice on financial matters for a fee

financial assistance /faɪˌnænʃəl əˈsɪstəns/ *noun* help in the form of money

financial resources /faɪˌnænʃəl rɪˈzɔːsɪz/ *plural noun* money which is available for investment ○ *a company with strong financial resources*

financial year /faɪˌnænʃəl ˈjɪə/ *noun* the twelve-month period for a firm's accounts

fine /faɪn/ *adjective* good, pleasant or sunny with no rain ○ *When the weather is fine, the view from the hotel is splendid.* ○ *Don't rely on having fine weather in the middle of November.* ■ *noun* money which you have to pay as a punishment for having done something wrong ○ *He was asked to pay a $25,000 fine.* ○ *We had to pay a $10 parking fine.* ■ *verb* to make someone pay money as a punishment for having done something wrong ○ *to fine someone £2,500 for obtaining money by false pretences* ■ *adverb* very thin or very small ○ *Chop the vegetables very fine.*

finely /ˈfaɪn(ə)li/ *adverb* very thin or very small ○ *finely chopped parsley*

finger /ˈfɪŋgə/ *noun* **1.** one of the five parts at the end of the hand, but usually not including the thumb ○ *She pressed the button with her finger.* **2.** CATERING a piece of food shaped like a finger ○ *a box of chocolate fingers* **3.** AIR TRAVEL same as **airbridge**

finger biscuit /ˈfɪŋgə ˌbɪskɪt/ *noun* BREAD, ETC. a biscuit shaped like a finger

finger bowl /ˈfɪŋgə bəʊl/ *noun* CATERING a bowl of water, often with a slice of lemon in it, put beside a guest's plate so that they can wash their hands after eating

finger buffet /ˈfɪŋgə ˌbʊfeɪ/ *noun* CATERING a buffet where snacks are served which guests eat with their fingers, as opposed to a 'fork buffet' or 'fork luncheon'

fire /faɪə/ *noun* something which is burning and gives off heat ○ *She lost all her belongings in the hotel fire.* □ **to catch fire** to start to burn ■ *verb* □ **to fire someone** to dismiss someone from a job (*informal*) ○ *The new proprietor fired half the hotel staff.* □ **to hire and fire** to engage new staff and dismiss existing staff very frequently

'…each room is equipped with a fire detector. The five floors, with 120 rooms each, are divided into 15 fireproof zones, individually ventilated, and equipped with a fire detector, a siren, a glass breaker and a fire door. Each floor has 5 fire hoses and an extinguisher every 10 metres. Finally, the hotel has 8 fire exits accessible from each floor' [*Hotel Security Worldwide*]

fire alarm /ˈfaɪər əˌlɑːm/ *noun* a bell or siren which gives a warning that a fire has started ○ *If you see smoke, break the glass to sound the fire alarm.*

fire damage /ˈfaɪə ˌdæmɪdʒ/ *noun* damage caused by a fire

fire detector /ˈfaɪə dɪˌtektə/ *noun* an apparatus which senses heat and notices if a fire breaks out and automatically sounds an alarm or sets off a sprinkler system

fire door /ˈfaɪə dɔː/ *noun* a special door to prevent fire going from one part of a building to another

fire drill /'faɪə drɪl/ *noun* a procedure to be carried out to help people to escape from a burning building ○ *We will be holding a fire drill this morning.*

fire exit /'faɪər ˌegzɪt/ *noun* same as **emergency exit**

fire extinguisher /'faɪər ɪkˌstɪŋgwɪʃə/ *noun* a device full of foam, water or chemicals, used for putting out fires

fire hazard /'faɪə ˌhæzəd/, **fire risk** /'faɪə rɪsk/ *noun* a situation, such as the improper storage of goods, which could easily start a fire ○ *That room full of old furniture is a fire hazard.*

fire hose /'faɪə həʊz/ *noun* a length of pipe ready to be attached to a water supply, used to put out fires

fire insurance /'faɪər ɪnˌʃʊərəns/ *noun* insurance against damage by fire

fire notice /'faɪə ˌnəʊtɪs/ *noun* HOTELS a notice pinned to a wall, telling guests what to do in case of fire

fire precautions /'faɪə prɪˌkɔːʃ(ə)nz/ *plural noun* safety measures to protect a building and its occupants if a fire breaks out

fireproof /'faɪəpruːf/ *adjective* treated so that it cannot burn ○ *All soft furniture is covered in fireproof fabric.*

fire safety /ˌfaɪə 'seɪfti/ *noun* measures to make a place safe for the customers and staff in case of fire

fire safety officer /faɪə 'seɪfti ˌɒfɪsə/ *noun* somebody responsible for seeing that the customers and staff are safe if a fire breaks out

firetrap /'faɪətræp/ *noun* a place which could easily catch fire, and in which people could be trapped because of inadequate fire safety equipment or because of its construction ○ *The hotel has no fire escape – it's a real firetrap.*

first /fɜːst/ *adjective* relating to number 1 in a series

first aid /ˌfɜːst 'eɪd/ *noun* MEDICAL help given rapidly to someone who is suddenly ill or hurt until full-scale medical treatment can be given ○ *She ran to the man who had been knocked down and gave him first aid until the ambulance arrived.*

'…how much first-aid equipment should be provided in a workplace depends on the number of people employed. For a small establishment a single first-aid box may be sufficient. It should be in the charge of a responsible person and should be properly stocked' [*Health and Safety in Kitchens (HSE)*]

first-aid hut /ˌfɜːst 'eɪd ˌhʌt/ *noun* a small building containing a first-aid post

first-aid kit /ˌfɜːst 'eɪd ˌkɪt/ *noun* a box with bandages and dressings kept ready to be used in an emergency

first-aid post /ˌfɜːst 'eɪd ˌpəʊst/, **first-aid station** /'steɪʃ(ə)n/ *noun* a tent or other small building in which first aid can be given to people at an exhibition, agricultural show, etc.

first-class /ˌfɜːst 'klɑːs/ *adjective, adverb* **1.** best-quality, most expensive ○ *The hotel has a first-class restaurant.* ○ *We had a first-class meal last night.* **2.** TOURISM referring to the most expensive and most comfortable type of travel or hotel ○ *to stay in first-class hotels* ○ *I prefer to travel first-class.* ○ *First-class travel provides the best service.* ○ *A first-class ticket costs more than twice as much as economy class.*

first-class hotel /ˌfɜːst klɑːs həʊ'tel/ *noun* HOTELS a very good hotel, with comfortable rooms and a wide range of services

first-class mail /ˌfɜːst klɑːs 'meɪl/ *noun* the most expensive mail service, designed to be faster than second-class ○ *A first-class letter should get to Scotland in a day.*

first freedom /ˌfɜːst 'friːdəm/ *noun* AIR TRAVEL the right to overfly a country without landing at an airport in that country

first in the field /ˌfɜːst ɪn ðə 'fiːld/ *noun* BUSINESS the first company to bring out a product or to start a service

first name /'fɜːst neɪm/ *noun* a person's Christian name or given name, as opposed to the surname or family name

first night /ˌfɜːst 'naɪt/ *noun* ENTERTAINMENT the official opening performance of a play or entertainment

first option /ˌfɜːst 'ɒpʃən/ *noun* the right to be able to be the first to decide whether to buy or take something

fiscal year /ˌfɪskəl 'jɪə/ *noun* BUSINESS same as **tax year**

fish /fɪʃ/ *noun* FOOD a cold-blooded animal with fins and scales, that lives in water (NOTE: There is no plural form when referring to the food: *You should eat some fish every week.*) ■ *verb* SPORT to try to catch fish

COMMENT: Fish is high in protein, phosphorus, iodine and vitamins A and D. White fish has very little fat. Certain constituents of fish oil are thought to help prevent the accumulation of cholesterol on artery walls.

fish and chips /ˌfɪʃ ən 'tʃɪps/ *noun* FOOD a traditional British food, obtained from special shops, where portions of fish fried in batter are sold with chips

fish-and-chip shop /ˌfɪʃ ən ˈtʃɪp ʃɒp/ noun CATERING a shop selling fried fish and chips, and usually other food such as pies ○ *Don't bother cooking – I'll just pop down to the fish-and-chip shop and get some plaice and chips.* Also called **chip shop**, **fish shop 2**

fishbone /ˈfɪʃbəʊn/ noun a bone in a fish

fishcake /ˈfɪʃkeɪk/ noun FOOD a round cake of fish and potato mixed together and fried

fish chef /ˈfɪʃ ʃef/ noun CATERING the chef in charge of preparing fish dishes. Also called **chef poissonnier**

fisherman /ˈfɪʃəmən/ noun SPORT a man who catches fish, either as a job or for sport

fisherman's pie /ˌfɪʃəmənz ˈpaɪ/ noun FOOD same as **fish pie**

fish farm /ˈfɪʃ fɑːm/ noun a place where fish are raised in large numbers in special tanks

fish fingers /ˌfɪʃ ˈfɪŋgəz/ plural noun FOOD pieces of white fish shaped into oblongs and coated with breadcrumbs and fried ○ *The children don't like fresh fish, but they do like fish fingers.* (NOTE: The US English is **fish sticks**.)

fish fork /ˈfɪʃ fɔːk/ noun CATERING a fork with flat prongs used with a fish knife for eating fish

fishing /ˈfɪʃɪŋ/ noun the sport or industry of catching fish ○ *The sign said 'no fishing'.*

fishing boat /ˈfɪʃɪŋ bəʊt/ noun a boat used for fishing

fishing harbour /ˌfɪʃɪŋ ˈhɑːbə/ noun a harbour which is used by fishing boats

fishing port /ˈfɪʃɪŋ pɔːt/ noun a port which is used mainly by fishing boats

fishing rod /ˈfɪʃɪŋ rɒd/ noun a long pole to which is attached a line and hook

fishing tackle /ˈfɪʃɪŋ ˌtæk(ə)l/ noun all the equipment used by a fisherman

fish kettle /ˈfɪʃ ˌket(ə)l/ noun CATERING a long metal container for cooking a whole fish

fish knife /ˈfɪʃ naɪf/ noun CATERING a special wide knife, with a blunt blade, used when eating fish

fish paste /ˈfɪʃ peɪst/ noun FOOD a soft mixture of dried or salted fish, sold in pots, and served spread on bread or in sandwiches

fish pie /ˈfɪʃ ˌpaɪ/ noun FOOD a dish of various types of fish, cooked in a white sauce with a topping of potatoes. Also called **fisherman's pie**

fish shop /ˈfɪʃ ˈʃɒp/ noun CATERING **1.** a shop selling raw fish ○ *The fish shop has*

some wonderful fresh salmon. **2.** same as **fish-and-chip shop**

fish slice /ˈfɪʃ slaɪs/ noun CATERING a wide flat utensil used for turning fish and removing it from a frying pan

fish sticks /ˈfɪʃ ˈstɪk/ plural noun US FOOD another spelling of **fish fingers**

fit /fɪt/ adjective **1.** suitable for something ○ *The meat was declared to be fit for human consumption.* **2.** healthy and having a lot of physical energy ○ *He keeps fit by jogging every day.* ■ verb to be the right size or shape ○ *The chef's cap doesn't fit me.* ■ noun MEDICAL a sudden attack of a disorder, especially convulsions and epilepsy

FIT abbreviation AIR TRAVEL frequent independent traveller

fitness centre /ˈfɪtnəs ˌsentə/, **fitness club** noun SPORT a special room or rooms in a hotel or other building with sauna, gymnasium, etc., where customers can go to take exercise

fitted carpet /ˌfɪtɪd ˈkɑːpɪt/ noun carpet cut to the exact size of the room and fixed to the floor

fitted cupboard /ˌfɪtɪd ˈkʌbəd/ noun a specially made cupboard which fits into a bedroom, bathroom or kitchen

fittings /ˈfɪtɪŋz/ plural noun objects in a property which are sold with the property but are not permanently fixed and can be removed, such as carpets or shelves

five-dollar bill /ˌfaɪv ˌdɒlə ˈbɪl/ noun FINANCE a bank note for five dollars

five-star hotel /ˌfaɪv stɑː həʊˈtel/ noun HOTELS a very good hotel, with luxurious rooms and higher prices

fix /fɪks/ verb **1.** to arrange something, or to come to an agreement with somebody about something ○ *The date for the reception has been fixed for 10th October.* **2.** to repair something ○ *The technicians are coming to fix the telephone switchboard.* ○ *Can you fix the flat tyre?*

fixed /fɪkst/ adjective permanent, which cannot be removed

fixed assets /ˌfɪkst ˈæsets/ plural noun BUSINESS same as **capital assets**

fixed capital /ˌfɪkst ˈkæpɪt(ə)l/ noun BUSINESS capital in the form of fixed assets

fixed costs /ˌfɪkst ˈkɒsts/ plural noun BUSINESS business costs which do not rise with the quantity of the product made or with the amount of business done by a restaurant or hotel

fixed expenses /ˌfɪkst ɪkˈspensɪz/ plural noun FINANCE money which is spent regularly on things such as rent, electricity and telephone

fixed interest /ˌfɪkst 'ɪntrəst/ *noun* BUSINESS interest which is paid at a set rate

fixed-price agreement /fɪkst 'praɪs əˌgriːmənt/ *noun* BUSINESS an agreement where a company provides a service or a product at a price which stays the same for the whole period of the agreement

fixed rate /ˌfɪkst 'reɪt/ *noun* a charge which cannot be changed

fixed scale of charges /ˌfɪkst skeɪl əv 't ʃɑːdʒɪz/ *noun* BUSINESS a rate of charging which cannot be altered

fixtures /'fɪkstʃəz/ *plural noun* objects in a property which are permanently attached to it, such as sinks and lavatories

fixtures and fittings /ˌfɪkstʃəz ən 'fɪtɪŋz/ *plural noun* objects in a property which are sold with the property, both those which cannot be removed and those which can

fix up with /ˌfɪks ʌp 'wɪð/ *verb* to arrange something for someone ○ *The travel desk fixed me up with a car at the airport.* ○ *Can you fix me up with a room for tomorrow night?*

fizz /fɪz/ *noun* BEVERAGES champagne (*informal*) ○ *Let's have a drink, there's a bottle of fizz in the fridge.*

fizzy /'fɪzi/ *adjective* BEVERAGES containing bubbles of gas ○ *I don't like fizzy orange – do you have any squash?*

flag /flæg/ *noun* a piece of cloth with a design on it which is the symbol of a country or company ○ *a ship flying a British flag* □ **ship sailing under a flag of convenience** a ship flying the flag of a country which may have no ships of its own, but allows ships of other countries to be registered in its ports

flag airline, flag carrier *noun* AIR TRAVEL the main national airline of a country, seen as the representative of the country abroad

flagship /'flægʃɪp/ *noun* SHIPS AND BOATS the main or largest ship belonging to a shipping line

flagship hotel /'flægʃɪp həʊˌtel/ *noun* HOTELS the main hotel belonging to a chain

flaky pastry /ˌfleɪki 'peɪstri/ *noun* BREAD, ETC. a type of soft pastry which breaks into flakes easily when cooked

flambé /'flɒmbeɪ/ CATERING *adjective* having had brandy or other alcohol poured over it and set alight ■ *verb* to pour brandy or other alcohol over food and set it alight ○ *pancakes flambéed in brandy*

flambé lamp /'flɒmbeɪ læmp/ *noun* CATERING same as **chafing lamp**

flan /flæn/ *noun* **1.** FOOD an open tart ○ *an apricot flan* **2.** DESSERTS a French word for a custard tart

flapjack /'flæpdʒæk/ *noun* BREAD, ETC. a flat cake made of oats, honey, nuts, etc.

flash-freeze /ˌflæʃ 'friːz/ *verb* CATERING to freeze produce very rapidly, just after it has been picked or caught ○ *We use a unique flash-freeze packaging process.*

flat /flæt/ *adjective* **1.** BEVERAGES (*of a drink*) not fizzy when it ought to be ○ *This beer is flat.* ○ *The champagne has gone flat.* **2.** fixed, not changing ○ *a flat fee* ■ *noun* **1.** a set of rooms, usually on one level, used as living accommodation ○ *He has a flat in the centre of town.* ○ *She is buying a flat close to her office.* (NOTE: The US English is **apartment**.) **2.** CATERING a flat dish with low straight sides, e.g. a ramekin

flat bed /'flæt bed/ *noun* AIR TRAVEL same as **sky bed**

flat rate /ˌflæt 'reɪt/ *noun* a charge which always stays the same ○ *We pay a flat rate for bed and breakfast.*

flat swap /'flæt swɒp/ *noun* TOURISM an arrangement where two families exchange flats for a holiday

flat tyre /ˌflæt 'taɪə/ *noun* ROAD TRAVEL a tyre which has a leak in it so that the air has come out

flatware /'flætweə/ *noun* **1.** CATERING same as **cutlery 2.** flat pieces of china, e.g. plates

flavour /'fleɪvə/ *noun* taste ○ *The dish has a distinctive Italian flavour.* ■ *verb* CATERING to add spices and seasoning in cooking to add a flavour to something (NOTE: [all senses] The US spelling is **flavor**.)

flavoured /'fleɪvəd/ *adjective, suffix* tasting of something ○ *a lemon-flavoured drink*

flavour enhancer /'fleɪvə ɪnˌhɑːnsə/ *noun* a substance added to processed food or drink to improve its flavour

flavouring /'fleɪvərɪŋ/ *noun* CATERING a substance added to food to give a particular taste

flavouring agent /ˌfleɪvərɪŋ 'eɪdʒ(ə)nt/ *noun* CATERING a substance added to give flavour

flea /fliː/ *noun* a tiny insect which sucks blood and is a parasite on animals and humans

COMMENT: Fleas can transmit disease, most especially bubonic plague which is transmitted by infected rat fleas.

fleabag /ˈfliːbæg/ *noun* a cheap shabby hotel or lodging house (*informal*)

flea market /ˈfliː ˌmɑːkɪt/ *noun* ENTERTAINMENT a market, usually in the open air, selling cheap second-hand goods

fleece /fliːs/ *verb* to charge someone too much ○ *The bars round the harbour are waiting to fleece the tourists.*

fleet /fliːt/ *noun* **1.** SHIPS AND BOATS a group of ships belonging together **2.** TRAVEL a group of vehicles belonging to the same owner ○ *the airline's fleet of Boeing 747s* ○ *The hotel has a fleet of limousines to take guests to the airport.*

flesh /fleʃ/ *noun* **1.** the soft part of the body covering the bones **2.** the soft part of a fruit ○ *a melon with pink flesh*

flexible /ˈfleksɪb(ə)l/ *adjective* adaptable, easily changed ○ *A fully flexible business-class ticket is £360.*

'…the lack of reasonably priced yet flexible tickets is one of the biggest complaints among European business people' [*Business Traveller*]

flight /flaɪt/ *noun* **1.** AIR TRAVEL a journey by an aircraft ○ *Flight AC267 is leaving from Gate 46.* ○ *He missed his flight.* ○ *I always take the afternoon flight to Rome.* ○ *If you hurry you will catch the six o'clock flight to Paris.* **2.** a series of straight steps between floors in a building ○ *There are two flights of stairs up to the bedrooms.*

flight attendant /ˈflaɪt əˌtendənt/ *noun* AIR TRAVEL somebody who looks after passengers during a flight. Also called **steward**, **stewardess**, **air hostess**

flight bag /ˈflaɪt bæg/ *noun* a soft suitcase of a size that can be carried on an aircraft

flight coupon /ˈflaɪt ˌkuːpɒn/ *noun* a portion of an airline ticket that indicates the departure and arrival points of a passenger for a single journey or each leg of a journey

flight crew /ˈflaɪt kruː/, **flight deck crew** *noun* AIR TRAVEL the captain, copilot, flight engineer and navigator, who are involved with the flying of an aircraft, as opposed to the 'cabin crew'

flight deck /ˈflaɪt dek/ *noun* AIR TRAVEL a section at the front of a large aircraft where the pilots sit

flight engineer /ˈflaɪt ˌendʒɪnɪə/ *noun* AIR TRAVEL a member of the flight deck crew who is responsible for the engines, hydraulics, electrical systems, etc., during flight

flight information /flaɪt ˌɪnfəˈmeɪʃ(ə)n/ *noun* AIR TRAVEL information about flight times

flight number /ˈflaɪt ˌnʌmbə/ *noun* AIR TRAVEL the number given to a specific flight, consisting of the airline designator code followed by three figures

flight recorder /ˈflaɪt rɪˌkɔːdə/ *noun* AIR TRAVEL a device carried in a plane which records what happens during a flight, including conversations between pilots and control tower. Also called **black box**

flightseeing /ˈflaɪtˌsiːɪŋ/ *noun* TOURISM the practice or business of transporting tourists to otherwise inaccessible wilderness areas by helicopter, for viewing the areas by air or for organised hikes

flip chart /ˈflɪp tʃɑːt/ *noun* a stand with large sheets of paper clipped together

COMMENT: Flip charts are a way of showing information to a group of people; a speaker writes on a sheet of paper which can then be turned over to show the next sheet.

float trip /ˈfləʊt trɪp/ *noun* a trip along a river on a raft

floor /flɔː/ *noun* **1.** the part of the room which you walk on **2.** all the rooms on one level in a building ○ *She got into the lift and pushed the button for the fourth floor.* ○ *The ladies' hair salon is on the first floor.* ○ *Her office is on the 26th floor.* ○ *We were given a bedroom on the top floor* or *a top-floor bedroom, overlooking the sea.* (NOTE: The numbering of floors is different in Britain and the USA. The floor at street level is the **ground floor** in Britain but the **first floor** in the USA. Each floor in the USA is one number higher than the same floor in Britain.)

floor attendant /ˈflɔː əˌtendənt/ *noun* HOTELS a waiter responsible for room service in a series of hotel rooms on the same floor. Also called **chef d'étage**

floor maid /ˈflɔː meɪd/ *noun* HOTELS a maid who cleans rooms on one floor of a hotel

floor manager /ˈflɔː ˌmænɪdʒə/ *noun* US BUSINESS somebody in charge of the sales staff in a department store

floor pantry /ˈflɔː ˌpæntri/ *noun* HOTELS a small room serving one floor of a hotel, where the floor waiter prepares trays to take to guests' bedrooms and brings back dirty plates and glasses after use

floor plan /ˈflɔː plæn/ *noun* a drawing of a floor in a building, showing where different rooms, stairs and emergency exits are

floor polish /ˈflɔː ˌpɒlɪʃ/ *noun* wax used to make wooden floors shiny

floor service /ˈflɔː ˌsɜːvɪs/ *noun* HOTELS service on one floor of a hotel

floorshow /'flɔː ʃəʊ/ *noun* ENTERTAIN-MENT a show of e.g. dancers, singers, comedians or a striptease in a club, bar, restaurant or other public place ○ *The floorshow starts at 10.30.*

floor space /'flɔː speɪs/ *noun* an area of floor in a building ○ *The hotel has 35,000 square metres of floor space on three floors.*

floor surface /'flɔː ˌsɜːfɪs/ *noun* the covering for the surface of a floor e.g. tiles, carpet, wood, etc.

flora /'flɔːrə/ *noun* the wild plants of an area ○ *The flora and fauna of the deserts.* Compare **fauna** (NOTE: The plural form is **florae**.)

floral sugarcraft /ˌflɔːrəl 'ʃʊɡəkrɑːft/ *noun* CATERING the art of making flowers out of icing sugar

floret /'flɒrət/ *noun* a little flower which is part of a flowerhead, such as a cauliflower

florist /'flɒrɪst/ *noun* somebody who sells flowers ○ *Florists are very busy in the days before Valentine's Day.*

florist's /'flɒrɪsts/ *noun* same as **flower shop** ○ *She bought some flowers at the florist's.*

flotel /fləʊ'tel/ *noun* HOTELS a floating hotel

flotilla /flə'tɪlə/ *noun* SHIPS AND BOATS a group of small ships sailing together ○ *We went flotilla cruising in the Aegean.*

flour /flaʊə/ *noun* FOOD a grain crushed to powder, used for making bread, cakes, etc. ○ *wheat flour* ○ *rice flour*

flourishing /'flʌrɪʃɪŋ/ *adjective* doing good business ○ *She runs a flourishing tour company.*

floury /'flaʊri/ *adjective* like flour

floury potatoes /ˌflaʊri pə'teɪtəʊz/ *plural noun* FOOD potatoes which become soft and powdery when cooked

flow /fləʊ/ *noun* the movement of things such as liquid or air, or of people ○ *The flow of tourists into the temple has worn away the steps.* ■ *verb* to move along smoothly ○ *The river flows very fast here, and bathing is forbidden.*

flow chart /'fləʊ tʃɑːt/, **flow diagram** /'fləʊ ˌdaɪəɡræm/ *noun* a diagram showing the arrangement of various work processes in a series

flower /'flaʊə/ *noun* the colourful part of a plant, which attracts insects and produces fruit or seeds ○ *A bouquet of flowers and a basket of fruit is left in each suite with the compliments of the management.* ○ *Fresh*

flowers are put on the dining room tables every evening.

flower garden /'flaʊə ˌɡɑːd(ə)n/ *noun* a garden with flowers growing in it, as opposed to a vegetable garden

flower shop /'flaʊə ʃɒp/ *noun* a shop which sells flowers. Also called **florist's**

flower show /'flaʊə ʃəʊ/ *noun* ENTERTAINMENT an exhibition of flowers

flume /fluːm/ *noun* a theme park ride in which small boats go down a water chute

flush /flʌʃ/ *verb* □ **to flush the toilet** to pull or push a knob or handle to get rid of the waste in a toilet bowl

flush toilet /ˌflʌʃ 'tɔɪlət/ *noun* a toilet where the waste matter is removed by a rush of water

flute /fluːt/ *noun* CATERING a tall narrow wineglass on a stem, used for serving champagne

fly /flaɪ/ *noun* a small insect with wings which eats food and spreads diseases ○ *There are clouds of flies around the meat stalls in the market.* ○ *Waiter, there's a fly in my soup!* (NOTE: The plural form is **flies**.) ■ *verb* AIR TRAVEL to move through the air in an aircraft ○ *The chairman is flying to Germany on business.* ○ *The overseas sales manager flies about 100,000 miles a year visiting the agents.* ○ *We fly to Athens, and then take a bus to the hotel.* (NOTE: **flies – flew – flown**)

fly-by-night /'flaɪ baɪ ˌnaɪt/ *adjective* referring to something, e.g. a company, which is not reliable and might disappear to avoid paying debts (*informal*) ○ *I want a reputable tour operator, not one of these fly-by-night outfits.*

fly-drive holiday /flaɪ draɪv/, **fly-drive package** *noun* AIR TRAVEL an arrangement where the traveller flies to an airport and has a rented car waiting for him or her to pick up, the rent of the car being paid in advance as part of the package price ○ *We have many fly-drive holidays still available.*

fly killer /'flaɪ ˌkɪlə/ *noun* a device or spray for killing flies

flypaper /'flaɪpeɪpə/ *noun* a special paper, treated with chemicals, which will kill flies which stick to its surface

fly-stay /ˌflaɪ 'steɪ/ *adjective* HOTELS referring to an arrangement where you book a hotel at the same time as booking a plane ticket ○ *Check out fly-stay deals which can provide considerable savings.*

fly swatter /'flaɪ ˌswɒtə/ *noun* a small fan, held in the hand, used to chase away and squash flies

focaccia /fə'kætʃə/ *noun* a flat Italian bread, often sprinkled with a topping before baking, and served hot or cold

fog /fɒg/ *noun* a thick mist through which it is difficult to see ○ *The airport was closed by fog.* ○ *Drivers are asked to drive slowly when there is fog on the motorway.*

fogbound /'fɒgbaʊnd/ *adjective* AIR TRAVEL prevented from travelling because of fog ○ *Six planes were fogbound at Heathrow.* ○ *Fogbound travellers were advised to take a bus.*

foggy /'fɒgi/ *adjective* covered in fog ○ *It's dangerous to drive fast when it's foggy.* ○ *It's often foggier than this in November.*

fog lights /'fɒg laɪts/ *plural noun* very bright red lights at the rear of a car, which are lit when driving in fog

foie gras /ˌfwɑː 'grɑː/ *noun* goose liver that is swollen because the bird has been forced to eat large amounts of maize

foil /fɔɪl/ *noun* a thin metal sheet □ (**cooking) foil** a thin sheet of aluminium or tin used especially to wrap food in □ **foil-wrapped** wrapped in foil ○ *foil-wrapped steamed fish* ○ *foil-wrapped butter portions*

fold away /ˌfəʊld ə'weɪ/ *verb* to bend something so that it takes less space

fold-away seats /ˌfəʊld ə,weɪ 'siːts/ *plural noun* seats which can be folded up to take less room

fold-away table /ˌfəʊld ə,weɪ 'teɪb(ə)l/ *noun* TRAVEL a table attached to the back of the seat in front of the passenger, which can be folded away after use

folder /'fəʊldə/ *noun* a cardboard envelope for holding papers

folding /'fəʊldɪŋ/ *adjective* possible to fold up, e.g. to store more easily ○ *They brought in some folding chairs as there were not enough chairs for all the guests.*

following wind /ˌfɒləʊɪŋ 'wɪnd/ *noun* TRAVEL same as **tailwind**

fondue /'fɒndjuː/ *noun* FOOD a dish eaten by dipping small pieces of food into a pot that contains e.g. melted cheese or hot oil

fondue bourguignonne /ˌfɒnduə ˌbɔːgɪn'jɒn/ *noun* FOOD same as **cheese fondue**

food /fuːd/ *noun* things which you eat ○ *He is very fond of Indian food.* ○ *The food in the staff restaurant is excellent.* ○ *This restaurant is famous for its food.* ○ *Do you like Chinese food?* ○ *This food tastes funny.*

food additive /'fuːd ˌædətɪv/ *noun* CATERING same as **additive**

food allergen /'fuːd ˌælədʒen/ *noun* CATERING a substance in food which produces an allergy

food allergy /'fuːd ˌælədʒi/ *noun* CATERING a reaction caused by sensitivity to particular foods, some of the commonest being strawberries, chocolate, milk, eggs and oranges

food and beverage /ˌfuːd ən 'bev(ə)rɪdʒ/ *noun* HOTELS food and drink as served in a hotel's restaurants, bars and room service. Abbr **F & B**

> 'F&B is a headache for all hoteliers. Doing away with F&B removes high operating costs and focuses management attention on room management and room sales' [*Caterer and Hotelkeeper*]
> '…the successful candidate will have full F&B responsibility for the golf clubhouse, the fitness club, the brasserie and conference centre' [*Caterer & Hotelkeeper*]

food and beverage facilities /ˌfuːd ən 'bev(ə)rɪdʒ fə,sɪlɪtiz/ *plural noun* CATERING facilities for serving food and drink in a hotel

food and beverage manager /ˌfuːd ən 'bev(ə)rɪdʒ ˌmænɪdʒə/ *noun* CATERING somebody who is in charge of ordering, preparing and serving food and drink in the restaurants, bars, and in the room service of a large hotel

Food and Drink Federation /ˌfuːd ən 'drɪŋk ˌfedəreɪʃ(ə)n/ *noun* an association that represents the interests of food and drink manufacturers in the United Kingdom. Abbr **FDF**

foodborne illness /ˌfuːdbɔːn 'ɪlnəs/ *noun* MEDICAL same as **food poisoning**

food cover /'fuːd ˌkʌvə/ *noun* CATERING any unit of food served to a guest, from a cup of tea to a full meal

food cycle /'fuːd ˌsaɪk(ə)l/ *noun* CATERING the cycle by which food passes from supplier to hotel or restaurant and then to the ultimate consumer

food handler /'fuːd ˌhændlə/ *noun* CATERING somebody who touches food, as part of his or her job

food handling /'fuːd ˌhændlɪŋ/ *noun* CATERING the act of touching food as part of your job

food hygiene /'fuːd ˌhaɪdʒiːn/ *noun* CATERING action to keep clean, healthy conditions for handling, storing and serving food

food poisoning /'fuːd ˌpɔɪz(ə)nɪŋ/ *noun* MEDICAL an illness caused by eating food which is contaminated with bacteria ○ *The hospital had to deal with six cases of food* *poisoning.* ○ *All the people at the party went down with food poisoning.*

COMMENT: Food poisoning, or foodborne illness, can be caused by chemicals present in food (some chemicals are naturally present in plants, but others, such as insecticides, get into the food chain from overuse by farmers). Most cases of food poisoning are biological, caused either by eating poisonous food (such as toadstools) or food which is contaminated by bacteria.

food processor /ˈfuːd ˌprəʊsesə/ *noun* CATERING a machine for chopping, cutting, slicing and mixing food

Food Protection Certificate /ˌfuːd prə ˈtekʃ(ə)n səˌtɪfɪkət/ *noun* CATERING a certificate awarded to an individual who has successfully completed a course in food protection

food sales /ˈfuːd seɪlz/ *plural noun* BUSINESS turnover from the sale of food

foodservice, food service *noun* CATERING the activity of providing food to customers □ **the foodservice industry** the industry comprising hotels, restaurants, caterers and their suppliers

Food Standards Agency /ˌfuːd ˈstændədz ˌeɪdənsi/ *noun* CATERING a British government agency set up in 2000 to offer advice on food safety, and make sure that food sold is safe to eat. Abbr **FSA**

foodstuffs /ˈfuːdstʌfs/ *plural noun* CATERING things which can be used as food

food vendor license /ˌfuːd ˈvendə ˌlaɪs(ə)ns/ *noun* US CATERING a licence to sell food, which is issued by the local authority and has to be bought by any person or company which sells food

fool /fuːl/ *noun* DESSERTS a type of creamed fruit dessert, usually made with acid fruit such as gooseberries or rhubarb

foot /fʊt/ *noun* **1.** a part of the body at the end of the leg □ **on foot** walking ○ *We visited the main temples on foot.* ○ *The rush-hour traffic is so bad that it is quicker to go to the museum on foot.* **2.** the bottom part of something ○ *He signed his name at the foot of the invoice.* **3.** a unit of measurement equal to about 30 centimetres ○ *a six-foot-wide rug* ○ *The piece of cloth is two feet long.* ○ *The hotel beds are less than 6 feet by three.* (NOTE: The plural form is **feet** for (1) and (3); there is no plural for (2). In measurements, **foot** is usually written **ft** or ' after figures: *10ft; 10'.*) ■ *verb* □ **to foot the bill** to pay the costs of something ○ *The airline will foot the bill for the hotel.*

'...the trail is mostly above 9,000ft and snow tends to lie on the passes until well into July' [*TGO – The Great Outdoors*]

footbridge /ˈfʊtbrɪdʒ/ *noun* RAIL TRAVEL a small bridge for people to walk across, e.g. over a stream or railway line ○ *To avoid accidents, children must use the footbridge to cross the road on their way to school.*

footpath /ˈfʊtpɑːθ/ *noun* a path for people to walk on, but not to ride on ○ *The footpath leads through the wood and along the edge of a field.*

forbid /fəˈbɪd/ *verb* to tell someone not to do something, to say that something must not be done ○ *Women are forbidden to go into the temple.* ○ *Swimming in the reservoir is forbidden.* ○ *We forbid the staff from using the front entrance.* (NOTE: **forbidding – forbade – forbidden**)

force /fɔːs/ *noun* **1.** strength □ **to be in force** to be operating or working ○ *The new schedules have been in force since January.* □ **to come into force** to start to operate or work ○ *The new regulations will come into force on January 1st.* **2.** an organised group of people ■ *verb* to make someone do something ○ *Competition has forced the tour company to lower its prices.*

force majeure /ˌfɔːs mæˈʒɜː/ *noun* something which happens which is out of the control of the parties who have signed a contract and which prevents the contract being fulfilled, e.g. strike, war or storm

forcemeat /ˈfɔːsmiːt/ *noun* FOOD a mixture of breadcrumbs, onions and flavouring, used to stuff meat and poultry

forcing bag /ˈfɔːsɪŋ bæg/ *noun* CATERING a soft bag of fabric or plastic, to which various nozzles can be attached, used to squeeze out a soft substance, such as icing or pureed potato, in a decorative way

fore and aft /ˌfɔː ən ˈɑːft/ *adverb* AIR TRAVEL at the front and at the back of an aircraft ○ *The toilets are located fore and aft.*

forecast /ˈfɔːkɑːst/ *noun* a description or calculation of what will probably happen in the future □ **medium-range weather forecast** a forecast covering two to five days ahead ■ *verb* to calculate or to say what will probably happen in the future ○ *They are forecasting rain for tomorrow.* ○ *Experts have forecast a steady rise in the number of tourists.* (NOTE: **forecasting – forecast**)

forecourt /ˈfɔːkɔːt/ *noun* ROAD TRAVEL an area in front of a building, into which vehicles can be driven ○ *There are taxis waiting in the station forecourt.* ○ *He drove into the* *petrol station forecourt and asked for some-one to wash his windscreen.*

foreign /ˈfɒrɪn/ *adjective* not from your own country ○ *Foreign tourists are all over the town for the Easter break.* ○ *We are increasing our trade with foreign countries.*

foreign currency /ˌfɒrɪn ˈkʌrənsi/ *noun* FINANCE money of another country

foreign currency account /ˌfɒrɪn ˈkʌrənsi əˌkaʊnt/ *noun* FINANCE a bank account in the currency of another country, e.g. a dollar account

foreigner /ˈfɒrɪnə/ *noun* somebody from another country

foreign exchange /ˌfɒrən ɪksˈtʃeɪndʒ/ *noun* FINANCE **1.** the business of exchanging the money of one country for that of another **2.** money of another country

foreign exchange broker /ˌfɒrɪn ɪks ˈtʃeɪndʒ ˌbrəʊkə/, **foreign exchange dealer** /ˈdiːlə/ *noun* FINANCE somebody who deals on the foreign exchange market

foreign exchange dealing /ˌfɒrɪn ɪks ˈtʃeɪndʒ ˌdiːlɪŋ/ *noun* FINANCE the business of buying and selling foreign currencies

foreign exchange market /ˌfɒrɪn ɪks ˈtʃeɪndʒ ˌmɑːkɪt/ *noun* FINANCE a market where people buy and sell foreign currencies

foreign exchange transfer /ˌfɒrɪn ɪks ˈtʃeɪndʒ ˌtrænsfɜː/ *noun* FINANCE the transfer of money from one country to another

foreign goods /ˌfɒrɪn ˈɡʊdz/ *plural noun* BUSINESS goods manufactured in other countries

foreign money order /ˌfɒrɪn ˈmʌni ˌɔːdə/ *noun* FINANCE a money order in a foreign currency which is payable to someone living in a foreign country. Also called **international money order**, **overseas money order**

foreign trade /ˌfɒrɪn ˈtreɪd/ *noun* BUSINESS same as **overseas trade**

foreign visitor /ˌfɒrɪn ˈvɪzɪtə/ *noun* same as **overseas visitor**

foresee /fɔːˈsiː/ *verb* to feel in advance that something will happen ○ *They foresee a big increase in tourism.* (NOTE: **foresees – foresaw**)

forest /ˈfɒrɪst/ *noun* a large area covered with trees ○ *The whole river basin is covered with tropical forest.* ○ *Forest fires are widespread in the dry season and can sometimes be started by lightning.* ○ *In winter bears come out of the forest to search for food.*

forester /ˈfɒrɪstə/, **forest ranger** /ˈfɒrɪst ˈreɪndʒə/ *noun* somebody in charge of the management and protection of a forest

forestry /ˈfɒrɪstri/ *noun* the management of forests, woodlands and plantations of trees ○ *We studied forestry at agricultural college.* ○ *Forestry is becoming an important skill in Third World countries.*

Forestry Commission /ˈfɒrɪstri kə ˌmɪʃ(ə)n/ *noun* a British government agency responsible for the management of state-owned forests

COMMENT: The Forestry Commission seeks to attract tourists by making picnic areas, nature trails, etc., in its forests.

forex /ˈfɔːreks/, **Forex** *abbreviation* FINANCE foreign exchange

'…the amount of reserves sold by the authorities were not sufficient to move the $200 billion Forex market permanently' [*Duns Business Month*]

forge /fɔːdʒ/ *verb* to copy money or a signature, so as to trick someone ○ *He paid his bill with a forged £50 note.* ○ *When paying with a stolen credit card, she forged the signature on the slip.*

forged knife /ˌfɔːdʒd ˈnaɪf/ *noun* CATERING the best-quality kitchen knife, made of a single piece of steel which forms the blade and centre of the handle

forget /fəˈɡet/ *verb* not to remember something ○ *She forgot to tell the group that breakfast was at 7.30 sharp.* ○ *Don't forget we're leaving the hotel early tomorrow.* (NOTE: **forgetting – forgot – forgotten**)

fork /fɔːk/ *noun* **1.** CATERING a piece of cutlery, with a handle at one end and sharp points at the other, used for picking food up **2.** ROAD TRAVEL a place where a road divides into two new roads ■ *verb* **1.** ROAD TRAVEL to turn off a road ○ *Fork right at the next junction.* **2.** (*of a road*) to split into two parts

fork buffet, **fork luncheon** *noun* CATERING a lunch where food is eaten from a plate with a fork when standing up, as opposed to a 'finger buffet'

form /fɔːm/ *noun* an official printed paper with blank spaces which have to be filled in with information ○ *You have to fill in form A20.* ○ *Before entering the USA, all passengers must fill out a customs declaration form.*

formality /fɔːˈmælɪti/ *noun* something which has to be done to obey the law (NOTE: The plural form is **formalities**.)

fortified wine /ˌfɔːtɪfaɪd ˈwaɪn/ *noun* BEVERAGES wine which has extra alcohol added, e.g. port or sherry

fortify /ˈfɔːtɪfaɪ/ *verb* to make something strong □ **a fortified town** a town with thick walls round it to protect it

fortnight /ˈfɔːtnaɪt/ *noun* two weeks ○ *I saw him a fortnight ago.* ○ *We will be on holiday during the last fortnight of July.* (NOTE: **Fortnight** is not used in US English.)

forward /ˈfɔːwəd/ *adjective* **1.** in advance **2.** to be paid at a later date **3.** TRAVEL towards the front part of a ship or plane ○ *the forward section of an aircraft* ○ *The stewardess is in the forward galley.* ○ *The passenger lounge is forward of the dining saloon.* ■ *adverb* **1.** □ **to date a cheque forward** to put a later date than the present one on a cheque □ **charges forward** charges which will be paid by the customer when delivery is taken of the goods **2.** □ **to buy forward** to buy foreign currency before you need it, in order to be certain of the exchange rate □ **to sell forward** to sell foreign currency for delivery at a later date **3.** TRAVEL towards the front part of a ship or plane ○ *Please move forward to the passenger lounge.* ■ *verb* □ **to forward something to someone** to send something to someone ○ *We will forward the visa application to the consulate.* □ **please forward**, **to be forwarded** words written on an envelope, asking the person receiving it to send it on to the person whose name is written on it

forward bookings /ˌfɔːwəd ˈbʊkɪŋz/ *plural noun* reservations made in advance

forward buying /ˌfɔːwəd ˈbaɪɪŋ/ *noun* FINANCE the act of buying currency at today's price for delivery at a later date. Also called **buying forward**

forwarding address /ˈfɔːwədɪŋ əˌdres/ *noun* the address to which a person's mail can be sent on after he or she has left the current address ○ *They left the hotel and didn't leave a forwarding address.*

forwarding agent /ˈfɔːwədɪŋ ˌeɪdʒənt/ *noun* BUSINESS a person or company which arranges shipping and customs documents

forward rate /ˈfɔːwəd reɪt/, **forward exchange rate** *noun* FINANCE the rate for purchase of foreign currency at a fixed price for delivery at a later date ○ *What are the forward rates for the pound?*

foster /ˈfɒstə/ *verb* to take action to help something such as an idea to become successful ○ *Tourism fosters interest in other countries.*

four /fɔː/ *number* □ **the four O's** a simple way of summarising the essentials of a marketing operation, which are objects, objectives, organisation and operations □ **the four P's** a simple way of summarising the essentials of the marketing mix, which are product, price, promotion and place

four-lane motorway /ˌfɔː leɪn ˈməʊtəweɪ/ *noun* ROAD TRAVEL a motorway with tracks for two rows of traffic in each direction

four-poster bed /ˌfɔː ˌpəʊstə ˈbed/ *noun* an old-fashioned bed with four posts, one at each corner, which support a cover with curtains

four-star hotel /ˌfɔː stɑː həʊˈtel/ *noun* HOTELS a good hotel, with comfortable rooms

fowl /faʊl/ *noun* a domestic bird kept for food or for its eggs, e.g. a chicken, duck, turkey or goose (NOTE: The plural form is **fowl** or **fowls**.)

foyer /ˈfɔɪeɪ/ *noun* the entrance lobby of a hotel, restaurant, theatre or cinema ○ *We'll meet in the foyer at 9 p.m.* ○ *The foyer was full of tourists waiting to register.*

Fr *abbreviation* franc

franc /fræŋk/ *noun* FINANCE the currency used in Switzerland and some other countries ○ *It costs twenty-five Swiss francs.*

franchise /ˈfræntʃaɪz/ BUSINESS *noun* a licence to trade using a brand name and paying money for it ○ *She has bought a hot dog franchise.* ■ *verb* to sell licences for people to trade using a brand name and paying money for it ○ *His sandwich bar was so successful that he decided to franchise it.* ○ *The family owns a franchised chain of restaurants.*

'…the company wants to franchise many of its restaurants away from the three big metropolitan areas of London, Birmingham and Manchester. Although it has some existing franchisees it also has regional headquarters which can easily manage local restaurants.' [*Caterer & Hotelkeeper*]

franchisee /ˌfræntʃaɪˈziː/ *noun* BUSINESS somebody who trades under a franchise

franchiser /ˈfræntʃaɪzə/ *noun* BUSINESS somebody who licenses a franchise

franchising /ˈfræntʃaɪzɪŋ/ *noun* BUSINESS the act of selling a licence to trade as a franchise ○ *She runs her sandwich chain as a franchising operation.*

franchisor /ˈfræntʃaɪzə/ *noun* BUSINESS same as **franchiser**

frangipane /ˌfrændʒɪˈpɑːni/ *noun* FOOD an almond-flavoured cream or paste used in pastries, cakes and other sweet foods

frankfurter /ˈfræŋkfɜːtə/ *noun* MEAT a long thin sausage of spicy pork meat ○ *We've brought some frankfurters for the barbecue.* Also called **wiener**

COMMENT: Frankfurters originally came from Frankfurt in Germany, but are now made all over the world. They are cooked in hot water, and are the sausages used in hot dogs.

frappé /'fræpeɪ/ *adjective* BEVERAGES referring to a drink that is chilled by being poured over crushed ice

free /fri:/ *adjective, adverb* **1.** not costing any money ○ *We were given free tickets to the exhibition.* ○ *The price includes free transport from the airport to the hotel.* ○ *Goods are delivered free to the customer's hotel.* ○ *Catalogue and price list sent free on request.* □ **admission free** visitors do not have to pay □ **free of charge** with no payment to be made **2.** with no restrictions **3.** not busy, not occupied ○ *Are there any free tables in the restaurant?* ○ *I shall be free in a few minutes.* ○ *We always keep Friday afternoon free for a game of bridge.*

'…can free trade be reconciled with a strong dollar resulting from floating exchange rates?' [*Duns Business Month*]

'…free traders hold that the strong dollar is the primary cause of the nation's trade problems' [*Duns Business Month*]

freecarving /'fri:ˌkɑːvɪŋ/ *noun* a style of snowboarding that focuses on carving deep tracks in the snow with tight cornering rather than on doing stunts

free climbing /ˌfri: 'klaɪmɪŋ/ *noun* mountain or rock climbing done without aids such as spikes and ladders, though usually with ropes and other safety equipment

free currency /ˌfri: 'kʌrənsi/ *noun* FINANCE a currency which is allowed by the government to be bought and sold without restriction

freediving /'fri:ˌdaɪvɪŋ/ *noun* the extreme sport of submerging into deep water for as long as possible without the aid of oxygen tanks

freedom /'fri:dəm/ *noun* the state of being free to do something □ **the freedoms of the air** special internationally agreed rights given to airlines to allow them to fly without interference

free gift /ˌfri: 'ɡɪft/ *noun* MARKETING a present given by a shop or business to a customer who buys a particular amount of goods

free house /'fri: haʊs/ *noun* BARS a public house which does not belong to a brewery and so can serve any beer or spirits which the owner decides to serve

free of charge /ˌfri: əv 'tʃɑːdʒ/ *adjective* free, with no payment to be made

free parking /ˌfri: 'pɑːkɪŋ/ *noun* parking facilities that customers do not have to pay for

freephone /'fri:fəʊn/ *noun* MARKETING a system where you can telephone to reply to an advertisement, to place an order or to ask for information and the seller pays for the call ○ *The advertisement gives a freephone number for you to call.* (NOTE: In the UK, freephone numbers have the code 0800.)

free port /ˌfri: 'pɔːt/, **free trade zone** /ˌfri: 'treɪd ˌzəʊn/ *noun* a port or area where there are no customs duties to be paid

freepost /'fri:pəʊst/ *noun* MARKETING a system where you can write to an advertiser to place an order, to ask for information to be sent, and the seller pays the postage

free-range eggs /ˌfri: reɪndʒ 'eɡz/ *plural noun* FOOD eggs from hens that are allowed to run about in the open and eat more natural food, as opposed to battery hens

freeriding /'fri:ˌraɪdɪŋ/ *noun* a basic style of snowboarding that involves travelling over the snow without performing stunts

free-soloing /ˌfri: 'səʊləʊɪŋ/ *noun* the sport of climbing boulders and rock faces without a safety line or a partner to catch or break a fall

free trade /ˌfri: 'treɪd/ *noun* BUSINESS a system where goods can go from one country to another without any restrictions ○ *The government adopted a free trade policy.*

free trade area /ˌfri: 'treɪd ˌeəriə/ *noun* a group of countries between which no customs duties are paid

free trader /ˌfri: 'treɪdə/ *noun* BUSINESS somebody who is in favour of free trade

free trial /ˌfri: 'traɪəl/ *noun* the testing of something such as a machine with no payment involved ○ *to send a piece of equipment for two weeks' free trial*

freeway /'fri:weɪ/ *noun* US a major expressway where no toll charge is made ○ *We took the interstate freeway to San Diego.*

freeze /fri:z/ *verb* **1.** to change the state of something from liquid to solid because of the cold **2.** (*of weather*) to become very cold ○ *It was freezing when we reached the hotel.* **3.** CATERING to store food at below freezing point ○ *You can freeze fresh produce easily.* ○ *Strawberries cannot be frozen.* ◊ **flash-freeze 4.** BUSINESS to keep prices, costs, etc., at their present level and not allow them to rise ○ *We have frozen our prices for two years.* (NOTE: **freezing – froze – has frozen**)

freeze-dry /'fri:z draɪ/ *verb* CATERING to preserve food by freeze-drying

freeze-drying /'fri:z ˌdraɪɪŋ/ *noun* CATERING a method of preserving food by freezing rapidly and drying in a vacuum

freezer /'fri:zə/ *noun* CATERING a deep-freeze, where food is kept at very low temperatures ○ *Put the ice cream back into the freezer before it starts to melt.*

freezer burn /'fri:zə bɜ:n/ *noun* the pale dry spots that form when moisture evaporates from frozen food that is not properly wrapped

freezing point /'fri:zɪŋ pɔɪnt/ *noun* the temperature at which a liquid becomes solid ○ *The freezing point of water is 0°C.*

freight /freɪt/ *noun* **1.** BUSINESS the cost of transporting goods by air, sea or land ○ *At an auction, the buyer pays the freight.* **2.** □ **air freight** the shipping of goods in an aircraft ○ *to send a shipment by air freight* **3.** BUSINESS goods which are transported □ **to take on freight** to load goods onto a ship, train or truck ■ *verb* □ **to freight goods** to send goods ○ *We freight goods to all parts of the USA.*

freight rates /'freɪt reɪts/ *plural noun* the prices charged for sending freight

French /frentʃ/ *adjective* referring to France ■ *noun* the language spoken in France, Belgium and other countries

COMMENT: Because of the importance of French cooking (or 'cuisine'), French words and phrases are widely used in kitchens and menus.

French beans /ˌfrentʃ 'bi:nz/ *plural noun* VEGETABLES same as **green beans**

French bread /ˌfrentʃ 'bred/ *noun* bread in the form of a long thin stick

French dressing /ˌfrentʃ 'dresɪŋ/ *noun* SAUCES, ETC. same as **vinaigrette**

French fries /'frentʃ 'fraɪz/, **French fried potatoes** /'frentʃ 'fraɪd pə'teɪtəʊz/ *plural noun* FOOD thin stick-shaped pieces of potato, fried in deep oil or fat ○ *She ordered a cheeseburger and French fries.*

French onion soup /ˌfrentʃ ˌʌnjən 'su:p/ *noun* FOOD soup made with onions and stock, served with croutons

French service /ˌfrentʃ 'sɜ:vɪs/ *noun* CATERING **1.** a style of laying a table, with a large round plate, called the 'show plate' in the centre of each setting, a folded napkin on it, and cutlery and glasses beside it. The plate is not used for food, and may be removed, or other plates such as a soup plate may be put on it. **2.** a way of serving at a meal, where the waiter or waitress offers the guest a dish from the left, and the guest helps himself or herself from it

French thyme /ˌfrentʃ 'taɪm/ *noun* SAUCES, ETC. same as **common thyme**

French toast /ˌfrentʃ 'təʊst/ *noun* FOOD a slice of bread, dipped in beaten egg and fried, usually served with syrup or sprinkled with sugar

French window /ˌfrentʃ 'wɪndəʊ/ *noun* a door with glass panels, usually opening onto a garden

frequent /'fri:kwənt/ *adjective* happening often, or doing something often

'…cabin layouts, as with cabin service, good timekeeping, and flight frequency, are important influences on frequent travellers' choice of carrier' [*Business Travel*]

frequent flyer /ˌfri:kwənt 'flaɪə/ *noun* AIR TRAVEL somebody who flies often with the same company, and so gets special treatment ○ *He has a frequent flyer card.* ○ *When making reservations, quote your frequent flyer number.*

frequent guest /ˌfri:kwənt 'gest/ *noun* somebody who often stays at the same hotel or hotel chain, especially while travelling on business, and is therefore offered free overnight stays and other benefits

frequent independent traveller /frɪ ˌkwent ˌɪndɪpəndənt 'træv(ə)lə/ *noun* AIR TRAVEL an independent traveller who travels often. Abbr **FIT**

frequently /'fri:kwəntli/ *adverb* often ○ *We frequently get requests for information about camping facilities.*

fresh /freʃ/ *adjective, adverb* **1.** referring to food which has been made recently, or which has been recently picked, killed or caught, or which is not frozen or tinned □ **oven-fresh loaves** bread which has just been baked **2.** not used, not dirty

'…meat that has been frozen and then thawed should not be described as 'fresh'' [*Food Standards Agency*]

fresh air /ˌfreʃ 'eə/ *noun* the open air ○ *They came out of the mine into the fresh air.*

freshly /'freʃli/ *adverb* recently ○ *freshly picked strawberries*

freshly-squeezed orange juice /ˌfreʃli skwi:zd 'ɒrɪndʒ ˌdʒu:s/ *noun* BEVERAGES orange juice which has just been squeezed from the fruit, not taken from a can or carton

freshness /'freʃ(ə)nəs/ *noun* the state of being fresh ○ *When you buy fruit and vegetables, remember to check them for freshness.* ○ *Freshness is the main selling point of this chain of fish restaurants.*

fresh water /ˌfreʃ ˈwɔːtə/ *noun* water in rivers and lakes which contains almost no salt, as opposed to water in the sea

freshwater /ˈfreʃwɔːtə/ *adjective* containing or having its habitat in fresh water ○ *Some freshwater fish such as pike can withstand levels of acidity.*

fricassee /ˈfrɪkəseɪ/ *noun* FOOD a dish of pieces of meat cooked in a rich white sauce ○ *chicken fricassee* ■ *verb* CATERING to stew meat, usually chicken, with vegetables in a little water, which is then used to make a rich white sauce

fridge /frɪdʒ/ *noun* CATERING a refrigerator, a machine for keeping food cold (*informal*) ○ *The fridge is empty – we must buy some more food.* ○ *Shall I put the milk back in the fridge?*

fried /fraɪd/ *adjective* CATERING cooked in a little oil or fat ○ *Add the fried onions to the meat.* ○ *We had fried rice with our sweet and sour pork.* ◊ **fry**

fried egg /ˌfraɪd ˈeg/ *noun* FOOD an egg which has been fried in hot fat ○ *I had two fried eggs and bacon for breakfast.*

-friendly /frendli/ *suffix* with facilities that make it suitable for or easy to use by somebody ○ *child-friendly* ○ *user-friendly*

fries /fraɪz/ *plural noun* FOOD same as **French fries**

fringe /frɪndʒ/ *noun* an edge ○ *hotels on the fringe of the desert* ■ *verb* □ **fringed with palm trees**, **palm-fringed** with palm trees growing along the side

Fringe Theatre /ˌfrɪndʒ ˈθɪətə/ *noun* ENTERTAINMENT a general term referring to small theatres which put on mainly experimental plays and do not form part of the theatre establishment

frisk /frɪsk/ *verb* to search someone by running the hands over his or her body ○ *When they frisked him at the airport, they found a knife hidden under his shirt.*

fritter /ˈfrɪtə/ *noun* FOOD a piece of fruit, meat or vegetable, dipped in a mixture of flour, egg and milk and fried ○ *apple fritters* ○ *banana fritters*

fromage /frɒˈmɑːʒ/ *noun* DAIRY a French noun meaning cheese

fromage frais /ˌfrɒmɑːʒ ˈfreɪ/ *noun* DAIRY a fresh cheese with a light creamy taste and a texture like thick cream or yoghurt

front /frʌnt/ *noun* 1. the part of something which faces forward □ **in front of** ahead of, in the direction in which you are facing, or outside the front part of ○ *I'll meet you in front of the hotel.* ○ *The safety instructions are in the pocket in front of your seat.* 2. same as **seafront** ○ *The hotel is on the front.* ■ *adjective* most important, first

front desk /ˌfrʌnt ˈdesk/ *noun* HOTELS a reception desk at the entrance to a hotel or restaurant

front door /ˌfrʌnt ˈdɔː/ *noun* the main door to a house or building ○ *The reception gave him a key to the front door* or *to the main door of the hotel.*

front door key /ˌfrʌnt ˈdɔː ˌkiː/ *noun* HOTELS the key to a front door such as the main door of a hotel

front hall /ˌfrʌnt ˈhɔːl/ *noun* 1. a room or passage through which you enter a building 2. the people who work in the front part of a hotel

front office /ˌfrʌnt ˈɒfɪs/ *noun* HOTELS the main office of a hotel, with the reservations department and the reception desk

front office manager /ˌfrʌnt ˈɒfɪs ˌmænɪdʒə/ *noun* the manager in charge of the front office

front of house, front-of-the-house *noun* BUSINESS the part of a hotel which deals with customers direct, including departments such as reception, porters, room service and housekeeping

'…a team of three part-time staff cover front-of-house operations under the direction of the head waiter' [Caterer & Hotelkeeper]

front-of-house manager /ˌfrʌnt əv haʊs ˈmænɪdʒə/ *noun* HOTELS somebody in charge of the front part of a hotel, i.e. the entrance, reception and reservations area

front-of-house services /ˌfrʌnt əv haʊs ˈsɜːvɪsɪz/ *plural noun* HOTELS services which are in the front of a hotel, such as reception and porters

front-of-house staff /ˌfrʌnt əv ˈhaʊs ˌstɑːf/ *noun* BUSINESS staff who deal with customers, e.g. the receptionist, doorman and porters

frost /frɒst/ *noun* 1. the weather when the temperature is below the freezing point of water □ **ten degrees of frost** ten degrees below freezing point 2. a white covering on the ground or trees when the temperature is below freezing

froze /frəʊz/ ♦ **freeze**

frozen /ˈfrəʊz(ə)n/ *adjective* 1. very cold 2. at a temperature below freezing point ○ *Use frozen prawns if you can't get fresh ones.*

frozen food /ˈfrəʊz(ə)n fuːd/ *noun* CATERING food stored at a temperature below freezing point

fructose /ˈfrʌktəʊs/ *noun* the sugar found in honey and fruits such as figs

fruit /fruːt/ *noun* FOOD the part of a plant which contains the seeds and which is often eaten raw

COMMENT: Fruit contains fructose and is a good source of Vitamin C and some dietary fibre. Dried fruit has a higher sugar content but less Vitamin C than fresh fruit.

fruitarian /fruːˈteəriən/ *noun* somebody who only eats fruit

fruitcake /ˈfruːtkeɪk/ *noun* BREAD, ETC. a cake with a lot of dried fruit in it

fruit cocktail /ˌfruːt ˈkɒkteɪl/ *noun* DESSERTS a mixture of fruit

fruit juice /ˈfruːt dʒuːs/ *noun* BEVERAGES juice from fruit, often served as an appetiser or starter ○ *She started breakfast with a glass of fruit juice.*

COMMENT: The commonest fruit juices are: orange juice, apple juice, pineapple juice and grapefruit juice.

fruit machine /ˈfruːt məˌʃiːn/ *noun* a gambling machine where pictures of different types of fruit appear when you press a button ○ *He's always playing the fruit machines in the pub.*

fruit salad /ˌfruːt ˈsæləd/ *noun* DESSERTS pieces of fresh fruit mixed and served cold

fry /fraɪ/ *verb* CATERING to cook in oil or fat in a shallow pan ○ *Fry the onions on a low heat so that they don't burn.* ○ *Fry the eggs in some fat.* ◊ **deep-fry** (NOTE: **fries – frying – fried**)

fryer /ˈfraɪə/ *noun* CATERING a large device for frying quantities of food at the same time

frying pan /ˈfraɪɪŋ pæn/ *noun* a shallow, open pan used for frying ○ *Put some butter in the frying pan and fry the mushrooms.*

FSA *abbreviation* CATERING Food Standards Agency

ft /fʊt/ *abbreviation* foot

fuel surcharge /ˈfjuːəl ˌsɜːtʃɑːdʒ/ *noun* AIR TRAVEL an extra amount added to an air fare, to cover increased fuel costs which have come into effect since the air fare was calculated

full /fʊl/ *adjective* **1.** with as much inside it as it can contain ○ *The train was full of commuters.* ○ *The hotel is full next week.* **2.** complete, including everything ○ *The full wine list has more than 100 different types of wine.* **3.** □ **in full** completely ○ *refund paid in full* ○ *Give your name and address in full.* ○ *She accepted all our conditions in full.*

full board /ˌfʊl ˈbɔːd/ *noun* HOTELS a special rate for guests staying in a hotel, who take all their meals in the hotel. Also called **en pension rate**

full costs /ˌfʊl ˈkɒsts/ *plural noun* all the costs of a service

full cover /ˌfʊl ˈkʌvə/ *noun* FINANCE insurance cover against all risks

full-cream /ˌfʊl ˈkriːm/ *adjective* referring to milk that has had none of the cream or fat removed, or to products made with this kind of milk

full English breakfast /ˌfʊl ˌɪŋglɪʃ ˈbrekfəst/ *noun* CATERING a breakfast of cereals, eggs, bacon, toast and marmalade, served with tea or coffee

COMMENT: A traditional 'full English breakfast' may include cereals, porridge, or stewed fruit (such as prunes), grilled fish (such as kippers), bacon and eggs, sausages, kidneys, fried or grilled tomatoes or mushrooms and fried bread, followed by toast and marmalade and tea or coffee.

full fare /ˌfʊl ˈfeə/ *noun* TRAVEL a ticket for a journey by an adult paying the full price

full-fare economy passengers /ˌfʊl feə ɪˈkɒnəmi ˌpæsɪndʒəz/ *plural noun* AIR TRAVEL economy passengers who pay the full rate, with no discounts ○ *Some airlines provide more leg-room for full-fare economy passengers.*

full house /ˌfʊl ˈhaʊs/ *noun* HOTELS a hotel with no vacancies

full-length mirror /ˌfʊl leŋθ ˈmɪrə/ *noun* a mirror in which you can see a reflection of your whole body

full occupancy /ˌfʊl ˈɒkjʊpənsi/ *noun* HOTELS a situation where a hotel is completely full ○ *We're busy all the time, with up to three or four parties a night and full occupancy.*

full on licence /ˌfʊl ɒn ˈlaɪs(ə)ns/ *noun* BARS same as **justices' full on licence**

full payment /ˌfʊl ˈpeɪmənt/ *noun* same as **payment in full**

full price /ˌfʊl ˈpraɪs/ *noun* a price with no discount ○ *He bought a full-price ticket.*

full rate /ˌfʊl ˈreɪt/ *noun* the full charge, with no reductions

full refund /ˌfʊl ˈriːfʌnd/ *noun* same as **refund in full** ○ *He got a full refund when he complained that there were mice in his bedroom.*

full repairing lease /ˌfʊl rɪˈpeərɪŋ ˌliːs/ *noun* a lease where the tenant has to pay for all repairs to the property

full Scottish breakfast /ˌfʊl ˌskɒtɪʃ ˈbrekfəst/ *noun* CATERING a breakfast similar to a full English breakfast, but with porridge, kippers or herrings, and oatcakes and very strong tea

full-service hotel /ˌful ˌsɜːvɪs həʊˈtel/ *noun* HOTELS a hotel offering all services, such as restaurants, bars, room service, cleaning, valeting, etc.

full-service restaurant /ˌful ˌsɜːvɪs ˈrest(ə)rɒnt/ *noun* CATERING a restaurant which offers full meals, alcohol and table service

full-time /ˈful taɪm/ *adjective, adverb* working for the whole normal working day, i.e. about eight hours a day, five days a week ○ *She is in full-time work* or *She works full-time* or *She is in full-time employment.* ○ *He is one of our full-time staff.*

full-time equivalent /ˌful taɪm ɪˈkwɪvələnt/ *noun* BUSINESS a way of calculating the cost of part-time employment for accounting purposes, by converting the hours worked by part-timers to their equivalent if they were working full-time

full up /ˌful ˈʌp/ *adjective* having all its rooms occupied

fully /ˈfuli/ *adverb* completely ○ *The hotel is fully booked for August.*

fully comprehensive insurance /ˌfuli ˌkɒmprɪhensɪv ɪnˈʃʊərəns/ *noun* an insurance policy which covers you against all risks which are likely to happen

fully-licensed /ˌfuli ˈlaɪs(ə)nst/ *adjective* BARS with a full liquor licence

function /ˈfʌŋkʃən/ *noun* ENTERTAINMENT a party, usually when a group of people gathers for a meal ○ *A club function is being held in the main restaurant.*

COMMENT: Functions can range from a small lunch party to a large wedding; they are arranged and booked some weeks or months in advance.

functional food /ˈfʌŋkʃ(ə)nəl fuːd/ *noun* food, often containing additives, that is said to be beneficial to health and able to prevent or reduce diseases such as tooth decay and cancer

function catering /ˈfʌŋkʃən ˌkeɪtərɪŋ/ *noun* catering for special functions such as weddings

function chart /ˈfʌŋkʃən tʃɑːt/ *noun* HOTELS a chart showing the function rooms in a hotel, with the functions which will be held in them over a period of time

function diary /ˈfʌŋkʃən ˌdaɪəri/ *noun* HOTELS a list of dates of functions to be held in a hotel

function room /ˈfʌŋkʃən ruːm/ *noun* ENTERTAINMENT a special room for holding functions such as private dinners or parties

fund /fʌnd/ *verb* to provide money for a special purpose

fun fair /ˈfʌn feə/ *noun* ENTERTAINMENT a small permanent amusement park where people can ride on roundabouts, shoot at targets, etc.

funicular railway /fjuːˌnɪkjʊlə ˈreɪlweɪ/ *noun* RAIL TRAVEL a cable railway going up the side of a mountain, often with one car going up as another is coming down ○ *Six of us decided to walk back down the mountain, but the others took the funicular railway.*

furnish /ˈfɜːnɪʃ/ *verb* **1.** to supply, to provide ○ *We can furnish all the equipment necessary for a hotel gym.* **2.** to put furniture in a room ○ *The hotel bedrooms are furnished with typical Spanish furniture.* ○ *He furnished the guesthouse with second-hand chairs and sofas.* ○ *The hotel spent £10,000 on furnishing the residents' lounge.*

furniture /ˈfɜːnɪtʃə/ *noun* chairs, tables, beds and similar items (NOTE: There is no plural form: for one item say *a piece of furniture.*) □ **bedroom furniture** the furniture found in a bedroom, e.g. beds and chests of drawers

furniture polish /ˈfɜːnɪtʃə ˌpɒlɪʃ/ *noun* wax used to make furniture shiny

fusion cuisine /ˌfjuːʒ(ə)n kwɪˈziːn/ *noun* CATERING the addition of a product from a different country to a particular type of cooking, or the mixing of dishes from different countries in the same menu

'…he adds a note of caution to any restaurant opting for fusion cuisine, because although some combinations may work, others clearly do not' [*Caterer and Hotelkeeper*]

'…prove that fusion food is nothing new by starting with taramasalata followed by escalope of veal Holstein' [*Evening Standard*]

futures /ˈfjuːtʃəz/ *plural noun* BUSINESS the activity of trading in shares or commodities for delivery at a later date

COMMENT: A futures contract is a contract to purchase; if an investor is bullish, he or she will buy a contract, but if they feel the market will go down, they will sell one.

G

g /dʒiː/ *abbreviation* gram

galangal /ˈɡælənɡəl/ *noun* the pungent underground stem of a ginger plant, sold fresh or dried and ground

gallery /ˈɡæləri/ *noun* a building which is open to the public and offers pieces of art to look at or for sale

galley /ˈɡæli/ *noun* TRAVEL a kitchen on a plane or ship ○ *The stewardess will get you some water from the galley.*

gallon /ˈɡælən/ *noun* **1.** a unit of measurement of liquids equalling 8 pints or 4.55 litres. Also called **imperial gallon** □ the car does twenty-five miles per gallon, the car does twenty-five miles to the gallon the car uses one gallon of petrol in travelling twenty-five miles **2.** *US* a unit of measurement of liquids equalling 3.79 litres (NOTE: **Gallon** is usually written **gal** after figures: *25gal.*)

game /ɡeɪm/ *noun* **1.** ENTERTAINMENT an activity in which people compete with each other using skill, strength or luck ○ *They all wanted to watch a game of football.* **2.** animals which are hunted and killed for sport and food **3.** MEAT food from animals such as deer or pheasants, which have been hunted and killed

COMMENT: Common types of game are rabbit, hare and venison; the commonest game birds in the UK are pheasant, partridge and grouse.

game bird /ˈɡeɪm bɜːd/ *noun* any bird which is hunted and killed for sport and food

gamekeeper /ˈɡeɪmkiːpə/ *noun* somebody working on a private estate who protects wild birds and animals bred to be hunted

game larder /ˈɡeɪm ˌlɑːdə/ *noun* a special larder for keeping game until it is ready to eat

game pie /ˌɡeɪm ˈpaɪ/ *noun* FOOD a pie made from the meat of a game animal, such as hare, rabbit or pheasant

game reserve /ˈɡeɪm rɪˌzɜːv/ *noun* ENTERTAINMENT an area of land where wild animals are kept to be hunted and killed for sport

game soup /ˌɡeɪm ˈsuːp/ *noun* FOOD soup made from game

games room /ˈɡeɪmz ruːm/ *noun* ENTERTAINMENT a special room in a hotel or pub where games such as darts or pool can be played

game warden /ˈɡeɪm ˌwɔːd(ə)n/ *noun* somebody who protects big game for photographers or for hunters

gamma rays /ˈɡæmə reɪz/ *plural noun* CATERING rays which are shorter than X-rays, given off by radioactive substances and used in food irradiation

gammon /ˈɡæmən/ *noun* MEAT smoked or cured ham, either whole or cut into slices

gammon steak /ˌɡæmən ˈsteɪk/ *noun* MEAT a thick slice of gammon ○ *grilled gammon steak with pineapple*

g & t, G & T *abbreviation* BEVERAGES gin and tonic

G&T *abbreviation* BEVERAGES gin and tonic

gangplank /ˈɡæŋplæŋk/ *noun* SHIPS AND BOATS a wooden walkway for going from the quay on board a ship ○ *The passengers walked across the gangplank carrying suitcases.*

gangway /ˈɡæŋweɪ/ *noun* **1.** TRAVEL (*in a theatre, cinema, etc.*) a passage between rows of seats **2.** SHIPS AND BOATS a little movable bridge for going on board a ship ○ *We went up the gangway carrying our cases.*

gantry /ˈɡæntri/ *noun* BARS a series of shelves to display bottles of alcohol behind a bar

gap year /ˈɡæp jɪə/ *noun* a long holiday usually taken after ending one stage in your life or education and before beginning another, especially between studying at school and studying at university, and usually involving foreign travel

garage /ˈɡærɪdʒ, ˈɡærɑːʒ/ *noun* ROAD TRAVEL **1.** a place where cars can be serviced and repaired, and where petrol can be bought ○ *The next garage is 50 miles from here.* ○

You can hire cars from the garage near the railway station. Also called **service station 2.** a building where one or several cars can be parked ○ *Get a ticket from the hotel desk which allows you to park in the hotel garage.* ○ *Each of the apartments has its own garage.*

garage attendant /ˈgærɪdʒ əˌtendənt/ *noun* ROAD TRAVEL somebody who works in a garage, filling customers' cars with petrol, etc.

garage facilities /ˈgærɪdʒɪŋ/, **garage space, garaging** *noun* a space in a garage for parking cars ○ *The hotel has garage space for thirty cars.*

garam masala /ˌgæræm məˈsɑːlə/ *noun* a mixture of spices used in South Asian cooking to give a hot pungent flavour to a dish

garbage /ˈgɑːbɪdʒ/ *noun* refuse or rubbish

garbage can /ˈgɑːbɪdʒ kæn/ *noun* US same as **trashcan**

garçon /ˈgɑːsɒn/ *noun* a waiter in a French restaurant or café

garden /ˈgɑːd(ə)n/ *noun* a piece of ground used for growing flowers, fruit or vegetables

COMMENT: Most large cities are well provided with public gardens, which are usually open free of charge; botanical gardens may belong to a university, or an academy of science, and are also usually open to the public, though a charge may be levied.

gardens /ˈgɑːd(ə)nz/ *plural noun* a large area of garden ○ *The hotel is surrounded by flower gardens.*

garden suite /ˈgɑːd(ə)n swiːt/ *noun* HOTELS a suite of rooms with doors leading to a garden

garden view /ˈgɑːd(ə)n vjuː/ *noun* HOTELS a view over a garden

garlic /ˈgɑːlɪk/ *noun* SAUCES, ETC. a plant whose bulb has a strong smell and taste, used as a flavouring

garlic bread /ˌgɑːlɪk ˈbred/ *noun* bread spread with a mixture of butter and crushed garlic, warmed in an oven

garlicky /ˈgɑːlɪki/ *adjective* CATERING tasting or smelling of garlic

garni /gɑːˈniː/ *noun* HOTELS same as **hôtel garni**

garnish /ˈgɑːnɪʃ/ *noun* CATERING a small piece of food used as a decoration ○ *fish served with a garnish of lemon slices and chopped chives* ■ *verb* to decorate, especially food ○ *slices of beef garnished with capers*

garoupa /gæˈruːpə/ *noun* SEAFOOD same as **grouper**

gas /gæs/ *noun* **1.** a chemical substance which is burnt to make heat, e.g. for cooking ○ *The flat is equipped with a gas cooker.* ○ *The hotel is heated by gas.* ○ *Each gas appliance should be installed in a well-lit and draught-free position.* **2.** US same as **gasoline**

gas flushed /ˈgæs flʌʃt/ *adjective* MARKETING referring to a type of packaging, where the package is flushed with gas and then sealed to keep the product in perfect condition ○ *The coffee is gas-flushed and packed in portions to suit each cafetière size.* Compare **vacuum-packed**

gasoline /ˈgæsəliːn/ *noun* US petrol

gastric /ˈgæstrɪk/ *adjective* referring to the stomach

gastric flu /ˌgæstrɪk ˈfluː/ *noun* MEDICAL any mild stomach disorder

gastroenteritis /ˌgæstrəʊentəˈraɪtɪs/ *noun* MEDICAL inflammation of the membrane lining the intestines and the stomach, caused by a viral infection and resulting in diarrhoea and vomiting

gastrointestinal tract /ˌgæstrəʊɪntestɪn(ə)l ˈtrækt/ *noun* the digestive tract, comprising the stomach and intestines

gastronome /ˈgæstrəʊnəʊm/ *noun* an expert on food and drink

gastronomic /ˌgæstrəˈnɒmɪk/ *adjective* referring to food and drink of particularly high quality ○ *The restaurant offers a special gastronomic menu.*

gastronomic tour /ˌgæstrənɒmɪk ˈtʊə/ *noun* TOURISM a tour which includes gastronomic meals of the special dishes of a region

gastronomy /gæʃˈtrɒnəmi/ *noun* CATERING the art of food and cooking

gastropub /ˈgæstrəʊpʌb/ *noun* a pub that serves good-quality food

gate /geɪt/ *noun* AIR TRAVEL a door leading to an aircraft at an airport ○ *Flight AF270 is now boarding at Gate 23.*

gâteau /ˈgætəʊ/ *noun* BREAD, ETC. a French noun meaning a large cream cake ○ *For dessert there is a chocolate gâteau.* ◊ **Black Forest gâteau** (NOTE: The plural form is **gâteaux**.)

gatecrash /ˈgeɪtkræʃ/ *verb* □ **to gatecrash a party** to get into a party without being invited ○ *A group of students tried to gatecrash her party.*

gatecrasher /ˈgeɪtkræʃə/ *noun* somebody who gatecrashes a party ○ *We had bouncers on the door to stop gatecrashers coming in.*

gateway /'geɪtweɪ/ *noun* a town which leads to an area ○ *Washington, gateway to the south*

'Narita is the major international gateway' [*Airliner World*]

gavel /'gæv(ə)l/ *noun* a small wooden hammer, used by an auctioneer to hit the table to show that a bid has been successful, or by a toastmaster to call the attention of guests to a speaker

gazpacho /gæz'pætʃəʊ/ *noun* FOOD a Spanish-style soup, made of tomatoes, onions, cucumber, garlic, oil and vinegar, served cold

GDS *abbreviation* global distribution system

geese /giːs/ *plural noun* ♦ **goose**

gelatin /'dʒelətɪn/ *noun* FOOD protein which is soluble in water, made from collagen

COMMENT: Gelatin is used in foodstuffs to make liquids such as desserts or meat jellies set into a semi-solid.

gelatinous /dʒə'lætɪnəs/ *adjective* referring to gelatin or something with a texture like jelly

general /'dʒen(ə)rəl/ *adjective* **1.** including or affecting everything or nearly all of something **2.** □ **in general** as a rule, normally

general clean /ˌdʒen(ə)rəl 'kliːn/ *noun* HOTELS the activity of cleaning all parts of a room

General Delivery /ˌdʒen(ə)rəl dɪ 'lɪv(ə)ri/ *noun* US a system where letters can be addressed to someone at a post office, where they can be collected (NOTE: The British English is **Poste Restante**.)

general expenses /ˌdʒen(ə)rəl ɪk 'spensɪz/ *plural noun* money spent on the day-to-day costs of a business

general manager /ˌdʒen(ə)rəl 'mænɪdʒə/ *noun* a manager who is in charge of the administration of a whole establishment ○ *the general manager of a hotel*

general office /'dʒen(ə)rəl ˌɒfɪs/ *noun* the main administrative office in a company

general strike /ˌdʒen(ə)rəl 'straɪk/ *noun* a strike of all the employees in a country

genetically modified /dʒə,netɪkli 'mɒdɪfaɪd/ *adjective* referring to a plant that has received genetic material from a totally different organism or to products made from such plants. Abbr **GM**

gentleman /'dʒent(ə)lmən/ *noun* a polite way of referring to a man ○ *Could you show this gentleman to his table?* ○ *Well, gentle-men, shall we begin the meeting?* (NOTE: The plural form is **gentlemen**.)

gentlemen /'dʒent(ə)lmən/ *noun* a public toilet for men

gents /dʒents/ *noun* a public toilet for men (*informal*) ○ *Can you tell me where the gents or the gents' toilet is?* ○ *The gents is down the corridor on the left.* (NOTE: **Gents** is singular, and takes a singular verb.)

German /'dʒɜːmən/ *adjective* referring to Germany

German sausage /ˌdʒɜːmən 'sɒsɪdʒ/ *noun* MEAT a frankfurter or other similar smooth meat sausage

German wine /ˌdʒɜːmən 'waɪn/ *noun* BEVERAGES wine from Germany

getaway /'getəweɪ/ *noun* a trip to somewhere different from the place where you live ○ *The brochure includes weekend getaways in the British Isles.*

get back /ˌget 'bæk/ *verb* **1.** to return to a place ○ *The coach leaves at 8.30 a.m., and we should get back to the hotel by 9 o'clock in the evening.* **2.** to get something again which you had before ○ *I got my money back after I had complained to the manager.*

get off /ˌget 'ɒf/ *verb* to come down from a vehicle ○ *She got off the bus at the post office.* ○ *You have to get off the Underground at South Kensington.*

get on /ˌget 'ɒn/ *verb* to board a train, a bus or an aircraft, or to mount a bicycle or horse ○ *She got on at Charing Cross.* ○ *He got on the plane at Frankfurt.*

get ready /ˌget 'redi/ *verb* **1.** to prepare yourself for something ○ *How long will it take you to get ready for the meeting?* ○ *All guests must get ready to leave the hotel at 7.30 a.m.* **2.** to get something prepared ○ *We need to get the bedrooms ready by 12.00.* ○ *The courier is trying to get the tour notes ready before the party leaves.*

get through /ˌget 'θruː/ *verb* **1.** to speak to someone on the phone ○ *I tried to get through to the complaints department.* **2.** to try to make someone understand ○ *I could not get through to her that I had to be at the airport by 2.15.*

get up /ˌget 'ʌp/ *verb* **1.** to get out of bed ○ *It is 9.30 and Mr Jones has still not got up. Can you give him a call?* **2.** to make someone get out of bed ○ *We must get all the party up by 7.30 if we are going to leave on time.*

geyser /'giːzə/ *noun* a hot spring, where water shoots up into the air at regular intervals ○ *There are famous geysers in Yellowstone National Park.*

gherkin /'gɜːkɪn/ *noun* VEGETABLES a small vegetable of the cucumber family used for pickling

giardiasis /ˌdʒiːɑːˈdaɪəsɪs/ *noun* MEDICAL a disorder of the intestine caused by the parasite *Giardia lamblia,* usually with no symptoms, but in heavy infections the absorption of fat may be affected, causing diarrhoea

giblets /'dʒɪbl(ə)ts/ *plural noun* MEAT the liver, heart and other internal organs of poultry, removed before the bird is cooked

gift /gɪft/ *noun* something given to someone as a present

gift shop /'gɪft ʃɒp/ *noun* a shop selling small items which are given as presents

gift token /'gɪft ˌtəʊkən/, **gift voucher** /'gɪft ˌvaʊtʃə/ *noun* a voucher bought in a shop which is given as a present and which must be exchanged in that shop for goods ○ *We gave her a gift token for her birthday.*

gift-wrap /'gɪft ræp/ *verb* to wrap a present in attractive paper ○ *Do you want this book gift-wrapped?*

gift-wrapping /'gɪft ˌræpɪŋ/ *noun* **1.** a service in a store for wrapping presents for customers **2.** attractive paper for wrapping presents

gigot /'ʒiːgəʊ/ *noun* a French or Scottish cut of lamb or mutton taken from the leg

gill /dʒɪl/ *noun* CATERING a measure of liquids, equal to a quarter of a pint

gin /dʒɪn/ *noun* BEVERAGES **1.** a strong colourless alcohol, distilled from grain and flavoured with juniper **2.** a glass of this alcohol ○ *She drank three gins before dinner.*

> COMMENT: Gin is usually drunk with tonic water (making a 'g & t'), but also forms the basis of dry martinis. The word 'gin' is also used to refer to Dutch 'genever', which is drunk cold and neat.

gin and French /ˌdʒɪn ən 'frentʃ/ *noun* BEVERAGES gin and French vermouth

gin and Italian /ˌdʒɪn ən ɪ'tæljən/ *noun* BEVERAGES gin and Italian vermouth. Abbr **gin and it**

gin and lime /ˌdʒɪn ən 'laɪm/ *noun* BEVERAGES a drink made with gin, lime juice and ice cubes

gin and tonic /ˌdʒɪn ən 'tɒnɪk/ *noun* BEVERAGES a drink made from gin, ice, a slice of lemon and tonic water ○ *Two gin and tonics, please.* Abbr **G&T**

ginger /'dʒɪndʒə/ *noun* **1.** SAUCES, ETC. a plant with a hot-tasting root used in cooking and medicine **2.** a spice made from the powdered root of this plant

ginger ale /ˌdʒɪndʒə 'eɪl/ *noun* BEVERAGES a fizzy drink flavoured with ginger, often served mixed with whisky or brandy. Also called **dry ginger**

ginger beer /ˌdʒɪndʒə 'bɪə/ *noun* a fizzy mildly alcoholic drink made by fermenting a mixture of syrup and ginger

ginger biscuit, ginger nut *noun* BREAD, ETC. a hard sweet biscuit, flavoured with ginger

gingerbread /'dʒɪndʒəbred/ *noun* BREAD, ETC. a cake made with treacle and flavoured with ginger

gin sling /ˌdʒɪn 'slɪŋ/ *noun* BEVERAGES a drink made from gin, ice, sweetened water and lemon or lime juice

gippy tummy /ˌdʒɪpi 'tʌmi/ *noun* MEDICAL diarrhoea which affects people travelling in foreign countries as a result of eating unwashed fruit or drinking water which has not been boiled (*humorous*)

GIT *abbreviation* TOURISM group inclusive tour

gîte /ʒiːt/ *noun* TOURISM a house or cottage in France which can be rented for self-catering holidays

given name /'gɪv(ə)n neɪm/ *noun* especially US the first name or Christian name of a person, as opposed to the surname or family name

glacier /'glæsiə/ *noun* a mass of ice like a frozen river which moves slowly down a mountain

glass /glɑːs/ *noun* **1.** a hard, smooth material which you can see through, used to make things such as windows, vases and bowls **2.** CATERING a vessel made of glass used especially for drinking ○ *Each place setting should have two glasses.* **3.** the contents of such a glass ○ *He drank six glasses of white wine.* ○ *Add a glass of red wine to the sauce.* □ **to sell wine by the glass** to sell single glasses of named wines ○ *You can have a bottle of house wine, or we sell wines by the glass.* ○ *The wine bar has a wine-by-the-glass list.*

> COMMENT: There are various shapes of glasses used for different drinks: champagne is served in tall tapering glasses (or 'flutes'), and also sometimes in wide flat glasses called 'coupes'. Bordeaux wines are served in taller narrower glasses than those for Burgundies, which are flatter. In Germany, wines are served in coloured glasses, usually pale yellow, with a green or orange stem. Draught beer is served in moulded glasses with handles, or in tall plain glasses without handles. Bottled beers are served in glasses on stems.

Water can be served in ordinary wine glasses or in tumblers. Sherry glasses have short stems. Brandy glasses (or 'balloons') have wide bodies tapering to a narrower mouth.

glass-bottomed boat /ˌglɑːs ˌbɒt(ə)md 'bəʊt/ *noun* TOURISM a boat with a bottom made of glass, so that tourists can see into the water under the boat

glass-breaker /'glɑːs ˌbreɪkə/ *noun* an alarm panel, with a glass window, which you have to break to sound the alarm

glassful /'glɑːsfʊl/ *noun* the amount contained in a glass ○ *Add two glassfuls of wine to the soup.*

glassware /'glɑːsweə/ *noun* HOTELS articles made of glass, especially drinking glasses used in a restaurant or hotel

glass washer /'glɑːs ˌwɒʃə/ *noun* CATERING a special washing machine for washing glasses

glaze /gleɪz/ *noun* CATERING a shiny surface on food ○ *The glaze on her gâteau was perfect.* ■ *verb* to cover with a shiny coating ○ *She glazed the cake and put six candles on it.*

global distribution system /ˌgləʊb(ə)l ˌdɪstrɪ'bjuːʃ(ə)n ˌsɪstəm/ *noun* a computer system which provides information for travel agencies, etc. so that people can reserve air tickets, theatre tickets, etc. Abbr **GDS**

globe artichoke /gləʊb 'ɑːtɪˌtʃəʊk/ *noun* VEGETABLES ♦ **artichoke**

globetrotter /'gləʊbtrɒtə/ *noun* someone who travels all around the world (*informal*)

Glorious Twelfth /ˌglɔːriəs 'twelfθ/ *noun* August 12th. See Comment at **grouse**

glucose /'gluːkəʊz/ *noun* a simple sugar found in some fruit, but also broken down from white sugar or carbohydrate and absorbed into the body or secreted by the kidneys

Glühwein /'gluːveɪn/ *noun* same as **mulled wine**

gm *abbreviation* gram

GM *abbreviation* genetically modified

GMT *abbreviation* Greenwich Mean Time

gnocchi /'nɒki/ *plural noun* FOOD in Italian cookery, dumplings made of potato, semolina or flour, usually boiled and served with soup or a sauce

go /gəʊ/ *verb* to move, or to make a journey or trip ○ *He's going on a tour of the south of Spain.* (NOTE: **going – went – has gone**) □ **to go on board** to move onto a ship, plane or train ○ *They went on board the boat at 10.00.*

goal /gəʊl/ *noun* an aim, the thing you are trying to achieve

goat /gəʊt/ *noun* a small farm animal with horns and a beard, giving milk and wool (NOTE: Males are called **bucks**, females are **does**, and the young are **kids**.)

COMMENT: In Europe, goats are important for milk production; goat's milk has a higher protein and butterfat content than cow's milk, and is used especially for making cheese. Elsewhere goats are reared for meat.

goat's cheese /'gəʊts tʃiːz/ *noun* DAIRY cheese made from the milk of a goat

goblet /'gɒblət/ *noun* CATERING a drinking glass with a stem, used for serving wine or beer

go down /ˌgəʊ 'daʊn/ *verb* to descend, to go to a lower level ○ *After having a rest in her bedroom, she went down to the hotel bar.* ○ *Part of the tour is a visit to the coal mines, and you go down into the mine in a little lift.*

going /'gəʊɪŋ/ *adjective* **1.** active or busy □ **to sell a business as a going concern** to sell a business as an actively trading company □ **it is a going concern** the company is working and making a profit **2.** □ **the going price** the usual or current price, the price which is being charged now ○ *What is the going price for two weeks in a three-star hotel in Cyprus?* □ **the going rate** the usual or current rate of payment ○ *We pay the going rate for waitresses.*

gold card /'gəʊld kɑːd/ *noun* FINANCE a credit card issued to important customers with a particular high level of income, which gives privileges such as a higher spending limit than ordinary credit cards

golden syrup /ˌgəʊld(ə)n 'sɪrəp/ *noun* FOOD thick golden juice from sugar, used to make dishes such as treacle tart

golden wedding /ˌgəʊld(ə)n 'wedɪŋ/ *noun* an anniversary of 50 years of marriage

Gold Ribbon award /ˌgəʊld 'rɪbən əˌwɔːd/ *noun* HOTELS an award given by the RAC to hotels which are committed to very high standards of service and accommodation

'…the RAC has given its Gold Ribbon accolade to 63 hotels and town houses in the UK and Ireland. Thirteen have received it for the first time' [*Caterer & Hotelkeeper*]

golf /gɒlf/ *noun* SPORT a game for two people, or two couples, where a small hard ball is struck with long-handled clubs into a series of holes, the object being to use as few strokes as possible □ **a round of golf** a game of golf, going round all 18 holes on the course ○ *The room price includes four rounds of golf.*

golf club /ˈɡɒlf klʌb/ *noun* **1.** ENTERTAINMENT a wooden- or metal-headed long-handled stick for striking a golf ball **2.** SPORT a group of people who play golf, and allow others to join them on payment of a fee **3.** ENTERTAINMENT a house where golfers meet

golf course /ˈɡɒlf kɔːs/ *noun* SPORT a large area of ground specially designed for playing golf ○ *They've cut down a lot of trees to make a new golf course.* ○ *The hotel is next to an 18-hole golf course.*

golfer /ˈɡɒlfə/ *noun* SPORT somebody who plays golf

golfing /ˈɡɒlfɪŋ/ *noun* SPORT the activity of playing golf ○ *a golfing holiday* ○ *They organise golfing tours of France.*

golf umbrella /ˈɡɒlf ʌmˌbrelə/ *noun* a large colourful umbrella used by golfers, and also by the general public

goods /ɡʊdz/ *plural noun* things that are produced for sale

goods vehicle /ˈɡʊdz ˌviːɪk(ə)l/ *noun* ROAD TRAVEL a lorry or other vehicle used to transport goods

goodwill /ɡʊdˈwɪl/ *noun* BUSINESS the good reputation of a business ○ *He paid £10,000 for the goodwill of the restaurant and £4,000 for the fittings.*

COMMENT: Goodwill can include the trading reputation, the patents, the trade names used, the value of a 'good site', etc., and is very difficult to establish accurately. It is an intangible asset, and so is not shown as an asset in a company's accounts, unless it figures as part of the purchase price paid when acquiring another company.

goose /ɡuːs/ *noun* **1.** a web-footed water bird, larger than a duck ○ *goose-liver pâté* **2.** MEAT meat from this bird ○ *roast goose* (NOTE: The plural form is **geese**.)

gooseberry /ˈɡʊzb(ə)ri/ *noun* FRUIT a small soft fruit from a small prickly bush, which is green or red in colour and is usually cooked or preserved ○ *gooseberry fool* ○ *gooseberry jam*

gorge-walking /ˈɡɔːdʒ ˌwɔːkɪŋ/ *noun* SPORT same as **canyoneering**

Gouda /ˈɡaʊdə/ *noun* a mild Dutch cheese, typically sold in a thick round shape covered in yellow wax

goujon /ˈɡuːʒɒn/ *noun* a long strip of fish or chicken coated in egg and breadcrumbs and deep-fried

goulash /ˈɡuːlæʃ/ *noun* FOOD a Hungarian dish of meat and vegetables, flavoured with paprika

gourmand /ˈɡɔːmɒnd/ *noun* somebody who is fond of eating, and eats and drinks too much. Compare **gourmet**

gourmet /ˈɡʊəmeɪ/ *noun* somebody who knows a lot about and appreciates food and wine ○ *a gourmet meal* ○ *The restaurant offers a gourmet menu.* Compare **gourmand**

government loan /ˌɡʌv(ə)nmənt ˈləʊn/ *noun* money lent by the government

government pension /ˌɡʌv(ə)nmənt ˈpenʃən/ *noun* a pension paid by the state. Also called **state pension**

government-regulated price /ˌɡʌv(ə)nmənt ˌreɡjʊleɪtɪd ˈpraɪs/ *noun* BUSINESS a price which is imposed by the government

grade /ɡreɪd/ *noun* a category of something which is classified according to quality or size ■ *verb* to sort things according to size or quality ○ *Eggs are graded into classes A, B, and C.*

COMMENT: There are various systems of grading hotels and restaurants; the English Tourism Council gives hotels and other accommodation stars or diamonds depending on the type of facilities offered. Restaurants are graded for quality (shown by stars) by the Michelin organisation. The French national system gives stars to hotels according to the facilities offered.

graded hotel /ˌɡreɪdɪd həʊˈtel/ *noun* HOTELS a good-quality hotel

grading system /ˈɡreɪdɪŋ ˌsɪstəm/ *noun* HOTELS a system of classifying hotels or restaurants into different levels of quality

grain whisky /ˌɡreɪn ˈwɪski/ *noun* whisky that is made from any fermented cereal other than malted barley

gram /ɡræm/, **gramme** /ɡræm/ *noun* a measure of weight equalling one thousandth of a kilo ○ *She bought 500g of butter.* ○ *Coffee is sold in 250g packs.* (NOTE: This is usually written **g** or **gm** after figures: *25g*.)

granadilla /ˌɡrænəˈdɪlə/ *noun* FRUIT same as **passion fruit**

granary /ˈɡrænəri/ *noun* a place where threshed grain is stored, now often used as a trade name for bread or flour containing malted wheat grain

grand total /ˌɡrænd ˈtəʊt(ə)l/ *noun* the final total made by adding several subtotals

granola /ɡrəˈnəʊlə/ *noun* a breakfast cereal consisting of rolled oats mixed with other ingredients such as dried fruit and nuts

granulated sugar /ˌɡrænjʊleɪtɪd ˈʃʊɡə/ *noun* FOOD refined sugar in small white crystals. Also called **white sugar**

grape /ɡreɪp/ *noun* the fruit of the grapevine

COMMENT: Grapes are grown in most areas of the world that have a Mediterranean climate, and even in temperate areas like southern England and central Germany. There are two main colours of grapes: black and white (actually they are very dark blue and pale green). Grapes are not usually cooked, but are eaten raw or in fruit salads. They are crushed to make grape juice and wine, and are also dried to produce currants, raisins and sultanas. In some parts of the world (such as Greece) bunches of very small currant grapes are sold as dessert grapes.

grapefruit /ˈɡreɪpfruːt/ *noun* the citrus fruit similar to and about twice as large as an orange, but not as sweet, that is lemon-yellow when ripe and very juicy, and has flesh that is usually pale greenish-yellow, but can also be pink ○ *a glass of grapefruit juice* (NOTE: The plural form is **grapefruit**.)

COMMENT: Grapefruit are usually served cut in half, with sugar; they are usually eaten at breakfast. They are also used to make marmalade.

grapefruit segments /ˈɡreɪpfruːt ˌseɡmənts/ *plural noun* FOOD sections of peeled grapefruit, served in a glass bowl as an hors d'oeuvre and at breakfast

grapevine /ˈɡreɪpvaɪn/ *noun* a plant with long flexible stems on which grapes grow

grate /ɡreɪt/ *verb* to shred something into very small pieces, using a metal tool with holes with rough edges ○ *Do you want grated cheese on your pasta?* ○ *There was a salad of grated carrot and French dressing.*

grater /ˈɡreɪtə/ *noun* CATERING a tool with a rough metal surface, or with rough holes, used for grating food such as cheese

gratin /ˈɡrætæŋ/ *noun* CATERING **1.** food which has been topped with breadcrumbs, cream sauce or cheese, and is then browned under a grill or in an oven ○ *cauliflower gratin* **2.** a low flat dish in which food can be browned under a grill

gratis /ˈɡrætɪs/ *adverb* free, without paying anything ○ *We got into the exhibition gratis.*

gratuity /ɡrəˈtjuːɪti/ *noun* FINANCE same as **tip** *noun* 1 ○ *The staff are instructed not to accept gratuities.*

gravity feed slicer /ˌɡrævɪti fiːd ˈslaɪsə/ *noun* CATERING a type of slicer for cooked meat such as ham, where the meat is placed on a sloping tray and slides further down after each slice is cut

gravlax, gravadlax *noun* FOOD a Scandinavian dish of raw salmon pickled in salt, sugar and herbs, served sliced thinly with brown bread

gravy /ˈɡreɪvi/ *noun* SAUCES, ETC. the juices which come from meat during cooking, or a brown sauce made using these which is served with meat ○ *She poured the gravy over the meat.*

COMMENT: In many British restaurants, gravy is prepared from dry powder, mixed with water and meat juices. Real gravy is made from the juices of the meat only.

grease /ɡriːs/ *noun* thick oil, used to make machines run smoothly

greasy /ˈɡriːsi/ *adjective* oily ○ *I don't like the chips they serve here – they're too greasy.* (NOTE: **greasy – greasier – greasiest**)

greasy spoon /ˌɡriːsi ˈspuːn/ *noun* a small, cheap and often dirty cafe

greedy /ˈɡriːdi/ *adjective* always wanting to eat a lot of food ○ *Don't be greedy – you've already had two pieces of cake.* (NOTE: **greedy – greedier – greediest**)

Greek /ɡriːk/ *adjective* referring to Greece

Greek coffee /ˌɡriːk ˈkɒfi/ *noun* BEVERAGES same as **Turkish coffee**

Greek salad /ˌɡriːk ˈsæləd/ *noun* FOOD a salad of tomatoes, lettuce, cucumber, olives, oregano and feta cheese

green /ɡriːn/ *adjective* referring to a concern about the environment ■ *noun* an area of public land covered with grass in the middle of a village

greenback /ˈɡriːnbæk/ *noun* US a dollar bill (*informal*)

green beans /ˌɡriːn ˈbiːnz/ *plural noun* VEGETABLES beans grown on low bushes and eaten when green in their pods. Also called **French beans, string beans**

Green Belt /ˈɡriːn belt/ *noun* an area of farming land or woods and parks, which surrounds a town, and on which building is restricted or completely banned ○ *They can't put houses in Old Oak Wood, it's Green Belt land.* ○ *The Green Belt is supposed to stop the remorseless advance of houses into the countryside.*

COMMENT: Green Belt land is protected and building is restricted and often prohibited completely. The aim of setting up a Green Belt is to prevent urban sprawl and reduce city pollution.

green card /ˌɡriːn ˈkɑːd/ *noun* **1.** FINANCE a special British insurance certificate to prove that a car is insured for travel abroad **2.**

a work permit for a person going to live in the USA

green channel /ˈgriːn ˌtʃæn(ə)l/ *noun* TRAVEL the exit from customs through which you pass if you are not importing goods which are liable to duty

greengage /ˈgriːngeɪdʒ/ *noun* FRUIT a bitter green plum, used for cooking, making pies, jam, etc. ○ *My mother makes jam with our greengages.*

greengrocer /ˈgriːngrəʊsə/ *noun* somebody who sells fruit and vegetables □ **the greengrocer's** a shop where you can buy fruit and vegetables ○ *Can you buy some potatoes at the greengrocer's?* ○ *I went to the greengrocer's in the High Street to buy some fruit.*

green holiday /ˌgriːn ˈhɒlɪdeɪ/ *noun* TOURISM a holiday spent in the countryside doing work which helps the environment

green olive /ˌgriːn ˈɒlɪv/ *noun* VEGETABLES an unripe olive

green pepper /ˌgriːn ˈpepə/ *noun* VEGETABLES an unripe sweet pepper with a green skin, eaten raw or cooked

green salad /ˌgriːn ˈsæləd/ *noun* FOOD a salad made of lettuce or other green leaves, sometimes including other raw green vegetables such as cucumber or green pepper

green space /ˌgriːn ˈspeɪs/ *noun* an area of land which has not been built on, containing grass, plants and trees

Greenwich Mean Time /ˌgrɪnɪtʃ ˈmiːn ˌtaɪm/ *noun* the local time on the 0° meridian where it passes through Greenwich, England, used to calculate international time zones ○ *At midnight Greenwich Mean Time it is 7 a.m. in Bangkok.* Abbr **GMT**

greeter /ˈgriːtə/ *noun* US CATERING somebody whose job it is to receive guests as they enter a restaurant and show them to their tables

griddle /ˈgrɪd(ə)l/ *noun* CATERING a flat metal sheet which is heated and on which food can be cooked, used for short-order breakfasts, Japanese food, etc. ○ *He fried the eggs on a griddle.*

'…cooking breakfast to order on the griddle provides guests with a more direct service and helps avoid the unattractive accumulation of fried food which can easily occur on breakfast buffets at large hotels' [*Caterer & Hotelkeeper*]

griddlecake /ˈgrɪd(ə)lkeɪk/ *noun* BREAD, ETC. a little pancake cooked on a griddle

gridlock /ˈgrɪdlɒk/ *noun* ROAD TRAVEL a traffic jam in which the vehicles cannot move for a very long time ○ *The gridlock stretched from Hyde Park Corner to the City.*

gridlocked /ˈgrɪdlɒkt/ *adjective* blocked by traffic jams ○ *Downtown New York was gridlocked for two hours.*

grill /grɪl/ CATERING *noun* **1.** an open metal surface with heat above or below, used to cook meat, fish and some vegetables **2.** food which has been cooked on a grill **3.** a restaurant, or part of a restaurant, which specialises in grilled food ○ *We didn't eat in the hotel but went across the road to a Mexican grill.* ■ *verb* to cook food on or under a grill ○ *I'll grill the sausages as it makes them less fatty.*

grilled /grɪld/ *adjective* CATERING cooked on a grill ○ *Grilled fish is drier and less greasy than fried fish.* ○ *I'll have a grilled chop, please.*

griller /ˈgrɪlə/ *noun* CATERING a kitchen device with an open metal rack with heat beneath, used to cook meat, fish and some vegetables

grillroom /ˈgrɪlruːm/ *noun* CATERING a restaurant which specialises in grilled food

grind /graɪnd/ *verb* CATERING to pass food through a machine which reduces it to powder or pulp (NOTE: **grinding – ground – ground**)

grinder /ˈgraɪndə/ *noun* CATERING **1.** a machine for grinding food such as coffee or spices **2.** US a machine for mincing meat (NOTE: The British English for this meaning is **mincer** or **mincing machine**.)

grip /grɪp/ *noun* TRAVEL same as **holdall**

grits /grɪts/ *plural noun* US FOOD ground maize, cooked in milk or water, then fried and eaten as a breakfast dish

grocer /ˈgrəʊsə/ *noun* somebody who sells many types of food and often general household goods ○ *The grocer weighed out 500 grams of coffee.* □ **the grocer's** a shop where you can buy many types of food and general household goods ○ *Can you buy some sugar at the grocer's?* ○ *We went to the grocer's in the High Street to get some tea.*

groom /gruːm/ *verb* to make something smart or neat ○ *They groom ski slopes before a competition.*

gross /grəʊs/ *noun* twelve dozen ○ *She ordered four gross of paper towels.* (NOTE: There is no plural form in this meaning.) ■ *adjective* total, with no deductions ■ *adverb* with no deductions ○ *Her salary is paid gross.* ■ *verb* to make a gross profit ○ *The group grossed £25m in 1993.*

gross earnings /ˌgrəʊs ˈɜːnɪŋz/ *plural noun* BUSINESS total earnings before tax and other deductions

gross income /ˌgrəʊs ˈɪnkʌm/ *noun* BUSINESS income before tax is deducted

gross profit /grəʊs ˈprɒfɪt/, **gross trading profit** /grəʊs ˈtreɪdɪŋ/ *noun* BUSINESS profit calculated as sales income less the cost of the goods sold, i.e. without deducting any other expenses

gross receipts /ˌgrəʊs rɪˈsiːts/ *plural noun* FINANCE the total amount of money received before expenses are deducted

gross salary /ˌgrəʊs ˈsæləri/ *noun* BUSINESS salary before tax is deducted

gross tonnage /ˌgrəʊs ˈtʌnɪdʒ/ *noun* SHIPS AND BOATS the total amount of space in a ship

gross turnover /ˌgrəʊs ˈtɜːnəʊvə/ *noun* BUSINESS the total turnover including discounts, VAT charged, etc.

gross weight /ˌgrəʊs ˈweɪt/ *noun* the weight of both a container and its contents

gross yield /ˌgrəʊs ˈjiːld/ *noun* BUSINESS the profit from investments before tax is deducted

grotto /ˈgrɒtəʊ/ *noun* a picturesque small cave or room decorated with shells to look like a cave

ground /graʊnd/ *noun* soil or earth □ **on the ground** not in the air ■ *verb* 1. □ **to ground an aircraft** to say that an aircraft must not fly, usually because of a mechanical failure ○ *After the crash, all planes were grounded until their engines were inspected.* 2. ♦ **grind**

ground beef /ˌgraʊnd ˈbiːf/ *noun* US MEAT finely minced beef, used for making hamburgers

ground coffee /ˌgraʊnd ˈkɒfi/ *noun* FOOD coffee beans which have been ground to small pieces, ready for making coffee

ground engineer /ˈgraʊnd ˌendʒɪnɪə/ *noun* AIR TRAVEL somebody who maintains and repairs aircraft on the ground, as opposed to a flight engineer

ground floor /ˌgraʊnd ˈflɔː/ *noun* a floor in a shop or office which is level with the ground ○ *The men's department is on the ground floor.* ○ *He has a ground-floor office.*

ground handling /ˈgraʊnd ˌhændlɪŋ/ *noun* AIR TRAVEL the activity of dealing with airline passengers on the ground, after they have arrived at an airport

ground hostess /ˈgraʊnd ˌhəʊstɪs/ *noun* AIR TRAVEL a woman who looks after passengers at the airport before they board the plane

grounds /graʊndz/ *plural noun* 1. gardens round a large house ○ *If the weather is fine,* the concert will be held in the grounds of the house. 2. basic reasons ○ *Does he have good grounds for complaint?* ○ *There are no grounds on which we can be sued for negligence.*

ground transportation /ˈgraʊnd trænspɔːˌteɪʃ(ə)n/ *noun* AIR TRAVEL vehicles such as buses and taxis, available to take passengers from an airport to the town

group /gruːp/ *noun* 1. several things or people together ○ *a group of Japanese tourists* 2. BUSINESS several companies linked together in the same organisation ○ *a major travel group* ○ *The group owns hotels in several European cities.* ■ *verb* □ **to group together** to put several items together ○ *Sales from six different agencies are grouped together under the heading 'European sales'.*

group booking /ˌgruːp ˈbʊkɪŋ/ *noun* HOTELS a reservation of seats, hotel rooms or restaurant places for a group of people made together at the same time

grouper /ˈgruːpə/ *noun* SEAFOOD a large tropical sea fish, used as food

group inclusive tour /ˌgruːp ɪnˌkluːsɪv ˈtʊə/ *noun* TOURISM a tour for a group of people, where the price per person includes all travel, accommodation and meals. Abbr **GIT**

group purchasing /ˌgruːp ˈpɜːtʃɪsɪŋ/ *noun* BUSINESS central purchasing for a whole group, which results in cost savings

group rate /ˈgruːp reɪt/ *noun* a special rate for larger groups of people travelling together

group rates /ˈgruːp reɪts/ *plural noun* HOTELS hotel room charges for groups

group results /ˌgruːp rɪˈzʌlts/ *plural noun* BUSINESS the financial accounts of a group of companies taken together

group travel /ˌgruːp ˈtræv(ə)l/ *noun* travel as a member of a group of people, as opposed to individual travel

grouse /graʊs/ *noun* 1. SPORT a small black game bird, found in the UK, especially in the north of England and in Scotland (NOTE: There is no plural form: two of the birds are called *a brace of grouse.*) 2. a complaint ○ *The manager is tired of listening to the guests' grouses.* ■ *verb* to complain ○ *The group was grousing about the service in the hotel restaurant.*

COMMENT: Grouse are shot and eaten in season; the season starts on August 12th, also called the 'Glorious Twelfth', and ends on December 10th.

grouse moor /ˈɡraʊs ˌmʊə/ *noun* an area of open land where grouse live

growth market /ˈɡrəʊθ ˌmɑːkɪt/ *noun* BUSINESS an area where sales are going to increase

GRS *abbreviation* global reservation system

grub /ɡrʌb/ *noun* food (*informal*)

guacamole /ˌɡwækəˈməʊleɪ/ *noun* SAUCES, ETC. pureed avocado with chillis, used as a dip or as a filling for tacos

guarantee /ˌɡærənˈtiː/ *noun* a legal document which promises that a machine will work properly, that an item is of good quality or that a service will be provided ○ *The tour company refused to give the guarantee that the group would be accommodated in the hotel mentioned in the brochure.* ○ *The guarantee lasts for two years.* ○ *It is sold with a twelve-month guarantee.* □ **the car is still under guarantee** the car is still covered by the maker's guarantee ■ *verb* to give a firm promise that something will work, that something will be done ○ *I guarantee that this will not happen again.* □ **the product is guaranteed for twelve months** the manufacturer says that the product will work well for twelve months, and he will mend it free of charge if it breaks down

guaranteed price /ˌɡærəntiːd ˈpraɪs/ *noun* a price which the seller promises will not change

guaranteed reservation /ˌɡærəntiːd ˌrezəˈveɪʃ(ə)n/ *noun* a reservation that must be paid for in advance and ensures that the hotel keeps a room free until the guest arrives

guaranteed wage /ˌɡærəntiːd ˈweɪdʒ/ *noun* BUSINESS a wage which a company promises will not fall below a particular figure

guard /ɡɑːd/ *noun* a person or group of people, whose job it is to protect someone or something ○ *The tourist bus carries armed guards when going into the bandit country.* ○ *The hotel grounds are patrolled by security guards.*

guava /ˈɡwɑːvə/ *noun* FRUIT an orange-coloured tropical fruit with pink flesh

guéridon /ˈɡerɪdɒn/ *noun* CATERING **1.** a French noun meaning side table, on which the waiter places dishes, and from which the guests are served **2.** a trolley for bringing food to the table

guest /ɡest/ *noun* **1.** somebody staying in a hotel or guesthouse **2.** a person who is invited to come to your home or to an event ○ *We're expecting 300 guests at the launch.* **3.** somebody who is visiting another person. ◊ **paying guest**

'…the relatively limited range of facilities offered by many small hotels does not necessarily mean that guest care suffers' [*Caterer & Hotelkeeper*]

guest account, guest bill *noun* HOTELS a bill made out to a guest in a hotel, for room, restaurant and other services

guest beer /ˈɡest bɪə/ *noun* a beer kept on draught in a bar for a limited period only as an addition to the usual beers

guest book /ˈɡest bʊk/ *noun* a book in which guests write their names and often make comments when visiting a hotel, guesthouse or place of interest

guest care /ˈɡest keə/ *noun* HOTELS the work of looking after guests in a hotel

guest flow /ˈɡest fləʊ/ *noun* the number of guests requiring assistance, e.g. for checking in or out

guest history /ˌɡest ˈhɪst(ə)ri/ *noun* HOTELS details of a guest, his or her previous stays in the hotel, room preferences, etc.

guesthouse /ˈɡesthaʊs/ *noun* **1.** TOURISM a privately owned house, which takes several guests, usually not more than ten **2.** HOTELS (*in the Far East*) a small state-owned hotel for official guests, but where other visitors may be offered accommodation

COMMENT: Guesthouses are similar to small hotels, but may not be licensed to serve alcohol, and may only offer bed and breakfast. Guesthouses are always family-owned and -run.

guest ledger /ˈɡest ˌledʒə/ *noun* **1.** a list of all the money owed by a guest to a hotel that must be paid before the guest checks out, including e.g. accommodation, bar bills and phone charges **2.** same as **guest book**

guest relations manager /ˌɡest rɪˈleɪʃ(ə)nz ˌmænɪdʒə/ *noun* a person whose job is to ensure that guests are well looked after while they are staying in a hotel

guest rooms /ˈɡest ruːmz/ *plural noun* HOTELS bedrooms and suites in a hotel which are used only by guests as opposed to public rooms

guest room technology /ˌɡest ruːm tekˈnɒlədʒi/ *noun* HOTELS technical equipment, such as Internet links, in a hotel bedroom ○ *Guest-room technology is very expensive.* Also called **in-room technology**

guest services directory /ˌɡest ˈsɜːvɪsɪz daɪˌrekt(ə)ri/ *noun* HOTELS a book in each bedroom of a hotel which lists the services available to guests, and the phone numbers to call

guide /gaɪd/ TOURISM *noun* **1.** somebody who shows tourists round a site or house ○ *Our guide took us into the castle chapel.* ○ *The guide to the museum spoke so rapidly that we couldn't understand what she was saying.* **2.** a guide book ○ *This is the best guide to the region.* ○ *You can get a small guide to walks round the town at the tourist information office.* ■ *verb* to show tourists round a site

guidebook /ˈgaɪdbʊk/ *noun* TOURISM a book for tourists, explaining what there is to see in a place, where to stay, how to travel around and where to eat ○ *The guidebook lists three hotels by the beach.*

guided tour /ˌgaɪdɪd ˈtʊə/ *noun* TOURISM a tour with a guide who shows places to tourists. Also called **conducted tour**

guinea fowl /ˈgɪni faʊl/ *noun* MEAT a small black bird with white spots, raised for its meat which has a delicate flavour similar to that of game birds

gulet /ˈgʌlət/ *noun* SHIPS AND BOATS a traditional Turkish wooden yacht with double cabin and a large sundeck, that carries around 15 passengers ○ *They advertise gulet cruises leaving from the harbour near the hotel.*

gullet /ˈgʌlɪt/ *noun* the tube down which food and drink passes from the mouth to the stomach ○ *She had a piece of bread stuck in her gullet.* Also called **oesophagus**

gumbo /ˈgʌmbəʊ/ *noun* **1.** CATERING same as **okra 2.** FOOD a type of thick soup or stew, made with meat or fish and okra, from the southern USA

gym /dʒɪm/, **gymnasium** /dʒɪmˈneɪziəm/ *noun* SPORT a hall for indoor athletics and exercises

H

haddock /ˈhædək/ *noun* SEAFOOD a common white sea fish

COMMENT: Smoked haddock is smoked until yellow on the bone (called 'Finnan haddock') or as fillets. Small whole haddock smoked until they are brown are called 'Arbroath smokies'. Smoked haddock is used in various recipes including kedgeree, and omelette Arnold Bennett.

haggis /ˈhægɪs/ *noun* FOOD a Scottish dish made of a sheep's stomach stuffed with a mixture of the sheep's heart, liver and other organs and oatmeal, which is boiled in water (NOTE: In Scotland haggis is served on special occasions, such as Burns' Night.)

haggle /ˈhæg(ə)l/ *verb* to discuss prices and terms and try to reduce them ○ *To buy anything in the local market you will have to learn to haggle.* ○ *After two hours' haggling over the price we bought the carpet.* (NOTE: You haggle **with** someone **over** something.)

hail /heɪl/ *noun* small pieces of ice which fall like frozen rain ■ *verb* **1.** to fall as frozen rain ○ *It hailed for ten minutes and then the sun came out.* **2.** to wave to a taxi to stop ○ *He whistled to hail a taxi.*

hailstone /ˈheɪlstəʊn/ *noun* a piece of frozen rain ○ *Hailstones bounced off the roof of the car.* ○ *Huge hailstones covered the road.*

hailstorm /ˈheɪlstɔːm/ *noun* a storm during which hail falls ○ *After the hailstorm, the road was white with hailstones.*

hair /heə/ *noun* **1.** a single long thread growing on the body of a human or animal ○ *Waiter, there's a hair in my soup!* **2.** a mass of hairs growing on the head ○ *Your hair is too long, you must get it cut.*

hairbrush /ˈheəbrʌʃ/ *noun* a special brush for keeping hair tidy (NOTE: The plural form is **hairbrushes.**)

haircut /ˈheəkʌt/ *noun* an act of making hair shorter by cutting it ○ *He went to the hairdresser's to get a haircut.*

hairdresser /ˈheəˌdresə/ *noun* a person who cuts and washes your hair □ **the hairdresser's** a shop where people can have their hair cut, dyed and styled

hairdressing /ˈheədresɪŋ/ *noun* the work of cutting, dyeing or styling hair

hairdressing salon /ˈheədresɪŋ ˌsælɒn/ *noun* a shop where people can have their hair cut, dyed and styled

hair drier, hair dryer *noun* a machine for drying wet hair ○ *Each bathroom is equipped with a hair dryer.*

hairnet /ˈheənet/ *noun* a very fine cover put over the hair to keep it tidy ○ *Kitchen staff with long hair must wear hairnets.*

hake /heɪk/ *noun* SEAFOOD a large white sea fish (NOTE: The plural form is **hake.**)

halal /həˈlɑːl/ *adjective* CATERING prepared according to Islamic law

halal butcher /həˌlɑːl ˈbʊtʃə/ *noun* CATERING a butcher who prepares meat according to Islamic law

half board /ˌhɑːf ˈbɔːd/ *noun* HOTELS a special rate for guests staying at a hotel, who take breakfast and dinner at the hotel, but not lunch. Also called **demi-pension**

half-carafe /ˌhɑːf kəˈræf/ *noun* CATERING a half-litre carafe ○ *He ordered a half-carafe of house wine.*

half-case /ˌhɑːf ˈkeɪs/ *noun* BARS a cardboard or wooden box containing six bottles of wine

half-day /ˈhɑːf deɪ/ *adjective* referring to the morning or afternoon ○ *a half-day tour of the island* ○ *A half-day excursion to the old town costs £10.00.*

half-day closing /ˌhɑːf deɪ ˈkləʊzɪŋ/ *noun* a system by which a shop closes, usually at lunchtime, and remains closed for the rest of that day

half-dollar /ˌhɑːf ˈdɒlə/ *noun* US fifty cents

half fare /ˌhɑːf ˈfeə/ *noun* TRAVEL a half-price ticket for a child

half-fat milk /ˌhɑːf fæt ˈmɪlk/ *noun* DAIRY milk from which some of the fat has been removed

halfpipe /'hɑːfpaɪp/ *noun* SPORT a structure in the shape of the bottom half of a pipe, built for freestyle snowboarding, in-line skating, and skateboarding

half price /ˌhɑːf 'praɪs/ *noun, adjective* 50% of the usual price ○ *Tour operators are offering tours at half price* or *half-price tours to people making last-minute bookings.* □ **to sell goods off at half price** to sell goods at 50% of the usual price

half-price sale /ˌhɑːf praɪs 'seɪl/ *noun* MARKETING a sale of all goods at 50% of the usual price

halibut /'hælɪbət/ *noun* SEAFOOD a type of flat white sea fish

hall /hɔːl/ *noun* **1.** a large building for public meetings **2.** ♦ **front hall**

hall of residence /ˌhɔːl əv 'rezɪd(ə)ns/ a building on a university campus in which students live while studying at the university

hall porter /'hɔːl ˌpɔːtə/ *noun* HOTELS somebody who is on duty in the hall of a hotel, especially somebody who stands near the main door of a hotel and deals with arriving or departing guests and their baggage

ham /hæm/ *noun* **1.** □ **a ham** the thigh of the back leg of a pig **2.** MEAT meat from this part of the pig, usually cured in brine and sometimes dried in smoke ○ *a ham sandwich* ○ *a plate of salad with two slices of ham*

> COMMENT: Ham is cooked by boiling or roasting, and may be bought ready-cooked in a piece or in slices. Some types of smoked ham, such as prosciutto and Parma ham are sliced very thinly and eaten raw; Parma ham is sometimes served with melon as an hors-d'oeuvre.

ham and eggs /ˌhæm ən 'egz/ *noun* FOOD fried ham with fried eggs

hamburger /'hæmbɜːgə/ *noun* MEAT a small flat cake of minced beef that is grilled or fried ○ *The children want hamburgers and fries for lunch.* Also called **beefburger**

> COMMENT: The hamburger is so called because it was originally minced beef steak cooked in the style of Hamburg, a town in Germany. It has nothing to do with ham. It is also called simply a 'burger' or 'beefburger'.

hamburger bar /'hæmˌbɜːgə bɑː/ *noun* CATERING a simple restaurant serving hamburgers

hamburger roll /'hæmbɜːgə rəʊl/ *noun* BREAD, ETC. a soft round bread roll suitable for serving a hamburger in

hamlet /'hæmlət/ *noun* a small village ○ *Villagers from the surrounding hamlets came to the town on market day.*

hand /hænd/ *noun* **1.** a part of the body at the end of each arm □ **to shake hands** to hold someone's hand when meeting to show you are pleased to meet him or her or to show that an agreement has been reached ○ *The visitors shook hands and sat down at the table.* ○ *The restaurant proprietor always shakes hands with regular customers.* □ **to shake hands on a deal** to shake hands to show that a deal has been agreed **2.** □ **by hand** using the hands, not a machine ○ *The chef makes all his pasta by hand.* **3.** □ **in hand** kept in reserve ○ *We have £10,000 in hand.* **4.** □ **to hand** here, present □ **I have the invoice to hand** I have the invoice in front of me **5.** □ **to change hands** to be sold to a new owner ○ *The hotel changed hands for £300,000.*

hand-dipped chocolates /ˌhænd dɪpt 'tʃɒkləts/ *plural noun* FOOD chocolates which are coated by hand, as opposed to those made by machines

hand dryer /'hænd ˌdraɪə/ *noun* a machine for drying the hands. It switches itself on when hands are placed under it or when a button is pressed, and blows hot air onto the hands.

handjug /'hænddʒʌg/ *noun* a small jug which you can hold in one hand ○ *Coffee is served in individual handjugs.*

handle /'hænd(ə)l/ *noun* a part of an object which is held in the hand ○ *Don't touch the pan – the handle is hot.* ○ *The handle has come off my suitcase.* ○ *Push the knob in the door handle if you want to lock the door from the inside.* ■ *verb* **1.** to deal with something, to organise something ○ *The accounts department handles all the cash.* ○ *We can handle up to 1,500 passengers per hour.* ○ *They handle all our overseas visitors.* **2.** MARKETING to sell or to trade in a sort of service or product ○ *We do not handle tours for old-age pensioners.* ○ *They handle tours to the Far East.*

handling /'hændlɪŋ/ *noun* **1.** the act of moving something by hand **2.** the act of dealing with something □ **baggage handling facilities** arrangements or machines for moving passengers' baggage

> '…shipping companies continue to bear the extra financial burden of cargo handling operations at the ports' [*Business Times (Lagos)*]

hand luggage /'hænd ˌlʌgɪdʒ/ *noun* AIR TRAVEL same as **carry-on baggage**

handmade /'hændmeɪd/ *adjective* made by hand, not by a machine ○ *handmade pasta*

hand towel /'hænd ˌtaʊəl/ *noun* a small towel for drying the hands

handy /'hændi/ *adjective* useful or convenient ○ *Paper handkerchiefs are sold in handy-sized packs.* ○ *This small case is handy for use when travelling.*

hang /hæŋ/ *verb* CATERING to suspend meat or a recently killed game animal until the flesh begins to decompose slightly and becomes more tender and highly flavoured (NOTE: **hangs – hanging – hung**)

hang-glider /'hæŋ ˌglaɪdə/ *noun* SPORT **1.** a large cloth wing stretched over a lightweight frame, like a giant kite, under which the pilot hangs in a harness, holding onto a bar which is used for steering ○ *His hang-glider got caught in a tree.* ◊ **paraglider 2.** somebody who flies a hang-glider

hang-gliding /'hæŋ ˌglaɪdɪŋ/ *noun* SPORT the sport of flying a hang-glider ○ *He goes hang-gliding every weekend.* ○ *I'd love to have a go at hang-gliding.* ◊ **paragliding**

COMMENT: To get a hang-glider into the air, it is necessary either to run down a hill or jump off a cliff into the prevailing wind; by pushing the bar away from you, the nose of the glider dips and the glider picks up speed as it descends; by pulling the bar towards you, the nose lifts up and the glider decreases speed until it reaches stalling point.

happy hour /'hæpi ˌaʊə/ *noun* BUSINESS a time, usually in the early evening, when a bar offers cheaper drinks to encourage customers to come in early ○ *There's a happy hour every day from 5 to 7.*

harassment /'hærəsmənt, hə'ræsmənt/ *noun* unpleasant behaviour towards somebody that usually involves persistently threatening or worrying them ○ *The bar owner complained of police harassment.* □ **anti-harassment policy** the policy of a work place which is strict about harassment

'…bullying and harassment at work can have an unsettling effect on the work force' [*Caterer & Hotelkeeper*]

harbour /'hɑːbə/ *noun* SHIPS AND BOATS a port, a place where ships come to load or unload (NOTE: The US spelling is **harbor**.)

harbour dues /'hɑːbə djuːz/ *plural noun* SHIPS AND BOATS a payment which a ship makes to the harbour authorities for the right to use the harbour

harbour facilities /ˌhɑːbə ˌɪnstə 'leɪʃ(ə)ns/, **harbour installations** *plural noun* SHIPS AND BOATS buildings or equipment in a harbour

hard /hɑːd/ *adjective* not soft, firm to the touch ○ *We prefer to have a hard mattress.*

hard-boiled /ˌhɑːd 'bɔɪld/ *adjective* CATERING (*refers to an egg*) cooked in boiling water until the white and yolk are set

hard cash /ˌhɑːd 'kæʃ/ *noun* FINANCE money in notes and coins, as opposed to cheques or credit cards

hard cheese /ˌhɑːd 'tʃiːz/ *noun* DAIRY cheese which has been pressed and so has a firm texture

COMMENT: Many German, British, Dutch and Swiss cheeses are hard. A very hard cheese is Parmesan from Italy, which is only used grated and sprinkled on pasta dishes, or sliced very thinly on salads.

hard currency /ˌhɑːd 'kʌrənsi/ *noun* FINANCE a currency which is issued by a country with a strong economy and which can be changed into other currencies easily

hare /heə/ *noun* a common field mammal, like a large rabbit

haricot beans /'hærɪkəʊ biːnz/ *plural noun* VEGETABLES dry white beans which are used to make baked beans

harissa /hə'rɪsə/ *noun* a spicy oily paste made from chilli and tomatoes, used as an ingredient in North African cooking

hash /hæʃ/ *noun* FOOD a dish prepared from chopped meat and vegetables

hash browns /ˌhæʃ 'braʊnz/ *plural noun* US FOOD boiled potatoes, diced or mashed and fried till crisp and brown

hat /hæt/ *noun* a covering for the head

hatch /hætʃ/ *noun* an opening in the floor or wall with a little door

haute cuisine /ˌəʊt kwɪ'ziːn/ *noun* CATERING high-class French cooking

HAV *abbreviation* MEDICAL hepatitis A virus

have /həv, əv, hæv/ *verb* **1.** to own something, or to be able to give somebody something ○ *Do you have a room for two people for one night?* ○ *Do you have a table for three, please?* **2.** to take something such as a meal or a bath ○ *We had breakfast on the balcony.* **3.** □ **have a nice day!** I hope the day passes pleasantly for you □ **have a good trip!** I hope your journey is pleasant

haze /heɪz/ *noun* mist, smoke or dust suspended in the atmosphere which reduces visibility ○ *The sun's rays filtered through the haze.*

hazelnut /'heɪz(ə)lnʌt/ *noun* NUTS a small round nut with a smooth shiny shell. Also called **cob nut**

hazy /'heɪzi/ *adjective* misty ○ *It was too hazy for us to get a good view from the top of the cliff.*

HBV *abbreviation* MEDICAL hepatitis B virus

HCIMA *abbreviation* Hotel & Catering International Management Association

head /hed/ *noun* **1.** the most important person **2.** one person, or one animal, when counting **3.** most important, main

head buyer /ˌhed ˈbaɪə/ *noun* BUSINESS the main person in a shop responsible for buying goods which are to be sold

headcheese /ˈhedtʃiːz/ *noun* US MEAT same as **brawn**

head chef /ˌhed ˈʃef/ *noun* CATERING the main chef in a restaurant

head concierge /ˌhed ˌkɒnsiˈeəʒ/ *noun* HOTELS the main concierge in a hotel ○ *He's the head concierge at the Savoy in London.*

head of department /ˌhed əv dɪˈpɑːtmənt/ *noun* somebody in charge of a department

head office /ˌhed ˈɒfɪs/ *noun* an office building where the board of directors works and meets. Also called **main office**

head porter /ˌhed ˈpɔːtə/ *noun* the porter who is in charge of all the other porters

headrest /ˈhedrest/ *noun* TRAVEL a cushion to support your head, attached to a seat in a car or plane ○ *You can adjust the headrest to the height you want.*

head waiter /ˌhed ˈweɪtə/ *noun* CATERING the person in charge of a restaurant, who is responsible for all the service and himself takes orders from customers

headwind /ˈhedwɪnd/ *noun* TRAVEL a wind blowing straight towards a ship or aircraft ○ *Strong headwinds over the Atlantic meant that the plane was half an hour late.*

health /helθ/ *noun* the fact of being well or being free from any illness □ **your health!**, **good health!** a wish said when raising your glass and drinking from it □ **to drink someone's health** to wish someone good health, and celebrate it by raising your glass and drinking from it

Health and Safety at Work Act /ˌhelθ ən ˌseɪfti ət ˈwɜːk ˌækt/ *noun* in the UK, an Act of Parliament which rules how the health of workers should be protected by the companies they work for

Health and Safety Executive /ˌhelθ ən ˈseɪfti ɪgˌzekjʊtɪv/ *noun* a British government organisation responsible for checking the conditions of work of workers. Abbr **HSE**

health club /ˈhelθ klʌb/ *noun* ENTERTAINMENT a club for people who want to improve their health by taking exercise, dieting, etc.

health diet /ˈhelθ ˌdaɪət/ *noun* CATERING a diet for someone who wants to improve his or her health

health farm /ˈhelθ fɑːm/ *noun* a clinic in the country where people go who want to improve their health and appearance by taking exercise, dieting, etc.

health food /ˈhelθ fuːd/ *noun* CATERING food with no additives or natural foods which are good for your health, e.g. cereals, yoghurt, dried fruit and nuts

health inspector /ˈhelθ ɪnˌspektə/ *noun* HOTELS an official who inspects the kitchens of hotels, restaurants, etc., to see if they are clean

health resort /ˈhelθ rɪˌzɔːt/ *noun* TOURISM a resort town which has special facilities to improve the health of its visitors

health spa /ˈhelθ spɑː/ *noun* HOTELS an exercise and health centre in a hotel

healthy /ˈhelθi/ *adjective* **1.** in good physical condition **2.** making you stay fit and well ○ *a healthy climate* ○ *a healthy diet*

heaped /hiːpt/ *adjective* containing something in an amount large enough to rise up in a small heap

heart /hɑːt/ *noun* VEGETABLES the compact central part of a vegetable such as lettuce, cabbage or celery, where the leaves or stalks curl in tightly

heart-smart /ˈhɑːt smɑːt/ *adjective* referring to food that is low in fat and cholesterol and therefore reduces the risk of heart disease

heat /hiːt/ *noun* the state of being hot ■ *verb* to make something hot ○ *The room was heated by a small gas fire.* ○ *Heat the water until it is almost boiling.*

heated pool /ˌhiːtɪd ˈpuːl/ *noun* ENTERTAINMENT a swimming pool where the water is warmed before it is pumped into the pool

heated towel rail /ˌhiːtɪd ˈtaʊəl ˌreɪl/ *noun* a towel rail which is heated, and so keeps towels warm and dry

heater /ˈhiːtə/ *noun* an apparatus which warms ○ *There is an electric heater in the bedroom.* ○ *Cyprus can be cool in the winter, so the flat has several portable electric heaters.*

heat exhaustion /ˈhiːt ɪgˌzɔːstʃ(ə)n/ *noun* MEDICAL collapse due to overexertion in hot conditions

heat haze /ˈhiːt heɪz/ *noun* a reduction in visibility caused by warm air rising from the ground ○ *It's hard to judge distances when you are driving and there's a heat haze.*

heating /ˈhiːtɪŋ/ *noun* a means of making something warm

heat-sealing /ˈhiːt ˌsiːlɪŋ/ *noun* CATER-ING a method of closing plastic food containers in which air is removed from a plastic bag with the food inside and the bag is then pressed by a hot plate which melts the plastic and seals the contents in the vacuum

heat wave /ˈhiːt weɪv/ *noun* a sudden period of high temperature

heavy contract carpet /ˌhevi ˌkɒntrækt ˈkɑːpɪt/ *noun* a type of carpet which is strong and can stand a lot of wear, such as is supplied under contract to public areas of hotels and restaurants

heavy goods vehicle /ˌhevi ˈɡʊdz ˌviːɪk(ə)l/ *noun* ROAD TRAVEL a very large truck ○ *Heavy goods vehicles can park in the loading bay.* Abbr **HGV**

heavy traffic /ˌhevi ˈtræfɪk/ *noun* ROAD TRAVEL a lot of cars, buses and lorries passing

helibiking /ˈhelɪˌbaɪkɪŋ/ *noun* a sport in which mountain-bike riders are taken by helicopter to the top of a mountain and then ride down

helicopter /ˈhelɪkɒptə/ *noun* AIR TRAVEL an aircraft with a large propeller on top which allows it to lift straight off the ground ○ *He took the helicopter from the airport to the centre of town.* ○ *It is only a short helicopter flight from the centre of town to the factory site.* ○ *Club class travellers have a free helicopter connection to the city centre.*

helipad /ˈhelipæd/ *noun* a small area of tarmac for helicopters to land on or take off from ○ *Visitors can land at the helipad next to the hotel.*

heliport /ˈhelipɔːt/ *noun* an airport used only by helicopters

help /help/ *noun* something or somebody that makes it easier for you to do something ○ *She finds the word-processor a great help in writing publicity material.* ○ *The safari park was set up with financial help from the government.* ○ *Her assistant is not much help in the office – he can't type or drive.* ■ *verb* to make it easy for someone to do something or for something to be done ○ *The porter helped the visitors to get off the coach.* ○ *The computer helps in the rapid processing of reservations* or *helps us to process reservations rapidly.* ○ *The government helps exporting companies with easy credit.* (NOTE: You help someone or something **to do** something.) □ **to help yourself** to serve yourself ○ *At the buffet, you are asked to help yourself to food.*

helping /ˈhelpɪŋ/ *noun* CATERING a portion of food served to one person ○ *She asked for a second helping of chips.* ○ *The helpings are very small, and seem even smaller because the plates are so large.*

hemisphere /ˈhemɪsfɪə/ *noun* one half of a sphere, or one of the two parts into which the Earth is divided □ **Northern Hemisphere, Southern Hemisphere** the two halves of the Earth, north and south, divided by the equator ○ *It is winter in the Northern Hemisphere when it is summer in the Southern.*

hepatitis /ˌhepəˈtaɪtɪs/ *noun* MEDICAL inflammation of the liver through disease or drugs

COMMENT: Infectious hepatitis and serum hepatitis are caused by different viruses (called A and B), and having had one does not give immunity against an attack of the other. Hepatitis B is more serious than the A form, and can vary in severity from a mild gastrointestinal upset to severe liver failure and death. Hepatitis C and D have also been identified.

hepatitis A /ˌhepətaɪtɪs ˈeɪ/ *noun* MEDICAL a relatively mild form of viral hepatitis that is transmitted through contaminated food and water. Also called **infectious virus hepatitis**

hepatitis A virus /ˌhepətaɪtɪs ˈeɪ ˌvaɪrəs/ *noun* MEDICAL a virus which causes hepatitis A. Abbr **HAV**

hepatitis B /ˌhepətaɪtɪs ˈbiː/ *noun* MEDICAL a severe form of viral hepatitis that is transmitted by contact with infected blood or other body fluids. Also called **serum hepatitis**

hepatitis B virus /ˌhepətaɪtɪs ˈbiː ˌvaɪrəs/ *noun* MEDICAL a virus which causes hepatitis B. Abbr **HBV**

herb /hɜːb/ *noun* CATERING a plant which can be used to give a particular taste to food or to give a particular scent ○ *Add some herbs to the sauce.* ○ *Rosemary, thyme and sage are some of the herbs that are grown in the hotel garden.*

herb garden /ˈhɜːb ˌɡɑːd(ə)n/ *noun* a garden where herbs are grown

heritage /ˈherɪtɪdʒ/ *noun* the history, traditions, environment and historic buildings of a country or area, seen as something to be passed on in good condition to future generations ○ *The Highland Games are part of Scotland's cultural heritage.*

heritage attraction /ˌherɪtɪdʒ ə ˈtrækʃ(ə)n/ *noun* TOURISM a tourist facility which is based on a country's historical or cultural background

herring /ˈherɪŋ/ *noun* SEAFOOD a common sea fish ○ *She had grilled herrings for dinner.* (NOTE: There is no plural form when referring to the live fish: *a shoal of herring.*)

HGV *abbreviation* ROAD TRAVEL heavy goods vehicle

high /haɪ/ *adjective* **1.** tall, situated or reaching up above other things ○ *The shelves are 30cm high.* ○ *The door is not high enough to let us get the wardrobe into the bedroom.* ○ *They are planning a 20-storey-high hotel next to the royal palace.* **2.** going far above other things ○ *A very high mountain overlooks the town.* **3.** greater than average, large, considerable ○ *High overhead costs increase the room price.* ○ *High prices put customers off.* ○ *They are budgeting for a high level of expenditure on renovation.* ○ *High interest rates are killing small businesses.* **4.** CATERING referring to meat, especially game, which has been kept until it is beginning to rot and has a strong flavour

high-altitude climbing /ˌhaɪ ˌæltɪtjuːd ˈklaɪmɪŋ/ *noun* SPORT the activity of climbing mountains over 5,000m

highball /ˈhaɪbɔːl/ *noun* US BEVERAGES any long drink, e.g. whiskey and soda ○ *The waiters passed round with trays of highballs.*

high chair /ˈhaɪ ˌtʃeə/ *noun* a little chair on tall legs, so that a baby or small child can sit and eat at a table ○ *Most restaurants provide high chairs these days.*

high-class /ˌhaɪ ˈklɑːs/ *adjective* of very good quality ○ *a high-class hotel or coach service*

High Commission /ˌhaɪ kəˈmɪʃ(ə)n/ *noun* the building where a High Commissioner lives and works ○ *the British High Commission in Ottawa* or *the UK High Commission in Ottawa* ○ *British Embassies, High Commissions and Consulates can issue emergency passport replacements.* (NOTE: A **High Commission** is the equivalent of an **embassy** in a non-Commonwealth country.)

High Commissioner /ˌhaɪ kəˈmɪʃ(ə)nə/ *noun* somebody who represents a Commonwealth country in another Commonwealth country, having the same rank and the same duties as an ambassador

high-energy food /ˌhaɪ ˌenədʒi ˈfuːd/ *noun* CATERING food containing a large number of calories, which give a lot of energy when they are broken down by the digestive system, e.g. fat or carbohydrate

high-fibre diet /haɪ ˌfaɪbə ˈdaɪət/ *noun* a diet which contains a high percentage of cereals, nuts, fruit and vegetables

high-grade /ˈhaɪ ɡreɪd/ *adjective* considered to be of very good quality

highlands /ˈhaɪləndz/ *noun* TOURISM an area of high hills or mountains ○ *the Scottish Highlands* ○ *the Cameron Highlands of Malaysia*

high official /ˌhaɪ əˈfɪʃ(ə)l/ *noun* an important person in a government department

high-quality /ˌhaɪ ˈkwɒlɪti/ *adjective* very good ○ *The store specialises in high-quality imported cheese.* Also called **top quality**

high-risk recreation /ˌhaɪ rɪsk ˌrekri ˈeɪʃ(ə)n/ *noun* SPORT a leisure activity that involves an element of danger, e.g. hang-gliding, skydiving, bungee jumping and white-water rafting

high season /ˌhaɪ ˈsiːz(ə)n/ *noun* TOURISM a period when there are lots of travellers and when fares are higher, usually the period from July to September ○ *Rates in high season are 30% higher than in low season.*

high-speed /ˈhaɪ spiːd/ *adjective* running or operating at a very high speed ○ *We took the high-speed train to Paris.*

high-speed rail link /ˌhaɪ spiːd ˈreɪl ˌlɪŋk/ *noun* RAIL TRAVEL a railway which links two cities with high-speed trains ○ *They are planning a high-speed rail link between Berlin and Warsaw.*

High Street /ˈhaɪ striːt/ *noun* the most important street in a British town, where the shops and banks are ○ *We'll meet at the pub in the High Street.* ○ *She runs a High Street travel shop.* □ **the High Street banks** the main British banks which accept deposits from individual customers

high tea /ˌhaɪ ˈtiː/ *noun* CATERING (*in the North of England and Scotland*) an early evening meal ○ *They arrived just in time for high tea.*

COMMENT: 'high tea' is common in hotels and guesthouses in the North, the Midlands, Wales and Scotland. It is eaten around 5 o'clock in the afternoon and may consist of cold meat, hot or cold pies, salad, cakes, scones and, of course, tea.

high temperature short time method /ˌhaɪ ˌtemprɪtʃə ʃɔːt ˈtaɪm ˌmeθəd/ *noun* CATERING the usual method of pasteurising milk, where the milk is heated to 72°C for 15 seconds and then rapidly cooled. Abbr **HTST method**

high-traffic site /ˌhaɪ ˌtræfɪk ˈsaɪt/ *noun* a place where a lot of people pass by ○ *You need high-quality carpeting for restaurants and other high-traffic sites.*

highway /'haɪweɪ/ *noun* ROAD TRAVEL a main road

Highway Code /ˌhaɪweɪ 'kəʊd/ *noun* ROAD TRAVEL a British government publication containing the rules for people travelling on roads ○ *You need to know the Highway Code if you're taking your driving test.*

hike /haɪk/ SPORT *noun* a strenuous walk ■ *verb* to go for a strenuous walk ○ *Most people hike north to south.* ○ *You still have to hike another 10 miles before you come to the village.*

hiker /'haɪkə/ *noun* SPORT somebody who goes for strenuous walks

hiking /'haɪkɪŋ/ *noun* SPORT strenuous walking as a sport

hill /hɪl/ *noun* a raised area of land, lower than a mountain ○ *The Cheviot Hills are between England and Scotland.*

hill station /'hɪl ˌsteɪʃ(ə)n/ *noun* TOURISM a resort town in a hill area, where the weather is cooler in the summer than on the plain

hill walking /'hɪl ˌwɔːkɪŋ/ *noun* SPORT walking in hills as a recreation

hinterland /'hɪntəlænd/ *noun* an area inland from a sea port or around a large town

hire /'haɪə/ *noun* **1.** the act of paying money to rent a car, boat or piece of equipment for a period of time □ **boat hire**, **cycle hire**, **car hire** the lending of boats, cycles, cars to people for money **2.** □ **'for hire'** sign on a taxi showing it is empty ■ *verb* **1.** □ **to hire staff** to engage new staff to work for you ○ *We have hired the best lawyers to represent us.* ○ *They hired a small company to repaint the dining room.* □ **to hire and fire** to engage new staff and dismiss existing staff frequently **2.** □ **to hire a car** *or* **a bus** to pay money to use a car or a bus for a period of time ○ *When their coach broke down, they hired a van to take them to the next hotel.* **3.** □ **to hire (out) cars** *or* **coaches** to own cars or coaches and lend them to customers who pay for their use

hire car /'haɪə kɑː/ *noun* ROAD TRAVEL a car which is rented ○ *He was driving a hire car when the accident happened.*

hitch /hɪtʃ/ *verb* □ **to hitch (a lift)** to ask a car driver or truck driver to take you as a passenger, usually by signalling with the thumb or by holding a sign with your destination written on it ○ *He hitched a lift to Birmingham.* ○ *Her car broke down and she hitched a lift from a passing motorist.* ◊ **thumb**

hitch-hike /'hɪtʃ haɪk/ *verb* TRAVEL to travel by hitching lifts from drivers ○ *He hitch-hiked his way all across the United*

States. ○ *Hitch-hiking is forbidden on motorways.*

hitch-hiker /'hɪtʃ ˌhaɪkə/ *noun* TRAVEL somebody who travels by hitching lifts from drivers ○ *He picked up two hitch-hikers who were going to Scotland.*

COMMENT: In the UK, hitch-hikers are not allowed on motorways. Although it is a cheap way of travelling, it can be dangerous, and is not recommended.

HIV *noun* a virus that destroys the human immune system and causes AIDS. Full form **Human Immunodeficiency Virus**

HLTT *abbreviation* hospitality, leisure, travel and tourism

hob /hɒb/ *noun* **1.** CATERING the flat top on a cooker ○ *Our new cooker has a ceramic hob.* ○ *Do not use abrasive cleaner on the hob.* **2.** a metal stand by a fire ○ *Put the kettle on the hob.*

hock /hɒk/ *noun* **1.** BEVERAGES any white wine from the Rhine valley in Germany ○ *We opened a bottle of hock.* **2.** FOOD the lower part of a leg of a pig, used for food

Hogmanay /'hɒgməneɪ/ *noun* ENTERTAINMENT a festival in Scotland on 31st December, celebrating the New Year ○ *We will be in Edinburgh for Hogmanay.*

COMMENT: It is a tradition that the first person who comes through the door on New Year's Day (i.e. after midnight on New Year's Eve) should bring luck. If possible the person should be a dark stranger, and should carry a piece of coal for the fire, as well as food and drink, usually whisky. This tradition also exists in the north of England and is called 'first-footing'.

hoisin sauce /ˌhɔɪsɪn 'sɔːs/ *noun* SAUCES, ETC. a thick dark sweet and spicy sauce made from fermented soya beans and used to flavour Chinese dishes

hold /həʊld/ *noun* TRAVEL the bottom part of a ship or an aircraft, in which cargo is stored ■ *verb* **1.** to support or grip something with your hands ○ *Would you mind holding my coat while I sign the register?* **2.** to be large enough to contain a certain quantity of things or people ○ *The plane holds 250 passengers.* ○ *Each box holds 250 sheets of paper.* **3.** to make an event happen ○ *to hold a reception* or *a party* ○ *The computer show will be held in London next month.* ○ *The wedding reception will be held in the Blue Room.* **4.** to keep or reserve something ○ *We will hold the room for you until 8.00.* **5.** □ **hold the line please** (*on telephone*) please wait ○ *The chairman is on the other line – hold the line please?* (NOTE: **holds – holding – held**)

holdall /'həʊldɔːl/ *noun* TRAVEL a soft bag for carrying clothes and other belongings when travelling. Also called **grip**

hold up /,həʊld 'ʌp/ *verb* **1.** to lift, to support ○ *The roof is held up by those pillars.* **2.** to make someone or something late ○ *The planes were held up by fog.* ○ *The traffic conditions will hold up deliveries.*

hold-up /'həʊld ʌp/ *noun* a delay ○ *Long hold-ups are expected as the air-traffic controllers go on strike.*

hold valet /'həʊld ,væleɪ/ *noun* a place where a guest's laundry is kept until he or she collects it

holiday /'hɒlɪdeɪ/ *noun* **1.** ENTERTAINMENT a day on which no work is done because of national or religious law **2.** ENTERTAINMENT a period when an employee does not work, but rests, goes away and enjoys himself or herself ○ *to take a holiday* or *to go on holiday* ○ *We always go on holiday* or *take our holidays in June.* ○ *When is the manager taking his holidays?* ○ *My head waiter is off on holiday tomorrow.* ○ *He will be away on holiday for two weeks.* (NOTE: The US English is **vacation**.) □ **the job carries five weeks' holiday** one of the conditions of the job is that you have five weeks' paid holiday each year

holiday camp /'hɒlɪdeɪ kæmp/ *noun* ENTERTAINMENT a permanent facility where people spend holidays in cabins and enjoy organised entertainment and sport

holiday centre /'hɒlɪdeɪ ,sentə/ *noun* TOURISM a town or area which is popular for holidays

holiday entitlement /'hɒlɪdeɪ ɪn,taɪt(ə)lmənt/ *noun* the number of days' paid holiday which an employee has the right to take

holiday home /'hɒlɪdeɪ həʊm/ *noun* TOURISM a small house or flat, used by a family for their holidays

holidaymaker /'hɒlɪdeɪmeɪkə/ *noun* somebody who is on holiday ○ *In August the town is full of holidaymakers.*

holiday pay /'hɒlɪdeɪ peɪ/ *noun* salary which is still paid during the holiday

holiday period /'hɒlɪdeɪ ,pɪəriəd/ *noun* the time when people take their holiday ○ *The restaurant will be closed for the holiday period.*

holiday resort /'hɒlɪdeɪ rɪ,zɔːt/ *noun* TOURISM a place where people often go on holiday

holiday season /'hɒlɪdeɪ ,siːz(ə)n/ *noun* TOURISM the time of year when most people take their holidays ○ *Late winter is the main holiday season in the Alpine resorts.* ○ *The holiday season on the North Italian coast lasts about three months.*

holiday village /'hɒlɪdeɪ ,vɪlɪdʒ/ *noun* TOURISM a specially built village of small houses for holidaymakers, usually on the sea or near a lake or river

hollandaise sauce /,hɒləndeɪz 'sɔːs/ *noun* SAUCES, ETC. a sauce for meat, fish or vegetables, made of egg yolks, butter, lemon juice and sometimes vinegar

hollowware /'hɒləʊweə/ *noun* CATERING metal or china dishes from which food is served

home /həʊm/ *noun* **1.** the place where a person lives ○ *Please send the letter to my home address, not my office.* **2.** □ **home country** the country where a person lives

'…people are far more appreciative of our efforts to provide freshly prepared, home-cooked meals' [*Caterer & Hotelkeeper*]

home address /,həʊm ə'dres/ *noun* the address of a house or flat where someone lives ○ *Please send the tickets to my home address.*

homebound /'həʊmbaʊnd/ *adjective* moving or travelling towards home

home consumption /,həʊm kən'sʌmpʃən/ *noun* same as **domestic consumption**

home-cooked meals /,həʊm kʊkt 'miːlz/ *plural noun* CATERING meals cooked on the premises or which are intended to appear to be cooked on the premises

home fries /'həʊm fraɪz/ *plural noun* US FOOD potatoes which have been boiled, sliced and then fried

homemade /,həʊm'meɪd/ *adjective* made at home and not bought from outside ○ *a pot of homemade marmalade* ○ *The restaurant offers homemade soup and roasts.*

''homemade' should be made at home, using traditional methods, prepared from first ingredients to final dish on the premises. If you buy frozen pastry and put a tin of meat into it, you cannot sell it as 'homemade'' [*Food Standards Agency*]

homestay /'həʊmsteɪ/ *noun* TOURISM a visit to stay in a private house ○ *We can arrange homestays in several houses in the residential neighbourhood.*

homeward /'həʊmwəd/ *adjective* going towards the home country ○ *homeward flight* ○ *homeward journey*

homewards /'həʊmwədz/ *adverb* towards the home country ○ *journey homewards*

hominy /'hɒmɪni/ *noun US* FOOD ground maize which can be cooked in milk or water

homogenisation /hə,mɒdʒənaɪ 'zeɪʃ(ə)n/, **homogenization** *noun* the treatment of milk so that the cream does not separate

homogenise /hə'mɒdʒənaɪz/ *verb* CATERING to mix various parts until they become a single whole, especially to treat milk so that the cream does not separate

homogenised milk /hə,mɒdʒənaɪzd 'mɪlk/ *noun* BEVERAGES milk which has been treated so that the cream is evenly mixed through the liquid ○ *I prefer homogenised milk, although it doesn't have cream on top.*

honey /'hʌni/ *noun* FOOD a sweet substance produced by bees ○ *Yoghurt served with honey is a popular Greek dessert.*

honeycomb /'hʌnikəʊm/ *noun* a construction of wax cells in which bees store honey

honeydew melon /,hʌnidju: 'melən/ *noun* FRUIT a type of melon which has yellow skin and pale green flesh

honeymoon /'hʌnimu:n/ *noun* TOURISM a holiday taken by a husband and wife immediately after their wedding ■ *verb* to go on a honeymoon

honeymoon couple /'hʌnimu:n ,kʌp(ə)l/ *noun* two people on their honeymoon

honeymoon suite /'hʌni,mu:n swi:t/ *noun* HOTELS a specially decorated suite of rooms for honeymoon couples

honeypot site /'hʌnipɒt saɪt/ *noun* a place that attracts a large number of tourists

hop /hɒp/ *noun* **1.** AIR TRAVEL a short trip, especially in an aircraft ○ *It's only a short hop from London to Paris.* **2.** FOOD a bitter fruit used in making beer ○ *Hops are used to give the bitter flavour to British beer.* (NOTE: Hops are not used in sweeter continental beers.)

hopping /'hɒpɪŋ/ *noun* the act of making short trips from one place to another

horizontal integration /,hɒrɪzɒnt(ə)l ,ɪntɪ'greɪʃ(ə)n/ *noun* BUSINESS the process of joining together similar companies in the same type of business, or of taking over another company in the same line of business

hors-d'oeuvre /,ɔ: 'dɜ:vrə/ *noun* CATERING cold food served at the beginning of a meal (NOTE: **Hors-d'oeuvre** is a French word, meaning 'outside the main work'. In English, the plural 'hors-d'oeuvres' can be used, although not in French.)

COMMENT: Hors-d'oeuvres can simply consist of pâté, prawns, radishes, etc., or can be a more complicated dish, such as a salad with scallops, or hard-boiled eggs with mayonnaise. Several items can be served together as 'mixed hors-d'oeuvres', and in some restaurants are brought to the table on an hors-d'oeuvre trolley.

hors-d'oeuvre trolley /,ɔ:'dɜ:v ,trɒli/ *noun* CATERING a trolley with various hors-d'oeuvres, from which the guest can choose

horse /hɔ:s/ *noun* a large animal used for riding or for pulling vehicles ○ *You can hire horses to go into the mountains.*

horseback /'hɔ:sbæk/ *noun* □ **on horseback** riding a horse ○ *There were ten policemen on horseback outside the football ground.*

horse-drawn /'hɔ:s drɔ:n/ *adjective* ENTERTAINMENT pulled by a horse ○ *holidays in Ireland in horse-drawn caravans* ○ *A horse-drawn sleigh met them at the hotel.* ○ *You can go for rides in the woods in horse-drawn sleighs.*

horseradish /'hɔ:srædɪʃ/ *noun* SAUCES, ETC. a plant with a large root which is grated to make a sharp sauce

COMMENT: Horseradish sauce is very sharp, similar to hot mustard. It is served with meat, particularly beef, and also with smoked fish, such as smoked eel. Jewish cuisine uses a type of red horseradish sauce flavoured with beetroot.

horse-riding /'hɔ:s raɪdɪŋ/ *noun* SPORT the activity of riding horses for pleasure ○ *We often go horse-riding in the summer.* ○ *The hotel offers horse-riding holidays in the mountains.* ◊ **pony-trekking**

hospitable /hɒ'spɪtəb(ə)l/ *adjective* welcoming and friendly to guests ○ *The people in the village were very hospitable.* ○ *As a rule, Americans are very hospitable people.*

hospitable climates /hɒ,spɪtəb(ə)l 'klaɪməts/ *plural noun* a system of keeping energy bills down while still providing a comfortable environment for guests

hospitality /,hɒspɪ'tælɪti/ *noun* friendly and welcoming treatment given to guests ○ *The town is famous for its old-fashioned American hospitality.*

'…respondents said hospitality was not taken seriously as a profession and still had a reputation for unsociable hours, poor salaries and lack of benefits' [*Caterer & Hotelkeeper*]

hospitality box /,hɒspɪ'tælɪti bɒks/ *noun* ENTERTAINMENT a special closed area at a function where corporate guests can be entertained ○ *They can organise any enter-*

tainment, from cocktail parties and hospitality boxes in sports venues to prestigious occasions such as Royal Ascot.

hospitality industry /ˌhɒspɪˈtælɪtɪ ˌɪndəstri/ *noun* HOTELS all the companies involved in providing services for guests, e.g. hotels, inns and restaurants, considered as a group

hospitality management /ˌhɒspɪˈtælɪtɪ ˌmænɪdʒmənt/ *noun* HOTELS the organisation of hotels, restaurants and other guest services ○ *Applicants for the job need a degree in Hospitality Management.*

hospitality pad /ˌhɒspɪˈtælɪtɪ pæd/ *noun* CATERING a small portable electronic pad on which a waiter or waitress can key orders for food or drink which are then relayed to the kitchen

hospitality suite /ˌhɒspɪˈtælɪtɪ swiːt/ *noun* BUSINESS a set of special reception rooms for entertaining business guests in a hotel or conference centre, or at a TV or radio station

hospitality tray /ˌhɒspɪˈtælɪtɪ treɪ/ *noun* a set of items such as an electric kettle, cups, milk and tea or coffee provided in a hotel room to enable guests to make a hot drink

host /həʊst/ *noun* **1.** a person who has invited guests ○ *He was the host at the reunion.* ○ *The waiter presented the bill to the guest, not to the host.* **2.** BARS the landlord of a hotel or inn, also sometimes of a restaurant □ **'mine host'** old-fashioned or humorous way of referring to the landlord of an inn ■ *verb* □ **to host a conference** *or* **a meeting** to be the place where a conference is held ○ *Geneva is hosting the IATA conference this year.* ○ *Barcelona hosted the Olympic games in 1992.*

hostel /ˈhɒst(ə)l/ *noun* TOURISM a building providing rooms for students, etc. □ **a student hostel** a building providing cheap lodgings for students

hosteller /ˈhɒst(ə)lə/ *noun* someone who stays at hostels while travelling for pleasure, especially a young person who stays at youth hostels

hostelling /ˈhɒst(ə)lɪŋ/ *noun* the practice of staying at hostels, especially youth hostels, while travelling for pleasure

hostelry /ˈhɒst(ə)lri/ *noun* BARS an inn ○ *We stayed at an old hostelry down by the river.* (NOTE: **Hostelry** is an 'old-fashioned' word, suggesting that the inn is very traditional.)

hostess /ˈhəʊstɪs/ *noun* **1.** TRAVEL a woman who looks after passengers or clients **2.** *US* CATERING a woman whose job it is to

receive guests as they enter a restaurant and show them to their tables

hot /hɒt/ *adjective* **1.** very warm ○ *The guests complain that the rooms are too hot in the daytime and too cold at night.* ○ *The drinks machine sells coffee, tea and hot soup.* ○ *Switch on the air-conditioner if you find the room too hot.* ○ *Travellers in hot countries are advised to take light clothes.* □ **room with hot and cold running water** a room with a washbasin, providing both hot and cold water from taps **2.** having a very strong and spicy taste ○ *This lime curry is particularly hot.*

hot-air balloon /hɒt ˈeə bəˌluːn/ *noun* AIR TRAVEL a very large balloon which rises into the air as the air inside it is heated, with people travelling in a basket attached underneath ○ *For my birthday, my father took me for a ride in a hot-air balloon.*

hot box /ˈhɒt bɒks/ *noun* an insulated storage trolley for plates with hot food

hot buffet /ˌhɒt ˈbʊfeɪ/ *noun* CATERING a buffet with hot dishes to choose from

hot chocolate /ˌhɒt ˈtʃɒklət/ *noun* BEVERAGES a hot drink made of powdered chocolate

hot cross bun /ˌhɒt krɒs ˈbʌn/ *noun* BREAD, ETC. a spiced bun, with a cross on top of it, eaten at Easter time, and especially on Good Friday

hot cupboard /ˌhɒt ˈkʌbəd/ *noun* CATERING a special cupboard for keeping food hot

hot dog /ˈhɒt dɒg/ *noun* FOOD a snack made of a hot frankfurter sausage in a long bun ○ *You can buy hot dogs at the food stall by the station.* □ **hot dog bun** long thin bread roll suitable for serving a sausage in

hotel /həʊˈtel/ *noun* TOURISM a building where travellers can rent a room for a night, or eat in a restaurant, or drink in the bar, and non-residents can eat and drink also ○ *The hotel is situated across the river from the Houses of Parliament.* ○ *He is a hotel manager in Moscow.* (NOTE: Although most people say **a hotel**, some people still use the older form **an hotel**.) □ **the hotel business, the hotel industry, the hotel trade** the business of running hotels ○ *She did not know anything about the hotel trade when she started her business.*

'…the hotel operator has called in the receiver after failing to come to terms with trading difficulties coupled with a fall in hotel property values' [*Caterer & Hotelkeeper*]

hotel accommodation /həʊˌtel əˌkɒməˈdeɪʃ(ə)n/ *noun* rooms available in hotels ○ *All hotel accommodation has been booked up for the exhibition.*

Hotel & Catering International Management Association *noun* an international organisation which represents hotels, caterers, restaurants, fast-food outlets, pubs, educational institutions, hospitals and all professionals involved in the hospitality industry. Abbr **HCIMA**

hotel bar /həʊˈtel bɑː/ *noun* HOTELS the bar in a hotel, usually open to non-residents as well as to guests staying at the hotel

hotel bus /həʊˈtel bʌs/ *noun* ROAD TRAVEL a special bus belonging to a hotel, which takes guests between the hotel and various destinations, often the airport or railway station

hotel chain /həʊˈtel tʃeɪn/ *noun* BUSINESS a group of hotels belonging to the same company

hotel division /həʊˈtel dɪˌvɪʒ(ə)n/ *noun* BUSINESS a division of a large company which runs hotels ○ *their profitable but slow-growing hotels division*

hôtel garni /həʊˌtel ɡɑːˈniː/ *noun* HOTELS a building with furnished rooms or apartments to let for periods of time, but usually with no restaurant, similar to an 'apartment hotel'

hotel group /həʊˈtel ɡruːp/ *noun* BUSINESS a large public company which owns a chain of hotels

hotelier /həʊˈtelieɪ/ *noun* HOTELS somebody who owns or manages a hotel ○ *Seaside hoteliers say that the season has been poor so far.*

'...hoteliers are emerging from the recession with a new energy and enthusiasm for their brands, marketing and customer service' [*Caterer & Hotelkeeper*]

hotel inspector /həʊˈtel ɪnˌspektə/ *noun* **1.** a person who visits a hotel to assess what grade it should have **2.** a person from an official body who visits hotels to check that they are observing health, hygiene and fire regulations

hotelkeeper /həʊˈtelˌkiːpə/ *noun* HOTELS same as **hotelier**

hotelman /həʊˈtelmən/ *noun* HOTELS somebody who owns or works in a hotel

hotel occupancy rate /həʊˌtel ˈɒkjʊpənsi ˌreɪt/ *noun* a figure that shows how many of the rooms in a hotel are used at a particular time or over a particular period

hotel plate /həʊˈtel pleɪt/ *noun* CATERING heavy EPNS cutlery, still used in some hotel restaurants

hotel premises /həʊˈtel ˈpremɪsɪz/ *noun* HOTELS a building which houses a hotel

hotel school /həʊˈtel skuːl/ *noun* HOTELS a college where students study hotel management

hotel security /həʊˌtel sɪˈkjʊərɪti/ *noun* HOTELS actions taken to protect a hotel against theft or fire

hotel tax /həʊˈtel tæks/ *noun* BUSINESS a local government tax added to the basic rate for a hotel room

hotel transfer /həʊˈtel ˌtrænsfɜː/ *noun* TRAVEL transport from an airport or railway station to a hotel

hotelware /həʊˈtelweə/ *noun* CATERING cups, saucers and plates specially made for hotel and restaurant use ○ *The factory manufactures several grades of hotelware.*

hotline /ˈhɒtlaɪn/ *noun* a phone line for giving urgent messages, or placing urgent orders ○ *Call the ticket hotline for reservations.*

hotplate /ˈhɒtpleɪt/ *noun* CATERING a piece of metal heated usually by electricity, used to cook food or to keep it hot

hotpot /ˈhɒtpɒt/ *noun* FOOD a meat stew with sliced potatoes on top, cooked in the oven

COMMENT: 'Lancashire hotpot' is a stew of lamb chops, onions and carrots, cooked in the oven with sliced potatoes on top. 'Mongolian hotpot' is a very hot broth, in a special container in the centre of the table, into which guests dip thin slices of meat to be cooked.

hot tub /ˈhɒt tʌb/ *noun* ENTERTAINMENT a large container full of hot water in which several people can sit at the same time ○ *The hotel has a heated outdoor pool and a hot tub.*

hot-water bottle /hɒt ˈwɔːtə ˌbɒt(ə)l/ *noun* a leakproof bag filled with hot water which is placed in a bed to warm it

hoummos /ˈhʊməs/ *noun* FOOD same as **hummus**

hour /aʊə/ *noun* **1.** a period of time lasting sixty minutes ○ *An hour's ski lesson costs $25.00.* □ **to work a thirty-five hour week** to work seven hours a day each weekday □ **the restaurant staff work an eight-hour day** they work for eight hours a day, e.g. from 8.30 to 4.30, or from 16.00 to 24.00 **2.** sixty minutes of work ○ *She earns £4 an hour.* ○ *We pay waiters £6 an hour.* □ **to pay by the hour** to pay people a fixed amount of money for each hour worked ○ *The chambermaids are paid by the hour.*

hourly /'aʊəli/ *adverb* per hour

hourly-paid workers /,aʊəli peɪd 'wɜːkəz/ *plural noun* workers paid at a fixed rate for each hour worked

hourly rate /,aʊəli 'reɪt/ *noun* the amount of money paid for an hour worked

house /haʊz/ *noun* **1.** a building in which people live ○ *We rented a house by the sea for the summer holidays.* **2.** BUSINESS a company or business **3.** a restaurant, hotel, bar or club □ **drinks are on the house** drinks are being offered free by the landlord or innkeeper ■ *verb* to provide a place for somebody or something to stay or be kept ○ *The art gallery is housed in a former cinema.* ○ *The group of students will be housed with Japanese families.*

housecraft /'haʊskrɑːft/ *noun* HOTELS skill at looking after a house or hotel

house doctor /'haʊz ,dɒktə/ *noun* MEDICAL a doctor who is on call to treat guests who become ill in a hotel

house fly /'haʊs flaɪ/ *noun* a common fly living in houses, which carries bacteria and other microorganisms onto food and can spread disease by laying its eggs in decaying meat and vegetables

household goods /,haʊshəʊld 'gʊdz/ *plural noun* items which are used in the home

housekeeper /'haʊskiːpə/ *noun* HOTELS somebody employed to look after the rooms in a hotel, be in charge of the cleaning staff, and make sure that linen is washed and ready

housekeeping /'haʊskiːpɪŋ/ *noun* HOTELS the work of looking after the rooms in a hotel ○ *Housekeeping in one of the most physically demanding jobs in hotels.*

'…housekeeping tends to be a department that is forgotten about. But it is very important, and gives employees a wonderful opportunity to contribute to a department that makes the most money for the hotel' [*Caterer & Hotelkeeper*]

housekeeping department /'haʊskiːpɪŋ dɪ,pɑːtmənt/ *noun* HOTELS the department in a hotel which deals with looking after the rooms, especially cleaning and providing linen

house laundry /'haʊs ,lɔːndri/ *noun* HOTELS a laundry which is part of a hotel, so that the dirty linen is not sent out for washing

housemaid /'haʊsmeɪd/ *noun* HOTELS a woman or girl who looks after the cleaning of a hotel room

houseman /'haʊsmən/ *noun* US HOTELS a man who does general jobs in a hotel

house moth /'haʊs mɒθ/ *noun* a small moth which sometimes lives in houses and whose larvae can destroy clothes and blankets, etc., kept in cupboards

house phone /,haʊs 'fəʊn/ *noun* HOTELS a telephone which links different rooms in a hotel, but is not connected to an outside line ○ *Call room service on the house phone.* Also called **internal phone**

house porter /,haʊz 'pɔːtə/ *noun* HOTELS a porter at the main entrance to a hotel or large restaurant

house special /,haʊs 'speʃ(ə)l/ *noun* CATERING a special dish for which a restaurant is famous

house swap /'haʊz swɒp/ *noun* TOURISM an arrangement where two families exchange houses for a holiday

house-swapping /'haʊs ,swɒpɪŋ/ *noun* TOURISM the activity of exchanging houses with someone living in another country

house wine /'haʊs waɪn/ *noun* BEVERAGES a cheaper wine which a restaurant buys in bulk, often with its own label on it

hovercraft /'hɒvəkrɑːft/ *noun* SHIPS AND BOATS a vehicle which moves over water or land on a cushion of air ○ *We are taking the hovercraft from Dover to Calais.*

HSE *abbreviation* Health and Safety Executive

HTST method /,eɪtʃ tiː es 'tiː ,meθəd/ CATERING same as **high temperature short time method**

hub /hʌb/ *noun* **1.** the centre of a wheel where it is connected to the axle ○ *The spokes of a wheel meet at the hub.* **2.** AIR TRAVEL a central airport, from which domestic flights called 'spokes' connect to international flights ○ *Chicago is the American hub for United Airlines.* **3.** BUSINESS a business centre ○ *Frankfurt is hoping to take the place of the City of London as the financial hub of Europe.*

'Orlando International Airport will become the hub for Vacation Express, the largest tour operator in the south of the USA. It is planned that the airport will then link six eastern and mid-western cities and five Caribbean destinations' [*Airliner World*]

human relations /,hjuːmən rɪ 'leɪʃ(ə)nz/ *plural noun* BUSINESS relations between people, especially between managers and staff, or between staff and customers

human resources /,hjuːmən rɪ'sɔːsɪz/ *plural noun* BUSINESS the workers which a company has available, seen from the point of view of their skills and experience

humid /'hjuːmɪd/ *adjective* damp, containing moisture vapour ○ *The climate in the summer is hot and humid.* ○ *I don't like* *humid weather – I much prefer a hot dry climate.*

humidifier /hjuːˈmɪdɪfaɪə/ *noun* a device for adding moisture to dry air, often used in centrally heated buildings where the air remains very dry ○ *We switch the humidifier on at night because the central heating makes the air too dry.*

humidify /hjuːˈmɪdɪfaɪ/ *verb* to make something damp ○ *The flat needs to be humidified in winter because the heating dries the air so much.*

humidity /hjuːˈmɪdɪti/ *noun* a measurement of how much water vapour is contained in the air ○ *The temperature is 32° with 90% humidity.*

humidity control /hjuːˈmɪdɪti kənˌtrəʊl/ *noun* a method of making the air humidity remain at a particular level, often by adding moisture to the air circulating in central heating systems

humidor /ˈhjuːmɪdɔː/ *noun* a special box for keeping cigars fresh, and preventing them from drying out

hummus /ˈhʊməs/ *noun* FOOD a thick paste made by combining mashed chickpeas, tahini, oil, lemon juice and garlic

hurricane /ˈhʌrɪkən/ *noun* a violent tropical storm with extremely strong winds, in the Caribbean or Eastern Pacific Ocean ○ *The hurricane damaged properties all along the coast.* (NOTE: In the Far East, this is called a **typhoon**.)

husky sledging /ˈhʌski ˌsledʒɪŋ/ *noun* SPORT the sport of riding on sledges pulled by huskies ○ *Are you going husky sledging in Canada?*

huss /hʌs/ *noun* SEAFOOD a large sea fish. Also called **dogfish**

hydro /ˈhaɪdrəʊ/ *noun* a hotel, resort or clinic offering hydrotherapy or other treatments involving water

hydrocooling /ˈhaɪdrəʊˌkuːlɪŋ/ *noun* CATERING the process of chilling food, especially fruit and vegetables, by putting them in chilled water, which stops the process of ripening. ◊ **refrigerate**

hydrofoil /ˈhaɪdrəʊfɔɪl/ *noun* SHIPS AND BOATS a boat which has aerodynamic wing-like structures which allow it to skim fast over water

hydrotherapy /ˌhaɪdrəʊˈθerəpi/ *noun* a type of physiotherapy where the patients are put in hot baths or are encouraged to swim ○ *a health spa offering beauty treatment, hydrotherapy, etc.* Compare **thalassotherapy**

hygiene /ˈhaɪdʒiːn/ *noun* **1.** actions to keep people and places clean and healthy ○ *The inspectors' report criticised the hygiene in the kitchen.* **2.** the science of health ○ *Food handlers have to maintain strict personal hygiene.*

hygienic /haɪˈdʒiːnɪk/ *adjective* **1.** clean and safe because all germs have been destroyed ○ *Don't touch the food with dirty hands – it isn't hygienic.* **2.** producing or fostering healthy conditions

hygienically /haɪˈdʒiːnɪkli/ *adverb* in a hygienic way

hypermarket /ˈhaɪpəmɑːkɪt/ *noun* a very large supermarket, usually on the outskirts of a large town

I

IAPA *abbreviation* AIR TRAVEL International Airline Passengers' Association

IATA *abbreviation* International Air Transport Association

ice /aɪs/ *noun* **1.** water which is frozen and has become solid ○ *Can we have some ice for the drinks, please?* **2.** FOOD ice cream ○ *She ordered a strawberry ice.* **3.** frozen water, as a surface for e.g. skating ■ *verb* **1.** to add ice to something, such as a drink ○ *She asked for a glass of iced water.* **2.** CATERING to put icing on a cake ○ *She ordered a dozen cup cakes to be iced with chocolate icing.*

iceberg lettuce /ˌaɪsbɜːg ˈletɪs/ *noun* a large round lettuce with a tight head of pale crisp juicy leaves

icebox /ˈaɪsbɒks/ *noun* **1.** the part of a refrigerator for making or storing ice in **2.** CATERING a box containing ice to keep food or drink cool **3.** *US* a refrigerator

ice bucket /ˈaɪs ˌbʌkɪt/ *noun* CATERING a container of crushed ice and water in which a wine bottle is placed to keep cool. Also called **wine bucket**

ice cream /ˌaɪs ˈkriːm/ *noun* DAIRY a mixture of cream, eggs, sugar and flavouring or of milk, sugar, water and flavouring, frozen until quite hard ○ *She ordered a strawberry ice cream.* ○ *What flavours of ice cream do you have?*

ice cream soda /ˌaɪs kriːm ˈsəʊdə/ *noun* BEVERAGES a sweet fizzy drink mixed with ice cream

ice cube /ˈaɪs kjuːb/ *noun* CATERING a little block of ice, used to cool a drink

ice lolly /ˈaɪs ˌlɒli/ *noun* DESSERTS a mixture of water and flavouring, frozen until solid with a stick in it (NOTE: The US English is **popsicle**.)

ice maker, icemaker *noun* a machine for making large quantities of ice

ice rink /ˈaɪs rɪŋk/ *noun* SPORT a special area of ice for ice skating or playing ice hockey. Also called **skating rink**

ice skate /ˈaɪs skeɪt/ *noun* SPORT a boot with a sharp blade for sliding on ice ○ *You can hire ice skates at the rink.*

ice skating /ˈaɪs ˌskeɪtɪŋ/ *noun* SPORT the sport or activity of skating on ice with skates fitted with blades

ice station /ˈaɪs ˌsteɪʃ(ə)n/ *noun* HOTELS a place in US hotels where you can get ice for the ice bucket in your room ○ *The ice station is along the corridor from your room.*

icing /ˈaɪsɪŋ/ *noun* FOOD a covering of sugar and flavouring, spread over a cake or biscuits

icing sugar /ˈaɪsɪŋ ˌʃʊgə/ *noun* FOOD a fine powdered white sugar, mixed with water or egg white and flavouring, used to cover cakes or biscuits

ID /ˌaɪ ˈdiː/ *noun* a document or card that proves that you are who you say you are ○ *Have you got any ID on you?*

ID card /ˌaɪ ˈdiː ˌkɑːd/ *noun* a card which shows a photograph of the holder, with the name, date of birth and other details ○ *Show your ID card when entering the Ministry.* ○ *In some European countries you are legally required to carry an ID card around with you.*

IDD *abbreviation* international direct dialling

ideal /aɪˈdɪəl/ *adjective* perfect, very good for something ○ *The cottage is an ideal place for birdwatching.* ○ *This is the ideal site for a new swimming pool.*

Ideal Home Exhibition /aɪˌdɪəl ˈhəʊm ˌeksɪbɪʃən/ *noun* an annual exhibition in London showing new houses, new kitchens, new products for the home, etc.

identification /aɪˌdentɪfɪˈkeɪʃ(ə)n/ *noun* **1.** the act of discovering or stating who someone is or what something is **2.** a document which shows who someone is ○ *The manager asked him for identification.*

identity /aɪˈdentɪti/ *noun* someone's name and personal details

identity document /aɪˈdentɪtɪ ˌdɒkjʊmənt/ *noun* a document which shows who someone is, e.g. a passport

IFTO *abbreviation* International Federation of Tour Operators

IHRA *abbreviation* International Hotel and Restaurant Association

ill /ɪl/ *adjective* sick, not well □ **to be taken ill** to become sick suddenly ○ *One of the guests was taken ill during the night and we had to call the doctor.*

illegal /ɪˈliːg(ə)l/ *adjective* not legal, against the law

illegal connection /ɪˌliːg(ə)l kə ˈnekʃən/ *noun* a connection between flights that would not allow a traveller enough time to change planes

illegal immigrant /ɪˌliːg(ə)l ˈɪmɪgrənt/ *noun* somebody who has entered a country illegally and wants to settle there

illegally /ɪˈliːgəli/ *adverb* in an illegal way ○ *He was accused of illegally importing arms into the country.*

illicit /ɪˈlɪsɪt/ *adjective* not legal, not permitted ○ *illicit sale of alcohol* ○ *trade in illicit alcohol*

illness /ˈɪlnəs/ *noun* sickness ○ *A lot of the staff are absent because of illness.*

immediate /ɪˈmiːdiət/ *adjective* **1.** happening at once ○ *He wrote an immediate letter of complaint.* ○ *Your order will receive immediate attention.* **2.** □ **immediate family member** a close family member, e.g. son, daughter, wife or husband, parent or grandparent

immediately /ɪˈmiːdɪətli/ *adverb* at once ○ *As soon as he heard the news he immediately phoned his wife.* ○ *Can you phone immediately the chalet becomes vacant?*

immigrant /ˈɪmɪgrənt/ *noun* somebody who comes to a country to settle ○ *Immigrants are rushing to Germany because the economy is booming.* Compare **emigrant**

immigrate /ˈɪmɪgreɪt/ *verb* to come into a country to settle. Compare **emigrate**

immigration /ˌɪmɪˈgreɪʃ(ə)n/ *noun* **1.** the act of settling in a new country ○ *The government is encouraging immigration because of the shortage of qualified staff in key industries.* Compare **emigration 2.** □ **Immigration** the section of an airport where new arrivals have to show their passports ○ *He was stopped at Immigration.* ○ *You will need to show all these documents when you go through Immigration.*

immigration control /ˌɪmɪˈgreɪʃ(ə)n kənˌtrəʊl/ *noun* restrictions placed by a country on the numbers of immigrants who are allowed to come to it ○ *Many countries have imposed immigration controls.*

immigration office /ˌɪmɪˈgreɪʃ(ə)n ˌɒfɪs/ *noun* an office dealing with immigrants

immunisation /ˌɪmjʊnaɪˈzeɪʃ(ə)n/, **immunization** *noun* MEDICAL treatment to give a person protection against an infection, either by injecting an antiserum or by giving the body the disease in such a small dose that the body does not develop the disease, but produces antibodies to counteract it ○ *Check what immunisation you need before you travel.*

'…no particular immunization is required for travellers to the United States, Europe, Australia or New Zealand' [*British National Formulary*]

immunisation centre /ˌɪmjʊnaɪ ˈzeɪʃ(ə)n ˌsentə/ *noun* MEDICAL a clinic where travellers can get immunisation before travelling

immunise /ˈɪmjʊnaɪz/ *verb* MEDICAL to give someone protection against an infection ○ *I was immunised against tetanus three years ago.* (NOTE: You immunise someone **against** a disease.)

import *noun* /ˈɪmpɔːt/ **1.** an article or type of goods brought into a country from abroad **2.** BUSINESS same as **importation** ■ *verb* /ɪmˈpɔːt/ BUSINESS to bring goods from abroad into a country for sale ○ *The company imports television sets from Japan,* ○ *This car was imported from France.* ○ *The union organised a boycott of imported cars.* Compare **export**

'European manufacturers rely heavily on imported raw materials which are mostly priced in dollars' [*Duns Business Month*]

importation /ˌɪmpɔːˈteɪʃ(ə)n/ *noun* BUSINESS the act of bringing goods from abroad into a country for sale ○ *The importation of arms is forbidden.*

import ban /ˈɪmpɔːt bæn/ *noun* a law forbidding imports ○ *The government has imposed an import ban on arms.*

import duty /ˈɪmpɔːt ˌdjuːti/ *noun* same as **customs duty**

importing /ɪmˈpɔːtɪŋ/ BUSINESS *adjective* that brings in or buys goods from other countries ○ *oil-importing countries* ○ *an importing company* ■ *noun* same as **importation** ○ *The importing of arms into the country is illegal.*

import levy /ˈɪmpɔːt ˌlevi/ *noun* BUSINESS a tax on imports, or, especially in the EU, a tax on imports of farm produce from outside the EU

import licence /'ɪmpɔːt ˌlaɪs(ə)ns/, **import permit** /'ɪmpɔːt ˌpɜːmɪt/ *noun* BUSINESS a document which allows goods to be imported

imports /'ɪmpɔːts/ *plural noun* BUSINESS goods brought into a country from abroad for sale ○ *Imports from Poland have risen to $1m a year.*

import surcharge /'ɪmpɔːt ˌsɜːtʃɑːdʒ/ *noun* BUSINESS an extra duty charged on imported goods, to try to prevent them from being imported and to encourage local manufacture

improve /ɪm'pruːv/ *verb* to make something better or to become better ○ *We are trying to improve our image with a series of TV commercials.* ○ *The general manager has promised that the bus service will improve.* ○ *They hope to improve the cash flow position by asking for payment in advance.* ○ *We hope the cash flow will improve or we will have difficulty in paying the suppliers' bills.* □ **bar takings have improved sharply during the first quarter** more money has been taken over the bar during the first quarter of the year

improved /ɪm'pruːvd/ *adjective* better ○ *Improved service has resulted in another star in the hotel's grade.*

improvement /ɪm'pruːvmənt/ *noun* **1.** the act of getting better ○ *There has been no improvement in the train service.* ○ *Hotel bookings are showing a sharp improvement over last year.* **2.** something which is better ○ *The new annexe is a great improvement over the old hotel.*

in /ɪn/ *abbreviation* inch

inaugural flight /ɪˌnɔːgjʊrəl 'flaɪt/ *noun* AIR TRAVEL the first flight over a new route, the first flight of a new aircraft, etc.

inbound /'ɪnbaʊnd/ *adjective* returning to the home country ○ *The inbound flights all leave on the hour.* ○ *The copilot flew the inbound leg from Durban to London.* Compare **outbound**

inbound tourism /ˌɪnbaʊnd 'tʊərɪz(ə)m/ *noun* tourism by visitors to the home country

incentive /ɪn'sentɪv/ *noun* BUSINESS something which encourages someone to work better

incentive bonus /ɪn'sentɪv ˌbəʊnəs/, **incentive payment** /ɪn'sentɪv ˌpeɪmənt/ *noun* BUSINESS extra pay offered to an employee to make him or her work better

incentive scheme /ɪn'sentɪv skiːm/ *noun* BUSINESS a plan to encourage better

work by paying higher commissions or bonuses ○ *Incentive schemes are boosting production.*

incentive travel /ɪn'sentɪv ˌtræv(ə)l/ *noun* AIR TRAVEL a travel scheme which gives cheap or free flights to someone who has earned them, e.g. to a salesperson for increased sales

incentive trip /ɪn'sentɪv trɪp/ *noun* BUSINESS a journey or holiday awarded to an employee to encourage him or her to work better

inch /ɪntʃ/ *noun* a measurement of length equalling 2.54cm (NOTE: This is usually written **in** or " after figures: *2in* or *2".*)

incidental expenses /ˌɪnsɪdent(ə)l ɪk'spensɪz/ *plural noun* FINANCE small amounts of money spent at various times, in addition to larger amounts

include /ɪn'kluːd/ *verb* to count something along with other things ○ *The charge includes VAT.* ○ *The total comes to £1,000 including service.* ○ *The total is £140 not including insurance and handling charges.* ○ *The room is £40 including breakfast.* ○ *Service is not included in the bill.*

inclusive /ɪn'kluːsɪv/ *adjective* counting something in with other things ○ *The total comes to £700, inclusive of VAT.* □ **the conference runs from the 12th to the 16th inclusive** it starts on the morning of the 12th and ends on the evening of the 16th

inclusive charge /ɪnˌkluːsɪv 'tʃɑːdʒ/, **inclusive sum** /ɪnˌkluːsɪv 'sʌm/ *noun* a charge which includes all costs

inclusive tour /ɪnˌkluːsɪv 'tʊə/ *noun* TOURISM a package holiday, where the price includes travel, hotel accommodation and meals and is cheaper than it would be if each item were bought separately. Abbr **IT**

income /'ɪnkʌm/ *noun* money which you receive

income tax /'ɪnkʌm tæks/ *noun* BUSINESS a tax on income

incoming call /ˌɪnkʌmɪŋ 'kɔːl/ *noun* a phone call coming into a building from someone outside

incoming mail /ˌɪnkʌmɪŋ 'meɪl/ *noun* mail which comes into an office

incoming tour /ˌɪnkʌmɪŋ 'tʊə/ *noun* TOURISM a group of tourists who are arriving at their destination, taking the place of another group which is just leaving

incorrect /ˌɪnkə'rekt/ *adjective* wrong, not correct ○ *The details of the tour were incorrect and the publicity had to be changed.*

incorrectly /ˌɪnkəˈrektli/ *adverb* wrongly, not correctly ○ *The suitcase was incorrectly labelled.*

increase /ˈɪnkriːs/ *noun* **1.** growth, the fact of becoming larger ○ *increase in tax* or *tax increase* ○ *increase in price* or *price increase* ○ *Profits showed a 10% increase* or *an increase of 10% on last year.* □ **increase in the cost of living** a rise in the annual cost of living **2.** a higher salary ○ *increase in pay* or *pay increase* ○ *increase in salary* or *salary increase* ○ *The government hopes to hold salary increases to 3%.* **3.** □ **on the increase** growing larger, becoming more frequent ○ *Overseas travel is on the increase.* ○ *Stealing from shops is on the increase.* ■ *verb* **1.** to grow bigger or higher ○ *The number of package holidays sold has increased by 20% over the last year.* ○ *Profits have increased faster than the increase in the rate of inflation.* ○ *The price of oil has increased twice in the past week.* □ **to increase in size** *or* **in value** to become larger or more valuable **2.** to make a level or amount higher ○ *Room charges were increased on January 1st.* ○ *The company have increased their fares by 10%.*

incubation period /ˌɪŋkjuˈbeɪʃ(ə)n ˌpɪəriəd/ *noun* MEDICAL a period during which a virus develops in your body after infection, before the symptoms of the disease appear ○ *The incubation period for measles is 12–14 days.*

independent /ˌɪndɪˈpendənt/ *adjective* **1.** not owned by a group, or not controlled by the state ○ *The big chains are squeezing the independent hotels out of the market.* **2.** not needing or not relying on anyone else ○ *She's eighteen and wants to be independent of her family.*

independent audit /ˌɪndɪpendənt ˈɔːdɪt/ *noun* same as **external audit**

independent traveller /ˌɪndɪpendənt ˈtræv(ə)lə/ *noun* TOURISM a traveller who organises his or her own trips, without buying package holidays

indicator board /ˈɪndɪkeɪtə ˌpæn(ə)l/, **indicator panel** *noun* TRAVEL a large device with letters or words on moving strips, used to show information about arrivals and departures at railway stations and airports

indirect tax /ˌɪndaɪrekt ˈtæks/ *noun* BUSINESS a tax such as VAT paid to someone who then pays it to the government

individual /ˌɪndɪˈvɪdʒuəl/ *noun* one single person ○ *We aim to cater for the private individual as well as for groups.* ■ *adjective* single, belonging to one person ○ *We sell individual portions of ice cream.*

individually-wrapped /ˌɪndɪvɪdʒuəli ˈræpt/ *adjective* with each piece of produce wrapped in its own wrapping ○ *The meat arrives from the butcher in individually-wrapped portions.*

individual travel /ˌɪndɪvɪdʒuəl ˈtræv(ə)l/ *noun* TOURISM the activity of travelling alone, or with a family group, but not in a group organised by a tour company

indoor /ˈɪndɔː/ *adjective* situated inside a building

indoor pool /ˈɪndɔː puːl/ *noun* a swimming pool which is indoors and usually has heated water

indoors /ɪnˈdɔːz/ *adverb* inside a building ○ *Since it is raining, we will hold the reception indoors.*

industrial dispute /ɪnˌdʌstriəl dɪˈspjuːt/ *noun* an argument between management and workers. Also called **labour dispute**

industrial training /ɪnˌdʌstriəl ˈtreɪnɪŋ/ *noun* the training of new employees to work in an industry

industry /ˈɪndəstri/ *noun* BUSINESS a business activity that many people and companies are involved in □ **the travel industry** all companies and services dealing with travel and tourism, e.g. trains, buses, planes, travel agents and hotels

inedible /ɪnˈedɪb(ə)l/ *adjective* not fit to be eaten ○ *The food was so burnt that it was inedible.*

inexpensive /ˌɪnɪkˈspensɪv/ *adjective* cheap, not expensive

inexpensively /ɪnɪkˈspensɪvli/ *adverb* without spending much money ○ *You can still eat quite inexpensively in Greece.*

infant passenger /ˌɪnfənt ˈpæsɪndʒə/ *noun* a child under 2 years of age

infect /ɪnˈfekt/ *verb* MEDICAL to contaminate someone or something with microorganisms that cause disease or toxins ○ *The disease infected his liver.* ○ *His whole arm soon became infected.*

infection /ɪnˈfekʃən/ *noun* MEDICAL the entry or introduction into the body of microorganisms, which then multiply

infectious /ɪnˈfekʃəs/ *adjective* MEDICAL possible to transfer from one person to another ○ *This strain of flu is highly infectious.* ○ *Chickenpox is infectious, so children who have it must be kept away from others.*

infectious virus hepatitis /ɪnˌfekʃəs ˈvaɪrəs ˌhepətaɪtɪs/ *noun* MEDICAL same as **hepatitis A**

infest /ɪnˈfest/ *verb* (*of parasite, vermin*) to be present in large numbers

infestation /ˌɪnfeˈsteɪʃ(ə)n/ *noun* the state of having large numbers of parasites or vermin ○ *The inspector reported cockroach infestation in the kitchens.*

inflexible /ɪnˈfleksɪb(ə)l/ *adjective* not possible to change

inflexible ticket /ɪnˌfleksɪb(ə)l ˈtɪkɪt/ *noun* TRAVEL a ticket which cannot be changed for another

in-flight /ˈɪn flaɪt/ *adjective* AIR TRAVEL during a flight

in-flight catering /ˌɪn flaɪt ˈkeɪtərɪŋ/ *noun* AIR TRAVEL food served during a flight

in-flight entertainment /ˌɪn flaɪt ˌentə ˈteɪnmənt/ *noun* AIR TRAVEL a film which passengers can watch, music which they can listen to or games which they can play during a long-distance flight

in-flight service /ˌɪn flaɪt ˈsɜːvɪs/ *noun* AIR TRAVEL service given to passengers during a flight

influx /ˈɪnflʌks/ *noun* the rapid entry of a crowd of people ○ *an influx of tourists in summer*

inform /ɪnˈfɔːm/ *verb* to tell someone details of something ○ *Please inform the group that the coach will leave the hotel at 10.30.*

information /ˌɪnfəˈmeɪʃ(ə)n/ *noun* details which explain something ○ *a piece of information* ○ *to answer a request for information* ○ *Please send me information on or about holidays in the United States.* ○ *Have you any information on or about discounts for groups of more than 10 people?* ○ *I enclose this leaflet for your information.* ○ *For further information, please write to Department 27.* (NOTE: There is no plural form: for one item say *a piece of information*.)

information bureau /ˌɪnfəˈmeɪʃ(ə)n ˌbjʊərəʊ/, **information office** /ˌɪnfə ˈmeɪʃ(ə)n ˌɒfɪs/ *noun* TOURISM same as **tourist information office**

information desk /ˌɪnfəˈmeɪʃ(ə)n desk/ *noun* a desk in a hotel, on a ship, at an exhibition, etc., where you can ask for information

infrastructure /ˈɪnfrəˌstrʌktʃə/ *noun* large-scale public systems and services, such as roads and railways, that are necessary for a country's economy to function properly

infuse /ɪnˈfjuːz/ *verb* to soak tea or herbs in liquid to extract the flavour or other qualities from them

infusion /ɪnˈfjuːʒ(ə)n/ *noun* BEVERAGES a drink made by pouring boiling water on a dry substance such as a herb tea or a powdered drug ○ *Instead of coffee could I have a camomile infusion?* ○ *My grandmother drinks a herbal infusion every evening before bed to help her get to sleep.*

ingredient /ɪnˈɡriːdiənt/ *noun* CATERING an item used in making a dish of food ○ *All the ingredients for the barbecue can be bought locally.* ○ *The ingredients are listed on the packet.*

inhabitant /ɪnˈhæbɪt(ə)nt/ *noun* somebody who lives in a place ○ *The local inhabitants do not like noisy tourists in summer.*

in-house /ˌɪn ˈhaʊs/ *adverb, adjective* working inside a company's building ○ *the in-house staff* ○ *We do all our catering in-house.*

in-house training /ˌɪn haʊs ˈtreɪnɪŋ/ *noun* BUSINESS training given to staff at their place of work

injure /ˈɪndʒə/ *verb* MEDICAL to hurt somebody in a fight or accident ○ *Six people were injured in the car crash.*

injury /ˈɪndʒəri/ *noun* MEDICAL a hurt or wound ○ *She received severe back injuries in the accident.* (NOTE: The plural form is **injuries**.)

inland /ˈɪnlənd/ *adjective, adverb* away from the coast of a country

inland port /ˌɪnlənd ˈpɔːt/ *noun* a port on a river or canal

Inland Revenue /ˌɪnlənd ˈrevənjuː/ *noun* BUSINESS a British government department which deals with taxes but not duties such as VAT. These duties are collected by Customs and Excise. (NOTE: The US equivalent is the **Internal Revenue Service (IRS)**.)

inland waterways /ˌɪnlənd ˈwɔːtəweɪz/ *plural noun* rivers and canals

in-line skates /ˌɪn laɪn ˈskeɪts/ *noun* SPORT roller skates that run on little wheels arranged in a line

in-line skating /ˌɪn laɪn ˈskeɪtɪŋ/ *noun* SPORT the sport of going on in-line skates

inn /ɪn/ *noun* BARS a building where alcoholic drinks are served, and which also has accommodation for visitors who wish to stay the night ○ *We stayed in a little inn in the mountains.*

inner /ˈɪnə/ *adjective* inside ○ *The capital has an inner ring road.*

inner city /ˌɪnə ˈsɪti/ *noun* the central part of a large town ○ *Inner city hotels are most convenient, but can be noisy.*

innkeeper /'ɪnkiːpə/ *noun* BARS somebody who runs an inn

inoculate /ɪ'nɒkjʊleɪt/ *verb* MEDICAL to introduce vaccine into a person's body in order to make the body create antibodies, so protecting the person against a disease ○ *The baby was inoculated against diphtheria.* (NOTE: You inoculate someone **with** or **against** a disease.)

inoculation /ɪˌnɒkjʊ'leɪʃ(ə)n/ *noun* MEDICAL **1.** the act of inoculating somebody **2.** an injection to stop somebody catching a disease ○ *Has the baby had a diphtheria inoculation?* ○ *Make sure you have the right inoculations before you go to the Far East.*

inquire /ɪn'kwaɪə/ *verb* to ask questions about something ○ *The chef inquired if anything was wrong.* ○ *She inquired about APEX fares to Canada.* □ **'inquire within'** ask for more details inside the office or shop

inquire into /ɪn'kwaɪər ˌɪntuː/ *verb* to investigate, to try to find out about something ○ *We are inquiring into the background of the new chef.*

inquiries desk /ɪn'kwaɪərɪz desk/ *noun* a desk in a hotel, train station, conference hall, etc., where an inquiries clerk sits to answer questions

inquiry /ɪn'kwaɪəri/ *noun* an official question ○ *I refer to your inquiry of May 25th.* ○ *All inquiries should be addressed to this department.*

inquiry office /ɪn'kwaɪəri ˌɒfɪs/ *noun* an office where somebody answers questions from members of the public

in-room technology /ˌɪn ruːm tek 'nɒlədʒi/ *noun* HOTELS same as **guest room technology** ○ *In-room technology is very expensive.*

in-seat power supply /ˌɪn siːt 'paʊə sə ˌplaɪ/, **in-seat power** *noun* an onboard power supply that enables passengers to use laptops or similar machines during the flight

insect /'ɪnsekt/ *noun* a small animal with six legs and a body in three parts, sometimes with wings ○ *Insects were flying round the lamp.* ○ *She was stung by an insect.*

insect bite /'ɪnsekt baɪt/ *noun* MEDICAL a sting caused by an insect which punctures the skin to suck blood, and in so doing introduces irritants

COMMENT: Most insect bites are simply irritating, but some patients can be extremely sensitive to certain types of insect bites (such as bee stings). Other insect bites can be more serious, as insects can carry the bacteria which produce typhus, sleeping sickness, malaria, filariasis, etc.

insecticide /ɪn'sektɪsaɪd/ *noun* a liquid or powder which kills insects ○ *They sprayed the bedrooms with insecticide.*

inside cabin /ˌɪnsaɪd 'kæbɪn/ *noun* a cabin with no window or porthole

inside lane /ˌɪnsaɪd 'leɪn/ *noun* ROAD TRAVEL the track nearest the side of the road, used by slower-moving vehicles, or by vehicles planning to turn off the road. Also called **slow lane**

insipid /ɪn'sɪpɪd/ *adjective* CATERING without much taste ○ *This sauce has no taste – it's really insipid.*

inspect /ɪn'spekt/ *verb* to examine something in detail ○ *to inspect a kitchen* or *a toilet* ○ *to inspect the accounts of a hotel* ○ *to inspect a bedroom to see if it has been cleaned*

inspection /ɪn'spekʃ(ə)n/ *noun* a close examination of something ○ *to make an inspection* or *to carry out an inspection of a kitchen* or *a toilet* ○ *inspection of a room to see if it has been cleaned* □ **to carry out a tour of inspection** to visit various places, hotels or restaurants and examine them in detail

inspector /ɪn'spektə/ *noun* an official who inspects

inspectorate /ɪn'spekt(ə)rət/ *noun* all inspectors

inspector of weights and measures /ɪnˌspektər əv ˌweɪts ən 'meʒəz/ *noun* BUSINESS a government official who inspects weighing machines and goods sold in shops to see if the quantities and weights are correct

instant /'ɪnstənt/ *adjective* referring to food that is quickly and easily prepared, and is usually sold in a premixed, precooked or powdered form

instant coffee /ˌɪnstənt 'kɒfi/ *noun* **1.** FOOD soluble freeze-dried granules or powder used to make coffee ○ *The bedroom has a kettle with tea bags and sachets of instant coffee.* **2.** BEVERAGES a drink made from freeze-dried granules of coffee or from powder, over which boiling water is poured ○ *She made a cup of instant coffee.*

instant purchase excursion fare /ˌɪnstənt ˌpɜːtʃɪs ɪk'skɜːʃ(ə)n ˌfeə/ *noun* AIR TRAVEL an excursion fare ticket which you purchase over the counter before boarding a flight. Abbr **IPEX**

instant tea /ˌɪnstənt 'tiː/ *noun* BEVERAGES tea made from freeze-dried granules or powder, onto which boiling water is poured

instruct /ɪnˈstrʌkt/ *verb* **1.** to give an order to someone □ **to instruct someone to do something** to tell someone officially to do something ○ *He instructed the restaurant to replace its kitchen equipment.* **2.** to show someone how to do something ○ *The hotel fire officer will instruct you in how to evacuate the building if a fire breaks out.*

instruction /ɪnˈstrʌkʃən/ *noun* something which explains how something is to be done or used □ **to await instructions** to wait for someone to tell you what to do □ **in accordance with** *or* **according to instructions** as the instructions show □ **failing instructions to the contrary** unless someone tells you to do the opposite

instructor /ɪnˈstrʌktə/ *noun* somebody who shows how something is to be done □ **aerobics instructor, ski instructor, swimming instructor** a person who teaches people how to do aerobics, to ski or to swim

instrument panel /ˈɪnstrʊmənt ˌpæn(ə)l/ *noun* ROAD TRAVEL the flat part of a car in front of the driver, with dials which show speed, etc.

insulate /ˈɪnsjʊleɪt/ *verb* to protect something against e.g. cold, heat or noise ○ *All the bedrooms are noise-insulated.*

insulation /ˌɪnsjʊˈleɪʃ(ə)n/ *noun* **1.** the act of protecting something against cold, heat or noise **2.** material which protects against cold, heat or noise

insurable /ɪnˈʃʊərəb(ə)l/ *adjective* FINANCE possible to insure ○ *The hotel is a firetrap and isn't insurable.*

insurance /ɪnˈʃʊərəns/ *noun* BUSINESS a contract stating that, in return for regular small payments, a company will pay compensation for loss, damage, injury or death (NOTE: For life insurance, British English prefers to use **assurance**, **assure**, **assurer**.) □ **to take out (an) insurance against fire** to make a small regular payment, so that if a fire happens, compensation will be paid □ **to take out (an) insurance on the building** to make a small regular payment, so that if the building is damaged compensation will be paid □ **the damage is covered by the insurance** the insurance company will pay for the damage □ **to pay the insurance on a car** to pay premiums to insure a car

insurance agent /ɪnˈʃʊərəns ˌeɪdʒənt/, **insurance broker** /ɪnˈʃʊərəns ˌbrəʊkə/ *noun* FINANCE somebody who arranges insurance for clients

insurance claim /ɪnˈʃʊərəns kleɪm/ *noun* FINANCE a request to an insurance company to pay compensation for loss, damage, injury or death

insurance company /ɪnˈʃʊərəns ˌkʌmp(ə)ni/ *noun* BUSINESS a company whose business is to receive payments and pay compensation for loss, damage, injury or death

insurance contract /ɪnˈʃʊərəns ˌkɒntrækt/ *noun* FINANCE an agreement by an insurance company to insure somebody or something

insurance cover /ɪnˈʃʊərəns ˌkʌvə/ *noun* FINANCE protection guaranteed by an insurance policy ○ *Do you have insurance cover against theft?*

insurance policy /ɪnˈʃʊərəns ˌpɒlɪsi/ *noun* FINANCE a document which shows the conditions of an insurance

insurance premium /ɪnˈʃʊərəns ˌpriːmiəm/ *noun* FINANCE a regular small payment made by the insured person to the insurer

insurance rates /ɪnˈʃʊərəns reɪts/ *plural noun* FINANCE the amount of premium which has to be paid per £1000 of insurance

insure /ɪnˈʃʊə/ *verb* BUSINESS to protect somebody or something by insurance ○ *to insure a building against fire* ○ *to insure someone's life* ○ *to insure baggage against loss* ○ *to insure against bad weather* ○ *to insure against loss of earnings* ○ *He was insured for £100,000.* □ **the life insured** the person whose life is covered by a life assurance policy □ **the sum insured** the largest amount of money that an insurer will pay under an insurance policy

insurer /ɪnˈʃʊərə/ *noun* BUSINESS a company which insures

intangible assets /ɪnˌtændʒɪb(ə)l ˈæsets/ *plural noun* BUSINESS assets which have a value, but which cannot be seen, such as goodwill, a patent or a trademark

integration /ˌɪntɪˈɡreɪʃ(ə)n/ *noun* BUSINESS the process of bringing several businesses together under a central control

intensive /ɪnˈtensɪv/ *adjective* involving a concentrated effort or the use of a lot of energy and materials

inter- /ɪntə/ *prefix* between

interchange /ˈɪntətʃeɪndʒ/ *noun* ROAD TRAVEL a large road junction where motorways cross ○ *There was a massive pile-up at the interchange.*

intercity /ˌɪntəˈsɪti/ *adjective* TRAVEL between two cities ○ *Intercity rail services* *have been disrupted by ice.* ○ *Hourly inter-city trains give a good service between London and Glasgow.*

intercontinental /ˌɪntəkɒntɪˈnent(ə)l/ *adjective* AIR TRAVEL between two continents

intercontinental **flight** /ˌɪntəkɒntɪnent(ə)l ˈflaɪt/ *noun* AIR TRAVEL a flight between two continents

interest /ˈɪntrəst/ *noun* **1.** a feeling of wanting to know about something ○ *The manager takes no interest in the guests.* **2.** FINANCE a payment made by a borrower for the use of money, calculated as a percentage of the capital borrowed □ **high** *or* **low interest** interest at a high or low percentage **3.** BUSINESS part of the ownership of something, e.g. money invested in a company giving a financial share in it □ **he has a controlling interest in the hotel** he owns more than 50% of the shares and so can direct how the hotel is run □ **majority interest**, **minority interest** a situation where someone owns a majority or a minority of shares in a company ○ *He has a majority interest in a supermarket chain.* □ **to acquire a substantial interest in a company** to buy a large number of shares in a company ■ *verb* to attract someone's attention ○ *She tried to interest the guests in a game of tennis.* □ **interested in** wanting to know about or do something ○ *The chef is not interested in Greek food.*

interest charges /ˈɪntrəst ˌtʃɑːdʒɪz/ *plural noun* BUSINESS the amount of interest paid

interest-free credit /ˌɪntrəst friː ˈkredɪt/, **interest-free loan** /ˈɪntrəst friː ləʊn/ *noun* FINANCE a credit or loan where no interest is paid by the borrower

interest rate /ˈɪntrəst reɪt/ *noun* FINANCE a percentage charge for borrowing money. Also called **rate of interest**

interior /ɪnˈtɪəriə/ *noun* the inner part of a building

interior decorator /ɪnˌtɪəriə ˈdekəreɪtə/, **interior designer** /ɪnˌtɪəriə dɪˈzaɪnə/ *noun* somebody who designs the inside of a building, including wall coverings, paint colours, furniture, fabrics, etc.

interline /ˈɪntəlaɪn/ *adjective* AIR TRAVEL between two airlines

internal /ɪnˈtɜːn(ə)l/ *adjective* inside

internal audit /ɪnˌtɜːn(ə)l ˈɔːdɪt/ *noun* BUSINESS an audit carried out by a department inside the company ○ *He is the manager of the internal audit department.*

internal auditor /ɪnˌtɜːn(ə)l ˈɔːdɪtə/ *noun* BUSINESS a member of staff who audits a company's accounts

internal flight /ɪnˌtɜːn(ə)l ˈflaɪt/ *noun* AIR TRAVEL same as **domestic flight**

internal phone /ɪnˌtɜːn(ə)l ˈfəʊn/ *noun* HOTELS same as **house phone**

Internal Revenue Service /ɪnˌtɜːn(ə)l ˈrevənjuː ˌsɜːvɪs/ *noun* BUSINESS in the US, the government department which deals with tax. Abbr **IRS**

international /ˌɪntəˈnæʃ(ə)nəl/ *adjective* between countries

international access code /ˌɪntənæʃ(ə)nəl ˈækses ˌkəʊd/ *noun* the first number dialled when making a telephone call to another country

International Airline Passengers Association *noun* AIR TRAVEL an organisation which represents passengers on airlines. Abbr **IAPA**

International Air Transport Association /ˌɪntənæʃ(ə)nəl eə ˈtrænspɔːt əˌsəʊsieɪʃ(ə)n/ *noun* AIR TRAVEL an organisation which regulates international air travel. Abbr **IATA**

international call /ˌɪntənæʃ(ə)nəl ˈkɔːl/ *noun* a telephone call to another country

International Date Line /ˌɪntənæʃ(ə)nəl ˈdeɪt ˌlaɪn/ *noun* a line of longitude in the Pacific Ocean which indicates the change in date from east to west

international dialling code /ˌɪntənæʃ(ə)nəl ˈdaɪəlɪŋ ˌkəʊd/ *noun* a special series of numbers used to make a call to another country, consisting of the international access code followed by the country code

international direct dialling /ˌɪntənæʃ(ə)nəl ˌdaɪrekt ˈdaɪəlɪŋ/ *noun* a system for calling telephone numbers in other countries yourself without asking the operator to do it for you. Abbr **IDD**

international driving licence /ˌɪntənæʃ(ə)nəl ˈdraɪvɪŋ ˌlaɪs(ə)ns/ *noun* ROAD TRAVEL a driving licence which allows you to drive legally in various countries provided you have a valid driving licence from your own country

international hotel /ˌɪntənæʃ(ə)nəl həʊˈtel/ *noun* HOTELS a hotel which is part of a chain which has hotels in several countries, and which caters for guests of many different nationalities

international law /ˌɪntənæʃ(ə)nəl ˈlɔː/ *noun* laws referring to the way countries deal with each other

international money order /ˌɪntənæʃ(ə)nəl ˈmʌni ˌɔːdːə/ *noun* FINANCE same as **foreign money order**

international operator /ˌɪntənæʃ(ə)nəl ˈɒpəreɪtə/ *noun* a telephone operator who deals with calls to other countries

international postal reply coupon /ˌɪntənæʃ(ə)nəl ˌpəʊst(ə)l rɪˈplaɪ kuːˌpɒn/ *noun* a document which can be used in another country to pay the postage of replying to a letter ○ *He enclosed an international postal reply coupon with his letter.*

international tourist /ˌɪntənæʃ(ə)nəl ˈtʊərɪst/ *noun* TOURISM a tourist who visits another country for at least one night's stay

international travel /ˌɪntənæʃ(ə)nəl ˈtræv(ə)l/ *noun* TRAVEL travel between different countries

Internet /ˈɪntənet/ *noun* an international network allowing people to exchange information on computers using telephone lines ○ *Much of our business is done on the Internet.* ○ *Internet sales form an important part of our turnover.* ○ *He searched the Internet for information on cheap tickets to Alaska.*

Internet access /ˈɪntənet ˌækses/ *noun* links to the Internet via computer terminals ○ *All business lounges are air-conditioned and feature workstations, Internet access, telephones, a bar and light refreshments.*

'…it also suggests that, by not capitalizing on guests' IT interest, the average 150-bedroom hotel is missing out on at least £50,000 of revenue a year from pay-per-view movies or metered Internet access' [*Caterer & Hotelkeeper*]

Internet check-in /ˌɪntənet ˈtʃek ˌɪn/ *noun* a procedure in which a passenger checks in for a flight online before departure

interpret /ɪnˈtɜːprɪt/ *verb* to translate what someone has said into another language ○ *The courier knows Greek, so he will interpret for us.*

interpretation /ɪnˌtɜːprɪˈteɪʃ(ə)n/ *noun* explanatory information to help people understand what they are seeing at a place of interest

interpretation centre /ɪnˌtɜːprə ˈteɪʃ(ə)n ˌsentə/ *noun* TOURISM same as **visitor centre**

interpreter /ɪnˈtɜːprɪtə/ *noun* somebody who translates what someone has said into another language ○ *The hotel porter will act as interpreter.* ○ *We need an Italian interpreter.*

interpretive centre /ɪnˈtɜːprətɪv ˌsentə/ *noun* TOURISM same as **visitor centre**

Inter rail /ɪnˈtɜː reɪl/ *noun* a pass that enables young people to travel free on railways throughout Europe

interstate /ˌɪntəˈsteɪt/ *adjective* US TRAVEL between two or more states in the USA ○ *interstate bus company*

interview /ˈɪntəvjuː/ *noun* **1.** a period spent talking to a person who is applying for a job ○ *We called six people for interview.* ○ *I have an interview next week* or *I am going for an interview next week.* **2.** ENTERTAINMENT a period spent asking a person questions on radio or television or for a magazine or newspaper ○ *The manager gave an interview to the local paper.* ■ *verb* to talk to a person applying for a job to see if they are suitable ○ *We interviewed ten candidates, but did not find anyone suitable.*

in tray /ˈɪn treɪ/ *noun* a container for letters or memos which have been received and are waiting to be dealt with

introductory offer /ˌɪntrədʌkt(ə)ri ˈɒfə/ *noun* BUSINESS a special price offered on a new product to attract customers

inventory /ˈɪnvənt(ə)ri/ *noun* **1.** especially US BUSINESS the goods kept in a restaurant or hotel, warehouse or shop ○ *The restaurant carries a high inventory.* ○ *Our aim is to reduce inventory.* (NOTE: The usual British English is **stock**.) **2.** a list of the contents of a house or hotel or restaurant for sale or for rent ○ *to draw up an inventory of fixtures* ○ *He checked the kitchen equipment against the inventory.* (NOTE: The plural form is **inventories**.) □ **to agree the inventory** to agree that all the items on the inventory are there and in the stated condition ■ *verb* to make a list of stock or contents

inventory control /ˈɪnvənt(ə)ri kən ˌtrəʊl/ *noun* US same as **stock control**

invest /ɪnˈvest/ *verb* **1.** BUSINESS to put money into shares or a business, hoping that it will produce interest and increase in value ○ *He invested all his money in a Chinese restaurant.* ○ *She was advised to invest in a fast-food franchise.* □ **to invest abroad** to put money into businesses in overseas countries **2.** FINANCE to spend money on something which you believe will be useful ○ *We invested in a new oven.* ○ *The hotel has invested in a fleet of courtesy cars.*

investment /ɪnˈvestmənt/ *noun* **1.** BUSINESS the act of placing of money so that it will increase in value and produce interest ○ *investment in hotel property* ○ *to make investments in travel companies* ○ *They called for more government investment in new industries.* **2.** FINANCE a thing bought with invested money □ **a long-term** *or* **short-term investment** an investment which is likely to increase in value over a long *or* short period □ **he is trying to protect his investments** he is trying to make sure that the money he has invested is not lost

investment income /ɪnˈvestmənt ˌɪnkʌm/ *noun* BUSINESS income from investments, e.g. interest and dividends

investor /ɪnˈvestə/ *noun* FINANCE somebody who invests money □ **the institutional investor** an organisation such as a pension fund or insurance company with large sums of money to invest □ **the small investor, the private investor** a person with a small sum of money to invest

invisible earnings /ɪnˌvɪzɪb(ə)l ˈɜːnɪŋz/ *plural noun* BUSINESS foreign currency earned by a country by providing services, not selling goods

invisible trade /ɪnˌvɪzəb(ə)l ˈtreɪd/ *noun* FINANCE services which are paid for in foreign currency or earn foreign currency without actually selling a product, e.g. banking, insurance or tourism

invoice /ˈɪnvɔɪs/ *noun* BUSINESS a note asking for payment for goods or services supplied ○ *your invoice dated November 10th* ○ *to make out an invoice for £250* ○ *to settle* or *to pay an invoice* ○ *They sent in their invoice six weeks late.* □ **the total is payable within thirty days of invoice date** the total sum has to be paid within thirty days of the date on the invoice ■ *verb* BUSINESS to send an invoice to someone ○ *to invoice a customer* □ **we invoiced you on November 10th** we sent you the invoice on November 10th

invoice price /ˈɪnvɔɪs praɪs/ *noun* BUSINESS the price of something as given on an invoice, including discount and VAT

IPEX /ˈaɪpeks/ *abbreviation* AIR TRAVEL instant purchase excursion fare

Irish coffee /ˌaɪrɪʃ ˈkɒfi/ *noun* BEVERAGES hot coffee, served in a glass, with Irish whiskey added to it and whipped cream poured on top

iron /ˈaɪən/ *noun* an electric household instrument for smoothing the creases from clothes ○ *Each room has an iron and ironing board.* ■ *verb* to make cloth smooth using an iron

ironer /ˈaɪənə/ *noun* a large machine for ironing big items like sheets and pillowcases

ironing /ˈaɪənɪŋ/ *noun* **1.** the work of pressing clothes, sheets, etc., with an electric iron **2.** clothes, sheets, etc., which need pressing

ironing board /ˈaɪənɪŋ bɔːd/ *noun* a high narrow table used for pressing clothes, sheets, etc., on

irradiate /ɪˈreɪdieɪt/ *verb* to treat food with electromagnetic radiation in order to kill germs and slow down the process of ripening and decay

irradiation /ɪˌreɪdiˈeɪʃ(ə)n/ *noun* CATERING the use of rays to kill bacteria in food

COMMENT: Food is irradiated with gamma rays from isotopes which kill bacteria. It is not certain, however, that irradiated food is safe for humans to eat, as the effects of irradiation on food are not known. In some countries irradiation is only permitted as a treatment of certain foods.

IRS *abbreviation* US BUSINESS Internal Revenue Service

island /ˈaɪlənd/ *noun* a piece of land entirely surrounded by water ○ *Greek island holidays* ○ *The Channel Islands are favourite holiday destinations.*

island-hop /ˈaɪlənd hɒp/ *verb* to travel from island to island within the same chain, especially as part of a holiday

island hopping /ˈaɪlənd ˌhɒpɪŋ/ *noun* TOURISM travel from island to island, staying only a short time on each one ○ *Greek island hopping can be a nightmare without an itinerary.*

IT *abbreviation* TOURISM inclusive tour

Italian dressing /ɪˌtæljən ˈdresɪŋ/ *noun* SAUCES, ETC. a salad dressing typically made with oil and vinegar, garlic and oregano

item /ˈaɪtəm/ *noun* **1.** a thing ○ *Do you have any items of jewellery in your luggage?* ○ *Valuable items should be left with the reception desk.* ○ *She declared several items to the customs.* **2.** a point on a list ○ *Items 6 and 7 on the fire drill instructions do not apply.*

itemise /ˈaɪtəmaɪz/ *verb* to make a detailed list of things

itemised account /ˌaɪtəmaɪzd əˈkaʊnt/ *noun* a detailed record of money paid or owed

itemised bill /ˌaɪtəmaɪzd ˈbɪl/ *noun* a piece of paper giving details of each object or service and the price

itemised invoice /ˌaɪtəmaɪzd ˈɪnvɔɪs/ *noun* BUSINESS an invoice which lists each item separately

itinerary /aɪˈtɪnərəri/ *noun* TOURISM a list of places to be visited on one journey ○ *The members of the group were given a detailed* *tour itinerary by the courier.* ○ *The itinerary takes us to six countries in ten days.*

IYHF *abbreviation* International Youth Hostel Federation

J

jab /dʒæb/ *noun* MEDICAL an injection (*informal*) ○ *Have you had your cholera jabs yet?*

jacket /'dʒækɪt/ *noun* a short coat ○ *You have to wear a jacket and tie to enter the restaurant.* ○ *Chef's jackets are mostly white, and worn with blue checked trousers.*

jacket potato /ˌdʒækɪt pə'teɪtəʊ/ *noun* FOOD same as **baked potato**

jacuzzi, jacuzzi bath *tdmk* a trademark for a type of bath with jets which circulate the water and keep it bubbling ○ *The health club has two jacuzzis and a whirlpool.*

jalapeño /'hæləpeɪnəʊ/ *noun* a small hot pepper that is picked when green and is used extensively in Mexican cooking

jam /dʒæm/ *noun* **1.** CATERING a sweet food made with fruit and sugar ○ *Each table has little pots of jam and honey.* ○ *Help yourself at the buffet to individual packs of butter and jam.* **2.** a blockage which prevents something moving ■ *verb* to stop working, to be blocked ○ *The traffic lights failed and the traffic was jammed for miles.* ○ *The switchboard was jammed with calls.* (NOTE: **jamming – jammed**)

jambalaya /ˌdʒæmbə'laɪjə/ *noun* FOOD a Creole dish of rice with a mixture of fish and meat such as shrimps, chicken, ham and spicy sausage

jar /dʒɑː/ *noun* a pot, usually glass, for keeping food in ○ *There was a jar of marmalade on the breakfast table.*

java /'dʒɑːvə/ *noun* US coffee, especially brewed coffee as opposed to instant coffee

Java /'dʒɑːvə/ *noun* a variety of rich coffee grown on Java and the surrounding islands

jaw /dʒɔː/ ♦ **open-jaw arrangement**

jeep /dʒiːp/ *tdmk* ROAD TRAVEL a trademark for a strongly built four-wheel-drive vehicle used for travelling over rough ground ○ *The convoy of jeeps crossed slowly over the bridge.*

jeep safari /'dʒiːp sə,fɑːri/ *noun* an organised sightseeing tour or excursion in a jeep or other four-wheel-drive vehicle

jell /dʒel/ *verb* (*of liquid*) to become a jelly ○ *Boil the jam until it jells.*

jellied /'dʒeliːd/ *adjective* FOOD cooked or preserved in a jelly ○ *jellied eels*

Jell-O /'dʒel əʊ/ *tdmk* US DESSERTS a trademark for a type of sweet food made of gelatine, water and fruit flavourings, etc. (NOTE: The British English is **jelly**.)

jelly /'dʒeli/ *noun* **1.** FOOD a semi-solid substance, especially a type of sweet food made of gelatine, water and fruit flavouring, etc. ○ *The children had fish fingers and chips followed by jelly and ice cream.* (NOTE: The plural form is **jellies**. In the USA this is often called by a trademark, **Jell-O**.) **2.** CATERING a type of preserve made of fruit juice boiled with sugar ○ *roast lamb served with mint jelly* **3.** US FOOD a sweet preserve, made with fruit and sugar ○ *She loves peanut butter and blackcurrant jelly sandwiches.* (NOTE: The British English is **jam**.)

jelly baby /'dʒeli ,beɪbi/ *noun* FOOD a sweet of coloured jelly, shaped like a little baby ○ *She gave the little girl a bag of jelly babies.*

jelly bean /'dʒeli biːn/ *noun* US FOOD a sweet of coloured jelly, shaped like a bean

jelly mould /'dʒeli məʊld/ *noun* CATERING a shape for making jelly

jelly roll /ˌdʒeli 'rəʊl/ *noun* US BREAD, ETC. a cake made by rolling a thin sheet of sponge cake covered with jam (NOTE: The British English is **Swiss roll**.)

Jerusalem artichoke /dʒə,ruːsələm 'ɑːtɪtʃəʊk/ *noun* VEGETABLES ♦ **artichoke**

jet /dʒet/ *noun* AIR TRAVEL an aircraft with jet engines ■ *verb* TRAVEL to travel by jet (*informal*) ○ *She jetted off to Los Angeles for a short holiday.* ○ *Nice airport was busy with stars jetting in for the Cannes Film Festival.*

jetbridge /'dʒetbrɪdʒ/ *noun* AIR TRAVEL same as **airbridge**

jet foil /'dʒet fɔɪl/ *noun* SHIPS AND BOATS a boat which skims fast over water, propelled by gas turbine engines

jet lag /'dʒet læg/ *noun* AIR TRAVEL a tired state after flying by jet aircraft across several time zones ○ *She suffered dreadful jet lag after the flight from New York.*

jet-propelled aircraft /,dʒet prə,peld 'eəkrɑːft/ *noun* AIR TRAVEL an aircraft with jet engines

jet set /'dʒet set/ *noun* wealthy people who frequently travel by jet ○ *What a party! – All the international jet set were there.*

jet-setter /'dʒet ,setə/ *noun* a member of the jet set

jetty /'dʒeti/ *noun* SHIPS AND BOATS a landing stage for smaller boats ○ *There were two boats tied up to the jetty.* (NOTE: The plural form is **jetties**.)

jetway /'dʒetweɪ/ *noun* AIR TRAVEL same as **airbridge**

jewel /'dʒuːəl/ *noun* a valuable stone such as a diamond ○ *She decided it was safer to lock up her jewels in the hotel safe.*

jewellery /'dʒuːəlri/ *noun* ornaments to be worn, made from precious stones or precious metals, or of imitation stones ○ *The burglar stole all her jewellery.* (NOTE: The US spelling is **jewelry**.)

JFK *abbreviation* AIR TRAVEL John Fitzgerald Kennedy International Airport

job /dʒɒb/ *noun* **1.** a task, a particular piece of work that has to be done □ **to do an excellent job (of work)** to work extremely well □ **to do odd jobs** to do general work ○ *He does odd jobs for us around the hotel.* **2.** regular paid work ○ *to apply for a job with an airline* ○ *He is looking for a job in the hotel industry.* ○ *She lost her job when the tourist office closed.* ○ *She got a job in a travel agency.* □ **to look for a job** to try to find work

job analysis /'dʒɒb ə,næləsɪs/ *noun* a detailed examination and report on the duties of a job

job application /'dʒɒb æplɪ,keɪʃ(ə)n/ *noun* a written request for a job ○ *You have to fill in a job application form.*

job classification /'dʒɒb klæsɪfɪ ,keɪʃ(ə)n/ *noun* the work of sorting jobs into various categories

job description /'dʒɒb dɪ,skrɪpʃən/ *noun* an official document from the management which says in detail what a job involves

job evaluation /'dʒɒb ɪvælju,eɪʃ(ə)n/ *noun* BUSINESS the work of examining different jobs within an organisation to see what skills and qualifications are needed to carry them out

job of work /,dʒɒb əv 'wɜːk/ *noun* a piece of work

job satisfaction /'dʒɒb sætɪs,fækʃən/ *noun* a feeling which employees have of being happy in their place of work and pleased with the work they do

job security /'dʒɒb sɪ,kjʊərɪti/ *noun* a feeling which employees have that they have a right to keep their jobs, or that they can stay in their jobs until they retire

job sharing /'dʒɒb ,ʃeərɪŋ/ *noun* a situation where a job is done by more than one person, each working part-time

job specification /'dʒɒb ,spesɪfɪkeɪʃ(ə)n/ *noun* a very detailed description of what is involved in a job

job title /'dʒɒb ,taɪt(ə)l/ *noun* the name given to a person doing particular work ○ *Her job title is 'Chief Reservations Clerk'.*

job vacancies /'dʒɒb ,veɪkənsi/ *plural noun* jobs which are available and need people to do them

jog /dʒɒg/ *noun* SPORT a rather slow run, especially taken for exercise ○ *She goes for a jog each morning.* ■ *verb* **1.** □ **to go jogging**, **to jog** to run at an easy pace, especially for exercise ○ *He was jogging round the park.* ○ *She goes jogging for half an hour every morning.* **2.** to shake or to push lightly ○ *When the turbulence started, my neighbour jogged my arm and made me spill my drink.*

jogger /'dʒɒgə/ *noun* SPORT somebody who jogs for exercise ○ *Joggers run round the park every morning.*

jogging /'dʒɒgɪŋ/ *noun* SPORT the activity of running at an easy pace for exercise

jogging track /'dʒɒgɪŋ træk/ *noun* SPORT a track in the grounds of a hotel, health farm, etc., where guests can go jogging, without having to run on the street

join /dʒɔɪn/ *verb* **1.** to put things together ○ *The two bedrooms are joined together to make a suite.* **2.** □ **to join an association** *or* **a group** to become a member of an association or a group ○ *Two more people will join the group in Cairo.*

joint /dʒɔɪnt/ *noun* **1.** MEAT a piece of meat, especially one suitable for roasting ○ *a joint of beef* ○ *a bacon joint* □ **a cut off the joint** a slice cut from a piece of roast meat **2.** a low-class club or restaurant (*informal*) ○ *a hamburger joint* ■ *adjective* **1.** BUSINESS in which two or more organisations are linked together **2.** for two or more people

joint account /'dʒɔɪnt ə,kaʊnt/ *noun* FINANCE a bank account for two people

joint bill /,dʒɔɪnt 'bɪl/ *noun* two bills added together and paid by one person

joint discussions /ˌdʒɔɪnt dɪ
ˈskʌʃ(ə)nz/ *plural noun* talks between management and employees before something is
done

jointly /ˈdʒɔɪntli/ *adverb* together with one
or more other people ○ *to own a property
jointly* ○ *The brother and sister manage the
family hotel jointly.*

joint management /ˌdʒɔɪnt
ˈmænɪdʒmənt/ *noun* management done by
two or more people

joint ownership /ˌdʒɔɪnt ˈəʊnəʃɪp/
noun a situation where a property is owned
by several people or companies

joint venture /ˌdʒɔɪnt ˈventʃə/ *noun*
BUSINESS a very large business project where
two or more companies join together, often
forming a new joint company to manage the
project

journey /ˈdʒɜːni/ *noun* TRAVEL a period of
travelling that takes you from one place to
another ○ *He planned his journey to visit all
the capitals of Europe in two weeks.* ○ *The
car broke down and we had to complete our
journey on foot.*

jug /dʒʌg/ *noun* a container with a handle,
used for pouring liquids ○ *a jug of milk* ○
There is a jug of water by the bedside. ○
Could we have another jug of water, please?

jugged hare /ˌdʒʌgd ˈheə/ *noun* FOOD
hare cooked slowly in a covered dish

juice /dʒuːs/ *noun* FOOD the liquid inside a
fruit or vegetable, or inside meat or poultry ○
She had a glass of orange juice for breakfast.
○ *I'd like a tomato juice with Worcester
sauce.* ○ *Make gravy using the meat juices in
the roasting pan.*

juice bar /ˈdʒuːs bɑː/ *noun* a café serving
freshly prepared fruit juices and other
healthy foods and drinks

juice extractor /ˈdʒuːs ɪkˌstræktə/ *noun*
CATERING a device for extracting juice from
a fruit or vegetable

juicy /ˈdʒuːsi/ *adjective* full of juice ○ *a
juicy orange* ○ *slices of juicy roast chicken* ○
This grapefruit is not very juicy.

juke box /ˈdʒuːk bɒks/ *noun* ENTERTAIN-
MENT a machine which plays records when
money is inserted

julienne /ˌdʒuːliˈen/ *adjective* cut into
long thin matchstick strips ■ *verb* to cut vegetables into thin matchstick strips

jumbo jet /ˈdʒʌmbəʊ dʒet/, **jumbo**
/ˈdʒʌmbəʊ/ *noun* AIR TRAVEL the Boeing
747, a very large jet aircraft ○ *They live close
to the airport, with jumbos roaring overhead
all day long.* ○ *The airline is buying another
ten jumbo jets to add to its fleet.*

junior /ˈdʒuːniə/ *adjective* lower in rank ■
noun the son of the family (*humorous*) ○
Harry Markovitz Junior

junior clerk /ˌdʒuːniə ˈklɑːk/ *noun* a
clerk, usually young, who has lower status
than a senior clerk

junior executive /ˌdʒuːniə ɪgˈzekjʊtɪv/,
junior manager /ˈdʒuːniə ˈmænɪdʒə/
noun BUSINESS a young manager in a company

junior suite /ˈdʒuːniə swiːt/ *noun*
HOTELS a large hotel room divided into living
room and bedroom areas

junket /ˈdʒʌŋkɪt/ *noun* BUSINESS an
expensive business trip, paid for by a company or by a government

junk food /ˈdʒʌŋk fuːd/ *noun* CATERING
food of little nutritional value, e.g. high-fat
processed snacks, eaten between or instead
of meals ○ *They just spent their holiday
watching TV and living off junk food.*

justice /ˈdʒʌstɪs/ *noun* **1.** fair treatment in
law **2.** a magistrate

justices' full on licence /ˌdʒʌstɪsɪz fʊl
ɒn ˈlaɪs(ə)ns/ *noun* BARS a licence to sell
any type of alcohol for drinking on the
premises, such as in a bar or restaurant. Also
called **full on licence**

jut /dʒʌt/ *verb* □ **to jut out over something**
to stick out beyond something, usually horizontally ○ *The balcony juts out over the main
street.*

K

karaoke /ˌkæri'əʊki/ *noun* ENTERTAIN-MENT a type of entertainment, coming originally from Japan, where people sing to recorded music

karaoke machine /ˌkæri'əʊki məˌʃiːn/ *noun* ENTERTAINMENT a machine which plays the music of well-known songs, and displays the words on a screen so that people can sing along

karaoke night /ˌkæri'əʊki naɪt/ *noun* ENTERTAINMENT a night at a pub or club, when people can use the karaoke machine ○ *Friday night is karaoke night in our local pub.*

kayak /'kaɪæk/ *noun* SPORT a type of small canoe which is pointed at both ends, and almost completely covered, with only a narrow opening for the canoeist ○ *A group of kayaks from the canoe club raced up the river.*

kayaking /'kaɪækɪŋ/ *noun* SPORT the sport of going in kayaks ○ *The river is fast-flowing and ideal for kayaking.*

kebab /kɪ'bæb/ *noun* FOOD a dish of pieces of meat, fish or vegetables stuck on a skewer and cooked over a charcoal grill ○ *a lamb kebab* ○ *a pork kebab*

kedgeree /'kedʒəri/ *noun* FOOD a spicy mixture of rice, fish, curry and eggs, traditionally eaten at breakfast

keeper /'kiːpə/ *noun* somebody who looks after something □ **(zoo) keeper** somebody who looks after animals in a zoo

keg /keg/ *noun* BARS a small barrel, especially an aluminium barrel in which beer is stored with gas mixed in with it

keg beer /'keg bɪə/ *noun* BEVERAGES beer which is stored in a keg and served from a pressurised pump

kernel /'kɜːn(ə)l/ *noun* FOOD the softer edible part inside a nut

ketchup /'ketʃəp/ *noun* SAUCES, ETC. thick savoury tomato sauce, eaten especially with fried food ○ *The children asked for hamburgers with ketchup.* ○ *I know someone who likes ketchup on his omelettes.*

kettle /'ket(ə)l/ *noun* **1.** a metal or plastic container, with a lid and a spout, used for boiling water ○ *Each bedroom has a kettle, tea bags and packets of instant coffee.* **2.** a large container used in a kitchen for boiling soup, stew, etc.

key /kiː/ *noun* **1.** a piece of shaped metal used to open a lock **2.** a part of a computer keyboard which you press with your fingers ○ *There are sixty-four keys on the keyboard.*

key card /'kiː kɑːd/ *noun* **1.** an electronic card given to a guest at registration, which acts as a key to their room **2.** a card given to a guest on registration, which shows the number of their room and which they may need to show for identification purposes ▶ ◊ **card**

'…staff create key cards for guests using a card programming unit, linked to a point of sale system. The door lock updates itself with the guest identity code each time a new card authorized for that room is used.' [*Caterer & Hotelkeeper*]

COMMENT: There are two main types of magnetic key card: the 'dip' card, which is pushed down into a slot and then pulled out again when the door unlocks, and a 'swipe' card, which you run down a slot to unlock the door.

key-drop box /'kiː drɒp ˌbɒks/ *noun* a box at reception for guests to put their keys in as they leave the hotel

key lime pie /ˌkiː laɪm 'paɪ/ *noun* a pie made from thickened sweetened condensed milk flavoured with juice from key limes

key money /'kiː ˌmʌni/ *noun* BUSINESS a premium paid when taking over the keys of a flat or office which you are renting

key rack /'kiː ræk/ *noun* HOTELS a board with hooks or a series of pigeonholes where room keys are put near the front desk of a hotel

kg *abbreviation* kilogram

kidney /'kɪdni/ *noun* **1.** one of a pair of organs in animals that extract impurities from the blood **2.** FOOD this organ used as food ○ *grilled kidneys with bacon*

COMMENT: Lamb's kidney, ox kidney and pig's kidneys are all used in cooking; they can be cooked in a red wine sauce, or used in kebabs. The best-known English dishes using kidneys are steak and kidney pie or pudding.

kidney bean /'kɪdni biːn/ *noun* VEGETABLES a type of bean with reddish seeds, shaped like kidneys, used e.g. in 'chilli con carne'

kilo /'kiːləʊ/, **kilogram** /'kɪləgræm/, **kilogramme** *noun* a measure of weight equalling one thousand grams ○ *She bought a kilo of tomatoes.* ○ *You need two kilos of potatoes to serve six people.* Abbr **kg** (NOTE: This is usually written **kg** after figures: *4kg.*)

kilometre /kɪ'lɒɪtə/ *noun* a measure of distance equal to one thousand metres. Abbr **km** (NOTE: This is usually written **km** after figures: *25km.* The US spelling is **kilometer**.) □ **the car does fifteen kilometres to the litre** the car uses a litre of petrol to travel fifteen kilometres

king prawn /ˌkɪŋ 'prɔːn/ *noun* SEAFOOD a type of very large prawn, the type which is served as scampi

king room /'kɪŋ ruːm/ *noun* a room with a king-sized bed

king-sized bed /ˌkɪŋ saɪzd 'bed/, **king size bed** *noun* a double bed which is wider and longer than normal

kiosk /'kiːɒsk/ *noun* a small wooden shelter, for selling goods out of doors ○ *a newspaper kiosk*

kipper /'kɪpə/ *noun* SEAFOOD a smoked herring, which has been opened up and is flat

COMMENT: Kippers are traditionally eaten for breakfast, grilled, and then served hot with butter.

kippered /'kɪpəd/ *adjective* CATERING smoked

kir /kɪə/ *noun* BEVERAGES a drink of cold white wine, served with a dash of blackcurrant liqueur

kir royal /ˌkiːr rɔɪ'jɑːl/ *noun* BEVERAGES kir made with sparkling white wine

kit /kɪt/ *noun* TRAVEL clothes and personal equipment, usually packed for travelling

kitchen /'kɪtʃɪn/ *noun* a room in which food is prepared before serving ○ *The inspector found cockroaches in the hotel kitchens.*

COMMENT: The kitchen of a large restaurant will be organised in brigades: the chef (or chef de cuisine) is in charge of all sections of the kitchen; various sections (each under a chef de partie) include sauces, vegetables, pastries, etc. A clerk (the 'aboyeur') takes orders from the waiters and shouts them out to the various sections. Kitchen staff will also include assist-

ants (or commis chefs), porters, plate washers (plongeurs), etc.

kitchen assistant /'kɪtʃɪn əˌsɪst(ə)nt/ *noun* somebody who does general work in a kitchen

kitchen clerk /'kɪtʃɪn klɑːk/ *noun* CATERING the person in the kitchen who shouts the order from the waiter to the chefs, and pins the waiter's written order on a hook relating to the particular table. Also called **aboyeur**

kitchenette /ˌkɪtʃɪ'net/ *noun* a small kitchen in a corner of a living room ○ *Each studio flat is equipped with a bathroom, kitchenette and balcony.*

kitchen garden /ˌkɪtʃɪn 'gɑːd(ə)n/ *noun* a garden where vegetables and fruit are grown ○ *The hotel has its own kitchen garden.*

kitchen porter /ˌkɪtʃɪn 'pɔːtə/ *noun* somebody who carries things about in a kitchen

kitchen roll /'kɪtʃɪn rəʊl/ *noun* CATERING a roll of absorbent paper, used e.g. for mopping up spilled liquids and wiping pans

kitchen staff /'kɪtʃən stɑːf/ *noun* the people who work in a kitchen

kitchen utensils /ˌkɪtʃən juː'tens(ə)lz/ *plural noun* pans, knives, spoons, etc., used for work in the kitchen

kitchenware /'kɪtʃənweə/ *noun* CATERING frying pans, saucepans and other cooking or preparing containers, used in a kitchen

kite /kaɪt/ *noun* SPORT a large, often crescent-shaped, device, consisting of fabric stretched over a light frame, used by participants in kiteboarding or kitesurfing to give propulsion and lift

kiteboarding /'kaɪtbɔːdɪŋ/ *noun* a sport in which the participants ride on skateboards or snowboards with a kite attached to their bodies to give propulsion and lift

kite mark /'kaɪt mɑːk/ *noun* BUSINESS a mark on goods to show that they meet official standards

kitesurfing /'kaɪtbɜːfɪŋ/ *noun* a water sport in which the participants ride on surfboards with a kite attached to their bodies to give propulsion and lift

kiwi fruit /'kiːwi fruːt/ *noun* FRUIT a subtropical woody climbing plant *Actinidia chinensis* which bears brownish oval fruit with a green juicy flesh. The plant was developed in New Zealand, and is now grown in many subtropical regions including southern Europe. Also called **Chinese gooseberry**

Kleenex /ˈkliːneks/ *tdmk* a trademark for a paper handkerchief ○ *There is a box of Kleenex in the bathroom.* (NOTE: There is a plural form **Kleenexes** which is used when referring to several handkerchiefs, but the word **Kleenex** can also be used as the plural form: *a box of Kleenex.*)

kloofing /ˈkluːfɪŋ/ *noun* SPORT the extreme sport of following the course of a river through a gorge by climbing, swimming and jumping

km *abbreviation* kilometre ○ *It is 2km from here to the Post Office.* ○ *The furthest distance I have travelled by train is 800km.* ○ *The road crosses the railway line about 2km from here.*

knead /niːd/ *verb* CATERING to press and fold dough before it is cooked to make bread ○ *Pizza dough must be kneaded for five minutes.*

knife /naɪf/ *noun* an implement with a sharp blade, used for cutting and spreading

COMMENT: All chefs say that their knives (each one owns a set of several knives, which they take with them from job to job) are the most important part of their equipment. The best knives are forged (i.e. the blade, bolster and centre part of the handle are made from one piece of metal). A good knife needs to balance easily and so has to have a heavy handle: the tang is the central metal part of the handle, to which wooden or plastic grips are attached with rivets. The tang is the part which gives the weight to the handle.

knot /nɒt/ *noun* TRAVEL a unit of measurement of speed of ships, aircraft, water currents or wind, equivalent to 1.85km per hour ○ *wind speed of 60 knots* ○ *The ship was travelling at 23 knots.*

knowledge /ˈnɒlɪdʒ/ *noun* the general facts or information that people know □ **the Knowledge** familiarity with the street plan of London, which taxi drivers have to know by heart, and on which they are tested before getting their licence (*informal*)

knuckle /ˈnʌk(ə)l/ *noun* MEAT a joint on the leg of an animal

korma /ˈkɔːmə/ *noun* FINANCE in South Asian cooking, a mildly spiced dish of meat, seafood or vegetables cooked in a cream or yoghurt sauce

kosher /ˈkəʊʃə/ *adjective* CATERING prepared according to Jewish law ○ *There's a kosher restaurant on 21st Street.*

krona /ˈkrəʊnə/ *noun* FINANCE the currency used in Iceland

krone /ˈkrəʊnə/ *noun* FINANCE the currency used in Denmark and Norway

L

l /el/ *abbreviation* litre

label /'leɪb(ə)l/ *noun* **1.** a piece of paper or card attached to something to show its price, an address or instructions for use, etc. **2.** □ **address label** a label with an address on it ■ *verb* to attach a label to something ○ *All hand baggage must be labelled.* □ **incorrectly labelled parcel** a parcel with the wrong information on the label

labelling /'leɪb(ə)lɪŋ/ *noun* the work of putting labels on products, especially food products, to show what the products contain or how or where they are made

COMMENT: Government regulations cover the labelling of food. The label should show not only the price and weight of the food, but also where it comes from, the quality grade, the ingredients, listing the main ingredient first, and a sell-by date.

Labor Day /'leɪbə deɪ/ *noun* a US national holiday celebrated on the first Monday in September

labor union /'leɪbə ˌjuːnjən/ *noun US* BUSINESS same as **trade union**

labour /'leɪbə/ *noun* **1.** work, especially heavy work (NOTE: The US spelling is **labor.**) □ **to charge for materials and labour** to charge for both the materials used in a job and also the hours of work involved □ **labour is charged at £10 an hour** each hour of work costs £10 **2.** workers, the workforce (NOTE: The US spelling is **labor.**)

labour costs /'leɪbə kɒsts/ *plural noun* BUSINESS the cost of the staff employed to make a product or provide a service, not including materials or overheads

labour dispute /'leɪbə dɪˌspjuːt/ *noun* same as **industrial dispute**

labour force /'leɪbə fɔːs/ *noun* BUSINESS same as **workforce**

labour laws /'leɪbə lɔːz/, **labour legislation** /ˌleɪbə ˌledʒɪ'sleɪʃ(ə)n/ *noun* laws concerning the employment of workers

labour-saving /'leɪbə ˌseɪvɪŋ/ *adjective* that makes hard work easier ○ *a labour-saving device*

labour shortage /'leɪbə ˌʃɔːtɪdʒ/ *noun* a situation where there are not enough employees to fill jobs

labour turnover /'leɪbə ˌtɜːnəʊvə/ *noun* BUSINESS changes in staff, when some leave and others join. Also called **employee turnover**, **staff turnover**

lactovegetarian /ˌlæktəʊvedʒɪ'teəriən/ *noun* somebody who eats vegetables, grains, fruit, nuts and milk products but not meat or eggs

ladle /'leɪd(ə)l/ *noun* a spoon with a large bowl, used for serving soup ■ *verb* □ **to ladle (out)** to serve with a ladle ○ *She ladled the soup out into bowls.*

lady /'leɪdi/ *noun* **1.** a polite way of referring to a woman ○ *Could you show this lady to her table, please?* ○ *There are two ladies waiting for you in reception.* **2.** □ **'ladies' (toilet)** a public toilet for women (*informal*) ○ *Can you tell me where the ladies* or *the ladies' toilet is?* ○ *The ladies is down the corridor on the right.*

lady's finger /ˌleɪdiz 'fɪŋgə/ *noun* VEGETABLES same as **okra**

COMMENT: Also called 'bhindi' or 'gumbo'. Used in Caribbean and Indian cooking; also used in the south of the USA.

lager /'lɑːgə/ *noun* BEVERAGES **1.** a German type of beer, which is pale yellow in colour, highly carbonated, and relatively sweet **2.** a glass of this beer ○ *He came to the bar and ordered six lagers.*

COMMENT: Lager is served cold, and usually from a pressurized metal keg. It is also available in bottles and cans.

lagoon /lə'guːn/ *noun* an area of sea water almost completely surrounded by land, especially by coral reefs ○ *You can swim safely in the lagoon, the sharks are out in the ocean.*

laid /leɪd/ ♦ **lay**

laid-up table /ˌleɪd ʌp 'teɪb(ə)l/ *noun* CATERING a table which has been prepared ready for the guests

'…the meal was served course by course on laid-up tables (the tray appears only for the hot entrée) and the bar service was more than generous' [*Business Traveller*]

lain /leɪn/ ♦ **lie**

lake /leɪk/ *noun* a large inland stretch of fresh water ○ *Let's take a boat out on the lake.* ○ *We can sail across the lake.* ○ *The hotel stands on the shores of Lake Windermere.* □ **the Lake District** an area of northwest England where there are several large lakes

lakeside /'leɪksaɪd/ *adjective* situated on the shores of a lake ○ *a lakeside villa*

lamb /læm/ *noun* MEAT meat from a sheep, especially from a young sheep ○ *roast leg of lamb* ○ *lamb kebabs* ○ *lamb chops*

COMMENT: Strictly speaking, meat from an older sheep is called 'mutton', but this term is rarely used. The commonest forms of lamb in British cooking are lamb chops or roast lamb. Traditionally, lamb is served with mint sauce.

lamp /læmp/ *noun* an electric device which produces light

lampshade /'læmpʃeɪd/ *noun* a decorative cover over a light ○ *The dining room looks very elegant with dark red lampshades.*

land /lænd/ *verb* **1.** TRAVEL to put goods or passengers on to land after a voyage by sea or by air ○ *to land goods at a port* ○ *to land passengers at an airport* **2.** AIR TRAVEL to come down to the ground after a flight ○ *The plane landed ten minutes late.*

landau /'lændɔː/ *noun* TOURISM a wide horse-drawn carriage with a top which can be lowered, often used for taking tourists on trips round old towns

landing /'lændɪŋ/ *noun* the arrival of an aircraft on the ground after a flight

landing card /'lændɪŋ kɑːd/ *noun* **1.** TRAVEL a card given to passengers who have passed customs and can land from a ship **2.** AIR TRAVEL a card given to passengers to fill in before passing through immigration and passport control

landing charges /'lændɪŋ ˌtʃɑːdʒɪz/ *plural noun* BUSINESS payments made to a government for the right to put goods on land and for any customs duties payable on the goods

landing fees /'lændɪŋ fiːz/ *plural noun* AIR TRAVEL payments made to an airport for landing there. Airlines usually include the fee in the ticket price.

landing rights /'lændɪŋ raɪts/ *plural noun* AIR TRAVEL the right of an airline to land its aircraft

landing stage /'lændɪŋ steɪdʒ/ *noun* SHIPS AND BOATS a wooden platform built out into a river, lake, or the sea for boats to tie up to

landlady /'lændleɪdi/ *noun* **1.** a woman who owns a property which is let **2.** HOTELS a woman who runs a public house or hotel

landlord /'lændlɔːd/ *noun* **1.** a person or company which owns a property which is let **2.** HOTELS a man who runs a public house or hotel

landscape /'lændskeɪp/ *noun* the countryside and its hills, valleys, woods and fields, considered as something beautiful to look at

landscape gardening /ˌlændskeɪp 'gɑːd(ə)nɪŋ/ *noun* the work of making a garden more beautiful by shaping the ground, planting trees and bushes, making pools and waterfalls etc.

landside /'lændsaɪd/ *adjective* AIR TRAVEL referring to the area of the airport before the security checks, etc.

landslide /'lændslaɪd/ *noun* a situation where large amounts of earth and rock slip down a hillside ○ *After the rains, landslides buried several houses.* ○ *Landslides have blocked several roads through the mountains.*

land tax /'lænd tæks/ *noun* BUSINESS a tax on the amount of land owned

lane /leɪn/ *noun* **1.** ROAD TRAVEL a narrow road, often in the country ○ *a lane with hedges on both sides* **2.** a part of a road for traffic going in a particular direction or at a certain speed ○ *Motorways usually have three lanes on either side.* ○ *One lane of the motorway has been closed for repairs.*

langlauf /'læŋlaʊf/ *noun* SPORT a German noun meaning cross-country skiing

langoustine /ˌlɒŋguːˈstiːn/ *noun* SEAFOOD a very large prawn

language /'læŋgwɪdʒ/ *noun* the words spoken or written by people in a particular country ○ *The guidebook to the museum is written in three languages: English, German and Japanese.*

language school /'læŋgwɪdʒ skuːl/ *noun* a school that offers courses in the native language of a country for visitors from abroad, or a course in foreign languages for people travelling abroad

laptop computer /ˌlæptɒp kəmˈpjuːtə/, **laptop** /'læptɒp/ *noun* a small computer which can be held on the knees when sitting ○ *I take my laptop with me onto the plane so that I can write my reports.* ○ *Each of the businessmen arrived with one bag and a laptop.*

lard /lɑːd/ *noun* FOOD pig fat used in cooking ○ *You need lard to make the pastry for* *pies.* ■ *verb* CATERING to cover meat with bacon, lard or other fat before cooking in the oven

larder /'lɑːdə/ *noun* CATERING a cool room or cupboard for storing food ○ *Old houses often have big larders.*

larder chef /'lɑːdə ʃef/ *noun* CATERING the chef in charge of cold dishes, salads and salad sauces, sandwiches, and who cuts meat and fish ready for cooking in the kitchen. Also called **chef garde-manger**

larder fridge /'lɑːdə frɪdʒ/ *noun* CATERING a fridge for keeping food in until needed

lardy cake /'lɑːdi ˌkeɪk/ *noun* BREAD, ETC. a type of cake, made with fat and dried fruit and covered with sticky sugar

larva /'lɑːvə/ *noun* a stage in the development of an insect, after the egg has hatched but before the animal becomes adult (NOTE: The plural form is **larvae**.)

larval /'lɑːv(ə)l/ *adjective* referring to larvae

lasagne /lə'zænjə/, **lasagna** *noun* FOOD flat sheets of pasta, arranged in layers in a dish, often with meat, sauce and cheese, and baked in the oven

last call /ˌlɑːst 'kɔːl/ *noun* US same as **last orders** (*informal*)

last minute /ˌlɑːst 'mɪnɪt/ *noun* the latest time that it is possible to do something and still be in time

last-minute /ˌlɑːst 'mɪnɪt/ *adjective* very very late ○ *Tour operators are offering tours at half price* or *half-price tours to people making last-minute bookings.*

last orders /ˌlɑːst 'ɔːdəz/ *plural noun* the final orders which a bar or restaurant will accept before closing time ○ *Last orders: 10.30 pm.*

late /leɪt/ *adjective* **1.** after the usual or expected time **2.** at the end of a period of time □ **latest date for purchase of APEX tickets** the last acceptable date for buying APEX tickets, usually 21 days before the date of departure **3.** □ **the latest** the most recent ○ *He always drives the latest model of car.* ○ *Here are the latest figures for passengers carried.* ○ *The latest snow reports are published each day in the papers.* ■ *adverb* after the time stated or agreed ○ *The train arrived late, and we missed the connection to Paris.* ○ *The plane was two hours late.*

late arrival /ˌleɪt ə'raɪv(ə)l/ *noun* **1.** TRAVEL the arrival of a plane or train after the scheduled time ○ *We apologise for the late arrival of the 14.25 Intercity express from Edinburgh.* **2.** HOTELS a guest who arrives at

a hotel after the time when they were expected or after the date for which they had booked ○ *Most of the tour party arrived on time, but there were two late arrivals who were delayed in traffic.*

late availability /ˌleɪt əˌveɪlə'bɪlɪti/ *noun* AIR TRAVEL cheaper airline tickets which are available when booking close to the time of departure

late booking /ˌleɪt 'bʊkɪŋ/ *noun* a booking made after the final date allowed

late cancellation /ˌleɪt ˌkænsə'leɪʃ(ə)n/ *noun* the cancellation of a booking made after the normal time limit

late checkout /ˌleɪt 'tʃekaʊt/ *noun* HOTELS a checkout that takes place after the time at which hotel guests are usually required to check out

latecomer /'leɪtkʌmə/ *noun* somebody who arrives after others or after the appointed time

late-night /'leɪt naɪt/ *adjective* happening late at night ○ *He had a late-night meeting at the airport.* ○ *There is a late-night bus which leaves at 23.45.*

late-night opening /ˌleɪt naɪt 'əʊp(ə)nɪŋ/ *noun* an extension of the time when a shop is open until late in the evening

late-night shopping /ˌleɪt naɪt 'ʃɒpɪŋ/ *noun* shopping in the late evening, with shops opening much later than usual

latitude /'lætɪtjuːd/ *noun* a position on the Earth's surface measured in degrees north or south of the equator

COMMENT: Together with longitude, latitude is used to indicate an exact position on the earth's surface. Latitude is measured in degrees, minutes and seconds. The centre of London is latitude 51°30'N, longitude 0°5'W. The lines of latitude are numbered, and called 'parallels', and some of them act as national boundaries: the 49th parallel marks most of the border between the USA and Canada.

latte /'læteɪ/ *noun* an espresso coffee with frothy steamed milk

launch /lɔːntʃ/ *verb* **1.** SHIPS AND BOATS to put a new boat into the water for the first time **2.** MARKETING to put a new product on the market, usually spending money on advertising it ○ *The company is spending thousands of pounds to launch a new travel service.* ■ *noun* MARKETING the act of putting a new product on the market ○ *The launch of the new caravan model has been put back three months.* ○ *The company is geared up for the launch of the new package holiday.* ○ *The management has decided on a September launch date.*

launder /ˈlɔːndə/ *verb* to wash clothes, sheets, etc. ○ *He asked to have two shirts laundered.*

launderette /ˌlɔːndəˈret/, **laundromat** *US* /ˈlɔːndrəmæt/ *noun* a shop with coin-operated washing machines for public use ○ *I take my washing to the launderette once a week.*

laundering /ˈlɔːndərɪŋ/ *noun* the washing of clothes, sheets, etc. ○ *A chute from the first floor will speed up the laundering process.*

laundress /lɔːnˈdres/ *noun* a woman who washes clothes, sheets, etc., for other people

laundry /ˈlɔːndri/ *noun* **1.** a room or building where clothes are washed ○ *The hotel's sheets and towels are sent to the laundry every day.* (NOTE: The plural form in this meaning is **laundries**.) **2.** clothes that need to be washed ○ *Please put any laundry into the bag provided and leave it at the desk on your hotel floor.* (NOTE: no plural)

laundry bag /ˈlɔːndri bæg/ *noun* HOTELS a special bag in a hotel room, into which you can put dirty clothes to be taken to be washed

laundry list /ˈlɔːndri lɪst/ *noun* HOTELS a printed form provided with a laundry bag, giving a list of items of clothing which you may want to have washed

laundry service /ˈlɔːndri ˌsɜːvɪs/ *noun* HOTELS a service in a hotel which takes away dirty clothing and returns it washed and ironed

laundry staff /ˈlɔːndri stɑːf/ *noun* the staff who run the laundry service

lavatory /ˈlævətri/ *noun* **1.** a room with a toilet, usually with a flushing bowl for getting rid of waste matter from the body ○ *The lavatories are situated at the rear of the plane.* ○ *There is a gentlemen's lavatory on the ground floor.* **2.** a bowl with a seat and a flushing system, for getting rid of waste matter from the body ○ *The drink was so awful that I poured it down the lavatory.*

lavatory attendant /ˈlævətri əˌtendənt/ *noun* somebody who is on duty in a public lavatory

lavatory paper /ˈlævətri ˌpeɪpə/ *noun* same as **toilet paper**

laver, laver bread *noun* VEGETABLES seaweed, used as a breakfast food in Wales

law /lɔː/ *noun* **1.** one of the rules by which a country is governed and the activities of people and organisations are controlled **2.** □ **inside the law, within the law** obeying the laws of a country □ **against the law, outside the law** not according to the laws of a country ○ *The company is operating outside the law.* □ **to break the law** to do something which is not allowed by law ○ *She is breaking the law by selling goods on Sunday.* ○ *You will be breaking the law if you try to take that computer out of the country without an export licence.* **3.** a general rule

laws /lɔːz/ *plural noun* the rules by which a country is governed and the activities of people and organisations controlled

lay /leɪ/ *verb* to put something down on a surface (NOTE: **laying – laid**) □ **to lay the table** to get a table ready for guests by putting out cutlery, glasses, napkins, etc. ○ *The table was laid for six people, so when only five guests arrived the waiter removed one of the settings.*

layby /ˈleɪbaɪ/, **lay-by** *noun* ROAD TRAVEL a place at the side of a road where vehicles can park

layover /ˈleɪəʊvə/ *noun* US TRAVEL same as **stopover**

lazy Susan /ˌleɪzi ˈsuːz(ə)n/ *noun* CATERING a revolving tray, placed in the centre of a dining table to hold condiments, extra dishes, hors d'oeuvres, etc.

lb /paʊndz/ *abbreviation* pound ○ *It weighs 26lb.*

L/C *abbreviation* FINANCE letter of credit

lead time /ˈliːd taɪm/ *noun* BUSINESS the time between placing an order and receiving the goods

leaflet /ˈliːflət/ *noun* MARKETING a sheet of paper giving information about something or used to advertise something ○ *to mail leaflets* or *to hand out leaflets describing services* ○ *They sent a leaflet mailing to 20,000 addresses.*

lean /liːn/ *adjective* referring to meat with little fat ■ *noun* same as **lean meat**

lean meat /ˌliːn ˈmiːt/ *noun* MEAT meat with very little fat ○ *Animals are bred to produce lean meat.* ○ *Venison is a very lean form of meat.*

lease /liːs/ *noun* a written contract for letting or renting a building, or a piece of land or a piece of equipment for a period against payment of a fee □ **the lease expires** *or* **runs out in 1999** the lease comes to an end in 1999 □ **on expiration of the lease** when the lease comes to an end ■ *verb* **1.** to let or rent a building, a piece of land or a piece of equipment for a period ○ *to lease offices to small firms* ○ *to lease equipment* **2.** to use a building, a piece of land or a piece of equipment for a period and pay a fee ○ *to lease hotel premises from an insurance company* ○ *All the airline's aircraft are leased.*

leasehold /'li:shəʊld/ *noun, adjective, adverb* the right to live in or use property on the basis of a lease ○ *to buy a property lease-hold* ○ *The company has some valuable leaseholds.*

leaseholder /'li:shəʊldə/ *noun* somebody who use or lives in property on the basis of a lease

leasing /'li:sɪŋ/ *noun* **1.** the letting or renting a building, a piece of land or a piece of equipment for a period ○ *an aircraft leasing company* **2.** the use of a building, a piece of land or a piece of equipment for a period after paying a fee ○ *to run a copier under a leasing agreement*

leave /li:v/ *noun* permission to be away from work □ **six weeks' annual leave** six weeks' holiday each year ■ *verb* to go away from a place ○ *He left his hotel early to go to the airport.* ○ *The next plane leaves at 10.20.* (NOTE: **leaving – left**)

leave out /,li:v 'aʊt/ *verb* not to include ○ *She left out the date on the cheque.* ○ *The brochure leaves out all details of travelling arrangements from the airport to the hotel.*

lectern /'lektɜ:n/ *noun* a stand with a sloping surface on which you can put a book or papers from which you are going to read aloud in public ○ *The conference room is equipped with a lectern.*

lecture /'lektʃə/ *noun* a talk on a particular subject given to people such as students

lecture tour /'lektʃə ,tʊə/ *noun* TOURISM a tour with lectures on the places or buildings visited and the paintings or other objects seen ○ *The museum has a programme of lecture tours on 20th-century art.* ○ *The group went on a lecture tour of sites in Greece.*

lee /li:/ *noun* the sheltered side of a hill or ship ○ *They rested on the lee of the hill, so as to be out of the wind.*

leek /li:k/ *noun* VEGETABLES a vegetable related to the onion, with a white stem and long green leaves ○ *a bowl of leek soup*

leeward /'li:wəd/ *adjective, adverb* SHIPS AND BOATS on or to the sheltered side of a ship, i.e. not the side onto which the wind is blowing ○ *We anchored to the leeward of the island.* ○ *The boat tied up on the leeward side of the jetty.* Compare **windward**

left /left/ *adjective* opposite of right ○ *The flight destinations run down the left side of the page.* ○ *They put the subtotals in the left column, and the final figure is at the bottom of the right-hand column.* ◊ **leave** (NOTE: On ships and aircraft, the left side is called the **port side**.)

left-hand /,left 'hænd/ *adjective* belonging to the left side ○ *The subtotals are in the left-hand column of the bill.* ○ *He keeps the personnel files in the left-hand drawer of his desk.*

left luggage office /,left 'lʌgɪdʒ ,ɒfɪs/ *noun* TRAVEL a room at a railway station, coach station, ferry terminal or airport where suitcases, bags and parcels can be left. Also called **baggage room** (NOTE: The US English is **baggage room**.)

leftovers /'leftəʊvəz/ *plural noun* what is not used, especially food which has not been eaten ○ *The children will eat the leftovers tomorrow morning.*

leg /leg/ *noun* **1.** one of the parts of the body with which a person or animal walks. ◊ **legroom 2.** a stage of a journey ○ *The last leg of the trip goes from Paris to the final destination, Amsterdam.*

legal currency /,li:g(ə)l 'kʌrənsi/ *noun* FINANCE money which can be legally used in a country

legal expenses /'li:g(ə)l ɪk,spensɪz/ *plural noun* money spent on fees paid to lawyers

legal tender /,li:g(ə)l 'tendə/ *noun* FINANCE coins or notes which can be legally used to pay a debt ○ *These notes are not legal tender any more.*

legionnaires' disease /,li:dʒə'neəz dɪ,zi:z/ *noun* MEDICAL a bacterial disease similar to pneumonia

COMMENT: The disease is thought to be transmitted in droplets of moisture in the air, and the bacterium is often found in central air-conditioning systems. It can be fatal to old or sick people, and so is especially dangerous if present in a hospital.

leg of lamb /,leg əv 'læm/ *noun* MEAT the leg of a sheep, considered as food ○ *a slice of roast leg of lamb*

legroom /'legru:m/, **leg room, leg-room** *noun* TRAVEL the amount of space available for the legs of a person sitting down, as between the rows of seats in a cinema or aircraft or inside a car ○ *There's not much legroom in tourist class.*

'...virtually every airline's Boeing 747 will seat passengers ten abreast (3–4–3) with a tight 31–33 inches of legroom' [*Business Traveller*]

legume /'legju:m/ *noun* VEGETABLES a seed, pod, or other part of a plant such as a pea or bean, used as food

leisure /'leʒə/ *noun* free time to do what you want □ **at your leisure** when there is an opportunity, without hurrying

'...when hiring a car in Europe for three days or more, never overlook the so-called 'holiday rate' in the belief that it is intended for leisure customers only' [*Business Traveller*]

leisure centre /'leɪʒə ˌsentə/ *noun* ENTERTAINMENT a public building that provides the space and equipment for recreational activities such as sports, games and hobbies

leisure club /'leʒə klʌb/ *noun* ENTERTAINMENT a club where hotel guests can use leisure facilities, usually without payment ○ *The price includes the use of the hotel leisure club.*

'…a leisure club, including a 14-metre pool, spa pool, sauna, steam room, gym and sunbeds' [*Evening Standard*]

leisure complex /'leʒə ˌkɒmpleks/ *noun* ENTERTAINMENT a series of buildings with various leisure facilities

leisure facilities /'leʒə fəˌsɪlətiz/ *plural noun* ENTERTAINMENT facilities for enjoying yourself, e.g. a swimming pool, putting green, or cinema

leisure industry /'leʒə ˌɪndəstri/ *noun* all the companies that provide goods and services used during people's leisure time, such as holidays, cinema, theatre and amusement parks

leisurely /'leʒəli/ *adjective* without hurrying ○ *The group toured the museum at a leisurely pace.* ○ *We enjoyed a leisurely lunch before going round the Prado.*

leisure pursuits /'leʒə pəˌsjuːts/ *plural noun* ENTERTAINMENT hobbies, things you do during your free time, for relaxation or enjoyment

leisure traveller /'leʒə ˌtræv(ə)lə/ *noun* TOURISM somebody who is going on holiday and is not travelling on business

lemon /'lemən/ *noun* FRUIT the yellow edible fruit of an evergreen citrus tree, with sour-tasting flesh and juice ○ *a gin and tonic with a slice of lemon in it* ○ *She ordered a lemon sorbet.*

lemonade /ˌleməˈneɪd/ *noun* BEVERAGES **1.** a drink made from fresh lemon juice, sugar and water **2.** a ready-made fizzy drink, flavoured with lemon, also used to mix with beer to make shandy ○ *Can I have a glass of lemonade with ice, please?*

lemon curd /'lemən kɜːd/ *noun* FOOD a preserve made with eggs and lemons, used to spread on bread

lemon grass /'lemən grɑːs/ *noun* SAUCES, ETC. a green lemon-flavoured herb, used especially in Thai cooking

lemon meringue pie /ˌlemən məˌræŋ 'paɪ/ *noun* DESSERTS pastry filled with lemon-flavoured filling, topped with soft meringue

lemon sole /'lemən səʊl/ *noun* SEAFOOD a common flatfish used as food

lemon squash /ˌlemən 'skwɒʃ/ *noun* BEVERAGES a drink made of concentrated lemon juice and water

lemon-squeezer /'lemən ˌskwiːzə/ *noun* CATERING a device for pressing slices of lemon, to make the juice run out

lemon tea /'lemən tiː/ *noun* BEVERAGES black tea, served in a glass with a slice of lemon and sugar

lemon thyme /'lemən taɪm/ *noun* SAUCES, ETC. a variety of thyme which smells of lemon

length /leŋθ/ *noun* a measurement of how long something is from end to end □ **a stay of some length** quite a long stay

length of service /ˌleŋθ əv 'sɜːvɪs/ *noun* BUSINESS the number of years someone has worked for a company

length of stay /ˌleŋθ əv 'steɪ/ *noun* HOTELS the number of days a guest stays in a hotel

lentil /'lentɪl/ *noun* VEGETABLES the small round dried yellow or green seed of a plant of the pea family, used as food, especially in soups and stews ○ *a bowl of lentil soup* ○ *fried sea bass and lentils*

let /let/ *verb* to allow someone to use a house or office in return for payment (NOTE: **letting – let**) □ **to let a cottage** to allow someone to use a cottage for a period against payment of rent □ **holiday flats to let** furnished flats which are available to be leased by people on holiday ■ *noun* a period during which somebody leases a property ○ *They took the house on a short let.*

let-out clause /'let aʊt ˌklɔːz/ *noun* BUSINESS a section in a contract which allows someone to avoid doing something in the contract ○ *He added a let-out clause to the effect that the payments would be revised if the exchange rate fell by more than 5%.*

letter /'letə/ *noun* **1.** a piece of writing sent from one person to another to pass on information □ **circular letter** a letter sent to many people **2.** □ **to acknowledge receipt by letter** to write a letter to say that something has been received **3.** a written or printed symbol representing a language sound or part of a sound, e.g. A, B, C ○ *Write your name and address in block letters* or *in capital letters.*

letterbox /'letəbɒks/ *noun* **1.** same as **postbox** ○ *There's a letterbox at the corner of the street.* **2.** a hole in a front door through which the postman pushes letters ○ *The Sunday paper is too big to go through the letterbox.*

letterhead /'letəhed/ *noun* BUSINESS the name and address of a company printed at the top of a piece of notepaper

letter of acknowledgement /ˌletər əv əkˈnɒlɪdʒmənt/ *noun* a letter which says that something has been received

letter of application /ˌletər əv æplɪ ˈkeɪʃ(ə)n/ *noun* a letter in which someone applies for something

letter of appointment /ˌletər əv ə ˈpɔɪntmənt/ *noun* a letter in which someone is appointed to a job

letter of complaint /ˌletər əv kəm ˈpleɪnt/ *noun* a letter in which someone complains

letter of credit /ˌletə əv ˈkredɪt/ *noun* FINANCE a document issued by a bank on behalf of a customer authorising payment to a supplier when the conditions specified in the document are met. Abbr **L/C** □ **irrevocable letter of credit** a letter of credit which cannot be cancelled

letter of reference /ˌletər əv ˈref(ə)rəns/ *noun* BUSINESS a letter in which a former employer recommends someone for a new job

letting /'letɪŋ/ *noun* the business of leasing property

letting agency /'letɪŋ ˌeɪdʒənsi/ *noun* an office which deals in property to let

letting agent /'letɪŋ ˌeɪdʒənt/ *noun* an agent who is responsible for letting accommodation to visitors, and receives a fee or commission from the owners for this service

letting bedrooms /'letɪŋ ˌbedruːmz/ *plural noun* bedrooms which are let, as opposed to private bedrooms where the owner and staff sleep ○ *The pub has 20 en-suite letting bedrooms.*

'…the guest house has 3 letting bedrooms plus four private bedrooms' [*Caterer & Hotelkeeper*]

lettuce /'letɪs/ *noun* VEGETABLES a green salad plant

COMMENT: The commonest varieties of lettuce in Europe have relatively soft green leaves: round lettuces, and tall cos lettuces (or Romaine) are the commonest in the United Kingdom. Lettuces are not always green: Italian varieties, such as lollo rosso, have red leaves. In the United States, iceberg lettuces, with stiff crunchy leaves, are preferred.

levy /'levi/ *noun* money which is demanded and collected by the government (NOTE: The plural form is **levies.**) □ **levies on luxury items** taxes on luxury items ■ *verb* BUSINESS

to demand payment of a tax or an extra payment, and to collect it ○ *to levy a duty on the import of luxury items* ○ *The government has decided to levy a tax on imported cars.* □ **to levy members for a new club house** to ask members of the club to pay for the new building

'…royalties have been levied at a rate of 12.5% of full production' [*Lloyd's List*]

liaison /liˈeɪz(ə)n/ *noun* a thickening agent used in soups and sauces, e.g. egg yolks or flour

library /'laɪbrəri/ *noun* **1.** a place where books are stored to be read, borrowed or consulted **2.** a collection of things such as books or records ○ *Passengers can use the ship's library.* ○ *The hotel has an excellent library of romantic novels.*

licence /'laɪs(ə)ns/ *noun* an official document which allows someone to do something. ◊ **off-licence, on licence** (NOTE: The US spelling is **license.**)

license /'laɪs(ə)ns/ *noun* US same as **licence** ■ *verb* to give someone official permission to do something ○ *The store is licensed to sell beers, wines and spirits.* ○ *The club is licensed for music.* □ **licensed hotel, licensed restaurant** a hotel or restaurant which has a licence to sell alcohol

licensed premises /ˌlaɪs(ə)nst ˈpremɪsɪz/ *noun* CATERING a shop, restaurant or public house which has a licence to sell alcohol

licensee /ˌlaɪs(ə)nˈsiː/ *noun* BARS somebody who has a licence, especially a licence to sell alcohol

license plate /'laɪs(ə)ns pleɪt/ *noun* US a plate on a car, with its number (NOTE: The British English is **number plate.**)

licensing /'laɪs(ə)nsɪŋ/ *noun* referring to licences ○ *a licensing agreement* ○ *licensing laws*

COMMENT: In England and Scotland, pubs and bars can serve alcohol throughout the day, from 10.30 to 11 p.m., though not all are open as long as this; some only open for the full day on Fridays and Saturdays. Hotels can serve drinks to residents at any time. In the USA and Canada, local districts can vote to allow the sale of alcohol, and some vote to ban it altogether (these are said to be 'dry').

licensing hours /'laɪs(ə)nsɪŋ ˌaʊəz/ *plural noun* BARS the hours of the day when alcohol can be sold

lichee /laɪˈtʃiː/ *noun* FRUIT same as **litchi**

lie /laɪ/ *verb* to be in a position ○ *The town lies at the end of the valley.*

life assurance /'laɪf ə,ʃʊərəns/ *noun* same as **life insurance**

life belt, life buoy *noun* a ring which can float, used to throw to someone who has fallen into water ○ *They threw life belts to the passengers from the sinking ferry.* (NOTE: The US English is **life preserver**.)

lifeboat /'laɪfbəʊt/ *noun* SHIPS AND BOATS a boat used to rescue passengers from sinking ships

lifeguard /'laɪfgɑːd/ *noun* somebody who is on duty on a beach or at a swimming pool, and who rescues people who get into difficulty in the water ○ *Lifeguards have raised red flags to show that the sea is dangerous.* ○ *Two lifeguards came to rescue us.*

life insurance /'laɪf ɪn,ʃʊərəns/ *noun* FINANCE an insurance policy which pays a sum of money when someone dies

life jacket /'laɪf ,dʒækɪt/ *noun* **1.** SHIPS AND BOATS a jacket with blocks of light material which allows it to float, provided for sailors and passengers on boats ○ *Children must all wear life jackets on the river.* **2.** AIR TRAVEL a jacket which can be inflated and will make the wearer float in water, provided by airlines for each passenger ○ *Instructions for donning the life jacket are in the pocket in front of your seat.* (NOTE: The US English is **life preserver**.)

life preserver /'laɪf prɪ,zɜːvə/ *noun* US same as **life belt, life jacket**

life raft /'laɪf rɑːft/ *noun* SHIPS AND BOATS a construction which can float, carried by a ship, and used to carry passengers if the ship sinks

lift /lɪft/ *noun* **1.** a machine which takes people or goods from one floor to another in a building ○ *He took the lift to the 27th floor.* ○ *The guests could not get to their rooms when the lift broke down.* (NOTE: The US English is **elevator**.) **2.** □ **to give someone a lift** to allow a pedestrian to ride in your car or lorry ○ *Do you want a lift?* ○ *Several people stopped to offer us lifts.* ■ *verb* **1.** to go away ○ *The fog had lifted by lunchtime.* **2.** to take away, to remove ○ *to lift trade barriers* ○ *The government has lifted the ban on imports from Japan.* ○ *The minister has lifted the embargo on the export of computers to East European countries.*

lift attendant /'lɪft ə,tendənt/ *noun* HOTELS somebody, usually a young man, who operates a lift

light /laɪt/ *adjective* not heavy ○ *You need light clothing for tropical countries.* ○ *He only has a light holdall with him.* (NOTE: **light – lighter – lightest**) ■ *noun* **1.** bright-

ness, the opposite of darkness □ **candlelight** light given out by a candle **2.** an electric bulb which gives light ○ *a bedside light* ○ *There is an overhead light in the bathroom.* ■ *adverb* □ **to travel light** to travel with very little luggage ○ *If you're hitching across Australia, it's best to travel light.*

lighthouse /'laɪthaʊs/ *noun* SHIPS AND BOATS a tall building on a coast containing a light to guide ships

lighting-up time /,laɪtɪŋ 'ʌp taɪm/ *noun* the time at which street lamps and car lights have to be switched on ○ *In the autumn, lighting-up time is earlier each day.*

light pen /'laɪt pen/ *noun* a pen with a tip which is sensitive to light and can 'read' lines or images and transfer them to a computer, used to read bar codes on products

lightship /'laɪtʃɪp/ *noun* SHIPS AND BOATS a ship which carries a large light to guide ships, acting as a floating lighthouse

light show /'laɪt ʃəʊ/ *noun* a form of entertainment in which coloured lights move and flash in time with recorded music

lime /laɪm/ *noun* FRUIT a green citrus fruit similar to, but smaller than, a lemon

lime juice /'laɪm dʒuːs/ *noun* BEVERAGES **1.** the juice of a lime **2.** a concentrated drink which tastes of lime

lime pickle /,laɪm 'pɪk(ə)l/ *noun* SAUCES, ETC. a very hot-tasting Indian condiment

lime tea /,laɪm 'tiː/ *noun* BEVERAGES a drink made from the dried flowers of the lime tree

limit /'lɪmɪt/ *noun* the point at which something ends, or where you can go no further

limo /'lɪməʊ/ *noun* ROAD TRAVEL same as **limousine** (*informal*)

limousine /lɪmə'ziːn/ *noun* ROAD TRAVEL a large luxurious car □ **limousine transfer to hotel** the transfer of passengers from an airport to their hotel in a limousine, provided free by the hotel or airline

limousine service /,lɪmə'ziːn ,sɜːvɪs/ *noun* HOTELS service to and from a hotel or airport by limousine

line /laɪn/ *noun* **1.** a long thin mark ○ *paper with thin blue lines* ○ *I prefer notepaper without any lines.* ○ *She drew a thick line across the bottom of the column to show which figure was the total.* **2.** a row of written or printed words **3.** a wire along which telephone messages pass □ **the line is bad** it is difficult to hear clearly what someone is saying □ **the line is engaged** the person is already speaking on the phone □ **the chairman is on the other line** the chairman is speaking on his or her second telephone **4.** *US* a row of people or vehicles waiting one behind the other (NOTE: The British English is **queue**.) □ **to stand in line** to wait in a line with other people **5.** to put a lining in something

lined /laɪnd/ *adjective* **1.** with lines on it ○ *a pad of A4 lined paper* **2.** □ **lined with trees**, **tree-lined** with trees along both sides ○ *the tree-lined avenues of Phnom Penh*

line management /'laɪn ˌmænɪdʒmənt/ *noun* BUSINESS the organisation of a business where each manager is responsible for doing what their superior tells them to do

linen /'lɪnɪn/ *noun* **1.** a cloth made from flax ○ *He was wearing a linen jacket.* **2.** □ **(household) linen** sheets, pillowcases, tablecloths, etc.

linen cupboard /'lɪnɪn ˌkʌbəd/ *noun* a cupboard for keeping linen

linen keeper /'lɪnɪn ˌkiːpə/ *noun* HOTELS somebody who is in charge of the linen in a hotel, and makes sure it is clean and ready for use when needed

linen room /'lɪnɪn ruːm/ *noun* HOTELS a room where clean linen is kept

liner /'laɪnə/ *noun* **1.** SHIPS AND BOATS a large passenger ship **2.** CATERING a dish on which another dish is placed containing food ready for serving

lining /'laɪnɪŋ/ *noun* a layer of material used to cover the inner surface of something, especially a piece of clothing ○ *a jacket with a lining of silk*

link /lɪŋk/ *noun* something which connects two things or places ■ *verb* to join or to attach something to something else ○ *to link bonus payments to productivity* ○ *His salary is linked to the cost of living.* ○ *All rooms are linked to the main switchboard.*

linoleic acid /ˌlɪnəʊliːɪk 'æsɪd/ *noun* CATERING one of the essential fatty acids, found in grains and seeds

liqueur /lɪ'kjʊə, lɪ'kɜː/ *noun* BEVERAGES a strong sweet alcohol, made from fruit or herbs ○ *a glass of raspberry liqueur*

> COMMENT: Liqueurs are served after a meal as a digestif. The most popular are Bénédictine, Chartreuse, Cointreau, Drambuie, Grand Marnier, Kirschwasser, Sambucca, Tia Maria.

liqueur chocolate /lɪˌkjʊə 'tʃɒklət/ *noun* FOOD a small chocolate containing a liqueur filling ○ *My favourite liqueur chocolates are the ones with cherries in brandy.*

liqueur trolley /lɪ'kjʊə ˌtrɒli/ *noun* CATERING a trolley brought to the table at the end of a meal, with liqueurs, brandy, cigars, etc.

liquid /'lɪkwɪd/ *noun* a substance which flows easily like water, and which is neither a gas nor a solid ■ *adjective* neither gas nor solid, flowing easily ○ *In the desert you must take plenty of liquids to avoid dehydration.*

liquid assets /ˌlɪkwɪd 'æsets/ *plural noun* BUSINESS cash, or investments which can be quickly converted into cash

liquidise /'lɪkwɪdaɪz/, **liquidize** *verb* CATERING to reduce fruit or vegetables to liquid ○ *Liquidise the oranges and carrots.*

liquidiser /'lɪkwɪdaɪzə/, **liquidizer** *noun* CATERING a machine which liquidises ○ *Put the oranges and carrots in the liquidiser.*

liquidity /lɪ'kwɪdɪti/ *noun* BUSINESS liquid assets, or the fact of having enough liquid assets to meet your needs

liquidity crisis /lɪ'kwɪdɪti ˌkraɪsɪs/ *noun* BUSINESS a situation where somebody does not have enough liquid assets

liquor /'lɪkə/ *noun* **1.** BARS alcohol **2.** CATERING liquid produced in cooking

liquor licence /'lɪkə ˌlaɪs(ə)ns/ *noun* CATERING a document given by the Magistrates' Court allowing someone to sell alcohol

liquor store /'lɪkə stɔː/ *noun* US a shop which sells alcohol (NOTE: The British English is **off-licence**.)

list /lɪst/ *noun* **1.** several items written one after the other ○ *to add an item to a list* ○ *to cross an item off a list* **2.** a catalogue ■ *verb* to write several items one after the other ○ *to list products by category* ○ *to list representatives by area* ○ *The guidebook lists twenty-five cheap hotels in the Bournemouth area.*

listed building /ˌlɪstɪd 'bɪldɪŋ/ *noun* a building which is considered important because of its architecture or associations, and which cannot be demolished or altered without the consent of the local authority

Listeria /lɪ'stɪəriə/ *noun* MEDICAL bacteria found in some prepared foods and in domestic animals, which can cause infections such as meningitis

> COMMENT: Listeria can be present in ready-prepared meals which are reheated; it also occurs in cooked meats and ready-made salads. Listeria is killed by heating to at least 70°C.

listings /'lɪstɪŋz/ *noun* ENTERTAINMENT a published list of information about events such as films, plays and concerts ○ *Cinema listings are found on the back page of the local paper.*

list price /'lɪst praɪs/ *noun* the price of something as marked in a catalogue or list. Also called **catalogue price**

litchi /laɪ'tʃiː/, **lichee**, **lychee** /'laɪtʃiː/ *noun* FRUIT a subtropical fruit from China with a hard red skin and a soft white juicy pulp surrounding a hard shiny brown seed

literature /'lɪt(ə)rətʃə/ *noun* written information about something ○ *Please send me literature about your tours to Italy.*

litre /'liːtə/ *noun* a unit of measurement for liquids, equal to 1000 millilitres (NOTE: This is usually written **l** after figures: *25l.* The US spelling is **liter.**) □ **the car does fifteen kilometres to the litre** *or* **fifteen kilometres per litre** the car uses one litre of petrol to travel fifteen kilometres

litter /'lɪtə/ *noun* rubbish on streets or in public places ○ *The council tries to keep the main street clear of litter.*

litterbasket /'lɪtəbɑːskɪt/ *noun* a special basket for rubbish

litterbin /'lɪtəbɪn/ *noun* a special metal container for rubbish ○ *The men from the council come to empty the litter bins every morning.*

Little Gem /ˌlɪt(ə)l 'dʒem/ *noun* HOTELS the highest award given by RAC inspectors to guesthouses

live *adjective* /laɪv/ carrying an electric current ○ *Do not touch the live wires.* ■ *verb* /lɪv/ to have your home in a place ○ *They live in the centre of Paris.* ○ *Where do you live?*

live in /ˌlɪv 'ɪn/ *verb* to live in the building where you work ○ *Most of the restaurant staff live in.*

live-in /'lɪv ɪn/ *adjective* living in the building where they work ○ *We have six live-in staff.*

live-in doctor /ˌlɪv ɪn 'dɒktə/ *noun* MEDICAL a doctor who lives in a hotel and is employed by the hotel to treat guests who become ill

lively /'laɪvli/ *adjective* very active ○ *It's the liveliest nightspot in town.*

live off /'lɪv ɒf/ *verb* to earn money from ○ *The whole population of the village lives off tourism.*

liver /'lɪvə/ *noun* **1.** an organ in the body which helps the digestion by producing bile **2.** MEAT an animal's liver used as food □ **calf's liver, lamb's liver, ox liver, pig's liver** liver from a calf, a lamb, an ox or a pig

COMMENT: The traditional English way of eating liver is fried with bacon and onions.

liver pâté /ˌlɪvə 'pæteɪ/ *noun* FOOD a cooked paste made from livers of animals ○ *chicken-liver pâté*

livery /'lɪvəri/ *noun* **1.** special clothing worn by the employees of an organisation ○ *Every employee has to wear the hotel's distinctive livery.* **2.** BUSINESS a special design used to show that something belongs to an organisation ○ *British Airways have changed the livery of all their planes.*

livery cab /'lɪvəri kæb/ *noun* US ROAD TRAVEL a limousine-style cab, which is available for telephone booking, as opposed to the ordinary 'yellow cabs'

living /'lɪvɪŋ/ *noun* money that you need for things such as food and clothes ○ *He earns his living from selling postcards to tourists.*

living room /'lɪvɪŋ ruːm/ *noun* a room in a house for general use ○ *They were sitting in the living room watching TV.*

living standards /'lɪvɪŋ ˌstændədz/ *plural noun* the quality of people's home life, looking at factors such as the amount of food or clothes that they buy and the size of the family car

Lloyd's register /ˌlɔɪdz 'redʒɪstə/ *noun* SHIPS AND BOATS a classified list showing details of all the ships in the world

load /ləʊd/ *noun* ROAD TRAVEL goods which are transported in a vehicle □ **load of a truck** *or* **of a container** goods carried by a truck or container ■ *verb* **1.** □ **to load a truck** *or* **a ship** to put goods into a truck or a ship for transporting ○ *a truck loaded with boxes* ○ *a ship loaded with iron* **2.** (*of ship, aircraft*) to take on cargo ○ *The ferry will start loading in 15 minutes.*

load-carrying capacity /'ləʊd ˌkæriɪŋ kəˌpæsɪti/ *noun* ROAD TRAVEL the amount of goods which a truck is capable of carrying

load factor /'ləʊd ˌfæktə/ *noun* TRAVEL the number of seats in a bus, a train or an aircraft which are occupied by passengers who have paid the full fare

loading /'ləʊdɪŋ/ *noun* the act of putting goods into a ship, aircraft or vehicle

loading dock /'ləʊdɪŋ dɒk/ *noun* SHIPS AND BOATS the part of a harbour where ships can load or unload

loaf /ləʊf/ *noun* BREAD, ETC. a large single piece of bread, which is cut into slices before being eaten

loan /ləʊn/ *noun* money which has been lent □ **bank loan** money lent by a bank □ **short-term loan, long-term loan** loans which have to be repaid within a few weeks or some years □ **interest on a loan** interest which the borrower has to pay on the money borrowed ■ *verb* to lend ○ *The furniture has been loaned by the museum.*

lobby /'lɒbi/ *noun* the main entrance hall of a hotel, large restaurant or theatre

lobster /'lɒbstə/ *noun* SEAFOOD a shellfish with a long body, two large claws, and eight legs, used as food

COMMENT: Lobster can be served cold (with mayonnaise, as 'lobster salad'), and in this case the customer is provided with a pick and a pair of crackers to break the shell. Lobster is also served hot without its shell, for example as 'lobster Newburg' or cooked and served in its open shell as, for example, 'lobster Thermidor'.

lobster bisque /ˌlɒbstə 'biːsk/ *noun* FOOD a thick rich soup made with lobster

lobster chowder /ˌlɒbstə 'tʃaʊdə/ *noun* FOOD milk soup made with lobster ○ *We had a bowl of lobster chowder.*

local /'ləʊk(ə)l/ *adjective* relating to a place or district near where you are or where you live ■ *noun* BARS the nearest pub to where someone lives (*informal*) ○ *He took us all to his local for lunch.*

'...each cheque can be made out for the local equivalent of £100 rounded up to a convenient figure' [*Sunday Times*]

'EC regulations insist that customers can buy cars anywhere in the EC at the local pre-tax price' [*Financial Times*]

local authority /ˌləʊk(ə)l ɔː'θɒrɪti/ *noun* an elected section of government which runs a small area of the country such as a town or county

local call /ˌləʊk(ə)l 'kɔːl/ *noun* a telephone call to a number in the same area as the person making the call

local labour /ˌləʊk(ə)l 'leɪbə/ *noun* BUSINESS workers recruited near a business, not brought in from somewhere else

locally /'ləʊk(ə)li/ *adverb* in the area near a hotel, restaurant or office ○ *We recruit all our restaurant staff locally.*

local time /'ləʊk(ə)l ˌtaɪm/ *noun* the time of day in a particular area ○ *It will be 1 a.m. local time when we land.*

locate /ləʊ'keɪt/ *verb* □ **to be located** to be in a particular place ○ *The hotel is conveniently located near the motorway.* □ **centrally located** located in the centre of a town ○ *We are staying in a centrally located hotel.*

location /ləʊ'keɪʃ(ə)n/ *noun* a place where something is ○ *The hotel is in a very central location.*

lock /lɒk/ *noun* **1.** a device for closing a door or box so that it can be opened only

with a key ○ *The lock is broken on the safe.* ○ *She left her room key in the lock.* ○ *I have forgotten the combination of the lock on my briefcase.* ○ *We changed the locks on the doors after a set of keys were stolen.* **2.** SHIPS AND BOATS a section of a canal or river with barriers which can be opened or closed to control the flow of water, so allowing boats to move up or down to different levels ■ *verb* to close something with a key, so that it cannot be opened ○ *The manager forgot to lock the door of the reception office.* ○ *The petty cash box was not locked.*

locker /'lɒkə/ *noun* a small cupboard for personal belongings which you can close with a key ○ *Luggage lockers can be rented at the airport.* ○ *You will need a 20p coin for the lockers at the swimming pool.*

lock-in /'lɒk ɪn/ *noun* BARS a session of after-hours drinking inside a pub

lock-up garage /ˌlɒk ʌp 'gærɪdʒ/ *noun* HOTELS a garage attached to a hotel, which is locked at night

lock-up premises /ˌlɒk ʌp 'premɪsɪz/ *noun* BUSINESS a restaurant or shop which has no living accommodation and which the proprietor locks at night when it is closed

lodge /lɒdʒ/ *noun* **1.** TOURISM a small house in the country used for parties of hunters or ramblers **2.** a type of motel, especially one where buildings are made of wood, and are, or appear to be, simple and rustic ■ *verb* TOURISM to rent a room in a boarding house

lodge hotel /'lɒdʒ həʊˌtel/ *noun* **1.** a large main hotel building in a park or sports complex **2.** a hotel with rooms in separate wooden or rustic buildings

lodger /'lɒdʒə/ *noun* somebody who rents a room ○ *She has taken in three lodgers for the summer.*

lodging /'lɒdʒɪŋ/ *noun* accommodation

lodgings /'lɒdʒɪŋz/ *plural noun* rented rooms ○ *Are you still looking for lodgings or have you found somewhere to stay?*

loganberry /'ləʊgənb(ə)ri/ *noun* FRUIT a soft red fruit, a cross between a blackberry and a raspberry

loggia /'lɒdʒiə/ *noun* (*in southern Europe*) a covered gallery which is open on one side

logo /'ləʊgəʊ/ *noun* BUSINESS a symbol, design or group of letters used by a company as a distinctive mark on its products and in advertising ○ *The hotel group uses a small pine tree as its logo.*

loin /lɔɪn/ *noun* MEAT a cut of meat taken between the neck and the leg ○ *We had roast loin of pork for dinner.*

lollo rosso /ˌlɒləʊ ˈrɒsəʊ/ VEGETABLES a type of lettuce with curly red-tipped leaves

long /lɒŋ/ adjective for a large period of time ○ The hot season is very long. □ **in the long term** over a long period of time

long-distance /ˌlɒŋ ˈdɪstəns/ adjective travelling or extending to a point that is far away

long-distance call /ˌlɒŋ dɪstəns ˈkɔːl/ noun a telephone call to a number which is in a different zone or area. Also called **trunk call**

long-distance flight /ˌlɒŋ ˌdɪstəns ˈflaɪt/ noun AIR TRAVEL a flight to a destination which is a long way away

long-distance footpath /ˌlɒŋ ˌdɪstəns ˈfʊtpɑːθ/ noun TOURISM a path laid out by an official organisation, which goes for a very long way

long-distance skiing /ˌlɒŋ ˌdɪstəns ˈskiːɪŋ/ noun SPORT skiing for long distances following marked tracks across country

long-distance ski trail /ˌlɒŋ ˌdɪstəns ˈskiː ˌtreɪl/ noun SPORT a marked path for skiers over a long distance

long drink /ˈlɒŋ drɪŋk/ noun BEVERAGES **1.** a drink with a lot of liquid, such as a drink of spirits (gin, whisky, etc.) to which soda water, tonic water, fruit juice, etc., is added **2.** a drink of beer, cider, shandy, diluted fruit juice, etc.

long-grain rice /ˌlɒŋ ɡreɪn ˈraɪs/ noun FOOD rice with long grains used in savoury dishes

long-haul /ˌlɒŋ ˈhɔːl/ adjective relating to travel or transport over long distances

long-haul flight /ˌlɒŋ hɔːl ˈflaɪt/ noun AIR TRAVEL a long-distance flight, especially one between continents

long-haul market /ˌlɒŋ hɔːl ˈmɑːkɪt/ noun AIR TRAVEL the market for long-haul flights ○ The long-haul market is booming.

long-haul visitors /ˌlɒŋ hɔːl ˈvɪzɪtəz/ plural noun TOURISM visitors who come from other continents

longhouse /ˈlɒŋhaʊs/ noun a communal dwelling place, especially on the island of Borneo

longitude /ˈlɒŋɡɪtjuːd/ noun a position on the Earth's surface measured in degrees east or west

COMMENT: Longitude is measured from Greenwich (a town in England, just east of London) and, together with latitude, is used to indicate an exact position on the earth's surface. Longitude is measured in degrees, minutes and seconds. The cen-

tre of London is latitude 51°30'N, longitude 0°5'W.

long lease /ˌlɒŋ ˈliːs/ noun a lease which runs for fifty years or more

long-range weather forecast /ˌlɒŋ reɪndʒ ˈweðə ˌfɔːkɑːst/ noun a forecast covering a period of more than five days ahead

long-standing customer /lɒŋ ˌstændɪŋ ˈkʌstəmə/ noun BUSINESS somebody who has been a customer for many years

long-stay /ˈlɒŋ steɪ/ adjective referring to a stay of weeks or months

long-stay car park /ˌlɒŋ steɪ ˈkɑː ˌpɑːk/ noun TRAVEL a car park, especially at an airport, for people who will leave their cars there for several days or weeks

long-stay guest /ˈvɪzɪtə/, **long-stay visitor** noun HOTELS somebody who stays in a hotel for some weeks or months, rather than just a few days

long-term /ˌlɒŋ ˈtɜːm/ adjective planned to last for a long time ○ a long-term project like building a new tunnel through the Alps

long-term car park /ˌlɒŋ tɜːm ˈkɑː ˌpɑːk/ noun ROAD TRAVEL same as **long-stay car park**

long weekend /ˌlɒŋ wiːkˈend/ noun the period from Friday to Monday

loo /luː/ noun a toilet (informal) ○ Where's the loo? ○ She's gone to the loo. (NOTE: This is the term which is used most often in Britain.)

loose /luːs/ adjective not packed or packaged together □ **to sell sth loose** to sell e.g. biscuits, sweets, flour or sugar in small quantities which are separately weighed, not in packets

loose change /ˌluːs ˈtʃeɪndʒ/ noun money in coins

loose tea /ˌluːs ˈtiː/ noun BEVERAGES tea which is not in teabags

lorry /ˈlɒri/ noun ROAD TRAVEL a large vehicle used to transport goods. Also called **truck**

lorry driver /ˈlɒri ˌdraɪvə/ noun ROAD TRAVEL somebody who drives a lorry

lose /luːz/ verb **1.** not to have something any more □ **to lose customers** to have fewer customers ○ Their service is so slow that they have been losing customers. **2.** to have less ○ **the pound has lost value** the pound is worth less □ **to lose weight** to become thinner ○ She spent a week at a health farm trying to lose weight. **3.** to drop to a lower price ○ The dollar lost two cents against the yen. **4.** □ **to**

lose your way to get lost, to be unable to find the way to where you were going

loss /lɒs/ *noun* **1.** not having something which you had before ○ *She reported the loss of her passport to the police.* **2.** having less money than before, not making a profit □ **the company suffered a loss** the company did not make a profit □ **at a loss** making a loss, not making any profit ○ *The company is trading at a loss.* ○ *He sold the shop at a loss.* □ **to cut one's losses** to stop doing something which was losing money

lost /lɒst/ *adjective* that cannot be found □ **to get lost** to lose your way, to be unable to find the way to where you were going ○ *They got lost in the fog and mountain rescue teams had to be sent out to find them.*

lost and found office /ˌlɒst ən ˈfaʊnd ˌɒfɪs/ *noun US* same as **lost property office**

lost property /ˌlɒst ˈprɒpəti/ *noun* personal belongings which have been lost by their owners

lost property office /lɒst ˈprɒpəti ˌɒfɪs/ *noun* an office which collects objects which people have left behind and keeps them until the owners claim them. Also called **lost and found office** (NOTE: The US English for this is **lost and found office**.)

lounge /laʊndʒ/ *noun* a comfortable room in a hotel, cruise liner, etc.

lounge bar /ˈlaʊndʒ bɑː/ *noun* a bar in a pub or hotel which is more comfortable than the public bar, and where the drinks may be slightly more expensive

'British Airways is to open a £1.6 million lounge at Heathrow for arriving passengers. The lounge, which is claimed to be the first of its kind in the world, will enable passengers to freshen up after an overnight intercontinental flight with a shower while a valet irons their clothes' [*The Times*]

'…business passengers departing Heathrow Terminal 3 with hand luggage only, can avoid the queues and hurry straight through to the airline's new airside lounge to check in' [*Business Traveller*]

low /laʊ/ *adjective* small, not high ○ *Low overhead costs keep the room price low.* ○ *We try to keep our wages bill low.* ○ *By restricting the choice of dishes, the restaurant can keep its prices lower than those of the competition.* ○ *The pound is at a very low rate of exchange against the dollar.* ○ *Our aim is to buy at the lowest price possible.* (NOTE: **low – lower – lowest**) □ **low sales** a small amount of money produced by sales □ **low volume of sales** a small number of items sold

low-alcohol /ˌlaʊ ˈælkəhɒl/ *adjective* BEVERAGES containing very little alcohol ○ *I'm driving, so I'll have a low-alcohol lager.*

low-alcohol beer /ˌlaʊ ˌælkəhɒl ˈbɪə/ *noun* BEVERAGES beer containing very little alcohol

low-cal /ˈlaʊ kæl/ *adjective* same as **low-calorie**

low-calorie /ˌlaʊ ˈkæləri/ *adjective* containing very few calories or fewer calories than normal ○ *She's on a low-calorie diet.*

low-cost /ˈlaʊ kɒst/ *adjective* cheap ○ *low-cost accommodation*

low-cost travel /ˌlaʊ kɒst ˈtræv(ə)l/ *noun* TRAVEL cheap travel

lower berth /ˌlaʊə ˈbɜːθ/ *noun* a bottom bed

lower deck /ˈlaʊə dek/ *noun* ROAD TRAVEL the ground level section of a double-decker bus

low-fat /ˌlaʊ ˈfæt/ *adjective* CATERING containing very little fat ○ *Do you have any low-fat yoghurt?*

low-grade /ˈlaʊ greɪd/ *adjective* of not very good quality

low season /ˌlaʊ ˈsiːz(ə)n/ *noun* TOURISM same as **off-season** ○ *Tour operators urge more people to travel in the low season.* ○ *Air fares are cheaper in the low season.*

loyal toast /ˌlɔɪəl ˈtəʊst/ *noun* a toast to the Queen, at the end of a banquet

COMMENT: The loyal toast is drunk before coffee is served, and after it, guests are allowed to smoke. The loyal toast comes before speeches and other toasts. During the time when toasts are being called and speeches made, waiters make sure that guests' glasses are filled.

LRV *abbreviation* AIR TRAVEL light refreshment voucher

luge /luːʒ/ *noun* SPORT a sledge for downhill competition racing, on which two or more people lie on their backs, with their feet going first

luggage /ˈlʌgɪdʒ/ *noun* TRAVEL suitcases or bags for carrying clothes when travelling (NOTE: There is no plural form: to show one suitcase, etc., you can say **a piece of luggage**. Note also that US English uses **baggage** more often than **luggage**.)

luggage allowance /ˈlʌgɪdʒ əˌlaʊəns/ *noun* AIR TRAVEL the weight of luggage which an air passenger is allowed to take free when they travel. Also called **free luggage allowance**

luggage claim /ˈlʌgɪdʒ kleɪm/ *noun* TRAVEL a place in an airport where luggage comes off the plane onto a carousel to be claimed by the passengers. Also called **baggage claim**

luggage lift /'lʌgɪdʒ lɪft/ *noun* HOTELS a special lift for taking guests' luggage up to different floors of a hotel. Also called **baggage lift**

luggage lockers /'lʌgɪdʒ ˌlɒkəz/ *plural noun* TRAVEL series of small cupboards in e.g. an airport or railway station where passengers can leave luggage locked away safely

luggage rack /'lʌgɪdʒ ræk/ *noun* RAIL TRAVEL a device above the seats in a train for holding luggage. Also called **baggage rack**

luggage reclaim /'lʌgɪdʒ ˌriːkleɪm/ *noun* TRAVEL same as **luggage claim**

luggage stand /'lʌgɪdʒ stænd/ *noun* HOTELS a special low bench for holding luggage in a hotel room. Also called **baggage stand**

luggage trolley /'lʌgɪdʒ ˌtrɒli/ *noun* TRAVEL a trolley at an airport, railway station, ferry terminal, etc. on which passengers can put their luggage. Also called **baggage trolley**, **baggage cart**

lukewarm /ˌluːk'wɔːm/ *adjective* slightly warm, not hot enough ○ *The bathwater is only lukewarm.* ○ *We sent back the coffee because it was lukewarm.*

lunch /lʌntʃ/ *noun* CATERING a meal eaten in the middle of the day ○ *The hours of work are from 9.30 to 5.30 with an hour off for lunch.* ○ *The chairman is out at lunch.* ○ *The restaurant serves 150 lunches a day.* ○ *Take your seats for the first sitting for lunch.*

luncheon /'lʌntʃən/ *noun* same as **lunch** (*formal*) ○ *Luncheon is served in the small dining room from 12.30 to 2 p.m.* (NOTE: The word **luncheon** is usually used in formal menus.)

luncheon club /'lʌntʃən klʌb/ *noun* a group of people who meet regularly to eat

lunch together and listen to someone make a speech after the meal

luncheon meat /'lʌntʃən miːt/ *noun* MEAT a tinned meat loaf containing mostly minced pork

luncheon voucher /'lʌnʃtən ˌvaʊtʃə/ *noun* CATERING a ticket given by an employer to an employee in addition to their wages, which can be exchanged for food in a restaurant

lunch hour /'lʌntʃ aʊə/, **lunchtime** /'lʌntʃtaɪm/ *noun* the time when people have lunch ○ *a series of lunchtime concerts in the public gardens* ○ *The office is closed during the lunch hour or at lunchtimes.*

luscious /'lʌʃəs/ *adjective* sweet and juicy

luxurious /lʌg'zjʊəriəs/ *adjective* very comfortable ○ *The guest rooms have been refurnished with luxurious carpets and fittings.* ○ *Business class is not as luxurious as first class.*

luxury /'lʌkʃəri/ *noun* an expensive thing which is not necessary but which is good to have ○ *a black market in luxury articles*

luxury goods /'lʌkʃəri gʊdz/ *plural noun* expensive items which are not basic necessities

luxury hotel /ˌlʌkʃəri həʊ'tel/ *noun* HOTELS a very good hotel, with luxurious rooms and higher prices

luxury rating /'lʌkʃəri ˌreɪtɪŋ/ *noun* HOTELS a rating system which grades hotels according to their comfort

luxury suite /ˌlʌkʃəri 'swiːt/ *noun* HOTELS a series of extremely comfortable rooms in a hotel, apartment block or on a ship

lychee /'laɪtʃiː/ *noun* FRUIT same as **litchi**

lyophilise /laɪ'ɒfɪlaɪz/ *verb* CATERING to freeze-dry, a method of preserving food by freezing it rapidly and drying in a vacuum

M

m *abbreviation* metre *or* mile *or* million

macaroni /ˌmækəˈrəʊni/ *noun* FOOD short thick tubes of pasta, often served with a cheese sauce

macaroon /ˌmækəˈruːn/ *noun* BREAD, ETC. a small sweet almond biscuit

macchiato /ˌmækiˈɑːtəʊ/ *noun* BEVERAGES a drink of espresso coffee with a small amount of steamed milk on top

mackerel /ˈmækrəl/ *noun* SEAFOOD a sea fish with dark flesh, eaten grilled or smoked and also used for canning ○ *We had smoked mackerel as a starter.*

macrobiotic /ˌmækrəʊbaɪˈɒtɪk/ *adjective* referring to a vegan diet of seeds, grains, and organically grown fruit and vegetables, said to prolong life and balance the body's systems

mad cow disease /mæd ˈkaʊ dɪˌziːz/ *noun* same as **bovine spongiform encephalopathy**

made to measure /ˌmeɪd tə ˈmeʒə/ *adjective* made specially to fit ○ *He has his clothes made to measure.*

madras /məˈdrɑːs/ *noun* FOOD a fairly hot curried dish made with meat, spices, chillies, and lentils

maggot /ˈmægət/ *noun* the soft-bodied, legless larva of a fly, such as a bluebottle, warble fly or fruit fly ○ *The meat was covered in maggots.*

maid /meɪd/ *noun* **1.** a girl or woman who helps in the house, especially doing cleaning and serving at meals ○ *The maid forgot to change the towels.* **2.** HOTELS same as **chambermaid** ○ *The chalet has a daily maid to do the cleaning.*

maiden flight /ˌmeɪd(ə)n ˈflaɪt/, **maiden voyage** /ˌmeɪd(ə)n ˈvɔɪdʒ/ *noun* TRAVEL the first flight by an aircraft or first voyage by a ship ○ *The 'Titanic' sank on her maiden voyage across the Atlantic in 1912.*

maiden name /ˈmeɪd(ə)n neɪm/ *noun* the surname of a woman before she married

mail /meɪl/ *noun* **1.** a system of sending letters and parcels from one place to another ○ *to put a letter in the mail* ○ *The cheque was lost in the mail.* ○ *The invoice was put in the mail yesterday.* ○ *Mail to some of the islands in the Pacific can take six weeks.* Also called **post** □ **by mail** using the postal services, not sending something by hand or by messenger □ **by sea mail** sent by post abroad, using a ship □ **we sent the order by first-class mail** by the most expensive mail service, designed to be faster **2.** letters sent or received ○ *Has the mail arrived yet?* ○ *Your cheque arrived in yesterday's mail.* ○ *My assistant opens my mail as soon as it arrives.* ○ *The receipt was in this morning's mail.* ■ *verb* to send something by post ○ *to mail a letter confirming the booking* ○ *We mailed our confirmation last Wednesday.*

mailbox /ˈmeɪlbɒks/ *noun* **1.** one of several boxes where incoming mail is put in a large building, or a box for putting letters and packages in which you want to post **2.** an address where e-mail messages are received

mailing list /ˈmeɪlɪŋ lɪst/ *noun* same as **address list**

mail rack /ˈmeɪl ræk/ *noun* HOTELS a rack where letters for guests or occupants are put

main /meɪn/ *adjective* most important ○ *main post office* ○ *main dining room* ○ *main lounge* ○ *main bar*

main course /ˈmeɪn kɔːs/, **main dish** *noun* CATERING the largest and most important part of a meal

main deck /ˌmeɪn ˈdek/ *noun* SHIPS AND BOATS the deck with the most important facilities, such as the restaurant and bars

main door, main entrance *noun* HOTELS the most important door or entrance to a hotel

main office /ˌmeɪn ˈɒfɪs/ *noun* same as **head office**

main post office /ˌmeɪn ˈpəʊst ˌɒfɪs/ *noun* a large post office in a big town, which handles all the services available through post offices. Also called **central post office**

main road /meɪn ˈrəʊd/, **main thoroughfare** *noun* ROAD TRAVEL an important road, used by a lot of traffic ○ *The hotel is noisy as it stands at the crossing of two main roads.*

mainstream tourism /ˌmeɪnstriːm ˈtʊərɪz(ə)m/ *noun* tourism to well-established holiday destinations using ordinary means of transport and not requiring special arrangements

Main Street /ˈmeɪn striːt/ *noun US* the most important street in a town, where the shops and banks are (NOTE: In British English, this is **High Street**.)

maintain /meɪnˈteɪn/ *verb* **1.** to keep something in good working order ○ *to maintain good relations with one's customers* ○ *to maintain contact with a courier overseas by phone* **2.** to make something stay the same ○ *The restaurant has maintained the same volume of business in spite of the recession.*

maintenance /ˈmeɪntənəns/ *noun* **1.** actions intended to keep things going or working ○ *maintenance of contacts* ○ *maintenance of supplies* **2.** the work of keeping a machine in good working order

maintenance contract /ˈmeɪntənəns ˌkɒntrækt/ *noun* BUSINESS a contract by which a company keeps a piece of equipment in good working order ○ *We offer a full maintenance service.* Also called **service contract**

maintenance staff /ˈmeɪntənəns stɑːf/ *noun* people employed to keep something in good working condition

maître d'hôtel /ˈmetrədəʊˈtel/, **maître d'** *US* /metrəˈdiː/ *noun* CATERING the person in charge of a restaurant, who is responsible for all the service and takes orders himself from customers ○ *The maître d'hôtel showed us to our table.* Also called **head waiter**

maître d'hôtel de carré /ˌmeɪtrə dəʊ ˌtel diː ˈkæreɪ/ *noun* CATERING a chief waiter who is in charge of a station, and takes the orders from customers. Also called **station head waiter**

maize /meɪz/ *noun* FOOD a widely grown cereal crop. Also called **corn** (NOTE: The US English is **corn**.)

COMMENT: In Europe only a small proportion of the crop is sold for human consumption as 'corn on the cob'. Maize is the only grain crop which was introduced into the New World into the Old World, and it owes its name of Indian corn to the fact that it was cultivated by American Indians before the arrival of European settlers. It is the principal crop grown in the United States; in Mexico it is the principal food of the people, being coarsely ground into flour from which tortillas are made.

make /meɪk/ *verb* **1.** to prepare or to do □ **to make the beds** to tidy the beds after they have been slept in **2.** □ **to make a call** to use the telephone □ **to make a deposit** to pay money as a deposit □ **to make a payment** to pay

make up /ˌmeɪk ˈʌp/ *verb* □ **to make up a room** to prepare a room in a hotel for the next guest, by cleaning it, putting clean sheets and pillowcases on the bed and putting fresh towels, shampoo and soap in the bathroom □ **to make up the beds** to put clean sheets and pillowcases on beds

makeup /ˈmeɪkʌp/ *noun* cosmetic products, e.g. lipstick, foundation and eye shadow, used on the face

malaria /məˈleəriə/ *noun* MEDICAL a mainly tropical disease caused by a parasite which enters the body after a bite from the female anopheles mosquito ○ *Some people going on holiday to African countries come back with malaria.*

COMMENT: Malaria is a recurrent disease which produces regular periods of shivering, vomiting, sweating and headaches as the parasites develop in the body; the patient also develops anaemia. Malaria can be treated with Chloroquine, although some types of malaria are resistant to the drug. Such cases are treated with quinine. Prevention of malaria is not 100% certain, but travellers to Africa, the Middle East, India, the Far East and Central and South America should take a course of drugs before, during and after their trip.

malarious /məˈleəriəs/ *adjective* MEDICAL referring to a region where malaria is endemic

mall /mɔːl/ *noun US* same as **shopping mall**

malt /mɔːlt/ *noun* BEVERAGES **1.** a grain which has been prepared for making beer or whisky by being allowed to sprout and then dried **2.** *US* same as **malted milk**

malted /ˈmɔːltɪd/ *adjective* tasting of malt

malted milk /ˌmɔːltɪd ˈmɪlk/ *noun* BEVERAGES **1.** dried milk powder, flavoured with malt **2.** a drink made by adding fresh milk to this powder

malt whisky /ˌmɔːlt ˈwɪski/ *noun* BEVERAGES a whisky made from barley which has been allowed to sprout and then dried

manage /ˈmænɪdʒ/ *verb* **1.** to direct, to be in charge of ○ *She manages a restaurant.* ○ *He manages one of our hotel chains.* **2.** □ **manage property** to look after rented property for the owner **3.** □ **to manage to** to be able to do something ○ *Did you manage to catch the train?* ○ *She managed to confirm* *six flight bookings and take three phone calls all in two minutes.*

management /'mænɪdʒmənt/ *noun* **1.** BUSINESS the work of being in charge of a business ○ *to study management* ○ *good management* or *efficient management* ○ *bad management* or *inefficient management* ○ *a management graduate* or *a graduate in management* **2.** a group of managers or directors ○ *The management has decided to give an overall pay increase.*

management accountant /'mænɪdʒmənt ə,kaʊntənt/ *noun* BUSINESS an accountant who prepares financial information for managers so that they can take decisions

management accounts /'mænɪdʒmənt ə,kaʊnts/ *plural noun* BUSINESS financial information such as sales, expenditure, credit, and profitability, prepared for a manager so that he or she can take decisions

management committee /'mænɪdʒmənt kə,mɪti/ *noun* a committee which manages a club, block of flats, pension fund, etc.

management consultant /'mænɪdʒmənt kən,sʌltənt/ *noun* BUSINESS somebody who gives advice on how to manage a business

management contract /'mænɪdʒmənt ,kɒntrækt/ *noun* HOTELS a contract with a person or group of people to run a hotel, restaurant, etc., for a fee which is fixed in advance for a particular period of time

management course /'mænɪdʒmənt kɔːs/ *noun* BUSINESS a training course for managers

management team /'mænɪdʒmənt tiːm/ *noun* BUSINESS a group of managers working together

management techniques /'mænɪdʒmənt tek,niːks/ *plural noun* BUSINESS ways of managing a business

management trainee /,mænɪdʒmənt treɪ'niː/ *noun* BUSINESS somebody being trained to be a manager

management training /,mænɪdʒmənt 'treɪnɪŋ/ *noun* BUSINESS training for staff who want to be managers which makes them study problems and work out ways of solving them

manager /'mænɪdʒə/ *noun* **1.** the head of a department in a company ○ *personnel manager* ○ *sales manager* ○ *purchasing manager* **2.** somebody in charge of a hotel, inn, branch or shop ○ *Mr Smith is the manager of our*

local pub. ○ *The manager of our New York hotel is in London for a series of meetings.*

manageress /,mænɪdʒə'res/ *noun* a woman in charge of a shop or department

managerial /,mænə'dʒɪəriəl/ *adjective* referring to managers ○ *managerial staff* □ **to be appointed to a managerial position** to be appointed a manager

managing director /,mænədʒɪŋ daɪ'rektə/ *noun* BUSINESS a director who is in charge of the whole company

mandatory meeting /,mændət(ə)ri 'miːtɪŋ/ *noun* a meeting which everyone has to attend

mandolin /,mændə'lɪn/ *noun* CATERING a kitchen tool for slicing vegetables, consisting of adjustable blades in a frame

mangetout /'mɒnʒtuː/ *noun* VEGETABLES a variety of pea in which the whole pod is eaten

mango /'mæŋgəʊ/ *noun* FRUIT a tropical fruit, which is large, yellow or yellowish-green with a soft orange pulp surrounding the very large flat seed

mango chutney /,mæŋgəʊ 'tʃʌtni/ *noun* SAUCES, ETC. a spicy chutney made from mangoes, eaten with Indian dishes ○ *They served mango chutney with the curry.*

mangosteen /'mæŋgəstiːn/ *noun* FRUIT a fruit that has a dark shiny rind and a soft sweet white flesh

Manhattan /mæn'hæt(ə)n/ *noun* BEVERAGES a cocktail of rye whisky, Italian vermouth and angostura bitters

manifest /'mænɪfest/ *noun* TRAVEL a list of goods, cargo, or passengers

manpower /'mænpaʊə/ *noun* the workers employed in a business or industry or who are available to be employed □ **manpower shortage, shortage of manpower** lack of workers

manpower planning /'mænpaʊə ,plænɪŋ/ *noun* planning to obtain the right number of employees in each job

manpower requirements /'mænpaʊə rɪ,kwaɪəmənts/ *plural noun* the number of employees needed

manufacturer's recommended price /,mænjʊfæktʃərəz ,rekəmendɪd 'praɪs/ *noun* BUSINESS the price which a manufacturer suggests the product should be sold at on the retail market, though it is often reduced by the retailer. Abbr **MRP**. Also called **recommended retail price**

map /mæp/ *noun* a diagram of a town or country as if seen from above ○ *The hotel has maps of the centre of the town.* ○ *Do you*

MAP 190

have any maps of the region? ○ I'll draw you a map of the town, otherwise you can easily get lost.

MAP *abbreviation* HOTELS modified American Plan

maple syrup /ˌmeɪp(ə)l ˈsɪrəp/ *noun* SAUCES, ETC. a sweet syrup made from the sap of the sugar maple tree

maraschino /ˌmærəˈʃiːnəʊ/ *noun* FOOD a cherry preserved in liqueur, used to decorate a drink or cake

marble /ˈmɑːb(ə)l/ *noun* a very hard type of stone which can be polished so that it shines ○ *The entrance hall has a marble floor.*

Mardi Gras /ˌmɑːdi ˈɡrɑː/ *noun* ENTERTAINMENT a festival at the beginning of Lent celebrated in many Catholic countries with elaborate festivals. Also called **Shrove Tuesday**

margarine /ˌmɑːdʒəˈriːn/ *noun* FOOD a mixture of animal or vegetable fat which is used instead of butter

marge /mɑːdʒ/ *noun* FOOD same as **margarine** (*informal*)

margin /ˈmɑːdʒɪn/ *noun* BUSINESS the difference between the money received when selling a product and the money paid for it

marginal pricing /ˌmɑːdʒɪn(ə)l ˈpraɪsɪŋ/ *noun* BUSINESS basing the selling price of a product on its variable costs of production plus a margin, but excluding fixed costs

marina /məˈriːnə/ *noun* SHIPS AND BOATS a harbour with floating jetties where a large number of pleasure boats can be tied up ○ *Her yacht was moored in the marina.*

marinade /ˈmærɪneɪd/ *noun* SAUCES, ETC. a mixture of wine and herbs in which meat or fish is soaked before cooking ■ *verb* CATERING to soak meat or fish in a mixture of wine and herbs ○ *Marinade the meat for twelve hours before cooking.*

marinate /ˈmærɪneɪt/ *verb* CATERING same as **marinade**

marinated /ˈmærɪnteɪtɪd/ *adjective* CATERING soaked in a mixture of wine and herbs before being cooked ○ *Anchovies are not cured but are marinated in-house.*

marine park /məˈriːn pɑːk/ *noun* TOURISM a natural park created on the bottom of the sea, as on a tropical reef, where visitors go into observation chambers under the sea to look at the fish and plant life

marital /ˈmærɪt(ə)l/ *adjective* referring to marriage

marital status /ˌmærɪt(ə)l ˈsteɪtəs/ *noun* the state of being married, single, divorced, widowed or separated

maritime /ˈmærɪtaɪm/ *adjective* referring to the sea and ships

maritime law /ˌmærɪtaɪm ˈlɔː/ *noun* SHIPS AND BOATS laws referring to ships, ports and conduct at sea

marjoram /ˈmɑːdʒərəm/ *noun* SAUCES, ETC. a herb used in Mediterranean cooking, especially pizzas

mark /mɑːk/ *noun* a sign put on an item to show something ■ *verb* to make a mark or write on something ○ *to mark a product 'for export only'* ○ *an article marked at £1.50* ○ *to mark the price on something*

mark down /ˌmɑːk ˈdaʊn/ *verb* to reduce the price of something ○ *The holiday package has been marked down to £224.* ○ *We have marked all prices down by 30% for the sale.* □ **to mark down a price** to reduce the price of something ○ *The holiday package has been marked down to £224.* ○ *We have marked all prices down by 30% for the sale.*

mark-down /ˈmɑːk daʊn/ *noun* **1.** a reduction of the price of something **2.** a percentage amount by which a price is lowered ○ *We have used a 30% mark-down to fix the sale price.*

market /ˈmɑːkɪt/ *noun* **1.** a place, often in the open air, where farm produce is sold ○ *fish market* ○ *flower market* ○ *open-air market* □ **antiques market** a series of shops or stalls under one roof where antiques are sold **2.** BUSINESS demand for or possible sales of a particular type of product ○ *The market for fly-drive holidays has risen sharply.* ○ *We have 20% of the British caravan market.* ○ *There is no market for expensive package tours in November.* **3.** □ **the black market** a system of buying and selling goods in a way which is not allowed by law, as in a time of rationing ○ *There is a flourishing black market in spare parts for cars.* □ **to pay black-market prices** to pay high prices to get items which are not easily available **4.** □ **up market, down market** more expensive or less expensive □ **to go up market, to go down market** to make products which appeal to a wealthy section of the market or to a wider, less wealthy, section of the market ■ *verb* to sell something ○ *This product is being marketed in all European countries.*

market day /ˈmɑːkɪt deɪ/ *noun* a day when a market is regularly held ○ *Tuesday is market day, so the streets are closed to traffic.*

market dues /ˌmɑːkɪt ˈdjuːz/ *plural noun* rent for a stall in a market

market forces /ˌmɑːkɪt ˈfɔːsɪz/ *plural noun* BUSINESS influences on the sales of a product

marketing /ˈmɑːkɪtɪŋ/ *noun* techniques used in selling a product, e.g. packaging and advertising

marketing department /ˈmɑːkɪtɪŋ dɪ ˌpɑːtmənt/ *noun* BUSINESS the department in a company which specialises in ways of selling a product

marketing manager /ˈmɑːkɪtɪŋ ˌmænɪdʒə/ *noun* MARKETING somebody in charge of a marketing department

marketing mix /ˈmɑːkɪtɪŋ mɪks/ *noun* MARKETING a combination of elements that make up marketing, e.g. price, distribution and advertising

market leader /ˌmɑːkɪt ˈliːdə/ *noun* BUSINESS the company with the largest market share ○ *We are the market leader in self-catering packages to Spain.*

market opportunities /ˌmɑːkɪt ɒpə ˈtjuːnɪtiz/ *plural noun* BUSINESS the possibility of finding new sales in a market

market penetration /ˌmɑːkɪt ˌpenɪ ˈtreɪʃ(ə)n/ *noun* BUSINESS same as **market share**

market price /ˈmɑːkɪt praɪs/ *noun* BUSINESS the price at which a product can be sold

market research /ˌmɑːkɪt rɪˈsɜːtʃ/ *noun* BUSINESS the work of examining the possible sales of a product before it is put on the market

market segment /ˌmɑːkɪt ˈsegmənt/ *noun* a section of a market defined by particular criteria

market share /ˌmɑːkɪt ˈʃeə/ *noun* BUSINESS the percentage of a total market which the sales of a company cover ○ *We hope our new product range will increase our market share.* Also called **market penetration**

market square /ˌmɑːkɪt ˈskweə/ *noun* a square where a market is held ○ *The hotel is in the square opposite the town hall.*

market survey /ˌmɑːkɪt ˈsɜːveɪ/ *noun* MARKETING a general report on the state of a market

market town /ˈmɑːkɪt taʊn/ *noun* TOURISM a town which has a regular market

market trend /ˌmɑːkɪt ˈtrend/ *plural noun* MARKETING gradual changes taking place in a market

mark up /ˌmɑːk ˈʌp/ *verb* to increase the price of something □ **to mark a price up** to

increase a price ○ *These prices have been marked up by 10%.*

mark-up /ˈmɑːk ʌp/ *noun* **1.** an increase in the price of something ○ *We put into effect a 10% mark-up of all prices in June.* **2.** BUSINESS an amount added to the cost price to give the selling price □ **we work to a 3.5 times mark-up** *or* **to a 350% mark-up** we take the unit cost and multiply by 3.5 to give the selling price

marmalade /ˈmɑːməleɪd/ *noun* SAUCES, ETC. jam made of oranges, or other citrus fruit such as lemon or grapefruit □ **Seville orange marmalade** marmalade made with bitter oranges

COMMENT: Marmalade is eaten with toast at breakfast, and not at any other time of day.

marquee /mɑːˈkiː/ *noun* ENTERTAINMENT a very large tent, used for wedding receptions, prize-givings, etc. ○ *The wedding reception was held in a marquee in the garden.*

marquise /mɑːˈkiːz/ *noun* **1.** a cold French dessert consisting of whipped cream folded into fruit-flavoured ice **2.** a French dessert consisting of either a rich chocolate mousse or a spongy chocolate cake, or a combination of chocolate mousse and cake

marrow /ˈmærəʊ/ *noun* VEGETABLES a large green cylindrical vegetable with spongy white flesh from a plant of the melon family (NOTE: Usually marrows are picked when very small; at this stage they are called **courgettes** or **zucchini**.)

marsala /mɑːˈsɑːlə/ *noun* BEVERAGES a sweet Italian wine

marshmallow /mɑːʃˈmæləʊ/ *noun* FOOD a soft spongy sweet made from sugar syrup, egg whites, and flavouring

martini /mɑːˈtiːni/ *noun* BEVERAGES a drink made of gin or vodka and dry or sweet vermouth

marzipan /ˈmɑːzɪpæn/ *noun* FOOD a paste made from ground almonds, sugar and egg, used to cover a fruit cake before icing or to make individual little sweets

masala /məˈsɑːlə/ *noun* FOOD a mixture of spices ground into a paste, used to flavour South Asian dishes, or a dish flavoured with this kind of paste

mash /mæʃ/ *noun* FOOD mashed potatoes (*informal*) ○ *a plate of sausage and mash* or *bangers and mash* ■ *verb* CATERING to crush food to a soft paste

mashed potatoes /ˌmæʃt pəˈteɪtəʊz/ *plural noun* FOOD potatoes which have been peeled, boiled and then crushed with butter and milk until they form a soft cream. Also called **creamed potatoes**

mass /mæs/ *noun* **1.** a large group of people **2.** a large number or quantity of things ○ *We have a mass of letters* or *masses of letters to write.* ○ *They received a mass of inquiries* or *masses of inquiries after the TV commercials.*

massage /ˈmæsɑːʒ/ ENTERTAINMENT *noun* an act of rubbing the body to relieve pain or to improve circulation ○ *She went to the sauna for a massage and a bath.* ■ *verb* to rub someone's body to relieve pain or to improve circulation

masseur /mæˈsɜː/ *noun* a man who massages ○ *The health club employs a qualified masseur.* ○ *A session with the masseur leaves you feeling really fit.*

masseuse /mæˈsɜːz/ *noun* a woman who massages

mass leisure /ˌmæs ˈleʒə/ *noun* the everyday leisure pursuits of the majority of a population

mass marketing /ˌmæs ˈmɑːkɪtɪŋ/ *noun* MARKETING marketing which aims at reaching large numbers of people

mass media /ˌmæs ˈmiːdiə/ *noun* ENTERTAINMENT the various means of communicating information to the public, e.g. television, radio and newspapers, considered together

mass tourism /ˌmæs ˈtʊərɪz(ə)m/ *noun* TOURISM tourism involving large numbers of people

master /ˈmɑːstə/ *adjective* main, which controls ○ *the master copy of the guest list*

master bedroom /ˌmɑːstə ˈbedruːm/ *noun* the main bedroom

master franchise /ˈmɑːstə ˌfræntʃaɪz/ *noun* BUSINESS the main franchise for an area, from which other outlets are sub- franchised

master key /ˈmɑːstə kiː/ *noun* the main key which opens all doors in a building

Master of Ceremonies /ˌmɑːstə əv ˈserəməniːz/ *noun* ENTERTAINMENT somebody who introduces the speakers at a dinner, or at some official meeting. Abbr **MC**

Master of Culinary Arts /ˌmɑːstə əv ˈkʌlɪn(ə)ri ˌɑːts/ *noun* CATERING an award made every four years by the Academy of Culinary Arts to senior restaurant personnel. Abbr **MCA**

'…the Master of Culinary Arts (MCA) has been awarded to just 20 chefs and restaurant managers since its inception in 1987' [*Caterer & Hotelkeeper*]

master switch /ˈmɑːstə swɪtʃ/ *noun* a switch which controls all other switches

mat /mæt/ *noun* a small piece of carpet or woven straw, etc., used as a floor covering

mature /məˈtʃʊə/ *verb* to develop a fuller flavour over time ■ *adjective* old enough to have acquired the maximum flavour

maximum load /ˌmæksɪməm ˈləʊd/ *noun* the largest weight of goods which a lorry or aircraft can carry

Maximum Permitted Mileage *noun* AIR TRAVEL the distance calculated according to the IATA mileage allowance for a direct flight between two towns. Abbr **MPM**

Mayday /ˈmeɪdeɪ/ *noun* TRAVEL an international signal to show that you are in distress ○ *The ship sent out a Mayday call.* □ **the aircraft captain put out a Mayday** the captain radioed a message to air traffic control to say the aircraft was in danger

mayo /ˈmeɪəʊ/ *noun* same as **mayonnaise**

mayonnaise /ˌmeɪəˈneɪz/ *noun* SAUCES, ETC. a sauce for cold dishes, made of oil, eggs and lemon juice or vinegar ○ *Would you like some mayonnaise on your salad?* ○ *We bought tuna mayonnaise sandwiches.*

COMMENT: Mayonnaise is served with cold boiled eggs (oeufs mayonnaise), with cold lobster (lobster mayonnaise), and other cold dishes; it is also used as a base for other sauces, such as tartare sauce, Thousand Island dressing, etc.

MC *abbreviation* ENTERTAINMENT Master of Ceremonies

MCA /ˌem siː ˈeɪ/ *abbreviation* CATERING Master of Culinary Arts

mead /miːd/ *noun* BEVERAGES an alcoholic drink made from honey

meal /miːl/ *noun* CATERING **1.** food eaten at a particular time of day ○ *Full board includes three meals: breakfast, lunch and dinner.* ○ *You can have your meals in your room at a small extra charge.* **2.** roughly ground flour. ◊ **wholemeal flour**

meal service /ˈmiːl ˌsɜːvɪs/ *noun* AIR TRAVEL the serving of meals on a plane

meal time /ˈmiːl taɪm/ *noun* CATERING the time when a meal is usually served ○ *Meal times are shown on the noticeboard.*

measure /ˈmeʒə/ *noun* **1.** a way of calculating size or quantity **2.** BEVERAGES a serving of alcohol or wine when served by the glass □ **to give short measure** to serve smaller quantities of alcohol than is allowed by law. ◊ **inspector of weights and measures** ■ *verb* to find out the size or quantity of something ○ *to measure the size of a package* □ **to be measured for a suit** to have your measurements, e.g. arm length, chest, waist, taken by a tailor when making a suit for you

measurements /ˈmeʒəmənts/ *plural noun* size represented in inches or centimetres ○ *to take down a customer's measurements*

measuring tape /ˈmeʒərɪŋ teɪp/ *noun* same as **tape measure**

meat /miːt/ *noun* FOOD food from an animal's body □ **the meat course** the main course in a meal, consisting of meat and vegetables

COMMENT: The names of different types of meat are different from the names of the animals from which they come. Full-grown cows or bulls give 'beef'; calves give 'veal'; pigs give 'pork', or if salted, 'bacon' and 'ham'; sheep and lambs give 'lamb'; deer give 'venison'. Only the birds (chicken, duck, goose, and turkey) give meat with the same name. In menus, meat is often referred to by its French name: agneau (= lamb), boeuf (= beef), porc (= pork), jambon (= ham), etc.

meatball /ˈmiːtbɔːl/ *noun* FOOD a small ball of minced meat with flavourings ○ *meatballs in tomato sauce*

meat extender /ˈmiːl ɪkˌstendə/ *noun* CATERING any edible material or mixture added to meat preparations to increase their bulk

meat loaf /ˈmiːt ləʊf/ *noun* FOOD a solid block of minced meat, vegetables and flavourings cooked and usually served hot

meat products /ˈmiːt ˌprɒdʌkts/ *plural noun* CATERING foods made from meat, e.g. pies, sausages and pâtés

médaillon /ˈmedaɪɒn/ *noun* a round thin slice of meat or other food

media /ˈmiːdiə/ *noun* □ **the media**, **the mass media** the various means of communicating information to the public, e.g. television, radio and newspapers, considered as a group ○ *The restaurant has attracted a lot of interest in the media* or *a lot of media interest.*

media coverage /ˈmiːdiə ˌkʌv(ə)rɪdʒ/ *noun* reports about something in the media ○ *We got good media coverage for the launch of the new tour guide.*

medical /ˈmedɪk(ə)l/ *noun* referring to the study or treatment of illness

medical aid /ˈmedɪk(ə)l eɪd/ *noun* **1.** treatment of someone who is ill or injured, given by a doctor. ◊ **first aid 2.** medical supplies and experts sent to a country after a disaster

medical assistance /ˌmedɪk(ə)l əˈsɪst(ə)ns/ *noun* help given by a doctor or nurse

medical certificate /ˈmedɪk(ə)l səˌtɪfɪkət/ *noun* MEDICAL a document signed by a doctor to show that an employee has been ill

medical inspection /ˈmedɪk(ə)l ɪnˌspekʃ(ə)n/ *noun* MEDICAL an examination of a place of work to check that the conditions will not make the employees ill

medical insurance /ˈmedɪk(ə)l ɪnˌʃʊərəns/ *noun* MEDICAL insurance which pays the cost of medical treatment, especially when travelling abroad

medium /ˈmiːdiəm/ *adjective* CATERING cooked so that the meat is brown on the outside but slightly pink and moist inside

medium-haul /ˈmiːdiəm hɔːl/ *adjective* AIR TRAVEL covering a distance longer than a short-haul flight, but not as long as an intercontinental flight

medium-term /ˌmiːdiəm ˈtɜːm/ *adjective* for a period of one or two years

meet /miːt/ *verb* **1.** to come together with someone ○ *to meet a tour party at the airport* ○ *to meet an agent at her hotel* ○ *We're meeting our relatives at 2.00 at the main station.* **2.** to be satisfactory for e.g. needs or requirements (NOTE: **meeting – met**) □ **to meet the demand for a new service** to provide a new service which has been asked for □ **we will try to meet your price** we will try to offer a price which is acceptable to you

meeting /ˈmiːtɪŋ/ *noun* a coming together of a group of people ○ *The staff meeting will be held in the lounge.*

meeting place /ˈmiːtɪŋ pleɪs/ *noun* a room or area where people can meet

meeting point /ˈmiːtɪŋ pɔɪnt/ *noun* TRAVEL a point at an airport or railway station where people can arrange to meet

meeting room /ˈmiːtɪŋ ruːm/ *noun* same as **conference room**

meet with /ˈmiːt wɪð/ *verb US* to come together with someone □ **I hope to meet with him in New York** I hope to meet him in New York

Melba sauce /ˌmelbə ˈsɔːs/ *noun* SAUCES, ETC. raspberry sauce

melba toast /ˌmelbə ˈtəʊst/ *noun* BREAD, ETC. a toast made by grilling a slice of bread once, then slicing it in half and grilling it again quickly, so as to produce a sort of cracker

melon /ˈmelən/ *noun* FRUIT a sweet round or cylindrical fruit with flesh varying from green to orange or white ○ *We had melon and Parma ham as a starter.*

COMMENT: Melon may be served as a first course (sometimes with Parma ham), or as a dessert. The fruit can be cut into wedges or halves, with the seeds removed. The hole in a half melon can have port poured into it.

melt /melt/ *noun* an open toasted sandwich, usually with cheese melted on top

member /ˈmembə/ *noun* **1.** somebody who belongs to a group or a society **2.** BUSINESS an organisation which belongs to a group or a society ○ *the member countries of the EC* ○ *the member companies of ABTA*

ménage /meˈnɑːʒ/ *noun* CATERING the cleaning and preparing of a restaurant for guests (NOTE: **ménage** comes from the French noun meaning 'housework'.)

meningitis /ˌmenɪnˈdʒaɪtɪs/ *noun* MEDICAL inflammation of part of the brain, where the patient has violent headaches, fever, and stiff neck muscles, and can become delirious □ **aseptic meningitis** a relatively mild viral form of meningitis

COMMENT: Meningitis is a serious viral or bacterial disease which can cause brain damage and even death. The bacterial form can be treated with antibiotics.

men's room /menz ruːm/ *noun especially US* a public toilet for men

menu /ˈmenjuː/ *noun* CATERING a printed list of food available in a restaurant ○ *The breakfast menu is displayed on each table.* ○ *The menu changes every week.* ○ *Some special dishes are not on the menu, but are written on a special board.* ○ *The dinner menu starts at £30 per person.*

COMMENT: The normal menu for a three-course meal (lunch or dinner) will consist of an hors d'oeuvre, starter or soup, followed by a main course of fish, meat or a vegetarian dish, then a dessert or cheese. More elaborate menus will have a fish or pasta course as well as a meat course, and a dessert as well as cheese. Note that in English menus, the dessert course comes before the cheese, while in French menus, the cheese comes before the dessert.

menu card /ˈmenjuː kɑːd/ *noun* CATERING a card placed on the table at a formal dinner, showing the dishes which will be served

menu holder /ˈmenjuː ˌhəʊldə/ *noun* a little metal or plastic holder for a menu on a table

menu planning /ˈmenjuː ˌplænɪŋ/ *noun* CATERING planning menus for special occasions, as well as for daily use

menu pricing /ˈmenjuː ˌpraɪsɪŋ/ *noun* CATERING the work of giving prices to dishes

on the menu so as to produce a profit, but not so high as to deter customers

merchandising /ˈmɜːtʃəndaɪzɪŋ/ *noun* MARKETING the work of organising the display and promotion of goods for sale

merchant /ˈmɜːtʃənt/ *noun* BUSINESS **1.** a business person who buys and sells goods, especially imported goods, in bulk for retail sale ○ *wine merchant* **2.** a company or shop which accepts a particular type of credit card for purchases

merchant number /ˈmɜːtʃənt ˌnʌmbə/ *noun* FINANCE the number of the merchant, printed at the top of the report slip when depositing credit card payments

meringue /məˈræŋ/ *noun* DESSERTS a mixture of whipped egg white and caster sugar, dried slowly in the oven

COMMENT: Small individual meringues can be served with cream or fruit salad; meringue mixture can also be spread on top of a fruit pie before cooking.

meshuval /məˈʃʊvəl/ *noun* BEVERAGES wine which has been boiled to make it kosher. ◊ **kosher**

'…although a few Champagne houses already produce kosher Champagnes, Nicolas Feuillatte is the first Champagne brand to offer a meshuval cuvée. Meshuval wine undergoes a special vinification close to the pasteurisation process that enables it to be served by non-religious individuals' [*Caterer & Hotelkeeper*]

mess /mes/ *noun* a place where servicemen or policemen live and eat

message /ˈmesɪdʒ/ *noun* information which is sent to someone ○ *I will leave a message with the receptionist.* ○ *Can you give Mr Smith a message from his wife?* ○ *He says he never received the message.*

message board /ˈmesɪdʒ bɔːd/, **message rack** *noun* a special board or rack where messages are put

messenger /ˈmesɪndʒə/ *noun* somebody who brings a message ○ *She sent the package by special messenger* or *by motorcycle messenger.*

messing /ˈmesɪŋ/ *noun* ENTERTAINMENT arrangements for providing food, accommodation and leisure activities for servicemen

mess manager /ˈmes ˌmænɪdʒə/ *noun* somebody in charge of catering, housekeeping, etc., in a mess

metal detector /ˈmet(ə)l dɪˌtektə/ *noun* a device that sounds an alarm if it senses that metal is present and is used to check whether people are carrying weapons or other dangerous objects, e.g. at airports

meteorological /ˌmiːtiərəˈlɒdʒɪk(ə)l/ *adjective* referring to weather or climate

Meteorological Office /ˌmiːtiərə ˈlɒdʒɪk(ə)l ˌɒfɪs/, **Met Office** /met ˈɒfɪs/ *noun* a central government office which analyses weather reports and forecasts the weather

meteorological station /ˌmiːtiərə ˈlɒdʒɪk(ə)l ˌsteɪʃ(ə)n/ *noun* a research station which notes weather conditions

meteorologist /ˌmiːtiəˈrɒlədʒɪst/ *noun* a scientist who specialises in the study of the weather and the atmosphere

meteorology /ˌmiːtiəˈrɒlədʒi/ *noun* the science of studying the weather and the atmosphere

meter /ˈmiːtə/ *noun* **1.** a device for counting how much of something has been used **2.** *US* same as **metre**

metered Internet access /ˌmiːtəd ˈɪntənet ˌækses/ *noun* HOTELS access to the Internet via the telephone in a guest's room, which is paid for by the guest

method /ˈmeθəd/ *noun* a way of doing something ○ *What is the best method of payment?* ○ *What method of payment do you prefer?*

methylated spirits /ˌmeθəleɪtɪd ˈspɪrɪts/, **meths** /meθs/ *noun* CATERING alcohol, stained purple, used as fuel in small burners to keep food hot at table, or for cooking particular dishes at table

metre /ˈmiːtə/ *noun* a measure of length equalling 3.4 feet (NOTE: This is usually written **m** after figures: *The case is 2m wide by 3m long.* The US spelling is **meter**.)

metric /ˈmetrɪk/ *adjective* using the metre as a basic measurement □ **the metric system** a system of measuring using metres, litres and grams

metric ton /ˌmetrɪk ˈtʌn/, **metric tonne** *noun* 1000 kilograms

metro /ˈmetrəʊ/ *noun* RAIL TRAVEL an underground railway system, or overground tram system ○ *the Paris metro*

COMMENT: The Paris underground railway was called the 'métropolitain', shortened to 'le métro' or 'the metro' in English, and this name is used in several other countries, including Newcastle in the UK and Brussels in Belgium. In Germany, underground railways are called 'U-Bahn'. The London underground railway is called the 'underground', or simply, the 'tube'. In North American, an underground railway is called a 'subway'.

metropolis /mɪˈtrɒpəlɪs/ *noun* a very large town ○ *The plan will provide an integrated transport system suitable for a modern metropolis.*

metropolitan /ˌmetrəˈpɒlɪt(ə)n/ *adjective* referring to the whole of a large town ○ *Metropolitan New York covers 200 square miles.*

meunière /ˌmɜːniˈeə/ *adjective* CATERING referring to e.g. fish that is dredged in flour, fried in butter, and sprinkled with lemon juice and chopped parsley

meze /ˈmetsə/ *noun* FOOD an assortment of snacks, e.g. stuffed vine leaves, small pastries, or grilled sausages, served with drinks as an appetiser or a light meal in Greece and Southwest Asia

mezzanine /ˈmetsəniːn/ *noun* a floor between the ground floor and the first floor ○ *The chalet has an open-plan living room with a mezzanine bedroom above.*

mezze /ˈmetsə/ *noun* FOOD same as **meze**

mg *abbreviation* milligram

mi *abbreviation* mile

mice /maɪs/ ♦ **mouse**

Michelin /ˈmiːʃəlæn/ *noun* CATERING a French tyre company, which produces guide books and awards stars to the best restaurants

Michelin star /ˈmɪʃəlɪn stɑː/ *noun* CATERING an award made to the very best restaurants, graded from one to three stars

microbrewery /ˈmaɪrəʊˌbruːəri/ *noun* BARS a small brewery that produces specialised beers in small quantities, often selling them on the premises

microwave /ˈmaɪkrəweɪv/ CATERING *noun* an oven which heats by using very short-wave radiation ○ *Put the pie in the microwave for two minutes to heat it up.* ■ *verb* to heat a dish in a microwave (*informal*) ○ *The pie isn't very hot – can you microwave it a bit more?*

'…among the 300 frequent travellers questioned, microwave ovens were cited as the single most important item in a hotel room' [*Caterer & Hotelkeeper*]

microwaveable, microwavable *adjective* CATERING possible to cook in a microwave ○ *frozen microwaveable TV dinners*

mid- /mɪd/ *prefix* middle □ **from mid-1998** from the middle of 1998 ○ *The hotel is closed until mid-July.*

middle lane /ˌmɪd(ə)l ˈleɪn/ *noun* ROAD TRAVEL a track in the centre of a three-lane carriageway

middle management /ˌmɪd(ə)l ˈmænɪdʒmənt/ *noun* BUSINESS the department managers of a company who carry out the policy set by the directors and organise the work of a group of workers

mid-month /ˌmɪd 'mʌnθ/ *adjective* taking place in the middle of the month

mid-range /'mɪd reɪndʒ/ *adjective* □ **a mid-range hotel** a hotel which is neither very expensive and luxurious nor very cheap and simple

midweek /ˌmɪd'wiːk/ *adjective, adverb* happening in the middle of the week ○ *If you travel midweek, the fares are higher than if a Saturday night is included.* □ **midweek bargain break** a special holiday package for the middle of a week

mild /maɪld/ *noun* BEVERAGES formerly, a type of brown beer, which is less alcoholic and sweeter than 'bitter' ■ *adjective* **1.** not sharp or strong-tasting ○ *yoghurt-based sauces are milder* ○ *We'll choose the mildest curry on the menu.* Opposite **hot 2.** not severe, as of weather ○ *Winters in the south of the country are usually milder than in the north.* (NOTE: **milder – mildest**)

mile /maɪl/ *noun* a measure of length equalling 1.625 kilometres (NOTE: This is usually written **m** after figures.) □ **the car does twenty-five miles to the gallon, twenty-five miles per gallon** the car uses one gallon of petrol to travel twenty-five miles

mileage /'maɪlɪdʒ/ *noun* TRAVEL the distance travelled in miles

mileage allowance /'maɪlɪdʒ əˌlaʊəns/ *noun* BUSINESS money paid per mile as expenses to someone who uses their own car for business travel

milk /mɪlk/ *noun* DAIRY a white liquid produced by female mammals for feeding their young, especially the milk produced by cows ■ *verb* to take the milk from an animal

milk bar /'mɪlk bɑː/ *noun* CATERING a bar which serves milk, other milk products such as ice cream, and non-alcoholic drinks

milk chocolate /ˌmɪlk 'tʃɒklət/ *noun* FOOD a sweet pale brown chocolate made with milk

milk products /'mɪlk ˌprɒdʌkts/ *plural noun* CATERING milk and other foodstuffs produced from it, which are sold for human consumption e.g. liquid milk, butter, cheese, cream, ice cream, condensed milk and milk powder

milkshake /'mɪlkʃeɪk/ *noun* BEVERAGES a drink made from milk mixed with flavouring and sometimes ice cream

mill /mɪl/ *verb* **1.** to grind grain or seed by machine **2.** to whisk or shake something such as cream or chocolate until it is foamy

millefeuille /ˌmiːl'fɔɪ/ *noun* DESSERTS a dessert or pastry consisting of several layers of puff pastry with a filling of cream and jam, topped with icing sugar or icing

millet /'mɪlɪt/ *noun* FOOD a common cereal crop grown in many of the hot, dry regions of Africa and Asia, where it is a staple food

milligram /'mɪlɪɡræm/, **milligramme** /'mɪlɪɡræm/ *noun* one thousandth of a gram (NOTE: This is usually written **mg** after figures.)

millilitre /'mɪlɪliːtə/ *noun* one thousandth of a litre (NOTE: This is usually written **ml** after figures. The US spelling is **milliliter**.)

millimetre /'mɪlɪmiːtə/ *noun* one thousandth of a metre (NOTE: This is usually written **mm** after figures. The US spelling is **millimeter**.)

million /'mɪljən/ *noun* the number 1,000,000 ○ *The company lost £10 million on the North American route.* ○ *Our turnover has risen to $13.4 million.* ○ *The museum had over one million visitors in its first year.* (NOTE: **Million** can be written **m** after figures: **$5m** (say 'five million dollars').)

mince /mɪns/ *noun* MEAT meat, usually beef, which has been ground into very small pieces or into a paste ○ *She asked for a pound of mince.* ■ *verb* CATERING to grind meat into very small pieces or into a paste ○ *a pound of minced beef* or *minced pork* (NOTE: The US English for **minced beef** and **mince** is **ground beef**.)

mincemeat /'mɪnsmiːt/ *noun* FOOD a mixture of dried fruit, suet, nuts and spices, used to make pies at Christmas time

mince pie /ˌmɪns 'paɪ/ *noun* FOOD a small pie, filled with mincemeat, eaten at Christmas time, usually hot

mincer /'mɪnsə/, **mincing machine** /'mɪnsɪŋ məˈʃiːn/ *noun* CATERING a machine for grinding up meat into very small pieces ○ *Badly cleaned mincers are a source of contamination.* (NOTE: The US English is a **grinder**.)

mine host /ˌmaɪn 'həʊst/ BARS ♦ host

mineral water /'mɪn(ə)rəl ˌwɔːtə/ *noun* BEVERAGES water which comes naturally from the ground and is sold in bottles

COMMENT: There are thousands of types of mineral water, each with different properties. From France, the commonest are Evian, Vichy, Perrier, Badoit, etc.; from Italy: San Pelligrino; from Belgium: Spa water, etc. British waters include Malvern, Ashbourne, Highland Spring.

minestrone /ˌmɪnɪ'strəʊni/ *noun* FOOD a soup of Italian origin made of vegetables, beans, pasta and herbs and served with grated parmesan cheese

mini- /mɪni/ *prefix* very small

minibar /'mɪni,bɑː/ *noun* HOTELS a small refrigerator in a hotel bedroom, with drinks in it which are paid for on checking out of the hotel

minibar key /'mɪnibɑː kiː/ *noun* HOTELS a small key given to a guest with the room key, used to open a locked minibar

minibus /'mɪnibʌs/ *noun* ROAD TRAVEL a small bus, which carries approximately ten passengers, often used to take passengers from an airport to a hotel or vice versa

minicab /'mɪni,kæb/ *noun* ROAD TRAVEL a small car, used as a taxi

minimarket /'mɪni,mɑːkɪt/ *noun* a very small self-service store

minor official /,maɪnə ə'fɪʃ(ə)l/ *noun* somebody in a low position in a government department ○ *Some minor official tried to stop my request for building permission.*

mint /mɪnt/ *noun* SAUCES, ETC. a common herb *Mentha* used in cooking as a flavouring, and to flavour commercially made sweets

COMMENT: Mint is widely used in British cooking to flavour vegetables, such as new potatoes or boiled peas. It is also used as a garnish for iced drinks. In Mediterranean cooking it is used in lamb dishes, such as keftedes.

mint jelly /,mɪnt 'dʒeli/ *noun* SAUCES, ETC. jelly made from apples flavoured with mint, served with lamb

mint julep /,mɪnt 'dʒuːlɪp/ *noun* US BEVERAGES an alcoholic drink made from rye whiskey or brandy and sugar over crushed ice, garnished with leaves of mint

mint sauce /,mɪnt 'sɔːs/ *noun* SAUCES, ETC. chopped mint mixed with vinegar and sugar, the traditional accompaniment in Britain to roast lamb

mirror /'mɪrə/ *noun* a piece of glass with a metal backing which reflects an image □ **bathroom mirror** a mirror in a bathroom

miscellaneous charges order *noun* AIR TRAVEL a voucher given by an airline which can be used to pay for meals or accommodation at the airline's expense

mise en place /,miːz ɒn 'plæs/ *noun* CATERING **1.** the act of setting out chairs, tables and linen in a restaurant, ready for customers **2.** the act of preparing ovens, pans, etc., in a kitchen, ready to start cooking for the day **3.** the act of preparing the basic ingredients for sauces, chopping vegetables, etc., ready for cooking (NOTE: **mise en place** comes from the French phrase meaning 'putting in place'.)

miss /mɪs/ *verb* **1.** not to catch a bus, plane or train because you arrive late ○ *You will have to hurry if you don't want to miss the plane.* ○ *He missed the bus and had to wait thirty minutes for the next one.* **2.** not to meet somebody, e.g. because you arrive late □ **he missed the person he was supposed to meet by ten minutes** he arrived ten minutes after the person left, or he left ten minutes before the person arrived

Miss /mɪs/ *noun* a title given to a woman who is not married ○ *Miss Smith is our receptionist.*

mistake /mɪ'steɪk/ *noun* a wrong action or wrong decision □ **to make a mistake** to do something wrong ○ *The shop made a mistake and sent the wrong items.* ○ *There was a mistake in the address.* ○ *She made a mistake in addressing the letter.* □ **by mistake** in error, wrongly ○ *They sent the wrong items by mistake.* ○ *She put my letter into an envelope for France by mistake.*

misunderstanding /,mɪsʌndə'stændɪŋ/ *noun* a situation where somebody does not understand what another person is saying or doing, which can lead to an argument ○ *There was a misunderstanding over my tickets.*

mixed grill /,mɪkst 'grɪl/ MEAT a dish consisting of grilled chops or steaks of various kinds of meat, usually with grilled sausages, bacon, mushrooms and tomatoes

mixer /'mɪksə/ *noun* BEVERAGES a non-alcoholic drink, e.g. tonic water or ginger ale, used in a cocktail along with alcohol

ml *abbreviation* millilitre

mm *abbreviation* millimetre

mobile /'məʊbaɪl/ *adjective* able to move or be moved ■ *noun* a mobile phone ○ *I'll call him on his mobile.* ○ *He gave me the number of his mobile.*

mobile home /,məʊbaɪl 'həʊm/ *noun* a large caravan in which people can live permanently, and which is permanently based in a special park (NOTE: The US English is also **trailer.**)

COMMENT: Many 'mobile homes' are not mobile at all, but are firmly fixed in caravan parks.

mobile phone /,məʊbaɪl 'fəʊn/ *noun* a small telephone which you can carry around ○ *The sound is bad because I'm calling on my mobile phone.*

mobile shop /,məʊbaɪl 'ʃɒp/ *noun* CATERING a van fitted out like a small shop which travels round selling meat, fish, groceries or vegetables

mocha /'mɒkə/ *noun* **1.** BEVERAGES a dark-brown strong-tasting coffee from Yemen and some other countries on the Arabian peninsula **2.** FOOD a flavouring or drink made by mixing coffee and cocoa

mode /məʊd/ *noun* a way of doing something. ◊ **à la mode**

modem /'məʊdem/ *noun* a device which links a computer to the telephone lines, so as to send data ○ *You'll need a modem to connect to the Internet.*

modem point /'məʊdem pɔɪnt/ *noun* a special telephone point where a modem can be plugged in ○ *The hotel has 120 bedrooms, all with modem points.*

mode of payment /ˌməʊd əv 'peɪmənt/ *noun* FINANCE the way in which a payment is made, e.g. by cash or cheque

moderate /'mɒd(ə)rət/ *adjective* not very expensive ○ *The room rate is quite moderate in winter.*

moderately priced /ˌmɒd(ə)rətli 'praɪst/ *adjective* not very expensive

modified American Plan /ˌmɒdɪfaɪd ə 'merɪkən ˌplæn/ *noun* HOTELS a room rate which includes breakfast and one other meal, either lunch or dinner. Abbr **MAP**

molasses /mə'læsɪz/ *noun* US FOOD a thick dark-brown syrup produced when sugar is refined (NOTE: The British English is **treacle**.)

mold /məʊld/ *noun, verb* US same as **mouldy**

moldy /'məʊldi/ *adjective* US same as **mould**

mollusc /'mɒləsk/ *noun* FOOD an animal with a shell, e.g. an oyster or a snail ○ *Edible molluscs such as clams are often made into soup.* (NOTE: The US spelling is **mollusk**.)

monastery /'mɒnəst(ə)ri/ *noun* a group of buildings where monks live or lived ○ *The old monastery has been completely modernised and turned into a luxury hotel.* ○ *Women tourists are not allowed to visit some Greek monasteries.*

money /'mʌni/ *noun* coins and notes used for buying and selling □ **to earn money** to have a salary □ **to lose money** to make a loss, not to make a profit □ **the hotel has been losing money for months** the hotel has been operating at a loss □ **to get your money back** to get a refund of money which you have paid out □ **to make money** to make a profit □ **to put money down** to pay cash, especially as a deposit ○ *He put £25 down and paid the rest in instalments.* □ **they are worth a lot of money** they are valuable

money belt /'mʌni belt/ *noun* a belt with a purse attached, which is worn round the waist to prevent theft

moneylender /'mʌniˌlendə/ *noun* BUSINESS somebody who lends money at interest

money order /'mʌni ˌɔːdə/ *noun* FINANCE a document which can be bought for sending money through the post

monkey nut /'mʌŋki nʌt/ *noun* NUTS same as **peanut**

monopoly /mə'nɒpəli/ *noun* MARKETING a situation where one person or company controls all the market in the supply of a product ○ *to have the monopoly of alcohol sales* or *to have the alcohol monopoly* ○ *The hotel is in a monopoly situation – it is the only hotel in town.* ○ *The company has the absolute monopoly of imports of French wine.*

monosodium glutamate /ˌmɒnəʊsəʊdiəm 'gluːtəmeɪt/ *noun* CATERING a substance added to processed food to enhance the flavour, but causing a reaction in hypersensitive people. ◊ **Chinese restaurant syndrome**

monsoon /mɒn'suːn/ *noun* **1.** a season of wind and rain in tropical countries ○ *At last the monsoon brought relief after the hot dry summer.* **2.** a wind which blows in opposite directions according to the season, especially the wind blowing north from the Indian Ocean in the summer ○ *They sailed north with the monsoon.*

Montezuma's revenge /ˌmɒntɪzuːməz rɪ'vendʒ/ *noun* MEDICAL diarrhoea which affects people travelling in foreign countries as a result of eating unwashed fruit or drinking water which has not been boiled (*humorous*)

monument /'mɒnjʊmənt/ *noun* **1.** a stone, building or statue, built in memory of someone who is dead ○ *They put up a monument to the people from the village who died in the war.* □ **the Monument** a tall column put up in the City of London to commemorate the Great Fire of 1666 **2.** a building which is very old

moonlight /'muːnlaɪt/ (*informal*) *noun* □ **to do a moonlight flit** to go away at night, leaving behind responsibilities such as unpaid bills ■ *verb* to do a second job for cash, often in the evening, as well as a regular job

moonlighter /'muːnlaɪtə/ *noun* somebody who moonlights (*informal*)

moonlighting /'muːnlaɪtɪŋ/ *noun* doing a second job (*informal*) ○ *He makes thousands a year from moonlighting as a chef.*

moor /mʊə/ *noun* a large area of poor land covered with grass and small bushes ○ *The Lake District is wild country, full of moors and forests.* ■ *verb* SHIPS AND BOATS to attach a boat to something ○ *The boat was moored to the river bank.* ○ *He rowed up to the jetty and moored his boat with a piece of rope.*

mooring /'mʊərɪŋ/ *noun* SHIPS AND BOATS a place where a boat is moored ○ *The boat had been moved to new moorings.*

moorings /'mʊərɪŋz/ *noun* SHIPS AND BOATS **1.** a place where a boat is moored ○ *The boat had been moved to new moorings.* **2.** ropes used to attach a boat ○ *We cast off our moorings and rowed out into the river.*

morning /'mɔːnɪŋ/ *noun* the first part of the day, before 12 o'clock ○ *There are six flights to Frankfurt every morning.* ○ *She took the morning train to Edinburgh.*

morning call /,mɔːnɪŋ 'kɔːl/ *noun* a phone call or knock on the door to wake someone up in the morning ○ *He asked for an early morning call at 6.15.* Also called **early morning call**

morning coffee /,mɔːnɪŋ 'kɒfi/ *noun* BEVERAGES coffee served with biscuits as a mid-morning snack

morning dress /'mɔːnɪŋ dres/, **morning suit** /'mɔːnɪŋ suːt/ *noun* clothes for men consisting of a black tail coat, light grey waistcoat and striped black and grey trousers, worn by men at formal occasions such as weddings

mosquito /mɒ'skiːtəʊ/ *noun* a small flying insect which bites people and animals and sucks their blood ○ *I was woken up by a mosquito buzzing round my head.* ○ *Mosquitoes can be carriers of diseases such as malaria.* (NOTE: The plural form is **mosquitoes**.)

mosquito net /mɒ'skiːtəʊ net/ *noun* a thin net spread over a bed to prevent mosquitoes biting at night

mosquito repellent /mɒ'skiːtəʊ rɪ,pelənt/ *noun* MEDICAL a substance which is sprayed or applied to the skin, to keep off mosquitoes

motel /məʊ'tel/ *noun* HOTELS a hotel for car drivers, with special parking places near to the rooms ○ *They checked into the motel last Saturday.* ○ *The hotel is full, but there is a motel just out of town near the motorway junction.* Also called **motor hotel**, **motor inn**, **motor lodge**

COMMENT: Motels are found on main roads, and often on the outskirts of towns. They usually offer comfortable rooms, and sometimes have a small restaurant. Larger motels may have swimming pools and other facilities, but they are usually used for single-night stays.

motion sickness /,məʊʃ(ə)n 'sɪknəs/ *noun* MEDICAL same as **travel sickness**

motivate /'məʊtɪveɪt/ *verb* to encourage someone to do something, especially to work well ○ *It's the job of the chef to motivate his team.* □ **highly motivated** eager ○ *The staff are all highly motivated and keen to tackle the new job.*

'...if we don't motivate and update our staff, we can't deliver to our clients. Coming up with new ideas for attracting, retaining and motivating staff is a constant headache for all employers in the hospitality industry' [*Caterer & Hotelkeeper*]

motivation /,məʊtɪ'veɪʃ(ə)n/ *noun* encouragement to do something, especially to work well ○ *The staff lack motivation – hence the poor sales.* ○ *Staff recruitment, retention and motivation is extremely important.*

'...our ongoing investment in training is crucial to retaining the motivation of our staff' [*Caterer & Hotelkeeper*]

motor /'məʊtə/ *noun* same as **car** ■ *verb* ENTERTAINMENT to travel in a car for pleasure ○ *We motored down to the coast.*

motor caravan /'məʊtə ,kærəvæn/ *noun* ROAD TRAVEL a van with the back part made into a caravan, containing e.g. bunk beds, kitchen equipment and a table, in which people can drive around during the day and park to stay overnight

motor home /'məʊtə həʊm/ *noun* ROAD TRAVEL a large very well-equipped motor caravan

motor hotel /'məʊtə həʊ,tel/ *noun* same as **motel**

motoring assistance /'məʊtərɪŋ ə,sɪst(ə)ns/ *noun* ROAD TRAVEL help given to a motorist who has broken down ○ *You'd be wise to take out motoring assistance insurance cover before you go.*

motoring organisation /'məʊtərɪŋ ,ɔːɡənaɪzeɪʃ(ə)n/ *noun* ROAD TRAVEL an organisation which represents the interests of motorists, and provides services to motorists

COMMENT: Motoring organizations provide breakdown services for their members, and many other services, such as insurance, travel information, etc. The main motoring organizations in the UK are the AA, the RAC, and the RSAC; in Germany, the ADAC; in the USA, the AAA.

motor inn /'məʊtə ɪn/ same as **motel**

motor insurance /'məʊtər ɪn,ʃʊərəns/ *noun* FINANCE same as **car insurance**

motorist /'məʊtərɪst/ *noun* ROAD TRAVEL somebody who drives a car ○ *Motorists are warned of long delays on all roads leading to the coast.*

motor lodge /'məʊtə lɒdʒ/ same as **motel**

motorway /'məʊtəweɪ/ *noun* ROAD TRAVEL a main road, with few entrances and exits, constructed for high-speed long-distance travel ○ *We drove south along the new motorway.* ○ *You will get there faster if you take the motorway.* ○ *There is a lot of traffic on the motorway on bank holidays.* (NOTE: Motorways in the UK are indicated by the letter M and a number, e.g. the M25 is the motorway that runs in a circular route around London.)

COMMENT: Called in various ways in different countries: in France: 'autoroute'; in Germany 'Autobahn'; in Italy: 'autostrada', etc. In the USA, the term 'motorway' is not used, and the roads are called 'thruway', 'expressway' or 'turnpike'.

motorway services /ˌməʊtəweɪ 'sɜːvɪsɪz/ *plural noun* ROAD TRAVEL a facility next to a motorway, where drivers can buy petrol, shop, eat in a choice of restaurants, and in some cases, find hotel accommodation

'…the motorway services operator has admitted that it has a rat problem at one of its service stations' [*Caterer & Hotelkeeper*]

motorway services operator /ˌməʊtəweɪ 'sɜːvɪsɪz ˌɒpəreɪtə/ *noun* ROAD TRAVEL a company which runs motorway services

mould /məʊld/, **mold** *US noun* **1.** CATERING a hollow shape into which a liquid is poured, so that when the liquid becomes hard it takes that shape **2.** a greyish-green powdery fungus ○ *Throw the bread away – it has got mould on it.* ■ *verb* to shape something (NOTE: The US spelling is **mold**.)

moulded chocolates /ˌməʊldɪd 'tʃɒkləts/ *plural noun* FOOD chocolates which are made in moulds, not hand-dipped

mouldiness, moldiness *US noun* the state of being mouldy

mouldy /'məʊldi/ *adjective* covered with mould (NOTE: The US spelling is **moldy**.)

mountain /'maʊntɪn/ *noun* an area of very high land that often rises steeply to a sharp peak ○ *They spent August climbing in the mountains.*

mountain bike /'maʊntɪn baɪk/ *noun* SPORT a specially strong bike with thick tyres, designed for riding over rough ground but not necessarily used on mountains ○

Mountain bikes are great for going along country paths.

mountainboarding /'maʊntɪnˌbɔːdɪŋ/ *noun* SPORT the sport of travelling down hillsides on a board similar to a skateboard but with bigger wheels

mountain climber /'maʊntɪn ˌklaɪmə/ *noun* SPORT somebody who climbs mountains for pleasure

mountain climbing /'maʊntɪn ˌklaɪmɪŋ/ *noun* SPORT the activity of climbing mountains for pleasure

mountaineer /ˌmaʊntɪ'nɪə/ *noun* SPORT somebody who climbs mountains as a sport ○ *Three mountaineers were killed by the avalanche.*

mountaineering /ˌmaʊntɪ'nɪərɪŋ/ *noun* SPORT the sport of climbing mountains. Also called **climbing**

mountain guide /'maʊntɪn gaɪd/ *noun* a local person who leads groups of people climbing mountains

mountain hut /'maʊntɪn hʌt/ *noun* a small wooden or stone shelter on a mountain

mountainous /'maʊntɪnəs/ *adjective* having mountains ○ *It is a mountainous region, and very good for bird-watching.* ○ *Parts of Scotland are very mountainous.*

mountain rescue /ˌmaʊntɪn 'reskjuː/ *noun* a service which provides experienced climbers to help people in difficulties on mountains

mountain rescue service /ˌmaʊntɪn 'reskjuː ˌsɜːvɪs/ *noun* a group of trained people who are on duty to help climbers and skiers who get into difficulties on mountains

mountain resort /ˌmaʊntɪn rɪ'zɔːt/ *noun* TOURISM a holiday town in the mountains

mountain sickness /'maʊntɪn ˌsɪknəs/ *noun* MEDICAL same as **altitude sickness**

mountain stream /ˌmaʊntɪn 'striːm/ *noun* a little river in the mountains

mountain trail /ˌmaʊntɪn 'treɪl/ *noun* a path through mountains

mouse /maʊs/ *noun* a small animal with a long tail, often living in holes in the walls of houses (NOTE: The plural form is **mice**.)

mousetrap /'maʊstræp/ *noun* a device for catching and killing mice when they have become a pest

moussaka /muː'sɑːkə/ *noun* FOOD a Greek dish, made of aubergines and minced meat in layers

mousse /muːs/ *noun* DESSERTS a light food made of whipped egg whites and cream with a gelatine base, flavoured with fruit, vegetables, fish or shellfish and served as a cold dessert or as a starter ○ *You can have chocolate mousse for dessert.* ○ *We had salmon mousse as a starter.*

mousseline /'muːsəliːn/ *noun* SAUCES, ETC. a French noun meaning a type of light hollandaise sauce made with whipped cream and egg whites

mouth-watering /'mauθ ˌwɔːtərɪŋ/ *adjective* looking and smelling so delicious that it makes your mouth water ○ *a plate of mouth-watering cream cakes*

movie /'muːvi/ *noun usually US* ENTERTAINMENT moving pictures shown at a cinema or on TV ○ *We go to the movies most weekends.*

'…it also suggests that, by not capitalizing on guests' IT interest, the average 150-bedroom hotel is missing out on at least £50,000 of revenue a year from pay-per-view movies or metered Internet access' [*Caterer & Hotelkeeper*]

movie theater /'muːvi ˌθɪətə/ *noun US* ENTERTAINMENT a place where films are shown (NOTE: The British English is **cinema**.)

mozzarella /ˌmɒtsə'relə/ *noun* a rubbery white unsalted Italian cheese used in salads, cooking, and especially on pizza

mpg /'empiː'dʒiː/ *abbreviation* miles per gallon

MPM *abbreviation* Maximum Permitted Mileage

Mr /'mɪstə/ *noun* a title given to a man ○ *Mr Smith is the hotel manager.*

MRP /'emɑː'piː/ *abbreviation* manufacturer's recommended price

Mrs /'mɪsɪz/ *noun* a title given to a married woman ○ *The guide is Mrs Smith.*

Ms /məz, mɪz/ *noun* a title given to a woman where it is not known if she is married, or where she does not wish to indicate if she is married or not ○ *Ms Smith is the courier.*

MSA *abbreviation* ROAD TRAVEL motorway service area

MSG *abbreviation* monosodium glutamate

mud /mʌd/ *noun* wet earth

mud bath /'mʌd bɑːθ/ *noun* ENTERTAINMENT a therapeutic treatment where a person is covered in hot mud

muesli /'mjuːzli/ *noun* FOOD a breakfast food of flakes of cereal, dried fruit, etc., eaten with milk

muffin /'mʌfɪn/ *noun* BREAD, ETC. **1.** a small round flat bun eaten warm with butter ○ *We toasted some muffins for tea.* ○ *They had blueberry muffins for breakfast.* **2.** *US* a small sweet cake that often contains fruit

mulled wine /ˌmʌld 'waɪn/ *noun* BEVERAGES red wine and brandy heated together with sugar and spices. Also called **Glühwein**

mullet /'mʌlɪt/ *noun* SEAFOOD a small sea fish

mulligatawny /ˌmʌlɪgə'tɔːni/ *noun* FOOD a hot soup made with curry

multi-city /ˌmʌlti 'sɪti/ *adjective* referring to travel in which people visit several cities in the course of a trip

multigrain /'mʌltigreɪn/ *adjective* referring to bread that is made from several different types of grain

multigym /'mʌltiˌdʒɪm/ *noun* ENTERTAINMENT an apparatus on which you can do exercises and weight training ○ *The hotel has the very latest multigym in its fitness centre.*

multinational /ˌmʌlti'næʃ(ə)nəl/ *noun* BUSINESS a company which has branches or subsidiary companies in several countries ○ *The hotel chain has been bought by one of the big multinationals.*

multiple /'mʌltɪp(ə)l/ *adjective* many ■ *noun* BUSINESS a company with stores in several different towns

multiple entry visa /ˌmʌltɪp(ə)l 'entri ˌviːzə/ *noun* a visa allowing someone to enter a country as often as they like

multiple store /'mʌltɪp(ə)l stɔː/ *noun* one store in a chain of stores

multipot /'mʌltɪpɒt/ *noun* CATERING a large tea or coffee urn, in which the liquid can be prepared in advance and then kept hot

multi-terrain biking /ˌmʌlti təˌreɪn 'baɪkɪŋ/ *noun* SPORT the sport of riding bikes over different types of terrain

muscovado /ˌmʌskə'vɑːdəʊ/ *noun* FOOD a dark-brown sugar made by evaporating the molasses from sugar-cane juice

museum /mjuː'ziːəm/ *noun* ENTERTAINMENT a building in which a collection of valuable or rare objects are put on show ○ *We will visit the Victoria and Albert Museum this afternoon.* ○ *The Natural History Museum has a special exhibition of dinosaurs.*

mushroom /'mʌʃruːm/ *noun* VEGETABLES a small white fungus which grows wild in fields, but is usually grown commercially in mushroom farms ○ *bacon and grilled mushrooms for breakfast* ○ *Do you want fried mushrooms with your steak?* ○ *She ordered a mushroom omelette.*

COMMENT: In the UK, mainly white mushrooms are used in cooking. In other parts of Europe, very many types of mushroom are eaten, and are either picked wild or bought in markets. You need to know which types of mushroom are good to eat, those which have an unpleasant taste, and those which are poisonous. In English, the word 'fungus' is used for all types of mushroom which are not the common white variety.

music festival /'mjuːzɪk ˌfestɪv(ə)l/ *noun* ENTERTAINMENT a series of concerts and recitals given over a short period of time

mussel /'mʌs(ə)l/ *noun* SEAFOOD a small shellfish, with a blue shell ○ *We always eat mussels when we're in Belgium.*

COMMENT: The usual way of eating mussels is as 'moules marinière', where the mussels are cooked quickly with onions, parsley and white wine.

mustard /'mʌstəd/ *noun* SAUCES, ETC. a very spicy yellow condiment, eaten with meat ○ *Would you like some mustard on your beef sandwich?*

COMMENT: English mustard is yellow and can be extremely strong. It is either sold as powder made from finely ground seeds of the mustard plant, which is then mixed with water to make a paste, or as ready-made paste in jars or tubes. In England, it is eaten mainly with beef, ham, pork pies, sausages, etc. French and German mustards are milder and there are very many different varieties of mustard with flavourings such as cider, garlic, herbs, etc.

mustard and cress /ˌmʌstəd ən 'kres/ *noun* VEGETABLES seedlings of white mustard and garden cress plants, usually sold growing in small plastic boxes, used in salads and as a garnish. ◊ **cress**

muster station /'mʌstə ˌsteɪʃ(ə)n/ *noun* SHIPS AND BOATS a place where passengers on a ship must gather in an emergency

mutton /'mʌt(ə)n/ *noun* MEAT meat from a fully-grown sheep (NOTE: The word is not much used, as most meat from sheep is called **lamb** even when it comes from an older animal.)

mycoprotein /'maɪkəʊˌprəʊtiːn/ *noun* a food, especially a meat substitute, made by fermenting a fungus and heating, draining and texturing the resultant product

N

naan /nɑːn/ *noun* FOOD same as **nan**

nacho /'nætʃəʊ/ *noun* FOOD a tortilla chip, usually eaten in quantity covered with melted cheese, salsa, or sliced pickled jalapeño peppers

name /neɪm/ *noun* a word used to call a person or a thing ○ *What is the name in her passport?* ○ *His first name is John, but I am not sure of his other names.* □ **under the name of** using a particular name ○ *They registered under the names of Mr and Mrs Smith.*

name tag /'neɪm ˌtæg/ *noun* a label with a name printed on it ○ *Visitors to the factory are given name tags.*

nam pla /ˌnæm 'plɑː/ *noun* SAUCES, ETC. a thin sauce of fermented fish, which has a strong flavour and smell and a salty taste and is widely used in Southeast Asian cookery

nan /næn/ *noun* a flat round or oval bread served with South Asian food

napkin /'næpkɪn/ *noun* □ **(table) napkin** a square piece of cloth used to protect clothes and wipe your mouth at meal times. Also called **serviette**

COMMENT: Napkins are usually placed on the table as part of the setting, either simply folded in the centre of the setting (on the show plate, if there is one) or folded into elaborate shapes, like fans, etc.

napperon /'næpərɒn/ *noun* a small square tablecloth, placed over a larger tablecloth to keep it clean. Also called **slip cloth**

narrow /'nærəʊ/ *adjective* not wide

narrowboat /'nærəʊbəʊt/ *noun* SHIPS AND BOATS an especially long narrow boat, built for travelling on canals ○ *The company offers two-week narrowboat holidays.*

narrow-bodied /'nærəʊ ˌbɒdid/ *adjective* AIR TRAVEL having a narrow body, as opposed to a wide body

'…the new seating provides a five across (2–3) layout on narrow-bodied planes like the A320, compared with the current six across (3–3) layout' [*Business Traveller*]

narrow-bodied aircraft /ˌnærəʊ ˌbɒdid 'eəkrɑːft/ *noun* AIR TRAVEL an aircraft with a narrow body, less than 5 metres wide

national /'næʃ(ə)nəl/ *adjective* belonging to the people of a particular country ■ *noun* somebody from a particular country ○ *The passenger list included nationals of seven countries.*

national airline /ˌnæʃ(ə)nəl 'eəlaɪn/ *noun* AIR TRAVEL the most important airline in a country, often seen as a symbol for the country itself

National Forest /ˌnæʃ(ə)nəl 'fɒrɪst/ *noun* a large area of forest owned and managed by the government for the nation

nationality /ˌnæʃə'nælɪti/ *noun* the status of being a citizen of a state □ **he is of British nationality** he is a British citizen

National Nature Reserve /ˌnæʃ(ə)nəl 'neɪtʃə rɪˌzɜːv/ *noun* a nature reserve designated by the Nature Conservancy Council for the protection of plants and animals living in it

national park /ˌnæʃ(ə)nəl 'pɑːk/ *noun* a large area of unspoilt land, owned and managed by the government for recreational use by the public

National Trust /ˌnæʃ(ə)nəl 'trʌst/ *noun* TOURISM an organisation in England and Wales which preserves historic buildings, parks and special areas of natural beauty. Abbr **NT**

National Trust for Scotland /ˌnæʃ(ə)nəl trʌst fə 'skɒtlənd/ *noun* TOURISM an organisation similar to the National Trust that is based in Scotland

nationwide /'neɪʃ(ə)nwaɪd/ *adjective* all over a country ○ *We offer a nationwide delivery service.* ○ *The new camping van is being launched with a nationwide sales campaign.*

natural /'nætʃ(ə)rəl/ *adjective* coming from nature, not made by human beings ○ *the pure natural goodness of fresh apple juice*

'…processes such as freezing, pasteurization and sterilization do not accord with consumer expectations of natural foods' [*Food Standards Agency*]

natural heritage /ˌnætʃ(ə)rəl 'herɪtɪdʒ/ *noun* geographical features, wildlife and plant life that are thought of as being valuable to a country and interesting to visitors

nature /'neɪtʃə/ *noun* the world of plants and animals

Nature Conservancy Council /ˌneɪtʃə kən'sɜːv(ə)nsi ˌkaʊns(ə)l/ *noun* an official body in the UK, established in 1973, which takes responsibility for the conservation of wild animals and plants. Abbr **NCC**

nature reserve /'neɪtʃə rɪ,zɜːv/ *noun* a special area where the wildlife is protected

nature tourism /'neɪtʃə ,tʊərɪz(ə)m/ *noun* travel to unspoiled places to experience and enjoy nature

nature trail /'neɪtʃə treɪl/ *noun* TOURISM a path through a park or the countryside with signs to draw attention to important and interesting features, such as plants, trees, birds or animals

naturism /'neɪtʃərɪz(ə)m/ *noun* TOURISM a belief in the physical and mental advantages of going about naked. Also called **nudism**

naturist /'neɪtʃərɪst/ *adjective, noun* TOURISM a person who believes in not wearing clothes outside. Also called **nudist**

naturist beach /'neɪtʃərɪst biːtʃ/ *noun* TOURISM a beach where people are allowed to not wear clothes. Also called **nudist beach**

nautical /'nɔːtɪk(ə)l/ *adjective* SHIPS AND BOATS referring to ships and the sea

nautical mile /ˌnɔːtɪk(ə)l 'maɪl/ *noun* TRAVEL a unit of measurement of distance used at sea and in the air, equalling 1.852 kilometres

navel orange /'neɪv(ə)l ,ɒrɪndʒ/ *noun* a sweet seedless orange with a small bump at the top enclosing a smaller secondary fruit

navigator /'nævɪgeɪtə/ *noun* **1.** AIR TRAVEL a member of the flight deck crew, the person who calculates the distances and direction taken by the aircraft **2.** ROAD TRAVEL somebody who deals with the maps, signs and timing for a car rally driver

NCC *abbreviation* Nature Conservancy Council

neap tide /'niːp ,taɪd/ *noun* SHIPS AND BOATS a tide which occurs at the first and last quarters of the moon, when the difference between high and low water is less than normal

near miss /ˌnɪə 'mɪs/ *noun* ROAD TRAVEL an incident where two vehicles come very close by accident and almost crash into each other

neat /niːt/ *adjective* with no water or any other liquid added ○ *a glass of neat whisky* ○ *I prefer my whisky neat.* (NOTE: US English only uses **straight** in this meaning.)

neck /nek/ *noun* **1.** a part of the body connecting the head to the shoulders **2.** MEAT this part of an animal eaten as food □ **best end of neck** a joint of lamb consisting of the ribs nearest the neck

neckerchief /'nekətʃiːf/ *noun* CATERING a scarf worn by chefs round the neck to prevent sweat falling on food being prepared. ◊ **toque**

nectarine /'nektəriːn/ *noun* FRUIT a fruit like a peach with a smooth skin

negative cash flow /ˌnegətɪv 'kæʃ fləʊ/ *noun* BUSINESS a situation where more money is going out of a company than is coming in

neighbourhood /'neɪbəhʊd/, **neighborhood** *US noun* **1.** a district and its people ○ *The hotel is pleasantly situated in a quiet neighbourhood.* **2.** □ **in the neighbourhood of** near to in space or amount ○ *There are three hotels in the neighbourhood of the conference centre.* ○ *They spent in the neighbourhood of £12,000 on redecorating the restaurant.*

nestle /'nes(ə)l/ *verb* to be in a sheltered or comfortable position ○ *a chalet nestling in the hills* ○ *The cottage nestles at the bottom of the valley.*

net /net/ *adjective* **1.** BUSINESS after all deductions have been made ○ *net pay* ○ *net loss* (NOTE: The spelling **nett** is sometimes used on containers.) **2.** □ **terms strictly net** payment has to be the full price, with no discount allowed

net cash flow /ˌnet 'kæʃ ˌfləʊ/ *noun* FINANCE the difference between the money coming in and the money going out

net margin /ˌnet 'mɑːdʒɪn/ *noun* BUSINESS the percentage difference between received price and all costs, including overheads

net price /ˌnet 'praɪs/ *noun* BUSINESS a price which cannot be reduced by a discount

net profit /ˌnet 'prɒfɪt/ *noun* BUSINESS a result where income from sales is more than all expenditure

net receipts /ˌnet rɪ'siːts/ *plural noun* BUSINESS the total money taken after deducting commission, tax and discounts

net salary /ˌnet ˈsæləri/ noun BUSINESS salary which is left after deducting tax and national insurance contributions

net sales /ˌnet ˈseɪlz/ plural noun BUSINESS sales less damaged or returned items

net turnover /net ˈtɜːnˌəʊvə/ noun BUSINESS turnover before VAT and after trade discounts have been deducted

net weight /ˌnet ˈweɪt/ noun BUSINESS the weight of goods after deducting the weight of the packing material and container

network /ˈnetwɜːk/ noun **1.** a system of things such as roads or railways connecting different places ○ *the Belgian railway network* or *rail network* **2.** a system of computers which are connected together ○ *You can book at any of our hotels throughout the country using our computer network.*

new potatoes /ˌnju: pəˈteɪtəʊz/ plural noun VEGETABLES small potatoes picked at the beginning of the season

news /njuːz/ noun spoken or written information about what has happened □ **it's in the news** it is of topical interest

newspaper /ˈnjuːzpeɪpə/ noun a daily or weekly paper containing news and information ○ *Newspapers are available in the residents' lounge.* ○ *Do you want a newspaper with your morning tea?* ○ *He ordered a newspaper and a call at 6.45.*

next /nekst/ adjective **1.** (*in time*) coming after ○ *When's the next plane for Paris?* ○ *The next train to London leaves in ten minutes' time.* **2.** (*in space*) adjoining □ **the room next door to mine** the room next to mine ○ *She's in the room next door to her parents.* ○ *There was a lot of noise in the room next door* or *in the next-door room during the night.*

NGO abbreviation BUSINESS non-governmental organisation

niche /niːʃ/ noun BUSINESS a special place in a market, occupied by one company

niche market /ˌniːʃ ˈmɑːkɪt/ noun BUSINESS a market for a very special product or service, which can be exploited by only a few suppliers ○ *Holidays in the Antarctic are a niche market.*

nickel /ˈnɪk(ə)l/ noun US FINANCE a five-cent coin ○ *Can you lend me a nickel?*

night /naɪt/ noun **1.** the period of time from evening to morning **2.** HOTELS a night spent in a hotel ○ *The tour ends with a three-night stay in Madrid.* **3.** ENTERTAINMENT an evening's entertainment □ **a night on the town** an evening spent enjoying yourself in the restaurants, theatres, bars, etc. of a town

night audit /ˌnaɪt ˈɔːdɪt/ noun HOTELS the act of checking at night which rooms are occupied, and reconciling these with guest accounts

night bell /ˈnaɪt bel/ noun HOTELS a bell outside a hotel, which you ring to wake up the porter during the night after the front door has been locked

night clerk /ˈnaɪt klɑːk/ noun HOTELS somebody who is on duty at the reception desk during the night

nightclub /ˈnaɪtklʌb/ noun ENTERTAINMENT a club only open at night ○ *Our daughter will only come with us on holiday if we go to a resort with lots of nightclubs.*

night duty /ˈnaɪt ˌdjuːti/ noun a period of work done at night ○ *She is on night duty three days a week.*

night ferry /ˈnaɪt ˌferi/ noun SHIPS AND BOATS a boat which travels during the night

night flight /ˈnaɪt flaɪt/ noun AIR TRAVEL a flight which takes place during the night

night life /ˈnaɪt laɪf/ noun ENTERTAINMENT the entertainment available in a town at night ○ *The place is dead – there's no night life.* ○ *The beaches are fine, but the night life is very dull.*

night light /ˈnaɪt laɪt/ noun a weak electric light which gives a faint light and is used to light passages, stairs or a child's room at night

night manager /ˈnaɪt ˌmænɪdʒə/ noun HOTELS somebody in charge of a hotel during the night

night out /ˌnaɪt ˈaʊt/ noun an evening spent outside the home ○ *They're planning to have a night out tomorrow.*

night porter /ˈnaɪt ˌpɔːtə/ noun HOTELS a porter who is on duty at a hotel during the night, answering calls from guest rooms as well as dealing with any late arrivals

night rate /ˈnaɪt reɪt/ noun a cheap rate for telephone calls made at night

night safe /ˈnaɪt seɪf/ noun a safe with a special door in the outside wall of a bank, where money and documents can be deposited when the bank is closed

night shift /ˈnaɪt ʃɪft/ noun a shift worked during the night ○ *He works the night shift.*

nightspot /ˈnaɪtspɒt/ noun ENTERTAINMENT an entertainment place open at night, e.g. a nightclub ○ *It's the most expensive nightspot in town.*

nightstand /ˈnaɪtstænd/ noun a table next to a bed, often with a telephone, notepad, glass and water jug

night-time /'naɪt taɪm/ *noun* the period whe it is night

nightwatchman /naɪt'wɒtʃmən/ *noun* a man who guards a building at night. Also called **watchman**

nil /nɪl/ *noun* zero, nothing

nil return /ˌnɪl rɪ'tɜːn/ *noun* BUSINESS a report showing no sales, income or tax

nip /nɪp/ *noun* BARS a single measure of alcohol ○ *Scotch: £1 per nip*

NITB *abbreviation* TOURISM Northern Ireland Tourist Board

no /nəʊ/ *adjective, adverb* showing the negative □ **no admission, no admittance** entrance not allowed □ **no entry** you cannot go in □ **no parking** do not leave your car here □ **no smoking** do not smoke here □ **a 'no smoking' sign** a sign to show that smoking is not allowed ○ *The captain has switched on the 'no smoking' sign.* □ **'no vacancies'** a sign to show that the hotel or guesthouse is full

no-claims bonus /nəʊ 'kleɪmz ˌbəʊnəs/ *noun* FINANCE the reduction of premiums on an insurance policy because no claims have been made

no-frills /ˌnəʊ 'frɪlz/ *adjective* simple, with no special luxuries

no-frills airline /ˌnəʊ frɪlz 'eəlaɪn/ *noun* AIR TRAVEL an airline flying planes with simple cabins and not offering meals or drinks during flights

no-frills chain /ˌnəʊ frɪlz 'tʃeɪn/ *noun* HOTELS a chain of simple restaurants or hotels, without bars or room service

noise /nɔɪz/ *noun* a loud, usually unpleasant sound ○ *The noise of the street kept us awake at night.* ○ *Noise readings of 90–95 decibels are unacceptable.*

noise abatement notice /ˌnɔɪz ə'beɪtmənt ˌnəʊtɪs/ *noun* a court order telling someone to reduce the levels of noise which they make ○ *He pleaded guilty on six counts of breaching a noise abatement notice.*

noisette /nwɑː'set/ *noun* a piece of boned and rolled meat, especially the neck or loin of lamb

noisy /'nɔɪzi/ *adjective* making a lot of noise, or affected by a lot of noise ○ *The best rooms are quiet, and overlook a garden: unfortunately, the hotel also has some rooms overlooking a noisy crossroads.* ○ *She asked for her room to be changed, because it was too noisy.*

nominal rent /'nɒmɪn(ə)l rent/ *noun* a very small rent

non- /nɒn/ *prefix* not

non-alcoholic drink /ˌnɒn ˌælkəhɒlɪk 'drɪŋk/ *noun* BEVERAGES a drink which does not contain alcohol

non-budget hotel /ˌnɒn ˌbʌdʒɪt həʊ'tel/ *noun* HOTELS an up-market hotel, not catering for budget visitors ○ *They aim to raise more than £30m through the sale of the non-budget hotels.*

non-business guest /ˌnɒn 'bɪznɪs ˌgest/ *noun* BUSINESS a hotel guest who is a private individual and not on a business trip

nondairy /'nɒndeəri/ *adjective* referring to ingredients or foods that contain no dairy products and can be substituted for them, e.g. some kinds of margarine

nonfat /'nɒnfæt/ *adjective* without fat solids, or with the fat content removed

nonfattening /nɒn'fæt(ə)nɪŋ/ *adjective* not likely to cause a gain in weight

non-food items /ˌnɒn 'fuːd ˌaɪtəmz/ *plural noun* items for sale which are not food, such as cigarettes, hotel rooms, etc.

non-governmental organisation /ˌnɒn ˌgʌvənment(ə)l ˌɔːgənaɪ'zeɪʃ(ə)n/ *noun* BUSINESS an organisation such as a charity or voluntary agency, which is not funded by a government, but which works on an international as well as a national level. Abbr **NGO**

COMMENT: Oxfam, the Red Cross, Médecins sans Frontières and other NGOs work in many countries to bring aid to people in need.

nonperishable /nɒn'perɪʃəb(ə)l/ *adjective* referring to food products that remain edible, without spoiling, for long periods without special storage, e.g. in a refrigerator ■ *noun* a non-perishable item of food

non-refundable /ˌnɒn rɪ'fʌndəb(ə)l/ *adjective* not possible to refund

non-refundable deposit /ˌnɒn rɪ ˌfʌndəb(ə)l dɪ'pɒzɪt/ *noun* a deposit which will not be refunded under any circumstances

non-resident /ˌnɒn 'rezɪdənt/ *noun, adjective* **1.** HOTELS (somebody who is) not staying in a hotel **2.** (somebody who is) not living in a place

non-resident entry visa /ˌnɒn ˌrezɪdənt 'entri ˌviːzə/ *noun* TOURISM a visa allowing a person who is not a resident of a country to go into that country

non-revenue passenger /ˌnɒn ˌrevənjuː 'pæsɪndʒə/ *noun* AIR TRAVEL a passenger who travels free, e.g. an employee of the airline

non-smoker /ˌnɒn ˈsməʊkə/ *noun* somebody who does not smoke ○ *There is a special section of the restaurant for non-smokers.*

non-smoking room /ˌnɒn ˌsməʊkɪŋ ˈruːm/ *noun* a room in which smoking is not allowed

non-stick /ˌnɒn ˈstɪk/ *adjective* CATERING covered with a substance which prevents food from sticking when cooking

non-stop /ˌnɒn ˈstɒp/ *adjective, adverb* TRAVEL travelling from departure point to destination without stopping ○ *a non-stop flight to Tokyo* ○ *to fly to Tokyo non-stop*

non-transferable /ˌnɒn trænsˈfɜːrəb(ə)l/ *adjective* TRAVEL impossible to transfer to another person ○ *Almost all airline tickets are non-transferable.*

noodles /ˈnuːd(ə)lz/ *plural noun* FOOD flat strips of pasta ○ *I ordered spicy meatballs with noodles.* ○ *We started with chicken noodle soup.*

COMMENT: Noodles are widely used in oriental cooking, as well as in many western dishes.

Nordic skiing /ˌnɔːdɪk ˈskiːɪŋ/ *noun* SPORT competitive cross-country skiing and ski-jumping

norm /nɔːm/ *noun* the usual or standard pattern

north /nɔːθ/ *noun* **1.** one of the points of the compass, the direction to which a compass needle points **2.** the northern part of a country ■ *adjective* relating to the north ○ *the north coast of Scotland* ■ *adverb* towards the north ○ *Drive north along the motorway for ten miles.*

northbound /ˈnɔːθbaʊnd/ *adjective* going towards the north ○ *The northbound carriageway of the motorway is closed.*

north-east /ˌnɔːθ ˈiːst/ *adverb* in a direction between north and east ○ *They were travelling north-east at the time.* ○ *Our bedroom windows faced north-east.* ■ *noun* the part of a country to the north and east ○ *The North-East of England will have snow showers.*

north-easterly /ˌnɔːθ ˈiːstəli/, **north-eastern** /ˌnɔːθ ˈiːstən/ *adjective* referring to the north-east, especially towards or from the north-east

northerly /ˈnɔːðəli/ *adjective* **1.** towards the north **2.** blowing from the north

northern /ˈnɔːð(ə)n/ *adjective* from, of or in the north

northerner /ˈnɔːð(ə)nə/ *noun* somebody who lives in or comes from the northern part of a country

Northern Ireland Tourist Board /ˌnɔːð(ə)n ˌaɪələnd ˈtʊərɪst ˌbɔːd/ *noun* TOURISM an organisation which promotes tourism in Northern Ireland and promotes tourism to Northern Ireland from other parts of the UK. Abbr **NITB**

northernmost /ˈnɔːð(ə)nməʊst/ *adjective* furthest north

northward /ˈnɔːθwəd/ *adjective, adverb* towards the north

northwards /ˈnɔːθwədz/ *adverb* towards the north

north-west /ˌnɔːθ ˈwest/ *adverb* the direction between west and north ■ *noun* the part of a country to the north and west ○ *The North-West of England is wetter than the east coast.* ○ *We can expect rain when the wind blows from the north-west.* ○ *The old castle stood to the north-west of the cathedral.*

north-westerly /ˌnɔːθ ˈwestəli/, **north-western** /ˌnɔːθ ˈwestən/ *adjective* referring to the north-west, especially towards or from the north-west

no-show /ˌnəʊ ˈʃəʊ/ *noun* HOTELS somebody who has booked a room in a hotel or a table in a restaurant or a seat on an aircraft and does not come ○ *Seats were still available on the aircraft because there were several no-shows.*

no-smoking policy /ˌnəʊ ˈsməʊkɪŋ ˌpɒlɪsi/ *noun* a policy that smoking is not allowed in a place ○ *We have been saying that the pub went bankrupt because of its no-smoking policy.*

note /nəʊt/ *noun* **1.** a very short letter, or a very brief written or printed document **2.** same as **bank note** ○ *a £10 note* (NOTE: The US English is **bill**.)

notepaper /ˈnəʊtpeɪpə/ *noun* **1.** writing paper for letters ○ *There is some hotel notepaper in the drawer of the desk in the bedroom.* **2.** *US* rough paper for writing notes

notice /ˈnəʊtɪs/ *noun* **1.** advance information or warning about something ○ *You must give at least 24 hours' notice of cancellation.* □ **at short notice** giving only a few hours' warning ○ *She found it difficult to get a hotel room at short notice.* □ **without notice** without giving any warning ○ *The train times were changed without notice.* **2.** a piece of writing giving information, usually put in a place where everyone can see it ○ *The courier pinned a notice on the hotel noticeboard.*

noticeboard /'nəʊtɪsbɔːd/ *noun* a board fixed to a wall where notices can be put up ○ *Did you see the list of tours on the noticeboard?*

notifiable disease /ˌnəʊtɪfaɪəb(ə)l dɪ'ziːz/ *noun* MEDICAL a serious infectious disease which, in the UK, has to be reported by a doctor to the Department of Health so that steps can be taken to stop it spreading

COMMENT: The following are notifiable diseases: cholera, diphtheria, dysentery, encephalitis, food poisoning, jaundice, malaria, measles, meningitis, ophthalmia neonatorum, paratyphoid, plague, poliomyelitis, relapsing fever, scarlet fever, smallpox, tuberculosis, typhoid, typhus, whooping cough, yellow fever.

notify /'nəʊtɪfaɪ/ *verb* to inform someone officially ○ *The local doctor notified the Health Service of the case of cholera.* (NOTE: **notifies – notifying- notified**. Note also that you notify someone **of** something.)

Notting Hill Carnival /ˌnɒtɪŋ 'hɪl/ *noun* ENTERTAINMENT a big carnival held every year in August in Notting Hill, in the west of London ○ *Thousands of people take part in the Notting Hill Carnival every year.*

nought /nɔːt/ *noun* zero, nothing □ **nought-per cent finance** interest-free credit

nourishing /'nʌrɪʃɪŋ/ *adjective* providing the substances that people need to grow and be healthy

nourishment /'nʌrɪʃmənt/ *noun* food or the valuable substances in food that help people to grow and be healthy

nouvelle cuisine /ˌnuːvel kwɪ'ziːn/ *noun* CATERING a type of French cooking which aims at less heavy traditional dishes and attractive presentation and often served in very small portions

nt *abbreviation* night ○ *Stay 5 nts, only pay for 4.*

NT /ˌen 'tiː/ *abbreviation* National Trust

nudism /'njuːdɪz(ə)m/ *noun* TOURISM same as **naturism**

nudist /'njuːdɪst/ *noun, adjective* TOURISM same as **naturist**

nudist beach /'njuːdɪst biːtʃ/ *noun* TOURISM same as **naturist beach**

nudist colony /ˌnjuːdɪst 'kɒləni/ *noun* TOURISM a club or camp for those who want to go about naked

number /'nʌmbə/ *noun* **1.** the quantity of people or things ○ *The number of passengers carried has increased over the last year.* ○ *The number of days of rain is very small.* ○ *The number of tickets sold was disappointing.* **2.** □ **a number of** some ○ *A number of* the staff will be retiring this year. ○ *A number of guests fell ill after the banquet.* **3.** a written figure ○ *account number* ○ *seat number* ○ *phone number* or *telephone number* ○ *He was sitting in seat number 6A, but he had a ticket for 12B.* ■ *verb* to mark or identify something with a number ○ *The seats are numbered from the front of the aircraft to the back.* ○ *I refer to your invoice numbered 1234.*

COMMENT: Flight numbers are identified with the airline code (in letters) followed by a series of figures.

numbered account /ˌnʌmbəd ə'kaʊnt/ *noun* FINANCE a bank account, usually in Switzerland, which is referred to only by a number, the name of the person holding it being kept secret

number plate /'nʌmbə pleɪt/ *noun* ROAD TRAVEL one of two plates on a vehicle, one on the front and one on the back, which shows the individual number of the vehicle ○ *The thieves had changed the van's number plates.*

numerical order /njuːˌmerɪk(ə)l 'ɔːdə/ *noun* arrangement by numbers

nursery /'nɜːs(ə)ri/ *noun* a room or building where babies or young children are looked after ○ *There is a children's nursery on 'C' Deck.*

nursery slope /'nɜːs(ə)ri sləʊp/ *plural noun* snow-covered mountain slopes where people learn to ski

nut /nʌt/ *noun* FOOD a fruit with an edible centre inside a hard shell □ **to crack nuts** to open the shells to get at the edible centres

nut allergy /'nʌt ˌælədʒi/ *noun* an allergy to nuts, often quite serious

nutcracker /'nʌtˌkrækə/ *noun* CATERING a device for cracking the shells of nuts

nut cutlet /ˌnʌt 'kʌtlət/ *noun* FOOD a vegetarian cake, patty, or burger made from chopped nuts and other vegetable ingredients mixed together and sometimes formed into the shape of a meat chop or cutlet

nutmeg /'nʌtmeg/ *noun* SAUCES, ETC. the seed of a tropical tree, grated and used as a spice ○ *Add some grated nutmeg to the cake mixture.*

nutmeg grater /'nʌtmeg ˌgreɪtə/ *noun* CATERING a small device on which a nutmeg is rubbed, to produce fine nutmeg powder

nutrient /'njuːtriənt/ *noun, adjective* a substance that provides nourishment

nutriment /'njuːtrɪmənt/ *noun* something which is nourishing

nutrition /njuː'trɪʃ(ə)ⁿn/ *noun* **1.** the way in which food affects health ○ *a scheme to improve nutrition in the poorer areas* **2.** the study of food ○ *We are studying nutrition as part of the food science course.*

nutritionist /njuː'trɪʃ(ə)nɪst/ *noun* a person who specialises in the study of nutrition and advises on diets ○ *The nutritionist warned me not to eat too much red meat.*

nutritious /njuː'trɪʃəs/ *adjective* providing food which is necessary for growth ○ *Ice cream is not a very nutritious food.*

nutritive /'njuːtrətɪv/ *noun* a food which is necessary for growth ■ *adjective* providing food or nourishment

nut roast /ˌnʌt 'rəʊst/ *noun* FOOD a vegetarian loaf made from chopped or ground-up nuts with onions, herbs, and seasonings, bound with breadcrumbs and baked

nutshell /'nʌtʃel/ *noun* the hard outer covering of a nut

nutty /'nʌti/ *adjective* tasting of or containing nuts ○ *a nutty chocolate bar*

O

oatcake /ˈəʊtkeɪk/ *noun* BREAD, ETC. a dry biscuit made of oatmeal, often served with cheese or eaten for breakfast

oatmeal /ˈəʊtmiːl/ *noun* FOOD coarse flour made from oats

COMMENT: Oatmeal is used to make porridge.

oats /əʊts/ *plural noun* FOOD a cereal food, grown in northern European countries

COMMENT: Oats are widely grown and used in Scotland, where the most common use for them is in making porridge and biscuits.

obligatory /əˈblɪɡət(ə)ri/ *adjective* necessary according to the law or rules ○ *Is the medical examination obligatory?*

observation car /ˌɒbzəˈveɪʃ(ə)n kɑː/ *noun* RAIL TRAVEL a special wagon with a glass roof, so that passengers can enjoy the mountain scenery

occasional /əˈkeɪʒ(ə)n(ə)l/ *adjective* happening sometimes, but not very often

occasional labour /əˌkeɪʒ(ə)n(ə)l ˈleɪbə/ *noun* US workers hired for a short period (NOTE: The British English is **casual labour**.)

occasional licence /əˌkeɪʒ(ə)n(ə)l ˈlaɪs(ə)ns/ *noun* BARS a licence to sell alcohol at a given place and time only

occupancy /ˈɒkjʊpənsi/ *noun* the fact of living, working or staying in a property such as a house, an office or a hotel room □ **with immediate occupancy** empty and available to be moved into straight away

'…hotel occupancies in the high tariff B or four-star hotels recorded an average occupancy of 88.5 per cent for the first half of this year, compared with the previous year's 84 per cent' [*South China Morning Post*]

occupancy rate /ˈɒkjʊpənsi reɪt/ *noun* HOTELS same as **room occupancy** ○ *During the winter months the occupancy rate was down to 50%.*

'…while occupancy rates matched those of 1984 in July, August has been a much poorer month than it was the year before' [*Economist*]

occupation /ˌɒkjʊˈpeɪʃ(ə)n/ *noun* **1.** same as **occupancy 2.** a person's job or profession

occupational pension /ˌɒkjʊpeɪʃ(ə)nəl ˈpenʃə/ *noun* BUSINESS a pension which is paid by the company by which an employee has been employed

occupation density /ˌɒkjʊˈpeɪʃ(ə)n ˌdensɪti/ *noun* HOTELS the number of people in a hotel or restaurant, shown as a ratio of the floor area

occupy /ˈɒkjʊpaɪ/ *verb* to live in or work in ○ *All the rooms in the hotel are occupied.* ○ *The company occupies three floors of an office block.* (NOTE: **occupies – occupying – occupied**)

ocean /ˈəʊʃ(ə)n/ *noun* a large area of sea

COMMENT: The oceans are: the Atlantic, the Pacific, the Indian, the Antarctic (or Southern) and the Arctic.

oceanarium /ˌəʊʃəˈneəriəm/ *noun* TOURISM a type of large saltwater aquarium where marine animals are kept

ocean terminal /ˌəʊʃ(ə)n ˈtɜːmɪn(ə)l/ *noun* TRAVEL the main building at a port where passengers arrive and depart

odd /ɒd/ *adjective* **1.** (*of an amount*) almost, not exactly □ **a hundred-odd** approximately one hundred **2.** one of a group □ **an odd shoe** one shoe of a pair □ **we have a few odd boxes left** we have a few boxes left out of the total shipment

odd-job-man /ˌɒd ˈdʒɒb ˌmæn/ *noun* a man who does general work, such as repairs, in a building or on an estate

oddments /ˈɒdmənts/ *plural noun* items left over

off /ɒf/ *adjective* **1.** CATERING not on the menu any more ○ *Liver is off today.* **2.** not good, rotten ○ *That fish smells a bit off.* ○ *The milk has gone off.* ○ *I'm afraid these prawns are off.* **3.** away from work ○ *We have quite a few staff off today.* ■ *preposition* a particular distance from or quite close to ○ *They spent their holiday on an island off the coast of Brittany.* ○ *The restaurant is just off the High Street.*

off-airport car rental firm /ˌɒf ˌeəpɔːt kɑː ˈrent(ə)l ˌfɜːm/ *noun* a rental firm which is not based within an airport and so can offer cheaper rates

offal /ˈɒf(ə)l/ *noun* MEAT the inside parts of an animal when used as food, e.g. liver, kidney or intestines (NOTE: There is no plural form. The US English is **variety meats**.)

offer /ˈɒfə/ *noun* **1.** a statement that you are willing to pay a particular amount of money to buy something □ **we are open to offers** we are ready to discuss the price which we are asking □ **cash offer** an offer to pay in cash □ **or near offer**, **or nearest offer** or an offer of a price which is slightly less than the price asked ○ *The car is for sale at £2,000 or near offer.* **2.** a statement that you are willing to sell something for a particular amount of money ■ *verb* **1.** □ **to offer someone a job** to tell someone that he can have a job in your company ○ *He was offered a job as a receptionist.* **2.** to say that you are willing to pay a particular amount of money for something ○ *She offered £200 for the carpet.* **3.** to say that you are willing to sell something ○ *They are offering cheap weekend tours to European cities.*

office /ˈɒfɪs/ *noun* **1.** BUSINESS a set of rooms where a company works or where business is done **2.** □ **for office use only** that must only be used in an office, usually said of a part of a form which must only be filled in by the people in the office which issues the form **3.** BUSINESS a room where someone works and does business ○ *Come into my office.* ○ *The manager's office is on the third floor.* **4.** a government department □ **the Foreign Office** the ministry dealing with foreign affairs ○ *Foreign Office officials asked to see the prisoners.*

office hours /ˈɒfɪs ˈaʊəz/ *plural noun* the time when an office is open ○ *Do not telephone during office hours.*

office space /ˈɒfɪs speɪs/ *noun* a space available for offices or occupied by offices ○ *We are looking for extra office space.*

office staff /ˈɒfɪs ˈstɑːf/ *noun* people who work in offices. Also called **clerical staff**

official /əˈfɪʃ(ə)l/ *adjective* relating to an organisation, especially one which is part of a government or some other authority ○ *He is travelling on official business.* ○ *He left official documents in his car.* ○ *She received an official letter of explanation.* □ **speaking in an official capacity** speaking as a person with special knowledge or responsibilities □ **to go through official channels** to deal with

officials, especially when making a request □ **the official exchange rate** the exchange rate which is imposed by the government ○ *The official exchange rate is ten to the dollar, but you can get twice that on the black market.* ■ *noun* somebody working in a government department ○ *Airport officials inspected the shipment.* ○ *Government officials stopped the import licence.*

officially /əˈfɪʃ(ə)li/ *adverb* according to what is said in public ○ *Officially, you are not supposed to take money out of the country.* Compare **unofficially**

official return /əˌfɪʃ(ə)l rɪˈtɜːn/ *noun* BUSINESS an official report

official strike /əˌfɪʃ(ə)l ˈstraɪk/ *noun* BUSINESS a strike which has been approved by the main office of a union

off-licence /ˈɒf ˌlaɪs(ə)ns/ *noun* **1.** a shop which sells alcohol for drinking away from the shop (NOTE: The US English is **package store**.) **2.** BARS a licence to sell alcohol to be drunk away from the place where it is bought

off-peak /ˌɒf ˈpiːk/ *adjective* not during the busiest time □ **during the off-peak period** at the time when business is less busy

off-peak tariff /ˌɒf piːk ˈtærɪf/, **rate** /reɪt/ *noun* lower charges applied when a service is not busy

off-piste skiing /ˌɒf piːst ˈskiːɪŋ/ *noun* SPORT skiing away from the marked tracks. Compare **on-piste skiing**

off-season /ˌɒf ˈsiːz(ə)n/ *adjective* happening during the time of year when fewer people are travelling or using facilities ■ *noun* TOURISM the time of year when there are fewer travellers, and so fares and room prices are cheaper ○ *Tour operators urge more people to travel in the off-season.* ○ *Air fares are cheaper in the off-season.* Also called **low season**

off-season tariff /ˌɒf ˌsiːz(ə)n ˈtærɪf/, **rate** /reɪt/ *noun* TOURISM cheaper fares and room prices which are charged when there are fewer travellers

offshore /ˈɒfʃɔː/ *adjective*, *adverb* on an island or in the sea near to the coast ○ *an offshore floating casino*

offshore wind /ˌɒfˈʃɔː wɪnd/ *noun* a wind which blows from the coast towards the sea. Compare **onshore wind**

off the beaten track /ˌɒf ðə ˌbiːt(ə)n ˈtræk/ *adjective* in a place which is not usually visited by many people

off the bone /ˌɒf ðə ˈbəʊn/ *adjective* CATERING with the bones removed

off-the-road /ˌɒf ðə 'rəʊd/ *adjective* referring to a destination or sight not visited by the average tourist

off the tourist trail /ˌɒf ðə 'tʊərɪst ˌtreɪl/ *adjective* not in a place which is usually visited by many tourists

Ogen melon /'əʊgən ˌmel(ə)n/ *noun* FRUIT a type of melon which has yellowish skin striped with green, and pale yellow flesh

oil /ɔɪl/ *noun* FOOD a thick smooth-running liquid of various kinds used in cooking ■ *verb* to put oil on ○ *Oil the tin before putting the dough in.*

COMMENT: The commonest cooking oil is made from sunflower seeds; many others exist, such as olive oil, walnut oil, etc.

oiliness /'ɔɪlɪnəs/ *noun* the state of being oily

oily /'ɔɪli/ *adjective* like oil, containing oil or covered with oil ○ *Oily fish such as mackerel or sardines are good for you.*

okra /'ɒkrə/ *noun* VEGETABLES a vegetable with a green pod used in soups. Also called **gumbo 1**, **lady's finger**

COMMENT: Also called 'bhindi', 'gumbo' or 'lady's finger'. Used in Caribbean and Indian cooking; also used in the south of the USA.

old age pension /ˌəʊld eɪdʒ 'penʃən/ *noun* a state pension given to men over 65 or women over 60. Also called **retirement pension**, **pension**

olive /'ɒlɪv/ *noun* FRUIT a small black or green fruit from a Mediterranean tree, which is crushed to produce oil and is also eaten as food

olive oil /ˌɒlɪv 'ɔɪl/ *noun* FOOD oil made from olives

omelette /'ɒmlət/ *noun* FOOD a dish made of beaten eggs, cooked in a frying pan and folded over before serving. Various fillings may be added. ○ *I had a cheese omelette and chips for lunch.* (NOTE: The US spelling is **omelet**.)

COMMENT: The commonest forms of omelette are cheese omelette and ham omelette. A Spanish omelette is made with onion, tomato, peppers, potatoes, etc., and is not folded over, but served flat.

on-airport car rental firm /ˌɒn ˌeəpɔːt kɑː 'rent(ə)l ˌfɜːm/ *noun* ROAD TRAVEL a car rental firm with its base inside an airport complex, which is more convenient for travellers, although the rates may be higher

on board /ˌɒn 'bɔːd/ on a ship, plane or train

on-call time /ˌɒn 'kɔːl ˌtaɪm/ *noun* the time during which an employee is not actually on duty but may be called to do a job, if needed

one-way /ˌwʌn 'weɪ/ *adjective* involving or allowing travel in only one direction. Abbr **OW**

one-way fare /ˌwʌn weɪ 'feə/ *noun* TRAVEL same as **single fare**

one-way street /ˌwʌn weɪ 'striːt/ *noun* ROAD TRAVEL a street where the traffic is allowed to go only in one direction ○ *The shop is in a one-way street, which makes it very difficult for parking.*

one-way ticket /ˌwʌn weɪ 'tɪkɪt/ *noun* TRAVEL same as **single ticket**

onion /'ʌnjən/ *noun* VEGETABLES a strong-smelling vegetable with a round white bulb ○ *fried onion rings*

on licence /ˈɒn ˌlaɪs(ə)ns/ *noun* a licence to sell alcohol for drinking on the premises, e.g. in a bar or restaurant

online /ɒn'laɪn/, **on line**, **on-line** *adverb* through a direct link to a computer network or the Internet ○ *The sales office is online to the airline's headquarters.* ○ *You need to know the password to access the data online.* □ **to book online** to book a ticket or make a reservation by connecting to the company's computer system ○ *You can book your own ticket online.* □ **an on-line travel company** a travel company which does its business online

'…when it come to booking business travel, most people still opt for an agency or in-house travel arranger rather than going online' [*Evening Standard*]

o.n.o. *abbreviation* or near offer

on-piste skiing /ˌɒn piːst 'skiːɪŋ/ *noun* SPORT skiing along marked tracks. Compare **off-piste skiing**

onshore /'ɒnʃɔː/ *adjective* towards the coast

onshore wind /ˌɒnʃɔː 'wɪnd/ *noun* a wind which blows from the sea towards the coast. Compare **offshore wind**

on-site /ˌɒn 'saɪt/ *adjective* on the premises ○ *The on-site courier is completely reliable.*

on-the-rocks /ˌɒn ðə 'rɒks/ served in a glass with ice cubes

onward /'ɒnwəd/ *adjective* next, further forward ○ *Passengers with onward connections should check at the transit desk on arrival.*

onward destination /ˌɒnwəd ˌdestɪ'neɪʃ(ə)n/ *noun* the next destination after arriving here

'…arriving passengers move from the arrival gate, down one floor to pick up their bags, and out of the door to their onward destination, via their chosen method of ground transportation' [*Airliner World*]

onward flight /ˌɒnwəd 'flaɪt/ *noun* AIR TRAVEL a flight to the next destination

on-your-own package /ˌɒn jɔː 'əʊn ˌpækɪdʒ/ *noun* TRAVEL arrangements made by a travel agency for an independent traveller who only wants the airline reservation and a hotel

open /'əʊpən/ *adjective* doing business, not closed ○ *Most slopes are open on Sunday mornings.* ○ *Our offices are open from 9 to 6.* ○ *They are open for business every day of the week.* ■ *verb* **1.** BUSINESS to start a new business working ○ *She has opened a shop in the High Street.* ○ *We have opened an office in London.* **2.** to start work, to be at work ○ *The information office opens at 9 a.m.* ○ *We open for business on Sundays.* **3.** to make something begin officially ○ *The new hotel was opened by the Minister of Tourism.* ○ *We are opening a new courier service to Japan.*

open-air /ˌəʊpən 'eə/ *adjective* in the open, not in a building ○ *an open-air performance of 'Twelfth Night'* ○ *an open-air concert in Central Park*

open bar /ˌəʊpən 'bɑː/ *noun* a bar at a party, wedding, or other social function where the drinks are served free of charge

open-cap mushroom /ˌəʊpən kæp 'mʌʃruːm/ *noun* VEGETABLES a large flatter type of mushroom

open cheque /ˌəʊpən 'tʃek/ *noun* FINANCE same as **uncrossed cheque**

open deck /ˌəʊpən 'dek/ *noun* TOURISM the top deck of a bus without a roof, to allow tourists to see and take photographs more easily

opening time /'əʊp(ə)nɪŋ taɪm/ *noun* the time when a shop or office starts work

open-jaw arrangement /ˌəʊpən 'dʒɔː əˌreɪndʒmənt/ *noun* AIR TRAVEL **1.** a system where a passenger flies to one airport on the outward flight and returns from another airport, having travelled between the two by bus, train, car, etc. **2.** a system where a passenger leaves from one airport on the outward trip and returns to another on the return trip, or flies to one airport and then returns from another airport

open sandwich /ˌəʊpən 'sænwɪdʒ/ *noun* FOOD one slice of bread with meat, cheese or some other filling on it

open sea /ˌəʊpən 'siː/ *noun* SHIPS AND BOATS an area of sea away from land, with no islands or rocks

open space /ˌəʊpən 'speɪs/ *noun* an area of land which has no buildings or trees on it ○ *The parks provide welcome open space in the centre of the city.*

open ticket /ˌəʊpən 'tɪkɪt/ *noun* TRAVEL a ticket which can be used on any date

open up /ˌəʊpən 'ʌp/ *verb* □ **to open up a new air route** to start flying a regular service on a route where such a service has not operated before

open-view kitchen /ˌəʊpən vjuː 'kɪtʃɪn/ *noun* CATERING a kitchen where the customers can watch the chefs at work ○ *a restaurant with an open-view kitchen built around a rôtisserie*

opera /'ɒp(ə)rə/ *noun* ENTERTAINMENT **1.** a dramatic performance with music, in which the words are partly or wholly sung ○ *We are going to see the new production of an opera by Britten.* ○ *'The Marriage of Figaro' is one of Mozart's best-known operas.* **2.** a company which performs operas

opera glasses /'ɒp(ə)rə ˌglɑːsɪz/ *plural noun* ENTERTAINMENT small binoculars for looking at performers on the stage

opera house /'ɒp(ə)rə haʊs/ *noun* ENTERTAINMENT a theatre in which operas are performed

operate /'ɒpəreɪt/ *verb* to make a machine work ○ *He knows how to operate the glasswasher.*

'...the company gets valuable restaurant locations which will be converted to the family-style restaurant chain that it operates and franchises throughout most parts of the US' [*Fortune*]

operating profit /'ɒpəreɪtɪŋ ˌprɒfɪt/ *noun* BUSINESS a result where sales from normal business activities are higher than the costs

operation /ˌɒpə'reɪʃ(ə)n/ *noun* **1.** BUSINESS a business organisation and work ○ *The company's tour operations in West Africa.* ○ *He is in charge of our hotel operations in Northern Europe.* **2.** □ **in operation** working, being used ○ *The computerised booking system will be in operation by June.* ○ *The new schedules came into operation on June 1st.*

operational /ˌɒpə'reɪʃ(ə)nəl/ *adjective* **1.** referring to how something works **2.** □ **the system became operational on June 1st** the system started working on June 1st

operational costs /ˌɒpəreɪʃ(ə)nəl 'kɒsts/ *plural noun* BUSINESS same as **running costs**

operational planning /ˌɒpəreɪʃ(ə)nəl 'plænɪŋ/ *noun* BUSINESS planning how a business is to be run

operations director /ˌɒpəˈreɪʃ(ə)nz daɪ ˌrektə/ *noun* BUSINESS somebody in charge of the way in which a company works

operative /ˈɒp(ə)rətɪv/ *adjective* □ **to become operative** to start working ○ *The new ticketing system has been operative since June 1st.*

operator /ˈɒpəreɪtə/ *noun* **1.** somebody who works a machine ○ *a keyboard operator* **2.** same as **telephonist** ○ *switchboard operator* ○ *to call the operator* or *to dial the operator* ○ *to place a call through* or *via the operator*

operator-controlled call /ˌɒpəreɪtə kənˌtrəʊld ˈkɔːl/ *noun* a telephone call where the operator makes the connection, usually charged at a higher rate

option /ˈɒpʃən/ *noun* **1.** a choice or another possibility ○ *The tour offers several options as half-day visits.* ○ *When you hire a car, you have the option of a two-door or four-door model.* **2.** □ **option to purchase, to sell** a possibility to buy or sell something within a period of time

optional /ˈɒpʃ(ə)n(ə)l/ *adjective* possible to add if the customer wants ○ *The insurance cover is optional.*

optional extras /ˌɒpʃ(ə)n(ə)l ˈekstrəz/ *plural noun* items which can be added for an extra charge, e.g. a visit to a market when on a tour

orange /ˈɒrɪndʒ/ *noun* FRUIT a sweet citrus fruit with a reddish-yellow skin ○ *roast duck and orange sauce* ○ *We saw orange trees growing in California.* ○ *She asked for an orange sorbet.*

COMMENT: The orange's nutritional value is due mainly to its high vitamin C content; it is eaten as fresh fruit or used for juice and for making preserves. Blood oranges are coloured by the presence of anthocyanins; mandarin oranges such as satsumas and tangerines have loose peel. The Seville orange is a bitter orange, grown in Spain and used to make marmalade.

orange marmalade /ˌɒrɪndʒ ˈmɑːmələɪd/ *noun* SAUCES, ETC. marmalade made from oranges, usually bitter oranges

order /ˈɔːdə/ *noun* **1.** a state of neatness and tidiness or a logical arrangement of things such as records, filing cards or invoices □ **alphabetical order** arrangement by the letters of the alphabet A, B, C, etc. **2.** a state of working properly □ **machine in full working order** a machine which is ready and able to work properly □ **the telephone is out of order** the telephone is not working □ **is all the documentation in order?** are all the documents valid and cor-

rect? **3.** BUSINESS an official request for goods to be supplied ○ *to give someone an order* or *to place an order with someone for twenty loaves of bread* □ **to fill, to fulfil an order** to supply items which have been ordered □ **terms: cash with order** conditions of sale showing that payment has to be made in cash when the order is placed □ **on order** ordered but not delivered ○ *This item is out of stock, but is on order.* □ **items available to order only** items which will be manufactured only if someone orders them **4.** CATERING food or drink which a customer has asked for in a restaurant ○ *This is not my order.* ○ *We only had twenty orders for the chef's special.* □ **to take an order** (*of a waiter*) to write down the dishes and drinks which a guest orders ■ *verb* **1.** BUSINESS to ask for goods to be supplied ○ *The hotel has ordered a new set of dining room furniture.* **2.** CATERING to ask for food or drink in a restaurant ○ *He ordered a full English breakfast.*

order book /ˈɔːdə bʊk/ *noun* a record of orders

order taker /ˈɔːdə ˌteɪkə/ *noun* CATERING a person whose job is to take orders for e.g. food or drink that is to be served or delivered to customers

Ordnance Survey /ˌɔːdnəns ˈsɜːveɪ/ *noun* formerly, a British government agency, now a public company, which is responsible for producing detailed maps of the UK ○ *We used an Ordnance Survey map to plot our route.*

oregano /ˌɒrɪˈgɑːnəʊ/ *noun* SAUCES, ETC. a common herb, used in Italian dishes such as pizzas

organic /ɔːˈgænɪk/ *adjective* cultivated naturally, without any chemical fertilisers or pesticides

COMMENT: Organic farming uses natural fertilizers and rotates the raising of animals with crop farming.

organically grown, organically produced *adjective* grown or produced naturally, without any chemical fertilisers or pesticides

organic farming /ɔːˌgænɪk ˈfɑːmɪŋ/ *noun* a method of farming which does not involve using chemical fertilisers or pesticides

organisation /ˌɔːgənaɪˈzeɪʃ(ə)n/, **organization** *noun* **1.** a way of arranging something so that it works efficiently **2.** a group or institution which is arranged for efficient work

organisation chart /ˌɔːgənaɪˈzeɪʃ(ə)n(ə)l tʃɑːt/ noun BUSINESS a diagram of people working in various departments, showing how a company or office is organised

organise /ˈɔːgənaɪz/, **organize** verb to arrange something so that it works efficiently ○ to organise a tour of Egypt

organised /ˈɔːgənaɪzd/, **organized** adjective arranged in advance ○ They went on an organised tour of Sicily.

organised labour /ˌɔːgənaɪzd ˈleɪbə/ noun BUSINESS workers who are members of trade unions

organiser /ˈɔːgənaɪzə/, **organizer** noun somebody who arranges things efficiently ○ Address any queries about the venue to the conference organiser.

orienteering /ˌɔːriəˈntɪərɪŋ/ noun SPORT the sport of finding your way through rough terrain which you do not know, using maps and compasses ○ He skis with the orienteering team.

origin /ˈɒrɪdʒɪn/ noun TRAVEL where something comes from, or the place where a traveller has started his or her journey

original /əˈrɪdʒ(ə)n(ə)l/ adjective **1.** new and different ○ She produced some very original ideas for the design of the new town centre. **2.** that is not a copy ○ I kept the original invoice and sent a copy. **3.** first, or made for the first time ○ Bath is the home of the original Bath Oliver.

originate /əˈrɪdʒɪneɪt/ verb to come from or to start from

ounce /aʊns/ noun a measure of weight equalling 28 grams (NOTE: This is usually written **oz** after figures: 14oz.)

outboard motor /ˌaʊtbɔːd ˈməʊtə/ noun SHIPS AND BOATS an engine which is attached to the outside of a boat ○ If there's not enough wind to sail the yacht we will have to use the outboard motor.

outbound /ˈaʊtbaʊnd/ adjective going away from the home base ○ The outbound flight departs at 09.15. ○ The captain flew the outbound leg from London to Durban. Compare **inbound**

outbreak /ˈaʊtbreɪk/ noun MEDICAL a series of cases of a disease which start suddenly ○ Tourists have been advised to drink only bottled water, as there is an outbreak of typhoid fever or a typhoid outbreak in the town.

outdoor /aʊtˈdɔː/ adjective in the open air ○ The hotel offers all sorts of outdoor activities.

outdoor catering /ˌaʊtdɔː ˈkeɪtərɪŋ/ noun CATERING catering for large numbers of people in the open air, as at sporting events, shows, etc.

outdoors /aʊtˈdɔːz/ adverb in or to the open air ○ The concert will be held outdoors if the weather is good. ■ noun the open air

'...the initiative is aimed at encouraging interest in outdoor pursuits for those who have never experienced the outdoors' [TGO – The Great Outdoors]

outgoing call /ˌaʊtgəʊɪŋ ˈkɔːl/ noun a phone call going out of a building to someone outside

outgoing mail /ˌaʊtgəʊɪŋ ˈmeɪl/ noun mail which is sent out

out of season /ˌaʊt əv ˈsiːz(ə)n/ adjective FOOD more expensive because the growing season is over and it has to be imported, or which is not found on menus because the time for growing it is over

outside /ˈaʊtsaɪd/ adverb, adjective not in a company's office or building □ **to send work to be done outside** to send work to be done in other offices ■ preposition □ **outside office hours, outside restaurant hours** when the office or restaurant is not open

outside broadcast /ˌaʊtsaɪd ˈbrɔːdkɑːst/ noun ENTERTAINMENT a radio or television programme recorded in the open air, not in a studio

outside cabin /ˌaʊtsaɪd ˈkæbɪn/ noun SHIPS AND BOATS a cabin with a window or porthole ○ We asked for an outside cabin. ○ We booked an inside cabin since there were no outside cabins left.

outside caterer /ˌaʊtsaɪd ˈkeɪtərə/ noun CATERING a person or company who supplies food and drink to be consumed in a different place

outside catering /ˌaʊtsaɪd ˈkeɪtərɪŋ/ noun CATERING the work of preparing food to be eaten in a different place

outside lane /ˌaʊtˈsaɪd leɪn/ noun ROAD TRAVEL the track nearest the centre of a road, used by the fastest-moving vehicles. Also called **fast lane**

outside line /ˌaʊtsaɪd ˈlaɪn/ noun a line from an internal office telephone system to the main telephone exchange

out tray /ˈaʊt treɪ/ noun a container for letters or memos which have been dealt with and are ready to be sent out

outward /ˈaʊtwəd/ adjective going away from the home base ○ On the outward voyage the ship will call in at the Canary Islands.

outward-bound /'aʊtwəd baʊnd/ *adjective* SHIPS AND BOATS sailing away from its home port

outward mission /ˌaʊtwəd 'mɪʃ(ə)n/ *noun* BUSINESS a visit by a group of businesspeople to a foreign country

ouzo /'uːzəʊ/ *noun* BEVERAGES a Greek alcoholic drink flavoured with aniseed

oven /'ʌv(ə)n/ *noun* CATERING an enclosed box which can be heated for cooking ○ *The kitchen has three large gas ovens.* ○ *Cook the vegetables in a microwave oven.*

ovenproof /'ʌv(ə)n,pruːf/ *adjective* CATERING possible to put into a hot oven without it being damaged by the heat ○ *The potatoes are served in an ovenproof bowl.*

ovenware /'ʌvənweə/ *noun* CATERING dishes which can be put in a hot oven without being damaged by the heat

over- /əʊvə/ *prefix* more than □ **shop which caters for the over-60s** a shop which has goods which appeal to people who are more than sixty years old

overboard /'əʊvəbɔːd/ *adverb* SHIPS AND BOATS from a boat into the water □ **man overboard!** someone has fallen into the water!

overbook /ˌəʊvə'bʊk/ *verb* to book more people than there are rooms or seats available ○ *The hotel or the flight was overbooked.*

overbooking /ˌəʊvə'bʊkɪŋ/ *noun* the fact of booking more people than there are rooms or seats available

overcapacity /ˌəʊvəkə'pæsɪti/ *noun* TOURISM the state of having more seats or space than there are travellers or guests

'...with the present overcapacity situation in the airline industry the discounting of tickets is widespread' [*Business Traveller*]

overcast /'əʊvəkɑːst/ *adjective* dull or cloudy

overcharge *noun* /'əʊvətʃɑːdʒ/ a charge which is higher than it should be ○ *to pay back an overcharge* ■ *verb* /ˌəʊvə'tʃɑːdʒ/ to ask too much money ○ *They overcharged us for meals.* ○ *We asked for a refund because we had been overcharged.*

overcook /ˌəʊvə'kʊk/ *verb* CATERING to cook something so long that it loses its flavour and texture

overcrowded /ˌəʊvə'kraʊdɪd/ *adjective* containing too many people ○ *We need to travel in the middle of the day to avoid the overcrowded commuter trains.*

overdo /ˌəʊvə'duː/ *verb* CATERING to cook food for too long

overdone /ˌəʊvə'dʌn/ *adjective* CATERING having been cooked too long ○ *I complained because my steak was overdone.*

overdue /ˌəʊvə'djuː/ *adjective* not paid on time □ **interest payments are three weeks overdue** interest payments should have been made three weeks ago

over easy /ˌəʊvər 'iːzi/ *adjective* US CATERING an egg fried on both sides. Compare **sunny side up**

overfly /ˌəʊvə'flaɪ/ *verb* AIR TRAVEL to fly over a country

overhead /'əʊvəhed/ *adjective* above one's head

overhead budget /ˌəʊvəhed 'bʌdʒɪt/ *noun* BUSINESS a plan of probable overhead costs

overhead costs /ˌəʊvəhed 'kɒsts/, **overhead expenses** /ˌəʊvəhed ɪk'spensɪz/, **overheads** /'əʊvəhedz/ *plural noun* BUSINESS same as **running costs**

overhead reading light /ˌəʊvəhed 'riːdɪŋ ˌlaɪt/ *noun* AIR TRAVEL a small light directly over a passenger's head in an aircraft

overheads /'əʊvəhedz/ *plural noun* BUSINESS same as **running costs**

overland /ˌəʊvə'lænd/ *adjective, adverb* across land, as opposed to over the sea ○ *an overland journey to China* ○ *They went down the river in small boats, and then went overland for a day to reach the safari station.* ○ *They took the overland route to Egypt.*

overload /ˌəʊvə'ləʊd/ *verb* to put too heavy a load on something ○ *With so many people trying to get on board, there was a danger of the boat being overloaded.*

overlook /ˌəʊvə'lʊk/ *verb* **1.** to look out over ○ *We want a room which overlooks the gardens, not one overlooking the car park.* **2.** not to notice something, or not to penalise or punish somebody for something ○ *In this instance we will overlook the delay.*

overnight /ˌəʊvə'naɪt/ *adverb* for the whole night ○ *We will stay overnight in France on our way to Italy.* ○ *They stay in the boat overnight, and make trips ashore at each port.* ■ *adjective* lasting all night ○ *They took an overnight flight back from China.* ○ *There are three sleeping cars on the overnight express.*

overpass /'əʊvəpɑːs/ *noun* ROAD TRAVEL a place where one road is built over another. Compare **underpass**

overrider /'əʊvəraɪdə/, **overriding commission** /ˌəʊvəraɪdɪŋ kə'mɪʃ(ə)n/, **override** /ˌəʊvə'raɪd/ *noun* a special extra commission which is paid on top of other commissions

overripe /ˌəʊvəˈraɪp/ *adjective* too ripe and past its best flavour and texture

overseas *adjective* /ˈəʊvəsiːz/ relating to foreign countries ■ *noun* /ˌəʊvəˈsiːz/ foreign countries ○ *The profits from overseas are far higher than those of the home division.*

overseas call /ˌəʊvəsiːz ˈkɔːl/ *noun* a phone call to another country

overseas money order /ˌəʊvəsiːz ˈmʌni ˌɔːdə/ *noun* FINANCE same as **foreign money order**

overseas trade /ˌəʊvəsiːz ˈtreɪd/ *noun* BUSINESS trade with foreign countries. Also called **external trade**, **foreign trade**

overseas travel /ˌəʊvəsiːz ˈtræv(ə)l/ *noun* TOURISM travel to other countries

overseas visitor /ˌəʊvəsiːz ˈvɪzɪtə/ *noun* a visitor from another country. Also called **foreign visitor**

overtake /ˌəʊvəˈteɪk/ *verb* ROAD TRAVEL to go faster than another vehicle on the road and pass it to get in front ○ *The road is too narrow to overtake.* ○ *The coach overtook our car on the motorway.*

overtime /ˈəʊvətaɪm/ BUSINESS *noun* hours worked more than the usual working time ○ *Overtime is paid at one and a half times the standard rate.* ■ *adjective* working more than the usual working day ○ *Overtime pay is calculated at one and a half times the standard rate.* ○ *They worked overtime when the hotel was full.*

overweight /ˌəʊvəˈweɪt/ *adjective* heavier than the allowed weight limit

ovolactovegetarian /ˌəʊvəʊlaæktəʊˌvedʒɪˈteəriən/ *noun* a vegetarian who eats eggs and dairy products, but no products that involve the killing of animals

OW *abbreviation* TRAVEL one-way

own /əʊn/ *verb* to have or possess something ○ *He owns 50% of the shares in the hotel chain.* □ **a state-owned airline** airline which belongs to the state

owner /ˈəʊnə/ *noun* somebody who owns something ○ *a restaurant owner* ○ *She's the* *owner of the chain of hotels.* □ **goods sent at owner's risk** a situation where the owner has to insure the goods while they are being transported □ **cars parked here at owner's risk** if a car parked here is damaged or stolen, the owner will have to claim on his or her insurance

owner-managed hotel /ˌəʊnə ˌmænɪdʒd həʊˈtel/ *noun* HOTELS a hotel which is owned and managed by the same person

owner-manager /ˌəʊnə ˈmænɪdʒə/ *noun* HOTELS somebody who owns a hotel or restaurant and manages it

owner-occupier /ˌəʊnər ˈɒkjʊpaɪə/ *noun* somebody who owns and lives in a property

ownership /ˈəʊnəʃɪp/ *noun* the fact of owning something

oxtail /ˈɒksteɪl/ *noun* MEAT the tail of a cow or bull, used in stews or to make oxtail soup

oxygen bar /ˈɒksɪdʒən bɑː/ *noun* a place similar to a café where customers can pay to breathe in oxygen through a face mask for its reviving effects

oyster /ˈɔɪstə/ *noun* SEAFOOD a shellfish, with two rough, roundish shells

COMMENT: Oysters are usually served raw, opened, with the flat half of the shell removed; they are usually served with lemon and slices of brown bread and butter. Traditionally, Guinness or dry champagne can be served with oysters, though nowadays a dry white wine is more usual. In restaurants oysters are served by the dozen or half-dozen. British oysters are only available between September and April, leading to the belief that they may only be eaten 'when there is an 'r' in the month'.

oyster bar /ˈɔɪstə bɑː/ *noun* CATERING a bar serving oysters, white wine, and usually other types of shellfish

oyster sauce /ˈɔɪstə sɔːs/ *noun* a salty bottled sauce flavoured with oysters, used in Chinese cooking

oz *abbreviation* ounce ○ *According to the recipe I need 12oz flour and 5oz butter.* (NOTE: Say 'twelve ounces of flour', 'five ounces of butter'.)

P

pack /pæk/ *noun* **1.** same as **packet** □ **pack of items** items put together in a container for selling ○ *a pack of cigarettes* ○ *a pack of biscuits* ○ *a pack of envelopes* □ **items sold in packs of 200** sold in boxes containing 200 items **2.** a rucksack, a bag carried on the back. ◊ **backpack** ■ *verb* **1.** TRAVEL to put things into a case for travelling ○ *Did you remember to pack your winter underwear?* ○ *He didn't pack his toothbrush.* ○ *We're leaving tonight, and you haven't finished packing yet.* **2.** to put things into a container for selling or sending ○ *to pack goods into cartons* ○ *The biscuits are packed in plastic wrappers.*

package /'pækɪdʒ/ *noun* **1.** goods packed and wrapped for sending by mail ○ *The Post Office does not accept bulky packages.* ○ *The goods are to be sent in airtight packages.* **2.** a number of different things or operations grouped together and considered as a single item ○ *a package of financial incentives for the staff* ○ *Free use of the swimming pool and sauna is part of the package.*

package deal /ˌpækɪdʒ 'diːl/ *noun* a deal where several items are agreed at the same time

package holiday /ˌpækɪdʒ 'hɒlɪdeɪ/ *noun* TOURISM a holiday where the travel, the accommodation and sometimes meals are all included in the price and paid for in advance ○ *The travel company is arranging a package trip to the international computer exhibition.*

package plan /'pækɪdʒ plæn/ *noun* HOTELS a rate which includes the use of other facilities or services, e.g. meals, tennis lessons or massages, as well as accommodation

packed lunch /ˌpækt 'lʌntʃ/ *noun* CATERING cold food, such as sandwiches, fruit, etc., packed in a box or basket for eating when travelling ○ *The party took packed lunches went they set off on their walk in the mountains.* ○ *We will ask the hotel to prepare packed lunches for us tomorrow.*

packet /'pækɪt/ *noun* a wrapping, container or box ○ *Empty cigarette packets littered the floor of the compartment.*

packing case /'pækɪŋ keɪs/ *noun* a large wooden box for carrying items which can be easily broken

pad /pæd/ *noun* CATERING a small terminal with keys, linked to a central computer, allowing orders to be keyed directly by a waiter or waitress

> '…pads are part of a network, so that in outlets with two or more pads, servers can move from pad to pad, and their orders move with them. Orders entered on any pad can be transmitted to kitchen or bar printers' [*Caterer & Hotelkeeper*]

paddle steamer /'pæd(ə)l ˌstiːmə/ *noun* SHIPS AND BOATS a steam-driven boat which moves forward with two large paddle wheels, one on either side ○ *An old paddle steamer runs tours across the lake.* Compare **sternwheeler**

paella /paɪ'elə/ *noun* FOOD a Spanish dish of cooked rice with fish, shellfish and vegetables in it

page /peɪdʒ/ HOTELS *noun also* **pageboy** a young man who takes messages and carries luggage in a hotel ■ *verb* to call someone to the reception desk or to answer a telephone call in a hotel ○ *He is not in his room, so we will page him in the restaurant.*

pager /'peɪdʒə/ *noun* a small portable radio which makes a tone when it receives a message. Also called **radiopager**

COMMENT: Pagers are used in many situations: to call members of staff to take incoming messages on an outside line, to call a doctor to an emergency, etc. Some pagers have small screens on which short written messages can be displayed.

paid-up capital /ˌpeɪd ʌp 'kæpɪt(ə)l/ *noun* BUSINESS the amount of money paid for the issued share capital

palace /'pælɪs/ *noun* a large ornate building, in which a king or nobleman lives ○ *Blenheim Palace is the home of the Duke of Marlborough.* ○ *Buckingham Palace was opened to the public for the first time in 1993.*

COMMENT: Note that a 'palace' would often be called 'château' in French, and in German, 'Schloss'. See note at CASTLE.

palm oil /ˈpɑːm ɔɪl/ *noun* FOOD an edible oil produced from the seed or fruit of an oil palm

palm tree /ˈpɑːm triː/ *noun* a large tropical plant with branching fern-like leaves, producing fruits which give oil and other foodstuffs □ **coconut palm**, **date palm** a palm which produces coconuts or dates

paludism /ˈpæljuːdɪzm/ *noun* MEDICAL same as **malaria**

COMMENT: Paludism is a recurrent disease which produces regular periods of shivering, vomiting, sweating and headaches as the parasites develop in the body; the patient also develops anaemia.

pamper /ˈpæmpə/ *verb* to make sure that someone is very comfortable and very well treated and has everything he or she wishes for

pan /pæn/ *noun* CATERING a metal cooking container with a handle

panada /pəˈnɑːdə/ *noun* CATERING a very thick paste of flour and a liquid such as milk or stock, used as a base for sauces, or for binding for stuffing

pancake /ˈpænkeɪk/ *noun* BREAD, ETC. a thin soft flat cake made of flour, milk and eggs ○ *We ate pancakes and maple syrup for breakfast.*

Pancake Day /ˈpænkeɪk deɪ/ *noun* the Tuesday before Lent starts, when pancakes are traditionally eaten ○ *You must have pancakes on Pancake Day.* Also called **Shrove Tuesday**

COMMENT: It is the last day before Lent, and so a day when feasts are held. In Britain, pancakes are traditionally eaten on Pancake Day, usually with lemon and sugar, but also with other sweet fillings. In France and French-speaking countries, the festival is called 'Mardi Gras'; it is celebrated particularly in Brazil.

pancetta /pænˈtʃetə/ *noun* MEAT a salt-cured and spiced form of belly of pork, used in Italian dishes

panel /ˈpæn(ə)l/ *noun* **1.** a group of people who answer questions or who judge a competition ○ *She's on the panel that will interview candidates for the post.* **2.** a flat piece of something such as wood or metal, which forms part of something ○ *Unscrew the panel at the back of the washing machine.*

panettone /ˌpænəˈtəʊni/ *noun* BREAD, ETC. a tall Italian yeast cake flavoured with vanilla and dried and candied fruits, traditionally eaten at Christmas

pan-fried /ˈpæn fraɪd/ *adjective* CATERING cooked in shallow oil or fat in a frying pan ○ *pan-fried fillets of sole*

panini /pəˈniːni/ *plural noun* BREAD, ETC. Italian white bread rolls, or sandwiches made with them

panoramic /ˌpænəˈræmɪk/ *adjective* looking out over a large area or commanding a wonderful view of scenery ○ *a panoramic view from the top of the tower* ○ *There is a panoramic restaurant on the top floor of the hotel.*

pantry /ˈpæntri/ *noun* **1.** cool cupboard or room for keeping food in ○ *My grandmother didn't own a refrigerator and kept all her food in the pantry.* **2.** CATERING (*in a restaurant*) a small room where dirty plates, glasses and cutlery are put after being cleared from the table, and where hot plates, cruets, etc., can be kept for service to guests' tables. Also called **service room**

pantryman /ˈpæntrimæn/ *noun* CATERING somebody who deals with the dirty dishes and glasses in a restaurant pantry

papaya /pəˈpaɪə/, **pawpaw** *noun* FRUIT a greenish-yellow tropical fruit with a soft pulp which is eaten raw

paper /ˈpeɪpə/ *noun* **1.** thin, often white, material, which you write on, and which is used for wrapping or to make books, newspapers and magazines **2.** a newspaper ○ *The cottage was advertised in our local paper.* ○ *Check in the paper to find out the times of high tides.*

paper money /ˌpeɪpə ˈmʌni/ *noun* FINANCE money in notes, not coins

paper napkin /ˌpeɪpə ˈnæpkɪn/ *noun* a napkin made from paper

paper towel /ˌpeɪpə ˈtaʊəl/ *noun* absorbent paper used for drying the hands, wiping spilled liquids, etc. ○ *There is a paper towel dispenser in the bathroom.*

pappardelle /ˌpæpɑːˈdelə/ *noun* FOOD pasta in the shape of broad flat ribbons

paprika /ˈpæprɪkə/ *noun* SAUCES, ETC. a red spice made from powdered sweet peppers (NOTE: **Paprika** is used in Central European cooking, such as goulash.)

parador /ˈpærədɔː/ *noun* HOTELS in Spain, a hotel operated by the national government and usually located in a castle, monastery, convent, or other historic site

paraglider /ˈpærəglaɪdə/ *noun* SPORT a large glider formed like a segment of a parachute, under which the pilot hangs in a harness, holding onto a bar which is used for steering. ◊ **hang-glider**

paragliding /'pærəglaɪdɪŋ/ *noun* SPORT the sport of flying a paraglider. ◊ **hang-gliding**

parallel /'pærəlel/ *noun* an imaginary line running round the earth, linking points at an equal distance from the equator

COMMENT: The parallels are numbered and some of them act as national boundaries: the 49th parallel marks most of the border between the USA and Canada.

parapente /'pærəpɒnt/ *noun* SPORT a modified parachute used for paraskiing and paragliding, similar to a hang-glider

parasailing /'pærəseɪlɪŋ/ *noun* SPORT a sport in which somebody wearing a parachute rises high into the air at the back of a moving motorboat and is towed along

parascending /'pærəsendɪŋ/ *noun* SPORT a sport in which somebody wearing an open parachute is towed along by a speedboat or land vehicle, rises into the air, and descends independently using the parachute

parasite /'pærəsaɪt/ *noun* a plant or animal which lives on or inside a host plant or animal and derives its nourishment and other needs from it ○ *Many diseases are carried by parasites.*

COMMENT: The commonest parasites affecting animals are lice on the skin and various types of worms in the intestines. Many diseases of humans (such as malaria and amoebic dysentery) are caused by infestation with parasites. Viruses are parasites on animals, plants and even on bacteria.

parasitic /ˌpærə'sɪtɪk/ *adjective* MEDICAL referring to parasites ○ *fleas and other parasitic insects* ○ *a parasitic plant*

paraskiing /'pærəskiːɪŋ/ *noun* SPORT the sport of skiing off high mountains and descending through the air using a parapente

parasol /'pærəsɒl/ *noun* a light umbrella to protect you from the rays of the sun

paratyphoid fever /ˌpærə'taɪfɔɪd ˌfiːvə/ *noun* MEDICAL an infectious disease which has similar symptoms to typhoid and is caused by bacteria transmitted by humans or animals

COMMENT: There are three forms of paratyphoid fever, known by the letters A, B, and C. They are caused by three types of bacterium, *Salmonella paratyphi* A, B, and C. TAB injections give immunity against paratyphoid A and B, but not against C.

parboil /'pɑːbɔɪl/ *verb* CATERING to half-cook food in boiling water

pare /peə/ *verb* **1.** CATERING to cut the skin or peel off a fruit, vegetable, etc. **2.** to cut back expenses □ **margins have been pared**

to the bone to keep our prices low they have been reduced as much as possible

parfait /'pɑːfeɪ/ *noun* a rich dessert consisting of frozen whipped cream or rich ice cream flavoured with fruit

parings /'peərɪŋz/ *plural noun* CATERING pieces of peel or skin cut off a fruit, vegetable, etc.

park /pɑːk/ *noun* an open space with grass and trees. ◊ **national park** ■ *verb* ROAD TRAVEL to leave your car in a place while you are not using it ○ *The rep parked her car outside the shop.* ○ *You cannot park here during the rush hour.* ○ *Parking is difficult in the centre of the city.*

park and fly /ˌpɑːk ən 'flaɪ/ *verb* to leave your car at the airport while you are away on a trip

parking /'pɑːkɪŋ/ *noun* ROAD TRAVEL the act of leaving your car in a place while you are not using it, or places where cars can be left ○ *There is plenty of free parking behind the conference centre.* □ **'no parking'** do not leave your car here

parking attendant /'pɑːkɪŋ əˌtendənt/ *noun* ROAD TRAVEL somebody who looks after a car park, telling people where to park, guarding the empty vehicles, collecting payment, etc.

parking facilities /'pɑːkɪŋ fəˌsɪlɪtiz/ *plural noun* ROAD TRAVEL arrangements for parking cars, either in a covered or open car park ○ *The hotel has parking facilities for 60 cars.*

parking lights /'pɑːkɪŋ laɪts/ *plural noun* same as **side lights**

parking lot /'pɑːkɪŋ lɒt/ *noun* US ROAD TRAVEL a car park

parking space /'pɑːkɪŋ speɪs/ *noun* a space for parking a single car ○ *The restaurant has six parking spaces allocated in the public car park next door.*

parking ticket /'pɑːkɪŋ ˌtɪkɪt/ *noun* a piece of paper showing that you have parked illegally and must pay a fine

park keeper /ˌpɑːk 'kiːpə/ *noun* a keeper who looks after a park, especially a town park

park ranger /pɑːk 'wɔːd(ə)n/, **park warden** *noun* somebody who looks after a forest or national park

parkway /'pɑːkweɪ/ *noun* US ROAD TRAVEL a highway with a grass strip in the middle with trees and shrubs

Parmesan /ˌpɑːmɪ'zæn/ *noun* DAIRY a pale yellow hard Italian cheese, often served grated as a garnish on pasta dishes

parquet floor /ˌpɑːkeɪ ˈflɔː/ *noun* a floor surface made of small pieces of wood, stuck down and polished ○ *Ladies with high heels should wear slippers when visiting the house to avoid damaging the parquet floors.*

parsley /ˈpɑːsli/ *noun* SAUCES, ETC. a green herb with either curly or flat leaves, used in cooking as a flavouring or garnish ○ *Sprinkle some chopped parsley on top of the salad.*

parsley sauce /ˌpɑːsli ˈsɔːs/ *noun* SAUCES, ETC. a white sauce, flavoured with parsley, served with fish

parsnip /ˈpɑːsnɪp/ *noun* VEGETABLES a plant whose long white root is eaten as a vegetable

COMMENT: Parsnips are eaten roasted (with roast beef and roast potatoes) or can be boiled and made into a purée. They are not eaten in most European countries, except in Britain.

part exchange /ˌpɑːt ɪksˈtʃeɪndʒ/ *noun* an arrangement where an old product is given by a buyer to a seller as part of the payment for a new one ○ *to take a car in part exchange*

participant /pɑːˈtɪsɪpənt/ *noun* somebody who takes part in something

participate /pɑːˈtɪsɪpeɪt/ *verb* to take part ○ *Not all the hotels in the chain are participating in this special Christmas offer.*

partie /ˈpɑːti/ *noun* CATERING a specialised section of a restaurant kitchen, making sauces, pastries, etc.

partition /pɑːˈtɪʃ(ə)n/ *noun* a thin wall between two spaces, especially splitting a large room into two ○ *There's only a thin partition between the bedrooms, so we can hear everything that is said in the room next door.* ■ *verb* to divide by means of a partition ○ *Part of the old dining room has been partitioned off to make a small function room.*

partridge /ˈpɑːtrɪdʒ/ *noun* a large brown and grey bird, shot for sport and food, in season between September 1st and February 1st

part-time /ˌpɑːt ˈtaɪm/ *adjective, adverb* not for a whole working day ○ *She has a part-time job at the hotel reception desk.* ○ *We employ several people part-time at weekends.*

part-timer /ˌpɑːt ˈtaɪmə/ *noun* somebody who works part-time

party /ˈpɑːti/ *noun* **1.** ENTERTAINMENT a special occasion when several people meet, usually in someone's house ○ *We're having a party on New Year's Eve.* ○ *A number of Christmas parties are already booked.* ○ *She invited twenty friends to her birthday party.*
2. a group of people doing something together ○ *Parties of tourists walking round the gardens.* ○ *A party of four arrived for a booking we did not have.*

pass /pɑːs/ *noun* TRAVEL **1.** a lower area between two mountain peaks ○ *The trail crosses nine major passes.* **2.** a bus or train season ticket, or a permit to go in or out of a building, etc. ○ *A monthly pass costs less than four weekly passes.* ◊ **airpass, railpass** ■ *verb* to go past ○ *You pass the Post Office on your left as you go to the station.*

'…the snow tends to lie on the passes well into July' [*TGO – The Great Outdoors*]

passage /ˈpæsɪdʒ/ *noun* **1.** a long narrow corridor ○ *The toilets are at the end of the passage.* ○ *Go down the passage and turn left for the dining room.* **2.** SHIPS AND BOATS a voyage by ship □ **to work your passage** to work on a ship so as to get a free voyage to a particular destination

passata /pəˈsɑːtə/ *noun* SAUCES, ETC. a thick tomato sauce with a rough texture, sometimes flavoured with herbs

passenger /ˈpæsɪndʒə/ *noun* TRAVEL somebody who travels in a plane, bus, taxi, train, car or ship, but is not the driver or a member of the crew

passenger facility charge /ˌpæsɪndʒə fəˈsɪlɪti ˌtʃɑːdʒ/ *noun* US AIR TRAVEL a charge added to each ticket, levied by airports and collected by airlines as a way of paying for the cost of airports. Abbr **PFC**

passenger ferry /ˈpæsɪndʒə ˌferi/ *noun* SHIPS AND BOATS a ferry which carries only passengers

passenger manifest /ˌpæsɪndʒə ˈmænɪfest/ *noun* TRAVEL a list of passengers on a ship or plane

passenger name record /ˌpæsɪndʒə ˈneɪm ˌrekɔːd/ *noun* an electronic record which identifies every airline passenger and provides information on their itinerary and travel reservations. Abbr **PNR**

passenger terminal /ˈpæsɪndʒə ˌtɜːmɪn(ə)l/ *noun* AIR TRAVEL the main building at an airport or port for people

passenger train /ˈpæsɪndʒə treɪn/ *noun* RAIL TRAVEL a train which carries only passengers, as opposed to freight trains which carry only goods

passing trade /ˌpɑːsɪŋ ˈtreɪd/ *noun* BUSINESS customers who walk or drive past a restaurant or hotel, and decide to stop and eat or stay the night, without having booked

passion fruit /ˈpæʃ(ə)n fruːt/ *noun* FRUIT a purple fruit with a hard case filled with juicy pulp and many seeds. Also called **granadilla**

passito /pæ'siːtəʊ/ *noun* dried grapes for making sweet wines

passport /'pɑːspɔːt/ *noun* an official document with your photograph and various personal details, proving that you are a citizen of a country ○ *We had to show our passports at the customs post.* ○ *His passport is out of date.* ○ *The immigration officer stamped my passport.*

passport control /'pɑːspɔːt kən,trəʊl/ *noun* AIR TRAVEL a place where passengers' passports are checked ○ *We had to wait for half an hour in passport control.*

passport number /'pɑːspɔːt ,nʌmbə/ *noun* a serial number which is unique to each passport

passport photo /'pɑːspɔːt ,fəʊtəʊ/ *noun* TRAVEL a small photograph of a person's face, used in passports or on season tickets

pass through /,pɑːs 'θruː/ *verb* to go through something ○ *The road passes through the national park.* □ **we're just passing through** we are on our way to somewhere else □ **to pass through customs** to go through a customs checkpoint

pasta /'pæstə/ *noun* FOOD a type of food made from flour from durum wheat and shaped into forms such as lasagne, macaroni, noodles, ravioli and spaghetti ○ *Spaghetti, macaroni, etc., are all types of pasta.* ○ *I'll just have some pasta and a glass of wine.* (NOTE: There is no plural form: *some pasta, a bowl of pasta*. **Pasta** takes a singular verb: *The pasta is very good here*.)

COMMENT: Pasta is available both dried and freshly made. It can be coloured in various ways, flavoured with basil, spinach, tomato, etc. There are a large number of different forms of pasta and they form a basic part of Italian cooking.

paste /peɪst/ *noun* **1.** FOOD thin glue, usually made of flour and water **2.** a soft substance ■ *verb* to stick with glue ○ *The posters advertising the bullfight are pasted onto shop windows.*

pasteurisation /,pɑːstʃəraɪ'zeɪʃ(ə)n/, **pasteurization** *noun* CATERING heating food or food products to destroy bacteria, but without changing the flavour very much ○ *Pasteurisation kills off harmful bacteria.*

COMMENT: Pasteurisation is carried out by heating food for a short time at a lower temperature than that used for sterilisation: the two methods used are heating to 72°C for fifteen seconds (the high-temperature short-time method) or to 65° for half

an hour, and then cooling rapidly. This has the effect of killing tuberculosis bacteria. Pasteurisation is used principally in the preservation of milk, though cheese made from unpasteurised milk is thought to have a better flavour.

pasteurise /'pɑːstʃəraɪz/ *verb* CATERING to heat food to destroy bacteria ○ *The government is telling people to drink only pasteurised milk.*

'...a recommendation that caterers use pasteurized eggs for products such as mayonnaise, mousse and ice cream. In addition, lightly cooked dishes such as meringue, hollandaise sauce and Welsh rarebit should not be served to the elderly, sick, babies or pregnant women' [*Caterer & Hotelkeeper*]

pastis /'pæsti/ *noun* BEVERAGES a French alcoholic drink, flavoured with aniseed

pastrami /pæ'strɑːmi/ *noun* MEAT smoked and strongly seasoned beef, usually prepared from a shoulder cut, that is served cold in thin slices

pastry /'peɪstri/ *noun* BREAD, ETC. **1.** a paste made of flour, fat and water which is used to make pies **2.** a sweet cake made of pastry filled with cream or fruit

pastry case /'peɪstri keɪs/ *noun* FOOD a piece of pastry used to line a dish and filled either before or after baking

pastry chef /'peɪstri ʃef/ *noun* CATERING a chef who specialises in preparing pastries and sweet dishes. Also called **chef pâtissier**

pastry fork /'peɪstri fɔːk/ *noun* CATERING same as **cake fork**

pasty /'pæsti/ *noun* FOOD a small pie made with meat or vegetables wrapped in a pastry case and cooked

PA system /,piː 'eɪ 'sɪstəm/ same as **public address system**

pâté /'pæteɪ/ *noun* MEAT a paste made of cooked meat or fish finely minced ○ *I'll start with chicken liver pâté.* ○ *He brought some pâté home with him from France.*

pâté de foie gras /,pæteɪ də ,fwɑː 'grɑː/ *noun* MEAT a fine pâté made from goose or duck liver

path /pɑːθ/ *noun* a narrow way for walking, cycling or riding

pathway /'pɑːθweɪ/ *noun* a track for walking along ○ *A concrete pathway connects the two buildings.*

patisserie /pæ'tiːsəri/ *noun* **1.** BREAD, ETC. sweet pastries or cakes **2.** a shop which sells these pastries or cakes

patron /'peɪtrən/ *noun* BUSINESS a customer, especially a regular one, of a pub or restaurant, or a visitor to a theatre ○ *Patrons are asked not to smoke in the auditorium.* ○

The car park is for the use of hotel patrons only.

patty /'pæti/ *noun* FOOD a small flat individual cake made from minced meat, vegetables, or other food

pavlova /pæv'ləʊvə/ *noun* DESSERTS a large circle of meringue filled with fruit and whipped cream

COMMENT: Named after the Russian ballerina, Anna Pavlova (1885–1931).

pawpaw /'pɔːpɔː/ FRUIT same as **papaya**

PAX /pæks/ *abbreviation* TRAVEL passengers

pay /peɪ/ *noun* salary or wage, the money given to someone for regular work □ **holidays with pay** a holiday which an employee can take by contract and for which he or she is paid ■ *verb* **1.** to give money to buy an item or a service ○ *They paid £1,000 for the first-class tickets.* ○ *How much did you pay to have your suit cleaned?* □ **to pay in advance** to give money before you receive the item bought or before the service has been completed ○ *You have to pay a deposit in advance when buying a made-to-measure suit.* □ **to pay in instalments** to give money for an item or service by giving small amounts regularly ○ *We are paying for our holidays in instalments of £50 a month.* □ **to pay by credit card** to pay by using a credit card, and not a cheque or cash □ **to pay the difference** to pay an amount which is the difference between two prices ○ *The second-class fare is £35.00 and first-class £49.00, but you can move to first-class if you are willing to pay the difference.* **2.** to pay somebody money for work done ○ *The restaurant staff have not been paid for three weeks.* ○ *We pay good wages for skilled workers.* ○ *How much do they pay you per hour?* □ **to be paid by the hour** to get a fixed amount of money for each hour worked **3.** to give money which is owed or which has to be paid ○ *to pay a bill* ○ *to pay an invoice* ○ *to pay duty on imports* (NOTE: **paying – paid**)

payable /'peɪəb(ə)l/ *adjective* due to be paid □ **electricity charges are payable by the tenant** the tenant, not the landlord, must pay for the electricity

payable in advance /ˌpeɪəb(ə)l ɪn əd'vɑːns/ *adjective* FINANCE due to be paid before you receive the item bought or before the service has been finished

payable on demand /ˌpeɪəb(ə)l ɒn dɪ'mɑːnd/ *adjective* FINANCE due to be paid when payment is asked for

pay cheque /'peɪ tʃek/ *noun* FINANCE a monthly cheque which pays a salary to a worker

pay day /'peɪ deɪ/ *noun* BUSINESS the day on which wages are paid to employees, usually Friday for employees paid once a week, and during the last week of the month for employees who are paid once a month

pay desk /'peɪ desk/ *noun* a place in a store where you pay for the goods bought

pay down /ˌpeɪ 'daʊn/ *verb* □ **to pay money down** to make a deposit ○ *She paid £50 down and the rest in monthly instalments.*

paying /'peɪɪŋ/ *adjective* **1.** giving or providing money **2.** making a profit ○ *It is a paying business.* □ **it is not a paying proposition** it is not a business which is going to make a profit

paying guest /ˌpeɪɪŋ 'gest/ *noun* **1.** a person who stays with a family in their home and pays a rent **2.** a person who stays at a boarding house and pays for room and board

payload /'peɪləʊd/ *noun* AIR TRAVEL the load of an aircraft which produces income, i.e. the passengers and cargo

payment /'peɪmənt/ *noun* **1.** the act of giving money for something **2.** money paid

payment by results /ˌpeɪmənt baɪ rɪ'zʌlts/ *noun* BUSINESS a method of paying a worker in which the amount of money he or she receives increases with the amount of work done or goods produced

payment in full /ˌpeɪmənt ɪn 'fʊl/ *noun* FINANCE payment of all money owed. Also called **full payment**

payment on account /ˌpeɪmənt ɒn ə'kaʊnt/ *noun* FINANCE payment of part of the money owed

payment on invoice /ˌpeɪmənt ɒn 'ɪnvɔɪs/ *noun* FINANCE payment as soon as an invoice is received

payment receipt /'peɪmənt rɪˌsiːt/ *noun* FINANCE a piece of paper showing that money has been received

pay-per-view film /ˌpeɪ pɜː vjuː 'fɪlm/ *noun* ENTERTAINMENT a film which is available on the room TV, but which the guest is charged for watching

'…it also suggests that, by not capitalizing on guests' IT interest, the average 150-bedroom hotel is missing out on at least £50,000 of revenue a year from pay-per-view movies or metered Internet access' [*Caterer & Hotelkeeper*]

payphone /'peɪfəʊn/ *noun* a public phone where you insert money to make a call

pay slip /'peɪ slɪp/ *noun* BUSINESS a piece of paper showing the full amount of an employee's pay, and the money deducted as tax, pension and insurance contributions

pea /piː/ *noun* VEGETABLES a climbing plant with round green seeds that are eaten as vegetables

COMMENT: Peas are available fresh in season, or frozen or canned. Peas can be served out of their pods, or the whole pod is cooked rapidly as 'mangetout'.

peach /piːtʃ/ *noun* FRUIT a juicy fruit with a soft hairy yellow or red-and-yellow skin and sweet yellow flesh ○ *We had peaches and cream for dessert.*

COMMENT: Peaches grow particularly in Mediterranean areas, though they can be grown as far north as southern England. The fruit are large and juicy, with a downy skin; they cannot be kept for any length of time. Peaches are divided into two groups: the freestone (where the flesh is not attached to the stone), and the clingstone. The nectarine is a form of peach with a smooth skin.

peach Melba /ˌpiːtʃ ˈmelbə/ *noun* DESSERTS a dessert of sliced peaches with ice cream and raspberry sauce

peak /piːk/ *noun* 1. the top of a mountain 2. the highest point

peak period /ˈpiːk ˌpɪəriəd/ *noun* the period of the day when most electricity is used or when most traffic is on the roads

peak rate /ˈpiːk reɪt/ *noun* the most expensive tariff for something such as a telephone call

peak season /ˌpiːk ˈsiːz(ə)n/ *noun* same as **high season** (*US*)

peanut /ˈpiːnʌt/ *noun* NUTS a nut which grows in the ground in pods like a pea. Also called **monkey nut**

COMMENT: Roasted salted peanuts are commonly served as a cocktail snack.

peanut butter /ˌpiːnʌt ˈbʌtə/ *noun* FOOD a paste made from crushed peanuts

pear /peə/ *noun* FRUIT a fruit with a greenish or yellowish skin and soft white flesh

COMMENT: Pears are commonly used as dessert fruit, also for cooking. In the UK, William's Bon Chrétien, Conference and Doyenné du Comice are popular dessert varieties, while William's is also commonly used for canning. Pears are also used for fermenting to make perry.

pearl barley /ˌpɜːl ˈbɑːli/ *noun* FOOD grains of barley used in cooking

pebble /ˈpeb(ə)l/ *noun* a small round stone ○ *There's no sand on the beach – it's all pebbles.*

pebbly /ˈpebli/ *adjective* covered with pebbles ○ *The beach is pebbly.*

pecan /ˈpiːkən, pɪˈkæn/ *noun* NUTS a sweet nut from a tree which grows in the south of the USA

pecan pie /ˌpiːkən ˈpaɪ/ *noun* DESSERTS a pie made from corn syrup, cornflour, and pecans

pecorino /ˌpekəˈriːnəʊ/ *noun* DAIRY a hard pungent Italian cheese made from ewe's milk

pectin /ˈpektɪn/ *noun* CATERING a substance in fruit which helps jam to set

pedal /ˈped(ə)l/ *noun* a lever worked by your foot ○ *If you want to stop the car put your foot down on the brake pedal.*

pedal bin /ˈped(ə)l bɪn/ *noun* rubbish bin with a lid worked by a pedal

pedalo /ˈpedələʊ/ *noun* SHIPS AND BOATS a type of little boat, with seats for two people who make it go forward by pedalling to turn paddle wheels (NOTE: The plural form is **pedalos**.)

pedestrian /pəˈdestriən/ *noun* somebody who goes about on foot

pedestrian crossing /pɪˌdestriən ˈkrɒsɪŋ/ *noun* ROAD TRAVEL a place marked with white lines where pedestrians can cross a road. Also called **zebra crossing**

pedestrian precinct /pəˌdestriən ˈpriːsɪŋkt/ *noun* same as **shopping precinct**

peel /piːl/ *noun* FOOD the outer skin of a fruit, or the skin of a potato ○ *Oranges have a thick peel.* ○ *Lemon peel is used as flavouring.* ■ *verb* CATERING to take the skin off a fruit or vegetable ○ *Peel the potatoes and cut into chunks.*

peeler /ˈpiːlə/ *noun* a tool for taking the skins off fruit or vegetables

peelings /ˈpiːlɪŋz/ *plural noun* CATERING bits of skin from vegetables or fruit

Peking duck /ˌpiːkɪŋ ˈdʌk/ *noun* FOOD duck cooked in the Chinese style with a sweet brown glaze, eaten with pancakes and raw onions

pence /pens/ ♦ **penny**

penne /ˈpeneɪ/ *noun* FOOD short tube-shaped pasta cut diagonally at the ends

penny /ˈpeni/ *noun* FINANCE 1. a small coin, of which one hundred make a pound (NOTE: This is usually written **p** after figures: *26p* (say 'twenty-six pee'). The plural is **pennies** or **pence**.) 2. *US* a small coin, one cent (*informal*)

pension /ˈpenʃən/ *noun* 1. money paid regularly to someone who no longer works 2. /ˈpɒ̃sjɑ̃/ TOURISM a guesthouse or boarding house

pension contributions /'penʃən kɒntrɪˌbjuːʃ(ə)nz/ *plural noun* BUSINESS money paid regularly by a company or employee to be saved up to make a pension

pension entitlement /'penʃən ɪnˌtaɪt(ə)lmənt/ *noun* the amount of pension which someone has the right to receive on their retirement

pension plan /'penʃən plæn/, **pension scheme** /'penʃən skiːm/ *noun* FINANCE a plan worked out by an insurance company which arranges for an employee to pay part of his or her salary over many years and receive a regular payment when he or she retires

penthouse /'penthaʊs/ *noun* a flat on the top floor of a high building ○ *The family has booked the penthouse suite for two weeks.*

pepper /'pepə/ *noun* **1.** a condiment, made from the crushed seeds of the pepper plant ○ *Add salt and pepper to taste.* □ **black pepper, white pepper, green pepper, pink pepper** different types of pepper which are commonly available **2.** same as **capsicum** ○ *Add salt and pepper to taste.*
■ *verb* to sprinkle with pepper

COMMENT: There are two types of ground pepper: black and white (the white is not as strong as the black). The pepper vegetable is either green, yellow or red. It is also called 'sweet pepper' to distinguish it from the chilli pepper.

peppercorn /'pepəkɔːn/ *noun* SAUCES, ETC. a dried seed of the pepper plant

peppered steak /ˌpepəd 'staɪk/ *noun* FOOD a steak covered with crushed peppercorns before cooking

peppermill /'pepəmɪl/ *noun* CATERING a device which twists to crush peppercorns

peppermint /'pepəmɪnt/ *noun* SAUCES, ETC. a flavouring prepared from the oil of a mint plant

pepperpot /'pepəpɒt/ *noun* CATERING a pot with holes on the lid, filled with ground pepper

COMMENT: In the UK, a pepper pot has several holes in it, sometimes in the shape of the letter 'P' to differentiate it from the salt cellar; in the USA, the pepper pot will have only one hole while it is the salt cellar which has several.

pepper salami /ˌpepə sə'lɑːmi/ *noun* MEAT salami with crushed peppercorns covering the outside

peppery /'pepəri/ *adjective* CATERING tasting of pepper ○ *a very peppery soup*

per /pɜː, pə/ *preposition* **1.** □ **as per** according to ○ *as per the attached schedule* □ **as per invoice** as stated in the invoice **2.** at

a rate of □ **per hour, per day, per week, per year** for each hour, day, week or year ○ *The rate is £5 per hour.* ○ *He makes about £250 per month.* □ **we pay £10 per hour** we pay £10 for each hour worked □ **the car was travelling at twenty-five miles per hour** at a speed which covered 25 miles in one hour □ **per head, per person, per capita** for each person ○ *Allow £15 per head for lunch.* ○ *The total cost for the tour comes to £150 per person.*

per cent /pə 'sent/ *adverb* out of each hundred, for each hundred □ **10 per cent** ten in every hundred ○ *What is the increase per cent?* ○ *12 per cent is added to the bill for service.* ○ *The airline has reduced the number of seats in Business Class, so increasing the leg room by about 15%.*

percentage /pə'sentɪdʒ/ *noun* an amount shown as part of one hundred

percentage discount /pəˌsentɪdʒ dɪs'kaʊnt/ *noun* a discount calculated at an amount per hundred

percentage increase /pəˌsentɪdʒ 'ɪnkriːs/ *noun* an increase calculated at an amount per hundred

percentage of occupancy /pəˌsentɪdʒ əv 'ɒkjʊpənsi/ *noun* HOTELS same as **room occupancy** ○ *During the winter months the occupancy rate was down to 50%.*

percentage point /pə'sentɪdʒ pɔɪnt/ *noun* 1 per cent

perch /pɜːtʃ/ *noun* SEAFOOD a type of freshwater fish

percolate /'pɜːkəleɪt/ *verb* to filter through

percolation /ˌpɜːkə'leɪʃ(ə)n/ *noun* the act of making e.g. coffee by filtering

percolator /'pɜːkəleɪtə/ *noun* CATERING a coffeemaker where the water boils up through a tube and filters through ground coffee

COMMENT: In a percolator, the coffee is boiled again and again, as opposed to expresso-type coffeemakers where the hot water only rises once.

period /'pɪəriəd/ *noun* a length of time ○ *for a period of time* or *for a period of months* or *for a six-year period* ○ *Bookings for the holiday period are down on last year.*

period of validity /ˌpɪəriəd əv və'lɪdɪti/ *noun* BUSINESS the length of time for which a document may be used lawfully

perishable /'perɪʃəb(ə)l/ *adjective* CATERING likely to go bad quickly

perishables /'perɪʃəb(ə)lz/ *plural noun* CATERING perishable food

perishable stores /ˌperiʃəb(ə)l ˈstɔːz/ *noun* CATERING a storeroom for food which can go bad quickly, such as meat and fruit

permission /pəˈmɪʃ(ə)n/ *noun* the fact of being allowed to do something □ **to give someone permission to do something** to allow someone to do something ○ *She asked permission of the manager* or *she asked the manager's permission to take a day off.*

permit *noun* /ˈpɜːmɪt/ an official document which allows someone to do something □ **export permit, import permit** an official document which allows goods to be exported or imported ■ *verb* /pəˈmɪt/ to allow someone to do something ○ *This document permits you to import twenty-five cases of wine.* ○ *The ticket permits three people to go into the exhibition.*

perry /ˈperi/ *noun* BEVERAGES an alcoholic drink made from pear juice

person /ˈpɜːs(ə)n/ *noun* a human being

personal /ˈpɜːs(ə)n(ə)l/ *adjective* referring to one person

personal assets /ˌpɜːs(ə)n(ə)l ˈæsets/ *plural noun* moveable assets which belong to a person

personal call /ˈpɜːs(ə)n(ə)l kɔːl/ *noun* **1.** a telephone call not related to business **2.** a telephone call where you ask the operator to connect you with a named person ○ *Staff are not allowed to make personal calls during office hours.*

personal effects /ˌpɜːs(ə)n(ə)l ɪˈfekts/ *plural noun* same as **personal property** (*formal*) ○ *The hotel does not accept liability for any loss of personal effects of delegates attending the conference.*

personal hygiene /ˌpɜːs(ə)n(ə)l ˈhaɪdʒiːn/ *noun* actions to keep yourself clean and healthy, e.g. washing your body, hands and hair often, and keeping your clothes clean

personal message /ˌpɜːs(ə)n(ə)l ˈmesɪdʒ/ *noun* a message for a particular person

personal organiser /ˌpɜːs(ə)n(ə)l ˈɔːɡənaɪzə/ *noun* a very small pocket computer in which you can enter details of names, addresses, telephone numbers, appointments and meetings. Also called **electronic organiser**

personal property /ˌpɜːs(ə)n(ə)l ˈprɒpəti/ *noun* items which belong to a person ○ *The storm caused considerable damage to personal property.* ○ *The management is not responsible for property left in the hotel rooms.*

personnel /ˌpɜːsəˈnel/ *noun* BUSINESS the people who work in a particular place or for a particular company ○ *the personnel of the hotel* or *the hotel personnel* ○ *We are looking for experienced personnel for our tourist information office.* □ **the personnel department** the section of the company which deals with the staff

personnel management /ˌpɜːsənel ˈmænɪdʒmənt/ *noun* BUSINESS the organising and training of staff so that they work well and profitably

personnel manager /ˌpɜːsəˈnel ˌmænɪdʒə/, **personnel officer** /ˌpɜːsəˈnel ˌɒfɪsə/ *noun* the head of the personnel department (NOTE: This has been replaced in some cases by **human resources**: *human resources manager, human resources department.*)

person-to-person call /ˌpɜːs(ə)n tə ˈpɜːs(ə)n kɔːl/ *noun* a telephone call where you ask the operator to connect you with a named person

peso /ˈpeɪsəʊ/ *noun* FINANCE the currency used in Mexico and many other countries such as Argentina, Bolivia, Chile, Colombia, Cuba, Dominican Republic, Philippines and Uruguay

pest /pest/ *noun* a plant, animal or insect which causes problems ○ *a spray to remove insect pests*

COMMENT: The word is a relative term: a pest to one person may not be a pest to another, so foxes are pests to chicken farmers, but not to naturalists.

pest control /ˈpest kənˌtrəʊl/ *noun* action to restrict the spread of pests by killing them

pesticide /ˈpestɪsaɪd/ *noun* a poisonous substance used to destroy pests

COMMENT: There are three basic types of pesticide. **1.** organochlorine insecticides, which have a high persistence in the environment of up to about 15 years (DDT, dieldrin and aldrin). **2.** organophosphates, which have an intermediate persistence of several months (parathion, carbaryl and malathion). **3.** carbamates, which have a low persistence of around two weeks (Temik, Zectran and Zineb). Most pesticides are broad-spectrum, that is they kill all insects in a certain area and may kill other animals like birds and small mammals. Pesticide residue levels in food in the UK are generally low. Pesticide residues have been found in bran products, bread and baby foods, as well as in milk and meat. Where pesticides are found, the levels are low and rarely exceed international maximum residue levels.

pesto /'pestəʊ/ *noun* SAUCES, ETC. a sauce or paste made by crushing together basil leaves, pine nuts, oil, Parmesan cheese, and garlic

pet /pet/ *noun* an animal kept in the home to give pleasure, e.g. a cat or dog ○ *Pets are not allowed into the restaurant.* ○ *This little sign in the directory indicates hotels which welcome pets.*

petits fours /pə‚ti: 'fɔ:/ *plural noun* FOOD very small cakes and biscuits, often containing marzipan, served with coffee after a meal

petrol /'petrəl/ *noun* ROAD TRAVEL liquid, made from petroleum, used to drive a car engine ○ *The car is very economic on petrol.* ○ *We are looking for a car with a low petrol consumption.* (NOTE: The US English is **gasoline** *or* **gas**.)

petrol station /'petrəl ‚steɪʃ(ə)n/ *noun* a place where you can buy petrol ○ *He stopped at a petrol station to get some petrol before going on to the motorway.*

petrol tank /'petrəl tæŋk/ *noun* a container built into a car, for holding petrol

Pet Travel Scheme, 'pet passport' *noun* a scheme by which cats and dogs can be brought into the UK from Europe without having to spend six months in quarantine (NOTE: Before arrival the animal must be checked for worms and ticks, and then has a microchip implanted, giving it a unique number. The animal is then vaccinated against rabies and has to have regular blood tests after arrival to check if the vaccine has taken.)

petty cash /‚peti 'kæʃ/ *noun* FINANCE small amounts of money

PFC *abbreviation* AIR TRAVEL passenger facility charge

pheasant /'fez(ə)nt/ *noun* a large bird with a long tail, shot for sport and food and in season from October 1st to February 1st

COMMENT: The male bird is brightly coloured and larger than the female. They are usually sold as a pair or 'brace' – that is, one male and one female.

phone /fəʊn/ *noun* a telephone, a machine used for speaking to someone ○ *We had a new phone system installed last week.* □ **by phone** using the telephone ○ *to place an order by phone* □ **to be on the phone** to be speaking to someone by telephone ○ *She has been on the phone all morning.* ○ *He spoke to the manager on the phone.* □ **to make a phone call** to dial and speak to someone on the telephone ■ *verb* □ **to phone a person, a place** to call someone or a place by telephone ○ *Don't phone me, I'll phone you.* ○

His secretary phoned to say he would be late. ○ *She phoned the reservation through to the hotel.* ○ *The travel agency phoned to say that the tickets were ready for collection.* ○ *She phoned room service to order some coffee.* ○ *It's very expensive to phone Singapore at this time of day.* □ **to phone about something** to make a telephone call to speak about something ○ *She phoned about the table he had reserved for 8 p.m.* □ **to phone for something** to make a telephone call to ask for something ○ *He phoned for a taxi.*

phone back /‚fəʊn 'bæk/ *verb* to make a phone call in reply to another ○ *The manager is in a meeting, can you phone back in about half an hour?* ○ *Mr Smith called while you were out and asked if you would phone him back.*

phone book /'fəʊn bʊk/ *noun* a book which lists names of people and businesses in alphabetical order with their telephone numbers and addresses ○ *Look up her address in the phone book.* ○ *He looked up the number of the company in the phone book.* Also called **telephone directory**

phone booking /‚fəʊn 'bʊkɪŋ/ *noun* a reservation made by phone of something such as a room in a hotel, a table in a restaurant, etc. ○ *Phone bookings must be confirmed in writing.*

phone booth /'fəʊn bu:ð/, **phone box** /'fəʊn bɒks/ *noun* a small cabin for a public telephone

phone call /'fəʊn kɔ:l/ *noun* a conversation with someone on the telephone

phonecard /'fəʊnkɑ:d/ *noun* a plastic card which you can buy at a post office, and insert into a special slot in a public telephone booth to make a phone call

phone link /'fəʊn lɪŋk/ *noun* same as **telephone line**

phone number /'fəʊn ‚nʌmbə/ *noun* a series of numbers that you press on a telephone to contact a particular person ○ *He keeps a list of phone numbers in a little black book.* ○ *The phone number is on the hotel notepaper.* ○ *Can you give me your phone number?*

photocopier /'fəʊtəʊkɒpiə/ *noun* a machine which makes a copy of a document by photographing and printing it

photocopy /'fəʊtəʊkɒpi/ *noun* a copy of a document made by photographing and printing it ○ *Make six photocopies of the letter.* ■ *verb* to make a copy of a document by photographing and printing it ○ *She photocopied the town plan.*

photocopying /'fəʊtəʊkɒpiɪŋ/ *noun* the act of copying a document by photographing and printing it □ **there is a mass of photocopying to be done** there are many documents waiting to be photocopied

photocopying bureau /'fəʊtəkɒpiɪŋ ˌbjʊərəʊ/ *noun* an office which photocopies documents for companies which do not possess their own photocopiers

photocopying service /'fəʊtəʊkɒpiɪŋ ˌsɜːvɪs/ *noun* a service that makes photocopies for customers ○ *The business centre has a photocopying service.*

physical map /'fɪzɪk(ə)l mæp/ *noun* a diagram showing mountains, rivers and other geographical features

physician /fɪ'zɪʃ(ə)n/ *noun* US a doctor (*formal*) ○ *Consult your physician before taking this medicine.* ○ *The tour will be accompanied by a qualified physician.*

pichet /'piːʃeɪ/ *noun* CATERING a small jug for serving carafe wine, usually holding a quarter-litre or half-litre

pick /pɪk/ *noun* **1.** the act of choosing, or the thing, person or place chosen □ **take your pick** choose what you want □ **the pick of the bunch, of the group** the best item in the group **2.** CATERING a small metal tool, like a long needle, used to remove flesh from shellfish or from nutshells, or to break up ice ○ *a lobster pick* ■ *verb* to choose something ○ *The board picked the finance director to succeed the retiring MD.* ○ *The Association has picked Paris for its next meeting.*

pickle /'pɪk(ə)l/ *noun* FOOD vegetables preserved in vinegar ■ *verb* CATERING to preserve e.g. vegetables in vinegar □ **pickled gherkins, pickled onions, pickled walnuts** gherkins, onions or walnuts preserved by soaking in vinegar and herbs

pick up /ˌpɪk 'ʌp/ *verb* **1.** to take a passenger into a vehicle ○ *He picked up two hitchhikers at the entrance to the motorway.* ○ *The coach will call to pick up passengers at the hotel.* **2.** to get better, to improve ○ *business or trade is picking up*

pickup and delivery service /ˌpɪkʌp ən dɪ'lɪv(ə)ri ˌsɜːvɪs/ *noun* BUSINESS a service which takes goods from the warehouse and delivers them to the customer

pickup point /'pɪkʌp pɔɪnt/ *noun* TRAVEL a place where a group of people arranges to be collected by a coach, etc.

pick-up station /'pɪk ʌp ˌsteɪʃ(ə)n/ *noun* CATERING the place in a kitchen where the prepared meals are left ready for the waiters to collect and deliver them

pickup truck /'pɪkʌp trʌk/ *noun* ROAD TRAVEL a type of small van with an open area for transporting goods

picnic /'pɪknɪk/ *noun* **1.** TOURISM an excursion with a meal eaten in the open air ○ *We have organised a picnic in the woods.* **2.** CATERING a meal eaten outdoors ■ *verb* to eat a picnic ○ *Picnicking is not allowed in the botanical gardens.* (NOTE: **picnicking – picnicked**)

picnic area /'pɪknɪk ˌeəriə/ *noun* CATERING a place where people can have a picnic

picnicker /'pɪknɪkə/ *noun* CATERING somebody who goes on a picnic ○ *The river bank is a favourite spot for picnickers.*

picnic lunch /'pɪknɪk lʌntʃ/ *noun* CATERING lunch eaten in the open air, taken with you in a bag, box or basket

pie /paɪ/ *noun* FOOD a cooked dish of pastry with a filling of meat or fruit, eaten hot or cold ○ *a slice of veal and ham pie* ○ *apple pie with ice cream*

pie chart /'paɪ tʃɑːt/ *noun* a diagram where information is shown as a circle cut up into sections of different sizes

pied-à-terre /pɪˌeɪ dɑː'teə/ *noun* a small flat or studio, used by someone as a temporary place to live ○ *She lives in the country but has a pied-à-terre in London.*

pier /pɪə/ *noun* SHIPS AND BOATS a construction going out into the water, used as a landing place for ships

pigeon /'pɪdʒən/ *noun* a fat grey bird which is common in towns ○ *Let's go and feed the pigeons in Trafalgar Square.* ◊ **wood pigeon**

pigeonhole /'pɪdʒənhəʊl/ *noun* one of a series of small spaces for filing documents or for putting letters for delivery to separate rooms or for collection ○ *There was a message in his pigeonhole when he returned to the hotel.*

pilaff /'piːlæf/, **pilau** *noun* FOOD an Eastern dish of rice with vegetables, herbs and spices, and sometimes with meat ○ *We had lamb pilaff.*

pilchard /'pɪltʃəd/ *noun* SEAFOOD a small fish similar to a herring, sold in tins

pilgrim /'pɪlɡrɪm/ *noun* TOURISM somebody who travels to an important religious place ○ *a coach carrying a group of 50 pilgrims to Lourdes* ○ *Pilgrims travel to Mecca in specially chartered planes.*

pilgrimage /'pɪlɡrɪmɪdʒ/ *noun* TOURISM a journey to an important religious place ○ *The church is organising a pilgrimage to Rome in April.*

pillar box /ˈpɪlə bɒks/ *noun* (*in Britain*) a cylindrical red metal container into which mail is put to be collected and delivered ○ *There's a pillar box at the corner of the street.*

pillow /ˈpɪləʊ/ *noun* a soft cushion on a bed which the head lies on when the person is lying down ○ *I like to sleep with two pillows.*

pillowcase /ˈpɪləʊkeɪs/, **pillowslip** /ˈpɪləʊslɪp/ *noun* a cloth bag to cover a pillow ○ *The maids change the room and put clean sheets and pillowcases on the beds every morning.*

pilot /ˈpaɪlət/ *noun* **1.** TRAVEL somebody who flies a plane ○ *The pilot reported bad visibility over the airport.* ◊ **captain**, **copilot** **2.** a test which, if successful, will then be expanded into a full operation ○ *The hotel group set up a pilot project to see if the proposed staff training scheme was efficient.* ○ *He is directing a pilot scheme for training unemployed young people.*

pimento /pɪˈmentəʊ/, **pimiento** *US* /pɪˈmjentəʊ/ *noun* VEGETABLES same as **sweet pepper**

pin /pɪn/ *noun* a small thin sharp metal object with a round piece at the top, used for fastening things such as pieces of cloth or paper ■ *verb* □ **to pin up a notice** to attach a notice to a wall or noticeboard with pins

pineapple /ˈpaɪnæp(ə)l/ *noun* FRUIT a fruit of a tropical plant, which has a tough knobbly skin, pale yellow flesh, and leaves sprouting from the top

pink gin /ˌpɪŋk ˈdʒɪn/ *noun* BEVERAGES a drink made by putting a little Angostura bitters into a glass, swirling it round and pouring it out, then adding gin

pint /paɪnt/ *noun* BEVERAGES a measure of liquids equalling one eighth of a gallon ○ *Two pints of bitter, please.* ○ *The recipe takes half a pint of milk.*

COMMENT: A British pint is equal to 0.568 of a litre; an American pint is equal to 0.473 of a litre. The pint is also used to measure seafood, such as prawns or mussels.

pip /pɪp/ *noun* CATERING a small seed

pipe /paɪp/ *verb* CATERING to squeeze soft food mixture through a small tube, so as to make decorative shapes ○ *Duchesse potatoes are piped into spiral shapes and cooked.*

pistachio, **pistachio nut** *noun* NUTS a small green tropical nut, eaten salted as an appetiser or used as a flavouring in sweet dishes, especially ice cream ○ *She had pistachio ice cream for dessert.*

piste /piːst/ *noun* SPORT a track for skiing

pit /pɪt/ *noun* CATERING the stone in some fruit such as cherries, plums, peaches, or dried fruit such as prunes and dates. ◊ **pitted**

pitch /pɪtʃ/ *verb* (*of a ship*) to move up and down lengthwise. Compare **roll**

pitcher /ˈpɪtʃə/ *noun* CATERING a large jug, often used to serve beer or cocktails

pith /pɪθ/ *noun* CATERING the soft white material under the skin of a lemon, orange or other citrus fruit

pitta bread /ˈpɪtə ˌbred/ *noun* BREAD, ETC. flat white unleavened bread, served with Greek and Turkish food

pitted /ˈpɪtɪd/ *adjective* CATERING having had the stone taken out ○ *pitted dates*

pizza /ˈpiːtsə/ *noun* FOOD an Italian savoury dish, consisting of a flat round piece of dough cooked with tomatoes, onions, cheese, and often sliced meat or vegetables on top. ◊ **deep pan pizza**

pizzeria /ˌpiːtsəˈriːə/ *noun* CATERING a restaurant which sells pizzas

pizzeria chef /ˌpiːtsəˈriːə ˌʃef/ *noun* CATERING a chef who prepares pizzas in a restaurant

place /pleɪs/ *noun* **1.** where something is or where something happens □ **to take place** to happen ○ *The meeting will take place in the conference room.* **2.** a position in a competition ○ *Three companies are fighting for first place in the package holiday market.* **3.** a job ○ *He was offered a place with a restaurant chain.* ○ *She turned down three places before accepting the one we offered.* ■ *verb* **1.** to put something somewhere ○ *The soup spoon is placed on the right-hand side of the place setting.* □ **to place a contract** to decide that a particular company will have the contract to do work □ **to place something on file** to file something ○ *He placed an order for 250 tins of instant coffee.* **2.** □ **to place staff** to find jobs for staff □ **how are you placed for work?** have you enough work to do?

placemat /ˈpleɪsmæt/ *noun* CATERING a piece of cloth, cork, etc., which a person's plate is put on to protect the table where there is no tablecloth. Also called **table mat**

place of birth /ˌpleɪs əv ˈbɜːθ/ *noun* the town where a person was born

place of issue /ˌpleɪs əv ˈɪʃuː/ *noun* the town where a passport was issued

place of work /ˌpleɪs əv ˈwɜːk/ *noun* the place, e.g. an office or a hotel, where a person works

place setting /'pleɪs ˌsetɪŋ/ *noun* CATER-ING a set of knives, forks, spoons, glasses, etc., for one person

places of interest /ˌpleɪsɪz əv 'ɪntrəst/ *plural noun* TOURISM buildings or parts of the countryside which are interesting to visit ○ *a tour to visit places of interest in south Italy* ○ *There are lots of places to visit within 50 miles of central London.*

plaice /pleɪs/ *noun* SEAFOOD a flat white sea fish ○ *fried fillets of plaice* (NOTE: The plural form is **plaice**.)

plain chocolate /ˌpleɪn 'tʃɒklət/ *noun* FOOD a dark, bitter chocolate

plain flour /ˌpleɪn 'flaʊə/ *noun* FOOD flour that has had no baking powder added to it

plain yoghurt /ˌpleɪn 'jɒgət/ *noun* DAIRY a yoghurt without any sweetening or flavouring

plan /plæn/ *noun* **1.** an idea or description of how you intend to do something **2.** a drawing which shows how something is arranged or how something will be built ○ *The designers showed us the first plans for the new hotel.* ■ *verb* to arrange how you are going to do something (NOTE: **planning – planned**) □ **to plan for an increase in visitors to the music festival** to change a way of doing things because you think there will be more visitors to the music festival

plane /pleɪn/ *noun* AIR TRAVEL same as **aeroplane** ○ *I intend to take the 5 o'clock plane to New York.* ○ *He could not get a seat on Tuesday's plane, so he had to wait until Wednesday.* ○ *There are twenty planes a day from London to Paris.*

planetarium /ˌplænɪ'teəriəm/ *noun* ENTERTAINMENT a domed building in which you sit and watch as pictures of the stars are projected against the ceiling ○ *We visited the planetarium with a school party.*

plane ticket /'pleɪn ˌtɪkɪt/ *noun* AIR TRAVEL a ticket which allows a passenger to travel by plane

planner /'plænə/ *noun* **1.** somebody who plans something, especially what buildings are to be built in an area **2.** a chart or notebook where you can write down the dates of future events

planning /'plænɪŋ/ *noun* **1.** BUSINESS the work of organising how something should be done, especially how a company should be run to make increased profits □ **long-term planning, short-term planning** making plans for a long or short period **2.** □ **the planning department** the section of a local government office which deals with requests for planning permission

'…buildings are closely regulated by planning restrictions' [*Investors Chronicle*]

planning permission /'plænɪŋ pəˌmɪʃ(ə)n/ *noun* BUSINESS an official document allowing a person or company to construct new buildings ○ *The group was refused planning permission.* ○ *We are waiting for planning permission before we can start building the cinema.* ○ *The land is to be sold with planning permission for a motel.*

plantain /'plænteɪn/ *noun* VEGETABLES the name given to various types of large banana used for cooking, which have a lower sugar content than dessert bananas

plat du jour /ˌplɑː duː 'ʒɔː/ *noun* CATER-ING a special dish prepared for the day and not listed in the printed menu (NOTE: **plat du jour** comes from the French phrase meaning 'dish of the day'.)

plate /pleɪt/ *noun* a flat dish for putting food on

plateau /'plætəʊ/ *noun* CATERING a French noun meaning large dish with a display of food (NOTE: The plural form is **plateaux**.) □ **a plateau de fromages** a large plate with a selection of cheeses

plated /'pleɪtɪd/ *adjective* CATERING served on plates □ **plated six-course meal** a meal of six courses, each served ready on the plate

'…the competition gave chefs just 30 minutes to prepare, cook and present two plated portions of a free-interpretation dish centred on a boneless loin of lamb' [*Caterer & Hotelkeeper*]

plated cover /ˌpleɪtɪd 'kʌvə/ *noun* CATERING part of a meal served on a plate

plateful /'pleɪtfʊl/ *noun* the quantity held by a plate

plate rack /'pleɪt ræk/ *noun* CATERING a device for holding several plates side by side as in a dishwasher

plate room /'pleɪt ruːm/ *noun* CATERING a room in a hotel where plates, glasses and cutlery are stored, ready for use in the restaurant

plate service /'pleɪt ˌsɜːvɪs/ *noun* CATERING a type of restaurant service, where the food is put onto the plate before the plate is carried to each guest

platform /'plætfɔːm/ *noun* RAIL TRAVEL a high pavement in a station, running alongside the track, where passengers can get on or off trains ○ *The train for Birmingham leaves from Platform 12.* ○ *The ticket office is on Platform 2.*

platinum card /'plætɪnəm kɑːd/ *noun* BUSINESS a credit card issued to very important customers with a high level of income, which gives privileges such as a higher spending limit, but also costs more than ordinary credit cards

platter /'plætə/ *noun* **1.** CATERING a large flat serving plate ○ *A huge joint of meat was carried in on a platter.* **2.** CATERING a large plate of prepared food, arranged in a decorative way □ **cheese platter, seafood platter, shellfish platter** large plate with various cheeses, fish or shellfish ○ *We ordered a seafood platter.*

play /pleɪ/ *verb* to take part in an enjoyable activity, especially a game, simply for the sake of amusement

playground /'pleɪɡraʊnd/, **play area** *noun* ENTERTAINMENT an area, especially round a building, where children can play ○ *There is a children's play area near the motel.*

playing cards /'pleɪɪŋ kɑːdz/ *plural noun* ENTERTAINMENT ordinary cards, marked in either diamonds, hearts, clubs, spades

plongeur /plɒn'ʒɜː/ *noun* CATERING a French noun meaning person who washes dishes in a restaurant

plonk /plɒŋk/ *noun* BEVERAGES inferior wine (*informal*) ○ *I bought a bottle of Spanish plonk from the supermarket.*

plough /plaʊ/ ♦ **snowplough**

ploughman's lunch /ˌplaʊmənz 'lʌntʃ/ *noun* FOOD a cold lunch, typically served in a pub, consisting of a plate of bread, cheese, pickle or chutney, and a pickled onion

pluck /plʌk/ *verb* CATERING to take the feathers off a bird, before it is cooked ○ *Ask the butcher to pluck the pheasants for you.*

plug /plʌɡ/ *noun* **1.** a device at the end of a wire for connecting a machine to the electricity supply **2.** a flat round rubber object which covers the hole in a bath or sink ○ *There is no plug in my bath.* **3.** □ **to give a plug to a new leisure centre** to publicise a new leisure centre (*informal*) **4.** same as **socket** ■ *verb* **1.** □ **to plug in** to connect a machine to the electricity supply ○ *The TV was not plugged in.* **2.** MARKETING to publicise or advertise something (*informal*) ○ *They ran six commercials plugging holidays in Spain.* (NOTE: **plugging – plugged**)

plum /plʌm/ *noun* FRUIT a gold, red or purple fruit with a smooth skin and a large stone

plum pudding /ˌplʌm 'pʊdɪŋ/ *noun* DESSERTS a rich fruit pudding, cooked by steaming and usually eaten at Christmas

plum tomato /ˌplʌm tə'mɑːtəʊ/ *noun* VEGETABLES a variety of tomato which is

longer and egg-shaped, the variety most usually used for canning

p.m. /ˌpiː 'em/, **P.M.** *US abbreviation* referring to the period between midday and midnight, in the afternoon or in the evening ○ *The train leaves at 6.50 p.m.* ○ *If you phone New York after 8 p.m. the calls are at a cheaper rate.*

pn *abbreviation* per night

PNR *abbreviation* AIR TRAVEL passenger name record

PO *abbreviation* post office

poach /pəʊtʃ/ *verb* CATERING to cook something, e.g. eggs without their shells or fish, in gently boiling liquid ○ *sole poached in white wine*

poached egg /ˌpəʊtʃt 'eɡ/ *noun* FOOD an egg which is taken out of its shell and cooked whole in boiling water, usually eaten on toast at breakfast

pocket /'pɒkɪt/ *noun* a small bag attached to the inside of a piece of clothing to hold money, keys and other small articles

point /pɔɪnt/ *noun* **1.** a place or position **2.** □ **the dollar gained two points** the dollar increased in value against another currency by two hundredths of a cent ■ *verb* □ **to point out** to show ○ *The report of the fire department points out the mistakes made by the builders of the hotel.* ○ *He pointed out that the bookings for the Christmas season were better than in previous years.*

'...banks refrained from quoting forward US/Hongkong dollar exchange rates as premiums of 100 points replaced discounts of up to 50 points' [*South China Morning Post*]

point of sale /ˌpɔɪnt əv 'seɪl/ *noun* MARKETING a place where a product is sold, e.g. a shop. Abbr **POS**

point-of-sale material /ˌpɔɪnt əv 'seɪl mə,tɪəriəl/ *noun* MARKETING display material used to advertise a product where it is being sold. Also called **POS material**

poison /'pɔɪz(ə)n/ *noun* MEDICAL a substance which can kill or harm when eaten, drunk, breathed in or touched □ **poison ivy, poison oak** North American plants whose leaves can cause a painful and itchy rash if touched ■ *verb* MEDICAL to kill or harm someone or something with poison

poisoning /'pɔɪz(ə)nɪŋ/ *noun* MEDICAL killing or harming someone or something with a poison

poisonous /'pɔɪz(ə)nəs/ *adjective* MEDICAL full of poison ○ *Some mushrooms are good to eat and some are poisonous.*

COMMENT: The commonest poisons, of which even a small amount can kill, are arsenic, cyanide and strychnine. Many common foods and drugs can be poisonous if taken in large doses. Common household materials such as bleach, glue and insecticides can also be poisonous. Some types of poisoning, such as Salmonella, can be passed to other people through lack of hygiene.

poivre /ˈpwɑːvrə/ *noun* SAUCES, ETC. a French noun meaning pepper

polar bear /ˌpəʊlə ˈbeə/ *noun* a big white bear which lives in the snow near the North Pole ○ *The explorers were attacked by polar bears.*

pole /pəʊl/ *noun* a long wooden or metal rod

polenta /pəˈlentə/ *noun* FOOD in Italian cooking, fine yellow maize meal cooked to a mush with water or stock, sometimes set, sliced, and served baked or fried

police escort /pəˌliːs ɪˈskɔːt/ *noun* a group of policemen who escort someone ○ *The president had a police escort to the airport.*

policy /ˈpɒlɪsi/ *noun* **1.** a set of decisions or rules on the general way in which something should be done (NOTE: The plural form is **policies**.) **2.** a contract between an insurance company and a person or organisation that wants insurance □ **an accident policy** an insurance which will pay if an accident occurs □ **all-risks policy** an insurance policy which covers risks of any kind, with no exclusions □ **a comprehensive**, **an all-in policy** an insurance policy which covers you against all risks which are likely to happen □ **contingent policy** a policy which pays out only if something happens, such as if the person named in the policy dies before the person due to benefit □ **to take out a policy** to sign the contract for an insurance and start paying the premiums ○ *She took out a life insurance* or *a house insurance policy.*

policy holder /ˈpɒlɪsi ˌhəʊldə/ *noun* FINANCE somebody who is insured by an insurance company

polish /ˈpɒlɪʃ/ *noun* a substance used to make things shiny (NOTE: The plural form is **polishes**.) ■ *verb* to rub something to make it shiny ○ *She polished the table until it shone.* ○ *Each bedroom has a mending kit and a shoe polishing kit.*

polite /pəˈlaɪt/ *adjective* pleasant towards other people, not rude ○ *We stipulate that our salesgirls must be polite to customers.* ○ *We had a polite letter from the hotel manager.*

politely /pəˈlaɪtli/ *adverb* in a pleasant way ○ *She politely answered the guests' questions.*

polyunsaturated fat /ˌpɒliʌnsætʃəreɪtɪd ˈfæt/ *noun* CATERING a fatty acid capable of absorbing more hydrogen, typical of vegetable and fish oils ○ *Vegetable oils and fish oils are polyunsaturated.*

polyvinyl chloride /ˌpɒlivɪnɪl ˈklɔːraɪd/ *noun* a type of plastic that is not biodegradable, used for floor coverings, clothes, shoes, pipes, etc. Abbr **PVC**

pomegranate /ˈpɒmɪɡrænɪt/ *noun* FRUIT a fruit with yellowish pink or red skin, masses of seeds and sweet red flesh ○ *Pomegranate juice stains badly.*

pony /ˈpəʊni/ *noun* a small horse ○ *My best friend lets me ride her pony sometimes.* (NOTE: The plural form is **ponies**.)

pony-trekking /ˈpəʊni ˌtrekɪŋ/ *noun* SPORT the activity of riding ponies in the country for pleasure ○ *We often go pony-trekking in the summer.* ○ *The hotel offers pony-trekking holidays in the mountains.* ◊ **horse-riding**

pool /puːl/ *noun* **1.** same as **swimming pool 2.** ENTERTAINMENT a game similar to snooker

poolroom /ˈpuːlruːm/ *noun* US ENTERTAINMENT a public room where you can play pool

pool table /ˈpuːl ˌteɪb(ə)l/ *noun* ENTERTAINMENT a table on which pool is played

poor /pɔː/ *adjective* **1.** with little or no money ○ *It is one of the poorest countries in the world, but the scenery is magnificent.* **2.** not very good ○ *We all complained about the poor service in the hotel coffee lounge.* ○ *Poor turnround time of aircraft can affect schedules.* ○ *The restaurant is okay but has poor air-conditioning* or *poor noise insulation.*

poorly /ˈpɔːli/ *adverb* badly ○ *The reception area is poorly laid out.* ○ *The tour was poorly planned.* □ **poorly paid staff** staff with low wages

popcorn /ˈpɒpkɔːn/ *noun* FOOD corn seed which is heated, sometimes with sugar, until it bursts, eaten as a snack and often served in large cardboard containers at cinemas and fairgrounds ○ *We always buy a carton of popcorn when we go to the cinema.*

poppadom /ˈpɒpədɒm/ *noun* BREAD, ETC. a thin round crisp Indian pancake, fried or grilled

Popsicle /ˈpɒpsɪk(ə)l/ *tdmk* US FOOD a trademark for a mixture of water and flavouring, frozen until solid with a stick in it ○ *I keep some Popsicles in the freezer for the kids.* (NOTE: The British English is **ice lolly**.)

popular /ˈpɒpjʊlə/ *adjective* liked by many people ○ *This is our most popular resort.* ○ *The South Coast is the most popular area for holidays.* □ **popular prices** prices which are low and therefore liked

pork /pɔːk/ *noun* MEAT fresh meat from pigs, as opposed to cured meat, which is bacon or ham (NOTE: There is no plural form.)

COMMENT: Roast pork is traditionally served with apple sauce and sage and onion stuffing. In some countries pork and other meat from pigs is not eaten as it is considered unclean by the religion of the country (this applies to the Muslim and Jewish religions).

pork pie /ˌpɔːk ˈpaɪ/ *noun* FOOD minced pork in a pastry case, usually eaten cold ○ *Let's buy a pork pie to eat on the picnic.*

porridge /ˈpɒrɪdʒ/ *noun* FOOD oatmeal cooked in water ○ *She had a bowl of porridge for breakfast.*

COMMENT: Porridge is served at breakfast; in Scotland it is traditionally served with salt, but elsewhere it is served with sugar and milk or cream.

porridge oats /ˈpɒrɪdʒ əʊts/ *plural noun* FOOD oats which have been crushed ready to be made into porridge

port /pɔːt/ *noun* **1.** SHIPS AND BOATS a harbour, a place where ships come to load or unload ○ *the port of Rotterdam* □ **to call at a port** to stop at a port to load or unload cargo or drop or taken on passengers **2.** BEVERAGES a dessert wine from Portugal, usually served after a meal **3.** SHIPS AND BOATS the left-hand side of a ship when facing the bow, also used of the left-hand side of an aircraft

port authority /ˈpɔːt ɔːˌθɒrɪti/ *noun* BUSINESS an organisation which runs a port

port charges /ˈpɔːt ˌtʃɑːdʒɪz/, **port dues** *plural noun* SHIPS AND BOATS payments which a ship makes to the port authority for the right to use the port

porter /ˈpɔːtə/ *noun* **1.** AIR TRAVEL somebody who carries luggage for travellers at an airport, a railway station, in a hotel, etc. (NOTE: In the USA and Canada they are called **'redcaps'**, because they wear red caps as part of their uniform.) **2.** a person who is on duty at the entrance to a building and checks on or helps people who want to come in or go out **3.** BEVERAGES a type of dark sweet beer brewed from malt

port installations /ˌpɔːt ɪnstəˈleɪʃ(ə)nz/ *plural noun* TRAVEL the buildings and equipment of a port

portion /ˈpɔːʃ(ə)n/ *noun* CATERING a small quantity, especially enough food for one person ○ *We serve ice cream in individual portions.* ○ *Foil-wrapped butter portions are served in a dish of ice.*

portion control /ˈpɔːʃ(ə)n kənˌtrəʊl/ *noun* CATERING keeping a check on the amount of food served by splitting it up into individual portions, e.g. by serving butter in small individual packets or pots

port of call /ˌpɔːt əv ˈkɔːl/ *noun* SHIPS AND BOATS a port at which a ship often stops

port of embarkation /ˌpɔːt əv ˌɪmbɑːˈkeɪʃ(ə)n/ *noun* SHIPS AND BOATS a port at which you get onto a ship

port of entry /ˌpɔːt əv ˈentri/ *noun* a place where passengers and goods may enter a country under the supervision of customs officials, e.g. a port or an airport

p.o.s. /ˈpiːəʊˈes/, **POS** *abbreviation* MARKETING point of sale

posada /pəˈsɑːdə/ *noun* HOTELS in a Spanish-speaking country, a hotel, pension, or hostel

posh /pɒʃ/ *adjective* expensive and attractive, or suitable for special occasions (*informal*) ○ *He took us for lunch to one of the poshest restaurants in town.*

position /pəˈzɪʃ(ə)n/ *noun* **1.** a situation or state of affairs □ **what is the cash position?** what is the state of the company's current account? **2.** a site, the place where a building is ○ *The hotel occupies a central position in the town.* ○ *The restaurant's lakeside position makes it very popular in summer.* **3.** a job, or a rank in an organisation ○ *to apply for a position as hotel manager* ○ *We have several positions vacant in our front-of-the-house area.* ○ *All the vacant positions have been filled.* ○ *She retired from her position in the corporate reservations department.* □ **he is in a key position** he has an important job **4.** (*at a bank, post office, check-in*) a separate place where a customer is dealt with □ **'position closed'** a notice to show that a counter is not open

positive cash flow /ˌpɒzɪtɪv ˈkæʃ fləʊ/ *noun* BUSINESS a situation where more money is coming into a company than is going out

POS material /ˌpiː əʊ ˈes məˌtɪəriəl/ *noun* MARKETING same as **point-of-sale material**

post /pəʊst/ *noun* **1.** a system of sending letters and parcels from one place to another ○ *He put the letter in the post.* ○ *The cheque was lost in the post.* ○ *Post to the Falkland Islands can take up to a week.* Also called **mail** □ **by post** using the postal services, not sending something by hand or by messenger ○ *to send the tickets by post* □ **we sent the order by first-class post** by the most expensive mail service, designed to be faster □ **to send a reply by return of post** to reply by the next post service □ **letter post**, **parcel post** a service for sending letters or parcels **2.** letters and parcels that are sent and received ○ *Has the post arrived yet?* ○ *My assistant opens the post as soon as it arrives.* ○ *The receipt was in this morning's post.* ○ *The tickets did not arrive by first post this morning.* **3.** a job, paid work in a company ○ *She is going to apply for a post as cashier.* ○ *We have three posts vacant.* ○ *All our posts have been filled.* ○ *We advertised three posts in the 'Hotel Gazette'.* Also called **position** ■ *verb* **1.** to send a letter or parcel ○ *We posted our confirmation of the booking last Wednesday.* **2.** □ **to post up a notice** to put a notice on a wall or on a noticeboard ○ *The courier posted up a list of ski runs which were open.*

postage /'pəʊstɪdʒ/ *noun* payment for sending a letter or parcel by post ○ *What is the postage to New Zealand?*

postage paid /ˌpəʊstɪdʒ 'peɪd/ *adjective* words printed on an envelope to show that the sender has paid the postage even though there is no stamp on it

postage stamp /'pəʊstɪdʒ stæmp/ *noun* a small piece of gummed paper which you buy from a post office and stick on a letter or parcel so it can be sent through the post

postal /'pəʊst(ə)l/ *adjective* referring to the post

postal charges /'pəʊst(ə)l ˌtʃɑːdʒɪz/, **postal rates** *plural noun* money to be paid for sending letters or parcels by post ○ *Postal charges are going up by 10% in September.*

postal order /'pəʊst(ə)l ˌɔːdə/ *noun* FINANCE a document which can be bought at a post office for sending small amounts of money through the post

postbox /'pəʊstbɒks/ *noun* a public box into which mail is put to be collected and delivered. Also called **letterbox 1**

postcard /'pəʊstkɑːd/ *noun* a piece of cardboard for sending a message by post (NOTE: With a picture on one side it is called a **picture postcard**.)

postcode /'pəʊstkəʊd/ *noun* letters and numbers used to indicate a town or street in an address (NOTE: The US English is **ZIP code**.)

poster /'pəʊstə/ *noun* MARKETING a large notice or advertisement to be stuck up on a wall ○ *In the underground we saw posters advertising holidays in Spain.*

poste restante /'pəʊst ˌrestɑːnt/ *noun* a system where letters can be addressed to someone at a post office, where they can be collected ○ *Send any messages to 'Poste Restante, Athens'.* (NOTE: The US English for this is **General Delivery**.)

post-free /ˌpəʊst 'friː/ *adverb* without having to pay any postage ○ *The timetable is obtainable post-free from the airline offices.*

postmark /'pəʊstmɑːk/ *noun* a mark stamped by the post office on a letter, covering the postage stamp, to show that the post office has accepted it, and giving the name of the post office or town and the date ○ *a letter with a London postmark* ■ *verb* to stamp a letter with a postmark ○ *The letter was postmarked New York.*

post office /'pəʊst ˌɒfɪs/ *noun* **1.** a building where you can do such things as buying stamps, sending letters and parcels and paying bills □ **sub-post office** a small post office, often part of a shop **2.** □ **the Post Office** a national organisation which deals with sending letters and parcels ○ *Post Office officials* or *officials of the Post Office* ○ *A Post Office van comes to collect the mail.*

'…travellers cheques cost 1% of their face value and can be purchased from any bank, main post offices, travel agents and several building societies' [*The Sunday Times*]

Post Office box number /ˌpəʊst ˌɒfɪs 'bɒks ˌnʌmbə/ *noun* a reference number used when asking for mail to be sent to a post office. Abbr **P.O. box number**

post-paid /ˌpəʊst 'peɪd/ *adjective* with the postage already paid ○ *The price is £5.95 post-paid.*

postpone /pəʊst'pəʊn/ *verb* to arrange for something to take place later than planned ○ *He postponed the meeting for a week.* ○ *They asked if they could postpone payment until the cash situation was better.*

postponement /pəʊs'pəʊnmənt/ *noun* the act of arranging for something to take place later than planned ○ *I had to change my appointments because of the postponement of the board meeting.*

post room /'pəʊst ruːm/ *noun* a room in an office where the post is sorted and sent to each department or collected from each department for sending

pot /pɒt/ *noun* a container made of glass, metal or clay ○ *Can we have a pot of tea for two, please?* ■ *verb* to put in a pot

potable /ˈpɒtəb(ə)l/ *adjective* clean and safe to drink ○ *The hotel has a potable water supply.*

potage /pɒˈtɑːʒ/ *noun* FOOD thick soup, especially one made from vegetables

potato /pəˈteɪtəʊ/ *noun* VEGETABLES a vegetable that grows from the roots of a plant, has a brown skin and white flesh, and can be eaten boiled, roasted, fried or baked ○ *Do you want any more potatoes?* ○ *We're having roast lamb and potatoes for Sunday lunch.*

COMMENT: In Britain potatoes were traditionally eaten at every main meal, along with another vegetable, such as cabbage, carrots, peas, etc. The potato is an important source of carbohydrate, but nowadays is replaced at some meals by pasta, rice or bread. More than a dozen different varieties are grown commercially in Britain, and some are better than others for different cooking purposes.

potato peeler /pəˈteɪtəʊ ˌpiːlə/ *noun* CATERING a special tool for peeling potatoes and other vegetables

pothole /ˈpɒthəʊl/ *noun* **1.** a hole in rock worn away by water ○ *They were exploring a pothole in the Mendip Hills.* **2.** ROAD TRAVEL a hole in a road surface ○ *The council still hasn't filled in the potholes in our street.*

potholer /ˈpɒthəʊlə/ *noun* SPORT somebody who climbs down inside pot-holes as a sport ○ *Several potholers were trapped in the cave by a flash flood.*

potholing /ˈpɒthəʊlɪŋ/ *noun* SPORT the sport of climbing down inside pot-holes ○ *We spent the weekend potholing in the limestone hills.*

potluck /pɒtˈlʌk/ *noun* □ **to take potluck** to take whatever food is served, with no possibility of choice

potted /ˈpɒtɪd/ *adjective* CATERING cooked or preserved in a vessel such as a pot or jar

potted shrimps /ˌpɒtɪd ˈʃrɪmps/ *plural noun* FOOD shrimps which have been cooked and put in a small pot with melted butter, served with lemon and brown bread and butter

poultry /ˈpəʊltri/ *noun* MEAT a general term for domestic birds kept for meat and egg production, e.g. chickens, turkeys, ducks etc. (NOTE: The word is mainly used in butchers' shops and recipe books.)

pound /paʊnd/ *noun* **1.** a measure of weight, equal to about 450 grams ○ *to sell oranges by the pound* ○ *a pound of oranges* ○ *Oranges cost 50p a pound.* ○ *She weighs 140 pounds.* (NOTE: In the USA, body weight is given in pounds, while in Britain it is given in stones; **pound** is usually written **lb** after figures: *25lb.*) **2.** FINANCE the currency used in the UK and many other countries (NOTE: This is usually written **£** before the figure: *£25.*) □ **a ten-pound note** a banknote for ten pounds

pound sterling /ˌpaʊnd ˈstɜːlɪŋ/ *noun* FINANCE the official term for the unit of money used in the UK

poussin /ˈpuːsæn/ *noun* MEAT a chicken reared to be eaten when very young and tender

powdered /ˈpaʊdəd/ *adjective* CATERING crushed so that it forms a fine dry dust ○ *a tin of powdered milk* ○ *an omelette made with powdered eggs*

powder room /ˈpaʊdə ruːm/ *noun* a women's toilet in a public place such as a restaurant or shop

power /ˈpaʊə/ *noun* electricity used to drive machines or devices

power pack /ˈpaʊə pæk/ *noun* a portable source of electricity

power point /ˈpaʊə pɔɪnt/ *noun* a wall plug which supplies electricity ○ *There is a power point for shavers in the bathroom.* ○ *Each bedroom has a safe large enough for a laptop and with in-built power point for recharging.*

pp *abbreviation* HOTELS per person

pppn *abbreviation* HOTELS per person per night

PR *abbreviation* MARKETING public relations ○ *a PR man* ○ *the PR department*

praline /ˈpreɪliːn/ *noun* FOOD a sweet made of crushed nuts and caramelised sugar

prawn /prɔːn/ *noun* SEAFOOD a type of shellfish, like a large shrimp ○ *She ordered a prawn curry and rice.* ○ *I had a prawn and mayonnaise sandwich.*

prawn cocktail /ˌprɔːn ˈkɒkteɪl/ *noun* FOOD a starter consisting of shelled prawns in mayonnaise and tomato dressing, served in a glass

pre- /priː/ *prefix* before or in front of. ◊ **pre-booked, prepay, pre-theatre menu**

pre-booked /ˌpriː ˈbʊkt/ *adjective* booked in advance

precinct /ˈpriːsɪŋkt/ *noun* US an administrative district in a town ○ *the 10th precinct police station*

precipitation /prɪˌsɪpɪˈteɪʃ(ə)n/ *noun* water which falls from clouds as rain, snow or hail ○ *Precipitation in the mountain areas is higher than in the plains.*

precook /priːˈkʊk/ *verb* CATERING to cook food completely or partially in advance, especially before it is sold, so that it only need minimal cooking or reheating before it is eaten

predict /prɪˈdɪkt/ *verb* to say in advance what will happen

pre-existing /ˌpriː ɪɡˈzɪstɪŋ/ *adjective* existing from before, already present

pre-existing condition /ˌpriː ɪɡˌzɪstɪŋ kənˈdɪʃ(ə)n/ *noun* MEDICAL an illness from which someone was already suffering when he or she took out a medical insurance policy

preheat /priːˈhiːt/ *verb* CATERING to heat an oven, dish, or other item before using it

premises /ˈpremɪsɪz/ *plural noun* a building and the land it stands on □ **on the premises** in the building ○ *There is a doctor on the premises at all times.*

premium /ˈpriːmiəm/ *noun* **1.** same as **insurance premium 2.** a special prize **3.** BUSINESS the amount to be paid to a landlord or a tenant for the right to take over a lease ○ *flat to let with a premium of £10,000* ○ *Annual rent: £8,500, premium: £25,000.* **4.** an extra charge

premium cabin, premium section *noun* AIR TRAVEL part of a plane where the passengers have special service, usually the first-class section

premium offer /ˈpriːmiəm ˌɒfə/ *noun* MARKETING a free gift offered to attract more customers

premium quality /ˈpriːmiəm ˌkwɒlɪti/ *adjective* top quality ○ *The hamburger chain says it only uses premium-quality beef.*

premium rate /ˈpriːmiəm reɪt/ *noun* HOTELS a special rate for high-quality rooms

premix /ˈpriːmɪks/ *noun* a product consisting of previously mixed ingredients or elements

prepaid /priːˈpeɪd/ *adjective* paid in advance

prepaid reply card /ˌpriːpeɪd rɪˈplaɪ kɑːd/ *noun* MARKETING a stamped addressed card which is sent to someone so that they can reply without paying the postage

prepay /priːˈpeɪ/ *verb* to pay in advance (NOTE: **prepaying – prepaid**)

prepayment /priːˈpeɪmənt/ *noun* payment in advance □ **to ask for prepayment of a fee** to ask for the fee to be paid before the work is done

prep counter /ˈprep ˌkaʊntə/ *noun* CATERING a metal counter on which food is prepared

pre-plated /ˌpriː ˈpleɪtɪd/ *adjective* CATERING put on the plates in the kitchen before being served

'…a classier food and beverage service will be on offer. The airline will be experimenting with chefs on board to serve food as meals will no longer arrive pre-plated' [*Business Traveller*]

pre-plating /ˌpriː ˈpleɪtɪŋ/ *noun* CATERING a type of service where food is served ready on the plate

pre-register /ˌpriː ˈredʒɪstə/ *verb* HOTELS to register a guest before he or she actually checks into the hotel

pre-registration /ˌpriː ˌredʒɪˈstreɪʃ(ə)n/ *noun* HOTELS the registration of guests before they actually check into the hotel, so as to save time when a group of guests arrive all together

presentation /ˌprez(ə)nˈteɪʃ(ə)n/ *noun* **1.** the act of showing something, e.g. a document □ **free admission on presentation of the card** you do not pay to go in if you show this card **2.** a demonstration or exhibition of a proposed plan ○ *The manufacturer made a presentation of her new product line to possible hotel customers.* ○ *We have asked two PR firms to make presentations of proposed publicity campaigns.*

preservative /prɪˈzɜːvətɪv/ *noun* CATERING a substance, e.g. sugar or salt, added to food to preserve it by slowing natural decay caused by bacteria ○ *The label says that the jam contains no artificial preservatives.*

preserve /prɪˈzɜːv/ *noun* FOOD a food consisting of fruit or vegetables, cooked and kept in jars or cans for future use, e.g. jam or marmalade ○ *Small pots of grapefruit preserve were on the breakfast table.* ■ *verb* CATERING to treat something such as food so that it keeps for a long time

pre-service /ˌpriː ˈsɜːvɪs/ *adjective* CATERING before a meal is served

pre-service checks /ˌpriː ˈsɜːvɪs tʃeks/ *plural noun* CATERING checks to make sure that the tables and food are ready, before the meal is served

preserving pan /prɪˈsɜːvɪŋ pæn/ *noun* CATERING a very large pan for making jam or chutney

press /pres/ *noun* **1.** newspapers and magazines □ **the local press** newspapers which are sold in a small area of the country □ **the national press** newspapers which are sold in all parts of the country **2.** CATERING a device or machine for crushing fruit or vegetables to extract the juice ○ *garlic press* ■ *verb* **1.** to iron the creases from clothes **2.** CATERING to crush fruit or seeds to extract juice or oil

press conference /'pres ˌkɒnf(ə)rəns/ *noun* MARKETING a meeting where newspaper and TV reporters are invited to hear news of e.g. a new product, a takeover bid or a court case

press cutting /'pres ˌkʌtɪŋ/ *noun* a piece cut out of a newspaper or magazine, which refers to an item which you find interesting

pressing service /'presɪŋ ˌsɜːvɪs/ *noun* same as **valet service**

press release /'pres rɪˌliːs/ *noun* MARKETING a sheet giving news about something which is sent to newspapers and TV and radio stations so that they can use the information

pressure cooker /'preʃə ˌkʊkə/ *noun* CATERING a type of pan with a tight-fitting lid, which cooks food rapidly under pressure

pressure steaming /'preʃə ˌstiːmɪŋ/ *noun* CATERING a method of cooking vegetables or meat in which a purpose-built steamer is used to create steam under high pressure so that the food cooks rapidly ○ *Pressure steaming is much quicker than steaming in the usual way.*

pressure steam oven /ˌpreʃə 'stiːm ˌʌv(ə)n/ *noun* CATERING a special oven where food can be steamed under pressure

pressurisation /ˌpreʃəraɪ'zeɪʃ(ə)n/, **pressurization** *noun* AIR TRAVEL a system where the pressure inside an aircraft is increased for the comfort of the passengers

pressurise /ˌpreʃəraɪ'zeɪʃ(ə)n/, **pressurize** *verb* AIR TRAVEL to increase the pressure inside an aircraft to keep a safe and comfortable environment, even at very high altitude ○ *the pressurised cabin*

COMMENT: Jet passenger aircraft fly at very high altitudes for reasons of fuel economy. At around 30,000 to 40,000 feet the air is very cold and too thin to breathe. To make a safe and comfortable environment for passengers and crew, warm air is pumped into the cabin to increase the temperature and pressure.

pre-theatre menu /ˌpriː ˌθɪətə 'menjuː/ *noun* CATERING a special dinner menu of light dishes, prepared for quick service to customers who are going on to the theatre after dinner

prevention /prɪ'venʃən/ *noun* the act of stopping something from happening

price /praɪs/ *noun* **1.** money which has to be paid to buy something □ **bargain price** a very cheap price □ **cut price** a cheaper price

than usual □ **discount price** the full price less a discount □ **holidays in the £6–700 price range** different types of holidays, selling for between £600 and £700 **2.** □ **to increase in price** to become more expensive ○ *Petrol has increased in price* or *the price of petrol has increased.* □ **to increase prices, to raise prices** to make items more expensive □ **to cut prices** to make items suddenly cheaper □ **to lower prices, to reduce prices** to make items cheaper ■ *verb* to give a price to a product ○ *We sell mainly package tours priced at under £200.* □ **competitively priced** sold at a low price to compete with a rival product or service □ **the company has priced itself out of the market** the company has raised its prices so high that its products do not sell

price control /'praɪs kənˌtrəʊl/ *noun* BUSINESS legal measures to stop prices rising too fast

price cutting /'praɪs ˌkʌtɪŋ/ *noun* BUSINESS a sudden lowering of prices

price differential /'praɪs dɪfəˌrenʃəl/ *noun* BUSINESS the difference in price between products in a range

price fixing /'praɪs ˌfɪksɪŋ/ *noun* BUSINESS an illegal agreement between companies to charge the same price for competing products

price freeze /'praɪs friːz/ *noun* BUSINESS a period when prices are not allowed to be increased

price label /'praɪs ˌleɪb(ə)l/, **price tag** /'praɪs tæg/, **price ticket** /'praɪs ˌtɪkɪt/ *noun* a label which shows a price

price list /'praɪs lɪst/ *noun* BUSINESS a sheet giving prices of goods for sale

price per person /ˌpraɪs pɜː 'pɜːs(ə)n/ *noun* the price for one adult

price range /'praɪs reɪndʒ/ *noun* BUSINESS a series of prices for similar products from different suppliers

price war /'praɪs wɔː/ *noun* BUSINESS a competition between companies to get a larger market share by cutting prices

pricing /'praɪsɪŋ/ *noun* the work of deciding on the prices at which products are to be sold

primavera /ˌpriːmə'veərə/ *adjective* CATERING made with an assortment of fresh spring vegetables, especially sliced as an accompaniment to pasta, meat or seafood

prime /praɪm/ *adjective* most important, first-rate ○ *a fish restaurant in a prime seafront location* ○ *A prime Soho nightclub is for sale.*

prime costs /ˌpraɪm ˈkɒsts/ *plural noun* BUSINESS the cost of sales plus the cost of staff

principal /ˈprɪnsɪp(ə)l/ *noun* BUSINESS **1.** a person or company which is represented by an agent ○ *The agent has come to London to see his principals.* **2.** money invested or borrowed on which interest is paid ○ *to repay principal and interest*

print /prɪnt/ *noun* words made on paper with a machine □ **to read the small print**, **the fine print on a contract** to read the conditions of a contract which are often printed very small so that people will not be able to read them easily ■ *verb* **1.** to make letters on paper with a machine ○ *printed agreement* ○ *printed regulations* **2.** to write capital letters or letters which are not joined together ○ *Please print your name and address on the top of the form.*

printer /ˈprɪntə/ *noun* a machine which prints from instructions given by a computer system, as in a kitchen, where orders are instructed by a keypad and the printer prints tickets for each item of food ordered

print out /ˌprɪnt ˈaʊt/ *verb* to print information from a computer through a printer

private /ˈpraɪvət/ *adjective* **1.** belonging to one person, not to everyone □ **room with private bath** room with a bathroom attached to it, which is only used by the occupant of the room and by no one else **2.** belonging to individuals, but not to the state or the general public □ **'private'** belonging to a person, and not open to the public (*notice*) ○ *To see the manager, knock at the door marked 'private'.* **3.** not holding an official position in a government ○ *a private citizen* ○ *a private individual* □ **the private sector** all companies which are owned by private shareholders, not by the state

private enterprise /ˌpraɪvət ˈentəpraɪz/ *noun* BUSINESS businesses which are owned by private shareholders, not by the state ○ *The theme park is funded by private enterprise.*

private grounds /ˌpraɪvət ˈɡraʊndz/ *plural noun* HOTELS gardens round a hotel, which can only be used by the guests, and not by the public

private hotel /ˌpraɪvət həʊˈtel/ *noun* HOTELS a hotel which is family owned and run, in which the proprietor may refuse to accept someone as a guest

private ownership /ˌpraɪvət ˈəʊnəʃɪp/ *noun* BUSINESS a situation where a company is owned by private shareholders

private property /ˌpraɪvət ˈprɒpəti/ *noun* buildings or land which belong to a private person and not to the public

private sector /ˈpraɪvət ˌsektə/ *noun* BUSINESS all companies which are owned by private shareholders, not by the state ○ *The leisure centre is funded completely by the private sector.* ○ *Salaries in the private sector have increased faster than in the public.*

private transfer /ˌpraɪvət ˈtrænsfɜː/ a transfer from an airport to a hotel by a car rather than in a bus with other people

private view /ˌpraɪvət ˈvjuː/, **private viewing** *noun* ENTERTAINMENT a preview of an exhibition for a group of invited guests

PRO *abbreviation* MARKETING public relations officer

procedure /prəˈsiːdʒə/ *noun* a method for doing something

process /ˈprəʊses/ *verb* **1.** □ **to process figures** to sort out numbers to make them easily understood ○ *The sales figures are being processed by our accounts department.* ○ *Flight data is being processed by our computer.* **2.** to deal with something in the usual routine way ○ *to process a flight reservation* or *an insurance claim* ○ *Claims for missing baggage are processed in our insurance department.* **3.** CATERING to treat food in a way so that it will keep longer or become more palatable

COMMENT: Food can be processed in many different ways: some of the commonest are drying, freezing, canning, bottling and chilling.

processed cheese /ˌprəʊsest ˈtʃiːz/ *noun* DAIRY a product made by beating and mixing one or more types of cheese and adding colouring, flavouring and emulsifiers

processed meats /ˌprəʊsest ˈmiːts/ *plural noun* MEAT products made from meat that has been treated in some way, e.g. bacon or sausages

processing /ˈprəʊsesɪŋ/ *noun* **1.** the work of sorting information **2.** □ **the processing of a claim for insurance** the work of dealing with a claim for insurance through the usual office routine in the insurance company

processor /ˈprəʊsesə/ *noun* a machine or person that processes

product /ˈprɒdʌkt/ *noun* an item of goods that is made or a service that is offered

professional /prəˈfeʃ(ə)n(ə)l/ *adjective* **1.** referring to one of the professions ○ *The accountant sent in his bill for professional services.* ○ *We had to ask our lawyer for professional advice on the contract.* **2.** expert or skilled ○ *Her work is very professional.* ○ *They did a very professional job in designing the new reception area.* **3.** doing work for money ○ *a professional tennis player* ■ *noun* a skilled person, or a person who does skilled work for money ○ *A golf professional is attached to the hotel.*

professional body /prəˌfeʃ(ə)n(ə)l 'bɒdi/ *noun* BUSINESS an organisation representing members who work in one of the professions, such as lawyers, doctors or accountants

professional qualifications /prəˌfeʃ(ə)n(ə)l ˌkwɒlɪfɪ'keɪʃ(ə)nz/ *plural noun* BUSINESS documents showing that someone has successfully finished a course of study which allows him or her to work in one of the professions

proficiency /prə'fɪʃ(ə)nsi/ *noun* skill in doing something ○ *She has a certificate of proficiency in English.* ○ *To get the job he had to pass a proficiency test.*

proficient /prə'fɪʃ(ə)nt/ *adjective* skilled, capable of doing something well ○ *She is quite proficient in English.*

profit /'prɒfɪt/ *noun* BUSINESS money gained from a sale which is more than the money spent □ **to make a profit** to have more money as a result of a deal □ **to move into profit** to start to make a profit ○ *The restaurant is breaking even now, and expects to move into profit within the next two months.* □ **to show a profit** to make a profit and state it in the company accounts ○ *We are showing a small profit for the first quarter.*

profitability /ˌprɒfɪtə'bɪlɪti/ *noun* BUSINESS **1.** ability to make a profit **2.** the amount of profit made as a percentage of costs

profitable /'prɒfɪtəb(ə)l/ *adjective* BUSINESS making a profit

profitably /'prɒfɪtəbli/ *adverb* BUSINESS making a profit

profit and loss account /ˌprɒfɪt ən 'lɒs ə,kaʊnt/ *noun* BUSINESS a statement of a company's expenditure and income over a period of time, almost always one calendar year, showing whether the company has made a profit or loss. Abbr **P&L account** (NOTE: The US English is **profit and loss statement** or **income statement**.)

COMMENT: The balance sheet shows the state of a company's finances at a certain date; the profit and loss account shows the movements which have taken place since the end of the previous accounting period, that is, since the last balance sheet.

profit centre /'prɒfɪt ˌsentə/ *noun* BUSINESS a person or department which is considered separately for the purposes of calculating a profit

profiterole /prə'fɪtərəʊl/ *noun* DESSERTS a small ball of choux pastry filled with cream and usually served with chocolate sauce

profit margin /'prɒfɪt ˌmɑːdʒɪn/ *noun* BUSINESS the percentage difference between sales income and the cost of sales

profit-sharing /'prɒfɪt ˌʃeərɪŋ/ *noun* BUSINESS an arrangement where employees get a share of the profits of the company they work for ○ *The company runs a profit-sharing scheme.*

programme /'prəʊɡræm/ *noun* **1.** a plan of things which will be done ○ *the programme of events during the music festival* **2.** ENTERTAINMENT a printed list of items in an entertainment ○ *a theatre programme* **3.** ENTERTAINMENT a show or item on TV or radio ○ *Did you see the travel programme on Italy last night?* ○ *There's a new food programme starting tonight.* (NOTE: [all senses] The US spelling is **program**.)

prohibit /prəʊ'hɪbɪt/ *verb* to ban or forbid something ○ *Women wearing shorts are prohibited from visiting the monastery.*

prohibitive /prəʊ'hɪbɪtɪv/ *adjective* MARKETING referring to a price that is so high that you cannot afford to pay it ○ *The cost of travel to the Far East is prohibitive.*

projector /prə'dʒektə/ *noun* an apparatus for making pictures appear on a screen ○ *The projector broke down so we couldn't see the end of the film.*

promote /prə'məʊt/ *verb* **1.** to give someone a better job ○ *He was promoted from chef de rang to head waiter.* **2.** MARKETING to use methods such as publicity or special offers to persuade people to buy something □ **to promote a new product** to try to increase the sales of a new product by publicity, by a sales campaign or TV commercials or by free gifts

promotion /prə'məʊʃ(ə)n/ *noun* **1.** a move up to a more important job □ **to earn promotion** to work hard and efficiently and so be moved to a more important job **2.** □ **promotion of a product** the selling of a new product by publicity, a sales campaign, TV commercials or free gifts ○ *We have increased our promotion budget.* ○ *The store has a special promotion on French cheese.*

promotional /prə'məʊʃ(ə)n(ə)l/ *adjective* MARKETING used in an advertising campaign ○ *The admen are using balloons as promotional material.*

'…the promotional fare (now available until March) offers a £100 saving for passengers who book the airline's early morning flight and return the same day' [*Business Traveller*]

promotional trip /prəˈməʊʃ(ə)n(ə)l trɪp/ *noun* a trip during which passengers are offered the opportunity to buy cheap or duty-free goods

promotion chances, promotion prospects *plural noun* the possibility of being moved to a more important job ○ *He ruined his promotion prospects when he argued with the chef.*

proof /pruːf/ *noun* BEVERAGES the relative strength of an alcoholic drink expressed by a number that is twice the percentage of the alcohol present in the liquid ■ *adjective* having a particular alcoholic strength that is expressed by a proof number

-proof /pruːf/ *suffix* meaning 'not affected by'

proof of identity /ˌpruːf əv aɪˈdentɪti/ *noun* proof in the form of a document such as a driving licence that a person is who they say they are ○ *The police asked her for proof of identity.*

property /ˈprɒpəti/ *noun* **1.** the things that a person owns **2.** buildings or land ○ *After the storm, damage to property* or *property damage was considerable.* ◇ **the property market 1.** possibilities for letting offices ○ *The commercial property market is booming.* **2.** possibilities for developing offices as investments **3.** the buying or selling houses or flats by individual people

proprietor /prəˈpraɪətə/ *noun* the owner ○ *the proprietor of a hotel* or *a hotel proprietor*

prosciutto /prəˈʃuːtəʊ/ *noun* MEAT Italian cured ham, usually served cold and uncooked in thin slices

protect /prəˈtekt/ *verb* to keep someone or something safe from harm or danger ○ *Travellers are protected against unscrupulous hoteliers by international agreement.* ○ *The engine is protected by a plastic cover.* ○ *The cover is supposed to protect the machine from dust.*

protection /prəˈtekʃən/ *noun* something which protects ○ *The legislation offers no protection to part-time workers.*

protein /ˈprəʊtiːn/ *noun* CATERING a compound which is an essential part of living cells, one of the elements in food which is necessary to keep the human body working properly ○ *The doctor told her she needed more protein in her diet.*

COMMENT: Proteins are necessary for growth and repair of the tissue of the body; they are mainly formed of carbon, nitrogen and oxygen in various combinations as amino acids. Certain foods (such as beans, meat, eggs, fish and milk) are rich in protein.

protest strike /ˈprəʊtest straɪk/ *noun* a strike in protest at a particular grievance

Provençale /ˌprɒvɒnˈsɑːl/ *adjective* CATERING prepared with olive oil, garlic, herbs, and tomatoes

province /ˈprɒvɪns/ *noun* **1.** a large division of a country ○ *the ten provinces of Canada* **2.** □ **the provinces** the parts of any country away from the capital ○ *There are fewer retail outlets in the provinces than in the capital.*

provincial /prəˈvɪnʃəl/ *adjective* referring to a province or to the provinces ○ *a provincial government* ○ *a provincial branch of a national bank*

provisional /prəˈvɪʒ(ə)n(ə)l/ *adjective* temporary, not final or permanent ○ *She made a provisional booking for a table for ten people.* ○ *He drew up a provisional advertising budget.* ○ *They faxed through their provisional acceptance of the contract.*

provisionally /prəˈvɪʒ(ə)nəli/ *adverb* temporarily, not finally ○ *The contract has been accepted provisionally.*

prune /pruːn/ *noun* a dried plum

COMMENT: Stewed prunes in syrup are sometimes offered as part of a 'full English breakfast'.

pt *abbreviation* BEVERAGES pint

pub /pʌb/ *noun* BARS same as **public house** (*informal*) ○ *The hotel has no restaurant, but you can go to the pub next door for meals.*

pub grub /ˈpʌb grʌb/, **pub food** *noun* CATERING simple snacks which are typically available in most pubs, e.g. pies, sandwiches and salads

public /ˈpʌblɪk/ *adjective* **1.** referring to all the people in general **2.** referring to the government or the state ■ *noun* □ **the public**, **the general public** the people □ **in public** in front of everyone.

public address system /ˌpʌblɪk əˈdres ˌsɪstəm/ *noun* MARKETING a system of loudspeakers, by which messages can be given to the public in e.g. a supermarket, exhibition centre or airport. Also called **PA system**

publican /ˈpʌblɪkən/ *noun* BARS somebody who keeps a public house ○ *Publicans work very long hours.*

Public Analyst /ˌpʌblɪk ˈænəlɪst/ noun a government official who examines products to analyse their contents

public bar /ˌpʌblɪk ˈbɑː/ noun BARS a bar in a public house which is less comfortable than the saloon bar and where the drinks may be slightly cheaper

public baths /ˌpʌblɪk ˈbɑːðz/ plural noun ENTERTAINMENT a large public building with a swimming pool

public conveniences /ˌpʌblɪk kənˈviːniənsɪz/ plural noun toilets which are open for anyone to use

public funds /ˌpʌblɪk ˈfʌndz/ plural noun government money available for expenditure

public gardens /ˌpʌblɪk ˈgɑːd(ə)ns/ plural noun ENTERTAINMENT a space in a town where plants are grown and the public is allowed to visit, usually free of charge

Public Health Inspector /ˌpʌblɪk ˈhelθ ɪnˌspektə/ noun same as **Environmental Health Officer**

public holiday /ˌpʌblɪk ˈhɒlɪdeɪ/ noun ENTERTAINMENT a day when all employees rest and enjoy themselves instead of working

COMMENT: Public holidays in England and Wales are: New Year's Day, Good Friday, Easter Monday, the first Monday in May (May Day), the last Monday in May (Spring Bank Holiday), the last Monday in August (Summer Bank Holiday), Christmas Day and Boxing Day (December 26th). In Scotland, the first Monday in August and January 2nd are also public holidays, but Easter Monday and the last Monday in August are not. In the USA, New Year's Day, 21st January (Martin Luther King Day), February 12th (Lincoln's Birthday), the third Monday in February (Washington's birthday), the last Monday in May (Memorial Day), July 4th (Independence Day), the first Monday in September (Labor Day), the second Monday in October (Columbus Day), 11th November (Veterans' Day), the fourth Thursday in November (Thanksgiving) and Christmas Day are public holidays nationally, although there are other local holidays.

public house /ˌpʌblɪk ˈhaʊs/ noun BARS **1.** a licensed building selling beer, wines, spirits, and often food, to the public for consumption on the premises. Compare **bar**, **off-licence 2.** US a small hotel or inn

COMMENT: In Britain a public house (or pub) usually offers simple meals, soft drinks and coffee for people who do not want to drink alcohol. Most pubs do not offer accommodation, but some do. Pubs normally have at least two bars, often called the 'public bar' and the 'lounge bar' or 'saloon bar' (the second is more expensive, and has more comfortable seating). Children are usually allowed into pubs, especially if they are part of a group eating food, and some pubs have special children's rooms.

publicity /pʌˈblɪsɪti/ noun MARKETING efforts to attract the attention of the public to products or services by mentioning them in the media

publicity agency /pʌˈblɪsɪti ˌeɪdʒənsi/, **publicity bureau** /pʌˈblɪsɪti ˌbjʊərəʊ/ noun MARKETING an office which organises publicity for companies that do not have publicity departments

publicity budget /pʌˈblɪsɪti ˌbʌdʒɪt/ noun MARKETING money allowed for expected expenditure on publicity

publicity department /pʌˈblɪsɪti dɪˌpɑːtmənt/ noun BUSINESS a section of a company which organises the company's publicity

publicity expenditure /pʌˈblɪsɪti ɪkˌspendɪtʃə/ noun MARKETING money spent on publicity

public ownership /ˌpʌblɪk ˈəʊnəʃɪp/ noun BUSINESS ownership of industries by the state. Also called **state ownership**

public phone /ˌpʌblɪk ˈfəʊn/ noun a telephone which anyone can use, either by paying cash or by using a card ○ *There's a public phone in the hotel foyer.*

public relations /ˌpʌblɪk rɪˈleɪʃ(ə)nz/ plural noun BUSINESS the work of keeping good relations between an organisation and the public and ensuring that people know what the organisation is doing and are likely to approve of it ○ *a public relations man* ○ *She works in public relations.* ○ *A public relations firm handles all our publicity.* Abbr **PR** □ **a public relations exercise** a campaign to improve public relations

public relations officer /ˌpʌblɪk rɪˈleɪʃ(ə)nz ˌɒfɪsə/ noun BUSINESS somebody in an organisation who is responsible for public relations activities. Abbr **PRO**

public rooms /ˌpʌblɪk ˈruːmz/ plural noun HOTELS rooms in a hotel which are used by both non-residents and guests (as opposed to 'guest rooms')

public sector /ˈpʌblɪk ˌsektə/ noun nationalised industries and services ○ *a report on wage rises in the public sector* ○ *on public sector wage settlements*

public transport /ˌpʌblɪk ˈtrænspɔːt/ noun TRAVEL transport which is used by any member of the public

public transport system /ˌpʌblɪk ˈtrænspɔːt ˌsɪstəm/ noun TRAVEL a system of trains, buses, etc., used by the general public

published price /ˌpʌblɪʃd ˈpraɪs/ *noun* AIR TRAVEL the price which an airline suggests the ticket should be sold at, though it is often reduced by travel agencies, etc.

pud /pʊd/ *noun* FOOD same as **pudding** (*informal*) ○ *steak and kidney pud* ○ *What's for pud?* (NOTE: Very informal, used by children, but also sometimes by adults as a joke.)

pudding /ˈpʊdɪŋ/ *noun* **1.** CATERING same as **dessert** ○ *What do you want for pudding?* ○ *I've eaten too much, so I won't have any pudding.* ○ *What's on the menu for pudding?* **2.** FOOD food made with flour and suet, which is cooked by boiling or steaming ○ *steak and kidney pudding* ○ *treacle pudding*

pudding basin /ˈpʊdɪŋ ˌbeɪs(ə)n/ *noun* CATERING a bowl used for cooking steamed puddings

puff pastry /ˌpʌf ˈpeɪstri/ *noun* BREAD, ETC. a type of soft pastry made from flour and butter, in which air is trapped by repeated folding and rolling of the dough

pull /pʊl/ *verb* to move something towards you □ **to pull a pint** to serve a pint of beer from a cask in the cellar, by pulling on the beer pull

pull out /ˌpʊl ˈaʊt/ *verb* **1.** ROAD TRAVEL to drive away from the side of the road towards the middle ○ *The bus suddenly pulled out in front of us.* **2.** to start to leave a station (*train*) ○ *The train was pulling out as the party arrived on the platform.*

pulp /pʌlp/ *noun* a soft mass that results when something with liquid in it is crushed ■ *verb* **1.** to crush something into pulp **2.** to remove the soft fleshy tissue from fruit or vegetables

pulse /pʌls/ *noun* FOOD a general term for seeds that grow in pods ○ *Pulses are used a lot in Mexican cooking.*

> COMMENT: Very many species of vegetable have this type of fruit. The term is often applied to edible seeds of leguminous plants (lentils, beans and peas) used as food.

pump /pʌmp/ *noun* a device for transferring liquid from one place to another, such as for serving beer or petrol ■ *verb* to transfer liquid from one place to another using a pump ○ *All our beer is hand-pumped.*

pumpkin /ˈpʌmpkɪn/ *noun* VEGETABLES a large round orange-coloured vegetable

> COMMENT: Pumpkins are used as decorations for Halloween (31st October). Each pumpkin is hollowed out, and holes cut to imitate eyes, nose and a mouth with teeth.

A lighted candle is put inside so that the whole pumpkin glows orange.

pumpkin pie /ˌpʌmpkɪn ˈpaɪ/ *noun* DESSERTS a pie made of pumpkin flavoured with cinnamon, nutmeg and other spices ○ *Pumpkin pie is a favourite American dish.*

punch /pʌntʃ/ *noun* BEVERAGES a drink made with a mixture of fruit juice, spices, and often wine or spirits, usually served hot

punctual /ˈpʌŋktʃuəl/ *adjective* on time ○ *The commuter trains are never punctual.*

punctuality /ˌpʌŋktʃuˈælɪti/ *noun* the quality of being on time and never being late ○ *an airline with a reputation for punctuality*

punctually /ˈpʌŋktʃuəli/ *adverb* on time ○ *The train left punctually at 18.00.*

pungent /ˈpʌndʒənt/ *adjective* CATERING strong and sharp in flavour or odour ○ *a particularly pungent type of goat's cheese* ○ *The pungent odour of curry came from the kitchen.*

punt /pʌnt/ *noun* **1.** SHIPS AND BOATS a long flat-bottomed boat, which is pushed with a long pole **2.** FINANCE the currency used in the Republic of Ireland before the euro ■ *verb* to gamble, to bet on something

purchase /ˈpɜːtʃɪs/ *noun* an item which has been bought □ **to make a purchase** to buy something ■ *verb* to buy something □ **to purchase something for cash** to pay cash for something

purchase book /ˈpɜːtʃɪs bʊk/ *noun* BUSINESS a written record of purchases

purchase ledger /ˈpɜːtʃɪs ˌledʒə/ *noun* BUSINESS a book in which expenditure is noted

purchase order /ˈpɜːtʃɪs ˌɔːdə/ *noun* BUSINESS an official order made out by a purchasing department for goods which a company wants to buy

purchaser /ˈpɜːtʃɪsə/ *noun* somebody who buys something ○ *Purchasers should examine the goods bought before taking them away from the shop.*

purchase tax /ˈpɜːtʃɪs tæks/ *noun* BUSINESS a tax paid on things which are bought

purchasing /ˈpɜːtʃɪsɪŋ/ *noun* buying

purchasing department /ˈpɜːtʃɪsɪŋ dɪˌpɑːtmənt/ *noun* BUSINESS a section of a restaurant, hotel, or other business which deals with buying of stock, raw materials and equipment

purchasing manager /ˈpɜːtʃɪsɪŋ ˌmænɪdʒə/ *noun* BUSINESS the head of a purchasing department

purchasing officer /ˈpɜːtʃɪsɪŋ ˌɒfɪsə/ *noun* BUSINESS somebody in an organisation who is responsible for buying stock, raw materials or equipment

purchasing power /'pɜːtʃɪsɪŋ ˌpaʊə/ *noun* BUSINESS the quantity of goods which can be bought by a group of people or with a particular amount of money ○ *the decline in the purchasing power of the pound*

pure /pjʊə/ *adjective* with nothing added ○ *The drink is made from pure orange juice.*

'...the word 'pure' should be used only to describe a single food to which nothing has been added – sugar or honey, for instance' [*Food Standards Agency*]

puree, purée *noun* FOOD a semi-liquid pulp made by mashing and crushing a vegetable or fruit ○ *apple puree* ○ *She made some strawberry purée to serve with the ice cream.* ■ *verb* CATERING to make something into a puree ○ *pureed tomatoes* ○ *She decided to puree the potatoes.*

purser /'pɜːsə/ *noun* TRAVEL a member of the crew of an aircraft or ship who deals with financial matters and, on a ship, also helps to look after the passengers ○ *See the purser if you have a complaint about your cabin.*

pursuit /pə'sjuːt/ *noun* a pastime, hobby, or leisure activity

push /pʊʃ/ *verb* to press or to move something by pressing ○ *He pushed the button for the ground floor.*

pushbike /'pʊʃbaɪk/ same as **bicycle**

put /pʊt/ *verb* to lay or stand something in a particular place □ **to stay put** to stay where you are (*informal*)

put back /ˌpʊt 'bæk/ *verb* to move a watch or clock to an earlier time ○ *Put your watches back one hour when you cross from France to England.*

put forward /ˌpʊt 'fɔːwəd/ *verb* to move a clock or watch to a later time ○ *When crossing from England to France, watches should be put forward one hour.*

put off /ˌpʊt 'ɒf/ *verb* to delay ○ *The visit to the winery has been put off till Friday.*

putt /pʌt/ ENTERTAINMENT *noun* a short shot on a green in golf ○ *He sank a fifteen-foot putt to win the game.* ■ *verb* to hit a short shot in golf ○ *He putted much better than his opponent.*

putter /'pʌtə/ *noun* ENTERTAINMENT a golf club for putting

putting green /'pʌtɪŋ griːn/ *noun* ENTERTAINMENT **1.** an area on a golf course where the ground is even and the grass is very short, allowing short shots to be made close to the hole **2.** a small golf course where only short shots are needed

put up /ˌpʊt 'ʌp/ *verb* to find a place for someone to sleep ○ *When the blizzard closed the airport, stranded travellers were put up in local schools.*

PVC *abbreviation* polyvinyl chloride

Q

QAU *abbreviation* Quality Assurance Unit

quad room /'kwɒd ruːm/ *noun* HOTELS a room for four people, usually with four single beds

quail /kweɪl/ *noun* MEAT a little game bird, often eaten roasted or stuffed

quails' eggs /'kwaɪlz egz/ *plural noun* FOOD tiny eggs, which are hard-boiled and served as toppings on canapés

quaint /kweɪnt/ *adjective* picturesque, oddly old-fashioned ○ *We stopped at a quaint old pub.* ○ *They live in a quaint little village in Devon.*

qualification /ˌkwɒlɪfɪ'keɪʃ(ə)n/ *noun* an official recognition of a standard of achievement, e.g. a degree or diploma ○ *to have the right qualifications for the job*

qualify /'kwɒlɪfaɪ/ *verb* **1.** □ **to qualify for** to be in the right position for, to be entitled to ○ *The company does not qualify for a government grant.* ○ *She qualifies for unemployment pay.* **2.** □ **to qualify as** to follow a specialised course and pass examinations so that you can do a certain job ○ *She has qualified as a hotel manager.* ○ *He will qualify as a solicitor next year.*

quality /'kwɒlɪti/ *noun* what something is like, how good or bad something is ○ *There is a market for good quality secondhand bar equipment.* □ **we sell only quality farm produce** we sell only farm produce of the highest grade

'...having discussed the new quality assurance scheme with fellow hoteliers, tourist centres and quality assurance staff, I have found that many are deeply concerned about the effect of the harmonised standards on good-quality, mid-range hotels throughout the country. I have joined the AA scheme because it provides a quality percentage – 70% is good quality – to go with my hotel's two-star rating. It seems ridiculous that each hotel is still given a quality percentage by the Quality Assurance Unit at its annual inspection, but that this is kept secret. How can that benefit anyone?' [*Caterer & Hotelkeeper*]

Quality Assurance Unit /ˌkwɒləti ə 'ʃɔːrəns ˌjuːnɪt/ *noun* TOURISM inspectors from the English Tourism Council who visit hotels and give percentage marks for quality. Abbr **QAU**

quality control /'kwɒlɪti kən,trəʊl/ *noun* BUSINESS the work of checking that the quality of a product is good

quality controller /'kwɒlɪti kən,trəʊlə/ *noun* BUSINESS somebody who checks the quality of a product

quality label /'kwɒlɪti ,leɪb(ə)l/ *noun* BUSINESS a label stating the quality of something

quality percentage /ˌkwɒlɪti pə 'sentɪdʒ/ *noun* BUSINESS marks for quality given under an inspection scheme

quantity /'kwɒntɪti/ *noun* **1.** an amount or number of items ○ *a small quantity of illegal drugs* ○ *He bought a large quantity of spare parts.* **2.** a large amount ○ *The company offers a discount for quantity purchase.*

quantity discount /ˌkwɒntɪti 'dɪskaʊnt/ *noun* BUSINESS a price reduction given to someone who buys a large amount of goods

quantity survey /'kwɒntɪti ,sɜːveɪ/ *noun* BUSINESS a calculation of the amount of materials and cost of labour needed for a construction project

quantity surveyor /ˌkwɒntɪti sə'veɪə/ *noun* BUSINESS somebody who calculates the amount of materials and cost of labour needed for a construction project

quarantine /'kwɒrəntiːn/ *noun* MEDICAL a situation in which a person, animal or ship just arrived in a country is kept isolated for a period of time in case he, she or it carries a serious disease ○ *The animals were put in quarantine on arrival at the port.* ○ *A ship in quarantine shows a yellow flag.* ■ *verb* to put a person or animal in quarantine

COMMENT: Animals coming into Great Britain are quarantined for six months because of the danger of rabies. People who are suspected of having an infectious disease can be kept in quarantine for a period which varies according to the incubation period of the disease. The main diseases concerned are cholera, yellow fever and typhus.

quart /kwɔːt/ *noun* CATERING a measure of liquid equal to one quarter of a gallon

COMMENT: A British quart is equal to 1.136 litres; a US quart is equal to 0.946 of a litre.

quarter /'kwɔːtə/ *noun* **1.** one of four equal parts ○ *He paid only a quarter of the normal fare because he works for the airline.* □ **a quarter of a litre, a quarter litre** 250 millilitres □ **a quarter of an hour** 15 minutes □ **three quarters** 75% □ **three quarters of an hour** 45 minutes ○ *Three quarters of the staff are less than thirty years old.* **2.** a period of three months □ **first quarter, second quarter, third quarter, fourth quarter or last quarter** periods of three months from January to the end of March, from April to the end of June, from July to the end of September, from October to the end of the year **3.** *US* FINANCE a 25 cent coin

quarter day /'kwɔːtə deɪ/ *noun* a day at the end of a quarter, when rents or fees should be paid

quarterly /'kwɔːtəli/ *adjective* happening every three months, or four times a year

quarterly sales return /ˌkwɔːtəli 'seɪlz rɪˌtɜːn/ *noun* BUSINESS a report of sales made each quarter

quay /kiː/ *noun* SHIPS AND BOATS a place in a harbour where ships tie up

quayside /'kiːsaɪd/ *noun* SHIPS AND BOATS the edge of a dock where ships tie up ○ *Customs formalities are carried out on the quayside.*

queen size bed /ˌkwiːn saɪz 'bed/ *noun* a double bed which is wider and longer than normal, but slightly smaller than a king size bed

question /'kwestʃ(ə)n/ *noun* **1.** words which need an answer ○ *The manager refused to answer questions about the fire.* ○ *The market research team prepared a series of questions to test the public's reactions to the new uniform for the airline cabin crew.* **2.** a problem or matter ○ *He raised the question of what would happen if the tour company got into difficulties.* ○ *The main question is that of cost.* ○ *The tourist board has discussed the question of a national advertising campaign.* ■ *verb* **1.** to ask somebody questions ○ *The police questioned the bar staff for four hours.* **2.** to suggest that something may be wrong ○ *We all question how accurate the computer printout is.*

questionnaire /ˌkwestʃə'neə/ *noun* MARKETING a printed list of questions, especially used in market research ○ *to send out a questionnaire to test the opinions of users*

of the booking system ○ *to answer* or *to fill in a questionnaire about holidays abroad*

queue /kjuː/ *noun* **1.** a line of people or things such as cars, waiting one behind the other for something ○ *to form a queue* or *to join a queue* ○ *Queues formed at the ticket offices when the news of the fare reductions got out.* **2.** a series of documents or telephone calls which are dealt with in order □ **his order went to the end of the queue** his order was dealt with last ■ *verb* to stand in a line waiting for something ○ *groups of tourists queueing to get on their buses* ○ *When food was rationed, people had to queue for bread.* ○ *We queued for hours to get tickets.* (NOTE: The US English is **to stand in line**.)

quiche /kiːʃ/ *noun* FOOD a savoury tart made of a pastry case filled with a mixture of eggs and milk, with other ingredients such as onion, bacon, vegetables or cheese added ○ *a slice of ham and mushroom quiche* or *of spinach quiche*

quiche Lorraine /ˌkiːʃ lə'reɪn/ *noun* FOOD a quiche with a filling of small pieces of bacon and sometimes cheese

quick-freeze /ˌkwɪk 'friːz/ *verb* CATERING to preserve food by cooling it quickly to 0°C or less

quiet /'kwaɪət/ *adjective* not noisy ○ *The hotel is in the quietest part of the town.* ○ *Currency exchanges were quieter after the government's statement on exchange rates.* ○ *The brochure said that the rooms were quiet, but ours looked out over a busy main road.* ■ *noun* a state in which there is little or no noise ○ *We like the peace and quiet of the little mountain villages.*

quince /kwɪns/ *noun* FRUIT a hard yellow or orange fruit, shaped like an apple or pear and used for making jelly

quinine /kwɪ'niːn/ *noun* MEDICAL an alkaloid drug made from the bark of cinchona, a South American tree

COMMENT: Quinine was formerly used to treat the fever symptoms of malaria, but is not often used now because of its side-effects. Symptoms of quinine poisoning are dizziness and noises in the head. Small amounts of quinine have a tonic effect and are used in tonic water.

quiz /kwɪz/ *noun* ENTERTAINMENT a game where questions are put to competitors

quiz night /'kwɪz naɪt/ *noun* ENTERTAINMENT a night at a pub when a quiz is held

Quorn /kwɔːn/ *tdmk* FOOD a trademark for a vegetable protein used in cooking as a meat substitute

quota /ˈkwəʊtə/ *noun* a fixed amount of something which is allowed ○ *The government has imposed an import quota on cars.*

quote /kwəʊt/ *verb* **1.** to repeat words used by someone else, especially to repeat a reference number ○ *In reply please quote this number.* ○ *When making a complaint please quote the batch number printed on the box.* ○ *He replied, quoting the number of the account.* **2.** to calculate the probable cost of something ○ *to quote a price for supplying 100 chairs* ○ *Their prices are always quoted in dollars.* ○ *He quoted me a price of £1,026.* ○ *Can you quote for supplying 200 cases of wine?* ■ *noun* an estimate of the probable cost of something (*informal*) ○ *to give someone a quote for supplying a computer system* ○ *We have asked for quotes for refitting the bar.* ○ *His quote was the lowest of three.* ○ *We accepted the lowest quote.*

R

rabbit /'ræbɪt/ *noun* a common wild animal with grey fur, long ears and a short white tail, used as food

COMMENT: Most rabbit on sale in Britain is farmed. Wild rabbit has a gamey flavour but is not commonly offered on menus. Rabbit stew or rabbit pie are the commonest ways of cooking it.

rabid /'ræbɪd/ *adjective* MEDICAL suffering from rabies ○ *She was bitten by a rabid dog.*

rabies /'reɪbiːz/ *noun* MEDICAL a very serious viral disease transmitted to humans by infected animals that causes convulsions and inability to move ○ *Dogs are put in quarantine in case they are infected with rabies.*

COMMENT: Rabies affects the mental balance, and the symptoms include difficulty in breathing or swallowing and an intense fear of water (hydrophobia) to the point of causing convulsions at the sight of water.

RAC /'ɑː 'eɪ 'siː/ *abbreviation* ROAD TRAVEL Royal Automobile Club

rack /ræk/ *noun* a frame to hold flat thin objects such as letters or pieces of toast

rack of lamb /ˌræk əv 'læm/ *noun* MEAT best end of neck of lamb, a joint for roasting

rack rate /'ræk reɪt/ *noun* HOTELS the price for rooms in a hotel which is advertised in the hotel, but which can be discounted

'The discount approach is typified by the hotel chain which is cutting its winter rack rates (the published tariff) by up to 50% for its European hotels' [*Business Travel*]

'...only 9.5% of customers paid full rack rate for a room last year, compared with 13.6% in the previous year and 28% four years ago' [*Caterer & Hotelkeeper*]

raclette /ræ'klet/ *noun* FOOD a Swiss dish consisting of slices of melted cheese served on boiled potatoes or bread

radiator /'reɪdieɪtə/ *noun* **1.** a water-filled metal panel for heating a room ○ *When we arrived at the hotel our room was cold, but we switched the radiators on.* ○ *Turn the radiator down – it's boiling in here.* **2.** ROAD TRAVEL a water-filled metal panel for cooling a car engine ○ *The radiator overheated causing the car to break down.*

radicchio /ræ'diːtʃiəʊ/ *noun* VEGETABLES a variety of chicory with reddish-purple and white leaves, usually eaten raw in salads

radio /'reɪdiəʊ/ *noun* a system for sending out or receiving messages using atmospheric waves, or an apparatus which does this ○ *They got the news by radio.* ○ *We always listen to BBC radio when we're on holiday.* ■ *verb* to send a message using a radio ○ *The stranded party radioed for help.*

radio cab /'reɪdiəʊ kæb/, **radio taxi** /'reɪdiəʊ 'tæksi/ *noun* ROAD TRAVEL a taxi which is in contact with its base by radio, and so can be called quickly to pick up a client ○ *It will be quicker to phone for a radio cab.*

radiopager /'reɪdiəʊˌpeɪdʒə/ same as **pager**

radish /'rædɪʃ/ *noun* VEGETABLES a small red root vegetable with a pungent flavour, eaten raw in salads

raft /rɑːft/ *noun* SHIPS AND BOATS a flat boat made of pieces of wood or logs tied together

rafting /'rɑːftɪŋ/ *noun* SPORT the activity of floating down a river on a raft. ◊ **whitewater canoeing**

RAGB *abbreviation* CATERING Restaurateurs Association of Great Britain

rail /reɪl/ *noun* RAIL TRAVEL a system of travel using trains ○ *Six million commuters travel to work by rail each day.* ○ *Rail travellers are complaining about rising fares.* ○ *Rail travel is cheaper than air travel.*

railcar /'reɪlkɑː/ *noun* RAIL TRAVEL a single coach with its own motor, carrying passengers by rail

railcard /'reɪlkɑːd/ *noun* RAIL TRAVEL an identity card which you can buy which allows you to buy rail tickets at specially reduced prices

railpass /'reɪlpɑːs/ *noun* RAIL TRAVEL a special ticket, paid for in advance, which allows unlimited travel by train in a country, over a limited period of time

railroad /'reɪlrəʊd/ *noun US* same as **railway**

railroad schedule /'reɪlrəʊd ˌʃedjuːl/ noun RAIL TRAVEL a train timetable, a list showing times of arrivals and departures of trains

railway /'reɪlweɪ/, **railroad** US /'reɪlrəʊd/ noun RAIL TRAVEL a system using trains to carry passengers and goods ○ *a railway station* ○ *a railway line* ○ *the British railway network* □ **the railway(s)** a country's railway system

railway line /'reɪlweɪ laɪn/ noun RAIL TRAVEL a set of metal rails on which trains run ○ *Please cross the railway line by the footbridge.*

railway lost property office /ˌreɪlweɪ lɒst 'prɒpəti ˌɒfɪs/ noun RAIL TRAVEL an office which collects objects which people have left behind in trains and keeps them until their owners collect them

railway station /'reɪlweɪ ˌsteɪʃ(ə)n/ noun RAIL TRAVEL a place where trains stop and passengers get on and off. Also called **train station**

rain /reɪn/ noun drops of water which fall from the clouds ○ *The rain stopped us from visiting the archaeological site.* ■ *verb* to fall as rain ○ *It rained all day, so we could not visit the gardens.*

rained off /ˌreɪnd 'ɒf/ adjective cancelled, because of rain ○ *The cricket match was rained off.*

rainfall /'reɪnfɔːl/ noun the amount of water which falls as rain on a particular area over a given period ○ *The annual rainfall on the mountains is higher than in the valley.*

rainstorm /'reɪnstɔːm/ noun heavy rain accompanied by wind ○ *The rainstorm last night caused some flooding.*

rainy /'reɪni/ adjective with a lot of rain (NOTE: **rainier – rainiest**)

rainy season /'reɪni ˌsiːz(ə)n/ noun a period of the year when it rains a lot ○ *The rainy season lasts from April to August.*

COMMENT: The phrase 'rainy season' is only used of areas where there is a very marked difference between the seasons. It is not used of Britain or any other European country.

raisin /'reɪz(ə)n/ noun FRUIT a dried grape

COMMENT: Raisins are larger than currants or sultanas, and can have seeds in them; they are all forms of dried grapes.

raki /'rɑːki/ noun BEVERAGES a Turkish alcoholic drink, flavoured with aniseed

Ramadan /'ræmədæn/ noun ENTERTAINMENT a Muslim religious festival, the ninth month of the Muslim year, during which believers are not allowed to eat or drink between sunrise and sunset

ramble /'ræmbəl/ ENTERTAINMENT noun a walk for pleasure in the country ○ *We're going for a ramble through the beech woods.* ■ *verb* to go for a walk for pleasure in the country ○ *We went rambling last weekend.*

rambler /'ræmblə/ noun ENTERTAINMENT somebody who goes for walks for pleasure in the country ○ *A group of ramblers came into the pub.*

rambutan /'ræmbuːtæn/ noun FRUIT a tropical fruit grown in South-East Asia, which is similar to the lychee but has a rough hairy skin

ramekin /'ræməkɪn/ noun CATERING a small dish for baking food in an oven, or food cooked in this type of dish

ramp /ræmp/ noun a sloping part of the ground, going from one level to another ○ *The pub has had a ramp installed so that people in wheelchairs can get into the garden.*

ranch /rɑːntʃ/ noun (*in America*) a farm where horses or cattle are reared

rancher /'rɑːntʃə/ noun somebody who owns or runs a ranch

ranch holiday /'rɑːntʃ ˌhɒlɪdeɪ/ noun TOURISM a holiday spent on a ranch, usually riding horses

rancid /'rænsɪd/ adjective CATERING referring to butter that tastes bad because it is stale ○ *This butter tastes rancid.*

rancidity /ræn'sɪdɪti/ noun the state of being rancid

rang /rɒŋ/ noun CATERING a section of a restaurant comprising a group of tables served by one waiter, the 'chef de rang' (NOTE: **rang** comes from a French noun meaning 'position' or 'station'.)

range /reɪndʒ/ noun **1.** a series of buildings or mountains in line **2.** a choice or series of things which are available ○ *We have a range of holidays at all prices.* **3.** CATERING a large cooking stove, usually with two or more ovens ■ *verb* to spread or to vary ○ *Holidays range in price from £150 to £850 per person, depending on the type of accommodation provided.*

ranger /'reɪndʒə/ noun somebody who looks after a forest or park

rangette /rɒn'get/ noun a small portable cooker that can be used for cooking in a hotel room

rank /ræŋk/ noun the degree of importance or superiority of somebody or something in relation to others ■ *verb* to classify in order of importance ○ *Hotels are ranked in order of luxury in the guidebook.*

rapid /'ræpɪd/ *adjective* fast or quick □ **we offer 5% discount for rapid settlement** we take 5% off the price if the customer pays quickly

rapid transit system /,ræpɪd 'trænzɪt ,sɪstəm/ *noun* RAIL TRAVEL a transport system which allows passengers to travel rapidly around a metropolitan area, e.g. an underground train network

rare /reə/ *adjective* CATERING (*of meat or fish*) very lightly cooked ○ *How would you like your steak? – Rare!*

rasher /'ræʃə/ *noun* MEAT a slice of bacon ○ *'Two rashers of bacon and a sausage, please!'*

raspberry /'rɑːzb(ə)ri/ *noun* FRUIT a small red soft fruit shaped like a tiny cup ○ *Could I have some raspberries and cream, please?* ○ *We had scones with raspberry jam.*

rat /ræt/ *noun* a small furry animal like a large mouse which has a long tail and can carry disease ○ *Rats live in the sewers in the city.* ○ *Bubonic plague is a disease which is transmitted to people by fleas from rats.*

> COMMENT: The black rat (*Rattus rattus*) lives in attics and lofts; the brown rat (*Rattus norvegicus*) is larger and lives in holes under buildings and in sewers. Both species carry diseases such as typhoid.

ratafia /,rætə'fiə/ *noun* BREAD, ETC. a sweet biscuit or drink flavoured with almonds

ratatouille /,rætə'twiː/ *noun* FOOD a Mediterranean vegetable stew of onions, tomatoes, aubergines, peppers and courgettes cooked in olive oil

rate /reɪt/ *noun* **1.** the amount of money charged for something, e.g. for providing a service or for working for a particular period of time □ **the going rate** the usual or the current rate of payment □ **letter rate, parcel rate** the postage for sending a letter or a parcel, calculated by weight ○ *It is more expensive to send a parcel letter rate but it will get there quicker.* □ **the market rate** the normal price in the market **2.** □ **to calculate costs on a fixed exchange rate** to calculate costs on an exchange rate which does not change ■ *verb* to classify something ○ *The restaurant has been rated among the best in the town.*

rated /'reɪtɪd/ *adjective* classified as being of good quality ○ *a Michelin-rated establishment*

rate of exchange /,reɪt əv ɪks'tʃeɪndʒ/ *noun* FINANCE same as **exchange rate** ○ *The current rate of exchange is 0.6 euros to the pound.*

rate of interest /,reɪt əv 'ɪntrəst/ *noun* BUSINESS same as **interest rate**

rating /'reɪtɪŋ/ *noun* the act of classifying or valuing

rating system /'reɪtɪŋ ,sɪstəm/ *noun* HOTELS a way of classifying things such as hotels and restaurants according to the quality of the service that they provide

ravioli /,rævi'əʊli/ *noun* FOOD a dish made from small squares of pasta sealed around a meat, cheese, or vegetable filling

raw /rɔː/ *adjective* in its original state, uncooked ○ *Sushi is a Japanese dish of cold rice and raw fish.* ○ *I don't like raw onions in my salad.*

razor /'reɪzə/ *noun* an instrument with a very sharp blade for removing hair by shaving

razor socket /'reɪzə ,sɒkɪt/ *noun* a socket in a bathroom where an electric razor can be plugged in. Also called **shaver point**

reach /riːtʃ/ *verb* to arrive at a place or at a point ○ *The plane reaches Hong Kong at midday.* ○ *The coach reached its destination three hours late.* ○ *I did not reply because your letter never reached me.*

read /riːd/ *verb* to look at and understand written words

reader board /'riːdə bɔːd/ *noun* an information board for guests in a hotel's lobby

reading lamp /'riːdɪŋ læmp/ *noun* a small lamp on a desk or beside a bed, for use when reading or writing

ready /'redi/ *adjective* **1.** prepared ○ *Are you all ready to leave yet?* ○ *Why isn't the coach here? – the group are all ready and waiting to go.* **2.** fit to be used ○ *You can't go to your room yet, because it isn't ready.* ○ *Is my dry cleaning ready yet?*

ready cash /,redi 'kæʃ/, **ready money** /,redi 'mʌni/ *noun* FINANCE money which is immediately available for payment

ready-cooked /'redi kʊkt/ *adjective* CATERING cooked in advance

real ale /,rɪəl 'eɪl/ *noun* BEVERAGES traditional beer, served directly from a wooden barrel or pumped by hand

reality tourism /ri,æliti 'tʊərɪz(ə)m/ *noun* travel to areas of the world considered politically unstable or less developed, in order to experience the way of life there at first hand

rear-view mirror /,rɪə vjuː 'mɪrə/ *noun* ROAD TRAVEL a mirror inside a car which enables the driver to see what is behind without turning his or her head

rear windscreen wiper /ˌrɪə ˈwɪndskriːn ˌwaɪpə/ *noun* ROAD TRAVEL a device on a vehicle which wipes rain away from the rear window

reboard /riːˈbɔːd/ *verb* TRAVEL to go back onto a ship, plane, train or bus again ○ *After visiting the church, the party will reboard the coach and drive to the hotel.*

receipt /rɪˈsiːt/ *noun* **1.** a piece of paper showing that money has been paid or that something has been received ○ *Did you get a receipt for the items you purchased?* ○ *Please produce your receipt if you want to exchange items.* **2.** the act of receiving something ○ *Goods will be supplied within thirty days of receipt of order.* ○ *Invoices are payable within thirty days of receipt.* ○ *On receipt of the confirmation, the tickets were sent to the customer.* □ **to acknowledge receipt of a letter** to write to tell someone that you have received his or her letter ○ *We acknowledge receipt of your letter of the 15th.* ■ *verb* BUSINESS to stamp or to sign a document to show that it has been received, or to stamp an invoice to show that it has been paid

receipt book /rɪˈsiːt bʊk/ *noun* BUSINESS a book of blank receipts to be filled in when purchases are made

receipts /rɪˈsiːts/ *plural noun* BUSINESS money taken in sales ○ *to itemise receipts and expenditure* ○ *Receipts are down against the same period of last year.*

receive /rɪˈsiːv/ *verb* **1.** to get something which has been sent ○ *We only received our tickets the day before we were due to leave.* **2.** to meet or to welcome a visitor ○ *The group was received by the mayor.*

receiver /rɪˈsiːvə/ *noun* **1.** BUSINESS an official put in charge of a bankrupt company ○ *The receiver has been called in to run the hotel group.* **2.** the part of a telephone which you lift and speak into

receiving /rɪˈsiːvɪŋ/ *noun* HOTELS the task of taking in supplies purchased for use in a hotel or restaurant

receiving clerk /rɪˈsiːvɪŋ klɑːk/ *noun* HOTELS somebody whose job is to check supplies coming into a hotel or restaurant

reception /rɪˈsepʃən/ *noun* **1.** same as **reception area 2.** ENTERTAINMENT a big party held to welcome special guests ○ *There's a big reception at the embassy tonight.* ○ *There will be a champagne reception for the delegates.*

reception area /rɪˈsepʃən ˌeəriə/ *noun* HOTELS the reception desk and the area

round it, usually where seats are provided, current newspapers or magazines, and sometimes a coffee machine

reception clerk /rɪˈsepʃ(ə)n klɑːk/ *noun* HOTELS somebody who works at the reception desk

reception desk /rɪˈsepʃ(ə)n desk/ *noun* **1.** HOTELS a desk where guests or visitors register or say who they have come to see when arriving at a hotel or office **2.** CATERING a high desk at the entrance to a restaurant where the reception head waiter greets the guests and organises the reservation of tables

reception head waiter /rɪˌsepʃən hed ˈweɪtə/ *noun* CATERING somebody who is on duty at the reception desk in a restaurant, who greets guests and organises the reservation of tables

receptionist /rɪˈsepʃənɪst/ *noun* HOTELS somebody in a hotel, restaurant or office who meets guests or visitors and answers telephone enquiries

reception manager /rɪˈsepʃən ˌmænɪdʒə/ *noun* BUSINESS the person in a hotel who is responsible for organising formal functions

reception room /rɪˈsepʃən ruːm/ *noun* HOTELS a large room in a hotel suitable for big groups of people

reception staff /rɪˈsepʃən stɑːf/ *noun* HOTELS the people who work in the reception area

réchaud /ˈreɪʃəʊ/ *noun* CATERING a small heater, usually with a spirit lamp under it, for keeping food hot on the table or for cooking dishes rapidly next to the guest's table

recipe /ˈresəpi/ *noun* CATERING written details of how to cook a dish ○ *The restaurant sells postcards with recipes of its famous fish dishes.* ○ *The cake is made from an old recipe.*

recline *verb* to lie back

reclining seat /rɪˌklaɪnɪŋ ˈsiːt/ *noun* TRAVEL a seat which lies back, so that the traveller can sleep

recommend /ˌrekəˈmend/ *verb* **1.** to suggest that it would be a good thing if someone did something **2.** to say that someone or something is good ○ *He recommended a French restaurant in the High Street.* ○ *I certainly would not recommend Miss Smith for the job.* ○ *Can you recommend a good hotel in Amsterdam?*

recommendation /ˌrekəmenˈdeɪʃ(ə)n/ *noun* a statement saying that someone or something is good ○ *We appointed him on the recommendation of his former employer.*

recommended retail price /ˌrekəmendɪd ˈriːteɪl ˌpraɪs/ noun BUSI-NESS same as **manufacturer's recommended price.** Abbr **RRP**

record /rɪˈkɔːd/ verb **1.** to fix sound on a plastic disc or tape ○ *A recorded message is played when the airport bus approaches the terminal.* **2.** to keep note of something ○ *She recorded their details in the logbook.* ■ noun □ **records** a note of something from the past such as a person's medical details, guests in a hotel, transactions in a shop, etc. ○ *I'll look that up in the records and get back to you.* ○ *Could you fetch the patient's records, please?*

recorded delivery /rɪˌkɔːdɪd dɪˈlɪv(ə)ri/ noun a mail service where the letters are signed for by the person receiving them ○ *They sent the passport by recorded delivery.*

recorder /rɪˈkɔːdə/ noun an instrument which records sound

recording /rɪˈkɔːdɪŋ/ noun **1.** the act of fixing sounds on a plastic disc or tape **2.** music or speech which has been recorded

recreation /ˌrekriˈeɪʃ(ə)n/ noun enjoyable activities that people do for fun

recreational /ˌrekriˈeɪʃ(ə)n(ə)l/ adjective referring to recreation

recreational vehicle /ˌrekriˈeɪʃ(ə)n(ə)l ˌviːɪk(ə)l/ noun US ROAD TRAVEL a large camping van in which a family can live while touring. Abbr **RV**

recreation ground /ˌrekriˈeɪʃ(ə)n graʊnd/ noun SPORT a public sports ground

recruit /rɪˈkruːt/ verb to take on as an employee ○ *We have recruited six people to act as hosts at the Computer Show.*

recruitment /rɪˈkruːtmənt/, **recruiting** /rɪˈkruːtɪŋ/ noun the act of taking people on as employees □ **the recruitment of new staff** the task of finding new staff to join a company

'…five-star hotels were finding recruitment slightly harder than three- and four-star hotels' [*Caterer & Hotelkeeper*]

red /red/ noun □ **in the red** showing a debit or loss ○ *My bank account is in the red.* ○ *The company went into the red in 1998.* ○ *The company is out of the red for the first time since 1950.*

redcap /ˈredkæp/ US a porter at an airport or railway station

red carpet /ˌred ˈkɑːpɪt/ noun a carpet put down when an important visitor comes, signifying an official welcome ○ *He got the red-carpet treatment.*

red channel /ˈred ˌtʃæn(ə)l/ noun BUSI-NESS the exit from customs through which you pass if you are importing goods which are liable to duty

redcoat /ˈredkəʊt/ noun a uniformed attendant at a Butlin's holiday camp

redcurrant /redˈkʌrənt/ noun FRUIT a red soft fruit growing in small clusters, mainly used to make jam and jelly, or used as decoration on cold dishes such as pâté ○ *a jar of redcurrant jelly*

redesign /ˌriːdɪˈzaɪn/ verb to design something again so that it looks different or works differently ○ *The health club has been redesigned.*

red-eye /ˈred aɪ/ adjective referring to flights or journeys that take place overnight so that it is difficult for passengers to sleep (*informal*)

red-light district /red ˈlaɪt ˌdɪstrɪkt/ noun the part of a town where brothels and striptease clubs are situated ○ *The two old ladies complained that their hotel was in the red-light district of Frankfurt.* ○ *It's best to avoid the red-light district after dark.*

red mullet /ˌred ˈmʌlɪt/ noun SEAFOOD a small red sea-fish, used in Mediterranean cooking

red tape /ˌred ˈteɪp/ noun BUSINESS official paperwork which takes a long time to complete ○ *The South-East Asian joint venture has been held up by government red tape.*

reduce /rɪˈdjuːs/ verb **1.** to make something smaller or lower ○ *reduced-price menu for children* ○ *We have reduced prices on all our winter holidays.* **2.** CATERING to boil sauce, so as to make it smaller in quantity and more concentrated

'…only heating rooms when they are occupied, the system is said to reduce energy use in a hotel of 200 to 250 bedrooms by 700kWh per room per year' [*Caterer & Hotelkeeper*]

reduced rate /rɪˌdjuːst ˈreɪt/ noun a specially cheap charge

reduction /rɪˈdʌkʃən/ noun **1.** a lowering of a price ○ *'Price reductions on selected holidays in Spain.'* **2.** CATERING a sauce which has been reduced by boiling

red wine /ˌred ˈwaɪn/ noun BEVERAGES wine which becomes red because the grape skins are left for a time in the fermenting mixture

COMMENT: Red wine is usually served at 'room temperature'. Fine red wines (vintage Bordeaux or Burgundies) should be opened in advance to allow the air to enter the bottle; some fine red wines may also need to be decanted to remove sediment.

Light red wines (such as Beaujolais nouveau, and red wines from the Loire Valley)
should be served at cellar temperature
(i.e. cool), or can even be chilled. Red
wine is traditionally served with meat and
game, and also with cheese.

re-entry /ˌriː 'entri/ *noun* the act of coming back in again

re-entry permit /ˌriː 'entri ˌviːzə/, **re-
entry visa** *noun* a visa allowing someone to
leave a country and go back in again

referral system /rɪˈfɜːrəl ˌsɪstəm/ *noun*
HOTELS a system by which one hotel or restaurant recommends another, and may take
bookings for another on which commission
may be paid

refreshments /rɪˈfreʃmənts/ *plural noun*
CATERING snacks and drinks, available usually as a buffet, or served by waiters ○
*Refreshments will be served in a tent on the
lawn.* ○ *You can get refreshments at the foyer
bar during the interval.*

refreshment tent /rɪˈfreʃmənt tent/
noun ENTERTAINMENT a tent in which
refreshments are served, e.g at a horse show
or village fête.

refrigerate /rɪˈfrɪdʒəreɪt/ *verb* CATERING
to keep food cold, so that it will not go bad

COMMENT: Low temperature retards the
rate at which food spoils, because all the
causes of deterioration proceed more
slowly. In freeze-drying, the food is quick-
frozen and then dried by vacuum, so
removing the moisture. Pre-cooked foods
should be cooled rapidly down to −3°C
and eaten within five days of production.
Certain high-risk chilled foods should be
kept below 5°C; these foods include soft
cheese and various pre-cooked products.
Eggs in shells can be chilled for short-term
storage (i.e. up to one month) at temperatures between −10°C and −16°C. Bakery
products, including bread, have storage
temperatures between −18°C and −40°C;
bread goes stale quickly at chill temperatures which are above these. Potatoes in
the form of pre-cooked chips can be
stored at −18°C or colder, but ordinary
potatoes must not be chilled at all. Apples
and pears can be kept in air-cooled boxes
at between −1°C and +4°C (this is known
as controlled temperature storage). Lettuces and strawberries (which normally
must not be chilled) can be kept fresh by
vacuum cooling; celery and carrots can be
chilled by hydrocooling.

refrigerated display case /rɪ
ˌfrɪdʒəreɪtɪd dɪsˈpleɪ ˌkeɪs/ *noun* CATER-
ING a cabinet with glass sides and top, cooled
by a refrigerating plant underneath, used to
keep prepared food dishes such as salads and
desserts fresh and cool

refrigerator /rɪˈfrɪdʒəreɪtə/ *noun* CATER-
ING a machine for keeping food cold ○ *Milk
will keep for several days in a refrigerator.* ○
*Each bedroom has a small refrigerator with
ice and cold drinks.*

refund *noun* /ˈriːfʌnd/ money paid back ○
*She got a refund after she had complained to
the manager.* ■ *verb* /rɪˈfʌnd/ to pay back
money ○ *to refund the cost of postage* ○ *All
money will be refunded if the tour is cancelled.* ○ *They refunded £100 of the £400 I
had paid.*

refundable /rɪˈfʌndəb(ə)l/ *adjective* that
will or can be paid back ○ *A refundable
deposit of 10% is payable on booking.* ○ *The
entrance fee is refundable if you purchase £5
worth of goods.*

refund in full /ˌriːfʌnd ɪn ˈfʊl/ *noun*
FINANCE the return of all the money paid ○
*She got a refund in full when she complained
that there were mice in her bedroom.* Also
called **full refund**

refurbish /riːˈfɜːbɪʃ/ *verb* to repair and
redecorate e.g. a room or building so that it is
like new ○ *They spent thousands of pounds
refurbishing the 36 bedrooms.*

refurbishment /riːˈfɜːbɪʃmənt/ *noun* the
act of refurbishing something ○ *The hotel
has reopened after a £1.5m refurbishment.*

refusal /rɪˈfjuːz(ə)l/ *noun* a statement saying that you will not do something or will not
accept something □ **his request met with a
refusal** his request was refused □ **to give
someone first refusal of something** to allow
someone to be the first to decide if they want
something or not

refuse *noun* /ˈrefjuːs/ rubbish ○ *Please put
all refuse in the bin.* ○ *Refuse collection on
our road is on Thursdays.* ■ *verb* /rɪˈfjuːz/ to
say that you will not do something or will not
accept something ○ *They refused to pay.* ○
*The bank refused to lend the hotel any more
money.* ○ *He asked for a refund but it was
refused.* ○ *The customer refused the goods* or
refused to accept the goods. (NOTE: You
refuse **to do something** or refuse **something**.)

regatta /rɪˈɡætə/ *noun* SHIPS AND BOATS a
sporting event where rowing boats or sailing
boats race

COMMENT: The two main regattas in England are the Henley Regatta in June and
Cowes Week held in August.

regeneration /rɪˌgenəˈreɪʃ(ə)n/ *noun*
CATERING the task of preparing food from
frozen, e.g. by putting it in a microwave ○
*Students learn cooking and regeneration
techniques.*

region /'riːdʒən/ *noun* **1.** area □ **the London region** the area around London **2.** □ **in the region of £10,000** about £10,000 ○ *We're looking for a hotel in the region of £30 per night.*

regional /'riːdʒ(ə)nəl/ *adjective* referring to a region ○ *The restaurant serves regional specialities.*

regional airport /ˌriːdʒ(ə)nəl 'eəpɔːt/ *noun* AIR TRAVEL an airport serving a region of the country, and not the capital ○ *Flights are also available from sixteen other regional airports.* ○ *There are no regional departures to the Far East.*

register /'redʒɪstə/ *noun* **1.** an official list ○ *to enter something in a register* ○ *to keep a register up to date* **2.** a large book for recording details, such as in a hotel, where guests sign in, or in a registry where deaths are recorded ○ *They asked the guests to sign the register.* **3.** CATERING a computerised billing system in a restaurant, where each item ordered is keyed in by the waiter using a special code, and the till provides a printout which itemises all dishes bought, so that the guest can check the bill easily ■ *verb* **1.** to write something on an official list ○ *to register a sale* **2.** HOTELS to arrive at a hotel or at a conference and write your name and address on a list ○ *They registered at the hotel under the name of Macdonald.* **3.** HOTELS (*of the receptionist*) to fill in the details of a guest when he or she arrives at a hotel

registered letter /ˌredʒɪstəd 'letə/, **registered parcel** /ˌredʒɪstəd 'pɑːs(ə)l/ *noun* a letter or parcel which is sent by registered post

registered office /ˌredʒɪstəd 'ɒfɪs/ *noun* BUSINESS the office address of a company which is officially registered with the Companies' Registrar

registered post /ˌredʒɪstəd 'pəʊst/ *noun* a service where the post office makes a note of a letter or parcel before it is sent, so that compensation can be claimed if it is lost or damaged ○ *to send documents by registered post*

registration /ˌredʒɪ'streɪʃ(ə)n/ *noun* the act of writing something on an official list

registration card, registration form *noun* HOTELS a card or form which has to be filled in when registering at a hotel, conference, etc.

registration number /ˌredʒɪ'streɪʃ(ə)n ˌnʌmbə/ *noun* the official number of a car

registration plate /ˌredʒɪ'streɪʃ(ə)n pleɪt/ *noun* ROAD TRAVEL a plate on the front and back of a vehicle, showing its registration number (NOTE: The US English for this is **license plate**.)

registry /'redʒɪstri/ *noun* □ **country, port of registry** the country or port where a ship is registered

regret /rɪ'gret/ *verb* to be sorry about something ○ *I regret having to refuse entry to small children.* ○ *We regret the delay in the arrival of our flight from Amsterdam.* ○ *We regret to inform you of the cancellation of the tour.* (NOTE: You **regret doing something** or **regret something**. Note also: **regretting – regretted**.)

regular /'regjʊlə/ *adjective* **1.** happening or coming at the same time each day or week or month or year ○ *His regular train is the 12.45.* ○ *The regular flight to Athens leaves at 06.00.* □ **regular staff** full-time staff **2.** ordinary or standard ○ *The regular price is $1.25, but we are offering them at 99c.* □ **regular size** the ordinary size, smaller than economy size or family size

regular customer /ˌregjʊlə 'kʌstəmə/ *noun* BUSINESS a customer who always buys from the same shop or who goes to the same place for a service

regularly /'regjʊləli/ *adverb* usually, or at the same time each day, week, month or year ○ *The first train in the morning is regularly late.*

regulate /'regjʊleɪt/ *verb* **1.** to adjust something so that it works well or is correct **2.** to control something by law

regulation /ˌregjʊ'leɪʃ(ə)n/ *noun* the act of adjusting something so that it works well

regulations /ˌregjʊ'leɪʃ(ə)nz/ *plural noun* laws or rules ○ *regulations concerning the entry of tourists without visas* ○ *The new government regulations on hotel standards.* ○ *The restaurant contravenes fire regulations* or *safety regulations.*

'EC regulations which came into effect in July insist that customers can buy cars anywhere in the EC at the local pre-tax price' [*Financial Times*]

Regulo /'regjʊləʊ/ *tdmk* CATERING a trademark for a system of numbers indicating temperatures on a gas cooker ○ *Cook in the oven for one hour at Regulo 6.*

COMMENT: The Regulo system goes from 1/4 to 9. The approximate temperature equivalents are: 1/4–2 = 110–150°C, 3–4 = 160–190°C, 5 = 200°C, 6–7 = 210–230°C, 8–9 = 235–250°C.

reheat /riː'hiːt/ *verb* CATERING to heat again ○ *Food left over can be reheated and served again the next day.*

'...surplus hot food that is to be served again hot must be cooled as rapidly as possible and kept at or below 5°C until it is to be reheated for service. It is best to use a blast chiller to cool hot food rapidly. It must then be reheated thoroughly to temperatures in excess of 75°C and subsequently kept above 63°C until served' [*Caterer & Hotelkeeper*]

reheating /riː'hiːtɪŋ/ *noun* CATERING the act of heating food again ○ *Care must be taken when reheating fish dishes.*

reimburse /ˌriːɪm'bɜːs/ *verb* □ **to reimburse someone their expenses** to pay someone back for money which they have spent ○ *You will be reimbursed for your expenses* or *Your expenses will be reimbursed.*

reimbursement /ˌriːɪm'bɜːsmənt/ *noun* FINANCE the act of paying back money ○ *reimbursement of expenses*

reissue /riː'ɪʃuː/ *verb* AIR TRAVEL to change an airline ticket so that a passenger can fly on a different date or route, or at a different time. Compare **revalidate**

relation /rɪ'leɪʃ(ə)n/ *noun* a link between two things

relative humidity /ˌrelətɪv hjuː'mɪdɪti/ *noun* the ratio between the amount of water vapour in air and the amount which would be present if the air was saturated, shown as a percentage

relax /rɪ'læks/ *verb* to rest from work, or to become less tense ○ *They spent the first week of their holiday relaxing on the beach.* ○ *Guests can relax in the bar before going to eat in the restaurant.*

relaxation /ˌriːlæk'seɪʃ(ə)n/ *noun* time spent resting from work ○ *For relaxation he goes jogging in the park.* ○ *Do you consider gardening a form of relaxation?*

relevée /rə'levеɪ/ same as **remove**

reliability /rɪˌlaɪə'bɪlɪti/ *noun* the ability to be trusted to do something ○ *The product has passed its reliability tests.*

reliable /rɪ'laɪəb(ə)l/ *adjective* that or who can be trusted to do something, e.g. to work properly or to be on time ○ *a reliable tour company* ○ *The on-site courier is completely reliable.*

relief /rɪ'liːf/ *adjective* taking the place of another who is away

relief cook /rɪ'liːf kʊk/ *noun* CATERING a cook who takes the place of a cook who is absent

relieve /rɪ'liːv/ *verb* **1.** to take over from someone ○ *The day receptionist will be relieved at 21.00 when the night shift comes on.* **2.** □ **to relieve yourself** to urinate or defecate

relish /'relɪʃ/ *noun* SAUCES, ETC. a sharp or spicy sauce made with vegetables or fruit which adds extra flavour when eaten with other food

rely on /rɪ'laɪ ɒn/ *verb* to depend on somebody or something ○ *We rely on part-time staff for most of our business.* ○ *Do not rely on the agents for accurate market reports.*

remote /rɪ'məʊt/ *adjective* a long way away, distant ○ *The hotel is situated in a remote mountain village.*

remote control /rɪˌməʊt kən'trəʊl/ *noun* control of something from a distance, e.g. control of a TV set by using a handheld switch with an infrared ray

remote stand /rɪˌməʊt 'stænd/ *noun* AIR TRAVEL an area where an aircraft waits some distance away from the airport for passengers to board

rémoulade /ˌremə'leɪd/ *noun* FOOD mayonnaise with herbs, mustard, capers, and gherkins added, and sometimes chopped hard-boiled egg

remove /rɪ'muːv/ *noun* CATERING (*in old menus*) a dish served after the first course has been eaten and cleared away

render /'rendə/ *verb* to melt something in order to purify or extract substances from it, especially to heat solid fat slowly until as much liquid fat as possible has been extracted from it

rennet /'renət/ *noun* a substance made from the lining of calves's stomachs that is used in cheese making

renovate /'renəveɪt/ *verb* to repair and redecorate something completely in order to make it like new ○ *The hotel has been completely renovated.* ○ *The house is in good structural condition but the central heating needs renovating.*

renovation /ˌrenə'veɪʃ(ə)n/ *noun* the act of renovating something ○ *The hotel is closed for renovation.*

rent /rent/ *noun* money paid to use a room, an office or house for a period of time □ **high rent**, **low rent** expensive or cheap rent ○ *to pay three months' rent in advance* ○ *Rents are high in the centre of the town.* ○ *We cannot afford to pay high-season rents.* □ **the flat is let at an economic rent** at a rent which covers all costs to the landlord □ **income from rents**, **rent income** income from letting an office, a house, etc. ■ *verb* **1.** to pay money to hire a room, an office, a house or piece of equipment for a period of time ○ *We rented a car at the airport.* ○ *He rented a villa by the beach for three weeks.* ○ *They were driving a rented car when they* *were stopped by the police.* **2.** □ **to rent (out)** to own e.g. a car or an office and lend it to someone who pays for its use ○ *We rented the villa to an American couple.*

rental /'rent(ə)l/ *noun* money paid to use a flat, house, car or piece of equipment for a period of time

rental agency /ˌrent(ə)l 'eɪdʒənsi/ *noun* an office which specialises in letting flats or houses

rental income /'rent(ə)l ˌɪnkʌm/ *noun* income from letting offices, houses, etc.

reopen /riː'əʊpən/ *verb* to open something again ○ *The hotel will reopen next week after its £1 million renovation.*

reopening /riː'əʊp(ə)nɪŋ/ *noun* the act of opening something again

repack /riː'pæk/ *verb* to put things back again into a suitcase ○ *He had to repack his case after it had been opened by customs officials.*

repacking /riː'pækɪŋ/ *noun* the act of putting things back into a suitcase

repair /rɪ'peə/ *noun* an act of mending or making good something which is broken ○ *The hotel is closed while they are carrying out repairs to the air-conditioning system.* ○ *His car is in the garage for repair.* ■ *verb* to mend or to make good something which is broken ○ *The lift is being repaired.*

repair kit /rɪ'peə kɪt/ *noun* a kit for repairing a machine, especially a kit for repairing a car ○ *There is a repair kit provided in the boot of each car.*

repay /rɪ'peɪ/ *verb* to pay back □ **he repaid me in full** he paid me back all the money he owed me

repayment /rɪ'peɪmənt/ *noun* FINANCE the act of paying back, or the money which is paid back

repeat /rɪ'piːt/ *verb* to say something again □ **to repeat an order** to order something again

repeat booking /rɪˌpiːt 'bʊkɪŋ/ *noun* a booking of the same room, table, etc., again ○ *very high occupancy with repeat bookings*

repeat business /rɪˌpiːt 'bɪznɪs/ *noun* BUSINESS a business deal which is a repeat of an earlier deal, as when organising for a group to stay at a hotel again

replace /rɪ'pleɪs/ *verb* **1.** to put something back where it was before ○ *She replaced the glasses on the table.* **2.** to exchange one part for another ○ *He offered to replace the broken mirror.*

replacement /rɪ'pleɪsmənt/ *noun* **1.** the action of replacing something with some-

thing else **2.** a thing which is used to replace something

replacement part /rɪˌpleɪsmənt 'pɑːt/ *noun* same as **spare part**

reply /rɪ'plaɪ/ *noun* an answer ○ *There was no reply to my letter* or *to my phone call.* ○ *I am writing in reply to your letter of the 24th.* ■ *verb* to answer □ **to reply to a letter** to write a letter in answer to one which you have received

reply coupon /rɪ'plaɪ ˌkuːpɒn/ *noun* MARKETING a form attached to an advertisement in a newspaper or magazine, which has to be filled in and returned to the advertiser

report /rɪ'pɔːt/ *verb* to tell somebody about something officially ○ *Cases of cholera must be reported immediately to the local health authorities.* ○ *The guest reported that her wallet was missing from her room.* (NOTE: You report sth **to** somebody.)

reporting time /rɪ'pɔːtɪŋ taɪm/ *noun* AIR TRAVEL the time before a flight departs when a passenger should check in ○ *Reporting time for international flights is 2 hours before departure.*

represent /ˌreprɪ'zent/ *verb* BUSINESS to sell goods or a service on behalf of someone ○ *She represents an Australian bus company.*

representative /ˌreprɪ'zentətɪv/ *adjective* typical of all the people or things in a group ○ *The hotel displayed a representative selection of locally made products.* ○ *The sample chosen was not representative of the whole batch.* ■ *noun* **1.** BUSINESS a company which works for another company, selling their goods ○ *We have appointed Smith & Co our exclusive representatives in Europe.* **2.** somebody who acts on someone's behalf ○ *She is the local representative for a British tour operator.* ○ *Our representative will meet you at the airport.*

reputable /'repjʊtəb(ə)l/ *adjective* with a good reputation ○ *We only use reputable carriers.*

reputation /ˌrepjʊ'teɪʃ(ə)n/ *noun* the opinion that people have of someone or something ○ *an airline with a reputation for punctuality* ○ *The hotel has a reputation for being expensive.*

request /rɪ'kwest/ *noun* an act of asking for something politely ○ *She has put in a request to be transferred to another branch.* □ **on request** if asked for ○ *More blankets are available on request.* ■ *verb* to ask for something politely or formally ○ *The stranded party radioed to request help.*

request stop /rɪˈkwest stɒp/ *noun* ROAD TRAVEL a bus stop where a buses stop only if you signal to them

require /rɪˈkwaɪə/ *verb* **1.** to need something ○ *You will require a visa to go to Russia.* **2.** to demand that someone does something □ **to require someone to do something** to have to do something ○ *Tourists are required to register with the local police.*

requirement /rɪˈkwaɪəmənt/ *noun* something that is needed

re-route /ˌriː ˈruːt/ *verb* TRAVEL to arrange another route for e.g. a plane or coach ○ *Bad weather in the mountains meant that the coach had to be re-routed via the coast road.*

rescue /ˈreskjuː/ *noun* an act of saving somebody or the fact of being saved from a dangerous situation ■ *verb* to save somebody or something from a dangerous situation ○ *When the river flooded, the party of tourists had to be rescued by helicopter.*

rescuer /ˈreskjuːə/ *noun* somebody who saves or tries to save someone from a dangerous situation ○ *Rescuers were delayed by extremely high winds.* ○ *A team of rescuers arrived in time to save the skiers.*

reservation /ˌrezəˈveɪʃ(ə)n/ *noun* a request for a room, seat, table, etc. to be kept available for you □ **to make a reservation** to book a room, a table, a seat, etc. ○ *I want to make a reservation on the train to Plymouth tomorrow evening.*

reservation diary /ˌrezəˈveɪʃ(ə)n ˌdaɪəri/ *noun* HOTELS a ledger with a separate page for each day, giving a list of all the rooms in a hotel, and marks to show if they are booked or vacant

reservation form /ˌrezəˈveɪʃ(ə)n fɔːm/ *noun* HOTELS a form to be filled in by the clerk when a room reservation is made

reservations chart /ˌrezəˈveɪʃ(ə)nz tʃɑːt/ *noun* HOTELS a chart showing all the rooms in a hotel, with marks showing which are occupied or booked in advance, and which are vacant

reservations clerk /ˌrezəˈveɪʃ(ə)nz klɑːk/ *noun* HOTELS somebody in a hotel who deals with room reservations

reservations manager /ˌrezəˈveɪʃ(ə)nz ˌmænɪdʒə/ *noun* CATERING somebody in charge of the department in a hotel or at an airline where reservations are made

reservations rack /ˌrezəˈveɪʃ(ə)nz ræk/ *noun* HOTELS a special board or series of pigeonholes where cards are put to show which rooms have been booked

reserve /rɪˈzɜːv/ *noun* **1.** BUSINESS money from profits not paid as dividend, but kept back by a company in case it is needed for a special purpose □ **reserve for bad debts** money kept by a company to cover debts which may not be paid **2.** □ **in reserve** kept to be used later on □ **to keep something in reserve** to keep something so as to be able to use it later on if necessary ○ *We keep stores of tinned and frozen food in reserve for use in emergencies.* **3.** an area of unspoilt land where no commercial exploitation is allowed, kept for the wildlife – as in the National Parks in Africa ■ *verb* □ **to reserve a room, a table, a seat** to ask for a room, table or seat to be kept free for you ○ *I want to reserve a table for four people.* ○ *Can you reserve a seat for me on the train to Glasgow?*

reserved /rɪˈzɜːvd/ *adjective* BUSINESS kept for a customer ○ *You can't have the window table, it is reserved.* ○ *There are two reserved tables and one free one.* ○ *Is this seat reserved?*

reserves /rɪˈzɜːvz/ *plural noun* supplies kept to be used later on if necessary ○ *The hotel was cut off by snow and had to rely on its reserves of food.* ○ *Reserves of fuel fell during the winter.* ○ *The country's reserves of gas* or *gas reserves are very large.*

residence /ˈrezɪd(ə)ns/ *noun* **1.** a house or flat where someone lives ○ *He has a country residence where he spends his weekends.* **2.** the act of living or operating officially in a country

residence permit /ˈrezɪd(ə)ns ˌpɜːmɪt/ *noun* an official document allowing a foreigner to live in a country ○ *He has applied for a residence permit.* ○ *She was granted a residence permit for one year.*

residence tax /ˈrezɪd(ə)ns tæks/ *noun* BUSINESS a tax applied to people staying in a town

resident /ˈrezɪd(ə)nt/ *noun* **1.** a person or company living or operating in a country ○ *The company is resident in France.* **2.** HOTELS a person who stays in a hotel **3.** a member of staff who lives in ○ *a resident manager* ◊ **non-resident**

resident alien /ˌrezɪd(ə)nt ˈeɪliən/ *noun* a foreigner who has a residence permit and lives in a particular country

residential /ˌrezɪˈdenʃəl/ *adjective* referring to residence

residential area /ˌrezɪ'denʃəl ˌeəriə/ *noun* a part of a town which is mainly occupied with private houses and flats

residential hotel /ˌrezɪdenʃəl həʊ'tel/ *noun* HOTELS a hotel which caters for long-stay guests, usually on a full-board basis

residential licence /ˌrezɪdenʃəl 'laɪs(ə)ns/ *noun* HOTELS a licence given to a small hotel or guesthouse, allowing them to sell alcohol to residents only

residential street /ˌrezɪdenʃəl 'striːt/ *noun* a street of private houses and flats, with no offices or shops

residents' lounge /'rezɪd(ə)ns laʊndʒ/ *noun* HOTELS a room in a hotel which is only open to residents of the hotel and their guests

resort /rɪ'zɔːt/ *noun* TOURISM a place where people go on holiday

resort hotel /rɪ'zɔːt həʊˌtel/ *noun* HOTELS a hotel in a resort, catering for holidaymakers rather than business visitors

responsibility /rɪˌspɒnsɪ'bɪlɪti/ *noun* **1.** the state of being in charge of something ○ *The management refuses to accept responsibility for guests' personal belongings.* □ **he has taken on responsibility for the reception area** he has agreed to be in charge of the reception area **2.** something that someone is responsible for ○ *His main responsibility is seeing that the guests are safe.*

responsible /rɪ'spɒnsɪb(ə)l/ *adjective* **1.** causing ○ *The fog was responsible for the accident.* **2.** reliable and able to be trusted to be sensible ○ *We want staff who are responsible and good with money.* **3.** in charge of something, taking decisions for something or directing something ○ *She is responsible for the tour schedules.* ○ *The hotel management is not responsible for the restaurant in the adjoining building.* **4.** □ **responsible to someone** being under the authority of someone who expects you to carry out the work well

responsible tourism /rɪˌspɒnsɪb(ə)l 'tʊərɪz(ə)m/ *noun* travel that respects the laws and customs of local people and is not harmful to the environment

rest /rest/ *noun* **1.** a period of being quiet and peaceful, being asleep or doing nothing ○ *She's having a rest in her room.* ○ *The afternoon has been set aside for rest.* **2.** a support **3.** □ **the rest** the other people or things in a group apart from those already mentioned ○ *Six people decided to walk back down the mountain, but the rest of the party used the funicular.* ■ *verb* to spend time relaxing or sleeping ○ *They went upstairs to rest before dinner.*

rest area /'rest ˌeəriə/ *noun* ROAD TRAVEL an area near a motorway or other large road, provided with a public toilet and picnic tables and benches, where you can park and get out of the car to relax

restaurant /'rest(ə)rɒnt/ *noun* a place where you can buy and eat a meal ○ *She runs a French restaurant in New York.* □ **he's in the restaurant business** he owns or manages restaurants

restaurant car /'rest(ə)rɒnt kɑː/ *noun* RAIL TRAVEL a railway coach where passengers can sit and eat meals. Compare **buffet car**

restaurant guide /'rest(ə)rɒnt gaɪd/ *noun* CATERING a guidebook listing the restaurants in a town

restaurant manager /'rest(ə)rɒnt ˌmænɪdʒə/ *noun* CATERING somebody who runs a restaurant, but does not own it

restaurant owner /prə'praɪətə/, **proprietor** *noun* CATERING somebody who owns a restaurant

restaurant staff /'rest(ə)rɒnt stɑːf/ *noun* people who work in a restaurant

restaurateur /ˌrest(ə)rə'tɜː/ *noun* CATERING somebody who runs a restaurant

'…a London restaurateur was fined at the magistrates court last week for failing to quieten a noisy extractor fan' [*Caterer & Hotelkeeper*]

rest-camp /'rest kæmp/ *noun* TOURISM a campsite on a safari where you rest after travelling in the bush

restrict /rɪ'strɪkt/ *verb* to set limits to something ○ *We are restricted to twenty tables by the size of the restaurant.*

restricted access /rɪ'strɪktɪd ˌækses/ *noun* ENTERTAINMENT access which is limited to small groups of people at particular times of the day only, e.g. to a museum

restricted articles /rɪ'strɪktɪd ˌɑːtɪk(ə)lz/ *plural noun* AIR TRAVEL things which passengers must not carry onto planes, e.g. knives or aerosols

restricted fare /rɪˌstrɪktɪd 'feə/ *noun* TRAVEL a type of e.g flight ticket that is not exchangeable.

restriction /rɪ'strɪkʃ(ə)n/ *noun* **1.** a rule or action that limits or imposes controls on something □ **to impose restrictions on imports, on credit** to start limiting imports or credit □ **to lift credit restrictions** to allow credit to be given freely **2.** TRAVEL a limit to travel imposed as a condition when you buy some types of ticket ○ *When buying your ticket, make sure you understand which restrictions apply.*

rest room /'rest ruːm/ *noun* a public toilet

résumé /'rezjumeɪ/ *US* BUSINESS same as **curriculum vitae**

retail /'riːteɪl/ *noun* the sale of goods to the people who will own and use them

retail price /'riːteɪl ˌpraɪs/ *noun* BUSINESS the price at which the retailer sells to the final customer

retail shop /'riːteɪl ʃɒp/ *noun* BUSINESS a shop where goods are sold only to the public

retinol /'retɪnɒl/ *noun* CATERING a vitamin found in liver, vegetables, eggs and cod liver oil which is essential for good vision

retirement pension /rɪ'taɪəmənt ˌpenʃən/ *noun* same as **old age pension**

retsina /ret'siːnə/ *noun* BEVERAGES a Greek wine flavoured with pine resin, which was originally added to preserve the wine

return /rɪ'tɜːn/ *noun* **1.** a journey back to the place you have left **2.** the act of sending or giving something back □ **he replied by return of post** he replied by the next post service **3.** profit or income from money invested ○ *to bring in a quick return* ○ *What is the gross return on this line?* **4.** □ **to make a return to the tax office, to make an income tax return** to send a statement of income and allowances to the tax office □ **to fill in a VAT return** to complete the form showing VAT receipts and expenditure □ **daily, weekly, quarterly sales return** a report of sales made each day, week or quarter ■ *verb* **1.** to give or send something back ○ *to return unsold stock to the wholesaler* ○ *to return a letter to sender* **2.** to make an official statement to the tax authorities about income you have earned ○ *to return income of £15,000 to the tax authorities*

returnable /rɪ'tɜːnəb(ə)l/ *adjective* BUSINESS possible to take back to a shop or supplier ○ *These bottles are not returnable.*

return address /rɪ'tɜːn əˌdres/ *noun* an address to send something back to

return date /rɪ'tɜːn deɪt/ *noun* TRAVEL the day on which a traveller or a tour returns

returned empties /rɪˌtɜːnd 'emptiz/ *plural noun* BUSINESS empty bottles or containers which are taken back to a shop or supplier, where any deposit paid will be given back

return fare /rɪ'tɜːn feə/ *noun* TRAVEL the fare for a journey from one place to another and back again

return guest /rɪˌtɜːn 'gest/ *noun* HOTELS somebody who goes back to stay in a hotel a second time

return journey /rɪˌtɜːn 'dʒɜːni/ *noun* TRAVEL a journey back to where you came from

return on investment /rɪˌtɜːn ɒn ɪn'vestmənt/ *noun* BUSINESS interest or dividends shown as a percentage of the money invested. Abbr **ROI**

return rate /rɪ'tɜːn reɪt/ *noun* the percentage of e.g. guests who come back to stay a second time ○ *In the three months the hotel has been open, the return rate of guests has already reached 40%-45%.*

return ticket /rɪˌtɜːn 'tɪkɪt/ *noun* TRAVEL a ticket for a journey from one place to another and back again. Also called **round-trip ticket**

return visit /rɪˌtɜːn ˌvɪzɪt/ *noun* TOURISM a second visit to a town, tourist attraction, hotel, etc. ○ *Our own surveys show that well over 50% of our customers are British, most of them on return visits.*

re-use /ˌriː 'juːz/ *verb* to use again ○ *To save money, we try to re-use unused food from previous meals where possible.*

revalidate /riː'vælɪdeɪt/ *verb* AIR TRAVEL to change an airline ticket so that a passenger can fly on a different date or at a different time, but still on the same route as the original ticket. Compare **reissue**

revalidation /riːˌvælɪ'deɪʃ(ə)n/ *noun* TRAVEL the act of making a ticket valid again, after a change has been made

revalidation sticker /riːˌvælɪ'deɪʃ(ə)n ˌstɪkə/ *noun* SHIPS AND BOATS a little sticker put on a ticket to show a change made to the original reservation

revamp *verb* /riː'væmp/ to improve the appearance of something which is slightly old-fashioned (*informal*) ○ *The lobby, conference rooms and 68 bedrooms have been revamped.* ■ *noun* /'riːvæmp/ a change in the appearance of something ○ *The reception area has had a complete revamp.*

revenue /'revənjuː/ *noun* **1.** FINANCE money which is received **2.** BUSINESS money received by a government in tax

revenue accounts /'revənjuː əˌkaʊnts/ *plural noun* BUSINESS accounts of a business which record money received as e.g. sales or commission

reverse /rɪ'vɜːs/ *adjective* opposite ■ *noun* **1.** the opposite **2.** ROAD TRAVEL a gear which makes a vehicle go backwards □ **the car was in reverse** the reverse gear was engaged ■ *verb* **1.** ROAD TRAVEL to make a car go backwards **2.** □ **to reverse the**

charges (*on the phone*) to ask the person you are calling to pay for the call

reverse-charge call /rɪˌvɜːs ˈtʃɑːdʒ ˈkɔːl/ *noun* a telephone call where the person receiving the call agrees to pay for it. Also called **collect call**

revolving door /rɪˌvɒlvɪŋ ˈdɔː/ *noun* a door which turns round a central pillar ○ *Her luggage got stuck in the revolving door at the entrance to the hotel.*

rhubarb /ˈruːbɑːb/ *noun* FRUIT a plant with long red leaf stalks which are cooked and eaten as dessert ○ *We're having stewed rhubarb for pudding.*

rib /rɪb/ *noun* **1.** one of several bones forming a cage across the chest **2.** MEAT a piece of meat with the rib bone attached to it. Also called **chop**

ribbon /ˈrɪbən/ *noun* a long thin strip of material for tying things or used as decoration

riboflavine /ˌraɪbəʊˈfleɪvɪn/ *noun* CATERING Vitamin B2, found in eggs, liver, green vegetables and yeast and also used as an additive in processed food

rice /raɪs/ *noun* FOOD a cereal grass that produces edible grains, or these grains used as food

COMMENT: While rice is always served in Chinese and Indian meals, it is also used in European cooking, being served either as a main course (e.g. in paella or risotto) or as a vegetable with meat or fish. In English cooking, it is commonly served as a sweet pudding.

rice cooker /ˈraɪs ˌkʊkə/ *noun* CATERING a special electric pan for boiling rice

rice paper /ˈraɪs ˌpeɪpə/ *noun* FOOD very thin paper which you can eat and which is used in cooking

rice pudding /ˌraɪs ˈpʊdɪŋ/ *noun* DESSERTS a dessert made of short-grain rice, milk and sugar

rich /rɪtʃ/ *adjective* CATERING referring to food which has a high calorific value

Richter scale /ˈrɪktə skeɪl/ *noun* a scale of measurement of the force of an earthquake ○ *There were no reports of injuries after the quake which hit 5.2 on the Richter scale.*

COMMENT: The scale, devised by Charles Richter, has values from zero to ten, with the strongest earthquake ever recorded being 8.9. Earthquakes of 5 or more on the Richter scale cause damage.

ricotta /rɪˈkɒtə/ *noun* DAIRY a soft white mild-tasting Italian cheese made from whey and used mostly in cooking

ride /raɪd/ *noun* a pleasant trip, e.g. on a horse or a bike or in a car ○ *We went for a ride on an elephant.* □ **bus ride** a short trip in a bus ■ *verb* to go for a trip on a horse, on a bicycle, in a car, etc. (NOTE: **riding – rode – has ridden**)

rigatoni /ˌrɪgəˈtəʊni/ *noun* FOOD short rounded tubes of pasta with narrow ridges running along them

right /raɪt/ *adjective* **1.** good or correct ○ *The customer was right when he said that the bill did not add up.* ○ *This is not the right plane for Paris.* **2.** the opposite of left ○ *The hotel is on the right side of the street, going towards the station.* (NOTE: On ships and aircraft, the right side is called the **starboard side**.) ■ *noun* the fact of being legally entitled to do or to have something ○ *She has a right to the property.* ○ *The group said they had the right to know why the visit to the temples had been cancelled.*

right-hand /ˌraɪt ˈhænd/ *adjective* belonging to the right side ○ *The restaurant is on the right-hand side of the main street.* ○ *He keeps the address list in the right-hand drawer of his desk.*

right-hand man /ˌraɪt hænd ˈmæn/ *noun* a person's main assistant

right of way /ˌraɪt əv ˈweɪ/ *noun* the legal right to go across someone else's property ○ *There is a public right of way through the wood.*

rind /raɪnd/ *noun* CATERING the skin on fruit or meat or cheese ○ *Add the grated rind of a lemon.* ○ *Can you eat the rind of this cheese?*

ring /rɪŋ/ *verb* **1.** to make a noise like a bell ○ *The telephone was ringing in the reception area, but no one answered it.* □ **to ring a bell** to press a button to make an electric bell ring □ **'please ring for service'** a notice by a bell, asking a visitor to ring it if he or she wants a member of staff to come **2.** to telephone someone ○ *He rang (up) his wife from the conference hotel.* (NOTE: **ringing – rang – has rung**)

ring back /ˌrɪŋ ˈbæk/ *verb* to make a phone call in reply to another ○ *The manager is in a meeting, can you ring back in about half an hour?* ○ *Mr Smith called while you were out and asked if you would ring him back.* ○ *Your office rang – can you ring them back?*

ring road /ˈrɪŋ rəʊd/ *noun* ROAD TRAVEL a road which goes right round a town ○ *Instead of driving through the town centre, it will be quicker to take the ring road.*

rink /rɪŋk/ *noun* SPORT a large enclosed area with a smooth flat surface for ice skating, playing ice hockey or roller skating ○ *In the evening we all went to the skating rink.*

ripe /raɪp/ *adjective* **1.** mature and ready to be picked and eaten **2.** matured or aged enough to have developed the best flavour

risk capital /'rɪsk ˌkæpɪt(ə)l/ *noun* BUSINESS same as **venture capital**

risotto /rɪ'zɒtəʊ/ *noun* FOOD an Italian dish of cooked rice with meat, fish, or vegetables in it

rissole /'rɪsəʊl/ *noun* FOOD a fried ball of minced meat, fish, etc. ○ *We ordered lamb rissoles and potatoes.*

Riviera /rɪvi'eərə/ *noun* TOURISM the coast of a Mediterranean Sea in France and Italy, also used to describe any popular south coast in other countries ○ *winter holidays on the French Riviera.* ○ *They rented a villa on the Italian Riviera.* ○ *The Cornish Riviera is popular for family holidays.*

roach /rəʊtʃ/ *noun* **1.** SEAFOOD a small freshwater fish (NOTE: The plural form is **roach.**) **2.** a cockroach (*informal*) (NOTE: The plural form is **roaches.**)

road /rəʊd/ *noun* **1.** a way used by cars, lorries, etc., to move from one place to another ○ *The first part of the tour is by road.* ○ *Road transport costs have risen.* ○ *The main entrance is in London Road.* ○ *Use the Park Road entrance to get to the hotel car park.* **2.** □ **on the road** travelling ○ *We were on the road for thirteen hours before we finally reached the hotel.* ○ *The sales force are on the road thirty weeks a year.*

roadhouse /'rəʊdhaʊs/ *noun* a hotel or pub located beside a road

road map /'rəʊd mæp/ *noun* ROAD TRAVEL a map showing the main roads in a country

road network /'rəʊd ˌnetwɜːk/ *noun* ROAD TRAVEL a system of interconnecting roads in a country

road regulations /'rəʊd ˌregjʊleɪʃ(ə)nz/ *plural noun* ROAD TRAVEL rules applied to drivers using roads in a particular country

road sign /'rəʊd saɪn/ *noun* ROAD TRAVEL a plate by the side of a road, giving instructions or warnings

road user /'rəʊd ˌjuːzə/ *noun* ROAD TRAVEL somebody driving a car, bus or truck ·or riding a bicycle or motorcycle along a road

roast /rəʊst/ *noun* MEAT **1.** meat which will be cooked in an oven ○ *The chef is preparing a roast of lamb.* **2.** meat which has been cooked in an oven ○ *The special of the day is a roast of pork.* ■ *verb* CATERING to cook over a fire or in an open pan in an oven ■ *adjective* CATERING cooked over a fire or in an oven ○ *roast beef*

roast chef /'rəʊst ʃef/ *noun* CATERING the chef in charge of roast meats. Also called **chef rôtisseur**

roasted /'rəʊstɪd/ *adjective* CATERING cooked over a fire or in an open pan in an oven ○ *roasted trout with whiting mousseline and mussels*

roasting /'rəʊstɪŋ/ *noun* CATERING cooking over a fire or in an oven

roasting chicken /'rəʊstɪŋ ˌtʃɪkɪn/ *noun* MEAT a chicken which is tender enough to be cooked by roasting

roasting tin /'rəʊstɪŋ tɪn/ *noun* CATERING a large low-sided metal dish in which meat is roasted in the oven

roast joint /ˌrəʊst 'dʒɔɪnt/ *noun* MEAT a joint of meat such as lamb or beef, which has been roasted

roast potato /ˌrəʊst pə'teɪtəʊ/ *noun* FOOD a potato baked in fat in an oven

rock-climbing /'rɒk ˌklaɪmɪŋ/ *noun* SPORT the sport of climbing up rock faces on cliffs or mountainsides

rocket /'rɒkɪt/ *noun* VEGETABLES a green salad plant with a peppery flavour

rocks /rɒks/ *plural noun* □ **on the rocks** served in a glass with ice cubes

rock salmon /'rɒk ˌsæmən/ *noun* SEAFOOD a dogfish

rodent /'rəʊd(ə)nt/ *noun* an order of mammals including rats and mice, which have sharp teeth for gnawing. ◊ **mouse**, **rat**

rodenticide /rəʊ'dentɪsaɪd/ *noun* a poison which kills rats and mice

roe /rəʊ/ *noun* FOOD fish eggs ○ *herring roe* ○ *smoked cod's roe*

rogan josh /ˌrəʊgən 'dʒɒʃ/ *noun* FOOD in South Asian cooking, a dish of curried meat, usually lamb, in a thick tomato-based sauce

ROI *abbreviation* BUSINESS return on investment

roll /rəʊl/ *noun* **1.** a tube of something which has been turned over and over on itself **2.** □ **(bread) roll** a small loaf of bread offered to the guests by the commis waiter while they are studying the menu ■ *verb* **1.** to turn something over and over **2.** to make something go forward by pushing it on wheels or by turning it over ○ *They rolled the bed into the corner of the room.* **3.** (*of a ship*) to move up and down from side to side. Compare **pitch**

rollaway bed /ˈrəʊləˌweɪ ˌbed/ *noun* HOTELS a bed which can be rolled under another

rolled joint /ˌrəʊld ˈdʒɔɪnt/ *noun* CATERING a joint of meat, made from a flat piece of meat which is turned over and over to make a roll and then tied with string

rollerblades /ˈrəʊləbleɪdz/ *noun* SPORT a trademark for a type of in-line skate ○ *The young man on rollerblades zoomed past us at great speed.*

rollerblading /ˈrəʊləbleɪdɪŋ/ *noun* SPORT the sport of going on rollerblades ○ *Rollerblading up and down the road is their 15-year-old son's favourite pastime.*

roller blind /ˈrəʊlə blaɪnd/ *noun* a blind made of a roll of thick cloth, which can be let down to cover a window

roller coaster /ˌrəʊlə ˈkəʊstə/ *noun* ENTERTAINMENT a fairground railway which goes up and down steep slopes ○ *We all went for a ride on the roller coaster.*

roller skate /ˈrəʊlə skeɪt/ *noun* SPORT a boot with wheels on it for roller skating

rolling contract /ˌrəʊlɪŋ ˈkɒntrækt/ *noun* BUSINESS a contract which continues from one period to the next, with only slight changes

rolling stock /ˈrəʊlɪŋ stɒk/ *noun* RAIL TRAVEL wagons and carriages used on the railway

roll on/roll off /ˌrəʊl ɒn ˌrəʊl ˈɒf/ *adjective* SHIPS AND BOATS where trucks and cars can drive straight on or off. Abbr **RORO**

roly-poly /ˌrəʊli ˈpəʊli/ *noun* DESSERTS a cooked pudding made of suet pastry spread with jam and rolled up

romaine /rəʊˈmeɪn/ *noun* VEGETABLES same as **cos**

roof /ruːf/ *noun* **1.** a covering over a building **2.** ROAD TRAVEL the top of a vehicle such as a car, bus or truck

roof box /ˈruːf bɒks/ *noun* ROAD TRAVEL a box which can be fitted to the roof of a car to carry luggage

roof garden /ˈruːf ˌɡɑːd(ə)n/ *noun* a garden on the roof of a building

roof rack /ˈruːf ræk/ *noun* ROAD TRAVEL a grid attached to the roof of a car for carrying luggage

roof terrace /ˈruːf ˌterəs/ *noun* a flat paved area on the roof of a building ○ *There is a bar on the roof terrace of the hotel.*

rooftop /ˈruːftɒp/ *noun* the top of a roof ○ *Our bedroom looks out over the rooftops of the village.* ■ *adjective* on the top of a roof

rooftop restaurant /ˌruːftɒp ˈrest(ə)rɒnt/ *noun* a restaurant on top of a roof ○ *The view from the rooftop restaurant is splendid.*

room /ruːm/ *noun* **1.** a part of a building, divided off from other parts by walls **2.** HOTELS a bedroom in a hotel □ **room with shower, with private bath** a bedroom with a shower room or bathroom attached ○ *I want a room with bath for two nights.*

room and board /ˌruːm ən ˈbɔːd/ *noun* HOTELS same as **board and lodging**

room attendant /ˈruːm əˌtendənt/ *noun* HOTELS somebody who looks after a hotel room, seeing that it is clean and ready for guests

room clerk /ˈruːm klɑːk/ *noun* US HOTELS somebody in a hotel who decides which bedrooms guests will stay in and keeps the register

room expenses /ˈruːm ɪkˌspensɪz/ *plural noun* HOTELS expenses on hotel bedrooms such as the cost of linen or cleaning materials, but not including staff costs

rooming house /ˈruːmɪŋ haʊs/ *noun* US TOURISM a house with furnished rooms to let

rooming slip /ˈruːmɪŋ slɪp/ *noun* HOTELS a piece of paper given to a guest, with the room number and price on it

room inspection /ˈruːm ɪnˌspekʃ(ə)n/ *noun* HOTELS an examination of a room after it has been cleaned, to see if it is ready for the next guest

room key /ˈruːm kiː/ *noun* HOTELS the key to a room, such as a bedroom in a hotel

room linen /ˈruːm ˌlɪnɪn/ *noun* HOTELS sheets, towels, etc., for use in a hotel bedroom

room maid /ˈruːm meɪd/ *noun* HOTELS same as **chambermaid**

room makeup /ˈruːm ˌmeɪkʌp/ *noun* HOTELS the work of preparing a room in a hotel for the next guest, by cleaning it, putting clean sheets and pillowcases on the bed and putting fresh towels, shampoo, soap, etc., in the bathroom

roomnight /ˈruːmnaɪt/ *noun* HOTELS one room occupied for one night ○ *The hotel industry has 84 million roomnights a year.*

room number /ˈruːm ˌnʌmbə/ *noun* HOTELS the number given to a room in a hotel

room occupancy /ˈruːm ˌɒkjʊpənsi/ *noun* HOTELS **1.** the act of staying in a room in a hotel **2.** the average number of rooms used in a hotel over a period of time, shown as a percentage of the total number of rooms ○ *During the winter months the occupancy* *rate was down to 50%.* Also called **occu-pancy rate**

room phone /'ruːm fəʊn/ *noun* HOTELS a telephone in a hotel room

room rate /'ruːm reɪt/ *noun* HOTELS the price for a hotel room for one night

room reservations /ruːm ˌrezə'veɪʃ(ə)nz/ *noun* HOTELS the department in a hotel which deals with bookings for rooms

room safe /'ruːm seɪf/ *noun* HOTELS a small safe in a hotel bedroom in which the guest can leave valuables

room sales /'ruːm seɪlz/ *plural noun* BUSINESS the turnover from letting rooms in a hotel

room service /'ruːm ˌsɜːvɪs/ *noun* CATERING an arrangement in a hotel where food or drink can be served in a guest's bedroom

'…he also draws attention to the growing use of good quality chinaware in room service. One factor in this is that more and more women guests use room service rather than dine alone in a hotel's main restaurant' [*Caterer & Hotelkeeper*]

rooms payroll /'ruːmz ˌpeɪrəʊl/ *noun* HOTELS the cost of the wages of hotel staff who deal with guest bedrooms

room status board /ˌruːm 'steɪtəs ˌbɔːd/ *noun* HOTELS a board in a hotel, showing each room, with its number and floor, and indicating whether it is vacant or occupied, or will be occupied or become vacant during the day

room tax /'ruːm tæks/ *noun* BUSINESS a visitor's tax levied by the local government or municipality on a visitor occupying a hotel room

room temperature /ˌruːm 'temprɪtʃə/ *noun* BEVERAGES the temperature in an ordinary room, usually around 20°C, at which most red wines should be served

root beer /'ruːt bɪə/ *noun* US BEVERAGES a dark fizzy drink, flavoured with the juice of roots, bark and herbs

root vegetable /ˌruːt 'vedʒtəb(ə)l/ *noun* a vegetable such as a carrot, turnip, or beet that is grown for its fleshy edible underground parts

RORO, ro-ro *abbreviation* SHIPS AND BOATS roll on/roll off

rosemary /'rəʊzməri/ *noun* SAUCES, ETC. a pungent herb with spiky green leaves, used in cooking ○ *We had roast lamb with rosemary.*

COMMENT: Rosemary is very often used when roasting lamb.

rosette /rəʊ'zet/ *noun* a ribbon bunched to look like a flower, used as a decoration or as a badge

rosé wine /ˌrəʊzeɪ 'waɪn/ *noun* BEVERAGES a pink wine which gets its colour from the grape skins being left for a time in the fermenting mixture

roster /'rɒstə/ *noun* a list showing employees and details of their periods of work ○ *The flight crew roster is issued on the 20th of the month.*

rösti /'rɜːsti/ *noun* FOOD a Swiss fried potato cake made from thinly sliced or grated potatoes, sometimes with added onions and bacon

rotisserie, rôtisserie *noun* CATERING a device in an oven, with a metal rod which can be passed through meat and turned so that the meat is evenly cooked

rotten /'rɒt(ə)n/ *adjective* **1.** that looks and smells bad because of decay **2.** terrible, unpleasant ○ *The service here is rotten!*

rouble /'ruːb(ə)l/, **ruble** US /'ruːb(ə)l/ *noun* FINANCE the currency used in Russia and Belarus

rough /rʌf/ *adjective* **1.** approximate, not very accurate **2.** not finished, or with no details

roughage /'rʌfɪdʒ/ *noun* CATERING same as **dietary fibre** ○ *Bran is an important source of roughage.* ○ *A diet that doesn't contain enough roughage is a possible cause of constipation.*

COMMENT: Roughage is found in cereals, nuts, fruit and some green vegetables. It is believed to be necessary to help digestion and avoid developing constipation, obesity, appendicitis and other digestive problems.

roughly /'rʌfli/ *adverb* approximately ○ *The number of visitors is roughly twice last year's.* ○ *The development cost of the marina will be roughly £25m.* ■ *adjective* in a way that is not gentle enough ○ *He was sacked for handling the animals roughly.*

rough out /ˌrʌf 'aʊt/ *verb* to make a first rough plan for something that will be planned in more detail later ○ *The tour guide roughed out a seating plan.*

rouille /rwiː/ *noun* SAUCES, ETC. a sauce made from chillies, garlic, and olive oil served as an accompaniment to Provençal foods such as bouillabaisse

roulade /'ruːlɑːd/ *noun* FOOD a dish in which a piece of food is coated with a sauce or filling and rolled up before being cooked, so that each slice has a spiral appearance

roulette /ruːˈlet/ *noun* ENTERTAINMENT a game of chance where bets are made on the numbers in boxes on a flat rotating wheel where a small ball will lodge when the wheel stops turning ○ *The casino has six roulette tables.*

round /raʊnd/ *adjective* shaped like a circle or ball □ **in round figures** not totally accurate, but correct to the nearest 10 or 100

roundabout /ˈraʊndəbaʊt/ *noun* **1.** ENTERTAINMENT a children's playing machine, which goes round when pushed and on which you can sit or stand **2.** ENTERTAINMENT (*in a fairground*) a large mechanical amusement machine, which turns round and plays music, usually with horses to sit on which move up and down **3.** ROAD TRAVEL a point where roads meet, and traffic has to turn in a circle, usually with each giving way to drivers coming from the right (NOTE: In US English, this is called a **traffic circle**.)

round down /ˌraʊnd ˈdaʊn/ *verb* to decrease to the nearest full figure ○ *The bill came to £164.62 but they rounded it down to £164.*

round-the-world /ˌraʊnd ðə ˈwɜːld/ *adjective* TRAVEL going round the world, returning to the original departure point ○ *Twenty yachts are taking part in the round-the-world yacht race.* ○ *A round-the-world ticket allows several stopovers.* Abbr **RTW**

round-the-world flight /ˌraʊnd ðə wɜːld ˈflaɪt/ *noun* AIR TRAVEL a flight which goes round the world, returning to the original departure airport. Abbr **RTW flight**

round-the-world ticket /ˌraʊnd ðə wɜːld ˈtɪkɪt/ *noun* AIR TRAVEL an airline ticket that entitles a passenger to travel to various destinations around the world, returning to the point of departure

round trip /ˈraʊnd trɪp/ *noun* TRAVEL a journey from one place to another and back again. Abbr **RT**

round-trip /ˈraʊnd trɪp/ *adjective* TRAVEL involving a journey to a place and back again. Abbr **RT**

round-trip ticket /ˌraʊnd trɪp ˈtɪkɪt/ *noun* TRAVEL same as **return ticket**

round up /ˌraʊnd ˈʌp/ *verb* to increase to the nearest full figure ○ *The bank cashier rounded up the figures to the nearest pound.*

'…each cheque can be made out for the local equivalent of £100 rounded up to a convenient figure' [*The Sunday Times*]

route /ruːt/ *noun* **1.** a way to be followed to get to a destination □ **bus route** way which is regularly taken by a bus from one place to another **2.** □ **en route** on the way ○ *We*

stopped for lunch en route for Scotland. ○ The pleasure ship sank when she was en route to the Gulf.* ■ *verb* ROAD TRAVEL to send a bus or aircraft by a particular route ○ *The train was routed via Berlin.* ◊ **re-route**

'…the consolidator is marketing perhaps the cheapest round-the- world Business class fare. It is charging a mere £1,389 for flights routed: London-Vienna-Bangkok-Taipei-Los Angeles-London' [*Business Traveller*]

roux /ruː/ *noun* SAUCES, ETC. a mixture of fat and flour cooked to make a base for a sauce

row /rəʊ/ *noun* **1.** a line of seats side by side, such as in a cinema or aircraft ○ *We had tickets for the front row of the stalls.* ○ *My seat is row 23A, so I must be next to a window.* **2.** SHIPS AND BOATS a short trip in a rowing boat ○ *We went for a row on the lake.* ■ *verb* SHIPS AND BOATS to make a small boat go forward by using oars

rowing boat /ˈrəʊɪŋ bəʊt/, **rowboat** US /ˈrəʊbəʊt/ *noun* SHIPS AND BOATS a small boat, which can be made to go forward using oars

Royal Automobile Club /ˌrɔɪəl ˈɔːtəməbiːl ˌklʌb/ *noun* ROAD TRAVEL a motoring organisation in Scotland. ◊ **AA**

Royal Scottish Automobile Association /ˌrɔɪəl ˌskɒtɪʃ ˈɔːtəməbiːl ə ˌsəʊsieɪʃ(ə)n/ *noun* ROAD TRAVEL a motoring organisation in the UK. Abbr **RSAC**

RRP *abbreviation* MARKETING recommended retail price

RSAC *abbreviation* ROAD TRAVEL Royal Scottish Automobile Club

RT *abbreviation* TRAVEL round trip

rtn *abbreviation* TRAVEL return ○ *fare from £30 rtn*

RTW *abbreviation* round-the-world

RTW flight *abbreviation* AIR TRAVEL round-the-world flight ○ *A round-the-world ticket allows several stopovers.*

rubber band /ˌrʌbə ˈbænd/ *noun* a thin ring of rubber for attaching things together ○ *Put a rubber band round the filing cards to stop them falling on the floor.*

rubber check /ˌrʌbə ˈtʃek/ *noun* FINANCE same as **bouncing cheque** (*informal*)

rubber stamp /ˌrʌbə ˈstæmp/ *noun* a stamp made of hard rubber cut to form words or numbers

rucksack /ˈrʌksæk/ *noun* a bag carried on the back of a walker ○ *She put extra clothes and a bottle of water in her rucksack.* ○ *A group of walkers with muddy boots and rucksacks came into the pub.* (NOTE: Larger bags are called **backpacks**.)

rug /rʌg/ *noun* **1.** a small carpet ○ *This beautiful rug comes from the Middle East.* **2.** a thick blanket, especially one used for travelling

rules /ruːlz/ *plural noun* regulations or laws, strict orders of the way to behave ○ *We apply strict rules of hygiene in the kitchen.* ○ *Did you read the rules about what to do in case of a fire?*

rum /rʌm/ *noun* BEVERAGES an alcoholic spirit made from sugar cane or molasses, usually coloured brownish-red

rump steak /ˌrʌmp ˈsteɪk/ *noun* MEAT a thick slice of beef cut from above the leg and considered to have the best flavour

run /rʌn/ *noun* TRAVEL a regular route of a plane, bus, train □ **he does the London-Paris run twice a week** he drives a coach from London to Paris twice a week ■ *verb* **1.** to manage e.g. a hotel or restaurant ○ *He runs a tourist guide service.* ○ *She runs the restaurant for her father.* **2.** (*of engine, transport*) to work or operate ○ *The bus does not run on Sundays.*

'…business is booming for airlines on the London to Manchester run' [*Business Traveller*]

running /ˈrʌnɪŋ/ *noun* BUSINESS the management of a business ○ *The day-to-day running of a large restaurant is complicated.*

running costs /ˈrʌnɪŋ kɒsts/, **running expenses** *plural noun* BUSINESS money spent on the day-to-day cost of a business. Also called **overhead costs**, **overhead expenses**, **overheads**, **operational costs**

run out of /ˌrʌn ˈaʊt əv/ *verb* to have nothing left of, to use up all the stock of ○ *The bureau de change has run out of dollars.* ○ *The hotel has run out of beer.*

run up /ˌrʌn ˈʌp/ *verb* to make a large debt quickly ○ *He quickly ran up a bill for £250.*

runway /ˈrʌnweɪ/ *noun* AIR TRAVEL a track on which planes land and take off at an airport ○ *The plane went out onto the runway and then stopped for half an hour.*

rupee /ruːˈpiː/ *noun* FINANCE the currency used in India, Mauritius, Nepal, Pakistan and Sri Lanka (NOTE: This is written **Rs** before the figure: *Rs. 250.*)

rush /rʌʃ/ *noun* a state in which you do something fast ■ *verb* to make something go fast ○ *to rush an order through the factory* ○ *to rush a shipment to Africa*

rush hour /ˈrʌʃ aʊə/ *noun* ROAD TRAVEL the time when most traffic is on the roads, when everyone is trying to travel to work or from work back home ○ *The taxi was delayed in the rush-hour traffic.*

rush job /ˈrʌʃ dʒɒb/ *noun* work which has to be done fast

rush order /ˌrʌʃ ˈɔːdə/ *noun* CATERING a request for something which has to be supplied fast

Russian /ˈrʌʃ(ə)n/ *adjective* referring to Russia (NOTE: Food served in the Russian way is called **à la russe**.)

Russian service /ˈrʌʃ(ə)n ˌsɜːvɪs/ *noun* CATERING **1.** a service similar to French service, where the waiter offers each guest a dish (from the left), and the guest helps himself from it **2.** a type of service at a banquet, where the food is carved at a sideboard, and served rapidly by the waiters to the guests so that the food does not get cold

Russian tea /ˌrʌʃ(ə)n ˈtiː/ *noun* BEVERAGES black tea, served in a glass

rustle up /ˌrʌs(ə)l ˈʌp/ *verb* to prepare a meal or snack quickly using any food that is immediately available

RV *abbreviation* ROAD TRAVEL recreational vehicle

rye /raɪ/ *noun* **1.** FOOD a hardy cereal crop grown in temperate areas **2.** same as **rye bread**

rye bread /ˈraɪ bred/ *noun* BREAD, ETC. bread made from rye, which is usually very dark in colour

rye whiskey /ˈraɪ ˌwɪski/, **rye whisky** *noun* BEVERAGES a type of whisky made in North America from rye

ryokan /riˈəʊkən/ *noun* CATERING a Japanese traditional inn

S

saccharin /'sækərɪn/ *noun* FOOD a substance used as a substitute for sugar

sachet /'sæʃeɪ/ *noun* a small plastic bag containing a portion of sauce, shampoo, etc. ○ *The fish is packaged with a sachet of sauce.*

saddle /'sæd(ə)l/ *noun* **1.** the rider's seat on a bicycle or on the back of a horse **2.** MEAT a cut of meat such as lamb, hare or venison, made up of both loins and part of the backbone

safari /sə'fɑːri/ *noun* ENTERTAINMENT an expedition in Africa to hunt or take photographs of wild animals ○ *He went on a safari in Kenya.*

safari holiday /sə'fɑːri ˌhɒlɪdeɪ/ *noun* TOURISM a holiday in a safari park

safari park /sə'fɑːri pɑːk/ *noun* ENTERTAINMENT a park where large wild animals such as lions, giraffes and elephants run free, and visitors can look at them from their cars, but cannot get out of the cars

safe /seɪf/ *noun* HOTELS a heavy metal box which cannot be opened easily, in which valuables, such as money, jewellery, and documents can be kept ○ *Put your valuables in the hotel safe.* ■ *adjective* uninjured, out of danger ○ *Three climbers were found safe after the avalanche.*

safe-deposit box /ˌseɪf dɪ'pɒzɪt ˌbɒks/ *noun* FINANCE a box in a hotel or bank in which valuables such as money, jewellery or documents can be kept

safe-keeping /ˌseɪf 'kiːpɪŋ/ *noun* the state of being looked after carefully ○ *We put the documents into the bank for safe-keeping.*

safety /'seɪfti/ *noun* **1.** the state of being free from danger or risk □ **to take safety precautions, safety measures** to act to make sure something is safe **2.** □ **for safety** so that something is safe ○ *Put the money in the hotel safe for safety.* ○ *Keep a note of the numbers of your traveller's cheques for safety.*

safety checklist /'seɪfti ˌtʃeklɪst/ *noun* a list of things which have to be checked as part of safety regulations

safety-deposit box /ˌseɪfti dɪ'pɒzɪt ˌbɒks/ same as **safe-deposit box**

safety margin /'seɪfti ˌmɑːdʒɪn/ *noun* time or space allowed for something to be safe

safety pin /'seɪfti pɪn/ *noun* a type of bent pin for attaching fabric, where the sharp point is held by a metal shield

safety regulations /'seɪfti ˌregjʊleɪʃ(ə)nz/ *plural noun* rules to make a place safe for the customers and staff

safflower /'sæflaʊə/ *noun* a plant which produces an oil used in cooking

saffron /'sæfrən/ *noun* SAUCES, ETC. an orange-coloured powder made from crocus flowers, from which colouring and flavouring are obtained

COMMENT: Saffron is used to colour food yellow; it is used in cooking rice and is an essential ingredient of bouillabaisse.

sage /seɪdʒ/ *noun* SAUCES, ETC. an aromatic herb with silvery-green leaves used in cookery

COMMENT: Sage and onion stuffing is often used in British cooking to stuff meat and poultry.

sago /'seɪgəʊ/ *noun* FOOD a white powder made from the sago palm, used as food and as a thickening agent

sail /seɪl/ SHIPS AND BOATS *noun* a trip in a boat ○ *They went for a sail down the Thames.* ■ *verb* to travel on water, or to leave harbour ○ *The ship sails at 12.00.*

sailing /'seɪlɪŋ/ *noun* **1.** SHIPS AND BOATS the departure of a ship ○ *There are no sailings to France because of the strike.* **2.** SPORT the activity of riding in or controlling a sailing boat, especially for pleasure ○ *We have booked to go on a sailing holiday in the Aegean.*

sailing boat /'seɪlɪŋ bəʊt/, **sailboat** /'seɪlbəʊt/ *noun* SHIPS AND BOATS a boat which uses mainly sails to travel

sailing time /ˈseɪlɪŋ taɪm/ *noun* SHIPS AND BOATS the time when a boat leaves

sake /ˈsɑːki/ *noun* BEVERAGES Japanese rice wine, usually drunk warm

salad /ˈsæləd/ *noun* FOOD a cold dish of various raw or cooked vegetables, often served with cold meat, fish or cheese ○ *cheese salad* ○ *prawn salad*

COMMENT: The commonest salad dressing is 'French dressing' or 'vinaigrette', made of olive oil, vinegar, salt, pepper, mustard and other flavourings; also common are 'Thousand Island dressing', made with mayonnaise and chopped onions, olives, etc., and 'blue-cheese' or 'Roquefort dressing', made with mayonnaise or vinaigrette and blue cheese or Roquefort cheese.

salad bar /ˈsæləd bɑː/ *noun* CATERING a self-service bar, where customers help themselves to a wide variety of meat, fish or vegetable salads

salad cream /ˈsæləd kriːm/ *noun* SAUCES, ETC. a commercially-prepared sauce made of eggs, oil and vinegar, used on salad and usually available in bottles or sachets

salad dressing /ˈsæləd ˌdresɪŋ/ *noun* SAUCES, ETC. a liquid sauce put on lettuce and other cold raw or cooked vegetables to give them additional flavour

salade niçoise /ˌsælæd ˈniːswɑːs/ *noun* FOOD a French salad, made with lettuce, hard-boiled eggs, cold boiled potatoes, anchovy fillets, black olives and tomatoes, with garlic in the dressing

salad servers /ˈsæləd ˌsɜːvəz/ *plural noun* a spoon and fork for serving salad

salamander /ˈsæləmændə/ *noun* CATERING **1.** a type of high-powered cooking grill used in restaurants, where food is grilled in a more or less enclosed box, as opposed to an open griller **2.** a very hot iron block, formerly used to grill the surface of food

salamander-glazed /ˌsæləmændə ˈgleɪzd/ *adjective* CATERING heated in a salamander until the coating melts and becomes shiny

salami /səˈlɑːmi/ *noun* MEAT a dry spicy pork sausage, originally from Italy

salary /ˈsæləri/ *noun* BUSINESS payment for work, made to an employee with a contract of employment, usually in the form of a monthly cheque ○ *She got a salary increase in June.* ○ *The company froze all salaries for a six-month period.*

salary cheque /ˈsæləri tʃek/ *noun* FINANCE a monthly cheque by which an employee is paid

sale /seɪl/ *noun* **1.** the act of selling, the act of giving an item or doing a service in exchange for money **2.** □ **for sale** ready to be sold **3.** □ **on sale** ready to be sold in a shop ○ *These items are on sale in most chemists.* **4.** BUSINESS a period during which goods are sold at specially low prices ○ *The shop is having a sale to clear old stock.* ○ *The sale price is 50% of the normal price.* □ **clearance sale** a sale of items at low prices to get rid of the stock

sales /seɪlz/ *plural noun* **1.** the money received from selling products ○ *Sales have risen over the first quarter.* **2.** the number of items sold

sales book /ˈseɪlz bʊk/ *noun* BUSINESS a book containing records of sales

sales campaign /ˈseɪlz kæmˌpeɪn/ *noun* BUSINESS a period of planned work to achieve higher sales

sales chart /ˈseɪlz tʃɑːt/ *noun* BUSINESS a diagram showing how sales vary from month to month

sales conference /ˈseɪlz ˌkɒnf(ə)rəns/ *noun* BUSINESS a meeting of sales managers, representatives and publicity staff to discuss results and future sales plans

sales force /ˈseɪlz fɔːs/ *noun* BUSINESS a group of salespeople

sales forecast /ˈseɪlz ˌfɔːkɑːst/ *noun* BUSINESS a calculation of future sales

sales manager /ˈseɪlz ˌmænɪdʒə/ *noun* BUSINESS somebody in charge of a sales department

sales representative /ˈseɪlz reprɪˌzentətɪv/ *noun* BUSINESS somebody who works for a company, showing goods or services for sale and trying to sell them ○ *They have vacancies for sales representatives to call on accounts in the north of the country.*

sales slip /ˈseɪlz slɪp/ *noun* BUSINESS a piece of paper showing that an article was bought at a particular shop ○ *Goods can be exchanged only on production of a sales slip.*

sales targets /ˈseɪlz ˌtɑːgɪts/ *plural noun* BUSINESS the amount of sales which a business is expected to achieve

sales tax /ˈseɪlz tæks/ *noun* BUSINESS a tax to be paid on each item sold

salmon /ˈsæmən/ *noun* SEAFOOD a large sea fish, with pink flesh ○ *cold poached salmon and salad*

Salmonella /ˌsælməˈnelə/ *noun* MEDICAL a genus of bacteria in the intestines, which are usually acquired by eating contaminated food, and cause typhoid or paratyphoid fever, gastroenteritis or food poisoning

'…according to Public Health Laboratory figures, infection in humans by Salmonella enteriditis stood at 16,981 last year. This comprised nearly half of all Salmonella figures' [*Caterer & Hotelkeeper*]

COMMENT: Salmonellae are found in meat, offal, eggs, milk and fish. The bacteria are killed by temperatures over 65°C, and so are killed by cooking. They survive freezing, and revive when frozen food is defrosted.

salmonella poisoning /ˌsælməˈnelə ˌpɔɪz(ə)nɪŋ/ *noun* MEDICAL an illness caused by eating food which is contaminated with Salmonella bacteria which develop in the intestines

salmon steak /ˈsæmən steɪk/ *noun* FOOD a slice of salmon cut across the body of the fish

salmon trout /ˈsæmən traʊt/ *noun* SEAFOOD a large sea trout with pink flesh like that of a salmon

salon /ˈsælɒn/ *noun* a shop where people can have their hair cut or styled, or have beauty treatments ○ *The hairdressing salon is on the fifth floor.* ○ *She went to the beauty salon for a manicure.*

saloon /səˈluːn/ *noun* US BARS a place which sells alcoholic drinks

saloon bar /səˈluːn bɑː/ *noun* BARS a bar in a pub which is more comfortable than the public bar, and where the drinks may be slightly more expensive

saloon keeper /səˈluːn ˌkiːpə/ *noun* US BARS somebody who runs a saloon

salsa /ˈsælsə/ *noun* SAUCES, ETC. a pungent Mexican sauce made of tomatoes, onions and chillis

salsify /ˈsælsəfi/ *noun* VEGETABLES a plant with a long, white root and green leaves, all of which are eaten as vegetables

COMMENT: Salsify has a flavour similar to that of oysters.

salt /sɔːlt/ *noun* small white tangy-tasting crystals consisting mainly of sodium chloride, used to flavour or preserve food ■ *adjective* **1.** containing common salt **2.** CATERING cured or preserved or seasoned with salt ○ *salt cod* ■ *verb* CATERING **1.** to add salt to ○ *You forgot to salt the soup.* **2.** to preserve food by keeping it in salt or in salt water

salt beef /ˌsɔːlt ˈbiːf/ *noun* MEAT beef which has been preserved in brine, then cooked and usually served cold in thin slices, in rye bread sandwiches

salt cellar /ˈsɒlt ˌselə/ *noun* CATERING a small pot containing salt usually with a hole in the top so that it can be sprinkled on food (NOTE: The US term is **salt shaker**.)

COMMENT: In the UK, a salt cellar has a single hole, to differentiate it from the pepper pot which has several; in the USA, the pepper pot will have only one hole while a salt cellar will have several. Table salt is ground to finer grains than cooking salt; kitchen salt may be treated with anti- caking agents to make it flow more freely.

salted /ˈsɔːltɪd/ *adjective* CATERING covered in salt ○ *There were bowls of salted nuts on the bar.*

salt-free /ˌsɔːlt ˈfriː/ *adjective* CATERING without salt ○ *a salt-free diet*

salt-free diet /ˌsɔːlt friː ˈdaɪət/ *noun* CATERING a diet in which no salt is allowed

saltiness, saltness *noun* CATERING the state of tasting strongly of salt

saltmill /ˈsɔːlmɪl/ *noun* CATERING a device which twists to crush salt crystals

salt water /ˌsɔːlt ˈwɔːtə/ *noun* water which contains salt, like sea water, as opposed to fresh water in rivers and lakes

saltwater /ˈsɔːltwɔːtə/ *adjective* containing salt water like the sea ○ *a saltwater swimming pool*

salty /ˈsɔːlti/ *adjective* containing or tasting strongly of salt ○ *We had a bowl of very salty pea and ham soup.*

salvage /ˈsælvɪdʒ/ *noun* income from the sale of waste materials from a hotel or restaurant, such as kitchen waste

salver /ˈsælvə/ *noun* CATERING a large flat serving plate, usually made of metal such as silver or stainless steel

samosa /səˈməʊsə/ *noun* FOOD an Indian dish consisting of a small triangular pastry containing spiced meat or vegetables, usually deep-fried and served as a starter or snack

samovar /ˈsæməvɑː/ *noun* CATERING an urn used in Russia for boiling water for tea

sample /ˈsɑːmpəl/ *noun* **1.** MARKETING a small quantity of something used for testing ○ *Can I see a sample of the cloth* or *a cloth sample?* ○ *Try a sample of the local cheese.* **2.** MARKETING a small representative group of people questioned to show what the reactions of a much larger group would be ○ *We interviewed a sample of potential customers.* □ **a random sample** a sample taken without any selection ■ *verb* **1.** to try something by taking a small amount ○ *to sample a product before buying it* ○ *You can sample the wine before placing your order.* **2.** MARKETING to question a small representative group of people to find out what the reactions of a much larger group would be ○ *They sampled 2,000 people at random to test the new orange drink.*

sanctuary /'sæŋktʃuəri/ *noun* a place for the protection of wild animals or birds ○ *They established several bird sanctuaries near the sea.*

sand /sænd/ *noun* a mass of very small bits of rock found on beaches and in the desert ○ *a beach of fine white sand* ○ *the black sand beaches of the Northern coast of New Zealand*

sand dunes /'sænd djuːnz/ *plural noun* grass-covered sandy ridges by the seashore

sandpit /'sændpɪt/ *noun* ENTERTAINMENT a place with sand where children can play

sandstorm /'sændstɔːm/ *noun* a high wind in the desert, which carries large amounts of sand with it

sandwich /'sænwɪdʒ/ *noun* **1.** FOOD two slices of bread with a filling such as meat, cheese between them **2.** BREAD, ETC. a type of cake, formed of two pieces of sponge cake, one on top of the other, with a cream or jam filling in between

sandwich bar /'sænwɪdʒ bɑː/ *noun* CATERING a small shop where you can buy sandwiches to take away

sandy /'sændi/ *adjective* like sand, or made of sand ○ *The resort has miles of safe sandy beaches.*

sanitary /'sænɪt(ə)ri/ *adjective* **1.** clean **2.** referring to hygiene or to health

sanitary towel /'sænɪt(ə)ri ˌtaʊəl/, **sanitary napkin** /'sænɪt(ə)ri ˌnæpkɪn/ *noun* a pad of absorbent paper worn during menstruation ○ *Do not put sanitary towels in the toilet, use the special bags provided.*

sanitation /ˌsænɪ'teɪʃ(ə)n/ *noun* the practice of being hygienic, especially referring to public hygiene ○ *Poor sanitation in crowded conditions can result in the spread of disease.*

sanitation officer /ˌsænɪ'teɪʃ(ə)n ˌɒfɪsə/ *noun* somebody responsible for ensuring that premises are kept in a hygienic condition

sardine /sɑː'diːn/ *noun* SEAFOOD a small fish of the herring family

SARS /sɑːz/ *noun* a serious disease of the lungs and bronchial tubes that was first reported in Asia in 2003. Full form **severe acute respiratory syndrome**

sarsaparilla /ˌsɑːsəpə'rɪlə/ *noun* BEVERAGES a non-alcoholic drink made from the root of an American plant

sashimi /sæ'ʃiːmi/ *noun* FOOD a Japanese dish consisting of slices of raw fish, usually served with a dipping sauce, e.g. a seasoned soy sauce

satay /'sæteɪ/ *noun* FOOD an appetiser served in South-East Asian cooking, made of marinaded meat cooked on a little skewer, and served with peanut sauce

satellite /'sætəlaɪt/ *noun* an object in space which goes round the Earth and sends and receives signals, pictures and data

satellite broadcast /ˌsætəlaɪt 'brɔːdkɑːst/ *noun* a radio or TV broadcast transmitted via a satellite

satellite dish /'sætəlaɪt dɪʃ/ *noun* an aerial, shaped like a dish used to capture satellite broadcasts

satellite TV /ˌsætəlaɪt tiː 'viː/ *noun* ENTERTAINMENT a television system, where pictures are sent via space satellites

satsuma /sæt'suːmə/ *noun* FRUIT a type of small sweet orange which peels easily

saturated fat /ˌsætʃəreɪtɪd 'fæt/ *noun* CATERING fat which has the largest amount of hydrogen possible. Compare **unsaturated fat**

COMMENT: Animal fats such as butter and fat meat are saturated fatty acids. It is known that increasing the amount of unsaturated and polyunsaturated fats (mainly vegetable fats and oils, and fish oil), and reducing saturated fats in the food intake helps reduce the level of cholesterol in the blood, and so lessens the risk of hardened arteries.

Saturday /'sætədeɪ/ *noun* the sixth day of the week, between Friday and Sunday □ **Saturday night stay fare** a special fare for someone who is staying Saturday night in a particular place

'...most destinations require a Saturday night stay but some in France can also be booked with a minimum two-night mid-week stay which makes them suitable for businessmen' [*Business Traveller*]

COMMENT: Discounted flights usually mean the passenger has to stay over a Saturday night. This is because most business people do not stay in hotels on Saturday, so rooms are more easily available.

sauce /sɔːs/ *noun* CATERING liquid with a particular taste poured over food to give it an extra flavour ○ *chicken in mushroom sauce* ○ *spaghetti with a tomato and meat sauce*

COMMENT: Common prepared sauces served in British restaurants include: tomato sauce (served with fried food);

horseradish sauce (served with roast beef and some smoked fish); mint sauce (served with lamb); and sauce tartare (served with fish). These are often commercially prepared and served in bottles or sachets.

sauceboat /'sɔːsbəʊt/ *noun* CATERING a vessel in which sauce is served

sauce chef /'sɔːs ʃef/ *noun* CATERING the chef in charge of preparing sauces. Also called **chef saucier**

saucepan /'sɔːspən/ *noun* CATERING a deep metal cooking pot with a long handle

saucer /'sɔːsə/ *noun* a shallow dish placed under a cup

sauce tartare /ˌsɔːs tɑːˈtɑː/ *noun* SAUCES, ETC. same as **tartare sauce**

saucisson /'sɒsiːsɒn/ *noun* MEAT a dry spicy pork sausage from France

sauerkraut /'saʊəkraʊt/ *noun* FOOD a German dish of pickled cabbage, often served with sausages

sauna /'sɔːnə/ *noun* ENTERTAINMENT **1.** a bath taken by sitting in a room filled with very hot steam ○ *We all had a sauna and then went for a swim in the lake.* **2.** a room where you can have a very hot steam bath ○ *There is a sauna in the basement of the hotel.*

sausage /'sɒsɪdʒ/ *noun* MEAT a tube of edible skin filled with minced and seasoned pork or other meat ○ *I'll have sausages and eggs for breakfast.*

sausagemeat /'sɒsɪdʒmiːt/ *noun* MEAT a mixture of meat, bread and flavourings for making sausages, sold separately, and used in pies and sausage rolls

sausage roll /ˌsɒsɪdʒ 'rəʊl/ *noun* FOOD a savoury snack made of pastry with a small sausage or piece of sausage meat inside it

sauté /'səʊteɪ/ CATERING *adjective* fried quickly in a little fat ■ *verb* to fry in a little fat (NOTE: **sautéeing – sautéed**)

sauté potatoes /ˌsəʊteɪ pəˈteɪtəʊz/ *plural noun* FOOD slices of potato, fried in a little fat ○ *Do you want sauté potatoes or new potatoes with your fish?*

save /seɪv/ *verb* **1.** to keep or not to spend money ○ *He is trying to save money by walking to work.* ○ *She is saving for a holiday in Spain.* **2.** not to waste or to use less ○ *To save time, let's continue the discussion in the taxi to the airport.* ○ *The government is encouraging companies to save energy.*

saver /'seɪvə/ *noun* TRAVEL an airline, coach, or train ticket that is cheaper than the normal price and usually places a number of restrictions on the date and time of travel

savings /'seɪvɪŋz/ *plural noun* FINANCE money which is not spent but put aside ○ *She spent all her savings on a trip to Egypt.* ○ *There are incredible savings on flights to Florida.*

savory /'seɪvəri/ *noun* SAUCES, ETC. a herb used in cooking, especially with beans

savoury /'seɪvəri/ CATERING *adjective* with a salty or other flavour which is not sweet ■ *noun* a snack, served at the end of a large meal, which is salty, or made of cheese (NOTE: The US spelling is **savory**. Note also that the plural is **savouries**.)

COMMENT: The savoury course in a large formal meal is normally served at the end, after the sweet course (or instead of it) and before the cheese. Common savouries in English cooking are 'Welsh rarebit' (grilled cheese on toast) or 'angels on horseback' (oysters cooked wrapped in rashers of bacon).

scald /skɔːld/ *verb* CATERING to plunge a fruit or vegetable into boiling water for a short time in order to loosen the skin or to prepare it for freezing

scale of charges /ˌskeɪl əv 'tʃɑːdʒɪz/ *noun* a list showing various prices

scallion /'skæliən/ *noun* US VEGETABLES same as **spring onion**

scallop /'skɒləp/ *noun* SEAFOOD a type of shellfish with a semi-circular ridged shell

scalloped potatoes /ˌskæləpt pə 'teɪtəʊz/ *noun* FOOD potatoes which are sliced and cooked in a shallow dish in the oven

scampi /'skæmpi/ *noun* FOOD large prawns usually served fried in batter (NOTE: The plural form is **scampi**.)

scenery /'siːnəri/ *noun* attractive countryside ○ *the beautiful scenery of the Lake District*

scenic /'siːnɪk/ *adjective* that has or runs through attractive countryside ○ *Welcome to scenic Nova Scotia.*

scenic railway /ˌsiːnɪk 'reɪlweɪ/ *noun* AIR TRAVEL a miniature railway running through artificial picturesque scenery at an amusement park

scenic route /'siːnɪk ruːt/ *noun* ROAD TRAVEL a road running through attractive countryside

schedule /'ʃedjuːl/ *noun* **1.** a timetable, a plan of times drawn up in advance ○ *The managing director has a busy schedule of appointments.* ○ *His secretary tried to fit me into his schedule.* □ **to be ahead of schedule** to be early ○ *The building of the hotel complex was completed ahead of schedule.* □ **to**

be on schedule to be on time ○ *The flight is on schedule.* □ **to be behind schedule** to be late ○ *I am sorry to say that we are three months behind schedule.* **2.** TRAVEL a list of times of departure and arrivals of trains, planes or coaches ○ *The summer schedules have been published.* **3.** a list, especially of additional documents attached to a contract ○ *Please find enclosed our schedule of charges.* ○ *For restrictions on use, see the attached schedule.* ■ *verb* **1.** to list officially ○ *scheduled prices* or *scheduled charges* **2.** to plan the time when something will happen ○ *The building is scheduled for completion in May.*

scheduled flight /ˌʃedʒuːld 'flaɪt/ *noun* AIR TRAVEL a regular flight which is in the airline timetable, as opposed to a charter flight ○ *She left for Helsinki on a scheduled flight.*

scheduling /'ʃedjuːlɪŋ/ *noun* drawing up a timetable or a plan

Schengen country /'ʃeŋgən ˌkʌntri/ *noun* a country that has signed the Schengen treaty

Schengen treaty /'ʃeŋgən ˌtyriːti/ *noun* an agreement signed by certain European Union Countries, plus Norway and Iceland, to end border controls and allow the free movement of goods and people within the treaty area and to harmonise external border controls

Schistosoma /ˌʃɪstə'səʊmə/ MEDICAL same as **Bilharzia**

schistosomiasis /ˌʃɪstəsəʊ'maɪəsɪs/[[SCAPS]] MEDICAL same as **bilharziasis**

schnapps /ʃnæps/ *noun* BEVERAGES a strong alcoholic spirit, resembling gin, made in Germany and the Netherlands

schnitzel /'ʃnɪts(ə)l/ *noun* FOOD a thin flat piece of veal or pork dipped in egg and breadcrumbs and fried. ◊ **Wiener schnitzel**

schooner /'skuːnə/ *noun* CATERING a large upright glass, used for serving sherry

scone /skɒn/ *noun* BREAD, ETC. a type of small crusty bread, sometimes with dried fruit in it, eaten with butter and jam or with cream. ◊ **cream tea**

scoop /skuːp/ *noun* CATERING **1.** a deep round spoon for serving ice cream ○ *You must wash the scoop each time you use it.* **2.** a portion of ice cream or vegetables served with a scoop ○ *I'll have one scoop of strawberry and one scoop of vanilla, please.*

Scotch /skɒtʃ/ *adjective* used for referring to some things, especially food and drink,

from Scotland ■ *noun* BEVERAGES **1.** a whisky made in Scotland ○ *a bottle of scotch* **2.** a glass of this whisky ○ *a large scotch, please*

Scotch broth /ˌskɒtʃ 'brɒθ/ *noun* FOOD a thick soup with barley, vegetables and lamb

Scotch egg /ˌskɒtʃ 'eg/ *noun* FOOD a hard-boiled egg, covered in sausage meat and fried and usually eaten cold

Scotch pancake /ˌskɒtʃ 'pænkeɪk/ *plural noun* BREAD, ETC. very small pancakes, cooked on a griddle

Scotch woodcock /ˌskɒtʃ 'wʊdkɒk/ *noun* FOOD a savoury consisting of small squares of toast spread with anchovy paste and topped with a mixture of scrambled egg yolks, cream and cayenne pepper

Scottish Natural Heritage /ˌskɒtɪʃ 'nætʃ(ə)rəl/ *noun* an official organisation which promotes the care and enjoyment of the national parks and other natural assets in Scotland

Scottish Tourist Board /ˌskɒtɪʃ 'tʊərɪst ˌbɔːd/ *noun* TOURISM an organisation which promotes tourism in Scotland and promotes tourism to Scotland from other parts of the UK. Abbr **STB**

scrambled eggs /ˌskræmbəld 'egz/, **scrambled egg** *noun* FOOD eggs which are beaten with salt and pepper and cooked in butter, often served on toast as part of an English breakfast ○ *We had a starter of scrambled egg with smoked salmon.*

scrambling /'skræmblɪŋ/ *noun* ROAD TRAVEL the sport of racing on motorbikes on rough terrain ○ *They arrange scrambling holidays in the Welsh mountains.*

screen /skriːn/ *noun* **1.** a flat surface which protects something or divides two things **2.** a flat panel which acts as protection against something, e.g. draughts, fire or noise **3.** a flat surface for projecting films onto **4.** a flat surface as on a television set or computer monitor, on which images are shown ○ *I'll call flight details up on the screen.*

screwdriver /'skruːdraɪvə/ *noun* BEVERAGES a cocktail of vodka and orange juice

scrumpy /'skrʌmpi/ BEVERAGES a type of strong cider traditionally made in south-west England

scuba /'skuːbə/ *noun* SPORT an underwater breathing apparatus

scuba-diver /'skuːbə ˌdaɪvə/ *noun* SPORT somebody who goes scuba-diving

scuba-diving /'skuːbə ˌdaɪvɪŋ/ *noun* SPORT the sport of swimming underwater, using breathing apparatus ○ *We went scuba diving in the Mediterranean.*

sea /siː/ *noun* an area of salt water

sea crossing /ˈsiː ˌkrɒsɪŋ/ *noun* a journey across a sea ○ *The sea crossing between Denmark and Sweden can be quite rough.*

seafood /ˈsiːfuːd/ *noun* SEAFOOD fish and shellfish which can be eaten (NOTE: There is no plural form.) □ **a seafood restaurant** a restaurant which specialises in seafood

seafront /ˈsiːfrʌnt/ *noun* ROAD TRAVEL a road which runs beside the sea in a seaside town ○ *We went for a walk along the seafront.* ○ *Our hotel was right on the seafront.* ○ *We stayed in a seafront hotel.* Also called **front** *noun* 2

sea level /ˈsiː ˌlev(ə)l/ *noun* the level of the sea, taken as a point for measuring altitude ○ *The resort is in the mountains, over 1,000ft above sea level.*

seaport /ˈsiːpɔːt/ *noun* a port by the sea

sear /sɪə/ *verb* CATERING to cook in a pan at a very high temperature for a short time, before grilling or roasting ○ *Sear the steak for a few seconds in a pan.*

seared /ˈsɪəd/ *adjective* CATERING cooked at the high temperature in a pan for a short time ○ *seared salmon and salad*

sea resort /ˈsiː rɪˌzɔːt/ *noun* TOURISM a holiday town near the seaside

sea salt /ˈsiː sɔːlt/ *noun* FOOD crystals of sodium chloride, extracted from sea water

seashell /ˈsiːʃel/ *noun* the shell of a shellfish which lives in the sea ○ *She walked along the beach collecting seashells.*

seashore /ˈsiːʃɔː/ *noun* land along the edge of the sea ○ *These types of plants grow on the seashore.*

seasick /ˈsiːsɪk/ *adjective* MEDICAL feeling sick because of the movement of a ship ○ *He gets seasick every time he crosses the Channel.* ○ *She didn't enjoy the cruise because she was seasick all the time.* ○ *I'll stay on deck because I feel seasick when I go down to my cabin.*

seasickness /ˈsiːsɪknəs/ *noun* MEDICAL sickness caused by the movement of a ship

seaside /ˈsiːdsaɪd/ *noun* an area near the sea where people go to have a holiday ○ *We always take the children to the seaside in August.* ○ *They'd like a seaside holiday instead of a holiday in the mountains.*

seaside town /ˈsiːsaɪd taʊn/ *noun* TOURISM a town by the sea ○ *Seaside towns are empty in the winter.*

season /ˈsiːz(ə)n/ *noun* **1.** TOURISM one of the four parts into which a year is divided,

namely spring, summer, autumn or winter **2.** TOURISM a period of time when something usually takes place □ **end of season sale** an event where goods are sold cheaply because the season in which they would be used is over, e.g. a sale of summer clothes in autumn **3.** □ **in season** which is fresh and plentiful and easy to buy ○ *Grouse isn't in season until 12th August.* ○ *Strawberries are cheaper in season.* ■ *verb* CATERING to add flavouring, spices, etc., to a dish ○ *Goulash is seasoned with paprika.*

seasonal /ˈsiːz(ə)n(ə)l/ *adjective* only lasting for a season

seasonal adjustments /ˌsiːz(ə)n(ə)l əˈdʒʌstmənt/ *plural noun* changes made to figures to take account of seasonal variations

seasonal demand /ˌsiːz(ə)n(ə)l dɪˈmɑːnd/ *noun* TOURISM a demand which exists only during the high season

seasonal labour /ˌsiːz(ə)nəl ˈleɪbə/ *noun* TOURISM workers who work for a season only

seasoned /ˈsiːz(ə)nd/ *adjective* CATERING flavoured with a particular type of seasoning ○ *highly seasoned Indian food*

seasoning /ˈsiːz(ə)nɪŋ/ *noun* CATERING salt, pepper, herbs or spices used to give flavour to food ○ *The meat seems to lack seasoning.*

season ticket /ˈsiːz(ə)n ˌtɪkɪt/ *noun* ROAD TRAVEL a rail or bus ticket which can be used for any number of journeys over a period, usually 1, 3, 6 or 12 months ○ *Season-ticket holders will receive a refund if their train is cancelled.*

seat /siːt/ *noun* a chair in a cinema, plane, restaurant, train, etc. ○ *They asked for six seats in row E.* ○ *Seats are available at all prices.* ○ *Take your seats for the first lunch.* ○ *Passengers are requested to remain in their seats until the plane has come to a standstill.* ○ *Seats in the first-class section are wider than in the tourist class.* ■ *verb* to have room for people to sit down ○ *The restaurants seats 75.* ○ *The hotel has a conference room seating up to 60 people.*

'…from April this year, passengers will be able to experience an upgraded Business class. Whether seat pitch (currently 104cm/40ins) will be improved upon has yet to be decided. There are several carriers which offer quite a few inches more' [*Business Traveller*]

'…the hotel has a 100-seat dining room, an 86-seat terrace and a 50-seat bar area' [*Caterer & Hotelkeeper*]

seat-back television /ˌsiːt bæk ˌtelɪˈvɪʒ(ə)n/ *noun* AIR TRAVEL a small television screen set into the back of the seat on an aircraft

seat belt /'siːt belt/ *noun* TRAVEL a belt worn in a car or aircraft as protection in case of accident ○ *The sole survivor of the crash had been wearing a seat belt.* ○ *The 'fasten seat belts' sign came on.*

-seater /siːtə/ *suffix* TRAVEL referring to a vehicle with a particular number of seats ○ *a 20-seater coach* ○ *a 10-seater executive jet*

seating /'siːtɪŋ/ *noun* seats available for people ○ *The hall has seating for three hundred people.*

seating capacity /'siːtɪŋ kə,pæsɪti/ *noun* the number of seats in a bus, cinema, etc.

seating plan /'siːtɪŋ plæn/ *noun* CATERING a chart showing where each guest sits at a big banquet

seat pitch /'siːt pɪtʃ/ *noun* TRAVEL the distance between the front edge of a seat and the front edge of the seat in front

seat recline /'siːt rɪ,klaɪn/ *noun* TRAVEL the distance by which a seat reclines

seat width /'siːt wɪdθ/ *noun* TRAVEL the distance between the armrests of a seat

sea voyage, sea cruise *noun* SHIPS AND BOATS a voyage or cruise on the sea

seaweed /'siːwiːd/ *noun* a plant which grows in the sea, a general name for several species of large algae (NOTE: There is no plural form.)

seaworthiness /'siːwɜːðinəs/ *noun* SHIPS AND BOATS the state of a boat that is able and safe to sail

seaworthy /'siːwɜːði/ *adjective* SHIPS AND BOATS able and safe to sail ○ *The old ferry is scarcely seaworthy.*

sec /sek/ *adjective* BEVERAGES a French adjective meaning dry (*used of wine*) (NOTE: For dry champagne, the word used is **brut**.)

second /'sekənd/ *adjective* coming after the first and before the third

second chef /,sekənd 'ʃef/ *noun* CATERING a deputy for a chef, who replaces the chef when he or she is on holiday, etc.

second-class /,sekənd 'klɑːs/ *adjective, adverb* TRAVEL referring to a less expensive and less comfortable type of travel than first-class ○ *to travel second-class* ○ *The price of a second-class ticket is half that of a first-class.* ○ *I find second-class hotels are just as comfortable as the best ones.*

second freedom /,sekənd 'friːdəm/ *noun* AIR TRAVEL the right to land at an airport for refuelling or repairs

second helping /,sekənd 'helpɪŋ/ *noun* CATERING another portion of the same dish ○ *After we had finished, the waiter came round with a second helping of fish.*

seconds /'sekəndz/ *plural noun* **1.** CATERING another portion of the same dish (*informal*) ○ *Can I have seconds, please?* **2.** items which have been turned down by the quality controller as not being top quality ○ *The shop has a sale of seconds.*

secretarial /,sekrɪ'teəriəl/ *adjective* referring to the work of a secretary ○ *She is taking a secretarial course.* ○ *He is looking for secretarial work.* ○ *We need extra secretarial help to deal with the correspondence.*

secretary /'sekrət(ə)ri/ *noun* a person who does work such as writing letters, answering the phone and filing documents for someone ○ *My secretary deals with incoming orders.* ○ *Her secretary phoned to say she would be late.*

section waiter /'sekʃən ,weɪtə/ CATERING same as **station waiter**

sector /'sektə/ *noun* BUSINESS part of the economy or business organisation of a country ○ *All sectors of the economy suffered from the fall in the exchange rate.* ○ *Tourism is a booming sector of the economy.*

'…government services form a large part of the tertiary or service sector' [*Sydney Morning Herald*]

security /sɪ'kjʊərɪti/ *noun* safety or protection against harm □ **airport security** actions taken to protect aircraft and passengers against attack

security bond /sɪ,kjʊərɪti dɪ'pɒzɪt/, **security deposit** *noun* TRAVEL money deposited by a tour company with a government organisation, which is to be used to repay travellers with tickets issued by the company if the company goes into liquidation

security guard /sɪ'kjʊərɪti gɑːd/ *noun* somebody who protects an office or factory against burglars

security manager /sɪ'kjʊərɪti ,mænɪdʒə/ *noun* a person who is in charge of efforts to protect a business against crime

security officer /sɪ'kjʊərɪti ,ɒfɪsə/ *noun* HOTELS somebody who protects a hotel against burglars

sediment /'sedɪmənt/ *noun* BEVERAGES a solid substance which forms in liquids such as red wine, and which can be removed by decanting the wine ○ *You could see a thick sediment at the bottom of the bottle of wine.*

seed /siːd/ *noun* part of a plant which germinates and grows to produce a new plant

seedless /'siːdləs/ *adjective* CATERING with no seeds in it ○ *seedless grapes*

segment /'segmənt/ *noun* part of a circle or sphere

'…different market segments and, ultimately, individual consumers must be addressed separately' [*Financial Times*]

segmentation /ˌsegmən'teɪʃ(ə)n/ *noun* the state of being divided into separate parts □ **segmentation of a market** the division of the market or consumers into categories according to their buying habits

seize /siːz/ *verb* to take hold of something or take possession of something by force ○ *The customs seized the shipment of books.*

seizure /'siːʒə/ *noun* **1.** the act of taking possession of something by force ○ *The court ordered the seizure of the shipment.* **2.** MEDICAL a fit, convulsion or sudden contraction of the muscles, especially in a heart attack, stroke or epileptic fit

Sekt /sekt/ *noun* BEVERAGES a sparkling German wine

COMMENT: Also familiarly called 'German champagne'; the best quality wine comes from the Rhine valley.

selection /sɪ'lekʃən/ *noun* **1.** a range ○ *There is a huge selection of farm produce in the market.* **2.** something which has been chosen ○ *a selection of French cheeses*

self-catering /ˌself 'keɪt(ə)rɪŋ/ *noun* TOURISM cooking for yourself

self-catering holiday /ˌself 'keɪtərɪŋ ˌhɒlɪdeɪ/ *noun* TOURISM a holiday where you rent accommodation, but cook your own meals ○ *self-catering villa holidays in Portugal*

self-contained /ˌself kən'teɪnd/ *adjective* HOTELS having its own kitchen, bathroom, etc., and not sharing these facilities with others

self-drive /ˌself 'draɪv/ *adjective* TOURISM involving a vehicle which you drive yourself ○ *The holiday includes a self-drive tour of the island.* □ **a 16-day self-drive package** a package holiday including a self-drive car for 16 days

self-employed /ˌself ɪm'plɔɪd/ *adjective* working for yourself, not being on the payroll of a company ○ *a self-employed accountant* ○ *He worked for a bank for ten years but now is self-employed.* ■ *noun* □ **the self-employed** people who work for themselves

self-financed /ˌself faɪ'nænst/ *adjective* □ **the project is completely self-financed** the project pays its development costs out of its own revenue, with no subsidies

self-raising /ˌself 'reɪzɪŋ/ *adjective* CATERING with a raising agent mixed in, so that baking powder need not be added when baking

self-service /ˌself 'sɜːvɪs/ *adjective* CATERING where the customers serve themselves

'…research revealed that customers wanted self-service restaurants for a quick meal, waitress service restaurants, takeaways and sandwich bars' [*Caterer & Hotelkeeper*]

self-service buffet /ˌself ˌsɜːvɪs 'bʌfɪt/ *noun* CATERING a buffet where guests help themselves to food from various dishes provided

self-service petrol station /ˌself ˌsɜːvɪs 'petrəl ˌsteɪʃ(ə)n/ *noun* ROAD TRAVEL a petrol station where the customers put the petrol in their cars themselves

self-service restaurant /ˌself ˌsɜːvɪs 'rest(ə)rɒnt/ *noun* CATERING a restaurant such as a cafeteria, where guests take a tray and help themselves to food

self-service store /ˌself 'sɜːvɪs ˌstɔː/ *noun* BUSINESS a shop where customers take goods from the shelves and pay for them at the checkout

sell-by date /'sel baɪ ˌdeɪt/ *noun* CATERING a date stamped on the label of a food product, which is the last date on which the product should be sold to guarantee good quality. Compare **best-before date**, **use-by date**

seller /'selə/ *noun* somebody who sells ○ *There were a few postcard sellers by the cathedral.*

seller's market /ˌseləz 'mɑːkɪt/ *noun* BUSINESS a market where a person selling goods or a service can ask high prices because there is a large demand for the product. Opposite **buyer's market**

semidry /'semidraɪ/ *adjective* BEVERAGES referring to wine that is partially or moderately dry

semihard /'semihɑːd/ *adjective* DAIRY referring to cheese that has a consistency firm enough to slice but that is moist and pliable

seminar /'semɪnɑː/ *noun* BUSINESS a class given to a small group of students who meet to discuss a subject with a teacher, or a organised discussion involving a small group of people ○ *The training seminar is being held in the conference room.*

seminar room /'semɪnɑː ruːm/ *noun* BUSINESS a small room with tables, audiovisual equipment, etc., used for holding seminars

semi-skimmed /ˌsemi ˈskɪmd/ *adjective* DAIRY from which some of the fat has been removed

semi-skimmed milk /ˌsemi skɪmd ˈmɪlk/ *noun* DAIRY milk from which some of the fat has been removed

semisoft /ˈsemɪsɒft/ *adjective* CATERING softer than most foods of its type

semisweet /ˈsemɪswiːt/ *adjective* CATERING slightly sweet, or having only a small amount of sugar or other sweetening ingredient added

semolina /ˌseməˈliːnə/ *noun* FOOD hard grains of wheat left when flour is sifted, used in puddings, stews, etc.

send /send/ *verb* to make someone or something go from one place to another ○ *to send a letter* or *an order* ○ *The company is sending the injured skiers back home by air.* ○ *Send the letter airmail if you want it to arrive next week.* (NOTE: **sending – sent**)

send away for /ˌsend əˈweɪ fɔː/ *verb* to write asking for something to be sent to you ○ *We sent away for the new brochure.*

send off /ˌsend ˈɒf/ *verb* to put in the post

send off for /ˌsend ˈɒf fɔː/ *verb* to write asking for something to be sent to you ○ *We sent off for the new catalogue.*

senior /ˈsiːniə/ *adjective* older, higher in rank ■ *noun* the father of the family ○ *Harry Markovitz Senior*

senior citizen /ˌsiːniə ˈsɪtɪz(ə)n/ *noun* an old retired person

senior executive /ˌsiːniər ɪgˈzekjʊtɪv/, **senior manager** /ˌsiːniə ˈmænɪdʒə/ *noun* BUSINESS a more experienced and higher-ranking manager in a company

senior passenger /ˌsiːniə ˈpæsɪndʒə/ *noun* TRAVEL a passenger over the age of 65

senior steward /ˌsiːniə ˈstjuːəd/ *noun* same as **chief steward**

separate *adjective* /ˈsep(ə)rət/ not together or attached □ **to send something under separate cover** to send something in a different envelope ■ *verb* /ˈsepəreɪt/ to divide ○ *The staff are separated into part-timers and full-time staff.*

separately /ˈsep(ə)rətli/ *adverb* individually, rather than together or as a group ○ *Each member of the group will pay separately.*

serum hepatitis /ˌsɪərəm ˌhepəˈtaɪtɪs/ *noun* MEDICAL same as **hepatitis B**

serve /sɜːv/ *verb* **1.** CATERING to bring food or drink to a customer ○ *She served the soup in small bowls.* ○ *Fish is served with a white sauce.* ○ *You should serve red wine with meat.* ○ *I can't serve six tables at once.* **2.** to deal with a customer in a shop or bar ○ *Will you serve this lady next, please?* ○ *I waited ten minutes before being served.* **3.** CATERING (*of a recipe*) to make enough food for ○ *The packet serves six.* ○ *A bottle of champagne should serve four people easily.*

server /ˈsɜːvə/ *noun* CATERING **1.** somebody who serves at table or a buffet **2.** a large flat knife for serving food

servery /ˈsɜːvəri/ *noun* CATERING a place where waiters pick up dishes ready to be taken to the guests' tables

service /ˈsɜːvɪs/ *noun* **1.** a period spent working for a company, in a shop, etc. **2.** the work of dealing with customers ○ *The service in that restaurant is extremely slow.* **3.** same as **service charge** ○ *to add on 10% for service* □ **the bill includes service** it includes an amount added to cover the work involved ○ *Is the service included?* **4.** CATERING a style of serving in a restaurant **5.** work to keep a machine in good working order ○ *the routine service of equipment* ○ *The machine has been sent in for service.* **6.** BUSINESS a business or office which gives help when it is needed **7.** □ **to put a new bus, plane into service** to start using a new bus or plane for the first time **8.** BUSINESS a system or arrangement of things that the public can use ○ *The postal service is efficient.* ○ *The bus service is very irregular.* ○ *We have a good train service to London.* **9.** a religious ceremony ■ *verb* **1.** to keep a machine in good working order ○ *The car needs to be serviced every six months.* ○ *The computer has gone back to the manufacturer for servicing.* **2.** to deal with somebody or something □ **to service arrivals** to deal with people arriving at a hotel, by looking after their luggage, etc. □ **to service a room** to clean a room after a guest has left, changing the beds and linen, etc.

service area /ˈsɜːvɪs ˌeəriə/ *noun* ROAD TRAVEL a place by a motorway where you can stop and buy petrol or get food, etc.

service bureau /ˈsɜːvɪs ˌbjʊərəʊ/ *noun* an office which specialises in helping other offices

service centre /ˈsɜːvɪs ˌsentə/ *noun* an office or workshop which specialises in keeping machines in good working order

service charge /ˈsɜːvɪs tʃɑːdʒ/, **service** /ˈsɜːvɪs/ *noun* **1.** CATERING an amount added to a bill to cover the work involved in dealing with a customer ○ *A 10% service charge is added.* ○ *Does the bill include a service charge?* **2.** an amount paid by tenants in a block of flats for general cleaning and maintenance

service cloth /'sɜːvɪs klɒθ/ *noun* CATERING a white cloth which a waiter carries over his or her arm and uses to hold hot plates when serving guests

service contract /'sɜːvɪs ˌkɒntrækt/ *noun* same as **maintenance contract**

serviced apartments /ˌsɜːvɪst ə'pɑːtmənts/ *plural noun* apartments where the rooms are cleaned daily, the beds are changed and new linen is put out

service department /'sɜːvɪs dɪ ˌpɑːtmənt/ *noun* BUSINESS a section of a company which keeps customers' machines in good working order

service engineer /'sɜːvɪs endʒɪˌnɪə/ *noun* somebody who specialises in keeping machines in good working order

service flat /'sɜːvɪs flæt/ *noun* a furnished flat which can be rented, together with the services of a cleaner and cook

service industry /'sɜːvɪs ˌɪndəstri/ *noun* BUSINESS an industry which does not make products, but offers a service such as banking, insurance, transport etc.

service manual /'sɜːvɪs ˌmænjʊəl/ *noun* a book which shows how to service a machine

service room /'sɜːvɪs ruːm/ *noun* CATERING same as **pantry**

service station /'sɜːvɪs ˌsteɪʃ(ə)n/ *noun* ROAD TRAVEL a garage where you can buy petrol and have small repairs done to a car

serviceware /'sɜːvɪsweə/ *noun* CATERING serving plates and trays, knives, forks and spoons which form part of a service ○ *stainless steel serviceware*

serviette /ˌsɜːviˈet/ *noun* CATERING a square piece of cloth used to protect clothes and wipe your mouth at meals ○ *He always tucks a large white serviette into his collar before each meal.* ○ *The restaurant is quite down-market – it has paper serviettes.* Also called **napkin**

serving /'sɜːvɪŋ/ *noun* CATERING **1.** the amount of food served to one person ○ *500g is enough for two servings.* **2.** the act of serving a customer

serving area /'sɜːvɪŋ ˌeəriə/ *noun* CATERING a place where food is served

serving hatch /'sɜːvɪŋ hætʃ/ *noun* CATERING a small opening in a wall for passing food and crockery from a kitchen to a dining room

serving suggestion /'sɜːvɪŋ sə ˌdʒestʃən/ *noun* CATERING the way a manufacturer suggests that you serve the product

sesame /'sesəmi/ *noun* FOOD a tropical plant whose seeds are eaten, usually scattered on the crust of bread or cakes

sesame oil /'sesəmi ɔɪl/ *noun* a strongly flavoured oil from sesame seeds, widely used in East and Southeast Asian cooking

sesame seed oil /'sesəmi siːd ˌɔɪl/ *noun* FOOD oil obtained from crushed sesame seeds, used in oriental cooking

session /'seʃ(ə)n/ *noun* a meeting to study, to discuss or to practise

set /set/ *verb* **1.** to put something in its place □ **to set the table** to put the cutlery, glasses, etc. on the table ready for a meal **2.** CATERING (*of food*) to become solid ○ *The jelly will set if you boil it long enough.* ■ *adjective* impossible to change □ **set times for meals** times for meals where everyone has to eat at the same time

set menu /ˌset 'menjuː/ *noun* CATERING a menu which cannot be changed, i.e., you cannot choose a dish from another part of the menu

setting /'setɪŋ/ *noun* the scenery around, or background for, a building

settle /'set(ə)l/ *verb* □ **to settle a bill, an account** to pay all the money owed on an account

settle up /ˌset(ə)l 'ʌp/ *verb* to pay the total of everything that is owed

Seville orange /sə,vɪl 'ɒrɪndʒ/ *noun* FRUIT an orange which is not sweet, and is used to make marmalade. Also called **bitter orange**

sew /səʊ/ *verb* to attach, make or repair something by using a needle and thread ○ *The button was not sewn on properly.* ○ *Can you sew my button back on, please?*

sewage /'suːɪdʒ/ *noun* waste water and other refuse such as faeces, carried away in sewers ○ *Exposure to sewage may cause disease transmission.* ○ *Food contaminated by sewage or liquid waste can cause typhoid.* □ **sewage disposal** the removal of sewage from buildings through pipes to places where it can be treated or got rid of ○ *Councils are fined for improper or unapproved sewage disposal systems.*

sewing /'səʊɪŋ/ *noun* the act of attaching by using a needle and thread

sewing kit /'səʊɪŋ kɪt/ *noun* a small wallet with needle, thread, etc., which can be used for making repairs to clothing in an emergency such as sewing on a button

sex tourism /ˈseks ˌtʊərɪz(ə)m/ *noun* travel undertaken to take advantage of the relatively relaxed laws on prostitution in some countries

sexual discrimination /ˌsekʃuəl dɪskrɪmɪˈneɪʃ(ə)n/ *noun* BUSINESS the act of treating men and women in different ways

sexual harassment /ˌsekʃuəl ˈhærəsmənt, həˈræsmənt/ *noun* BUSINESS harassment by making unwanted sexual approaches to somebody ○ *She complained of sexual harassment by her manager.*

shade /ʃeɪd/ *noun* a dark area which is not in the sunlight ○ *I would like a seat in the shade.* ○ *She was sitting in the shade of a big olive tree.*

shades /ʃeɪdz/ *plural noun* sunglasses (*informal*)

shady /ˈʃeɪdi/ *adjective* sheltered from the sun ○ *At midday in Madrid, it's better to walk on the shady side of the street.*

shake /ʃeɪk/ BEVERAGES same as **milk-shake**

shallot /ʃəˈlɒt/ *noun* VEGETABLES a small variety of onion, used in sauces, etc.

shallow-draught vessel /ˌʃæləʊ drɑːft ˈves(ə)l/ *noun* SHIPS AND BOATS a boat which can sail in shallow water

shampoo /ʃæmˈpuː/ *noun* **1.** liquid soap for washing the hair with ○ *There are sachets of shampoo in the bathroom.* **2.** the act of washing the hair ○ *She went to the hairdresser's for a shampoo.*

shandy /ˈʃændi/ *noun* BEVERAGES a drink made by mixing beer and lemonade

share /ʃeə/ *verb* **1.** □ **to share something with someone** to allow someone to use something which you also use ○ *The flat shares a front door with the flat next door.* **2.** to use something which someone else also uses ○ *We shared a taxi to the airport.* □ **prices are based on two people sharing**, **on twin share** prices are based on two people sharing the room

shared /ˈʃeəd/ *adjective* used by two or more people

shared bathroom /ˌʃeəd ˈbɑːθruːm/ *noun* HOTELS a bathroom which is shared by two or more rooms

sharp /ʃɑːp/ *adjective* **1.** having a thin edge which cuts easily ○ *You need a very sharp knife to slice vegetables.* **2.** MEDICAL hurting in a sudden and intense way ○ *He's suffering from sharp pains in his chest.* ■ *adverb* exactly ○ *The coach will leave the hotel at 7.30 sharp.*

shave /ʃeɪv/ *noun* the act of cutting off the hair on the face with a razor ○ *He went to have a shave at the barber's next to the hotel.* ■ *verb* to cut off the hair on the face with a razor

shaver /ˈʃeɪvə/ *noun* an electric instrument with a very sharp blade for removing hair on the face

shaver point /ˈʃeɪvə pɔɪnt/, **shaver socket** /ˈʃeɪvə ˈsɒkɪt/ *noun* same as **razor socket**

sheet /ʃiːt/ *noun* **1.** a piece of thin cloth, put on a bed ○ *Guests are asked to bring their own towels and sheets.* ○ *The maids change the sheets every day.* **2.** □ **sheet of paper** a piece of paper

shelf /ʃelf/ *noun* a plank attached to a wall or in a cupboard on which things can be put (NOTE: The plural form is **shelves**.)

shelf life /ˈʃelf laɪf/ *noun* CATERING the length of time food can be kept in a shop before it goes bad

shell /ʃel/ *noun* **1.** the hard outside part of an egg or a nut **2.** the hard outside part which covers some animals such as crabs or lobsters ○ *Snails are usually served in their shells.*

shellfish /ˈʃelfɪʃ/ *noun* SEAFOOD animals such as mussels, oysters, lobsters, and prawns, which have shells and live in them (NOTE: There is no plural form: *a dish of shellfish, a shellfish restaurant.*)

shelter /ˈʃeltə/ *noun* a place where you can go for protection ○ *There is no shelter from the pouring rain.* □ **to take shelter** to go under something for protection ○ *We took shelter in the hotel cellars when the civil war started.* ■ *verb* to go somewhere for protection ○ *They were sheltering from the snow in a small cave in the mountains.*

sheltered /ˈʃeltəd/ *adjective* protected from wind or cold ○ *The cottage is in a sheltered valley.*

shepherd's pie /ˌʃepədz ˈpaɪ/ *noun* FOOD minced lamb cooked in a dish with a layer of mashed potatoes on top. Compare **cottage pie**

sherry /ˈʃeri/ *noun* BEVERAGES a fortified wine from Spain

COMMENT: The word comes from the Spanish 'xerez', former name of the town Jerez in Southern Spain where the wine is made. Sherry can range from very dry to very sweet. The names used are 'manzanilla', the driest, 'fino', 'amontillado', 'oloroso' and 'cream sherry', which is the sweetest. In Spain, sherry is served cold, and very dry sherries are usually served in this way in Britain. Sweet sherries are served at room temperature. Sherry can be served in a small upright glass or, for large measures, in a schooner.

sherry glass /'ʃeri glɑːs/ *noun* CATERING a small glass suitable for serving sherry in

sherry trifle /ˌʃeri 'traɪf(ə)l/ *noun* DESSERTS a cold dessert of cake covered with jam and fruit, soaked in sherry and then covered with custard sauce, whipped cream, candied fruit and nuts

shift /ʃɪft/ *noun* a group of employees who work for a period, and then are replaced by another group, or a period of time worked by a group of employees ○ *We work an 8-hour shift.* ○ *The management is introducing a shift system* or *shift working.* □ **they work double shifts** two groups of employees are working shifts together

ship /ʃɪp/ *noun* SHIPS AND BOATS a large boat for carrying passengers and cargo on the sea

shipboard /'ʃɪpbɔːd/ *adjective* SHIPS AND BOATS on a ship ○ *shipboard entertainment*

ship chandler /ˌʃɪp 'tʃɑːndlə/ *noun* SHIPS AND BOATS somebody who supplies goods such as food to ships

shipping /'ʃɪpɪŋ/ *noun* **1.** BUSINESS the act or business of sending goods ○ *The shopkeeper will arrange for the shipping of the carpet.* **2.** ships

shipping company /'ʃɪpɪŋ ˌkʌmp(ə)ni/ *noun* BUSINESS a company which specialises in the sending of goods

shipping lanes /'ʃɪpɪŋ leɪnz/ *plural noun* SHIPS AND BOATS routes followed by ships

shipping line /'ʃɪpɪŋ laɪn/ *noun* SHIPS AND BOATS a company which owns ships

ship's doctor /ˌʃɪps 'dɒktə/ *noun* MEDICAL a doctor who travels on a ship and so is ready to treat passengers who become ill

shipwreck /'ʃɪprek/ *noun* SHIPS AND BOATS **1.** a ship which has been sunk or badly damaged on rocks. Also called **wreck 2.** the event of a ship being wrecked

shipwrecked /'ʃɪprekt/ *adjective* SHIPS AND BOATS involved in a shipwreck, or having been sunk or badly damaged on rocks

shish kebab /ˌʃɪʃ kɪ'bæb/ *noun* FOOD a kebab made of lamb, with peppers, onions and tomatoes, cooked on a skewer over a charcoal grill

shoe cleaner, shoe polisher *noun* HOTELS a machine for cleaning shoes

shoe polish /'ʃuː ˌpɒlɪʃ/ *noun* wax used to make shoes shiny

shoeshine /'ʃuːʃaɪn/ *noun* polishing of shoes

shooting /'ʃuːtɪŋ/ *noun* the act of shooting or killing with a gun

shooting party /'ʃuːtɪŋ ˌpɑːti/ *noun* ENTERTAINMENT a group of people who come together to shoot game as a sport ○ *The hotel caters for shooting parties, fishermen and golfers.*

shop /ʃɒp/ *noun* BUSINESS a place where goods are stored and sold ○ *All the shops in the centre of town close on Sundays.* (NOTE: US English usually uses **store**.) ■ *verb* □ **to shop (for)** to look for and buy things in shops

shop around /ˌʃɒp ə'raʊnd/ *verb* to go to various shops or offices and compare prices before making a purchase or before placing an order ○ *You should shop around before getting your car serviced.* ○ *He is shopping around for a new computer.* ○ *It pays to shop around when you are planning to fly to the States.*

shop assistant /'ʃɒp əˌsɪstənt/ *noun* somebody who serves customers in a shop

shop front /'ʃɒp frʌnt/ *noun* the part of a shop which faces the street, including the entrance and windows

shopkeeper /'ʃɒpkiːpə/ *noun* somebody who owns or runs a shop

shopping /'ʃɒpɪŋ/ *noun* **1.** the activity of looking for and buying goods in a shop ○ *She's not in her room – she must have gone shopping.* **2.** goods bought in a shop ○ *We buy our shopping* or *We do our shopping in the local supermarket.* ○ *She was carrying two baskets of shopping.*

shopping bag /'ʃɒpɪŋ bæg/ *noun* a bag used for carrying shopping

shopping basket /'ʃɒpɪŋ ˌbɑːskɪt/ *noun* a basket used for carrying shopping

shopping centre /'ʃɒpɪŋ ˌsentə/ *noun* ENTERTAINMENT a group of shops linked together with car parks and restaurants

shopping list /'ʃɒpɪŋ lɪst/ *noun* a list of things which you need to buy

shopping mall /'ʃɒpɪŋ mɒl/ *noun* ENTERTAINMENT an enclosed covered area for shopping, with shops, restaurants, banks and other facilities ○ *The new shopping mall is taking customers away from the stores in the town centre.*

shopping precinct /'ʃɒpɪŋ ˌpriːsɪŋkt/ *noun* ENTERTAINMENT part of a town which is closed to traffic so that people can walk about and shop

shop window /ˌʃɒp 'wɪndəʊ/ *noun* BUSINESS a window in a shop where goods are displayed so that customers can see them, place where goods or services can be exhibited ○ *The shop windows are all decorated for Christmas.*

shore /ʃɔː/ *noun* a beach or sandy area at the edge of the sea or of a lake □ **to go on shore, to go ashore** to go on land from a ship

short /ʃɔːt/ *adjective* 1. not long 2. for a small period of time □ **in the short term** in the near future, quite soon 3. not as much as should be ○ *The shipment was three items short.* □ **when we cashed up we were £10 short** we had £10 less than we should have had 4. □ **short of** with less than needed, with not enough of ○ *we are short of staff* or *short of money.* ■ *noun* BEVERAGES a drink of spirits such as gin, whisky, etc., with not much liquid

short black /ˌʃɔːt ˈblæk/ *noun* BEVERAGES a strong black coffee served in a small cup

shortbread /ˈʃɔːtbred/ *noun* BREAD, ETC. a thick sweet crumbly biscuit

short break /ˌʃɔːt ˈbreɪk/ *noun* TOURISM a holiday lasting only a few days

shortcake /ˈʃɔːtkeɪk/ *noun* US BREAD, ETC. a sponge cake with fruit filling, covered with whipped cream ○ *strawberry shortcake*

shortchange /ʃɔːtˈtʃeɪndʒ/ *verb* to give a customer less change than is right, either by mistake or in the hope that they will not notice

short credit /ˌʃɔːt ˈkredɪt/ *noun* FINANCE terms which allow the customer only a little time to pay

shortcrust pastry /ˌʃɔːtkrʌst ˈpeɪstri/ *noun* BREAD, ETC. the most commonly used type of pastry made with fat and flour

shorten /ˈʃɔːt(ə)n/ *verb* CATERING to make pastry more crumbly by adding more fat

shortening /ˈʃɔːt(ə)nɪŋ/ *noun* US FOOD a fat used in pastry, cakes and bread

short-grain rice /ˌʃɔːt ɡreɪn ˈraɪs/ *noun* FOOD rice with short grains used in rice pudding

short-handed /ˌʃɔːt ˈhændɪd/ *adjective* with not enough staff ○ *We are rather short-handed at the moment.*

short haul /ˈʃɔːt hɔːl/ *adjective* travelling or used for travelling a short distance ■ *noun* a short journey or distance

short-haul flight /ˌʃɔːt hɔːl ˈflaɪt/ *noun* AIR TRAVEL a flight over a short distance

short lease /ˌʃɔːt ˈliːs/ *noun* a lease which runs for up to two or three years ○ *We have a short lease on our current premises.*

short-life products /ˌʃɔːt laɪf ˈprɒdʌkts/ *adjective* CATERING products which have a short shelf life, especially fruit, vegetables, fish and meat

short measure /ˌʃɔːt ˈmeʒə/ *noun* a smaller amount than is legally allowed

short order /ˌʃɔːt ˈɔːdə/ *noun* US CATERING an order given for something which can be cooked quickly to order, such as ham and eggs

short-order chef /kʊk/, **cook** *noun* CATERING a cook who specialises in short orders

short-order diner /ˌʃɔːt ˌɔːdə ˈdaɪnə/ *noun* CATERING a café serving simple meals which can be cooked quickly to order

shorts /ʃɔːts/ *plural noun* short trousers which do not go below the knee ○ *Ladies are not allowed into the monastery in shorts.* □ **Bermuda shorts** longer shorts which go to knee length

short-sleeved shirt /ˌʃɔːt sliːvd ˈʃɜːt/ *noun* a shirt with short sleeves ○ *Women are not allowed into the monastery in short-sleeved shirts.*

short sleeves /ˌʃɔːt ˈsliːvz/ *plural noun* sleeves which do not go below the elbow

short-staffed /ˌʃɔːt ˈstɑːft/ *adjective* with not enough workers ○ *The restaurant is short-staffed and the service is slow.*

short-stay /ˈʃɔːt steɪ/ *adjective* referring to a stay of a few days □ **short-stay car park** a car park at an airport for travellers who will leave their cars there for a few hours or days □ **short-stay guest, visitor** a person who stays a few days in a hotel or a town. Compare **long-stay**

short-stay accommodation /ˌʃɔːt steɪ əˌkɒməˈdeɪʃ(ə)n/ *noun* accommodation for travellers who wish to stay for only a few nights

short take-off and landing /ˌʃɔːt teɪk ɒf ən ˈlændɪŋ/ *adjective* AIR TRAVEL needing a much shorter runway than other aircraft to take off or land. Abbr **STOL**

short-term /ˌʃɔːt ˈtɜːm/ *adjective* for a short period ○ *She is employed on a short-term contract.* □ **on a short-term basis** for a short period

short weight /ˌʃɔːt ˈweɪt/ *noun* a weight less than is legally allowed or than the customer has paid for

shoulder season /ˈʃəʊldə ˌsiːz(ə)n/ *noun* TOURISM a season between high and low, i.e., May and June, and October and November

show /ʃəʊ/ *noun* 1. an exhibition or display ○ *The Computer Show is on at Olympia.* 2. ENTERTAINMENT a performance, especially with music ○ *The show starts at 10.30.* ○ *Let's have dinner early and go to a show.* ■ *verb* to let somebody see something or point out something to somebody ○ *He showed us the sights of the town.* ○ *The guide will show you round the museum.*

show business /'ʃəʊ ˌbɪznəs/ *noun* the entertainment industry, including films, radio, television, theatre, and music recording

shower /'ʃaʊə/ *noun* **1.** a slight fall of rain or snow ○ *There was a shower this morning, but it is sunny again now.* **2.** a spray device for washing your whole body ○ *We have two single rooms with showers, or a double room with bath.* **3.** an occasion when you wash your body with a shower ○ *She went up to her room and had a shower.* ■ *verb* to wash yourself under a shower ○ *He had showered and was back in the lobby to greet his guests at 7.00 p.m.*

shower bath /'ʃaʊə bɑːθ/ *noun* **1.** a spray device for washing your whole body **2.** a bath taken in a spray of water

shower cap /'ʃaʊə kæp/ *noun* a waterproof cap to prevent the hair getting wet when taking a shower

shower cubicle /'ʃaʊə ˌkjuːbɪk(ə)l/ *noun* HOTELS a small box, with a shower in it, usually fitted into a corner of a small bathroom

shower curtain /'ʃaʊə ˌkɜːt(ə)n/ *noun* a piece of waterproof material around a shower

shower gel /'ʃaʊə dʒel/ *noun* liquid soap used for washing in a shower

shower room /'ʃaʊə ruːm/ *noun* HOTELS a room with a shower in it

show plate /'ʃəʊ pleɪt/ *noun* CATERING a plate placed in the centre of the setting in French service, removed before serving

show platter /'ʃəʊ ˌplætə/ *noun* CATERING a large plate of meat, etc., arranged decoratively as an example of how the dish can look ○ *a show platter of meat*

shred /ʃred/ *verb* CATERING to cut into very thin strips ○ *The dish is served with a salad of shredded carrot.*

shredder /'ʃredə/ *noun* CATERING a device for cutting vegetables into very thin strips

shrimp /ʃrɪmp/ *noun* SEAFOOD a small shellfish with a long tail

Shrove Tuesday /ˌʃrəʊv 'tjuːzdeɪ/ *noun* the last Tuesday before Lent, celebrated in Britain by eating pancakes ○ *Tomorrow is Shrove Tuesday, so we'll be having pancakes.* Also called **Mardi Gras**, **Pancake Day**

COMMENT: Also called 'Pancake Day', it is the last day before Lent, and so a day when feasts are held. In Britain, pancakes are traditionally eaten on Shrove Tuesday, usually with lemon and sugar, but also with other sweet fillings. In France and French-speaking countries, the festival is called 'Mardi Gras'.

shuck /ʃʌk/ *verb US* CATERING to remove the shell of an oyster, nut, etc. ○ *She sat on the quay shucking oysters.*

shucked /ʃʌkt/ *adjective US* CATERING removed from its shell, said of oysters ○ *We serve oysters either shucked or in the shell.*

shut /ʃʌt/ *adjective* closed ○ *We tried to get into the museum but it was shut.* ■ *verb* to close for business ○ *In Germany, shops shut on Saturday afternoons.*

shutter /'ʃʌtə/ *noun* **1.** a folding wooden or metal cover on a window ○ *Open the shutters and see what the weather is like.* **2.** a part in a camera which opens and closes very rapidly to allow the light to go on to the film

shuttle /'ʃʌt(ə)l/ *noun* ROAD TRAVEL a bus or plane which goes backwards and forwards between two places ○ *There's a shuttle bus from the hotel to the exhibition grounds.* □ **the Glasgow shuttle** the plane going regularly backwards and forwards between London and Glasgow

shuttle service /'ʃʌt(ə)l ˌsɜːvɪs/ *noun* ROAD TRAVEL a transport service which goes regularly backwards and forwards between two places ○ *The ferry operates a shuttle service between the islands.*

sick /sɪk/ *adjective* MEDICAL **1.** ill ○ *We have five staff off sick.* **2.** vomiting ○ *The greasy food made her feel sick.*

sick bag /'sɪk bæg/ *noun* AIR TRAVEL a strong paper bag provided in the pocket in front of each seat on planes or hovercraft, so that passengers suffering from airsickness can vomit without leaving their seats

sickness /'sɪknəs/ *noun* MEDICAL the state of being ill

side /saɪd/ *noun* **1.** the part of something near the edge ○ *She leant over the side of the ship.* ○ *The hitchhikers were standing by the side of the road.* **2.** one of the surfaces of a flat object ○ *Please write on one side of the paper only.* **3.** □ **on the side** separate from your normal work, and sometimes hidden from your employer ○ *He works in the hotel bar, but he runs a tour company on the side.* ○ *Her salary is too small to live on, so the family lives on what she can make on the side.*

sideboard /'saɪdbɔːd/ *noun* **1.** (*in a house*) a piece of furniture in a dining room, used to put plates or dishes on **2.** (*in a restaurant*) a piece of furniture for keeping articles for use on the tables, such as cloths, napkins, cruets, cutlery, etc., but not plates or glasses

sidecar /'saɪdkɑː/ *noun* BEVERAGES a cocktail of brandy, Cointreau and lemon juice

side dish /'saɪd dɪʃ/ *noun* CATERING a small plate or bowl of food eaten to accompany a main course ○ *We had a side dish of spinach to go with the fish.*

side lights /'saɪd laɪts/ *plural noun* ROAD TRAVEL small lights on a car or truck which show the outline of a vehicle in the dark. Also called **parking lights**

side order /'saɪd ˌɔːdə/ *noun* CATERING an order for something as a side dish ○ *Can I have a side order of chips?*

side plate /'saɪd pleɪt/ *noun* CATERING a small plate placed beside the main plate and cutlery, used for bread

side towel /'saɪd ˌtaʊəl/ *noun* CATERING a special towel used by a waiter for handling hot plates or to wipe the side of a plate

sidework /'saɪdwɜːk/ *noun* CATERING additional work assigned to waiters, e.g. glass polishing

siesta /si'estə/ *noun* ENTERTAINMENT a rest period in the middle of the day, common in Mediterranean countries

sieve /sɪv/ CATERING *noun* a kitchen utensil made of metal or plastic net, used to strain liquids to remove lumps ■ *verb* to pass something such as flour, liquid, etc. through a sieve to remove lumps

sift /sɪft/ *noun* CATERING to pass something such as flour, liquid, etc. through a sieve to remove lumps

sight /saɪt/ *noun* ENTERTAINMENT a spectacle, something which you ought to see ○ *They went off on foot to see the sights of the town.*

sightseeing /'saɪtsiːɪŋ/ *noun* ENTERTAINMENT visiting the sights of a town ○ *The bus company has sightseeing tours of the town every afternoon.* ○ *I'm too tired to go sightseeing* or *to do any sightseeing today.* ○ *Queue here for the London sightseeing bus.*

sightseer /'saɪtsiːə/ *noun* TOURISM a tourist who visits the sights of a town ○ *There were fewer sightseers than usual at the Tower of London.*

sign /saɪn/ *noun* **1.** a movement of the hand or head, etc. which means something **2.** MAR-

KETING an advertising board or panel showing the name of a shop **3.** ROAD TRAVEL a panel showing directions on a road ■ *verb* to write your name in a special way on a document to show that you have written it or approved it ○ *to sign a letter* or *a contract* or *a document* or *a cheque* ○ *They signed the hotel register using the name of Smith.* ○ *She sent the cheque as a deposit, but forgot to sign it.*

signage /'saɪnɪdʒ/ *noun* HOTELS all the signs, logos, etc., which identify a business such as hotel group or chain of restaurants ○ *All external hotel signage is being changed.*

'…if planning permission is granted and the Department of Transport is happy to grant motorway signage and access permission, you can buy or lease the land and start building' [*Caterer & Hotelkeeper*]

signal /'sɪgn(ə)l/ *noun* **1.** a movement of the hand or head which tells someone to do something **2.** a light or mechanical flag used to tell someone to do something ○ *The signal was at red so we had to stop.* ■ *verb* to make signs to tell someone to do something ○ *The driver signalled to show that he was turning right.* ○ *At a request stop you have to signal to the driver, otherwise he won't stop.* (NOTE: The British English is **signalling – signalled**; the US spelling is **signaling – signaled**.)

signal box /'sɪgn(ə)l bɒks/ *noun* RAIL TRAVEL a building by the side of the railway where the signalman controls the signals

signalman /'sɪgn(ə)lmən/ *noun* RAIL TRAVEL somebody who controls railway signals (NOTE: The plural form is **signalmen**.)

signature /'sɪgnɪtʃə/ *noun* somebody's name written by them in a special way ○ *He found a pile of cheques on his desk waiting for signature.* ○ *The signature on the form did not match that on the back of the credit card.*

signature dish /'sɪgnɪtʃə dɪʃ/ *noun* CATERING a special dish for which a particular restaurant is well known

signboard /'saɪnbɔːd/ *noun* a panel with a sign

sign language /'saɪn ˌlæŋgwɪdʒ/ *noun* a set of agreed signs made with the fingers and hands, used to communicate by or for people who cannot hear or speak

sign on /ˌsaɪn 'ɒn/ *verb* to start work

signpost /'saɪnpəʊst/ *noun* a post with a sign showing directions to a place

silver /'sɪlvə/ *noun* **1.** a precious grey metal often used for making jewellery **2.** coins made of light grey metal

Silver Award for Quality /ˌsɪlvə ə ˌwɔːd fə 'kwɒləti/ *noun* TOURISM an annual award given by one of the regional tourist boards to a hotel or restaurant

silver foil /'sɪlvə fɔɪl/, **silver paper** /'sɪlvə 'peɪpə/ *noun* CATERING a sheet of thin shiny metal which looks like silver, used for wrapping food in

silver plate /ˌsɪlvə 'pleɪt/ *noun* CATERING cutlery which is made of ordinary metal, but covered with silver, giving the impression that it is made of solid silver and used in high-class restaurants as being superior to stainless steel. Also called **electroplated nickel silver**

silver service /ˌsɪlvə 'sɜːvɪs/ *noun* CATERING a type of restaurant service, especially for banquets, where the waiter or waitress serves each guest from a flat dish

silverside /'sɪlvəsaɪd/ *noun* MEAT a cut of beef taken from behind and below the rump and topside, usually used for roasting or pot-roasting

Silver Thistle Award /ˌsɪlvə 'θɪs(ə)l ə ˌwɔːd/ *noun* TOURISM an annual award given by the Scottish Tourist Board to an outstanding hotel or restaurant

silverware /'sɪlvəweə/ *noun* **1.** articles made of silver **2.** (*in a restaurant*) cutlery and other articles made of silver plate (NOTE: There is no plural form.)

silver wedding /ˌsɪlvə 'wedɪŋ/ *noun* an anniversary of 25 years of marriage

simmer /'sɪmə/ *verb* CATERING to boil gently

simnel cake /'sɪmnəl keɪk/ *noun* BREAD, ETC. a fruit cake covered with marzipan, traditionally eaten in Lent or at Easter

simple interest /ˌsɪmpəl 'ɪntrəst/ *noun* BUSINESS interest calculated on the capital only, and not any sums later added to the capital

single /'sɪŋg(ə)l/ *adjective, noun* one alone

single bed /'sɪŋg(ə)l bed/ *noun* a bed for one person

single cream /ˌsɪŋg(ə)l 'kriːm/ *noun* DAIRY liquid cream, with a lower fat content

singledecker /ˌsɪŋg(ə)l 'dekə/ *noun* ROAD TRAVEL a bus with only one deck ○ *The airport bus is a singledecker.* Compare **double-decker**

single-entry visa /ˌsɪŋg(ə)l ˌentri 'viːzə/ *noun* TRAVEL a visa which allows you to enter a country once ○ *A single-entry visa costs £35 for adults.*

single fare /'sɪŋg(ə)l feə/ *noun* TRAVEL the fare for one journey from one place to another. Also called **one-way fare**

single measure /ˌsɪŋg(ə)l 'meʒə/ *noun* BEVERAGES one measure of spirits

single occupancy /ˌsɪŋg(ə)l 'ɒkjʊpənsi/ *noun* HOTELS one person in a room

single room /ˌsɪŋg(ə)l 'ruːm/ *noun* HOTELS a room for one person

single room supplement /ˌsɪŋg(ə)l ruːm 'sʌplɪmənt/ *noun* TOURISM an extra charge for a single person travelling with a group where charges are calculated on the basis of two people sharing each room

singles bar /'sɪŋg(ə)lz bɑː/ *noun* a bar where unmarried or divorced people go, hoping to meet others

single supplement /ˌsɪŋg(ə)l 'sʌplɪmənt/ *noun* HOTELS an extra sum charged for accommodation when it is occupied by only one person

single ticket /ˌsɪŋg(ə)l 'tɪkɪt/ *noun* TRAVEL a ticket for one journey from one place to another ○ *I want two singles to London.* Also called **one-way ticket**

single-track railway /ˌsɪŋg(ə)l træk 'reɪlweɪ/ *noun* RAIL TRAVEL a railway line on which trains go in either direction on the same rails, with passing places at intervals

single trip /'sɪŋg(ə)l trɪp/ *noun* TRAVEL one trip in one direction only ○ *The insurance offers single-trip policies for both families and individuals.*

sink /sɪŋk/ *noun* a basin for washing in a kitchen ■ *verb* to go down to the bottom of something such as water or mud ○ *The ferry sank in 30m of water.* ○ *All the passengers were saved when the liner sank in the tropical storm.* (NOTE: **sinking – sank – has sunk**)

sink unit /'sɪŋk ˌjuːnɪt/ *noun* an arrangement of sinks, taps and waste pipes forming a single piece of equipment

sirloin /'sɜːlɔɪn/ *noun* MEAT the best cut of beef from the back of the animal ○ *We bought a sirloin of beef for our Sunday roast.*

sirloin steak /ˌsɜːlɔɪn 'steɪk/ *noun* MEAT a thick piece of beef cut from a sirloin

sister company /'sɪstə ˌkʌmp(ə)ni/ *noun* BUSINESS a company which is part of the same group as another company

sister ship /'sɪstə ʃɪp/ *noun* SHIPS AND BOATS a ship which is of the same design and belongs to the same company as another ship

sit-down meal /ˌsɪt daʊn 'miːl/ *noun* CATERING a meal where the guests sit and eat at tables, as opposed to a 'stand-up meal' ○ *After the meeting a sit-down lunch will be served to the delegates.*

sit-down strike /ˈsɪt daʊn ˌstraɪk/ *noun* BUSINESS a strike where employees stay in their place of work and refuse to work or leave

site /saɪt/ *noun* **1.** a place where a building stands □ **on site** at the place where a building is or is being constructed **2.** ENTERTAINMENT a place where an event takes place ○ *They visited the sites of First World War battles.* **3.** MARKETING same as **website** ○ *How many hits did we have on our site last week?* ■ *verb* to place a building on a particular piece of land ○ *The hotel will be sited between the airport and the new exhibition centre.*

'…this site is designed for holidaymakers, so the cheapest flights pop up first' [*Evening Standard, travel section*]

Site of Special Scientific Interest /ˌsaɪt əv ˌspeʃ(ə)l ˌsaɪəntɪfɪk ˈɪntrəst/ *noun* a small area of land which has been noted as particularly important by the Nature Conservancy Council, and which is preserved for its fauna, flora or geology. Abbr **SSSI**

sitting /ˈsɪtɪŋ/ *noun* CATERING the time when a group of people eat together ○ *Take your seats for the second sitting.*

sitting room /ˈsɪtɪŋ ruːm/ *noun* a room with comfortable chairs where people can rest, talk, watch television, etc. ○ *The suite has a bedroom, bathroom and a private sitting room.*

situated /ˈsɪtʃueɪtɪd/ *adjective* placed ○ *The hotel is situated at the edge of the town.* ○ *The tourist office is situated near the railway station.*

situation /ˌsɪtʃuˈeɪʃ(ə)n/ *noun* a place where something is ○ *The hotel is in a very pleasant situation by the lake.*

situations vacant /ˌsɪtʃueɪʃ(ə)nz ˈveɪkənt/ *noun* a list in a newspaper of jobs which are available

six-pack /ˈsɪks pæk/ *noun* a box containing six items

sixth freedom /ˌsɪksθ ˈfriːdəm/ *noun* AIR TRAVEL the right of a carrier of one country to carry passengers from another country, stopping in its own country, and then continuing to a third country

size /saɪz/ *noun* the measurements of something, how big something is, or how many there are of something ○ *What size shoes do you take?* ○ *This packet is the maximum size allowed by the post office.* ○ *She's looking for something in a smaller size.*

skate /skeɪt/ *noun* SEAFOOD a large flat sea fish with white flesh (NOTE: The plural form is **skate**.) ■ *verb* SPORT to slide on ice wearing skates

skateboard /ˈskeɪtbɔːd/ SPORT *noun* a short narrow board with a set of small wheels fitted underneath, used to move rapidly or to perform jumps and stunts ■ *verb* to ride on a skateboard

skateboarding /ˈskeɪtbɔːdɪŋ/ *noun* SPORT the sport or pastime of riding a skateboard

skatepark /ˈskeɪtpɑːk/ *noun* SPORT an area specially designed and constructed for people practising and performing on skateboards and in-line skates

skater /ˈskeɪtə/ *noun* SPORT somebody who goes skating ○ *There were dozens of skaters on the frozen pond.*

skating /ˈskeɪtɪŋ/ *noun* SPORT the activity of sliding on the ice, wearing skates ○ *Skating is very popular in Canada.*

skating rink /ˈskeɪtɪŋ rɪŋk/ *noun* SPORT same as **ice rink** ○ *There used to be an indoor skating rink in Richmond.*

skeleton key /ˌskelɪt(ə)n ˈkiː/ *noun* a key which will fit any lock in a building

skeleton staff /ˈskelɪt(ə)n stɑːf/ *noun* a few staff left to carry on essential work while most of the workforce is away

skewer /ˈskjuːə/ *noun* CATERING a long thin metal rod for putting through pieces of meat when cooking ○ *She put some pieces of chicken and onion on the skewer.* ○ *The main course was a skewer of lamb with rice.* ■ *verb* to stick a long metal rod through something ○ *He skewered bits of meat and green peppers and grilled them.* ○ *The fish was skewered on a stick.*

ski /skiː/ *noun* one of two long flat objects which are attached to your boots for sliding over snow ○ *Skis can be hired at the chairlift.* ○ *We always hire skis when we get to the ski resort.* ○ *Someone stole my new pair of skis.* ■ *verb* to move over snow on skis ○ *The mountain rescue team had to ski to the site of the avalanche.* ○ *We go skiing in Switzerland every winter.*

'…the newest and best thing in snow sport is the twin-tip: a free-ride ski that is compact, bent up at both ends and can turn on a sixpence' [*The Sunday Times*]

ski area /ˈskiː ˌeəriə/ *noun* ENTERTAINMENT part of a mountain range or part of a club's land where you can ski

skiboots /ˈskiː buːts/, **ski boots** *plural noun* SPORT special boots worn when skiing, which attach to the skis

ski equipment, ski gear *noun* SPORT all the things needed to go skiing, e.g. skis, boots, goggles and poles

skier /'skiːə/ *noun* SPORT somebody who moves over snow on skis ○ *Not a single skier was out on the slopes.*

ski goggles /'skiː ˌɡɒɡ(ə)lz/ *plural noun* SPORT goggles worn when skiing

ski holiday /'skiː ˌhɒlɪdeɪ/ *noun* TOURISM a holiday when you ski

skiing /'skiːɪŋ/ *noun* SPORT the sport of moving over snow on skis ○ *Skiing is a very popular sport.* ○ *I did some skiing when I was younger.* ○ *We're going on a skiing holiday.*

skiing instructor /'skiːɪŋ ɪnˌstrʌktə/ *noun* SPORT somebody who teaches people how to ski

ski jump /'skiː dʒʌmp/ *noun* SPORT a slope with a sudden drop at the bottom from which skiers jump in a competition to see who can jump the furthest

ski lift /'skiː lɪft/ *noun* a device to take skiers to the top of a slope ○ *They had a marvellous view from the ski lift.* ○ *The hotel is within walking distance of the ski lifts.*

skill /skɪl/ *noun* the ability to do something well ○ *Making meringues requires a lot of skill.* ○ *Skills can be taught and that is where good teachers are important.*

skilled /skɪld/ *adjective* having a particular skill ○ *We need skilled staff in the reception area.* Compare **unskilled**

skilled labour /ˌskɪld 'leɪbə/ *noun* workers who have special knowledge or qualifications

skillet /'skɪlɪt/ *noun* US CATERING a frying pan

skim /skɪm/ *verb* CATERING to remove things floating on the surface of a liquid ○ *Skim the soup to remove the fat.*

skimmed milk /ˌskɪmd 'mɪlk/ *noun* DAIRY milk from which most of the fat has been removed

skin /skɪn/ *noun* **1.** the outer covering of the body ○ *She got sunburnt and her skin began to peel.* **2.** CATERING the outer surface of fruit, vegetable or meat ○ *Take the skin off the peach with a knife.*

skin-dive /'skɪn daɪv/ *verb* SPORT to swim underwater using breathing apparatus, as a sport

skin-diver /'skɪn ˌdaɪvə/ *noun* SPORT somebody who goes skin-diving ○ *From the boat we could see skin-divers on the reef.*

skin-diving /'skɪn ˌdaɪvɪŋ/ *noun* SPORT the sport of swimming underwater using breathing apparatus ○ *They went on a skin-diving holiday on the coast of Mexico.*

skip /skɪp/ *verb* (*informal*) **1.** to miss part of something ○ *We decided to skip the tour to the Roman ruins.* ○ *I'm not hungry, I'll skip the pudding.* **2.** to leave quickly, without paying ○ *The couple in Room 14 skipped during the night.*

ski pants /'skiː pænts/ *plural noun* SPORT trousers with an elastic strap under the foot, worn when skiing

ski pass /'skiː pɑːs/ *noun* SPORT a card which allows a skier to use the ski runs or ski lifts for a particular number of times ○ *They offer free tuition, equipment and ski passes to beginners.*

ski poles /'skiː pəʊlz/ *plural noun* SPORT a pair of long sticks used to push the skier along

skipper /'skɪpə/ *noun* **1.** TRAVEL the captain of a ship or an aircraft □ **a day-skipper certificate** certificate which allows someone to sail a boat in coastal waters ○ *A day-skipper certificate is required when booking.* **2.** HOTELS somebody who leaves a hotel quickly, without paying (*informal*)

ski resort /'skiː rɪˌzɔːt/ *noun* TOURISM a town in the mountains where people stay when on a skiing holiday

skirt /skɜːt/ *noun* FOOD a stewing cut of beef taken from the flank, below the sirloin and rump

ski run /'skiː sləʊp/, **ski slope** *noun* SPORT a specially prepared and marked slope for skiing down a mountain

ski tow /'skiː təʊ/ *noun* SPORT a device to take skiers to the top of a slope by dragging them along with their skis on the ground

ski trail /'skiː treɪl/ *noun* SPORT a marked path for skiers

skiwear /'skiːweə/ *noun* SPORT clothes worn when skiing (NOTE: There is no plural form.)

skull-cap /'skʌl kæp/ *noun* a small cap which covers your hair and the top of your head closely ○ *Some chefs wear skull-caps.* ◊ **toque**

sky /skaɪ/ *noun* the area above the Earth which is blue during the day, and where the moon and stars appear at night ○ *the beautiful deep blue sky of a Mediterranean evening* ○ *It's going to be a beautiful day – there's not a cloud in the sky.* ○ *The wind carried the glider high up into the sky.*

sky bed /'skaɪ bed/, **skybed** *noun* a seat on a passenger aircraft that transforms into a bed. Also called **flat bed**

skycap /'skaɪkæp/ *noun* a porter who works at an airport

skydive /'skaɪdaɪv/ *verb* to jump from an aeroplane and descend in free fall, sometimes performing acrobatic manoeuvres, before pulling the ripcord of a parachute

skyline /'skaɪlaɪn/ *noun* the shape of buildings seen against the sky ○ *The Chicago skyline is very distinctive.*

sky marshal /'skaɪ ˌmɑːʃ(ə)l/ *noun* an armed guard providing security during flights on commercial passenger aircraft

skyscraper /'skaɪskreɪpə/ *noun* a very tall building ○ *They're planning a 100-storey skyscraper near the park.*

skysurfing /'skaɪsɜːfɪŋ/ *noun* SPORT the sport of jumping from an aircraft and performing a series of moves before descending by parachute

slack /slæk/ *adjective* not busy ○ *November is a slack month in the hotel.* ○ *Tuesday is our slackest day.*

slack season /'slæk ˌsiːz(ə)n/ *noun* TOURISM a period when a hotel or resort is not very busy

slash /slæʃ/ *verb* to cut, to reduce sharply ○ *Prices have been slashed in all departments.* ○ *The company has slashed prices on tours to Turkey.*

sled /sled/ *noun* US SPORT same as **sledge**

sledge /sledʒ/ SPORT *noun* a small vehicle with runners for sliding over snow ■ *verb* to slide on the snow on a sledge as a sport

sledging /'sledʒɪŋ/ *noun* SPORT the sport of going on sledges □ **to go sledging** to play at sliding on the snow on a sledge

sleep /sliːp/ *noun* the state of resting naturally and unconsciously □ **to go, to get to sleep** to start sleeping ○ *She found it difficult to get to sleep because of the noise of the traffic.* ■ *verb* to be in a state of natural rest and unconsciousness ○ *Did you sleep well?* ○ *I can't sleep sitting upright.* (NOTE: **sleeping – slept**)

sleeper /'sliːpə/ *noun* **1.** RAIL TRAVEL a sleeping car **2.** RAIL TRAVEL an overnight train with sleeping cars ○ *The Edinburgh sleeper leaves at 11.30 p.m.* ○ *The sleeper from Moscow to St Petersburg is one of Russia's great rail journeys.* **3.** HOTELS an empty room which is shown as being occupied on the reservations board

sleeper seat /'sliːpə siːt/ *noun* TRAVEL a comfortable seat on an aircraft, boat or train which can be reclined so that you can sleep more easily

sleep in /ˌsliːp 'ɪn/ *verb* to sleep in the building where you work ○ *Most of the restaurant staff sleep in.*

sleeping bag /'sliːpɪŋ bæg/ *noun* a quilted bag for sleeping in a tent, etc.

sleeping car /'sliːpɪŋ kɑː/ *noun* RAIL TRAVEL a special coach on a railway train, with beds where passengers can sleep

sleeping pill /'sliːpɪŋ pɪl/, **sleeping tablet** /'sliːpɪŋ ˌtæblət/ *noun* MEDICAL a pill which makes you go to sleep or keeps you asleep

sleeping sickness /'sliːpɪŋ ˌsɪknəs/ *noun* MEDICAL an African disease, spread by the tsetse fly, where trypanosomes infest the blood

COMMENT: Symptoms are headaches, lethargy and long periods of sleep. The disease is fatal if not treated.

sleep out /'sliːp aʊt/ *verb* HOTELS not to sleep in a hotel room, even if it has been paid for

sleep-out staff /ˌsliːp aʊt 'stɑːf/ *noun* HOTELS staff who do not sleep in a hotel

sleigh /sleɪ/ *noun* ENTERTAINMENT a large sledge pulled by horses or reindeer, etc. ○ *At the ski resort you can go out for sleigh rides.*

slice /slaɪs/ *noun* a thin piece cut off something ○ *a slice of bread* ○ *two slices of cake* ○ *Can you cut me another slice of beef, please?* ■ *verb* to cut into slices

sliced bread /ˌslaɪst 'bred/ *noun* BREAD, ETC. a loaf of bread which has already been sliced mechanically before it is sold

slice of bread /ˌslaɪs əv 'bred/ *noun* CATERING a thin piece cut from a loaf

slicer /'slaɪsə/ *noun* CATERING a machine for slicing meat, bread, etc.

slide /slaɪd/ *noun* **1.** ENTERTAINMENT a slippery surface on ice **2.** a slippery metal or plastic slope for children to slide down **3.** a small piece of film which can be projected onto a screen ■ *verb* to move smoothly over a slippery surface (NOTE: **sliding – slid**)

slide projector /'slaɪd prəˌdʒektə/ *noun* an apparatus for making pictures from slides appear on a screen

slip /slɪp/ *noun* **1.** a small, often careless mistake ○ *He made a couple of slips in adding up the bill.* **2.** a small piece of paper ■ *verb* to slide by mistake ○ *She slipped on the polished floor and broke her leg.*

slip cloth /'slɪp klɒθ/ *noun* CATERING same as **napperon**

slip road /'slɪp rəʊd/ *noun* ROAD TRAVEL a road which leads onto or off a motorway ○ *You must not park on the slip road.*

sloe gin /ˌsləʊ 'dʒɪn/ *noun* BEVERAGES gin flavoured with the juice of blackthorn berries

slop basin /'slɒp ˌbeɪs(ə)n/ *noun* CATERING a bowl placed on a table into which waste liquid such as cold dregs from teacups can be put

slope /sləʊp/ *noun* a slanting piece of ground

slot /slɒt/ *noun* **1.** a narrow opening for putting a coin into **2.** a set time and place available for doing something ○ *The airline had requested more takeoff and landing slots at the airport.*

'...airlines, airports and even governments are arguing about the best way of allocating slots at congested airports' [*Airliner World*]

slot machine /'slɒt məˌʃiːn/ *noun* same as **vending machine**

slow lane /'sləʊ leɪn/ *noun* ROAD TRAVEL same as **inside lane**

slush /slʌʃ/ *noun* half-melted snow ○ *The snow has started to melt and the roads are covered with slush.*

small ads /'smɔːl ædz/ *plural noun* same as **classified ads** ○ *Look in the small ads to see if there are any cottages to let in Wales.*

small change /ˌsmɔːl 'tʃeɪndʒ/ *noun* coins

small to medium-sized enterprise, small to medium-size enterprise *noun* a business with 1 to 250 employees. Abbr **SME**

smart card /'smɑːt kɑːd/ *noun* FINANCE a credit card with a microchip, used for withdrawing money from cash dispensers or for buying at automatic terminals

SME *abbreviation* small to medium-sized enterprise

smell /smel/ *noun* something which you can sense with the nose ○ *the smell of coffee coming from the restaurant* ■ *verb* **1.** to sense something through the nose ○ *I can smell burning* **2.** to have a particular smell ○ *The room smells of cheese.* (NOTE: **smelling – smelt** or **smelled**)

COMMENT: The senses of smell and taste are closely connected, and together give the real taste of food. Smells are sensed by receptors in the nasal cavity which transmit impulses to the brain. When food is eaten, the smell is sensed at the same time as the taste is sensed by the taste buds, and most of what we think of as taste is in fact smell, which explains why food loses its taste when someone has a cold and a blocked nose.

smelt /smelt/ *noun* SEAFOOD a small edible sea fish (NOTE: There is no plural form.)

smoke /sməʊk/ *noun* vapour and gas given off when something burns ■ *verb* **1.** CATERING to preserve food such as meat, fish, bacon, cheese, by hanging it in the smoke from a fire ○ *As soon as the fish are caught, we select some for smoking.* **2.** to breathe in smoke from something such as a cigarette ○ *He asked if he could smoke his pipe in the restaurant.*

smoked /sməʊkt/ *adjective* CATERING preserved by hanging in the smoke of a fire ○ *We had smoked reindeer as an entrée.*

smoke detector /'sməʊk dɪˌtektə/ *noun* a device which is sensitive to smoke, and sets off alarms or sprinklers when it senses smoke ○ *Smoke detectors are fitted in all the rooms.* ○ *All the men smoked cigars, and this set off the smoke detectors.*

smoked haddock /ˌsməʊkt 'hædək/ *noun* SEAFOOD a common smoked fish, which is yellow in colour

smoked salmon /ˌsməʊkt 'sæmən/ *noun* SEAFOOD salmon which has been cured by smoking, and is served in very thin slices, usually with brown bread and lemon, as an hors d'oeuvre

smoke-free /'sməʊk friː/ *adjective* without anyone smoking ○ *The landlord is pressing for the right to run a smoke-free pub.* ○ *Each restaurant has to designate a smoke-free area.*

smokeless /'sməʊkləs/ *adjective* making no smoke

smokeless zone /ˌsməʊkləs 'zəʊn/ *noun* an area of a town where you are not allowed to make any smoke

smoker /'sməʊkə/ *noun* **1.** somebody who smokes cigarettes, etc. ○ *We only have two members of staff who are smokers.* **2.** RAIL TRAVEL a railway carriage where you can smoke

'...a report published in the Journal of the American Health Association found that restaurant staff were exposed to up to four-and-a-half times the level of atmospheric smoke as people who live with smokers, while exposure for bar staff was up to six times as great' [*Caterer & Hotelkeeper*]

smoking /'sməʊkɪŋ/ *noun* the act of smoking a cigarette □ **'no smoking'** do not smoke here ○ *Please extinguish your cigarettes when the 'no smoking' signs light up.*

'...the ruling came into force last week, making Los Angeles the largest city in the USA to make smoking in eating places a punishable offence' [*Caterer & Hotelkeeper*]

smoking area, smoking section *noun* a section of a restaurant, plane, etc., where smoking is allowed

smoking room /'sməʊkɪŋ ruːm/ *noun* ENTERTAINMENT a special room in a hotel or club where people can smoke, and which is also often used for playing cards

smoothie /'smuːði/ *noun* BEVERAGES a drink made from puréed fruit, sometimes with milk, yoghurt, or ice cream

smorgasbord /'smɔːbəzbɔːd/ *noun* CATERING Swedish buffet of many cold dishes ○ *For lunch there will be a smorgasbord.*

smuggle /'smʌg(ə)l/ *verb* BUSINESS to take goods into a country illegally without declaring them to the customs ○ *They had to smuggle the computer disks into the country.*

smuggler /'smʌglə/ *noun* somebody who smuggles

smuggling /'smʌglɪŋ/ *noun* BUSINESS the act of taking goods illegally into a country ○ *He made his money in cigarette smuggling.*

snack /snæk/ *noun* CATERING a light meal, or a small amount of food eaten ○ *We didn't have time to stop for a proper lunch, so just had a snack on the motorway.*

snack bar /'snæk bɑː/ *noun* CATERING a small simple restaurant where you can have a light meal, usually sitting at a counter ○ *He met the girl by chance in a snack bar at Waterloo Station.*

snapper /'snæpə/ *noun* SEAFOOD a type of Pacific fish

snood /snuːd/ *noun* CATERING a cloth bag which is worn over the hair, especially by people preparing or selling food

snooker /'snuːkə/ *noun* ENTERTAINMENT a game like billiards played with twenty-two balls of various colours, the object being to hit a white ball so that it sends a ball of another colour into one of the 'pockets' at the edge of the table

snooker table /'snuːkə ˌteɪb(ə)l/ *noun* ENTERTAINMENT a table on which snooker is played

snooze /snuːz/ *noun* a short sleep ■ *verb* to sleep lightly for a short time

snooze button, snooze control *noun* a button on an alarm clock which resets the alarm to go off again after a short time

snorkel /'snɔːk(ə)l/ *noun* SPORT a tube which goes from the mouth or mask of an underwater swimmer to the surface to allow him to breathe in air

snorkelling /'snɔːk(ə)lɪŋ/, **snorkeling** *US* /'snɔːklɪŋ/ *noun* □ **to go snorkelling** to go swimming with a snorkel ○ *Snorkelling has become my favourite holiday sport.*

snow /snəʊ/ *noun* water which falls as white flakes of ice crystals in cold weather ○ *Snow fell all night on the mountains.* ■ *verb* to fall as snow ○ *It snowed heavily during the night.*

snowblindness /'snəʊblaɪndnəs/ *noun* MEDICAL a temporary painful blindness caused by bright sunlight shining on snow

snowboard /'snəʊbɔːd/ *noun* SPORT a type of board similar to a surfboard, on which you slide down snow slopes

snowboarder /'snəʊbɔːdə/ *noun* SPORT somebody who slides down snow slopes on a snowboard

'…skiers think snowboarders are responsible for an increasing number of collisions but there is no statistical evidence to support this contention. On the other hand, snowboarders are about ten times more likely to injure themselves than skiers' [*The Sunday Times*]

snow cannon /'snəʊ ˌkænən/ *noun* a machine which makes snow when there is not enough snow on ski runs

snow conditions /'snəʊ kənˌdɪʃ(ə)nz/ *plural noun* the type and thickness of snow

snowdrift /'snəʊdrɪft/ *noun* a heap of snow which has been piled up by the wind ○ *The lane was blocked by a huge snowdrift.*

snowfall /'snəʊfɔːl/ *noun* the quantity of snow which comes down at any one time ○ *A heavy snowfall blocked the main roads.*

snowfield /'snəʊfiːld/ *noun* a permanent large flat area of snow

snowflake /'snəʊfleɪk/ *noun* a small piece of snow formed from a number of ice crystals

snowline /'snəʊlaɪn/ *noun* the level on a high mountain above which there is permanent snow

snowmobile /'snəʊməbiːl/ *noun* ROAD TRAVEL a vehicle with caterpillar tracks specially designed for driving on snow

snowplough /'snəʊplaʊ/ *noun* ROAD TRAVEL a heavy vehicle with a plough on the front for clearing snow off roads, railways, etc. (NOTE: The US spelling is **snowplow**.)

snow report /'snəʊ rɪˌpɔːt/ *noun* TOURISM a report from a resort, telling how much snow there is and of what type

snowshoeing /'snəʊʃuːɪŋ/ *noun* SPORT the sport of walking on snow-covered terrain wearing snowshoes

snowshoes /'snəʊʃuːz/ *plural noun* frames shaped like tennis rackets with a light web, which are tied under the feet for walking on snow

snowstorm /'snəʊstɔːm/ *noun* a heavy fall of snow accompanied by wind

snowtrain /'snəʊtreɪn/ *noun* RAIL TRAVEL a special train that goes direct to ski resorts

snow tyres /'snəʊ ˌtaɪəz/ *plural noun* ROAD TRAVEL special tyres with thick treads, for use when driving on snow

soap /səʊp/ *noun* a substance which you wash with, made from oils and usually with a pleasant smell ○ *Two small bars of soap are provided in the bathroom.* ○ *There is a liquid soap dispenser in the gents' toilets.*

soapdish /'səʊpdɪʃ/ *noun* a dish in which a bar of soap can be put ○ *Is there a soapdish in the shower cubicle?*

socio-economic group /ˌsəʊʃiəʊ ˌiːkənɒmɪk 'gruːp/ *noun* a group in society divided according to income and position, classified by letters A, B, C, D, and E

socket /'sɒkɪt/ *noun* □ **(electric) socket** a hollow device into which a light bulb can be fitted, or a set of holes into which an electric plug can be fitted ○ *There is a socket on the wall that you can plug your laptop into.* ○ *This plug doesn't fit that socket.*

COMMENT: Sockets vary considerably from country to country. In Europe, sockets usually have holes for two round pins. In the USA, Canada, Australia and Japan, sockets take two flat pins. In Britain, sockets take three flat pins. Travellers should always carry adaptor plugs.

soda /'səʊdə/ *noun* **1.** CATERING a compound of sodium **2.** *US* BEVERAGES any fizzy non-alcoholic sweet drink

soda biscuit /'səʊdə ˌbɪskɪt/ *noun* BREAD, ETC. a dry salty biscuit

soda fountain /'səʊdə ˌfaʊntɪn/ *noun* CATERING a bar where sweet drinks and ice cream are served

soda siphon /'səʊdə ˌsaɪf(ə)n/ *noun* BEVERAGES a bottle with a special spout, filled with water and gas under pressure, used for serving soda water at table or in a lounge

soda water /'səʊdə ˌwɔːtə/ *noun* BEVERAGES water made fizzy by putting gas into it, drunk with alcohol or fruit juice

sodium bicarbonate /ˌsəʊdiəm baɪ 'kɑːbənət/ *noun* CATERING a chemical compound, formula $NaHCO_3$, used as a raising agent in baked goods and to make fizzy drinks fizzy

sofa /'səʊfə/ *noun* a long seat with a soft back on which several people can sit ○ *He had to sleep on the sofa.*

sofabed /'səʊfəbed/ *noun* a type of sofa which can fold out to form a bed ○ *The children can sleep on the sofabed in the lounge.*

soft /sɒft/ *adjective* not hard ○ *The beds are too soft: I prefer a hard bed.*

soft-boiled egg /ˌsɒft bɔɪld 'eg/ *noun* FOOD an egg which has been cooked in boiling water for a short time so that the yolk is hot, but still liquid

soft cheese /ˌsɒft 'tʃiːz/ *noun* DAIRY cheese which is soft or soft in the middle, e.g. Camembert or Brie

soft currency /ˌsɒft 'kʌrənsi/ *noun* FINANCE the currency of a country which has a weak economy, so that the currency is cheap to buy and difficult to exchange for other currencies

soft drink /'sɒft drɪŋk/ *noun* BEVERAGES a drink which is not alcoholic, sold either ready prepared in a bottle or can or in concentrated form which can be mixed with water

soft fruit /ˌsɒft 'fruːt/ *noun* FRUIT a general term for all fruits and berries that have a relatively soft flesh, and so cannot be kept, except in some cases by freezing, e.g. raspberries, strawberries, blueberries and blackberries

soft ice cream /ˌsɒft aɪs 'kriːm/ *noun* DESSERTS ice cream mixed with air, dispensed from a machine

solarium /sə'leəriəm/ *noun* ENTERTAINMENT a room where you can enjoy real or artificial sunlight

sold out /ˌsəʊld 'aʊt/ *adjective* no longer available because all the items have been sold

sole /səʊl/ *adjective* only ■ *noun* SEAFOOD a type of flat sea fish with delicate white flesh ○ *She ordered a grilled sole and a glass of white wine.*

COMMENT: The two types of sole are 'Dover sole' and 'lemon sole'; Dover soles are more oval in shape, lemon soles are more rounded.

sole agency /ˌsəʊl 'eɪdʒənsi/ *noun* BUSINESS an agreement to be the only person to represent a company or to sell a product in a particular area ○ *He has the sole agency for the tour company.*

sole agent /ˌsəʊl 'eɪdʒənt/ *noun* BUSINESS somebody who has the sole agency for a company or a product in an area ○ *She is the sole agent for the airline.*

sole owner /ˌsəʊl 'əʊnə/, **sole proprietor** /ˌsəʊl prə'praɪətə/ *noun* BUSINESS somebody who owns a business on his or her own, with no partners, without forming a company

sole trader /ˌsəʊl ˈtreɪdə/ *noun* BUSINESS somebody who runs a business by themselves but has not registered it as a company

sommelier /sɒˈmeliə/ *noun* CATERING a French noun meaning wine waiter, the person in charge of serving the wines in a restaurant

son et lumière /ˌsɒn eɪ ˈluːmieə/ *noun* ENTERTAINMENT an entertainment consisting of sound and lighting effects, shown in the open air at night and usually based around a historic building ○ *The son et lumière begins at 22.00.* ○ *All the tickets for the son et lumière have been sold.*

sorbet /ˈsɔːbeɪ/ *noun* DESSERTS sweet flavoured ice made with water and flavouring and sometimes cream ○ *a raspberry sorbet* (NOTE: The US English is **sherbet**.)

SOS /ˌes əʊ ˈes/ *noun* 1. an international signal to show that you are in distress, in which the letters 's', 'o', and 's' are repeated in Morse code ○ *They sent out SOS messages.* 2. a message broadcast to say that someone is ill and asking a relative to get in contact ○ *This is an SOS for Mr Smith, at present holidaying in Scotland, to say that his mother is dangerously ill.*

soufflé /ˈsuːfleɪ/ *noun* FOOD a light cooked dish, made from beaten egg whites and cream or custard, with sweet or savoury flavouring, eaten hot ○ *a cheese soufflé* ○ *a lemon soufflé*

souk /suːk/ *noun* ENTERTAINMENT a market in an Arab country ○ *You must visit the souk in Marrakech.*

soundproof /ˈsaʊndpruːf/ *adjective* not allowing sound to pass through ○ *The radio commentators sit in a soundproof cabin.* ■ *verb* to make a building soundproof ○ *All the bedrooms in the hotel are soundproofed.*

soundproofing /ˈsaʊndpruːfɪŋ/ *noun* 1. the act of protecting something against noise 2. material which protects against noise

soundproof window /ˌsaʊndpruːf ˈwɪndəʊ/ *noun* a window which prevents noise from outside getting into a room

soup /suːp/ *noun* FOOD a liquid dish usually eaten at the beginning of a meal

COMMENT: Note various words for soup: thick vegetable soup is a 'potage'; soup made from shellfish is a 'bisque'; clear meat soup is 'consommé'; cream soup is 'crème' or 'velouté'.

soup bowl /ˈsuːp bəʊl/ *noun* CATERING a special deep dish in which soup is served

soup chef /ˈsuːp ʃef/ *noun* CATERING the chef in charge of making soups. Also called **chef potager**

soupçon /ˈsuːpsɒn/ *noun* CATERING a very small amount ○ *Just add a soupçon of curry powder.*

soup plate /ˈsuːp pleɪt/ *noun* CATERING a wide deep plate in which soup is served, as opposed to a soup bowl

soup spoon /ˈsuːp spuːn/ *noun* CATERING a specially large flat spoon, for eating soup

sour /ˈsaʊə/ *adjective* 1. not sweet, sharp-tasting 2. CATERING having gone bad

sourness /ˈsaʊənəs/ *noun* CATERING the state of being sour

sous-chef /ˈsuː ʃef/ *noun* CATERING a chef with less experience, who is the assistant to the main chef in a restaurant kitchen (NOTE: **sous-chef** comes from the French noun meaning 'under-chef'.)

soused herring /ˌsaʊst ˈherɪŋ/ *noun* SEAFOOD herring which has been pickled in vinegar and herbs

sous vide /ˌsuː ˈviːd/ *noun* CATERING a method of preparing ready-cooked food for resale, where the food is heat-sealed in plastic trays or in plastic bags with some of the air removed from the container

south /saʊθ/ *noun* 1. the direction facing towards the sun at midday ○ *Look south from the mountain, and you will see the city in the distance.* ○ *The city is to the south of the mountain range.* ○ *The wind is blowing from the south.* 2. the part of a country to the south of the rest ○ *The south of the country is warmer than the north.* ○ *She went to live in the south of England.* ■ *adjective* referring to the south ○ *The south coast is popular for holidaymakers.* ○ *Cross to the south side of the river.* ■ *adverb* towards the south ○ *Go due south for two kilometres, and you will see the village on your left.* ○ *The river flows south into the Mediterranean.*

southbound /ˈsaʊθbaʊnd/ *adjective* going towards the south ○ *There has been an accident on the southbound carriageway of the motorway.* ○ *All southbound trains have been cancelled.*

south-east /ˌsaʊθ ˈiːst/ *adjective, adverb, noun* the direction between south and east ○ *South-East Asia is an important trading area.* ○ *The river runs south-east from here.*

south-easterly /ˌsaʊθ ˈiːstəli/ *adjective* 1. blowing from the south-east 2. towards the south-east ○ *The plane was following a south-easterly route.*

south-eastern /ˌsaʊθ ˈiːstən/ *adjective* referring to the south-east or situated in the south-east ○ *Kent is a south-eastern county where apples grow well.*

southerly /'sʌðəli/ *adjective* **1.** towards the south **2.** situated in the south

southern /'sʌð(ə)n/ *adjective* of the south ○ *The southern part of the country is warmer than the north.*

southerner /'sʌð(ə)nə/ *noun* somebody who lives in or comes from the south ○ *He was a southerner who had never been to New York before.*

southernmost /'sʌð(ə)nməʊst/ *adjective* furthest south

southward /'saʊθwəd/ *adjective, adverb* towards the south

southwards /'saʊθwədz/ *adverb* towards the south

south-west /ˌsaʊθ 'west/ *adjective, adverb, noun* the direction between south and west ○ *We need to head south-west for two miles.* ○ *Arizona is in the south-west of the United States.*

south-westerly /ˌsaʊθ 'westəli/ *adjective* **1.** blowing from the south-west ○ *A south-westerly wind was blowing.* **2.** towards the south-west ○ *We were following a south-westerly direction.*

south-western /ˌsaʊθ 'westən/ *adjective* referring to the south-west or situated in the south-west ○ *The south-western corner of England includes Cornwall and Devon.*

south wind /ˌsaʊθ 'wɪnd/ *noun* a wind which blows from the south

souvenir /ˌsuːvə'nɪə/ *noun* ENTERTAINMENT something bought which reminds you of the place where you bought it ○ *I bought a tartan scarf as a souvenir of Scotland.* ○ *Keep it as a souvenir of your visit.* ○ *They were selling souvenir programmes of the Test Match.*

souvenir shop /ˌsuːvə'nɪə ʃɒp/ *noun* ENTERTAINMENT a shop which sells souvenirs ○ *There are too many souvenir shops on the seafront.*

soya /'sɔɪə/ *noun* FOOD a plant which produces edible beans which have a high protein and fat content and very little starch

soya milk /'sɔɪə mɪlk/ *noun* a milk substitute made from soya beans, often with vitamins and sugar added

soya sauce /ˌsɔɪə 'sɔːs/ *noun* SAUCES, ETC. a salty dark Chinese sauce made from soya beans

soybean /'sɔɪbiːn/, **soya bean** /'sɔɪə biːn/ *noun* FOOD a bean from a soya plant

soy sauce /ˌsɔɪ 'sɔːs/ SAUCES, ETC. same as **soya sauce**

spa /spɑː/ *noun* ENTERTAINMENT a place where mineral water comes out of the ground naturally and where people go to drink the water or bathe in it because of its medicinal properties ○ *He spends two weeks every summer at a French spa.*

'…the spa ranges over three floors with all the equipment that the modern exercise fanatic could desire, including a rooftop bar that overlooks Fifth Avenue' [*Business Traveller*]

space /speɪs/ *noun* an area which is available for something ○ *We still have some space on the flight.*

space availability /ˌspeɪs əˌveɪlə'bɪlɪti/ *noun* AIR TRAVEL how many empty seats there are on a flight

spacesaving /'speɪsseɪvɪŋ/ *adjective* compact or which folds, and so saves space

spaghetti /spə'geti/ *noun* FOOD long thin strips of pasta ○ *I ordered spaghetti with a special cream sauce.*

COMMENT: Spaghetti is boiled in salt water, and eaten either simply with butter or olive oil, or with certain sauces.

spaghetti bolognese /spəˌgeti ˌbɒlə'neɪz/ *noun* FOOD spaghetti with meat and tomato sauce

spaghetti carbonara /spəˌgeti ˌkɑːbə'nɑːrə/ *noun* FOOD spaghetti with egg and bacon sauce

spare /speə/ *adjective* available but not being used ○ *There is a spare toilet roll in the bathroom cupboard.* □ **spare battery**, **spare bulb** a battery or electric bulb which is kept to replace another one which is worn out or broken

spare part /ˌspeə 'pɑːt/ *noun* a piece of machinery used instead of a piece which is broken or worn out. Also called **replacement part**

spare ribs /ˌspeə 'rɪbz/ *noun* FOOD pork ribs cooked in a savoury sauce ○ *We are having spare ribs for the barbecue.*

spare room /ˌspeə 'ruːm/ *noun* a bedroom which a family does not use

spare time /ˌspeə 'taɪm/ *noun* the time when you are not at work ○ *He built himself a car in his spare time.*

sparkling /'spɑːklɪŋ/ *adjective* BEVERAGES with bubbles in it

sparkling water /ˌspɑːklɪŋ 'wɔːtə/ *noun* BEVERAGES mineral water which has bubbles in it

sparkling wine /ˌspɑːklɪŋ 'waɪn/ *noun* BEVERAGES wine which has bubbles in it ○ *Champagne is a sparkling wine from France.*

spatchcock /'spætʃkɒk/ *noun* MEAT a chicken or other fowl that is split, dressed and grilled

spa town /'spɑː taʊn/ *noun* TOURISM a town which has a spa ○ *Bath is the oldest spa town in England.*

speak /spiːk/ *verb* **1.** to say words, to talk ○ *She spoke to me when the meeting was over.* ○ *He walked past me without speaking.* ○ *I will speak to the manager about the service.* **2.** to be able to say things in a foreign language ○ *Our restaurant staff can all speak French.* ○ *Is there anyone in the hotel who can speak Russian?*

speaker /'spiːkə/ *noun* **1.** somebody who speaks ○ *There is an Arabic speaker to help the tour guide.* □ **he is a popular speaker** many people come to hear him give speeches at meetings **2.** a loudspeaker ○ *One of the speakers in the car doesn't work.*

-speaking /spiːkɪŋ/ *suffix* able to speak a language ○ *a Japanese-speaking tour guide*

special /'speʃ(ə)l/ *adjective* not ordinary, or designed for a specific purpose ■ *noun* CATERING a particular dish on a menu □ **today's special**, **special of the day** a special dish prepared for the day and not listed in the printed menu

special interest holiday /ˌspeʃ(ə)l ˌɪntrəst 'hɒlɪdeɪ/ *noun* TOURISM a holiday arranged for people with particular hobbies, such as bird-watching, sketching, etc.

speciality /ˌspeʃi'æləti/ *noun* something which you are known for, which you are good at ○ *The speciality of the restaurant is its fish soup.*

speciality restaurant /ˌspeʃiæləti 'rest(ə)rɒnt/ *noun* CATERING a restaurant which specialises in one type of food

special offer /ˌspeʃ(ə)l 'ɒfə/ *noun* MARKETING goods put on sale at a specially low price ○ *We have a range of luggage on special offer.*

special rates, special terms *plural noun* a cheaper tariff offered for a particular reason ○ *The hotel has special rates for families.* ○ *We offer special terms for groups.*

specific humidity /spəˌsɪfɪk hjuː'mɪdəti/ *noun* the ratio between the amount of water vapour in air and the total mass of the mixture of air and water vapour

speed /spiːd/ *noun* the rate at which something moves or is done ■ *verb* ROAD TRAVEL to drive a car faster than the legal speed ○ *He was stopped for speeding.*

speedboat /'spiːdbəʊt/ *noun* SHIPS AND BOATS a racing motor boat ○ *The windsurfers were almost killed by the speedboat.*

speed limit /'spiːd ˌlɪmɪt/ *noun* the legal speed which is enforced in some areas ○ *The speed limit is 30 mph in towns.*

spend /spend/ *verb* **1.** ROAD TRAVEL to pay money ○ *They spent all their savings on buying the shop.* **2.** to use time ○ *The average visitor spends about two hours in the museum.* (NOTE: **spending – spent**) ■ *noun* same as **expenditure** ○ *The number of long-haul visitors from the USA and their spend also declined by 1%.* ○ *The café is attracting an average food and drink spend of $25 per person.*

spice /spaɪs/ *noun* FOOD a substance made from the roots, flowers, seeds or leaves of plants, used to flavour food ○ *Cloves, cinnamon and nutmeg are the main spices I use.* ○ *You need lots of spices for Indian cookery.* ■ *verb* CATERING to add spice to a dish ○ *A pinch of mustard will spice up the sauce.*

COMMENT: The commonest spices are salt, pepper and mustard. Others often used are cinnamon, cloves, ginger, nutmeg, paprika, turmeric (in pickles), and the various spices which make up curry powders.

spiced /spaɪst/ *adjective* CATERING with spices added ○ *spiced chicken wings*

spiciness /'spaɪsɪnəs/ *noun* CATERING the taste of spices

spicy /'spaɪsi/ *adjective* CATERING tasting of spices ○ *She loves spicy Indian food.* ○ *Mexican cooking is hot and spicy.*

spill /spɪl/ *noun* the act of letting liquid fall by mistake ○ *Waiters should know how to deal with spills.* ■ *verb* to pour a liquid or a powder out of a container by mistake ○ *He spilt coffee over the tablecloth.* ○ *The waiter spilt white wine down the front of the guest's dress.* (NOTE: **spilling – spilled** or **spilt**)

spinach /'spɪnɪdʒ/ *noun* VEGETABLES a common green-leaved vegetable ○ *We had chicken, potatoes and spinach.* (NOTE: There is no plural form: *some spinach*; *a spoonful of spinach*.)

spirit /'spɪrɪt/ *noun* BEVERAGES a strong alcoholic drink, e.g. whisky, gin or brandy ○ *The club is licensed to sell beers, wines and spirits.*

spirit burner, spirit lamp *noun* CATERING apparatus in which methylated spirits is burned, used to keep food hot on the table, or to cook food rapidly next to the table

spit /spɪt/ *noun* CATERING a long metal rod passed through meat which turns so that the meat is evenly cooked ○ *spit-roasted pork*

split menu /ˌsplɪt 'menjuː/ *noun* CATERING a menu which offers two or more menu options, which are pre-agreed with the guests before arrival

split shift /'splɪt ʃɪft/ *noun* BUSINESS a system where working shifts are divided

spoil /spɔɪl/ *verb* **1.** to make something bad or unpleasant ○ *The trip was spoilt by the bad weather.* ○ *Rain spoiled our picnic.* **2.** to go bad ○ *The dish will spoil quickly unless you keep it in the fridge.* (NOTE: **spoiling – spoilt** or **spoiled**)

spoilage /'spɔɪlɪdʒ/ *noun* CATERING food going bad, such as fruit rotting when over-ripe

spoke /spəʊk/ *noun* AIR TRAVEL a domestic flight from a central airport connecting with international flights

sponge bag /'spʌndʒ bæg/ *noun* a small bag for carrying soap, flannel, toothbrush and other toilet articles

sponge cake /'spʌndʒ keɪk/, **sponge pudding** /spʌndʒ 'pʊdɪŋ/ *noun* BREAD, ETC. a light soft cake or pudding made from flour, eggs, sugar and fat ○ *You need slices of sponge cake to make a trifle.*

sponsor /'spɒnsə/ BUSINESS *noun* **1.** a company which pays to help a sport, in return for advertising rights **2.** a company which pays for a radio or TV programme as a way of advertising its products ■ *verb* to pay money to help business development in return for advertising ○ *to sponsor a television programme* ○ *The company has sponsored the football match.*

sponsorship /'spɒnsəʃɪp/, **sponsoring** *noun* BUSINESS the act of paying to help business development in return for advertising

spoon /spuːn/ *noun* **1.** an eating utensil with a bowl and a long handle ○ *Use a spoon to eat your pudding.* ○ *We need a big spoon to serve the soup.* **2.** same as **spoonful** ○ *Put three spoons of coffee into the cafetière.* ■ *verb* □ **to spoon something into something** to put something in with a spoon

spoonful /'spuːnfʊl/ *noun* the amount which a spoon can hold ○ *She always takes her coffee with two spoonfuls of sugar.* Also called **spoon**

sport /spɔːt/ *noun* a game or activity that involves physical exercise and skill, e.g. football, hockey or tennis

sports centre /'spɔːts ˌsentə/ *noun* a group of connected buildings in which there are facilities for various sports

sports facilities /'spɔːtz fəˌsɪlətiz/ *plural noun* the equipment and buildings for playing sports, e.g. tennis courts and swimming pools ○ *The club has extensive sports facilities.*

sports hall /'spɔːts hɔːl/ *noun* a large building where indoor sports such as basketball are played

sportswear /'spɔːtsweə/ *noun* clothes worn to play sports (NOTE: There is no plural form.)

spot /spɒt/ *noun* a place □ **on the spot** on duty, at one's post ○ *The fire services were on the spot in a few minutes.*

spot check /'spɒt tʃek/ *noun* a check made suddenly and at random ○ *Customs officers carry out* or *make spot checks on cars entering the country.*

spotlight /'spɒtlaɪt/ *noun* a bright light which shines on one small area

spouse /spaʊs/ *noun* a husband or wife

spouse fare /ˌspaʊs 'feə/ *noun* TRAVEL a specially discounted fare for a husband or wife of a passenger travelling on a full-fare ticket

sprat /spræt/ *noun* SEAFOOD a very small herring-like fish

spread /spred/ *noun* FOOD a soft food consisting of meat, fish or cheese, which you can spread on something such as bread ○ *As snacks, they offered us water biscuits with cheese spread.* ■ *verb* to cover with a layer of something ○ *He spread the butter thickly on his bread.*

spring /sprɪŋ/ *noun* **1.** a small stream of water coming out of the ground ○ *The spa was built in Roman times around hot mineral springs.* **2.** a season of the year following winter when plants begin to grow and put out leaves ○ *The travel company has brought out its spring catalogue.* ○ *We offer spring tours to the bulb fields of Holland.*

Springboard UK /ˌsprɪŋbɔːd juː 'keɪ/ *noun* an organisation in the UK that educates people about job opportunities in the hospitality, leisure, travel and tourism industries

spring onion /ˌsprɪŋ 'ʌnjən/ *noun* VEGETABLES a very small onion with long green leaves, used in salads and in cooking ○ *I chopped some spring onions into the salad.* (NOTE: The US English is **scallion**.)

spring roll /ˌsprɪŋ 'rəʊl/ *noun* FOOD a hot snack or starter of mixed savoury ingredients formed into a slightly flattened cylindrical shape, wrapped in thin dough and fried until crisp and golden

spring tide /ˌsprɪŋ ˈtaɪd/ *noun* a tide which occurs at the new and full moon when the influence of the sun and moon act together and the difference between high and low water is more than normal

spring water /ˈsprɪŋ ˌwɔːtə/ *noun* BEV-ERAGES water which comes from a natural spring

sprinkle /ˈsprɪŋkəl/ *verb* CATERING to scatter water, sugar, etc. ○ *The chef sprinkled poppy seeds on the cake.*

sprinkler /ˈsprɪŋklə/ *noun* a device for sprinkling water

sprinkler system /ˈsprɪŋklə ˌsɪstəm/ *noun* a system of automatic fire control which sprinkles water on a fire and is set off by rising heat

spritzer /ˈsprɪtsə/ *noun* BEVERAGES a drink of white wine and soda water

sprout /spraʊt/ *noun* **1.** a young shoot of a plant **2.** VEGETABLES same as **Brussels sprout**

square /skweə/ *noun* **1.** a shape with four equal sides and four right-angled corners **2.** an open area in a town, surrounded by buildings

square measure /ˌskweə ˈmeʒə/ *noun* area in square feet or metres, calculated by multiplying width and length

squash /skwɒʃ/ *noun* **1.** BEVERAGES con-centrated juice of a fruit to which water is added to make a long drink ○ *a glass of orange squash* **2.** SPORT a fast game played with rackets in a room with high walls **3.** VEGETABLES a vegetable like a marrow or pumpkin, etc. ■ *verb* to crush or to squeeze something ○ *Hundreds of commuters were squashed into the train.*

squash court /ˈskwɒʃ kɔːt/ *noun* SPORT a room with high walls for playing squash

squeeze /skwiːz/ *noun* □ **a squeeze of lemon** a few drops of lemon juice ■ *verb* to crush, to press ○ *Ten people tried to squeeze into the lift.*

squeezer /ˈskwiːzə/ *noun* CATERING a device for pressing lemons, oranges, etc., to let the juice run out

squid /skwɪd/ *noun* SEAFOOD a sea animal like a small octopus (NOTE: There is no plu-ral form: *a plate of fried squid.*)

SSSI *abbreviation* TOURISM Site of Special Scientific Interest

stabiliser /ˈsteɪbɪlaɪzə/, **stabilizer** *noun* **1.** CATERING an artificial substance added to processed food to stop the mixture from

changing, as in sauces containing water and fat **2.** SHIPS AND BOATS a piece put on the hull of a ship to prevent it from rolling

stabilising agent /ˈsteɪbɪlaɪzɪŋ ˌeɪdʒənt/ *noun* CATERING same as **stabi-liser**

stack /stæk/ *noun* a pile or heap of things on top of each other ○ *There is a stack of replies to our advertisement.* ■ *verb* **1.** to pile things on top of each other ○ *The skis are stacked outside the chalet.* **2.** AIR TRAVEL (*of aircraft*) to circle round waiting in turn for permission to land at a busy airport ○ *We have had aircraft stacking for over fifteen minutes on busy days.*

stacking /ˈstækɪŋ/ *adjective* designed to be piled one on top of another ○ *The hall is furnished with 200 stacking chairs.*

stadium /ˈsteɪdiəm/ *noun* a place where people watch sports, usually having a flat central playing area surrounded by rising rows of seats

staff /stɑːf/ *noun* BUSINESS the people who work for an organisation □ **to be on the staff** *or* **a member of staff** *or* **a staff member** to be employed permanently by a company □ **accounts staff** people who work in the accounts department □ **senior staff**, **junior staff** older or younger members of staff, or people in more important or less important positions in a company ■ *verb* BUSINESS to provide employees for an organisation ○ *The bar is staffed with skilled part-timers.* ○ *We had difficulty in staffing the hotel.*

staff accommodation /ˌstɑːf əˌkɒmə ˈdeɪʃ(ə)n/ *noun* HOTELS the rooms in a hotel where members of staff live

staff agency /ˈstɑːf ˌeɪdʒənsi/ *noun* BUSINESS an agency which looks for staff for organisations

staff appointment /ˈstɑːf əˌpɔɪntmənt/ *noun* a job on the staff

staff association /ˈstɑːf əsəʊsiˌeɪʃ(ə)n/ *noun* BUSINESS a society formed by mem-bers of staff of a company to represent them to the management and to organise entertain-ments

staff catering /ˌstɑːf ˈkeɪtərɪŋ/ *noun* the work of preparing meals for the staff of a hotel or restaurant

staff cook /ˌstɑːf ˈkʊk/ *noun* CATERING a chef who cooks meals for the staff of a hotel or restaurant

staff discount /ˌstɑːf ˈdɪskaʊnt/ *noun* a discount given to people working in the com-pany

staff incentives /ˌstɑːf ɪnˈsentɪvz/ *plural noun* BUSINESS better pay or conditions offered to employees to make them work better

staffing /ˈstɑːfɪŋ/ *noun* BUSINESS the work of providing employees for an organisation □ **the hotel's staffing policy** the hotel's views on staff: how many are needed for each department, if they should be full-time or part-time, what the salaries should be, etc.

staffing levels /ˈstɑːfɪŋ ˌlev(ə)lz/ *plural noun* BUSINESS the numbers of members of staff required in departments for them to work efficiently

staffing problems /ˈstɑːfɪŋ ˌprɒbləmz/ *plural noun* problems to do with staff

staff meals /ˌstɑːf ˈmiːlz/ *plural noun* BUSINESS meals provided for the staff of a hotel or restaurant, noted as a cost in the accounts

staff restaurant /ˌstɑːf ˈrest(ə)rɒnt/ *noun* BUSINESS a special restaurant for the staff of a hotel, club or other organisation

staff training /ˌstɑːf ˈtreɪnɪŋ/ *noun* BUSINESS the activity of teaching staff better and more profitable ways of working ○ *The shop is closed for staff training.*

staff turnover /ˌstɑːf ˈtɜːnəʊvə/ *noun* BUSINESS same as **labour turnover** ○ *We hope to motivate staff and achieve a reduction in staff turnover.*

stage /steɪdʒ/ *noun* **1.** ENTERTAINMENT the part of the theatre where the actors perform **2.** part of a journey ○ *The tour crosses India by easy stages.* ■ *verb* to put on or arrange a play, a show, a musical or other performance or event ○ *The exhibition is being staged in the conference centre.*

stagger /ˈstægə/ *verb* to arrange holidays, working hours etc. so that they do not all begin and end at the same time ○ *Staggered holidays help the tourist industry.* ○ *We have to stagger the lunch hour so that there is always someone on the switchboard.*

staggering /ˈstægərɪŋ/ *noun* HOTELS a method of staffing a hotel in which employees start and end their shifts at different times so as to ensure that there are always staff available to help guests

stainless steel /ˌsteɪnləs ˈstiːl/ *noun* metal made of steel with a high percentage of chromium, which makes it resistant to stains or rust ○ *a set of stainless steel pans* ○ *a stainless steel teapot* ○ *stainless steel cutlery*

stair /steə/ *noun* **1.** one step in a series of steps, going up or down inside a building **2.** □ **(flight of) stairs** a series of steps leading from one floor of a building to the next

staircarpet /ˈsteəkɑːpɪt/ *noun* a long narrow piece of carpet for covering stairs

staircase /ˈsteəkeɪs/ *noun* a set of stairs which go from one floor in a building to another ○ *The staircase is at the back of the building.* ○ *You have to go up a spiral staircase to get to the top of the tower.*

stairwell /ˈsteəwel/ *noun* the part of a building in which the staircase is fitted ○ *The lift is fitted in the centre of the stairwell.*

stale /steɪl/ *adjective* no longer fresh ○ *If you don't eat the cakes soon they'll go stale.* ○ *Nobody likes the smell of stale cigarette smoke.*

stall /stɔːl/ *noun* **1.** a wooden stand in a market, where a trader displays and sells his or her goods **2.** a section of a urinal for one person

stamp /stæmp/ *noun* **1.** a device for making marks on documents, or a mark made in this way ○ *The invoice has the stamp 'received with thanks' on it.* ○ *The customs officer looked at the stamps in her passport.* **2.** □ **(postage) stamp** a small piece of gummed paper which you buy from a post office and stick on a letter or parcel so that it can be sent through the post ○ *You'll need a £1 stamp to send the letter to Australia.* ■ *verb* **1.** to stick a stamp on a letter or parcel ○ *All the envelopes need to be sealed and stamped.* **2.** to mark something with a stamp ○ *They stamped my passport when I entered the country.*

stamp machine /ˈstæmp məˌʃiːn/ *noun* a machine which sells stamps automatically

stamp pad /ˈstæmp pæd/ *noun* a soft pad of cloth with ink, on which a stamp is pressed before marking paper

stand /stænd/ *noun* AIR TRAVEL a place where an aircraft waits for passengers to board

'…ten nose-in stands are available and are capable of handling aircraft up to Airbus A320 size' [*Airliner World*]

standard /ˈstændəd/ *noun* the usual quality or usual conditions which other things are judged against ■ *adjective* **1.** usual, recommended or established ○ *We make a standard charge of £25 for a thirty-minute session.* **2.** on a tall pole

standard lamp /ˈstændəd læmp/ *noun* a lamp in a room on a tall pole

standard letter /ˌstændəd 'letə/ noun a letter which is sent without any change to various correspondents

standard rate /'stændəd reɪt/ noun the normal charge for something such as a phone call

Standard Time /'stændəd taɪm/ noun normal local time as in the winter months

stand-by /'stænd baɪ/ adjective AIR TRAVEL referring to a ticket sold at a lower price shortly before the departure of a flight when there are empty seats remaining on the aircraft ■ noun AIR TRAVEL same as **standby ticket** ■ adjective referring to a passenger who travels with a standby ticket

standby fare /'stændbaɪ feə/ noun TRAVEL a cheaper fare for a standby ticket

standby ticket /'stændbaɪ ˌtɪkɪt/ noun AIR TRAVEL a cheaper air ticket which allows the passenger to wait until the last moment to see if there is an empty seat on the plane

standing /'stændɪŋ/ noun good reputation ○ a restaurant of good standing ○ the financial standing of a company

standing order /ˌstændɪŋ 'ɔːdə/ noun BUSINESS an instruction given by a customer asking a bank to make a regular payment. Also called **banker's order**

standing time /'stændɪŋ taɪm/ noun CATERING the time which a dish should be left in the microwave oven after cooking and before serving

stand-up buffet /ˌstænd ʌp 'bʊfeɪ/ noun CATERING a buffet where the guests stand to eat, holding their plates in their hands

star /stɑː/ noun 1. a small bright light which you see in the sky at night 2. a shape with several regular points, used as a system of classification □ **one-star, two-star, three-star, four-star hotel** a hotel which has been classified with one, two, three or four stars, under a classification system

'…they have been careful to stay well within the three-star market and not overload bedrooms with soft furnishings' [Caterer & Hotelkeeper]

COMMENT: Hotels in the UK are given stars by the English Tourism Council, together with the RAC and AA; other grading systems include rosettes, ribbons and crowns. Hotels can also be given stars by international guide books such as the Michelin Red Guides. Stars are also used to indicate how long frozen food can be kept and the temperature of freezers. One star means that food can be kept at −6°C for one week, two stars at −12°C for four weeks, and three stars at −18°C for three months. Similarly for freezers, each star is equal to −6°C, so a freezer marked or will keep food at −12°C, which is cold enough to keep food for one month.

starboard /'stɑːbəd/ noun SHIPS AND BOATS the right-hand side of a ship when facing the bow, also used of the right-hand side of an aircraft ○ We turned to starboard to avoid the ferry. ○ People on the starboard side of the plane can see the Statue of Liberty.

starch /stɑːtʃ/ noun CATERING the usual form in which carbohydrates exist in food, especially in bread, rice and potatoes

starchy /'stɑːtʃi/ adjective CATERING containing a lot of starch ○ He eats too much starchy food.

COMMENT: Starch is present in common foods, and is broken down by the digestive process into forms of sugar.

starlight /'stɑːlaɪt/ noun light from the stars

starlit /'stɑːlɪt/ adjective lit by the light of the stars

star rating /'stɑː ˌreɪtɪŋ/ noun a rating under a star system

'Business travellers accustomed to de luxe accommodation in Spain will appreciate the fact that several Spanish hoteliers have dropped their five-star rating to four, so that guests need only pay a 6% value added tax instead of the usual luxury rate of 15%' [Business Traveller]

'…star ratings symbolize the level of service, range of facilities and quality of guest care you can expect. Hotels are required to meet progressively higher standards as they move up the scale from one to five stars' [Caterer & Hotelkeeper]

starred /stɑːd/ adjective given a star as a sign of approval ○ a Michelin-starred restaurant

start /stɑːt/ noun the beginning of something □ **to make an early start** to set off early on a trip ■ verb 1. to begin ○ The main film starts at 8.15. ○ The tour starts from the castle gate. 2. to set a machine going ○ It is difficult to start a car in cold weather. ○ The car won't start – the battery must be flat. 3. □ **to start to** to begin ○ The weather is starting to become warmer. ○ It was starting to get dark and we were still miles from the chalet.

starter /'stɑːtə/ noun CATERING the first course in a meal ○ What do you want as a starter? ○ We don't want starters, we'll go straight onto the main course.

starter motor /'stɑːtə ˌməʊtə/ noun ROAD TRAVEL an electric motor in a car which sets the main engine going

starting /'stɑːtɪŋ/ noun beginning

starting date /'stɑːtɪŋ deɪt/ noun the date on which something begins

starting point /ˈstɑːtɪŋ pɔɪnt/ *noun* the place where something starts ○ *The starting point for the excursion is the Post Office.*

starting salary /ˈstɑːtɪŋ ˌsæləri/ *noun* BUSINESS the annual wage given to an employee when starting work with a company ○ *He was appointed at a starting salary of £10,000.*

starve /stɑːv/ *verb* not to have enough to eat □ **I'm starving** I'm very hungry (*informal*)

state ownership /ˌsteɪt ˈəʊnəʃɪp/ *noun* BUSINESS same as **public ownership**

state pension /ˌsteɪt ˈpenʃən/ *noun* same as **government pension**

stateroom /ˈsteɪtruːm/ *noun* SHIPS AND BOATS a large cabin on a liner

station /ˈsteɪʃ(ə)n/ *noun* **1.** the regular place where someone works **2.** *US* a place in a hotel, shop or other workplace where a service is available ○ *The restaurant has a baby-changing station.* ○ *The ice station is along the corridor from your room.* **3.** □ **TV station, radio station** a building where TV or radio programmes are produced ○ *The station broadcasts hourly reports on snow conditions.*

stationery /ˈsteɪʃ(ə)n(ə)ri/ *noun* **1.** things such as paper, envelopes, pens and ink which you use for writing ○ *You can buy food, toiletries and stationery at the hotel shop.* **2.** HOTELS in particular, notepaper, envelopes, etc., with the hotel's name and address printed on them ○ *The letter was typed on the hotel stationery.*

station head waiter /ˌsteɪʃ(ə)n hed ˈweɪtə/ *noun* CATERING a chief waiter who is in charge of a station, and takes the orders from customers

station manager /ˈsteɪʃən ˈmænədʒə, **stationmaster** /ˈsteɪʃ(ə)nmɑːstə/ *noun* RAIL TRAVEL somebody in charge of a railway station

station waiter /ˌsteɪʃ(ə)n ˈweɪtə/ *noun* CATERING a waiter who serves a particular group of four or five tables in a restaurant

statue /ˈstætʃuː/ *noun* a figure of a person carved in stone or made of metal, etc. ○ *The statue of King John is in the centre of the square.*

status /ˈsteɪtəs/ *noun* a position or condition

status inquiry /ˈsteɪtəs ɪnˌkwaɪəri/ *noun* BUSINESS a check on a customer's credit rating

statutory /ˈstætʃʊt(ə)ri/ *adjective* fixed by law ○ *There is a statutory period of probation of thirteen weeks.*

statutory holiday /ˌstætʃʊt(ə)ri ˈhɒlɪdeɪ/ *noun* a holiday which is fixed by law ○ *All employees have at least 2 days' statutory holiday over the Christmas period.*

stay /steɪ/ *noun* a length of time spent in one place ○ *a three-night stay at a centrally located hotel* ○ *The tourists were in town only for a short stay.* ○ *Did you enjoy your stay in London?* ■ *verb* to spend time in a place ○ *The party is staying at the Hotel London.* ○ *We always stay at the same resort.* ○ *Occupancy rates have stayed below 60% for two years.*

stay over /ˌsteɪ ˈəʊvə/ *verb* to stay in a place for at least one night

'…the numbers of stay-over visitors increased by two per cent, following a six per cent fall in the preceding year' [*Daily Telegraph*]

STB *abbreviation* TOURISM Scottish Tourist Board

STD *abbreviation* subscriber trunk dialling

steak /steɪk/ *noun* **1.** MEAT a thick slice of beef cut from the best part of the animal **2.** CATERING a thick slice cut across the body of an animal or fish ○ *a gammon steak* ○ *a salmon steak*

steak and kidney /ˌsteɪk ən ˈkɪdni/ *noun* FOOD a typically English combination of cubes of beef and kidney, which are cooked together with onions in a thick sauce in a pie or pudding ○ *a serving of steak and kidney pie* ○ *an individual steak and kidney pudding*

steak au poivre /ˌsteɪk əʊ ˈpwɑːvrə/ *noun* FOOD a steak which has been grilled and has a sauce made with pepper and peppercorns poured over it

steak bar /ˈsteɪk bɑː/ *noun* CATERING a restaurant which only serves steak, with seating for customers at counters

steakhouse /ˈsteɪkhaʊs/ *noun* CATERING a restaurant serving steak and other grilled food

steak knife /ˈsteɪk naɪf/ *noun* CATERING a very sharp knife or a knife with a serrated edge, used when eating meat (NOTE: The plural form is **steak knives**.)

steak tartare /ˌsteɪk tɑːˈtɑː/ *noun* FOOD a dish of raw minced steak, served mixed with raw eggs, raw onion and herbs

steal /stiːl/ *verb* to take and keep something that belongs to another person without permission ○ *A burglar broke into the hotel room and stole my wallet.* ○ *Keep your purse in your bag or it may get stolen.* ○ *The car* *was stolen from the hotel car park.* (NOTE: **stealing – stole – stolen**)

steam /stiːm/ *noun* vapour which comes off hot water ■ *verb* CATERING to cook something using the steam from boiling water

COMMENT: Vegetables, fish and poultry can be cooked by steaming in a container with holes in the bottom, placed over a pan of boiling water. Juices and vitamins are retained in the food during cooking. Puddings, such as steak-and-kidney pudding, are steamed by standing the basin containing the pudding in a pan of boiling water.

steamboat /ˈstiːmbəʊt/ *noun* SHIPS AND BOATS a boat powered by steam ○ *Steamboats criss-crossed the lake.*

steamed /stiːmd/ *adjective* CATERING cooked in steam ○ *One of the desserts on the menu is steamed treacle pudding.*

steam engine /ˈstiːm ˌendʒɪn/ *noun* an engine which is powered by steam pressure

steamer /ˈstiːmə/ *noun* **1.** *also* **steamship** SHIPS AND BOATS a large passenger ship powered by steam ○ *We took the steamer from Cape Town to Mombasa.* **2.** CATERING a type of pan with holes in the bottom which is placed over boiling water for steaming food ○ *The best way to cook vegetables is in a steamer.*

steaming oven, steaming cabinet *noun* CATERING an oven in a restaurant kitchen, used to steam large quantities of food at the same time

steam railway /ˌstiːm ˈreɪlweɪ/ *noun* RAIL TRAVEL a railway where the engines are powered by steam pressure

steel /stiːl/ *noun* a rod of rough metal with a handle, used for sharpening knives

steep /stiːp/ *adjective* **1.** rising or falling sharply ○ *There's a very steep hill at the entrance to the town.* **2.** excessive (*informal*) ○ *Their prices are a bit steep.*

stem ginger /ˌstem ˈdʒɪndʒə/ *noun* FOOD round portions of the underground stem of a ginger plant, cooked until tender and preserved in syrup

step /step/ *noun* a stair on a staircase, or a flat rung on a ladder ○ *There are 75 steps to the top of the tower.* □ **mind the step** be careful, because the floor level changes and goes up or down with a step

stereo /ˈsteriəʊ/ *noun* a machine which plays music or other sound through two different loudspeakers ○ *I bought a new pair of speakers for my stereo.*

sterilisation /ˌsterɪlaɪˈzeɪʃ(ə)n/, **sterilization** *noun* MEDICAL the act of making something free from bacteria or microbes

sterilise /ˈsterɪlaɪz/, **sterilize** *verb* MEDICAL to make something free from bacteria or microbes

sterilised milk /ˌsterəlaɪzd ˈmɪlk/ *noun* DAIRY milk prepared for human consumption by heating in sealed airtight containers to kill all bacteria

sterling /ˈstɜːlɪŋ/ *noun* FINANCE the standard currency used in the United Kingdom ○ *to quote prices in sterling* or *to quote sterling prices*

stern /stɜːn/ *noun* SHIPS AND BOATS the rear part of a ship

sternwheeler /ˈstɜːnwiːlə/ *noun* SHIPS AND BOATS a large steamboat with one large paddle-wheel at the back, as used on the Mississippi ○ *We took a trip up the Mississippi on an old-fashioned sternwheeler.* Compare **paddle steamer**

stew /stjuː/ *noun* FOOD a dish of meat and vegetables cooked together for a long time ○ *rabbit stew* ■ *verb* CATERING to cook for a long time in liquid ○ *stewed apples and cream* ○ *pears stewed in red wine*

steward /ˈstjuːəd/ *noun* TRAVEL somebody who looks after passengers and serves drinks and food on a ship, plane, or other vehicle, or a similar person who deals with guests in a club, restaurant, hotel, etc.

stewardess /ˌstjuːəˈdes/ *noun* TRAVEL a woman who looks after passengers and serves drinks and food on a ship or plane, or a similar person who deals with guests in a club, restaurant, hotel, etc. Also called **air hostess**, **flight attendant**

stewed apple /ˌstjuːd ˈæp(ə)l/ *plural noun* DESSERTS apples which have been cooked until they are soft, served as a dessert

stewing steak /ˈstjuːɪŋ steɪk/ *noun* MEAT pieces of beef used to make stews

stick /stɪk/ *noun* something long and thin

sticking plaster /ˈstɪkɪŋ ˌplɑːstə/ *noun* an adhesive plaster or tape used to cover a small wound or to attach a pad of dressing to the skin (NOTE: The US English calls this by a tradename: **Band-Aid**.)

still /stɪl/ *adjective* (*of drinks*) with no gas bubbles in it ○ *still water* ○ *still orange drink* Opposite **fizzy**

stillroom /ˈstɪlruːm/ *noun* (*in a hotel*) a room where coffee, tea, and some light meals such as afternoon tea are prepared

Stilton /ˈstɪltən/ *noun* DAIRY either of two strong-flavoured British white cheeses made from whole milk, one veined with blue mould, the other plain

stir /stɜː/ *verb* CATERING to mix up a liquid or food ○ *Keep stirring the porridge, or it will stick to the bottom of the pan.*

stir-fry /ˈstɜː fraɪ/ *verb* CATERING to cook vegetables or meat quickly in hot oil in a wok, while rapidly stirring ○ *Stir-fry the vegetables separately, not all together.* ■ *noun* FOOD vegetables or meat cooked quickly in a little hot oil ○ *She made a stir-fry of vegetables and bamboo shoots.*

stock /stɒk/ *noun* **1.** BUSINESS the quantity of goods or raw materials kept by a business ○ *Even if it is cut off by snow, the hotel has sufficient stocks of food to last a week.* **2.** BUSINESS the goods in a warehouse or shop □ **in stock, out of stock** available or not available in the warehouse or shop ○ *to hold 2,000 lines in stock* ○ *The item went out of stock just before Christmas but came back into stock in the first week of January.* ○ *We are out of stock of this item.* **3.** FOOD liquid made from boiling bones, etc., in water, used as a base for soups and sauces ○ *The soup is made with fish stock.* ■ *verb* BUSINESS to hold goods for sale in a warehouse or store ○ *to stock 200 lines*

stock code /ˈstɒk kəʊd/ *noun* BUSINESS a set of numbers and letters which refers to an item of stock

stock control /ˈstɒk kənˌtrəʊl/ *noun* a system of checking that there is not too much stock in a warehouse, but just enough to meet requirements (NOTE: The US term is **inventory control**.)

stock size /ˈstɒk saɪz/ *noun* BUSINESS a usual size that fits a lot of people or is needed for many tasks ○ *We only carry stock sizes of shoes.*

stock up with /ˌstɒk ˈʌp wɪð/ *verb* to buy goods to hold in case of emergency ○ *We'll stock up with food to last us over the holiday weekend.*

stodgy /ˈstɒdʒi/ *adjective* CATERING heavy and filling to eat and usually fairly tasteless

STOL /stɒl/ *abbreviation* AIR TRAVEL short take-off and landing

stone /stəʊn/ *noun* **1.** rock ○ *The church is built of the local grey stone.* **2.** a small piece of rock ○ *Stop a moment, I've got a stone in my foot.* **3.** a hard seed inside a fruit ○ *Count the cherry stones on the side of your plate.* **4.** a measure of weight equalling 14 pounds or 6.35 kilograms ○ *I've put on weight – I weigh 12 stone.* (NOTE: In the USA, human body weight is always given in pounds.)

stool /stuːl/ *noun* a seat with no back □ **bathroom stool** a stool placed in a bathroom

stop /stɒp/ *noun* **1.** □ **to come to a stop** not to go any further ○ *Work on the new marina came to a stop when the company could not pay the workers' wages.* ○ *The brakes failed and the car came to a stop against a wall.* **2.** a place where a bus or train lets passengers get on or off ○ *The bus stop is opposite the Town Hall.* ○ *There are six stops between here and Marble Arch.* **3.** □ **his account is on stop** he will not be supplied with anything until he pays what he owes □ **to put a stop on a cheque** to ask a bank not to pay a cheque you have written ■ *verb* **1.** to cause something not to move any more ○ *Does this bus stop near the Post Office?* ○ *The tourist coach was stopped by customs.* ○ *The government has stopped the import of cars.* ○ *He stopped his car by the side of the lake.* **2.** not to do anything any more ○ *The operator has stopped offering tours to Greece.* ○ *The restaurant stopped serving meals at 12.00 midnight.* ○ *The hotel staff stopped work when the company could not pay their wages.* ○ *The cleaning staff stop work at 5.30.* ○ *We have stopped supplying Smith & Co.* **3.** to stay in a place ○ *They stopped for five nights at the Grand Hotel.* **4.** □ **to stop an account** to stop supplying a customer until they have paid what they owe □ **to stop payments** not to pay any more money **5.** □ **to stop someone's wages** to take money out of someone's wages before he or she receives them ○ *We stopped £25 from his pay because he was rude to the guests.*

stop-off /ˈstɒp ɒf/ *noun* TRAVEL same as **stopover**

stop-off point /ˈstɒp ɒf ˌpɔɪnt/ *noun* TOURISM a place where you can stop and leave a tour ○ *The trails through the park are easy to follow and the stop-off points are well organised and comfortable.*

stop over /ˌstɒp ˈəʊvə/ *verb* to stay for a short time in a place during a long journey ○ *We stopped over in Hong Kong on the way to Australia.*

stopover /ˈstɒpəʊvə/ *noun* TRAVEL a short stay in a place during a long journey ○ *The ticket allows you two stopovers between London and Tokyo.* Also called **layover** (NOTE: The US English for this is **layover**.)

storage /ˈstɔːrɪdʒ/ *noun* the keeping of goods in store or in a warehouse ○ *We put our furniture into storage.*

store /stɔː/ *noun* **1.** a supply of food or other materials kept for later use **2.** BUSINESS a place in which goods are kept **3.** *US* a shop

○ *There's a department store next to the hotel.* (NOTE: British English usually uses **shop** for small businesses.) ■ *verb* **1.** to keep for future use **2.** to put in a warehouse

store card /'stɔː kɑːd/ *noun* BUSINESS a credit card issued by a department store which can only be used for purchases within that store

storekeeper /'stɔːkiːpə/, **storeman** /'stɔːmən/ *noun* CATERING somebody who looks after stores of food, drink, and other supplies in a hotel's storeroom

storeroom /'stɔːruːm/ *noun* a room where things such as foodstuffs are stored

storm /stɔːm/ *noun* violent weather, with wind and rain or snow

storm damage /'stɔːm ˌdæmɪdʒ/ *noun* damage caused by a storm

stout /staʊt/ *noun* BEVERAGES strong dark beer

stove /stəʊv/ *noun* same as **cooker**

straight /streɪt/ *adjective* with no turns ○ *The road goes in a straight line across the plain for two hundred kilometres.* ■ *adverb* **1.** without turning ○ *The road goes straight across the plain for two hundred kilometres.* □ **go straight on** continue along this road without turning off it ○ *Go straight on past the crossroads and then turn left.* **2.** without stopping ○ *The plane flies straight to Washington.* **3.** BARS with no water or any other liquid added ○ *He drinks his whisky straight.* (NOTE: British English also uses **neat**.)

straight up /ˌstreɪt 'ʌp/ *adjective* served without ice

strain /streɪn/ *verb* CATERING to pour liquid through a sieve to separate solids from it ○ *Boil the peas for ten minutes and then strain.*

strainer /'streɪnə/ *noun* CATERING a utensil made with metal or nylon mesh, used to separate solids from a liquid □ **a tea strainer** a small utensil placed over a cup to separate tea leaves from the liquid, used when making tea with loose tea leaves

strand /strænd/ *verb* to leave someone alone and helpless ○ *Her handbag was stolen and she was stranded without any money.*

stranded /'strændɪd/ *adjective* left alone and helpless ○ *The tourist group was stranded in the mountain hut by a sudden snowstorm.* ○ *The collapse of the holiday company left thousands of holidaymakers stranded in Turkey.*

straw /strɔː/ *noun* a long thin tube used for sucking up a drink

strawberry /'strɔːb(ə)ri/ *noun* FRUIT a common red heart-shaped soft summer fruit, used in desserts and also preserved as jam

stream /striːm/ *noun* **1.** a small flow of water, a small river **2.** a continuous flow of things ○ *Crossing the road is difficult because of the stream of traffic.* ○ *Streams of guests ran out of the burning hotel.*

street /striːt/ *noun* ROAD TRAVEL a road in a town □ **the High Street banks** main British banks which accept deposits from individual customers

streetcar /'striːtkɑː/ *noun* US RAIL TRAVEL a form of public transport, with carriages running on rails laid in the street ○ *You can take a streetcar from the station to the city centre.* (NOTE: The British English is **tram**.)

street directory /'striːt daɪˌrekt(ə)ri/ *noun* **1.** a map of a town with all the streets listed in alphabetical order in an index **2.** a list of the people living in a street

street map /'striːt mæp/, **street plan** /'striːt plæn/ *noun* a diagram showing the streets of a town, with their names

street market /'striːt ˌmɑːkɪt/ *noun* ENTERTAINMENT a market held in a street, with stalls along both sides of the roadway

stress /stres/ *noun* nervous tension or worry ○ *People in positions of responsibility often complain of stress-related illnesses.* ○ *The new work schedules caused too much stress on the shop floor.*

stressed /strest/ *adjective* worried and tense, suffering from stress ○ *When you're feeling stressed it's better to try to get to bed early.* ○ *You must be very careful in dealing with stressed customers.* □ **stressed out** very worried and tense (*informal*)

stressful /'stresf(ə)l/ *adjective* causing stress ○ *She left his job in the kitchen because he found it too stressful.*

stress management /'stres ˌmænɪdʒmənt/ *noun* BUSINESS a way of coping with stress-related problems at work

stress relief /'stres rɪˌliːf/ *noun* methods of relieving the effects of stress ○ *He said that the workshop on stress relief could be useful for his staff, who were having to cope with increasingly difficult and stressed customers.*

stretch /stretʃ/ *noun* a long piece of land, water or road ○ *For long stretches of the Transsiberian Railway, all you see is trees.* ○ *Stretches of the river have been so polluted that bathing is dangerous.* ■ *verb* **1.** □ **to stretch to** to be enough for ○ *Will your* *money stretch to the visit to the temple?* □ **dinner won't stretch to seven** there won't be enough food for seven people **2.** to spread out for a great distance ○ *White sandy beaches stretch as far as the eye can see.*

stretch limo /ˌstretʃ 'lɪməʊ/ *noun* ROAD TRAVEL a luxurious hire car, which is much longer than the normal models, used to carry important passengers (*informal*)

strike /straɪk/ *noun* **1.** BUSINESS a situation where employees refuse to work, because of e.g. bad pay or a lack of agreement with management ○ *All flights are delayed due to a strike by air traffic controllers.* **2.** □ **to take strike action** to go on strike **3.** □ **to come out on strike, to go on strike** to refuse to work ○ *The baggage handlers are on strike for higher pay.* □ **to call the workforce out on strike** to tell the employees to stop work ○ *The union called its members out on strike.* ■ *verb* BUSINESS to stop working because there is no agreement with management ○ *to strike for higher wages* or *for shorter working hours* ○ *to strike in protest against bad working conditions* (NOTE: **striking – struck**)

strikebound /ˈstraɪkbaʊnd/ *adjective* not able to work or to move because of a strike ○ *The cruise ship is strikebound in the docks.*

strikebreaker /ˈstraɪkbreɪkə/ *noun* an employee who goes on working while everyone else is on strike

strike call /ˈstraɪk kɔːl/ *noun* BUSINESS a demand by a union for a strike

strike fund /ˈstraɪk fʌnd/ *noun* BUSINESS money collected by a trade union from its members, used to pay strike pay

strike pay /ˈstraɪk peɪ/ *noun* BUSINESS wages paid to striking employees by their trade union

striker /ˈstraɪkə/ *noun* an employee who is on strike ○ *Strikers marched to the company headquarters.*

string /strɪŋ/ *verb* CATERING **1.** to remove the stringy fibres from fruit or vegetables before cooking or eating **2.** to remove currants from their stalks by sliding them off between the prongs of a fork

string beans /ˌstrɪŋ 'biːnz/ *plural noun* VEGETABLES same as **green beans**

strip /strɪp/ *noun* an act of taking your clothes off, often as an entertainment for other people

strip light /ˈstrɪp laɪt/ *noun* a light made in the form of a tube

stroll /strəʊl/ *noun* a slow and short leisurely walk ○ *After dinner we went for a*

stroll through the village. ■ *verb* to walk slowly along ○ *On Sunday evenings, everyone strolls along the boulevard.*

strong /strɒŋ/ *adjective* with a lot of force or strength □ **strong coffee, strong tea** coffee or tea made with more coffee or tea than usual ○ *You need a cup of strong black coffee to wake you up.* ○ *I like my tea very strong.* □ **strong pound** the pound when it is has a high value against other currencies

studio /ˈstjuːdiəʊ/ *noun* a very small flat for one person, usually one room with a small kitchen and bathroom ○ *You can rent a studio overlooking the sea for £300 a week in high season.*

'…the hotel offers 120 studios and nine apartments. Each has a direct telephone line, satellite TV, sofabed and fully equipped kitchenette. A self-service laundry is located within the hotel. Studios are for single people or couples, while apartments can sleep as many as four guests' [*Inside Hotels*]

study /ˈstʌdi/ *noun* the act of examining something carefully to learn more about it □ **course of study** a course at school, college or university ■ *verb* to learn about a subject at school, college or university ○ *He's studying hotel management.*

study tour /ˈstʌdi ˌtʊə/ *noun* TOURISM a tour of a country or an area which includes visits, lectures and classes

stuff /stʌf/ *verb* CATERING to put stuffing inside meat, fish or vegetables and cook and serve them together as a special dish

stuffed tomatoes /ˌstʌft təˈmɑːtəʊz/ *plural noun* FOOD tomatoes cooked with a savoury mixture inside them

stuffed vine leaves /ˌstʌft 'vaɪn ˌliːvz/ *plural noun* FOOD vine leaves cooked with a savoury mixture inside them

stuffing /ˈstʌfɪŋ/ *noun* FOOD a mixture of chopped meat or vegetables with breadcrumbs or rice and herbs and spices, usually put inside meat or vegetables ○ *Chicken is often cooked with a sage and onion stuffing.*

sturgeon /ˈstɜːdʒən/ *noun* SEAFOOD a large edible fish whose eggs are caviar (NOTE: The plural form is **sturgeon**.)

sub- /sʌb/ *prefix* under, less important

sub-agency /ˈsʌb ˌeɪdʒənsi/ *noun* a small agency which is part of a large agency

subaqua /sʌbˈækwə/ *adjective* SPORT referring to underwater sports ○ *a subaqua club*

sub-franchise /ˌsʌb 'fræntʃaɪz/ BUSINESS *noun* a franchise held from a main franchise in an area ■ *verb* (*of a main franchise*) to license a franchise in an area ○ *The* *master franchise runs three units and sub-franchises two other outlets.*

sub-franchisee /ˌsʌb ˌfræntʃaɪˈziː/ *noun* BUSINESS somebody who trades under a sub-franchise

submarine /ˌsʌbməˈriːn/ *noun* FOOD a sandwich made with a long roll cut horizontally

sub-post office /ˌsʌb ˈpəʊst ˌɒfɪs/ *noun* a small post office, usually part of a general store

subscriber trunk dialling /səb ˌskraɪbə trʌŋk ˈdaɪəlɪŋ/ *noun* a telephone system where you can dial long-distance numbers direct from your own telephone without going through the operator. Abbr **STD**

subsidise /ˈsʌbsɪdaɪz/ *verb* to help by somebody or something by giving them money ○ *The government has agreed to subsidise the hotel industry.*

subsidy /ˈsʌbsɪdi/ *noun* **1.** money given to help something which is not profitable ○ *The country's hotel industry exists on government subsidies.* ○ *The government has increased its subsidy to the hotel industry.* **2.** money given by a government to make something cheaper ○ *the subsidy on butter* or *the butter subsidy*

subsistence /səbˈsɪstəns/ *noun* the minimum amount of food, money, housing, etc., which a person needs □ **to live at subsistence level** to have only just enough money to live on

subsistence allowance /səbˈsɪstəns əˌlaʊəns/ *noun* BUSINESS money paid by a company to cover the cost of accommodation and meals for a member of staff who is travelling on business

suburb /ˈsʌbɜːb/ *noun* a residential area on the outskirts of a city or town ○ *She lives in a quiet suburb of Boston.* □ **the suburbs** the residential areas all round a town ○ *People who live in the suburbs find the air quality is better than in the centre of town.*

suburban /səˈbɜːbən/ *adjective* referring to the suburbs ○ *This is a very a suburban area – almost all the men commute to London every day.*

suburban line /səˈbɜːbən laɪn/ *noun* RAIL TRAVEL a railway line between the suburbs to the centre of a town ○ *Services on suburban lines have been disrupted by the strike.*

suburban trains /səˌbɜːbən ˈtreɪnz/ *plural noun* RAIL TRAVEL trains which run between the suburbs and the town centre

subway /ˈsʌbweɪ/ *noun* **1.** ROAD TRAVEL a passage underground along which pedestrians can pass, as under a busy road **2.** *US* RAIL TRAVEL an underground railway system ○ *the New York subway* ○ *He took the subway to Grand Central Station.*

subzero temperatures /ˌsʌbzɪərəʊ ˈtemprɪtʃəz/ *noun* temperatures below zero, ie. below freezing point. ○ *When you go skiing in Norway you must be prepared for subzero temperatures.*

succulent /ˈsʌkjʊlənt/ *adjective* CATERING tender and juicy ○ *a slice of succulent ham* ○ *They served each of us a succulent piece of roast chicken.*

suet /ˈsuːɪt/ *noun* FOOD hard fat from an animal, used in cooking

suet dumplings /ˌsuːɪt ˈdʌmplɪŋz/ *plural noun* FOOD small balls of flour, suet and water, flavoured with herbs

suet pudding /ˌsuːɪt ˈpʊdɪŋ/ *noun* FOOD a dish made with flour and suet, cooked by steaming or boiling, with a sweet or savoury filling

sugar /ˈʃʊgə/ *noun* FOOD any of several sweet carbohydrates

COMMENT: There are several natural forms of sugar: sucrose (in plants), lactose (in milk), fructose (in fruit), glucose and dextrose (in fruit and in body tissue). Edible sugar used in the home is a form of refined sucrose. All sugars are useful sources of energy, though excessive amounts of sugar can increase weight and cause tooth decay. Diabetes mellitus is a condition where the body is incapable of absorbing sugar from food.

sugarcraft /ˈʃʊgəkrɑːft/ *noun* CATERING the art of decorating cakes with icing sugar, and making designs out of sugar

sugar crystals /ˈʃʊgə ˌkrɪst(ə)lz/ *plural noun* FOOD large pale brown sugar crystals, used for sweetening coffee

sugar cubes /ˈʃʊgə kjuːbz/ *plural noun* FOOD granulated sugar formed into hard cubes

sugar-free /ˈʃʊgə friː/ *adjective* CATERING not containing sugar

sugar lump /ˈʃʊgə lʌmp/ *noun* FOOD a cube of white sugar

suit /suːt/ *noun* two or three pieces of clothing made of the same cloth, usually a jacket and/or waistcoat and trousers or skirt

suitcase /ˈsuːtkeɪs/ *noun* a case or box with a handle for carrying clothes and personal belongings when travelling ○ *The customs officer made him open his three suitcases.*

suitcase stand /'suːtkeɪs stænd/ *noun* HOTELS a wooden stand in a hotel bedroom, on which you can place your suitcases

suite /swiːt/ *noun* HOTELS a series of rooms which make a set, e.g. bedroom, bathroom and sitting room ○ *The hotel has 91 rooms and suites.*

suite hotel /ˌswiːt həʊ'tel/ *noun* HOTELS a hotel where all the accommodation consists of suites of rooms

sultana /sʌl'tɑːnə/ *noun* FRUIT a type of seedless raisin ○ *We will need sultanas for the Christmas cake.* Compare **currant**, **raisin**

summary sheet /'sʌməri ʃiːt/ *noun* BUSINESS a piece of paper giving details of sales in a restaurant, itemised by the cashier

summer /'sʌmə/ *noun* the warmest season of the year following spring, when plants begin to make fruit ◇ **the summer holidays 1.** the period during the summer when children do not go to school, the longest holidays during the school year (in the UK about six weeks, but much longer in the USA) **2.** any holiday taken during the summer

summer camp /'sʌmə kæmp/ *noun* TOURISM a camp organised for children or teenagers during the summer holidays

summer pudding /ˌsʌmə 'pʊdɪŋ/ *noun* DESSERTS a dessert made from slices of bread lining a basin, which is filled with a mixture of soft fruit such as raspberries, strawberries and blackcurrants. It is chilled and usually served with cream.

summer schedule, summer timetable *noun* TRAVEL a special timetable for planes or trains or ferries, which applies during the high season

summer school /'sʌmə skuːl/ *noun* classes held at a school, college or university during the summer holiday ○ *She is organising a summer school in Florence on 'The Italian Renaissance'.*

Summer Time /'sʌmə taɪm/ *noun* same as **Daylight Saving Time**

summit /'sʌmɪt/ *noun* (*of a mountain*) top

sun /sʌn/ *noun* **1.** a very hot body around which the Earth revolves and which provides heat and daylight ○ *The sun wasn't shining when she took the photo.* **2.** same as **sunshine** ○ *She was sitting in the sun on the deck.* ○ *He prefers a table out of the sun.*

sunbathe /'sʌnbeɪð/ *verb* to lie in the sun to get your body brown

sunbather /'sʌnbeɪðə/ *noun* somebody who is sunbathing ○ *The pool was surrounded by sunbathers.*

sunbathing /'sʌnbeɪðɪŋ/ *noun* lying in the sun to get your body brown ○ *Sunbathing on the beach at midday is not advised.*

sunburn /'sʌnbɜːn/ *noun* MEDICAL a painful inflammation of the skin caused by being in the sun for too long

sunburnt /'sʌnbɜːnt/ *adjective* damaged or made red by the sun

sundae /'sʌndeɪ/ *noun* DESSERTS a dessert of ice cream, cream, fruit and nuts and a sweet sauce

Sunday closing /ˌsʌndeɪ 'kləʊzɪŋ/ *noun* the practice of not opening a shop on Sundays

sundeck /'sʌndek/ *noun* SHIPS AND BOATS the top deck of a passenger ship where people can sit in the sun

sun-drenched /'sʌn drentʃt/ *adjective* very sunny ○ *the sun-drenched beaches of the Italian Riviera*

sun-dried /'sʌn draɪd/ *adjective* CATERING dried in the sun to preserve it, a method usually used with fruit such as tomatoes or figs or with fish ○ *a jar of sun-dried tomatoes*

sundry /'sʌndri/ *adjective, noun* various

sundry items /ˌsʌndri 'aɪtəmz/, **sundries** /'sʌndriz/ *plural noun* small items which are not listed in detail

sunflower oil /'sʌnflaʊər ɔɪl/ *noun* FOOD an edible oil made from the seeds of the sunflower

sunglasses /'sʌnglɑːsɪz/ *plural noun* dark glasses to protect your eyes from the sun ○ *I always wear sunglasses when I'm driving.*

sunhat /'sʌnhæt/ *noun* a hat worn to protect you from the sun ○ *The baby keeps taking his sunhat off.*

sunlight /'sʌnlaɪt/ *noun* the light from the sun

sun lounge /'sʌn laʊndʒ/ *noun* ENTERTAINMENT a room with many large windows, where you can enjoy sunlight

sunny /'sʌni/ *adjective* **1.** full of sunlight ○ *The sunniest part of the garden is beyond the tennis courts.* **2.** with periods, especially long periods, during which the sun shines ○ *The weather forecast is for sunny spells during the morning.*

sunny side up /ˌsʌni saɪd 'ʌp/ *adjective* US FOOD fried without being turned over (*informal*)

sunroof /'sʌnruːf/ *noun* ROAD TRAVEL a part of a roof of a car which slides open

sunshade /'sʌnʃeɪd/ *noun* same as **parasol** ○ *Virginia was sitting in a deckchair under a sunshade, reading a book.*

sunshine /'sʌnʃaɪn/ *noun* light from the sun ○ *London has on average 7.6 hours of sunshine per day during May.* ○ *The west coast of France has more than 250 days of sunshine per annum.* Also called **sun**

sunspot /'sʌnspɒt/ *noun* a place that has a warm and sunny climate and is usually popular as a holiday destination

sunstroke /'sʌnstrəʊk/ *noun* MEDICAL an illness caused by being in the sunlight too much ○ *In cases of sunstroke patients should lie down in a dark room.*

suntan /'sʌntæn/ *noun* a brown colour of the skin caused by the sun ○ *I have to get a suntan before I go back to the office otherwise no one will think I have been on holiday.*

suntan lotion /'sʌntæn ˌləʊʃ(ə)n/ *noun* a substance which is rubbed on the body to prevent sunburn ○ *Can you put some suntan oil on my back?*

Super APEX /ˌsuːpə 'eɪpeks/ *noun* TRAVEL a special fare offering cheaper prices than the normal APEX

supermarket /'suːpəmɑːkɪt/ *noun* a large store, usually selling food, where customers serve themselves and pay at a checkout ○ *You can buy all the food you need in the supermarket next to the holiday apartments.* ○ *We've got no tea left, can you buy some from the supermarket?*

supersaver /'suːpəseɪvə/ *noun* an airline, coach, or train ticket that is cheaper than the usual price and must usually be bought a specific amount of time before the date of travel

superstore /'suːpəstɔː/ *noun* BUSINESS a very large self-service store which sells a wide range of goods

supervise /'suːpəvaɪz/ *verb* to watch work carefully to see if it is well done ○ *She supervises six girls in the reception area.*

supervision /ˌsuːpə'vɪʒ(ə)n/ *noun* the act of watching work carefully to see if it is well done ○ *New staff work under supervision for the first three months.* ○ *The cash was counted under the supervision of the head cashier.* ○ *She is very experienced and can be left to work without any supervision.*

supervisor /'suːpəvaɪzə/ *noun* a person whose job is making sure that other people are working well

supervisory /'suːpəvaɪzəri/ *adjective* involving supervision ○ *supervisory staff* ○ *He works in a supervisory capacity.*

supper /'sʌpə/ *noun* CATERING an evening meal, especially a light informal meal □ **to**

have supper to eat an evening meal ○ *We'll have supper on the terrace.*

supper menu /'sʌpə ˌmenjuː/ *noun* CATERING a menu containing various light dishes, served at a supper

supplement /'sʌplɪmənt/ *noun* something which is in addition to something else, especially an additional charge

supplementary /ˌsʌplɪ'ment(ə)ri/ *adjective* in addition ○ *There are no supplementary charges – the price is all-inclusive.*

supplier /sə'plaɪə/ *noun* BUSINESS a person or company which provides something which is needed ○ *He's our regular supplier of beverages* or *our regular beverage supplier.* ○ *They are major suppliers of equipment to the hotel trade.*

supply /sə'plaɪ/ *noun* **1.** the act of providing something which is needed ○ *We rely on him for our supply of cheese* or *for our cheese supply.* □ **in short supply** not available in large enough quantities to meet the demand ○ *Fresh vegetables are in short supply during the winter.* **2.** a stock of something which is needed ○ *The restaurant is running short of supplies of bread.* ○ *Supplies are running out – we'll have to order in some more stock.* ■ *verb* to provide something which is needed ○ *The brewery supplies all the beer to the hotel.* ○ *This company has the contract to supply the American Embassy.* ○ *He supplies the hotel with cheese* or *He supplies cheese to the hotel.* (NOTE: You **supply someone with something** or **supply something to someone**. Note also **supplies – supplying – supplied**)

surcharge /'sɜːtʃɑːdʒ/ *noun* an extra amount to pay ■ *verb* to ask someone to pay an extra amount

surf /sɜːf/ *noun* a line of breaking waves along a shore, or the foam from breaking waves ○ *The surf is too rough for children to bathe.* ■ *verb* to ride on large waves coming onto a beach on a surf board ○ *He goes surfing each weekend.* ○ *It's too dangerous to go surfing today.*

surface /'sɜːfɪs/ *noun* the top part of something □ **to send a package by surface mail** to send a package by land or sea, not by air

surface transport /'sɜːfɪs ˌtrænspɔːt/ *noun* TRAVEL transport on land or sea

surf and turf /ˌsɜːf ən 'tɜːf/ *noun* CATERING a meal, menu, or dish including both seafood and meat, especially steak and lobster

surfboard /'sɜːfbɔːd/ *noun* SPORT a board which you stand or lie on to ride on breaking waves ○ *When they went on holiday* *they took their surfboards on the roof of the car.*

surfboat /'sɜːfbəʊt/ *noun* SHIPS AND BOATS a light boat for riding on surf

surfer /'sɜːfə/, **surf-rider** *noun* SPORT somebody who surfs

surfing /'sɜːfɪŋ/, **surf-riding** /'sɜːfraɪdɪŋ/ *noun* SPORT the sport of riding on breaking waves on a board ○ *Surfing is the most popular sport in Hawaii.*

'…as surfing becomes more popular, competition to ride the waves has intensified, resulting in a rising number of violent assaults at beaches worldwide' [*The Sunday Times*]

surname /'sɜːneɪm/ *noun* same as **family name** ○ *Her Christian name or first name is Anne, but I don't know her surname.* ○ *Smith is the commonest surname in the London telephone directory.*

surround /sə'raʊnd/ *verb* to be all round something or someone ○ *When the floods came, the hotel was surrounded by water and the guests had to be rescued by boat.* ○ *The villa is outside the town, surrounded by vineyards.*

surrounding /sə'raʊndɪŋ/ *adjective* all around ○ *Standing on the terrace, you have a marvellous view over the surrounding countryside.*

surroundings /sə'raʊndɪŋz/ *plural noun* the area around a place ○ *The surroundings of the hotel are very peaceful.*

survey *noun* /'sɜːveɪ/ **1.** a general report on something ○ *The Tourist Office has produced a survey of local hotels and the facilities they offer.* **2.** the careful examination of a building to see if it is in good enough condition ○ *We have asked for a survey of the hotel before buying it.* ○ *The insurance company is carrying out a survey of the damage caused by the storm.* **3.** the work of taking exact measurements of something ■ *verb* /sə'veɪ/ to examine something to see if it is in good condition

surveyor /sə'veɪə/ *noun* somebody who examines buildings to see if they are in good condition

sushi /'suːʃi/ *noun Japanese* FOOD a dish consisting of rice, various pickles, and raw fish, made into little rolls and eaten cold

sushi bar /'suːʃi bɑː/ *noun* CATERING a bar where you eat sushi and drink sake

sustainable /sə'steɪnəb(ə)l/ *adjective* not damaging to natural resources, leaving the environment in good condition ○ *They make conservatories from sustainable timber.* ○ *The table is made of hardwood from a sustainable source.*

sustainable development /sə‚steɪnəb(ə)l dɪ'veləpmənt/ *noun* economic development that does not use up too much of the earth's natural resources or cause environmental pollution

swap /swɒp/ *noun* the exchange of one thing for another ■ *verb* to exchange one thing for another ○ *She swapped her old car for a new motorcycle.* (NOTE: **swapping – swapped**) □ **they swapped jobs** each of them took the other's job

swapping /'swɒpɪŋ/ *noun* the act of exchanging one thing for another

sweat /swet/ *verb* CATERING to cook something in a pan in its own juices with a small amount of fat or oil until tender

swede /swiːd/ *noun* VEGETABLES a common vegetable with a round root and yellow flesh, used mainly in soups and stews

sweet /swiːt/ *adjective* not sour, tasting like sugar ○ *With the fruit, we ordered a sweet white wine.* ○ *Just one spoon of sugar in my tea – I don't like it too sweet.* ■ *noun* **1.** FOOD a small piece of food made of sugar, eaten as a snack ○ *She bought a bag of sweets to eat during the film.* (NOTE: The US English is **candy**.) **2.** same as **dessert**

sweet-and-sour /‚swiːt ən 'saʊə/ *adjective* CATERING cooked in or served with a sauce that has sugar and vinegar among the ingredients

sweetbread /'swiːtbred/ *noun* the pancreas or thymus of a calf, lamb, or other young animal soaked, fried, and eaten as food

sweet chestnut /‚swiːt 'tʃesnʌt/ *noun* NUTS an edible chestnut ○ *roast turkey and chestnut stuffing*

sweet corn /'swiːt kɔːn/ *noun* VEGETABLES maize seeds, eaten as a vegetable either removed from or still attached to the cob ○ *sweet corn covered with melted butter*

sweeten /'swiːt(ə)n/ *verb* to make something taste sweet or sweeter by adding sugar or another natural or artificial substance

sweetener /'swiːt(ə)nə/ *noun* CATERING an artificial substance added to food to make it sweet, e.g. saccharin

sweetening /'swiːt(ə)nɪŋ/ *noun* same as **sweetener**

sweet pepper /‚swiːt 'pepə/ *noun* VEGETABLES the fruit of the *Capsicum*, which can be green, red or yellow and is eaten cooked or raw in salads ○ *We had stuffed green peppers for lunch.* Also called **pimento**, **capsicum**

sweet pickles /ˌswiːt ˈpɪk(ə)lz/ *plural noun* SAUCES, ETC. pickles made with a lot of sugar

sweet potato /ˌswiːt pəˈteɪtəʊ/ *noun* VEGETABLES a starchy root vegetable grown in tropical and subtropical regions

COMMENT: Called 'yams' in the Southern USA; the plant has no connection with the ordinary potato.

sweet trolley /ˈswiːt ˌtrɒli/ *noun* CATERING same as **dessert trolley**

sweet wine /ˌswiːt ˈwaɪn/ *noun* BEVERAGES wine which is sweet, as opposed to dry wine ○ *Are we right to believe that sweet wine must always go with dessert?*

sweltering /ˈswelt(ə)rɪŋ/ *adjective* very hot

swim /swɪm/ SPORT *verb* to move through water using your arms and legs to make you go forward ■ *noun* a period spent swimming ○ *Let's go for a swim before breakfast.*

swimmer /ˈswɪmə/ *noun* SPORT somebody who swims ○ *One of the swimmers got into difficulties and was saved by the lifeguard.*

swimming /ˈswɪmɪŋ/ *noun* SPORT the activity of moving in water by using your arms and legs

swimming baths /ˈsɪmɪŋ bɑːðz/ *plural noun* ENTERTAINMENT a large building with a public swimming pool ○ *The teacher took the whole class to the swimming baths for a swimming lesson.*

swimming costume /ˈswɪmɪŋ ˌkɒstjuːm/ *noun* SPORT a piece of clothing worn when swimming. Also called **bathing costume**

swimming pool /ˈswɪmɪŋ puːl/ *noun* ENTERTAINMENT an enclosed tank of water for swimming in ○ *The hotel has an indoor swimming pool.* ○ *She swam two lengths of the swimming pool.*

swimming trunks /ˈswɪmɪŋ trʌŋks/ *plural noun* SPORT shorts worn by a man when swimming

swimsuit /ˈswɪmsuːt/ *noun* SPORT a one-piece swimming costume for women and girls ○ *She was wearing her blue swimsuit.*

swing door /ˌswɪŋ ˈdɔː/ *noun* a door which is not attached with a catch, and which is opened by pushing from either side ○ *There is a swing door between the kitchen and the restaurant.*

swipe /swaɪp/ *verb* to put an electronic card through a reader by passing it quickly along a groove

swipe card /ˈswaɪp kɑːd/ *noun* a type of magnetic key card which you run down a slot to unlock the door

Swiss franc account /ˌswɪs ˈfræŋk əˌkaʊnt/ *noun* FINANCE a bank account in Swiss francs

Swiss roll /ˌswɪs ˈrəʊl/ *noun* BREAD, ETC. a cake made by rolling up a thin sheet of sponge cake covered with jam or cream (NOTE: The US English is **jelly roll**.)

switch /swɪtʃ/ *verb* to change from one thing to another ○ *The waiter had switched our glasses by mistake.* ○ *She switched flights in Montreal and went on to Calgary.* ■ *noun* an apparatus for starting or stopping an electric current ○ *The light switch is near the bed.*

switchboard /ˈswɪtʃbɔːd/ *noun* a central point in a telephone system, where all internal and external lines meet ○ *You should phone the switchboard if you want an early call.*

switchboard operator /ˈswɪtʃbɔːd ˌɒpəreɪtə/ *noun* somebody who works the central telephone system

switch off /ˌswɪtʃ ˈɒf/ *verb* to stop a piece of electrical equipment working ○ *Don't forget to switch off the air-conditioning when you go to bed.* ○ *The captain has switched off the 'fasten seat belts' sign.*

switch on /ˌswɪtʃ ˈɒn/ *verb* to start a piece of electrical equipment working ○ *The captain switched on the 'no smoking' sign.* ○ *He switched on the air-conditioner.* ○ *When you put the light on in the bathroom, the fan switches on automatically.*

switch over to /ˌswɪtʃ ˈəʊvə tuː/ *verb* to change to something quite different ○ *We have switched over to a French supplier.* ○ *The hotel has switched over to gas for heating.*

swizzlestick /ˈswɪz(ə)lstɪk/ *noun* BARS a small stick put into a glass of fizzy drink to make it less fizzy, or into a cocktail to mix the ingredients

swop /swɒp/ same as **swap**

SWOT analysis /ˈswɒt əˌnæləsɪs/ *noun* MARKETING a method of developing a marketing strategy based on an assessment of the Strengths and Weaknesses of the company and the Opportunities and Threats in the market

syllabub /ˈsɪləbʌb/ *noun* DESSERTS a sweet food made of cream whipped with wine

synergy /'sɪnədʒi/ *noun* a process where greater effects are produced by joining forces than by acting separately

synthesise /'sɪnθəsaɪz/, **synthesize** *verb* to produce a substance, especially a chemical compound, by combining other substances

syrup /'sɪrəp/ *noun* FOOD a thick sweet liquid ○ *fruit syrup* ○ *raspberry syrup*

systems analysis /'sɪstəmz ə,næləsɪs/ *noun* BUSINESS use of a computer to analyse the way in which a company works at present and suggest how it can work more efficiently in future (NOTE: The plural form is **analyses**.)

T

tab /tæb/ *noun* □ **to pick up the tab** to pay the bill (*informal*)

table /'teɪb(ə)l/ *noun* **1.** a piece of furniture with a flat top and legs **2.** CATERING a piece of furniture in a restaurant where guests sit to eat ○ *He asked for a table by the window.* ○ *She says she booked a table for six people for 12.30.* □ **at table** sitting at a dining table ○ *The last guest arrived when everyone else was at table.* **3.** a list of figures or facts set out in columns

tablecloth /'teɪb(ə)l,klɒθ/ *noun* CATERING a cloth for covering a table during a meal

table d'hôte menu /,tɑːblə 'dəʊt ,menjuː/ *noun* CATERING a menu which has a restricted number of dishes at a single price for the whole meal ○ *They chose from the table d'hôte menu.* Compare **à la carte menu**

table lamp /'teɪb(ə)l læmp/ *noun* a lamp on a table ○ *You can use the table lamp if the overhead light is too bright.*

table linen /'teɪb(ə)l ,lɪnɪn/ *noun* CATERING tablecloths, napkins, etc.

table mat /'teɪb(ə)l mæt/ *noun* CATERING same as **placemat** ○ *Put hot dishes on table mats, not directly on the table itself.*

table napkin /,teɪb(ə)l 'næpkɪn/ *noun* CATERING a square piece of cloth used to protect clothes and wipe your mouth at meal times

table plan /'teɪb(ə)l plæn/ *noun* CATERING the layout of the tables in a large room for a function to show where each person is to sit, and to allow for efficient service

table service /'teɪb(ə)l ,sɜːvɪs/ *noun* CATERING service by a waiter or waitress to people sitting at a restaurant table. Also called **waiter service**

table setting /'teɪb(ə)l ,setɪŋ/ *noun* CATERING same as **place setting**

tablespoon /'teɪb(ə)lspuːn/ *noun* CATERING a large spoon for serving food at table

tablespoonful /'teɪb(ə)lspuːnfʊl/ *noun* CATERING the amount contained in a tablespoon ○ *Add two tablespoonfuls of sugar.*

table tent /'teɪb(ə)l tent/ *noun* CATERING a folded card advertising special items on the menu or special wines, placed on a table in a restaurant

tableware /'teɪb(ə)lweə/ *noun* CATERING knives, forks, spoons, plates and other utensils used on the table (NOTE: There is no plural form.)

table wine /'teɪb(ə)l waɪn/ *plural noun* BEVERAGES a less expensive wine which is considered suitable for drinking with meals

TAB vaccine /,tiː eɪ 'biː ,væksiːn/ *noun* MEDICAL a former vaccine which immunised against typhoid fever and paratyphoid A and B ○ *He was given a TAB injection.* ○ *TAB injections give only temporary immunity against paratyphoid.*

tachograph /'tækəɡrɑːf/ *noun* ROAD TRAVEL a device in a truck, which shows details of distance travelled and time of journeys

taco /'tækəʊ/ *noun* FOOD in Mexican cooking, a little vegetable omelette which is rolled round a filling and eaten as a snack

Tafelwein /'tæf(ə)lwaɪn/ *noun* BEVERAGES a German noun meaning table wine. ◊ **vin de table**

tag /tæɡ/ *noun* a label

Tageskarte /'tæɡəskɑːt/ *noun* CATERING a list of special dishes prepared for the day and not listed in the printed menu. ◊ **carte du jour** (NOTE: **Tageskarte** comes from the German noun meaning 'menu of the day'.)

tagliatelle /,tæɡliː'teli/ *noun* FOOD pasta in the form of long narrow ribbons

tailback /'teɪlbæk/ *noun* ROAD TRAVEL a long line of cars held up by roadworks, an accident, etc. ○ *Because of the crash, there's a six-mile tailback on the motorway from junction 4.*

tailored /'teɪləd/ *adjective* adapted to fit a particular requirement ○ *This course is tailored to the needs of women going back to work.* ○ *Individually tailored holidays are also available to selected destinations.*

tailor-made /ˌteɪlə ˈmeɪd/ *adjective* made to fit particular needs ○ *a tailor-made all-inclusive 16-day trip*

tailwind /ˈteɪlwɪnd/ *noun* TRAVEL a wind blowing from behind a ship or aircraft ○ *The flight will be slightly early because of a tailwind across the Atlantic.*

take /teɪk/ *noun* BUSINESS money received from customers in a shop, restaurant, etc. ■ *verb* **1.** to carry something to another place **2.** □ **to take place** to happen ○ *The reception will take place on Saturday.* **3.** to eat or to drink usually ○ *Do you take sugar in your tea?* (NOTE: **taking – took – has taken**)

takeaway /ˈteɪkəweɪ/ *noun, adjective* CATERING (*informal*) **1.** a shop where you can buy cooked food to eat somewhere else ○ *There's an Indian takeaway round the corner.* **2.** a hot meal which you buy to eat at home ○ *We had a Chinese takeaway for supper.* ○ *We can phone for a takeaway pizza.* (NOTE: The US English is **takeout**.)

take-home pay /ˈteɪk həʊm ˌpeɪ/ *noun* BUSINESS pay left after tax and insurance have been deducted

take off /ˌteɪk ˈɒf/ *verb* **1.** to remove or to deduct ○ *He took £25 off the price.* **2.** (*of a plane*) to start to rise from the ground into the air ○ *The plane took off ten minutes late.* **3.** □ **she took the day off** she decided not to work for the day

takeoff /ˈteɪkɒf/ *noun* (*of a plane*) the procedure where an aircraft runs along a runway and rises from the ground into the air ○ *The hostess will serve drinks shortly after takeoff.*

'…a queue of planes at takeoff delayed our departure by ten minutes' [*Business Traveller*]

takeout /ˈteɪkaʊt/ *noun* US CATERING same as **takeaway**

takings /ˈteɪkɪŋz/ *plural noun* BUSINESS money received from customers in a shop, restaurant or hotel ○ *The day's takings were stolen from the cash desk.*

tall drink /ˈtɔːl drɪŋk/ *noun* BEVERAGES an alcoholic drink served with more ice and mixer and in a taller glass than a highball

tan /tæn/ *noun* same as **suntan** ○ *She got a tan from spending each day on the beach.*

tandoori /tænˈdʊəri/ *noun* CATERING a method of Indian cooking using a special oven, or food cooked in this way ○ *a tandoori restaurant* ○ *tandoori chicken*

COMMENT: Food is usually marinated in yoghurt and spices, then cooked in a traditional clay oven called a 'tandoor'.

tandoori oven /tænˌdʊəri ˈʌv(ə)n/ *noun* CATERING a traditional clay oven used in Indian restaurants to cook tandoori-style food

tang /tæŋ/ *noun* CATERING **1.** a sharp taste or smell ○ *I love to smell the tang of the sea.* **2.** a piece of flat metal which forms the centre of the handle of a knife

tangerine /ˌtændʒəˈriːn/ *noun* FRUIT a small orange with soft skin which peels easily ○ *There was a bowl of tangerines on the table.*

tangible assets /ˌtændʒɪb(ə)l ˈæsets/ *plural noun* BUSINESS assets which have a value and actually exist, such as buildings, machines and fittings

tank /tæŋk/ *noun* a large, usually metal container for liquids

tanned /tænd/ *adjective* made brown by the sun ○ *My white legs looked out of place among all the tanned bodies on the beach.*

tap /tæp/ *noun* an apparatus with a twisting knob or lever and a valve which allows liquid to come out of a pipe or container (NOTE: In Britain, the hot tap is usually on the right, and the cold tap on the left, but in other countries they are often the other way round.) □ **cold tap**, **hot tap** a tap which produces cold or hot water □ **to turn a tap on** to allow water to run □ **to turn a tap off** to stop water running

tapas /ˈtæpæs/ *noun* CATERING small plates of snacks such as fried squid, olives, cheese etc., served with beer or wine

tapas bar /ˈtæpəs bɑː/ *noun* BARS a bar where the speciality is serving tapas

tape measure /ˈteɪp ˌmeʒə/ *noun* a metal or plastic ribbon with centimetres and inches marked on it, used to measure how long something is

taphouse /ˈtæphaʊs/ *noun* BARS an inn, bar, public house or other place serving alcohol

taproom /ˈtæpruːm/ *noun* BARS a bar in a place such as a hotel or pub

tap water /ˈtæp ˌwɔːtə/ *noun* water which comes from the mains and not from a well or bottle ○ *Can I have a carafe of water, please? – ordinary tap water will do.*

taramasalata /ˌtærəməsəˈlɑːtə/ *noun* FOOD a creamy pink or beige paste made from smoked fish roe, usually served in the form of a pâté or dip as an appetiser or snack

target /ˈtɑːɡɪt/ *noun* something to aim for □ **to set targets** to fix amounts or sales which employees have to reach □ **to meet a target** to produce the sales which are expected □ **to miss a target** not to produce the sales which are expected ■ *verb* to aim to sell to someone

□ **to target a market** to aim to sell to a particular market

'...many pub chains are also targeting their menu offer to appeal to children in an attempt to compete in the family market with the ever-popular hamburger chains' [*Caterer & Hotelkeeper*]

target market /'tɑːgɪt ˌmɑːkɪt/ *noun* MARKETING the market to which a company is planning to sell its products or services

tariff /'tærɪf/ *noun* HOTELS the rate of charging for electricity, hotel rooms, train tickets, etc. ○ *The new winter tariff will be introduced next week.*

tariff barriers /'tærɪf ˌbæriəz/ *plural noun* BUSINESS customs duty intended to make imports more difficult ○ *to impose tariff barriers on* or *to lift tariff barriers from a product*

tarmac /'tɑːmæk/ *noun* **1.** ROAD TRAVEL a hard road surface made of tar mixed with small stones ○ *The sun was so hot, the tarmac was starting to melt.* **2.** AIR TRAVEL a runway in an airport ○ *The snow ploughs were working flat out to clear the snow from the tarmac.*

tarragon /'tærəgən/ *noun* SAUCES, ETC. a herb used in cooking, often to flavour chicken

tarragon vinegar /ˌtærəgən 'vɪnɪgə/ *noun* SAUCES, ETC. vinegar flavoured with tarragon, made by putting leaves of the plant in vinegar for a few weeks

tart /tɑːt/ *noun* FOOD a pastry case usually filled with sweet food, but sometimes also savoury ○ *jam tart* ○ *cheese tart* ■ *adjective* CATERING bitter in flavour ○ *These apples are very tart.*

tartare /tɑː'tɑː/ *adjective* ♦ **steak tartare**

tartare sauce /ˌtɑːtə 'sɔːs/ *noun* SAUCES, ETC. a sauce made of mayonnaise and chopped pickles, served with fish. Also called **sauce tartare**

tarte /tɑːt/ *noun* DESSERTS a French noun meaning open tart

tarte tatin /ˌtɑː 'tætæn/ *noun* DESSERTS an apple tart, cooked upside down, made of sliced apples cooked in butter with the pastry on top, then reversed in the serving dish

tartlet /'tɑːtlət/ *noun* FOOD a little tart

tartrazine /'tɑːtrəziːn/ *noun* CATERING a yellow substance added to food to give it an attractive colour

COMMENT: Although widely used, tartrazine provokes reactions in some children and hypersensitive people and is banned in some countries.

taste /teɪst/ *noun* **1.** the sense by which you can tell differences of flavour between things you eat, using the tongue **2.** the flavour of a food or drink ○ *The soup has no taste.* ○ *The pudding has a funny taste.* ○ *This wine has a taste of raspberries.* ■ *verb* **1.** to sense the flavour of something ○ *The chef tastes each dish to check the sauces.* ○ *Would you like a piece of cheese to taste?* **2.** to have a flavour ○ *This soup tastes of onions.* ○ *The pudding tastes very good.*

COMMENT: The taste buds can tell the difference between salt, sour, bitter and sweet tastes. The buds on the tip of the tongue identify salt and sweet tastes, those on the sides of the tongue identify sour, and those at the back of the mouth the bitter tastes. Note that most of what we think of as taste is in fact smell, and this is why when someone has a cold and a blocked nose, food seems to lose its taste.

taste buds /'teɪst bʌdz/ *plural noun* cells on the tongue which enable you to tell differences in flavour

tasteless /'teɪstləs/ *adjective* CATERING with no particular flavour

taste panel /'teɪst ˌpæn(ə)l/ *noun* a number of people who taste food to assess its quality

taster /'teɪstə/ *noun* CATERING **1.** somebody who tastes food or drink to see if it is good ○ *A panel of tasters tried the new line of cakes.* ○ *She is chief taster for a tea company.* **2.** a small piece of food which is eaten to see how it tastes

tasting /'teɪstɪŋ/ *noun* an event at which people taste different kinds of food or wine

tasty /'teɪsti/ *adjective* CATERING with a particular pleasant flavour

tavern /'tæv(ə)n/ *noun* BARS an inn or public house (*old name*)

taverna /tə'vɜːnə/ *noun* **1.** CATERING a Greek restaurant **2.** TOURISM (*in Greece*) a guesthouse with a bar, often also serving meals

tax /tæks/ *noun* **1.** money taken by the government or by an official body to pay for government services **2.** □ **to levy a tax, to impose a tax** to demand payment of a tax □ **to lift a tax** to remove a tax □ **tax deducted at source** tax which is removed from a salary or interest before the money is paid out ■ *verb* **1.** to make someone pay a tax ○ *to tax businesses at 50%* **2.** to impose a tax on something ○ *Income is taxed at 35%.* ○ *Luxury items are heavily taxed.* ◇ **tax deductions** US **1.** money removed from a salary to pay tax **2.** business expenses which can be claimed against tax ◇ **tax exemption** US **1.** the state of not being required to pay tax **2.**

part of income which a person is allowed to earn and not pay tax on

taxable /'tæksəb(ə)l/ *adjective* BUSINESS liable to tax

taxable income /ˌtæksəb(ə)l 'ɪnkʌm/ *noun* BUSINESS income on which a person has to pay tax

taxable items /'tæksəb(ə)l ˌaɪtəmz/ *plural noun* BUSINESS things on which a tax has to be paid

tax adjustments /'tæks əˌdʒʌstmənts/ *plural noun* BUSINESS changes made to tax

tax adviser /'tæks ədˌvaɪzə/, **tax consultant** /'tæks kənˌsʌltənt/ *noun* BUSINESS somebody who gives advice on tax problems

tax allowance /'tæks əˌlaʊəns/ *noun* BUSINESS a part of a person's income which he or she is allowed to earn and not pay tax on

tax avoidance /'tæks əˌvɔɪd(ə)ns/ *noun* BUSINESS legal efforts to minimise the amount of tax to be paid. Compare **tax evasion**

tax code /'tæks kəʊd/ *noun* BUSINESS a number given to indicate the amount of tax allowances a person has

tax concession /'tæks kənˌseʃ(ə)n/ *noun* BUSINESS a measure that allows less tax to be paid

tax credit /'tæks ˌkredɪt/ *noun* FINANCE the part of a dividend on which the company has already paid tax, so that the shareholder is not taxed on it again

tax declaration /'tæks dekləˌreɪʃ(ə)n/ *noun* BUSINESS same as **tax return**

tax-deductible /ˌtæks dɪ'dʌktɪb(ə)l/ *adjective* BUSINESS deducted from an income before tax is paid

tax deductions /'tæks dɪˌdʌkʃənz/ *plural noun* US **1.** money removed from a salary to pay tax **2.** business expenses which can be claimed against tax

tax evasion /'tæks ɪˌveɪʒ(ə)n/ *noun* BUSINESS illegal efforts not to pay tax. Compare **tax avoidance**

tax form /'tæks fɔːm/ *noun* BUSINESS a blank form to be filled in with details of income and allowances and sent to the tax office each year

tax-free /ˌtæks 'friː/ *adjective* BUSINESS on which tax does not have to be paid ○ *Children's clothes are tax-free.* ○ *She bought the watch tax-free at the airport.*

tax haven /'tæks ˌheɪv(ə)n/ *noun* BUSINESS a place where taxes are low, encouraging companies to set up their main offices there

tax holiday /'tæks ˌhɒlɪdeɪ/ *noun* BUSINESS the period when a new company pays no tax

taxi /'tæksi/ *noun* ROAD TRAVEL a car which takes people from one place to another for money ○ *He took a taxi to the airport.* ○ *Where can we get a taxi to take us to the beach?* Also called **cab** ■ *verb* (*of an aircraft*) to go along the ground before takeoff or after landing ○ *The aircraft taxied out onto the runway.* ◇ **taxi fare 1.** the price to be paid for a journey in a taxi **2.** a passenger in a taxi

taxicab, taxi cab *noun* same as **taxi**

taxi driver /'tæksi ˌdraɪvə/ *noun* ROAD TRAVEL somebody who drives a taxi ○ *The taxi driver helped me with my luggage.*

taxi fare /'tæksi feə/ *noun* ROAD TRAVEL **1.** the price to be paid for a journey in a taxi **2.** a passenger in a taxi

tax inspector /'tæks ɪnˌspektə/ *noun* BUSINESS a government official who examines tax returns and decides how much tax someone should pay

taxi rank /'tæksi ræŋk/ *noun* ROAD TRAVEL a place where taxis wait in line for customers ○ *There's a taxi rank just outside the hotel.*

taxiway /'tæksiweɪ/ *noun* AIR TRAVEL a lane across an airport along which aircraft can taxi

'…a taxiway leads aircraft to Terminal 2 which has a large parking area at its northern end' [*Airliner World*]

tax relief /'tæks rɪˌliːf/ *noun* BUSINESS measures to allow people not to pay tax on parts of their income

tax return /'tæks rɪˌtɜːn/ *noun* BUSINESS a completed tax form, with details of income and allowances. Also called **tax declaration**

tax year /'tæks ˌjɪə/ *noun* BUSINESS a twelve-month period on which taxes are calculated. Also called **fiscal year**

T-bar /'tiː baː/ *noun* SPORT a type of ski-lift where two skiers hold onto a T-shaped bar, one on each side, to be pulled up a slope

T-bone steak /ˌtiː bəʊn 'steɪk/ *noun* MEAT a thick slice of beef cut from the rib and having a bone shaped like a T in it

tea /tiː/ *noun* **1.** BEVERAGES a hot drink made by pouring boiling water onto the dried leaves of an Asian plant ○ *a cup of tea* ○ *To make tea, you need freshly boiled water.* **2.** BEVERAGES the dried leaves of an Asian plant used to make a hot drink ○ *Buy a pound of tea.* ○ *You put the tea into the pot before adding the hot water.* **3.** BEVERAGES the dried leaves or flowers of other plants, used to make a drink ○ *camomile tea* ○ *mint tea* **4.** CATERING a meal taken in the afternoon, usually between 4 and 5 o'clock. ◊ **cream tea, high tea**

COMMENT: Tea is the most common drink in Britain, although coffee is becoming almost as popular as tea. There are two main types of tea: Indian tea (black tea, usually mixed in various blends) and Chinese tea (or China tea) which is green. Chinese tea is never served with milk. In Britain, Indian tea is usually served with milk. In the USA and Canada, tea is also served with cream.

teabag /'tiːbæg/ *noun* CATERING a small paper bag full of tea which is put into a cup, or into the pot instead of loose tea ○ *I don't like weak tea – put another teabag in the pot.*

tea break /'tiː breɪk/ *noun* ENTERTAINMENT a short rest time during work when the employees can drink tea or coffee

teacake /'tiːkeɪk/ *noun* BREAD, ETC. a type of bun with raisins in it, usually eaten toasted with butter ○ *We ordered toasted teacakes.*

tea ceremony /'tiː ˌserɪməni/ *noun* ENTERTAINMENT the formal serving of tea, especially in Japan

teacup /'tiːkʌp/ *noun* a large cup for tea ○ *She put the teacups and saucers on a tray.*

tea garden /'tiː ˌgɑːd(ə)n/ *noun* ENTERTAINMENT an outdoor place for having tea

tea party /'tiː ˌpɑːti/ *noun* ENTERTAINMENT a small gathering in the afternoon where tea may be drunk

teapot /'tiːpɒt/ *noun* a special pot with a handle and spout for making tea in and for serving it ○ *Put two teabags into the teapot and add boiling water.*

tearoom /'tiːruːm/, **teashop** /'tiːʃɒp/ *noun* CATERING a small restaurant which serves mainly tea, coffee, sandwiches, scones and cakes ○ *There's a tearoom attached to the baker's shop.* ○ *Our village teashop has the best chocolate cake I've ever tasted.*

teaspoon /'tiːspuːn/ *noun* **1.** a small spoon for stirring tea or other liquid ○ *Can you bring me a teaspoon, please?* **2.** same as **teaspoonful** ○ *I take one teaspoon of sugar in my coffee.*

teaspoonful /'tiːspuːnful/ *noun* the amount contained in a teaspoon ○ *Put a teaspoonful of salt into the pan.*

tea strainer /'tiː ˌstreɪnə/ *noun* CATERING a small sieve, which fits over a tea cup, used to prevent tea leaves from getting into the cup

teatime /'tiːtaɪm/ *noun* CATERING the time when tea is served, between 4 and 5.30 p.m.

○ *Hurry up, it'll soon be teatime!* ○ *The children's TV programmes are on at teatime.*

tea trolley /'tiː ˌtrɒli/ *noun* CATERING a table on wheels for carrying food

technology /tek'nɒlədʒi/ *noun* the application of scientific knowledge to industrial processes

'European hotels invest more than £150m a year on interactive guest room technology' [*Caterer & Hotelkeeper*]

tel *abbreviation* telephone

telegram /'telɪgræm/ *noun* a message sent by telegraph ○ *He went into the post office to send a telegram.* ○ *We sent a telegram to my grandmother on her birthday.*

telephone /'telɪfəʊn/ *noun* a machine used for speaking to someone who is a long way away ○ *We had a new telephone system installed last week.* (NOTE: The word **telephone** is often shortened to **phone**: **phone call, phone book**, etc., but not in the expressions **telephone switchboard, telephone operator, telephone exchange**.) □ **to be on the telephone** to be speaking to someone by telephone ○ *The receptionist is on the telephone all the time.* ○ *She's on the telephone at the moment. Can I take a message?* □ **by telephone** using the telephone ○ *He wanted to book his plane ticket by telephone.* ○ *We reserved a room by telephone.* □ **house telephone, internal telephone** a telephone which links different rooms in a hotel, but is not connected to an outside line □ **to make a telephone call** to dial and speak to someone on the telephone □ **to answer the telephone, to take a telephone call** to lift the telephone when it rings and listen to what the caller is saying ■ *verb* □ **to telephone a person, a place** to call someone or a place by telephone ○ *We telephoned the reservation through to the hotel.* ○ *The travel agent telephoned to say that the tickets are ready for collection.* ○ *It's very expensive to telephone Singapore at this time of day.* □ **to telephone about something** to make a telephone call to speak about something ○ *He telephoned about the bill.* □ **to telephone for something** to make a telephone call to ask for something ○ *He telephoned for a taxi.*

telephone booking /'telɪfəʊn ˌbʊkɪŋ/ *noun* HOTELS a booking made by phone for something such as a room in a hotel, a table in a restaurant etc.

telephone booth /'telɪfəʊn buːð/ *noun* a small cabin for a public telephone

telephone call /'telɪˌfəʊn kɔːl/ *noun* a conversation with someone on the telephone

telephone check-in /ˌtelɪfəʊn tʃek ˈɪn/ *noun* AIR TRAVEL a check-in made by phoning the airline, usually only available to passengers with hand baggage

telephone directory /ˈtelɪfəʊn daɪˌrekt(ə)ri/ *noun* same as **phone book** ○ *She looked up the number of the company in the telephone directory.*

telephone exchange /ˈtelɪfəʊn ɪksˌtʃeɪndʒ/ *noun* a central office where the telephones of a whole district are linked

telephone kiosk /ˈtelɪfəʊn ˌkiːɒsk/ *noun* a shelter with a public telephone in it

telephone line /ˈtelɪfəʊn laɪn/ *noun* a wire along which telephone messages travel

telephone link /ˈtelɪˌfəʊn lɪŋk/ *noun* a direct line from one telephone to another. Also called **phone link**

telephone number /ˈtelɪfəʊn ˌnʌmbə/ *noun* a number which you dial to speak to a particular person on the telephone ○ *Can you give me your telephone number?*

telephone order /ˈtelɪfəʊn ˌɔːdə/ *plural noun* an order received over the telephone

telephone subscriber /ˈtelɪfəʊn səbˌskraɪbə/ *noun* somebody who has a telephone

telephone switchboard /ˌtelɪfəʊn ˈswɪtʃbɔːd/ *noun* a central point in a telephone system, where internal and external lines meet

telephonist /təˈlefənɪst/ *noun* somebody who works a telephone switchboard. Also called **operator 2**

television /ˌtelɪˈvɪʒ(ə)n/ *noun* **1.** ENTERTAINMENT a system for broadcasting pictures by radio waves. Abbr **TV 2.** the pictures broadcast in this way ○ *He stayed in his room all evening, watching television.* **3.** same as **television set** ○ *Is there a television in the room?*

television set /ˌtelɪˈvɪʒ(ə)n set/ *noun* ENTERTAINMENT a piece of electrical equipment which shows pictures broadcast by television ○ *My father has bought a new television set* or *a new TV.*

temperance /ˈtemp(ə)rəns/ *noun* the practice of not drinking alcohol

temperance hotel /ˌtemp(ə)rəns həʊˈtel/ *noun* HOTELS a hotel which does not serve alcohol

temperate /ˈtemp(ə)rət/ *adjective* neither very hot nor very cold

temperature /ˈtemprɪtʃə/ *noun* **1.** a measurement of heat in degrees ○ *The temperature outside is below 30° Centigrade.* ○

What is the temperature in the sauna? ○ *The sea temperature is 18° in the summer.* **2.** an illness where your body is hotter than normal

tempura /tempˈpjʊərə/ *noun* FOOD a Japanese dish of vegetables or seafood coated in light batter and deep-fried

tenant /ˈtenənt/ *noun* BUSINESS somebody who rents or leases premises from a landlord

tenanted pub /ˌtenəntɪd ˈpʌb/ *noun* BARS a pub which is owned by a brewery and where the manager is a tenant of the brewery

tender /ˈtendə/ *noun* **1.** an offer to work for a particular price □ **to put a project out to tender, to ask for, to invite tenders for a project** to ask contractors to give written estimates for a job □ **to put in a tender, to submit a tender** to make an estimate for a job **2.** SHIPS AND BOATS a small boat used to take passengers and cargo to a ship which is not moored alongside a quay ■ *verb* **1.** □ **to tender for a contract** to put forward an estimate of cost for work to be carried out under contract ○ *to tender for the construction of a hotel* **2.** □ **to tender one's resignation** to resign from one's job ■ *adjective* CATERING easy to cut or chew, not tough ○ *a plate of tender young asparagus* ○ *The steak was so tender, you hardly needed a knife to cut it.*

tenderer /ˈtendərə/ *noun* BUSINESS a person or company which offers to work for an agreed price ○ *The company was the successful tenderer for the project.*

tendering /ˈtendərɪŋ/ *noun* BUSINESS the act of putting forward an estimate of cost ○ *To be successful, you must follow the tendering procedure as laid out in the documents.*

tenderise /ˈtendəraɪz/, **tenderize** *verb* CATERING to make meat tender by beating it, soaking it in a marinade, or sprinkling it with a special substance

tenderiser /ˈtendəraɪzə/, **tenderizer** *noun* CATERING a substance sprinkled on meat to break down its fibres and make it more tender

tenderloin /ˈtendərlɔɪn/ *noun* MEAT a fillet of pork, cut from the backbone

tennis /ˈtenɪs/ *noun* SPORT a game for two players or two pairs of players who use rackets to hit a ball backwards and forwards over a net ○ *Let's have a game of tennis before dinner.* ○ *She plays tennis every day when she is on holiday.*

tennis ball /ˈtenɪs bɔːl/ *noun* SPORT a ball used when playing tennis

tennis court /ˈtenɪs kɔːt/ *noun* SPORT a specially marked ground for playing tennis

tennis racket /ˌtenɪs 'rækɪt/ *noun* SPORT a type of bat with a long handle and a head made of mesh, used when playing tennis

tennis shoes /'tenɪs ʃuːz/ *plural noun* SPORT special shoes worn when playing tennis

tent /tent/ *noun* a canvas shelter held up by poles and attached to the ground with pegs and ropes □ **to pitch a tent** to put up a tent

tequila /tɪ'kiːlə/ *noun* BEVERAGES a strong Mexican spirit made by redistilling the fermented juice of the agave plant

teriyaki /ˌteri'jɑːki/ *noun* FOOD a Japanese dish consisting of grilled shellfish or meat brushed with a marinade of soy sauce, sugar, and rice wine

term /tɜːm/ *noun* **1.** a period of time □ **in the long term** over a long period of time □ **in the short term** in the near future, quite soon **2.** □ **cash terms** lower terms which apply if the customer pays cash □ **'terms: cash with order'** conditions of sale showing that payment has to be made in cash when the order is placed □ **on favourable terms** on especially good terms ○ *The shop is let on very favourable terms.* **3.** part of a legal or university year. ◊ **terms**

terminal /'tɜːmɪn(ə)l/ *noun* TRAVEL a building situated at the beginning or end of a transport route, with facilities for handling passengers or freight

terminal building /'tɜːmɪn(ə)l ˌbɪldɪŋ/ *noun* AIR TRAVEL same as **airport terminal**

terminate /'tɜːmɪneɪt/ *verb* to bring something to an end ○ *to terminate an agreement* ○ *his employment was terminated* ○ *The offer terminates on July 31st.* ○ *The flight from Paris terminates in New York.*

terminus /'tɜːmɪnəs/ *noun* TRAVEL a station at the end of a railway line, or a point at the end of a regular route of a bus or a coach (NOTE: The plural form is **termini** or **terminuses**.)

terms /tɜːmz/ *plural noun* BUSINESS conditions or duties which have to be carried out as part of a contract, arrangements which have to be agreed before a contract is valid ○ *to negotiate for better terms* ○ *He refused to agree to some of the terms of the contract.* ○ *By* or *Under the terms of the contract, the company is responsible for all damage to the property.* □ **terms of payment**, **payment terms** conditions for paying something □ **terms of sale** conditions attached to a sale □ **terms of employment** conditions set out in a contract of employment

'…companies have been improving communications, often as part of deals to cut down demarca-

tion and to give everybody the same terms of employment' [*The Economist*]

terrace /'terəs/ *noun* a flat outdoor area which is raised above another area ○ *The guests had cocktails on the terrace before going into dinner.*

terrazzo /tə'rætsəʊ/ *noun* a floor covering material made of small pieces of marble set in cement and then polished

terrine /tə'riːn/ *noun* FOOD a coarse pâté or similar cold food cooked and sometimes served in a small dish with a tight-fitting lid

terrorism /'terərɪz(ə)m/ *noun* violent acts such as kidnapping and bombing carried out for political purposes

tertiary industry /ˌtɜːʃəri 'ɪndəstri/ *noun* BUSINESS same as **service industry**

tertiary sector /'tɜːʃəri ˌsektə/ *noun* a section of the economy containing the service industries

TexMex /teks'meks/ *adjective* CATERING referring to the Texan and Mexican style of American cooking, based on steaks, barbecued meat and Mexican dishes such as chilli and tortillas

texture /'tekstʃə/ *noun* (*of food*) the quality in the structure of a food that makes it firm or soft or rough or smooth ○ *This bread has a light texture.* ○ *Flavour and texture are conserved by slow gentle cooking and then fast freezing.*

textured vegetable protein /ˌtekstʃəd 'vedʒtəb(ə)l ˌprəʊtiːn/ *noun* FOOD a substance made from processed soya beans or other vegetables, used as a substitute for meat

thalassotherapy /ˌθæləsə'θerəpi/ *noun* a type of physiotherapy where the patients are put in hot seawater baths or are encouraged to swim in the sea ○ *a large thalassotherapy spa near Bordeaux* Compare **hydrotherapy**

Thanksgiving /'θæŋks,ɡɪvɪŋ/ *noun* ENTERTAINMENT an American festival celebrating the first harvest of the pilgrims who settled in the United States, celebrated on the fourth Thursday in November ○ *All the family will be here for Thanksgiving.*

COMMENT: The traditional menu for Thanksgiving dinner is roast turkey with cranberry sauce, followed by pumpkin pie.

thaw /θɔː/ *verb* to melt something which is frozen

theatre /'θɪətə/ *noun* ENTERTAINMENT a building in which plays and shows are performed ○ *We'll have dinner early and then go to the theatre.* (NOTE: The US spelling is **theater**. Note also that in US English,

theater is also used to refer to a building where films are shown: in British English, this is a **cinema**.)

theatre bookings /'θɪətə ˌbʊkɪŋz/ *plural noun* ENTERTAINMENT the numbers of seats in theatres which are reserved

theatregoer /'θɪətəˌgəʊə/ *noun* ENTERTAINMENT somebody who goes to the theatre ○ *Shaftesbury Avenue was full of theatregoers trying to find taxis.* (NOTE: The US spelling is **theatergoer**.)

theatre seat /'θɪətə siːt/ *noun* ENTERTAINMENT a place to see a play or a show

theatre ticket /'θɪətə ˌtɪkɪt/ *noun* ENTERTAINMENT a ticket which allows you a seat in a theatre

theft /θeft/ *noun* the crime of stealing ○ *We have brought in security guards to protect the hotel against theft.* ○ *They are trying to cut their losses from theft by members of staff.*

theme /θiːm/ *noun* the main subject of a book or article

themed /θiːmd/ *adjective* having a special theme ○ *The hotel offers 18 individually themed rooms.*

theme park /'θiːm pɑːk/ *noun* ENTERTAINMENT an amusement park based on a single theme ○ *A visit to the theme park is included in the package tour.*

therapeutic /ˌθerə'pjuːtɪk/ *adjective* MEDICAL given in order to cure or ease a disorder or disease ○ *Massage of the back may be therapeutic in some cases.*

therapy /'θerəpi/ *noun* MEDICAL the treatment of a person to help cure a disease or disorder ○ *They use heat therapy to treat muscular problems.*

thermal /'θɜːm(ə)l/ *adjective* referring to heat

thermal baths /'θɜːm(ə)l bɑːθs/ *plural noun* ENTERTAINMENT baths of naturally hot water

thermal resort, thermal spa *noun* TOURISM a place where people go for treatment using naturally hot water or mud

thermal spring /'θɜːm(ə)l sprɪŋ/ *noun* ENTERTAINMENT a spring of naturally hot water coming out of the ground

thermometer /θə'mɒmɪtə/ *noun* an instrument for measuring temperature ○ *Put the thermometer in your mouth – I want to take your temperature.* ○ *The thermometer outside shows 20°.*

thermometer reading /θə'mɒmɪtə ˌriːdɪŋ/ *noun* the figure for the temperature given on a thermometer ○ *It's a cold morning – the thermometer reading was –25° at 6 a.m.*

Thermos flask, Thermos *noun* a trademark for a vacuum flask ○ *We took Thermoses of hot coffee to drink when we went cross-country skiing.*

third and fourth freedoms /ˌθɜːd ən fɔːθ 'friːdəmz/ *plural noun* AIR TRAVEL the right of an aircraft to land passengers or mail and the right to pick up passengers or mail

third party /ˌθɜːd 'pɑːti/ *noun* any person other than the two main parties involved in a contract

third-party insurance /ˌθɜːd ˌpɑːti ɪn 'ʃʊərəns/ *noun* FINANCE insurance which covers injury to or death of any person who is not one of the people named in the insurance contract

Third World /ˌθɜːd 'wɜːld/ *noun* the countries of Africa, Asia and South America which do not have highly developed industries and where people are generally poor ○ *We sell tractors into the Third World* or *to Third World countries.* ○ *Some Third World countries have asked for their debts to be rescheduled.*

thirsty /'θɜːsti/ *adjective* wanting to drink ○ *Running around on the beach makes me thirsty.*

thirty-day visa /ˌθɜːti deɪ 'viːzə/ *noun* a visa which allows you to stay in a country for 30 days

Thousand Island dressing /ˌθaʊz(ə)nd ˌaɪlənd 'dresɪŋ/ *noun* SAUCES, ETC. a type of salad dressing made with mayonnaise and chopped pimento, with chilli sauce, ketchup and paprika

thriving /'θraɪvɪŋ/ *adjective* doing well, lively, healthy ○ *a thriving seaside resort*

thrombosis /θrɒm'bəʊsɪs/ *noun* MEDICAL the blocking of an artery or vein by a mass of coagulated blood

'…the association between deep vein thrombosis (DVT) – a blood clot in the calf vein – and longhaul flights has long been recognised' [*Wanderlust*]

throng /θrɒŋ/ *noun* a great crowd of people ○ *throngs of Christmas shoppers* ■ *verb* to crowd together ○ *Crowds thronged the streets during the fiesta.* ○ *The shopping precinct was thronged with shoppers in the days before Christmas.*

through /θruː/ *adjective* TRAVEL going to the final terminus

throughput /'θruːpʊt/ *noun* BUSINESS the amount of work done, number of passengers who pass through or number of customers served

'…the peak times the departure lounge can be busy but the throughput of passengers is swift' [*Airliner World*]

through ticket /ˌθruː ˈtɪkɪt/ *noun* TRAVEL a ticket which allows you to travel to your final destination, even though you may change trains or planes en route

throughway /ˈθruːweɪ/, **thruway** *noun* US ROAD TRAVEL a main road with few entrances and exits (NOTE: The British English is **motorway**.)

thumb /θʌm/ *verb* □ **to thumb a lift** to ask a car driver or truck driver to take you as a passenger, usually by signalling with the thumb or by holding a sign with your destination written on it

thunder /ˈθʌndə/ *noun* a loud noise in the air following a flash of lightning ○ *a tropical storm accompanied by thunder and lightning* ○ *He was woken by the sound of thunder.*

thunderstorm /ˈθʌndəstɔːm/ *noun* a storm with rain, thunder and lightning ○ *There was a terrible thunderstorm last night and our house was struck by lightning.* ○ *Don't shelter under a tree during a thunderstorm.*

thyme /taɪm/ *noun* SAUCES, ETC. same as **common thyme**

tick /tɪk/ *noun* **1.** credit (*informal*) ○ *All the furniture in the house is bought on tick.* **2.** a mark written to show that something is correct ○ *If you want a receipt, put a tick in the box marked 'R'.* (NOTE: The US English for this is **check**.) **3.** MEDICAL a tiny parasite which sucks blood from the skin ■ *verb* to mark with a sign to show that something is correct ○ *The form is very easy to fill in – all you have to do is tick the boxes.*

ticket /ˈtɪkɪt/ *noun* **1.** a piece of paper which allows you to go into a place, e.g. a cinema or an exhibition **2.** a piece of paper or card which allows you to travel ○ *train ticket* or *bus ticket* or *plane ticket* **3.** a piece of paper which shows something ■ *verb* to issue tickets ○ *The new ticketing system has been operative since June 1st.*

ticket agency /ˈtɪkɪt ˌeɪdʒ(ə)nsi/ *noun* ENTERTAINMENT a shop which sells theatre tickets

ticket booth /ˈtɪkɪt buːð/ *noun* TOURISM a small cabin out of doors where entrance tickets, theatre tickets, bus tickets, etc., are sold

ticket collector /ˈtɪkɪt kəˌlektə/ *noun* RAIL TRAVEL somebody at a railway station who takes the tickets from passengers as they get off the train

ticket counter /ˈtɪkɪt ˌkaʊntə/ *noun* TRAVEL a place where tickets are sold

ticketing agent /ˈtɪkɪtɪŋ ˌeɪdʒənt/ *noun* TRAVEL an agent who is authorised to issue tickets, e.g. for travel by long-distance coach

ticket office /ˈtɪkɪt ˌɒfɪs/ *noun* TOURISM an office where tickets can be bought, either for travel or for theatres or other places of entertainment

tidal /ˈtaɪd(ə)l/ *adjective* referring to the tide □ **tidal stretch of the river** part of the river near its mouth where the movement of the tides is noticeable

tide /taɪd/ *noun* the regular rising and falling movement of the sea □ **high tide**, **low tide** points when the level of the sea is at its highest or at its lowest

tide tables /ˈtaɪd ˌteɪb(ə)lz/ *plural noun* lists which show exactly when high and low tide is at particular points on the coast

tie /taɪ/ *noun* **1.** a band of cloth which is worn knotted round the neck under the shirt collar ○ *You have to wear a jacket and tie to get into the restaurant.* **2.** BARS a system by which a pub belongs to a brewery and the landlord is obliged to buy his or her beer from that brewery ○ *The lease will be subject to a full tie on beer and ciders only.* ■ *verb* to attach something with string, rope or twine ○ *He tied the parcel with thick string.* ○ *She tied two labels onto the parcel.* □ **to tie up** (*of a boat*) to be attached by a rope to the quay

tied house /ˌtaɪd ˈhaʊs/ *noun* BARS a pub which belongs to a brewery and is let to a tenant landlord who is obliged to buy his or her beer from the brewery

tie-on label /ˌtaɪ ɒn ˈleɪb(ə)l/ *noun* a label with a piece of string attached so that it can be tied onto an item

tiger prawn /ˈtaɪgə prɔːn/ *noun* SEAFOOD a very large type of prawn

tight /taɪt/ *adjective* fitting closely ○ *My shoes hurt – they're too tight.* ○ *A biscuit tin should have a tight-fitting lid.* □ **a tight schedule** a schedule where many meetings are very close together ○ *The group has a very tight schedule today and is due to leave by coach for the airport in thirty minutes' time.*

tikka /ˈtiːkə/ *noun* FOOD a type of Indian cooking done in a hot clay oven with red curry sauce ○ *We ordered chicken tikka and rice.*

time /taɪm/ *noun* **1.** the period that is needed for something to take place, e.g. one hour, two days, fifty minutes **2.** the hour of the day, e.g. 9.00, 12.15, ten o'clock at night

○ *The time of arrival or arrival time is indicated on the screen.* ○ *Departure times are delayed by up to fifteen minutes because of the volume of traffic.* □ **on time** at the right time ○ *The plane was on time.* ○ *You will have to hurry if you want to get to the meeting on time or if you want to be on time for the meeting.* □ **opening time, closing time** the time when a shop or office starts or stops work, when a pub opens or closes **3.** a system of hours on the clock **4.** hours worked □ **the restaurant staff are paid time and a half on Sundays** they are paid the usual rate plus 50% extra when they work on Sundays **5.** a period before something happens □ **to keep within the time limits, within the time schedule** to complete work by the time stated

time and method study /ˌtaɪm ən ˈmeθəd ˌstʌdi/ *noun* BUSINESS an examination of the way in which something is done to see if a cheaper or quicker way can be found

time and motion expert /ˌtaɪm ən ˈməʊʃ(ə)n ˌekspɜːt/ *noun* BUSINESS somebody who analyses time and motion studies and suggests changes in the way work is done

time and motion study /ˌtaɪm ən ˈməʊʃ(ə)n ˌstʌdi/ *noun* BUSINESS an examination of how long it takes to do particular jobs and of the movements employees have to make to do them

time difference /ˈtaɪm ˌdɪf(ə)rəns/ *noun* the difference in time between one time zone and another ○ *There is a four-hour time difference between Moscow and London.*

time limit /ˈtaɪm ˌlɪmɪt/ *noun* the period during which something should be done

timeshare /ˈtaɪmʃeə/, **time sharing** *noun* TOURISM an arrangement where a share in the same flat or house is sold to several people, each having the right to stay in it for an agreed period each year ○ *They bought a timeshare apartment in Spain.*

time sheet /ˈtaɪm ʃiːt/ *noun* a piece of paper showing when an employee starts and finishes work and how they spend their time

timetable /ˈtaɪmteɪb(ə)l/ *noun* **1.** TRAVEL a list showing times of arrivals and departures of buses, trains or planes ○ *According to the timetable, there should be a train to London at 10.22.* ○ *The bus company has brought out its winter timetable.* **2.** ENTERTAINMENT a list of appointments or events ○ *The manager has a very full timetable, so I doubt if she will be able to see you today.* ■ *verb* to arrange the times for something to

happen ○ *You are timetabled to speak at 4.30.*

time zone /ˈtaɪm zəʊn/ *noun* one of 24 areas in the world in which the same standard time is used, divided by meridians roughly every 15°

tin /tɪn/ *noun* a metal container in which food or another substance is sold and can be kept for a long time (NOTE: The US English is **can.**) □ **biscuit tin** a tin with a tight-fitting lid for keeping biscuits in

tinfoil /ˈtɪnfɔɪl/ *noun* CATERING a thin sheet of aluminium, used to cover food ○ *Wrap the salmon in tinfoil and place in the oven.*

tinned /tɪnd/ *adjective* prepared in a tin, and kept until use ○ *Tinned food will keep for longer than frozen food.*

tin-opener /ˈtɪn ˌəʊp(ə)nə/ *noun* a device for opening tins ○ *We took several tins of soup with us when we went camping, but forgot the tin opener!* (NOTE: The US English is **can-opener.**)

tip /tɪp/ *noun* **1.** money given to someone who has helped you ○ *I gave the cab driver a 50-cent tip.* ○ *The staff are not allowed to accept tips.* Also called **gratuity 2.** a piece of advice on something to buy or to do which could be profitable ○ *He gave me a tip about a cheap restaurant just round the corner from the hotel.* ■ *verb* to give money to someone who has helped you ○ *He tipped the waitress £5.* (NOTE: **tipping – tipped**)

tip credit /ˈtɪp ˌkredɪt/ *noun* BUSINESS money removed from an employee's pay because he or she receives tips from customers

tipping /ˈtɪpɪŋ/ *noun* the act of giving money to someone who has helped you ○ *Tipping is not allowed in Singapore.*

TIR *abbreviation* ROAD TRAVEL Transports Internationaux Routiers

tiramisu /ˌtɪrəmiˈsuː/ *noun* DESSERTS an Italian dessert of sponge cake soaked in marsala wine and topped with cream

tisane /tɪˈzæn/ *noun* BEVERAGES a drink made by pouring boiling water on dried or fresh leaves or flowers, e.g. lime tea, camomile tea

tissue /ˈtɪʃuː/ *noun* a soft paper handkerchief ○ *There is a box of tissues beside the bed.*

T-junction /ˌtiː ˈdʒʌŋkʃ(ə)n/ *noun* ROAD TRAVEL a junction where one road joins another at right angles

toad-in-the-hole /ˌtəʊd ɪn ðə ˈhəʊl/ *noun* FOOD an English dish of sausages cooked in batter

toast /təʊst/ *noun* **1.** BREAD, ETC. a slice of bread which has been grilled ○ *You have toast and marmalade for breakfast.* ○ *She asked for scrambled eggs on toast.* □ **brown toast, white toast** toast made from brown bread or white bread **2.** the act of drinking to someone's health or success ○ *I'll give you a toast – the bride and groom!* ■ *verb* **1.** CATERING to grill bread, etc. until it is brown ○ *We had a pot of tea and toasted teacakes.* **2.** to drink to wish someone health or success

toaster /'təʊstə/ *noun* an electric device for toasting bread

toastie /'təʊsti/ *noun* FOOD same as **toasty**

toastmaster /'təʊstmɑːstə/ *noun* ENTERTAINMENT somebody at a banquet who announces the toasts and calls on people to speak

toast-rack /'təʊst ræk/ *noun* CATERING a device for holding slices of toast upright on the breakfast table ○ *The waiter brought a toast rack with six pieces of toast.* ○ *You should put the toast in the rack to prevent it getting soggy.*

toasty /'təʊsti/ *noun* FOOD a sandwich that has been toasted

toboggan /tə'bɒgən/ SPORT *noun* a long flat wooden sledge curved upwards at the front ■ *verb* to slide on a toboggan

tobogganing /tə'bɒgənɪŋ/ *noun* SPORT the sport of sliding on a toboggan

tofu /'təʊfuː/ *noun* FOOD bean curd, a soft white paste made from soya beans

toilet /'tɔɪlət/ *noun* **1.** a bowl with a seat on which you sit to pass waste matter from the body **2.** a room with this bowl in it ○ *The toilets are towards the rear of the plane.* ○ *The gents toilets are downstairs and to the right.*

toilet bowl /'tɔɪlət bəʊl/ *noun* the china basin of a toilet

toilet paper /'tɔɪlət ˌpeɪpə/, **toilet tissue** *noun* soft paper for wiping yourself after getting rid of waste matter. Also called **lavatory paper**

toilet paper dispenser, toilet paper holder *noun* a bracket or box, usually fixed to the wall, which holds toilet paper

toiletries /'tɔɪlətriz/ *plural noun* soap, cream, perfume, etc., used in washing the body

toilet roll /'tɔɪlət rəʊl/ *noun* a roll of soft paper in a toilet, used for wiping yourself after getting rid of waste matter

toilet seat /'tɔɪlət siːt/ *noun* the plastic or wooden part of a toilet on which you sit

token /'təʊkən/ *noun* **1.** something which acts as a sign or symbol **2.** □ **book token, flower token, gift token, record token** a card bought in a store which is given as a present and which must be exchanged in that store for goods ○ *We gave her a gift token for her birthday.*

token charge /ˌtəʊkən 'tʃɑːdʒ/ *noun* a small charge which does not cover the real costs ○ *A token charge is made for heating.*

token payment /'təʊkən ˌpeɪmənt/ *noun* a small payment which does not cover the real costs

token strike /ˌtəʊkən 'straɪk/ *noun* a short strike to show that employees have a grievance

toll /təʊl/ *noun* a payment for using a service, usually a bridge or a ferry ○ *We had to cross a toll bridge to get to the island.* ○ *You have to pay a toll to cross the bridge.*

toll call /'təʊl kɔːl/ *noun* US a long-distance telephone call

toll-free /ˌtəʊl 'friː/ *adverb, adjective* US without having to pay a charge for a long-distance telephone call ○ *to call someone toll-free* ○ *a toll-free number*

toll-free telephone /ˌtəʊl friː 'telɪfəʊn/ *noun* US MARKETING a system where one can telephone to reply to an advertisement, to place an order or to ask for information, and the seller pays for the call

tollway /'tɒlweɪ/ *noun* US ROAD TRAVEL same as **turnpike**

tomato /tə'mɑːtəʊ/ *noun* FRUIT a red fruit used in salads and sauces ○ *a glass of tomato juice*

tomato sauce /tə'mɑːtəʊ sɔːs/ *noun* SAUCES, ETC. a sauce made with tomatoes

ton /tʌn/ *noun* a measure of weight equal to 2,240 pounds or 907 kilos

tone /təʊn/ *noun* a noise made by a machine such as a telephone ○ *Please speak after the tone.*

tongue /tʌŋ/ *noun* the long organ in your mouth which can move and is used for tasting, swallowing and speaking

COMMENT: Tongue is used as food, ox tongue and lamb's tongue being the most common. It is available ready-cooked to be eaten sliced in salad or sandwiches.

tonic water /'tɒnɪk ˌwɔːtə/ *noun* BEVERAGES a fizzy drink of water and sugar, containing quinine

tonnage /'tʌnɪdʒ/ *noun* SHIPS AND BOATS the amount of space for cargo in a ship, measured in tons

tonne /tʌn/ *noun* a metric ton, 1,000 kilos

toothbrush /'tu:θbrʌʃ/ *noun* a small brush with a long handle used for cleaning the teeth ○ *I forgot to pack a toothbrush.*

toothpaste /'tu:θpeɪst/ *noun* a minty paste used with a toothbrush for cleaning the teeth ○ *I must buy a little tube of toothpaste to take when I'm travelling.*

toothpick /'tu:θpɪk/ *noun* a little pointed piece of wood, used for cleaning between the teeth

toothsome /'tu:θsəm/ *adjective* good to eat

top /tɒp/ *noun* **1.** the upper surface or the highest point of something ○ *We climbed to the top of the cathedral tower.* ○ *You can see three countries from the top of the mountain.* ○ *There is a roof garden on top of the hotel.* **2.** a cover for a container ○ *Make sure the top is screwed back tightly onto the jar.* **3.** *US* the roof of a car

top class /ˌtɒp 'klɑːs/ *adjective* top quality, most expensive ○ *It's a top class restaurant.* Also called **first class**

top deck /ˌtɒp 'dek/ *noun* ROAD TRAVEL the upstairs part of a double-decker bus ○ *Let's sit on the top deck to get a good view.* Also called **upper deck**

top floor /'tɒp flɔː/ *noun* the floor nearest the roof in a building ○ *The lift doesn't go to the top floor.*

top-grade /'tɒp greɪd/ *adjective* most important, of the best quality

top management /ˌtɒp 'mænɪdʒmənt/ *noun* BUSINESS the main directors of a company

top official /ˌtɒp ə'fɪʃ(ə)l/ *noun* a very important person in a government department

top-quality /ˌtɒp 'kwɒlɪti/ *adjective* same as **high-quality**

toque /təʊk/ *noun* CATERING a tall white hat worn by chefs

'…the formal toque is being superseded by coloured skull-caps and bandanas with matching neckerchiefs' [*Caterer & Hotelkeeper*]

torte /tɔːt/ *noun* DESSERTS a German noun meaning an open tart with various fillings ○ *The most popular dessert is a lemon and lime torte on a sponge base.*

tortellini /ˌtɔːtə'liːni/ *plural noun* FOOD small filled pasta that is shaped into rings, boiled, and served in a soup or sauce

tortilla /tɔː'tiːə/ *noun* FOOD a thin flat Mexican bread, cooked on a hot griddle and eaten folded, with a filling

tortilla chip /tɔː'tiːə tʃɪp/ *noun* FOOD a thin crunchy crisp made of maize meal, often

served with dips such as salsa and guacamole

tot /tɒt/ *noun* BEVERAGES a small glass of a spirit such as rum

total /'təʊt(ə)l/ *adjective* complete, with everything added together ○ *total amount* ○ *total cost* ○ *total expenditure* ○ *total revenue* □ **the car was written off as a total loss** the car was so badly damaged that the insurers said it had no value ■ *noun* an amount which is complete, with everything added up ○ *The total for one night came to more than £1,000.* ■ *verb* to add up to ○ *costs totalling more than £25,000* (NOTE: The British English is **totalling – totalled** but the US spelling is **totaling – totaled**.)

total invoice value /ˌtəʊt(ə)l 'ɪnvɔɪs ˌvæljuː/ *noun* BUSINESS the total amount on an invoice, including transport, VAT, etc.

touch down /ˌtʌtʃ 'daʊn/ *verb* (*of plane*) to land ○ *The plane touched down at 13.20.*

touchdown /'tʌtʃdaʊn/ *noun* AIR TRAVEL a landing by a plane ○ *The plane veered across the runway as one of its tyres burst on touchdown.* ○ *Touchdown was 15 minutes late.*

tough /tʌf/ *adjective* difficult to chew or to cut. Opposite **tender** (NOTE: **tough – tougher – toughest**) □ **it's as tough as old boots** it's extremely tough (*informal*)

tour /tʊə/ *noun* a holiday journey to various places coming back eventually to the place you started from ○ *The group went on a tour of Italy.* ○ *The minister went on a fact-finding tour of the region.* ■ *verb* to go on holiday, visiting various places ○ *We spent the holiday touring around Wales.*

tour guide /'tʊə gaɪd/ *noun* a person whose job is to accompany a group of tourists on a tour and give them information about the places they are visiting

tourism /'tʊərɪz(ə)m/ *noun* BUSINESS the business of providing travel, accommodation, food, entertainment, etc., for tourists ○ *Tourism is the country's main source of income.*

tourism industry /'tʊərɪz(ə)m ˌɪndəstri/ *noun* all the various businesses that provide services for tourists, considered together

tourism tax /'tʊərɪz(ə)m tæks/ *noun* FINANCE a tax on visitors to an area or country that is usually collected by the businesses who provide accommodation for them

tourist /'tʊərɪst/ *noun* a person who goes on holiday to visit places away from their home ○ *The tourists were talking German.* ○

There were parties of tourists visiting all the churches. ○ Trafalgar Square is always full of tourists.

tourist attraction /ˈtʊərɪst əˌtrækʃən/ *noun* a special sight or building which attracts a lot of tourists ○ *The main tourist attractions in London are the Tower of London and the Changing of the Guard.*

tourist board /ˈtʊərɪst bɔːd/ *noun* an official organisation which promotes tourism in a particular part of the world

tourist bus /ˈtʊərɪst bʌs/ *noun* a bus carrying tourists, visiting various places of interest

tourist centre /ˈtʊərɪst ˌsentə/ *noun* a town which caters for tourists who visit the surrounding area

tourist class /ˈtʊərɪst klɑːs/ *noun* TRAVEL same as **economy class** ○ *She always travels first class because tourist class is too uncomfortable.*

tourist class hotel /ˌtʊərɪst klɑːs həʊˈtel/ *noun* HOTELS same as **two-star hotel**

touristed /ˈtʊərɪstɪd/ *adjective* visited by a large number of tourists

tourist information /ˌtʊərɪst ˌɪnfəˈmeɪʃ(ə)n/ *noun* details of places visitors might like to visit, how to get there, opening times, available accommodation, etc.

tourist information office /ˌtʊərɪst ˌɪnfəˈmeɪʃ(ə)n ˌɒfɪs/ *noun* an office which gives information to tourists ○ *You can get a map of the town from the tourist bureau.* Also called **information bureau**

COMMENT: Tourist information offices are usually indicated by the international sign showing the letter 'i'.

tourist season /ˈtʊərɪst ˌsiːz(ə)n/ *noun* same as **holiday season** ○ *Late winter is the main holiday season in the Alpine resorts.* ○ *The tourist season on the North Italian coast lasts about three months.*

tourist trade /ˈtʊərɪst treɪd/ *noun* the business of tourism ○ *Tourist trade has fallen off sharply because of the recession.*

tourist trap /ˈtʊərɪst træp/ *noun* a place which attracts tourists and then makes them pay a lot of money for something which is not very good

tourist visa /ˈtʊərɪst ˌviːzə/ *noun* TRAVEL a visa which allows a person to visit a country for a short time on holiday

touristy /ˈtʊərɪsti/ *adjective* spoilt because of there being too many tourists, and because of having tried too hard to attract tourists ○ *The fishing village is pretty, but very touristy.*

tour leader /ˌtʊərə ˈliːdə/ *noun* TOURISM somebody who leads a tour and organises it locally

tournant /ˈtʊənɒn/ *adjective* CATERING a French adjective meaning 'turning'

tournedos /ˈtʊənədɒs/ *noun* MEAT a thick round piece of fillet steak

tour operator /ˈtuːər ˌɒpəreɪtə/ *noun* TRAVEL a travel agency which organises and sells package holidays or tours ○ *Hundreds of people were stranded in Spain when the tour operator went bust.*

'…a number of block bookings by American tour operators have been cancelled' [*Economist*]

tour organizer /tʊə ˈɔːɡəˌnaɪzə/ *noun* TOURISM company or person who arranges a tour

tour representative /ˈtʊə ˌreprɪzentətɪv/ *noun* TOURISM a representative of a tour operator available to assist its customers at a holiday destination

tour wholesaler /ˈtʊːə ˌhəʊlseɪlə/ *noun* TOURISM a company which organises tours and sells them through tour operators

tow /təʊ/ *verb* to pull something behind a vehicle ○ *The motorways were jammed with cars towing caravans.*

towel /ˈtaʊəl/ *noun* a large piece of soft cloth for drying something, especially your body ○ *There are piles of towels in the bathroom.* ○ *There's only one towel in the bathroom.*

towelling /ˈtaʊəlɪŋ/, **toweling** US *noun* an absorbent type of soft cloth used mainly for making towels ○ *He was wearing a yellow towelling bathrobe.*

towel rail /ˈtaʊəl reɪl/ *noun* a bar of metal or wood in a bathroom on which you can hang a towel

town /taʊn/ *noun* a place where people live and work, with shops, offices and factories

town centre /ˌtaʊn ˈsentə/ *noun* the central part of a town, where main shops, banks and places of interest are situated (NOTE: This is called **downtown** in US English.)

town crier /ˌtaʊn ˈkraɪə/ *noun* formerly, somebody employed to make public announcements in the street by ringing a bell and shouting in a loud voice

town guide /ˈtaʊn ɡaɪd/ *noun* TOURISM **1.** a guidebook with descriptions of the history of a town and what to visit **2.** a person who shows tourists round a town

town hall /ˌtaʊn ˈhɔːl/ *noun* a building in the centre of a town where the town council meets and where the town's administrative offices are

townhouse hotel /ˌtaʊnhaʊs həʊˈtel/ *noun* HOTELS a small privately-owned luxury hotel, usually with less than 50 rooms, situated in the middle of a town

track /træk/ *noun* **1.** a path ○ *They followed a track through the jungle.* **2.** RAIL TRAVEL a line of rails

trade /treɪd/ *noun* BUSINESS **1.** the business of buying and selling **2.** business done

trade cycle /ˈtreɪd ˌsaɪk(ə)l/ *noun* BUSINESS a period during which trade expands, then slows down and then expands again. Also called **economic cycle, business cycle**

trade directory /ˈtreɪd daɪˌrekt(ə)ri/ *noun* same as **commercial directory**

trade discount /ˌtreɪd ˈdɪskaʊnt/ *noun* BUSINESS a discount given to a customer in the same trade

trade fair /ˈtreɪd feə/ *noun* MARKETING a large exhibition and meeting for advertising and selling a particular type of product ○ *The fair is open from 9 a.m. to 5 p.m.* ○ *The computer fair runs from April 1st to 6th.* ○ *There are two trade fairs running in London at the same time – the carpet manufacturers' and the computer dealers'.*

trade terms /ˈtreɪd tɜːmz/ *plural noun* BUSINESS a special discount for people in the same trade

trade union /ˌtreɪd ˈjuːnjən/, **trades union** /ˌtreɪdz ˈjuːnjən/ *noun* BUSINESS an organisation which represents employees who are its members in discussions with employers about wages and conditions of employment ○ *The staff are all members of a trades union* or *are trade union members.* ○ *He has applied for trade union membership* or *applied to join a trades union.* (NOTE: The US English is **labor union**.)

trading loss /ˌtreɪdɪŋ ˈlɒs/ *noun* BUSINESS a situation where the company's receipts are less than its expenditure

trading profit /ˈtreɪdɪŋ ˌprɒfɪt/ *noun* BUSINESS a result where the company's receipts are higher than its expenditure

tradition /trəˈdɪʃ(ə)n/ *noun* customs, habits or stories passed from generation to generation

traditional /trəˈdɪʃ(ə)n(ə)l/ *adjective* following tradition, which has existed for a long time ○ *On Easter Day it is traditional to give chocolate eggs.* ○ *Villagers still wear the traditional costumes on Sundays.*

"traditional' should be used to describe a recipe or method for a product that has existed for a significant period" [*Food Standards Agency*]

traditionally /trəˈdɪʃ(ə)nəli/ *adverb* following tradition ○ *Brightly coloured clothing is traditionally worn during the parade.*

traffic /ˈtræfɪk/ *noun* **1.** ROAD TRAVEL cars and other vehicles which are moving ○ *There is an increase in commuter traffic* or *goods traffic on the motorway.* **2.** ROAD TRAVEL the movement of cars, trucks, trains, planes, or the movement of people or goods in vehicles ○ *Passenger traffic on the commuter lines has decreased during the summer.* **3.** BUSINESS illegal trade ○ *drugs traffic* or *traffic in drugs* **4.** BUSINESS the number of sales made by a business

'...just under ten million passengers travelled through the airport last year, and with a steady increase in the volume of traffic predicted, the airport has decided to build a new terminal to meet this demand' [*Airliner World*]

traffic circle /ˈtræfɪk ˌsɜːk(ə)l/ *noun US* ROAD TRAVEL same as **roundabout**

traffic congestion /ˈtræfɪk kənˈdʒestʃ(ə)n/ *noun* ROAD TRAVEL a situation where the streets are difficult to move through because there is a lot of traffic ○ *Traffic congestion makes it almost impossible for buses to run on time.*

traffic island /ˈtræfɪk ˌaɪlənd/ *noun* ROAD TRAVEL a small raised piece of pavement in the centre of the road where pedestrians can safely stand

traffic jam /ˈtræfɪk dʒæm/ *noun* ROAD TRAVEL a situation where there is so much traffic on the road that it moves only very slowly ○ *Traffic jams are common in the rush hour.*

traffic lights /ˈtræfɪk laɪts/ *plural noun* ROAD TRAVEL red, amber and green lights on a pole by a road, telling traffic when to stop or go ○ *Turn left at the next set of lights.*

traffic policeman /ˈtræfɪk pəˌliːsmən/ *noun* ROAD TRAVEL a policeman who directs traffic or who rides a motorcycle to supervise traffic

traffic sheet /ˈtræfɪk ʃiːt/ *plural noun* BUSINESS a list showing daily sales

traffic warden /ˈtræfɪk ˌwɔːdən/ *noun* ROAD TRAVEL a uniformed official who gives parking tickets to cars which are parked illegally

trail /treɪl/ *noun* ENTERTAINMENT a path or track ○ *a long-distance ski trail* ○ *The island has a great network of tracks and trails.*

trailer /ˈtreɪlə/ *noun* ROAD TRAVEL **1.** a small vehicle like a box on wheels which is towed behind a car, and which can be used for carrying luggage, camping equipment, etc. **2.** *US* a caravan

trailer park /'treɪlə pɑːk/ *noun* ROAD TRAVEL same as **caravan park** ○ *We rent a caravan in a caravan park.*

trailhead /'treɪlhed/ *noun* the point where a trail starts ○ *The trailhead lies at the end of the road up the pass.*

train /treɪn/ *noun* RAIL TRAVEL a set of coaches or wagons pulled by an engine along railway lines ○ *to take the 09.30 train to London* ○ *to ship goods by train* ○ *He caught his train* or *he missed his train.* ■ *verb* to teach somebody to do something, or to learn how to do something ○ *The tour will be accompanied by a trained nurse.* ○ *He trained as a scuba-diving instructor.*

'American Airlines offers a through connection by train for passengers arriving by air in Brussels. Expect to see a new generation of 'airline trains'' [*Evening Standard*]

trainee /treɪ'niː/ *noun* somebody who is learning how to do something ○ *We employ trainee waiters to help in the restaurant at peak periods.* ○ *Graduate trainees come to work in the head office when they have finished their courses at university.*

traineeship /treɪ'niːʃɪp/ *noun* a post as a trainee

training /'treɪnɪŋ/ *noun* the process of being taught a skill ○ *During training, students work in a restaurant for three days a week.* ○ *There is a ten-week training period for new staff.* □ **off-the-job training** training given to employees away from their place of work, such as at a college or school

training course /'treɪnɪŋ kɔːs/ *noun* BUSINESS a series of lessons to teach someone how to do something

training levy /'treɪnɪŋ ˌlevi/ *noun* BUSINESS a tax to be paid by companies to fund the government's training schemes

training officer /'treɪnɪŋ ˌɒfɪsə/ *noun* BUSINESS somebody in a company who deals with the training of staff

training unit /'treɪnɪŋ ˌjuːnɪt/ *noun* BUSINESS a special group of teachers who organise training for companies

train station /'treɪn ˌsteɪʃ(ə)n/ *noun* RAIL TRAVEL same as **railway station**

train timetable /treɪn 'taɪmˌteɪb(ə)l/ *noun* RAIL TRAVEL a list showing times of arrivals and departures of trains

traiteur /treɪ'tɜː/ *noun* CATERING a French noun meaning 'outside caterer'

tram /træm/ *noun* RAIL TRAVEL a form of public transport, consisting of carriages running on rails laid in the street (NOTE: The US English is **streetcar**.)

COMMENT: Although common in European countries (Germany, Switzerland, and Scandinavia, for example), trams are now rare in British towns, though some new tram systems have recently been installed (as in Croydon and Manchester). In the USA, the best-known streetcar system is in San Francisco.

tramcar /'træmkɑː/ *noun* RAIL TRAVEL a single carriage of a tram ○ *In Germany, most trams consist of two tramcars linked together.*

tramlines /'træmlaɪnz/ *plural noun* RAIL TRAVEL rails along which a tram runs

tramway /'træmweɪ/ *noun* RAIL TRAVEL same as **tramlines**

trancheur /trɒn'ʃɜː/ *noun* CATERING the person in the kitchen who cuts meat (NOTE: **trancheur** comes from the French noun meaning 'carver'.)

tranquillizer /'træŋkwɪlaɪzə/, **tranquilliser** *US noun* MEDICAL a drug which makes a person calm

transatlantic /ˌtrænzət'læntɪk/ *adjective* AIR TRAVEL across the Atlantic

transfer *noun* /'trænsfɜː/ TRAVEL **1.** a means of transport to take travellers from an airport to a hotel and back ○ *Included in the price are transfers from airport to hotel.* **2.** a change from one form of transport to another **3.** a piece of paper taken from a machine or given by a ticket collector, allowing a passenger on one form of transport to change to another ■ *verb* /træns'fɜː/ to pass from one place to another, or cause someone or something to pass from one place to another ○ *On arrival at the station, the party will transfer to a coach for the rest of the journey to the hotel.*

transfer coach /'trænsfɜː kəʊtʃ/ *noun* AIR TRAVEL a coach which takes travellers from the airport to their hotel

transfer passengers /'trænsfɜː ˌpæsɪndʒəz/ *plural noun* AIR TRAVEL travellers who are changing from one aircraft, train or bus to another, or to another form of transport

transferred-charge call /ˌtrænsfɜːd tʃɑːdʒ 'kɔːl/ *noun* a phone call where the person receiving the call agrees to pay for it

transformer /træns'fɔːmə/ *noun* a device for changing the voltage of electric current, so that electrical devices from one country can be used in countries with different voltage systems. ◊ **adaptor**

transient /'trænziənt/ *adjective* lasting or staying only for a short time

transients /'trænziənts/ *plural noun US* HOTELS people who stay in a hotel or guest house for a short time

transit /'trænzit/ *noun* TRAVEL the movement of passengers or goods on the way to a destination ○ *to pay compensation for damage suffered in transit* ○ *Some of the party's luggage was lost in transit.*

transit lounge /'trænzit laʊndʒ/ *noun* AIR TRAVEL a room in an airport where passengers wait for connecting flights

transit passenger /'trænzit ˌpæsindʒə/ *noun* a passenger who is at an airport simply in order to change flights and is not required to go through customs or immigration formalities

transit visa /'trænsit ˌviːzə/ *noun* TRAVEL a visa which allows someone to spend a short time in one country while travelling to another country

translate /træns'leit/ *verb* to put something which is said or written in one language into another language ○ *He asked his secretary to translate the letter from the German agent.* ○ *We have had the brochure translated from French into Japanese.* ○ *The guide will translate the instructions for you.*

translation /træns'leiʃ(ə)n/ *noun* **1.** the act of putting something which is said or written in one language into another language **2.** a text which has been translated ○ *The translation of the fire instructions was not correct.*

translator /træns'leitə/ *noun* somebody who translates ○ *She works as a translator for the European Parliament.*

transmissible /trænz'misəb(ə)l/ *adjective* MEDICAL possible to pass on or transmit ○ *a disease transmissible by food*

transmission /trænz'miʃ(ə)n/ *noun* ROAD TRAVEL the part of the mechanism of a vehicle which passes the power from the engine to the wheels

transport /'trænspɔːt/ *noun* the act or business of moving of goods or people from one place to another ○ *air transport* or *transport by air* ○ *rail transport* or *transport by rail* ○ *road transport* or *transport by road* ○ *passenger transport* or *the transport of passengers* ○ *What means of transport will you use to get to the museum?* □ **the visitors will be using public transport** or **private transport** the visitors will be coming by bus, train, etc., or in their own cars, etc. ■ *verb* to move goods or people from one place to another in a vehicle ○ *The company transports millions*

of tons of goods by rail each year. ○ *The visitors will be transported to the factory by air* or *by helicopter* or *by taxi.*

transportation /ˌtrænspɔː'teiʃ(ə)n/ *noun* BUSINESS **1.** same as **transport 2.** vehicles used to move goods or people from one place to another ○ *The company will provide transportation to the airport.*

'...arriving passengers move from the arrival gate, down one floor to pick up their bags, and out of the door to their onward destination, via their chosen method of ground transportation' [*Airliner World*]

transport café /'trænspɔːt ˌkæfei/ *noun* CATERING a restaurant where truck-drivers eat

Transports Internationaux Routiers *noun* ROAD TRAVEL a French term referring to a system of international documents which allows dutiable goods to cross several European countries by road without paying duty until they reach their final destination. Abbr **TIR**

trashcan /'træʃkæn/ *noun US* a large plastic or metal container for household rubbish ○ *They come to empty the trashcans once a week.* ○ *She put the rest of the dinner in the trashcan.*

travel /'træv(ə)l/ *noun* the action of moving from one country or place to another ○ *Business travel is a very important part of our overhead expenditure.* □ **the travel business** ♦ **business** □ **the travel trade** all businesses which organise travel for people ■ *adjective* specially made for use when travelling ○ *a travel pillow* ■ *verb* **1.** to move from one country or place to another ○ *He travels to the States on business twice a year.* ○ *In her new job, she has to travel abroad at least ten times a year.* **2.** BUSINESS to go from one place to another, showing a company's goods to buyers and taking orders from them ○ *He travels in the north of the country for a pharmaceutical company.* (NOTE: The British English is **travelling – travelled** but American English is **traveling – traveled**.)

travel advisory /'træv(ə)l əd,vaiz(ə)ri/ *noun* a notice published by a government or international agency giving advice on travel to particular areas or countries where travellers may encounter danger or difficulties

travel agency /'træv(ə)l ˌeidʒənsi/ *noun* TRAVEL an office which arranges tickets and accommodation for travellers ○ *Can you get foreign currency from the travel agency?* ○ *I have to collect my tickets from the travel agency.*

travel agent /'træv(ə)l ˌeidʒənt/ *noun* TRAVEL a person or company that arranges tickets and accommodation for its customers ○ *I asked the travel agent for details of tours to Greece.* ○ *The tour was arranged by our local travel agent.* ○ *The travel agent called to say that the tickets were ready.* ○ *See your travel agent for details of our tours to Spain.*

travel alarm clock /ˌtræv(ə)l əˈlɑːm ˌklɒk/ *noun* a small alarm clock which folds, and can easily be carried when travelling

travel allowance /ˈtræv(ə)l əˌlaʊəns/ *noun* money which an employee is allowed to spend on travelling

travelator /ˈtræv(ə)leɪtə/ *noun* a type of moving carpet, which you stand on to be taken from one place to another on the same level. Compare **escalator**, **lift**

travel bureau /ˈtræv(ə)l ˌbjʊərəʊ/ *noun* TRAVEL same as **travel agency**

travelcard /ˈtræv(ə)lkɑːd/ *noun* a ticket entitling the user to an unlimited number of journeys on a public transport system within a particular area for a fixed period of time

travel data /ˈtræv(ə)l ˌdeɪtə/ *noun* information about a person's travel arrangements or accommodation, which is stored on computer

travel document /ˈtræv(ə)l ˌdɒkjʊmənt/ *noun* TRAVEL a passport or visa which a person must have to be able to travel between countries

travel insurance /ˈtræv(ə)l ɪnˌʃʊərəns/ *noun* FINANCE insurance taken out by a traveller against accident, loss of luggage, illness, etc.

travel iron /ˈtræv(ə)l ˌaɪən/ *noun* a small iron which you can carry with you when you travel

traveller /ˈtræv(ə)lə/ *noun* TRAVEL somebody who travels (NOTE: The US spelling is **traveler**.)

traveller's cheque /ˈtræv(ə)ləz ˌtʃek/ *noun* FINANCE a cheque which you buy at a bank before you travel and which you can then use in a foreign country ○ *Most shops in the USA accept traveller's cheques.* ○ *The hotel will cash traveller's cheques for you.* (NOTE: The US term is **traveler's check**.) □ **dollar traveler's check, sterling traveller's cheque** a traveller's cheque in dollars or pounds sterling

travellers' diarrhoea /ˌtrævələz ˌdaɪəˈriːə/ *noun* MEDICAL diarrhoea caused by eating unwashed vegetables or fruit, or drinking unboiled water, contracted by travellers

travelling companion /ˈtræv(ə)lɪŋ kəmˌpænjən/ *noun* TRAVEL somebody who is travelling with another

travelling expenses /ˈtræv(ə)lɪŋ ekˌspensɪz/ *plural noun* TRAVEL money spent on travelling and hotels for business purposes

travel literature /ˈtræv(ə)l ˌlɪt(ə)rətʃə/ *noun* TRAVEL magazines, leaflets, etc., which give information about travel

travel magazine /ˈtræv(ə)l mægəˌziːn/ *noun* TRAVEL a magazine with articles on holidays and travel

travel management /ˈtræv(ə)l ˌmænɪdʒmənt/ *noun* TRAVEL the organisation and running of a travel system ○ *The aim of travel management is to make sure that business travel is both cost-effective and productive.*

'…travel management means meeting the demands and expectations of travellers, be they individuals or part of a group' [*Heathrow International Traveller*]

travel organisation /ˈtræv(ə)l ˌɔːgənaɪzeɪʃ(ə)n/ *noun* TRAVEL a body representing companies in the travel business

travel sickness /ˈtræv(ə)l ˌsɪknəs/ *noun* MEDICAL sickness caused by the movement of a car, aircraft, bus or train. Also called **motion sickness**

travel sickness pills /ˈtræv(ə)l ˌsɪknəs ˌpɪlz/ *plural noun* MEDICAL tablets taken to prevent travel sickness

travel warning /ˈtræv(ə)l ˌwɔːnɪŋ/ *noun* a notice published by a government warning its citizens against travelling to a particular country or area

tray /treɪ/ *noun* **1.** a flat board for carrying glasses or cups and saucers, etc. ○ *He had his lunch on a tray in his bedroom.* ○ *She bumped into a waiter carrying a tray of glasses.* ○ *The waiter brought round a tray of sandwiches and coffee.* ◊ **in tray, out tray 2.** □ **in tray** a container for letters or memos which have been received and are waiting to be dealt with

tray table /ˈtreɪ ˌteɪb(ə)l/ *noun* a small table that folds down from the back of the seat in front of you in a plane or train

treacle /ˈtriːk(ə)l/ *noun* FOOD a thick dark-brown syrup produced when sugar is refined, used to make treacle toffee (NOTE: The US English is **molasses**.)

'…syrup and treacle are both solutions of invert sugar in water, uncrystallized by-products of sugar refining. They contain approximately equal proportions of dextrose and fructose' [*The Sunday Times*]

treacle tart /ˈtriːk(ə)l ˌtɑːt/ *noun* DESSERTS a tart made with golden syrup

trek /trek/ TOURISM *noun* a long and difficult journey ○ *a four week trek in the Andes*

■ *verb* to make a long and difficult journey ○ *They trekked across the desert in search of water.*

trekker /'trekə/ *noun* SPORT somebody who goes on long and difficult journeys, usually on foot ○ *Will Nepal remain a safe destination for international trekkers?*

trekking /'trekɪŋ/ *noun* SPORT the activity of going on long and difficulty journeys, usually on foot ○ *This is one of the world's classic trekking routes.* ◊ **pony-trekking**

trestle /'tres(ə)l/ *noun* a pair of folding legs which can be used to hold up a table

trestle table /'tres(ə)l ,teɪb(ə)l/ *noun* a table made of planks resting on folding legs

trial /'traɪəl/ *noun* a test to see if something is good □ **on trial** being tested ■ *verb* to test something to see if it is good ○ *The restaurant is still only trialling farm cod.* ○ *We are trialling a new ticketing system.* (NOTE: **trialling – trialled**)

trim /trɪm/ *noun* **1.** the act of cutting something short to make it tidy ○ *He went to the barber's for a trim.* **2.** decoration on a car ■ *verb* **1.** CATERING to cut off parts of meat or fish because they are not needed ○ *The chef trimmed the meat to remove most of the fat and gristle.* **2.** to cut something short to make it tidy ○ *Ask the hairdresser to trim your beard.* **3.** to cut back or reduce ○ *They have trimmed their staff to the absolute minimum.* **4.** to ornament or to decorate

trimmings /'trɪmɪŋz/ *noun* CATERING **1.** pieces cut off when preparing meat or fish ○ *Keep any trimmings for stocks and soups.* **2.** sauces and garnishes which are usually served with a dish ○ *We had roast turkey with all the trimmings.*

trip /trɪp/ *noun* a journey ■ *verb* to catch your foot in something so that you stagger and fall down

trip dossier /,trɪp 'dɒsieɪ/ *noun* a collection of documents relating to the trip that a traveller is going to make

tripe /traɪp/ *noun* MEAT part of a cow's stomach used as food ○ *The local dish is tripe and onions.*

COMMENT: Tripe is sold bleached and boiled; the best quality tripe is that called 'honeycomb tripe'; it can be eaten cold or stewed with onions.

triple /'trɪp(ə)l/ *adjective* three times

triple occupancy /,trɪp(ə)l 'ɒkjʊpənsi/ *noun* HOTELS three people sharing one hotel room

tripper /'trɪpə/ *noun* TOURISM somebody who goes on a journey, especially a day's excursion by coach or by train

trocken /'trɒkən/ *adjective* BEVERAGES a German word meaning 'dry', used of wine

trolley /'trɒli/ *noun* **1.** a basket on wheels for carrying shopping, luggage, etc. **2.** CATERING a table on wheels for carrying food

trolley-bus /'trɒli bʌs/ *noun* ROAD TRAVEL a bus which works on electricity taken from overhead wires by contact poles ○ *Trolley-buses are an energy-efficient method of public transport.*

tronc /trɒŋk/ *noun* BUSINESS a French noun meaning a system where all tips from customers are put into a common pool, and then shared out among the staff at the end of the day

tropic /'trɒpɪk/ *noun* □ **the tropics** the region between the Tropic of Cancer and the Tropic of Capricorn where it is very hot, and the countries and areas that are situated there ○ *He lives in the tropics.* ○ *Yellow fever is endemic in parts of the tropics.*

tropical /'trɒpɪk(ə)l/ *adjective* situated in or coming from the tropics ○ *You will need a mosquito net to keep off the tropical insects.*

tropical disease /,trɒpɪk(ə)l dɪ'ziːz/ *noun* MEDICAL a disease which is found in tropical countries, e.g. malaria, dengue or Lassa fever

tropical medicine /,trɒpɪk(ə)l 'med(ə)sɪn/ *noun* MEDICAL the branch of medicine which deals with tropical diseases

tropical storm /,trɒpɪk(ə)l 'stɔːm/ *noun* a violent storm occurring in the tropics

Tropic of Cancer /,trɒpɪk əv 'kænsə/ *noun* a parallel running round the Earth at latitude 23°28N

Tropic of Capricorn /,trɒpɪk əv 'kæprɪkɔːn/ *noun* a parallel running round the Earth at latitude 23°28S

trotters /'trɒtəz/ *noun* MEAT pig's feet cooked for food ○ *Pig's trotters are on the menu tonight.*

trouble /'trʌb(ə)l/ *noun* problems or any situation that causes people worry or difficulties ○ *He's having trouble getting his visa.* ○ *The plane seems to have engine trouble.* ■ *verb* to create problems for someone or to bother someone ○ *Can I trouble you for a light?*

trouser press /'traʊzə pres/ *noun* a device for pressing trousers with two boards which clamp down on the trousers to remove creases, sometimes heated electrically ○ *Every room in the hotel has an electric trouser press.*

trousers /'traʊzəz/ *noun* □ **(pair of) trousers** outer clothes which cover the legs and the lower part of the body

trout /traʊt/ *noun* SEAFOOD a type of edible freshwater fish ○ *grilled trout with almonds*

truck /trʌk/ *noun* ROAD TRAVEL same as **lorry**

truck driver /'trʌk ˌdraɪvə/ *noun* ROAD TRAVEL somebody who drives a truck

truffle /'trʌf(ə)l/ *noun* FOOD **1.** an edible underground fungus that is regarded as a delicacy **2.** a rich ball-shaped chocolate with a centre of soft chocolate

trunk /trʌŋk/ *noun* a large case for carrying luggage, especially by sea or rail

trunk call /'trʌŋk kɔːl/ *noun* a telephone call to a number in a different zone or area

tsatsiki /tsæt'tsiːki/ *noun* FOOD a Greek dish of cucumber, mint and yoghurt

T-shirt, teeshirt *noun* a light shirt with no buttons or collar, usually with short sleeves ○ *She was wearing jeans and a T-shirt.* ○ *No wonder you're cold if you went out in just a T-shirt.*

tub /tʌb/ *noun* US same as **bathtub**

tube /tjuːb/ *noun* **1.** a long pipe for carrying liquids or gas ○ *a tube of toothpaste* **2.** □ **the Tube** the underground rail network in London **3.** BEVERAGES (*in Australia*) a can of beer

tulip glass /'tjuːlɪp glɑːs/ *noun* CATERING same as **flute**

tumbler /'tʌmblə/ *noun* CATERING a glass with a flat base and straight sides, used for serving water, etc.

tun /tʌn/ *noun* BARS a large barrel for wine or beer

tuna /'tjuːnə/ *noun* SEAFOOD a large edible sea fish with dark pink flesh (NOTE: The plural form is **tuna**.)

COMMENT: Fresh tuna is available in some countries, but in Britain is most easily available in tins. Tuna is often used in salads.

tunnel /'tʌn(ə)l/ *noun* a long hole in the ground ○ *The road round the lake goes through six tunnels.* ○ *The tunnel through the Alps is over 30km long.*

turbot /'tɜːbət/ *noun* SEAFOOD a large flat edible white sea fish (NOTE: The plural form is **turbot**.)

turbulence /'tɜːbjʊləns/ *noun* AIR TRAVEL a disturbance in the air causing an aircraft to rock suddenly

tureen /tjʊ'riːn/ *noun* CATERING a large serving dish for soup ○ *The waitress arrived* with a tureen of vegetable soup and put it on the table.

turkey /'tɜːki/ *noun* MEAT a large poultry bird raised for meat ○ *We're having roast turkey for Christmas dinner.*

COMMENT: Turkey is traditionally eaten at Christmas, with chestnut stuffing; it is also eaten in the US for Thanksgiving dinner.

Turkish /'tɜːkɪʃ/ *adjective* referring to Turkey

Turkish bath /ˌtɜːkɪʃ 'bɑːθ/ *noun* ENTERTAINMENT public baths with hot pools, cold baths, massages, etc.

Turkish coffee /ˌtɜːkɪʃ 'kɒfi/ *noun* BEVERAGES coffee heated with sugar and water. Also called **Greek coffee**

Turkish delight /ˌtɜːkɪʃ dɪ'laɪt/ *noun* DESSERTS a very sweet jelly, flavoured with essences of flowers, sometimes with nuts added, sprinkled with powdered sugar

turmeric /'tɜːmərɪk/ *noun* SAUCES, ETC. a yellow spice, used especially in pickles and curries

turn /tɜːn/ *noun* **1.** a change of direction, especially of a vehicle ○ *There's a sharp left turn about 250 metres further on.* **2.** movement in a circle **3.** ENTERTAINMENT a performance in a cabaret **4.** □ **the meat is done to a turn** the meat is properly cooked all through ■ *verb* **1.** to change direction, to go in another direction ○ *Turn left at the traffic lights.* **2.** to go round in a circle

turnaround /'tɜːnəˌraʊnd/ ♦ **turnround**

turndown service /'tɜːndaʊn ˌsɜːvɪs/ *noun* HOTELS the work of preparing a room in the evening, by removing the bedcovers and turning down a corner of the sheet to show the pillowcase

turning /'tɜːnɪŋ/ *noun* ROAD TRAVEL a point where a road leaves another road ○ *Take the second turning on the right.* ○ *After taking several wrong turnings we were hopelessly lost.*

turnip /'tɜːnɪp/ *noun* VEGETABLES a common vegetable with a round white root, used mainly in soups and stews

COMMENT: Boiled turnips or 'neaps' are the traditional accompaniment to Scottish haggis.

turnkey operation /'tɜːnkiː ɒpəˌreɪʃ(ə)n/ *noun* BUSINESS a deal where a company takes all responsibility for constructing, fitting and staffing a building such as a hotel, so that it is completely ready for the purchaser to take over

turnover /'tɜːnəʊvə/ *noun* **1.** FOOD pastry folded over a sweet filling, and baked or fried ○ *apple turnover* **2.** BUSINESS the amount of goods or services sold by an organisation ○ *The restaurant's turnover has increased by 23.5%.* ○ *We based our calculations on the forecast turnover.* (NOTE: The US English is **sales volume**.)

turnover tax /'tɜːnəʊvə tæks/ *noun* BUSINESS a tax on company turnover

turnpike /'tɜːnpaɪk/ *noun US* ROAD TRAVEL a motorway on which you pay a toll. Also called **tollway**

turnround /'tɜːnraʊnd/, **turnaround** *US* /'tɜːnə,raʊnd/ *noun* **1.** TRAVEL the act of unloading passengers and cargo from a ship or aircraft, cleaning, refuelling and reloading for the next trip ○ *Poor turnround time of aircraft can affect schedules.* **2.** the time taken to do this

turnstile /'tɜːnstaɪl/ *noun* a gate which turns round on a pivot, allowing only one person to go through at a time ○ *More than three thousand people went through the turnstiles in an hour.*

tutti frutti /,tuːti 'fruːti/ *noun* DESSERTS an Italian ice cream with pieces of preserved fruit in it

TV /,tiː 'viː/ *noun* ENTERTAINMENT **1.** television ○ *He loves to watch TV.* **2.** a television set ○ *There is a colour TV in each room.*

TV lounge /,tiː 'viː laʊndʒ/ *noun* ENTERTAINMENT a room in a hotel, college, hospital, etc., where residents can watch TV

TVP *abbreviation* FOOD textured vegetable protein

24-hour service /,twenti fɔːr aʊə 'sɜːvɪs/ *noun* help which is available for the whole day

twin /twɪn/ *verb* □ **to twin a town with another town** to arrange a special relationship between a town in one country and a similar town in another country ○ *Richmond is twinned with Fontainebleau.*

twin-bedded room /,twɪn ,bedɪd 'ruːm/ *noun* HOTELS a room with twin beds

twin beds /,twɪn 'beds/ *plural noun* two single beds placed in a bedroom

twinning /'twɪnɪŋ/ *noun* TOURISM a special arrangement between a town in one country and one of similar size or situation in another country ○ *The district council's town-twinning committee decided that Epping should be twinned with Eppingen in Germany.*

twin room /,twɪn 'ruːm/ *noun* HOTELS same as **twin-bedded room**

twin-tips skis, **twin-tipped skis** *plural noun* SPORT skis which are shorter and wider than conventional skis and are bent up at both ends

two-berth cabin /,tuː bɜːθ 'kæbɪn/ *noun* a cabin with two beds, usually one above the other

two-lane highway /,tuː leɪn 'haɪweɪ/ *noun US* ROAD TRAVEL a road in two parts, with a barrier between them ○ *The traffic on the two-lane highway was bumper-to-bumper.* (NOTE: The British English is **dual carriageway**.)

two-sink system /,tuː sɪŋk 'sɪstəm/ *noun* CATERING a system for washing dishes by hand, with two sinks, the first with warm water for washing, the second with very hot water for rinsing

two-star hotel /,tuː stɑː həʊ'tel/ *noun* HOTELS a hotel which provides quite basic accommodation at cheaper prices. Also called **tourist-class hotel**

type /taɪp/ *noun* sort or kind ○ *What type of accommodation are you looking for?*

typhoid fever /,taɪfɔɪd 'fiːvə/ *noun* MEDICAL an infection of the intestine caused by *Salmonella typhi* in food and water ○ *Contaminated water was probably the cause of the recent outbreak of typhoid fever.*

COMMENT: Typhoid fever gives a fever, diarrhoea and the patient may pass blood in the faeces. It can be fatal if not treated; patients who have had the disease may become carriers. Although a vaccine is available, travellers in countries where typhoid is endemic should avoid eating green salad, unpeeled fruit and drinking ordinary tap water; they should only drink bottled water or tap water which has been boiled.

typhoon /taɪ'fuːn/ *noun* a violent tropical storm with extremely strong winds, in the Far East (NOTE: In the Caribbean, this is called a **hurricane**.)

typhus /'taɪfəs/ *noun* MEDICAL one of several fevers caused by the Rickettsia bacterium, transmitted by fleas and lice ○ *Aid workers fear that a typhus epidemic may erupt if conditions in the refugee camps deteriorate any further.*

COMMENT: Typhus victims have a fever, feel extremely weak and develop a dark rash on the skin.

tyre /'taɪə/ *noun* a thick rubber cover round a wheel (NOTE: The US spelling is **tire**.)

U

ugli /'ʌgli/ *noun* FRUIT a citrus fruit similar to a grapefruit, but a little larger, of uneven shape and easy to peel

UHT *abbreviation* CATERING ultra heat treated

ultimate destination /ˌʌltɪmət ˌdestɪ'neɪʃ(ə)n/ *noun* TRAVEL same as **final destination**

ultra heat treated milk /ˌʌltrə hiːt ˌtriːtɪd 'mɪlk/ *noun* DAIRY milk which has been treated by sterilising at temperatures above 135°C, and then put aseptically into containers. Abbr **UHT milk**

ultraviolet lamp /ˌʌltrəvaɪələt 'læmp/ *noun* a lamp which gives off ultraviolet rays which tan the skin, help the skin produce Vitamin D and kill bacteria

ultraviolet radiation /ˌʌltrəvaɪələt ˌreɪdi'eɪʃ(ə)n/ *noun* short invisible rays, beyond the violet end of the colour spectrum, which form the tanning and burning element in sunlight

UM *abbreviation* TRAVEL unaccompanied minor

umbrella /ʌm'brelə/ *noun* a round frame covered with cloth which you hold over your head to keep off the rain

unaccompanied /ˌʌnə'kʌmpənid/ *adjective* TRAVEL not going with a passenger ○ *There are three unaccompanied children on the flight.*

unaccompanied baggage /ˌʌnəkʌmpənid 'bægɪdʒ/ *noun* TRAVEL baggage which is not accompanied by a passenger ○ *Unaccompanied baggage must be checked in at the airport 24 hours in advance.*

unaccompanied minor /ˌʌnəkʌmpənid 'maɪnə/ *noun* TRAVEL somebody below the age of majority travelling alone. Abbr **UM**

unappetising /ʌn'æpɪtaɪzɪŋ/ *adjective* not looking, smelling or tasting attractive

unbonded /ʌn'bɒndɪd/ *adjective* BUSINESS not having placed money as a surety against future potential loss

'…the booking of accommodation was organized through a US-based company which was not an ABTA member and so hotel bookings were unbonded' [*Sunday Times*]

unchecked /ʌn'tʃekt/ *adjective* that has not been checked ○ *unchecked figures* ○ *Three items of unchecked baggage remained in the check-in area.*

unclaimed /ʌn'kleɪmd/ *adjective* that has not been claimed

unclaimed baggage /ˌʌnkleɪmd 'bægɪdʒ/ *noun* cases which have been left with someone and have not been collected by their owners ○ *Unclaimed property* or *Unclaimed baggage will be sold by auction after six months.*

uncomfortable /ʌn'kʌmftəb(ə)l/ *adjective* not soft and relaxing ○ *Plastic seats are very uncomfortable on long journeys.*

uncooked /ʌn'kʊkt/ *adjective* CATERING raw, not cooked ○ *Some Japanese dishes consist of uncooked fish.* ○ *Shrimps are grey when uncooked and become pink when cooked.*

uncork /ʌn'kɔːk/ *verb* BARS to take the cork out of a bottle

uncrossed cheque /ˌʌnkrɒst 'tʃek/ *noun* FINANCE a cheque which can be cashed anywhere. Also called **open cheque**

uncured /ʌn'kjʊəd/ *adjective (of food)* not preserved by smoking, salting, pickling, or drying

undelivered /ˌʌndɪ'lɪvəd/ *adjective* that has not been delivered

underbooked /ˌʌndə'bʊkt/ *adjective* referring to a tour or flight which does not have enough bookings

undercharge /ˌʌndə'tʃɑːdʒ/ *verb* to ask for less money than you should ○ *I think we were undercharged for the meal.* ○ *He undercharged us by £5.*

undercloth /'ʌndəklɒθ/ *noun* CATERING a cloth, usually of baize, which covers a table before the tablecloth is put on

underdish /'ʌndədɪʃ/ *noun* CATERING a flat dish on which another deeper dish is placed before serving

underdone /ˌʌndə'dʌn/ *adjective* CATER-ING having not been cooked for very long ○ *a plate of underdone chicken* Opposite **over-done**

underground *adverb* /ˌʌndə'graʊnd/ under the ground ○ *The ordinary railway line goes underground for a short distance.* ■ *adjective* /'ʌndəgraʊnd/ under the ground ○ *There's an underground passage to the tower.* ○ *The hotel has an underground car park.* ■ *noun* /'ʌndəgraʊnd/ RAIL TRAVEL a railway system which runs in a tunnel under the ground ○ *He took the underground to the airport.* ○ *The underground can be very crowded during rush hour.* (NOTE: The US English is **subway**.)

underground train /'ʌndəgraʊnd treɪn/ *noun* RAIL TRAVEL a train which runs in a tunnel under the ground

underpass /'ʌndəpɑːs/ *noun* ROAD TRAVEL a place where one road goes under another ○ *Turn left at the lights when you come out of the underpass.* Compare **overpass**

underplate /'ʌndəpleɪt/ *noun* CATERING a flat plate on which another deeper dish is placed before serving, e.g. a plate under a soup plate or under a coffee cup and saucer

understaffed /ˌʌndə'stɑːft/ *adjective* with not enough staff ○ *Service is slow because the restaurant is understaffed.*

underwater /ˌʌndə'wɔːtə/ *adjective, adverb* below the surface of the water ○ *He dived and swam underwater for several seconds.* ○ *She goes on holiday to the Red Sea to do underwater photography.*

undesirable alien /ˌʌndɪzaɪrəb(ə)l 'eɪliən/ *noun* a foreigner who is not welcome in a country, and who can be expelled

undeveloped /ˌʌndɪ'veləpt/ *adjective* TOURISM where no facilities for tourists have been built ○ *The island is still undeveloped.*

undressed /ʌn'drest/ *adjective* **1.** (*of food*) not fully prepared for cooking or eating **2.** (*of food*) not covered with a dressing or sauce

unearned income /ˌʌnɜːnd 'ɪnkʌm/ *noun* BUSINESS money received from interest or dividends

unfair dismissal /ˌʌnfeə dɪs'mɪs(ə)l/ *noun* BUSINESS the removal of someone from a job by an employer who appears not to be acting in a reasonable way

unfilled /ʌn'fɪld/ *adjective* having not been filled ○ *We still have several unfilled places on the tour.* ○ *Almost 90% of hotels* had unfilled positions, especially among kitchen staff.

unfilled room /ˌʌnfɪld 'ruːm/ *noun* HOTELS a hotel room which is still vacant at the end of the day

unfit /ʌn'fɪt/ *adjective* not suitable □ **unfit for human consumption** not suitable for humans to eat, and possibly only be suitable to give to animals

unguaranteed reservation /ˌʌngærəntiːd ˌrezə'veɪʃ(ə)n/ *noun* a reservation for something which a company cannot promise will be available

uniform /'juːnɪfɔːm/ *noun* specially designed clothing worn by all members of a group ○ *The holiday camp staff all wear yellow uniforms.*

uniform allowance /'juːnɪfɔːm əˌlaʊəns/ *noun* money given to an employee to buy new items of uniform as old items wear out

uniformed /'juːnɪfɔːmd/ *adjective* wearing a uniform

uniformed services /ˌjuːnɪfɔːmd 'sɜːvɪsɪz/ *plural noun* HOTELS services in a hotel provided by staff who wear uniforms

uniformed staff /'juːnɪˌfɔːmd stɑːf/ *noun* HOTELS hotel staff who wear uniforms, e.g. porters and bellboys

uninsured /ʌnɪn'ʃʊəd/ *adjective* FINANCE not covered by an insurance policy ○ *After the fire, they discovered that the hotel was uninsured.*

union agreement /'juːnjən əˌgriːmənt/ *noun* BUSINESS a contract between management and a trade union concerning employment, pay, conditions of work, etc.

unit /'juːnɪt/ *noun* **1.** a single part of a larger whole ○ *The motel has sixteen units.* **2.** □ **bedroom unit** one cupboard, one set of shelves, etc., which can be matched with others to form a suite of furniture for a bedroom

unit of currency /ˌjuːnɪt əv 'kʌrənsi/ *noun* FINANCE the main element for counting the money of a country, e.g. dollar, pound, euro or yen

universal plug /ˌjuːnɪvɜːs(ə)l 'plʌg/ *noun* a form of plug with various types of pin, which can be used in several different types of socket

Universal Product Code /ˌjuːnɪvɜːs(ə)l 'prɒdʌkt ˌkəʊd/ *noun* BUSINESS same as **bar code**. Abbr **UPC**

universal time, universal time coordinated *noun* an international system for timekeeping ○ *The flight departs at 2040 UT* or *2040 UTC.* Abbr **UT, UTC**

unleavened /ʌn'levənd/ *adjective*
CATERING made without yeast or other raising agent

unleavened bread /ʌn'lev(ə)nd bred/
noun BREAD, ETC. bread made without using
a raising agent such as yeast, made in Mediterranean countries, and in India and Pakistan

unlimited /ʌn'lɪmɪtɪd/ *adjective* with no
limits

unlimited mileage /ʌn,lɪmɪtɪd
'maɪlɪdʒ/ *noun* ROAD TRAVEL an allowance
with a hired car, where the driver is not
charged for the number of miles covered

unload /ʌn'ləʊd/ *verb* to take goods off a
ship, etc. ○ *The ship is unloading at Ham-
burg.* ○ *We need a fork-lift truck to unload
the lorry.* ○ *We unloaded the spare parts at
Lagos.* ○ *There are no unloading facilities
for container ships.*

unlock /ʌn'lɒk/ *verb* to open something
which was locked

unmade /ʌn'meɪd/ *adjective* not yet made

unmade bed /,ʌnmeɪd 'bed/ *noun* a bed
which has not been made after someone has
slept in it

unmade room /,ʌnmeɪd 'ruːm/ *noun*
HOTELS a hotel room which has not been prepared by cleaning, changing the linen and
tidying, etc., since the last guest left it

unofficial /,ʌnə'fɪʃ(ə)l/ *adjective* not
approved by a department or organisation ○
*We have had some unofficial meetings with
people from the ministry.* Compare **official**

unofficially /ʌnə'fɪʃəli/ *adverb* in a way
which has not been approved by a department or organisation ○ *He was told by the
Foreign Office unofficially that it would be
better if he left the country.* Compare **officially**

unofficial strike /,ʌnəfɪʃ(ə)l 'straɪk/
noun BUSINESS a strike by local workers,
which has not been approved by the main
union

unpaid /ʌn'peɪd/ *adjective* having not
been settled

unpasteurised milk /ʌn,pæstʃəraɪzd
mɪlk/ *noun* DAIRY milk which has not been
treated by pasteurisation ○ *Cheese made
from unpasteurised milk has a better flavour.*

unrefined /,ʌnrɪ'faɪnd/ *adjective* CATER-
ING not processed to remove impurities or
unwanted substances

unsalted /ʌn'sɔːltɪd/ *adjective* CATERING
containing no salt

unsaturated fat /ʌn,sætʃəreɪtɪd 'fæt/
noun CATERING fat which does not have a

large amount of hydrogen, and so can be broken down more easily. Compare **saturated
fat**

unsecured loan /,ʌnsɪkjʊəd 'ləʊn/
noun BUSINESS a loan made with no security

unskilled /ʌn'skɪld/ *adjective* having no
particular skill

unskilled staff /ʌn'skɪld stɑːf/ *noun*
BUSINESS employees who have no particular
skill, and so may do general jobs such as
cleaning, washing dishes, carrying goods,
etc.

unskilled work /,ʌnskɪld 'wɜːk/ *noun*
work which does not require a particular
skill

unsocial /ʌn'səʊʃ(ə)l/ *adjective* □ **to
work unsocial hours** to work at times when
most people are not at work, i.e. in the
evening, at night or during public holidays

unspoilt /ʌn'spɔɪlt/ *adjective* TOURISM
not changed for the worse by modern development or tourism

unstrained /ʌn'streɪnd/ *adjective* CATER-
ING not put through a strainer to remove
lumps

unsweetened /ʌn'swiːtənd/ *adjective*
CATERING served, cooked, or manufactured
with no added sugar or other natural or artificial sweetening agent

untreated milk /ʌn'triːtɪd mɪlk/ *noun*
DAIRY milk which has not been processed in
any way

up /ʌp/ *adverb* not in bed ○ *At breakfast
time, the waitress still wasn't up.*

UPC *abbreviation* BUSINESS Universal
Product Code

update /'ʌpdeɪt/ *noun* information which
brings something up to date ○ *They issued an
update on the snow forecast.* ■ *verb* /ʌp
'deɪt/ to revise something so that it is more
up to date ○ *They have updated their guide to
Greece to include current prices.*

upgrade /ʌp'greɪd/ *noun* **1.** TRAVEL the
act of moving a passenger to a better class of
seat, without making him or her pay extra **2.**
work done to make facilities more luxurious
or more modern ■ *verb* **1.** TRAVEL to move a
passenger to a better class of seat, without
making him or her pay extra ○ *Because of a
mistake in the booking, he was upgraded to
first-class.* **2.** to make facilities more luxurious or more modern ○ *The new manager
plans to upgrade the residents' lounge.*

'...roads to and from the airport are being
upgraded while a new international terminal,
capable of handling 3,000 passengers an hour and
including a customs hall with seven baggage car-

ousels, should be ready by June 1996'
[*Business Traveller*]

'...a bedroom upgrade called superior is being rolled out, which includes contemporary furnishing, a work desk with modem point, and extra television channels. The upgrade to a superior room is just £20, but is forecast to generate £4m of additional revenue in the current financial year' [*Caterer & Hotelkeeper*]

upholstery /ʌp'həʊlst(ə)ri/ *noun* **1.** the work of covering chairs or other pieces of furniture with padded seats and covers ○ *He has an upholstery shop, repairing old chairs and sofas.* **2.** covers for chairs, or padded seats and cushions ○ *The upholstery matches the colour scheme in the sitting-room.*

up-market /ˌʌp 'mɑːkɪt/ *adjective* more expensive and appealing to a more sophisticated section of the population ○ *The company has decided to launch a more up-market version of the product.* ○ *The new shop is very up-market and everything is extremely expensive.* Compare **down-market**

upper berth /ˌʌpə 'bɜːθ/ *noun* a top bed

upper deck /ˌʌpə 'dek/ *noun* TRAVEL same as **top deck**

upright /'ʌpraɪt/ *adjective* vertical, not lying flat ○ *Put your seats into the upright position for landing.*

upstairs /ˌʌp'steəz/ *adverb* towards or in the upper part of a building or vehicle ○ *Let's go upstairs on the top deck: you can see London much better.* ■ *adjective* in the upper part of a building or vehicle ○ *There is an upstairs bar for guests.* ■ *noun* the upper part of a building or vehicle. Compare **downstairs**

urinal /jʊ'raɪn(ə)l/ *noun* **1.** a place where men can go to pass waste liquid from the body ○ *There's a public urinal at the corner of the street.* **2.** a bowl to catch waste liquid passed from the body by men ○ *The men's room is very modern, with stainless steel urinals.*

urn /ɜːn/ *noun* □ **tea urn, coffee urn** CATERING a large container with a tap, in which tea or coffee can be prepared in advance and then kept hot

use *noun* /juːs/ the act of taking something and making it serve a purpose, or the way in which something is used □ **to make use of** to put to a purpose ■ *verb* /juːz/ to put to a purpose ○ *Don't use the tap water for drinking.* ○ *Guests used the fire escape to get out of the building.*

use-by date /'juːz baɪ ˌdeɪt/ *noun* CATERING a date stamped on the label of a food product, which is the last date on which the food can be safely eaten. Compare **best-before date, sell-by date**

useful /'juːsf(ə)l/ *adjective* helpful □ **to make oneself useful** to do helpful things

usher /'ʌʃə/ *verb* □ **to usher in** to bring in

usual /'juːʒuəl/ *adjective* normal, happening, done or taken often ○ *The usual method of cooking onions is to fry them gently in a little oil.* ■ *noun* CATERING the drink or food which someone well-known to the waiter or barman has most often (*informal*) ○ *A pint of the usual, please.* ○ *Will you have your usual, sir?*

usually /'juːʒuəli/ *adverb* mostly, ordinarily, most often ○ *The restaurant is usually full on Friday evenings.*

UT *abbreviation* universal time

UTC *abbreviation* universal time coordinated

utensils /juː'tens(ə)lz/ *noun* a tool or container for use in the kitchen

U-turn /'juː tɜːn/ *noun* ROAD TRAVEL a turn made by a vehicle on a road, so as to face in the opposite direction ○ *She made a U-turn and went back to the hotel.* ○ *U-turns are not allowed on motorways.*

UV *abbreviation* ultraviolet

UV fly-killer /ˌjuː viː 'flaɪ ˌkɪlə/ *noun* a device which attracts flies to its UV rays and then kills them by electrocution

V

vacancy /ˈveɪkənsi/ *noun* **1.** an empty place or room □ **'vacancies'** empty rooms available □ **'no vacancies'** the hotel or guest-house is full **2.** a job which is not filled ○ *We advertised a vacancy in the local press.* ○ *We have been unable to fill the vacancy for an experienced sous-chef.* ○ *They have a vacancy for a secretary.*

vacancy rate /ˈveɪkənsi reɪt/ *noun* HOTELS the average number of rooms empty in a hotel over a period of time, shown as a percentage of the total number of rooms

vacant /ˈveɪkənt/ *adjective* empty or not occupied ○ *We have six rooms vacant in the annexe.*

vacate /vəˈkeɪt/ *verb* to leave a place ○ *Guests are asked to vacate their rooms before 12.00.* □ **to vacate the premises** to leave a building, offices or rooms so that they become empty

vacation /vəˈkeɪʃ(ə)n/ *noun* **1.** a period when the universities and colleges are closed **2.** *US* a holiday or period when people are not working ○ *The family went on vacation in Florida.* ■ *verb US* to go on holiday

vacationer /vəˈkeɪʃ(ə)nə/ *noun US* somebody who is on holiday

vacation hotel /vəˈkeɪʃ(ə)n həʊˌtel/ *noun US* a hotel which is used for holidays

vacation job /vəˈkeɪʃ(ə)n dʒɒb/ *noun US* a job taken by a student during the vacation to earn money to help pay for the costs of a university or college course

vacation rental /vəˈkeɪʃ(ə)n ˌrent(ə)l/ *noun US* any suite-type accommodation that has self-catering facilities

vaccinate /ˈvæksɪneɪt/ *verb* □ **to vaccinate someone against a disease** to use a vaccine to give a person immunisation against a specific disease ○ *She was vaccinated against smallpox as a child.*

vaccination /ˌvæksɪˈneɪʃ(ə)n/ *noun* MEDICAL the act of giving a vaccine to a person

vaccine /ˈvæksiːn/ *noun* MEDICAL a substance used to inoculate or vaccinate

COMMENT: A vaccine contains the germs of the disease, sometimes alive and sometimes dead, and this is injected into the patient so that his or her body will develop immunity to the disease. Vaccination is mainly given against cholera, diphtheria, rabies, smallpox, tuberculosis, and typhoid.

vacuum /ˈvækjuːm/ *noun* a space which is completely empty of all matter, including air ■ *verb* to clean e.g. a room or floor with a vacuum cleaner (*informal*)

vacuum cleaner /ˈvækjuəm ˌkliːnə/ *noun* a cleaning machine which sucks up dust

vacuum cooling /ˈvækjuːm ˌkuːlɪŋ/ *noun* CATERING a method of chilling food in a vacuum

vacuum flask /ˈvækjuəm flɑːsk/ *noun* a bottle with double walls which keeps liquids warm or cold. Also called **thermos flask**

vacuum-packed /ˈvækjuːm pækt/ *adjective* CATERING packed in a special plastic pack from which all air has been excluded, and then chilled or frozen. Compare **gas flushed**

valet /ˈvælɪt/ *noun* a male servant who looks after his master's clothes

valeting service /ˈvælɪtɪŋ ˌsɜːvɪs/ *noun* a service in a garage, for cleaning the outside and inside of a car

valet parking /ˈvælɪt ˌpɑːkɪŋ/ *noun* a service at a hotel or restaurant where a member of staff parks the guests' cars for them

valet service /ˈvælɪt ˌsɜːvɪs/ *noun* HOTELS a service in a hotel for cleaning and pressing clothes, especially for dry-cleaning. Also called **pressing service**

valid /ˈvælɪd/ *adjective* lawful, available for use ○ *Ticket which is valid for three months.* ○ *He was carrying a valid passport.* ○ *How long is the ticket valid for?*

validate /ˈvælɪdeɪt/ *verb* **1.** to check to see if something is correct ○ *The document was validated by the bank.* **2.** to make something valid ○ *The ticket has to be stamped by the airline to validate it.*

validator /ˈvælɪdeɪtə/ *noun* TRAVEL a metal stamp used to validate a ticket

validity /vəˈlɪdɪti/ *noun* being valid

valley /ˈvæli/ *noun* a long low area, usually with a river at the bottom, between hills or mountains ○ *Fog forms in the valleys at night.*

valuable /ˈvæljʊəb(ə)l/ *adjective* worth a lot of money, or very useful

valuables /ˈvæljʊəb(ə)lz/ *plural noun* items which are worth a lot of money ○ *Guests can deposit valuables with the manager for safe-keeping.*

value /ˈvælju:/ *noun* **1.** worth □ **to be good value for money** to be a good deal □ **to get value for money** to get a good deal □ **items of value** items which are worth a lot of money ○ *Items of value can be deposited in the hotel safe overnight.* **2.** a quantity shown as a number ■ *verb* to consider something as being valuable ○ *As a valued customer, you are entitled to a 10% discount.*

'…short break holidays continue to be driven by price and value for money, which will only continue to put pressure on us all to keep our prices down and our marketing well targeted' [*Caterer & Hotelkeeper*]

value added /ˌvælju: ˈædɪd/ *noun* same as **added value**

Value Added Tax /ˌvælju: ædɪd ˈtæks/ *noun* BUSINESS full form of **VAT**

van /væn/ *noun* a small closed goods vehicle ○ *The van will call this afternoon to pick up the goods.*

vanilla /vəˈnɪlə/ *noun* SAUCES, ETC. a flavouring made from the seed pods of a tropical plant ○ *This recipe uses vanilla-flavoured sugar.* ○ *I want vanilla ice cream with chocolate sauce.*

variable costs /ˌveəriəb(ə)l ˈkɒsts/ *plural noun* BUSINESS production costs which increase with the quantity of the product made or service provided, such as raw materials for meals, guest bedroom cleaning and linen or wages for extra casual staff

variety /vəˈraɪəti/ *noun* a mixture of different sorts ○ *There is a variety of different cereals for breakfast.*

variety show /vəˈraɪəti ʃəʊ/ *noun* ENTERTAINMENT an entertainment which includes several different types of performers such as singers, dancers, conjurors, ventriloquists, etc.

VAT /ˌvi: eɪ ˈti:, væt/ BUSINESS a tax imposed as a percentage of the invoice value of goods and services ○ *The invoice includes VAT at 17.5%.* ○ *Some items are still zero-rated for VAT.* ○ *A hotel has to charge VAT*

like any other business. ○ *The court heard how he failed to declare any VAT during the three years.* Full form **Value Added Tax**

VAT declaration /ˈvæt deklə,reɪʃ(ə)n/ *noun* BUSINESS a statement declaring VAT income to the VAT office

VAT inspection /ˈvæt ɪn,spekʃ(ə)n/ *noun* BUSINESS a visit by officials of the Customs and Excise Department to see if a company is correctly reporting its VAT

VAT inspector /ˈvæt ɪn,spektə/ *noun* BUSINESS a government official who examines VAT returns and checks that VAT is being paid

VAT invoice /ˈvæt ˌɪnvɔɪs/ *noun* BUSINESS an invoice which shows VAT separately

VAT invoicing /ˈvæt ˌɪnvɔɪsɪŋ/ *noun* BUSINESS the act of sending an invoice including VAT

VAT office /ˈvæt ˌɒfɪs/ *noun* BUSINESS a government office dealing with the collection of VAT in an area

VDQS *abbreviation* BEVERAGES vin délimité de qualité supérieure

VDU *abbreviation* visual display unit

veal /vi:l/ *noun* MEAT meat from a calf

COMMENT: Veal is not as popular in Britain as in other European countries.

veal and ham pie /ˌvi:l ən hæm ˈpaɪ/ *noun* FOOD a pie with a filling of veal and ham and hard-boiled eggs, eaten cold

veal cutlet /ˌvi:l ˈkʌt(ə)lət/ *noun* FOOD a flat cake of minced veal covered with breadcrumbs and fried

veal escalope /vi:l ˈeskə,lɒp/ *noun* FOOD a thin slice of veal, covered in breadcrumbs and fried

veg /vedʒ/ *noun* vegetables, or a vegetable (*informal*)

vegan /ˈvi:gən/ *noun, adjective* CATERING someone who does not eat meat, dairy produce, eggs or fish and eats only vegetables and fruit

vegetable /ˈvedʒtəb(ə)l/ *noun* FOOD a plant grown for food, not usually sweet, e.g. a potato, carrot, onion, cabbage, cauliflower, pea or bean ○ *The main course is served with a selection of vegetables.*

vegetable chef /ˈvedʒtəb(ə)l ʃef/ *noun* CATERING the chef in charge of preparing vegetables and pasta. Also called **chef entremétier**

vegetable oil /ˈvedʒtəb(ə)l ɔɪl/ *noun* FOOD an oil that has been extracted from a plant or the seeds of a plant, e.g. olive oil, sunflower oil, sesame oil, or rapeseed oil

vegetarian /ˌvedʒɪ'teəriən/ *noun, adjective* CATERING someone who does not eat meat, but eats mainly vegetables and fruit and sometimes dairy produce, eggs or fish ○ *She asked for a vegetarian meal.* ○ *Our children are all vegetarians.*

veggie /'vedʒi/ *noun* FOOD (*informal*) **1.** same as **vegetable 2.** same as **vegetarian**

veggieburger /'vedʒibɜːgə/ *noun* FOOD a flat cake made from vegetables, grains, or legumes, often served in the same way as a hamburger

vehicle /'viːɪk(ə)l/ *noun* ROAD TRAVEL a machine with wheels, used to carry goods or passengers on a road

vehicular /vɪ'hɪkjʊlə/ *adjective* referring to vehicles (*formal*) ○ *No vehicular traffic is allowed on the island.* □ **no vehicular access to the motorway** vehicles cannot get onto the motorway here

velouté /və'luːteɪ/ *noun* FOOD soup with a creamy texture

vending machine /'vendɪŋ məˌʃiːn/ *noun* a machine from which you can buy something, such as sweets, chocolate, cigarettes or drinks, by putting coins into a slot. Also called **slot machine**

venetian blind /vəˌniːʃ(ə)n 'blaɪnd/ *noun* a blind to shut out light, made of horizontal strips of plastic or wood, which can be opened and shut or raised and lowered by pulling a string

venison /'venɪs(ə)n/ *noun* MEAT meat from a deer

COMMENT: Venison is left to hang for at least one week before eating. It is dark red in colour and has very little fat.

venison pâté /ˌvenɪs(ə)n 'pæteɪ/ *noun* FOOD pâté made from venison

venison stew /ˌvenɪs(ə)n 'stjuː/ *noun* FOOD pieces of venison cooked in a liquid

ventilation /ˌventɪ'leɪʃ(ə)n/ *noun* a means or the act of bringing in fresh air

ventilation hood, ventilation canopy *noun* CATERING a device placed over an oven or other cooking surface, to remove smells and steam

'Ventilation hoods are needed to remove the smells, vapour and grease invariably produced in large quantities during cooking. The ventilation system should include a fan of sufficient extract capacity to cope with the expected fume load from the equipment it serves.' [*Health and Safety in Kitchens (HSE)*]

ventilation shaft /ˌventɪ'leɪʃ(ə)n ʃɑːft/ *noun* a tube which allows fresh air to go into a building

ventilator /'ventɪleɪtə/ *noun* an opening which allows fresh air to come in, or a machine which pumps fresh air into a room and extracts stale air

venture capital /ˌventʃə 'kæpɪt(ə)l/ *noun* BUSINESS capital for investment in the early stages of projects which may easily be lost. Also called **risk capital**

venue /'venjuː/ *noun* an agreed place where something will take place ○ *The venue for the conference has still to be booked.*

verdigris /'vɜːdɪgriː/ *noun* a green discoloration on things made of copper caused by contact with damp

vermicelli /ˌvɜːmɪ'tʃeli/ *noun* FOOD a type of pasta, like very thin spaghetti

vermin /'vɜːmɪn/ *noun* insects or animals, such as beetles, mice, etc., which are looked upon as pests by some people. ◊ **pest**

vermouth /'vɜːməθ/ *noun* BEVERAGES a type of strong wine flavoured with herbs

COMMENT: Vermouth can be either sweet or dry; Italian vermouth is used to make martinis.

vertical integration /ˌvɜːtɪk(ə)l ˌɪntɪ'greɪʃ(ə)n/ *noun* BUSINESS the joining together of businesses which deal with different stages in the production or sale of the same product, as when a restaurant chain takes over a wine importer

vessel /'ves(ə)l/ *noun* SHIPS AND BOATS a ship

vestibule /'vestɪbjuːl/ *noun* an entrance hall

via /'vaɪə/ *preposition* by or using a means or a route ○ *The shipment is going via the Suez Canal.* ○ *We are sending the information pack via our office in New York.* ○ *They sent the message via the courier.*

video /'vɪdiəʊ/ *noun, adjective* ENTERTAINMENT a system which records and shows pictures on a television screen

video camera /'vɪdiəʊ ˌkæm(ə)rə/ *noun* a camera which records video pictures

video cassette /'vɪdiəʊ kəˌset/ *noun* a plastic case containing videotape which can fit directly into a video cassette recorder

video-cassette recorder, video recorder *noun* ENTERTAINMENT a machine which records television or films pictures on tape, so that they can be played back later

video conference /'vɪdiəʊ ˌkɒnf(ə)rəns/ *noun* a meeting where some people take part by television

view /vjuː/ *noun* **1.** what you can see from a certain place ○ *a room with a view over the harbour* ○ *We asked for a room with a sea* *view and were given one looking out over the bus depot.* **2.** an opinion or a way of thinking about something ○ *We asked the sales manager for his views on the reorganisation of the reps' territories.* ○ *The chairman takes the view that credit should never be longer than thirty days.* □ **in view of** because of ○ *In view of the falling exchange rate, we have had to introduce surcharges on some of our tours.*

viewing area /'vjuːɪŋ ˌeərɪə/ *noun* a place, e.g. at an airport, where people can stand to watch what is happening

villa /'vɪlə/ *noun* TOURISM a large country or seaside house, usually in a warm country ○ *He is staying in a villa on the Mediterranean.* ○ *They are renting a villa in Greece for August.*

village /'vɪlɪdʒ/ *noun* a small group of houses in the country, like a little town, often with a church, and usually some shops

village fête /ˌvɪlɪdʒ 'feɪt/ *noun* ENTERTAINMENT a little local festival in a village

vin /væn/ *noun* BEVERAGES a French noun meaning wine

vinaigrette /ˌvɪnɪ'gret/ *noun* SAUCES, ETC. a salad dressing made with oil, vinegar, salt and other flavourings. Also called **French dressing**

vindaloo /ˌvɪndə'luː/ *noun* FOOD a very hot curry sauce made with coriander, red chilli, ginger, and other spices, or a dish cooked in this sauce

vin délimité de qualité supérieure /ˌvæn deɪˌlɪmɪteɪ də ˌkælɪteɪ suˌperi'ɜː/ *noun* BEVERAGES a French classification of wine, indicating that it comes from a particular region and is made from a particular variety of grape. Abbr **VDQS**

vin de pays /ˌvæn də 'peɪ/ *noun* BEVERAGES table wine from a particular region of France

vin de table /ˌvæn də 'tɑːblə/ *noun* BEVERAGES table wine

vinegar /'vɪnɪgə/ *noun* SAUCES, ETC. liquid made from sour wine or cider, used in cooking and for preserving food ○ *red wine vinegar* ○ *cider vinegar*

vineyard /'vɪnjəd/ *noun* BEVERAGES an area planted with vines for making wine ○ *There are some vineyards in southern England.* ○ *We visited vineyards along the Moselle and bought some wine.*

vino /'viːnəʊ/ *noun* BEVERAGES an Italian noun meaning wine

vino di tavola /ˌviːnəʊ ˌdiː 'tævələ/ *noun* BEVERAGES table wine

vintage /'vɪntɪdʒ/ *noun* **1.** BEVERAGES the work of collecting grapes to make wine, or the grapes which are collected **2.** BEVERAGES a fine wine made in a particular year ○ *This is a very good vintage.* ○ *What vintage is it? – it's a 1968.* □ **vintage wine**, **vintage port** a fine or expensive old wine or port which was made in a particular year

vinyl /'vaɪn(ə)l/ *noun* a plastic material, used especially to make floor coverings

VIP *abbreviation* very important person □ **we laid on VIP treatment for our visitors**, **we gave our visitors a VIP reception** we arranged for our visitors to be well looked after and entertained

VIP lounge /ˌviː aɪ 'piː laʊndʒ/ *noun* AIR TRAVEL a special room at an airport for important travellers

VIP suite /ˌviː aɪ 'piː ˌswiːt/ *noun* HOTELS a specially luxurious suite at an airport or in a hotel

virus /'vaɪrəs/ *noun* MEDICAL a tiny germ cell which can only develop in other cells, and often destroys them ○ *Scientists have isolated a new flu virus.*

COMMENT: Many common diseases such as measles or the common cold are caused by viruses; viral diseases cannot be treated with antibiotics.

visa /'viːzə/ *noun* a special document or special stamp in a passport which allows someone to enter a country ○ *You will need a visa before you go to the USA.* ○ *He filled in his visa application form.*

visa national /ˌviːzə 'næʃ(ə)nəl/ *noun* a person from a country whose citizens need a visa in order to enter the UK

visit /'vɪzɪt/ *noun* a short stay in a place ○ *We will be making a short visit to London next week.* ○ *He is on a business visit to Edinburgh.* ○ *We had a visit from the VAT inspector.* ■ *verb* to go to a place or to see someone or something for a short time ○ *He spent a week in Scotland, visiting museums in Edinburgh and Glasgow.* ○ *The trade delegation visited the Ministry of Commerce.*

visitor /'vɪzɪtə/ *noun* a person who comes to visit ○ *The coach brought a group of visitors to the exhibition.*

visitor centre /'vɪzɪtə ˌsentə/ *noun* TOURISM a building offering information and services to visitors in a city or at a historical or archaeological site, park, or nature reserve

visitor guide /'vɪzɪtə gaɪd/ *noun* TOURISM a guidebook for visitors to a place

visitors' book /'vɪzɪtəz bʊk/ *noun* a book in which visitors to a museum or guests to a hotel write comments about the place

visitors' ledger /ˈvɪzɪtəz ˌledʒə/ *noun* HOTELS a ledger in which itemised accounts for each guest in a hotel are kept

visitors' tax /ˈvɪzɪtəz tæks/ *noun* BUSINESS a tax to be paid to a local municipality for each visitor

vitamin /ˈvɪtəmɪn/ *noun* CATERING an essential substance not synthesised in the body, but found in most foods, and needed for good health

Vitamin A /ˌvɪtəmɪn ˈeɪ/ *noun* CATERING a vitamin which is soluble in fat and can be formed in the body, but is mainly found in food such as liver, vegetables, eggs and cod liver oil

COMMENT: Lack of Vitamin A affects the body's growth and resistance to disease and can cause night blindness.

Vitamin B₁ /ˌvɪtəmɪn biː ˈwʌn/ *noun* CATERING a vitamin found in yeast, liver, cereals and pork

Vitamin B₂ /ˌvɪtəmɪn biː ˈtuː/ *noun* CATERING a vitamin found in eggs, liver, green vegetables, milk and yeast

Vitamin B₆ /ˌvɪtəmɪn biː ˈsɪks/ *noun* CATERING a vitamin found in meat, cereals and molasses

Vitamin B₁₂ /ˌvɪtəmɪn biː ˈtwelv/ *noun* CATERING a vitamin found in liver and kidney, but not present in vegetables

Vitamin B complex /ˌvɪtəmɪn biː ˈkɒmpleks/ *noun* CATERING a group of vitamins such as folic acid, riboflavine and thiamine

COMMENT: Lack of vitamins from the B complex can have different results: lack of thiamine causes beriberi; lack of riboflavine affects a child's growth; lack of pyridoxine causes convulsions and vomiting in babies; lack of vitamin B₁₂ causes anaemia.

Vitamin C /ˌvɪtəmɪn ˈsiː/ *noun* CATERING a vitamin which is soluble in water and is found in fresh fruit, especially oranges and lemons, raw vegetables and liver

COMMENT: Lack of Vitamin C can cause anaemia and scurvy.

Vitamin D /ˌvɪtəmɪn ˈdiː/ *noun* CATERING a vitamin which is soluble in fat, found in butter, eggs and fish and also produced by the skin when exposed to sunlight

COMMENT: Vitamin D helps in the formation of bones, and lack of it causes rickets in children.

Vitamin E /ˌvɪtəmɪn ˈiː/ *noun* CATERING a vitamin found in vegetables, vegetable oils, eggs and wholemeal bread

vodka /ˈvɒdkə/ *noun* BEVERAGES **1.** a strong colourless alcohol distilled from grain or potatoes made originally in Russia and Poland **2.** a glass of this alcohol ○ *Two vodka and tonics, please.*

void /vɔɪd/ *adjective* invalid, which cannot lawfully be used ○ *The ticket is void.* ■ *verb* to mark a document to show that it cannot be used lawfully ○ *We will void the existing ticket and issue a new one.*

voiture /vwɑːˈtjʊə/ *noun* CATERING a trolley for food in a restaurant (NOTE: **voiture** comes from the French noun meaning 'car'.)

vol-au-vent /ˈvɒl əʊ ˌvɒŋ/ *noun* FOOD a small round case of pastry, usually filled with a savoury mixture, eaten hot or cold ○ *mushroom vol-au-vent*

vol-au-vent case /ˈvɒl əʊ vɒn ˌkeɪs/ *noun* FOOD a round case of pastry ready to be filled with a savoury filling

volcano /vɒlˈkeɪnəʊ/ *noun* a mountain with a hole on the top through which lava, ash and gas can exit

COMMENT: Volcanoes occur along faults in the earth's surface and exist in well-known chains. Some are extinct, but others erupt relatively frequently. Some are always active, in that they emit sulphurous gases and smoke, without actually erupting. Volcanic eruptions are a major source of atmospheric pollution. Volcanoes are popular tourist attractions: the best-known in Europe are Vesuvius, Stromboli and Etna in Italy and Helgafell in Iceland.

voltage /ˈvəʊltɪdʒ/ *noun* a measure of electrical force

COMMENT: The voltage in many countries is 110V (USA, Canada, Japan, etc.). In Europe, the Far East and Africa, voltage is usually 220V or 240V. Travellers should always carry a transformer to get electrical appliances to work.

volume catering /ˌvɒljuːm ˈkeɪtərɪŋ/ *noun* CATERING catering for large numbers of people, as at mass meetings or sports events

voucher /ˈvaʊtʃə/ *noun* a piece of paper which is given instead of money ○ *Each traveller has a book of vouchers to be presented at the reception desk in each hotel where the group stays.*

voyage /ˈvɔɪɪdʒ/ *noun* SHIPS AND BOATS a long journey by ship

voyager /ˈvɔɪɪdʒə/ *noun* SHIPS AND BOATS somebody who goes on a long journey by ship

W

wafer /'weɪfə/ *noun* BREAD, ETC. a thin sweet biscuit eaten with ice cream ○ *a bowl of vanilla and chocolate ice cream, with a wafer in it*

waffle /'wɒf(ə)l/ *noun* BREAD, ETC. a type of thick crisp pancake cooked in an iron mould and eaten with syrup ○ *We bought waffles at the stall in the fairground.* ○ *Waffles are very popular in Belgium.*

waffle-iron /'wɒf(ə)l ˌaɪən/ *noun* CATERING an iron mould used for making waffles

wage /weɪdʒ/ *noun* money paid, usually in cash each week, to an employee for work done ○ *She is earning a good wage* or *good wages in the bar.*

wage differentials /'weɪdʒ dɪfəˌrenʃəlz/ *plural noun* BUSINESS differences in salary between employees in similar types of jobs

wage packet /'weɪdʒ ˌpækɪt/ *noun* an envelope containing money and pay slip

wages book /'weɪdʒɪz bʊk/ *noun* BUSINESS a ledger in which details of all payments to staff are kept

wage scale /'weɪdʒ skeɪl/ *noun* BUSINESS a list of wages, showing different rates of pay for different jobs in the same company (NOTE: The plural **wages** is more usual when referring to the money earned, but **wage** is used before other nouns.)

wagon /'wægən/ *noun* RAIL TRAVEL a vehicle for carrying goods used on the railway

waistcoat /'weɪstkəʊt/ *noun* a short coat with buttons and without any sleeves, which is worn over a shirt and under a jacket ○ *The waiters' uniform is black trousers, white shirt and red waistcoats.*

wait /weɪt/ *verb* **1.** to stay where you are, and not do anything until something happens or someone comes ○ *We gave our order half an hour ago, but are still waiting for the first course.* ○ *If you wait here I expect a taxi will come along soon.* **2.** □ **to wait on someone** CATERING to serve food to someone at table

waiter /'weɪtə/ *noun* CATERING a man who serves food to people in a restaurant

waiter service, waitress service *noun* CATERING same as **table service**

waiting list /'weɪtɪŋ lɪst/ *noun* a list of people waiting to see someone or do something ○ *There is a waiting list of passengers hoping to get a flight.*

waiting room /'weɪtɪŋ ruːm/ *noun* TRAVEL a room where travellers wait for their trains, buses, etc.

waiting staff /'weɪtɪŋ stɑːf/ *noun* CATERING restaurant employees who serve the guests at table

waitlist /'weɪtlɪst/ same as **waiting list**

waitress /'weɪtrəs/ *noun* CATERING a woman who serves food to people in a restaurant

wake /weɪk/ *verb* to stop someone sleeping ○ *He asked to be woken at 7.00.* (NOTE: **waking – woke – has woken**)

wakeboarding /'weɪkbɔːdɪŋ/ *noun* SPORT a water sport in which somebody riding a single board is pulled behind a motor boat and performs jumps while crisscrossing the wake of the boat

wake up /ˌweɪk 'ʌp/ *verb* to stop sleeping ○ *She woke up at 7.30.* ○ *He asked to be woken up at 6.15.*

wake-up call /'weɪk ʌp ˌkɔːl/ *noun* HOTELS a phone call from the hotel switchboard to wake a guest up

Waldorf salad /ˌwɔːdɔːf 'sæləd/ *noun* FOOD a salad made of diced raw apples, celery, and walnuts with a mayonnaise dressing

Wales Tourist Board /ˌweɪlz 'tʊərɪst ˌbɔːd/ *noun* TOURISM an organisation which promotes tourism in Wales and promotes tourism to Wales from other parts of the UK. Abbr **WTB**

walk /wɔːk/ *noun* **1.** a usually pleasant journey on foot ○ *It's only a short walk to the beach.* **2.** an organised visit on foot ○ *Several London walks are advertised each Saturday.* ○ *He went on a Dickens walk.* ■ *verb* **1.** to go on foot ○ *He walks to the office every morning.* ○ *The visitors walked round the factory.* **2.** □ **to walk someone** HOTELS to move someone to a room in another hotel, even if they have a guaranteed reservation, because the hotel has been overbooked

walked guest /ˌwɔːkt 'gest/ plural noun HOTELS a guest who has made a reservation which cannot be honoured, so that he or she has to be accommodated somewhere else

walker /'wɔːkə/ noun SPORT somebody who goes walking for pleasure and exercise ○ She's a keen walker, and goes walking in Scotland every summer.

walk-in /'wɔːk ɪn/ adjective, noun large enough to walk into ○ We have a large walk-in fridge. ○ There's a walk-in wardrobe leading off the bedroom.

walk-in customer /'wɔːk ɪn/, **walk-in** noun BUSINESS a customer who eats at a hotel restaurant but is not staying at the hotel ○ Prices are accessible to both staying guests and walk-in customers.

walking /'wɔːkɪŋ/ noun SPORT the activity of going on foot as a relaxation ○ We spent two weeks on a walking holiday in North Italy.

walking boots /'wɔːkɪŋ ʃuːs/, **walking shoes** plural noun SPORT heavy boots or shoes, suitable for walking long distances

walking stick /'wɔːkɪŋ stɪk/ noun a stick used to support you when walking

walking tour /'wɔːkɪŋ ˌtʊə/ noun TOURISM a tour on which you walk from one place to another, spend the night, and then continue on foot the following day

wall /wɔːl/ noun **1.** a structure of brick, stone or wood, forming the side of a room or building or the boundary of a piece of land **2.** a thick stone construction round an old town ○ You can walk all round York on the town walls.

walled /wɔːld/ adjective with walls ○ Vegetables are grown in the hotel's walled garden. ○ They visited several old walled towns in South-West France.

wallet /'wɒlɪt/ noun a small leather case which fits into the pocket and is used for holding banknotes ○ His wallet was stolen from his back pocket. ○ Do not leave your wallet in the car.

wall planner /'wɔːl ˌplænə/ noun a chart which shows days, weeks or months so that the work of an office can be shown by diagrams

walnut /'wɔːlnʌt/ noun NUTS a hard round nut with a wrinkled shell

walnut oil /'wɔːlnʌt ɔɪl/ noun SAUCES, ETC. oil produced by crushing walnuts

wander /'wɒndə/ verb to walk about without any special direction □ **to wander off** to walk away from the correct path ○ Two of the group wandered off into the market and got lost.

want /wɒnt/ verb to need, to require ○ Do you want any more tea? ○ My little daughter wants to go to the toilet. ○ I want to go to Paris next Tuesday.

want ads /'wɒnt ædz/ plural noun same as **classified ads**

war /wɔː/ noun **1.** a period of fighting between countries or armies ○ Travel is dangerous in the south of the country because of the war. **2.** a period of strong competition between companies ○ a price war

warden /'wɔːd(ə)n/ noun somebody who looks after or guards something

wardrobe /'wɔːdrəʊb/ noun a large cupboard in which clothes may be hung ○ There are no hangers in my wardrobe.

warewashing /'weəwɒʃɪŋ/ noun CATERING the washing of kitchenware such as pans ○ They have installed a new warewashing system.

warm /wɔːm/ adjective quite hot, pleasantly hot ○ You must take plenty of warm clothing. ○ The winter sun can be quite warm in February. ■ verb CATERING to heat food until it is quite hot □ **to warm up** to heat food which has already been cooked, and has gone cold

warming cupboard /'wɔːmɪŋ ˌkʌbəd/ noun CATERING a specially heated cupboard in a kitchen, where food can be kept warm

warn /wɔːn/ verb to inform someone of a possible danger ○ The group was warned to look out for pickpockets. ○ The guide warned us that there might be snakes in the ruins. ○ They were warned not to go near the army base. (NOTE: You warn someone **of** something, or **that** something may happen, or **to do** or **not to do** something.)

warning /'wɔːnɪŋ/ noun notice of possible danger ○ The government issued a warning about travelling in the south of the country. ○ Warning notices were put up around the ruins.

warrant /'wɒrənt/ noun an official document which allows someone to do something ■ verb **1.** to guarantee ○ All the spare parts are warranted. **2.** to show that something is reasonable ○ The tour price is not warranted by the use of two-star hotels.

warranty /'wɒrənti/ noun **1.** BUSINESS a promise in a contract □ **breach of warranty** failure to do something which is a part of a contract **2.** a statement made by an insured person which declares that the facts stated by him or her are true

wasabi /wəˈsaːbi/ *noun* SAUCES, ETC. a strong-tasting green powder or paste from a plant root used as a condiment in Japanese cooking

wash /wɒʃ/ *noun* **1.** the act of cleaning something, somebody or yourself with water or another liquid ○ *I'll go and have a quick wash.* **2.** clothes which are being washed or which are dirty and need to be washed ■ *verb* to clean with water or another liquid ○ *She's washing her hair.* ○ *He washed the fruit before eating them.* ○ *Guests are asked not to wash clothes in hotel rooms.*

wash-basin, wash-hand basin *noun* a bowl in a bathroom with taps producing running hot and cold water for washing

washbowl /ˈwɒʃbəʊl/ *noun* a bowl for holding water, but not fixed and with no taps

wash cycle /ˈwɒʃ ˌsaɪk(ə)l/ *noun* a series of operations in a dishwasher to wash dishes, ending with the 'drain cycle'

washer /ˈwɒʃə/ *noun* **1.** a steel or rubber ring under a bolt or nut, or a rubber ring inside a tap which prevents water escaping when the tap is turned off **2.** a machine for washing ○ *a dishwasher* ◊ **glass washer**

washing /ˈwɒʃɪŋ/ *noun* **1.** the act of cleaning with water or another liquid **2.** clothes which are ready to be washed or which have been washed ○ *Put your washing in the plastic bag.* ○ *Washing left out in the morning will be delivered to the room within 12 hours.*

washing machine /ˈwɒʃɪŋ məˌʃiːn/ *noun* a machine for washing clothes

washing powder /ˈwɒʃɪŋ ˈpaʊdə/ *noun* a detergent powder for washing clothes

washing up /ˌwɒʃɪŋ ˈʌp/ *noun* CATERING **1.** the cleaning of dirty dishes, glasses, cutlery, pots and pans with water and detergent ○ *When he couldn't pay, he had to do the washing up.* **2.** dirty dishes, glasses, cutlery, pots and pans waiting to be cleaned ○ *There is a pile of washing up waiting to be put into the dishwasher.*

washroom /ˈwɒʃruːm/ *noun* US a room where you can wash your hands and use the toilet ○ *Where's the washroom, please?*

washstand /ˈwɒʃstænd/ *noun* **1.** a table on which a washbowl and jug of water stood in a bedroom (*dated*) **2.** US a fixed bowl, with taps, for holding water for washing the hands and face

wash up /ˌwɒʃ ˈʌp/ *verb* **1.** CATERING to clean dirty dishes, cutlery, glasses, pots and pans **2.** *US* to wash yourself ○ *I'll just go and wash up before lunch.*

wastage /ˈweɪstɪdʒ/ *noun* the act of wasting ○ *They have to reduce wastage in the kitchens.*

waste /weɪst/ *noun* material or matter which is useless, especially material that is left over after all the useful parts or substances have been used up ○ *kitchen waste* ■ *verb* to use more of something than is needed ○ *You shouldn't waste water.*

waste bin /ˈweɪst bɪn/ *noun* a container for putting rubbish in

waste compactor /ˈweɪst kəmˌpæktə/ *noun* a machine which crushes waste into small packs which are relatively easy to dispose of

waste disposal /ˈweɪst dɪˌspəʊz(ə)l/ *noun* HOTELS arrangements to get rid of rubbish, e.g. from a hotel or restaurant

COMMENT: Waste disposal units are not permitted in countries which do not allow ground waste products to be flushed into the sewage system.

waste disposal unit /ˈweɪst dɪ ˈspəʊz(ə)l ˌjuːnɪt/ *noun* CATERING a machine attached to a kitchen sink, which grinds waste food into pulp which can then be flushed away into the drainage system

waste paper basket /ˌweɪst ˈpeɪpə ˌbɑːskɪt/, **wastebasket** /ˈweɪstbɑːskɪt/ *noun* a container into which paper or pieces of rubbish can be thrown

waste pipe /ˈweɪst paɪp/ *noun* a pipe which takes dirty water from a sink to the drains

WATA *abbreviation* World Association of Travel Agencies

watch /wɒtʃ/ *noun* a small clock worn on the arm or carried in a pocket ■ *verb* to look at something that is happening or that is being shown ○ *to watch television* ○ *They went up to London to watch the changing of the guard.* ○ *Watch while I show you how to turn the pancake over.*

watchman /ˈwɒtʃmən/ *noun* somebody who guards a building, usually when it is empty. Also called **night watchman**

watch out /ˌwɒtʃ ˈaʊt/ *verb* to be alert and careful, especially to avoid danger ○ *Watch out, you nearly ran into that tree.* ○ *We've been warned to watch out for pickpockets.* (NOTE: You watch out **for** sth.)

water /ˈwɔːtə/ *noun* **1.** BEVERAGES the liquid essential to life which makes up a large part of the body ○ *Is the water safe to drink?* ○ *You are advised to drink only bottled water.* ○ *Each room has hot and cold running water.*

○ *The temperature of the water* or *The water temperature is* 60°. **2.** □ **to take the waters** to drink mineral water at a spa ■ *verb* □ **the display of cakes made my mouth water** the cakes looked and smelt so delicious that saliva came into my mouth

water biscuit /ˈwɔːtə ˌbɪskɪt/ *noun* BREAD, ETC. a thin unsweetened hard biscuit made of flour and water, eaten with cheese

water chestnut /ˌwɔːtə ˈtʃesnʌt/ *noun* VEGETABLES a round white crunchy stem base of a Chinese water plant, often used in Asian cooking

water closet /ˈwɔːtə ˌklɒzɪt/ *noun* a lavatory (*formal*) Abbr **WC**

water cooler /ˌwɔːtə ˈkuːlə/, **water fountain** *noun* a container which holds drinking water, which is cooled and may be drawn off through a tap

watercress /ˈwɔːtəkres/ *noun* VEGETABLES a creeping plant grown in water and eaten in salads and soup ○ *The chef has made a delicious watercress soup.* ◊ **cress**

waterfall /ˈwɔːtəfɔːl/ *noun* a drop in a river, etc., from a high level over the edge of a cliff ○ *Let's climb up to the waterfall and picnic there.* ○ *Is Niagara the largest waterfall in the world?*

waterfront /ˈwɔːtəfrʌnt/ *noun* the bank of a river or shore of the sea and the buildings along it ○ *Let's have lunch on the terrace of one of the waterfront restaurants.*

water glass /ˈwɔːtə glɑːs/ *noun* CATERING a glass on a table for drinking water, placed next to a wine glass in a table setting

water ice /ˈwɔːtə aɪs/ *noun* DESSERTS a type of light ice cream made of water and flavouring ○ *an orange water ice* ○ *The waiter brought round a tray of water ices.*

watering place /ˈwɔːtərɪŋ pleɪs/ *noun* **1.** a place where people go to drink or bathe in the local water for health reasons **2.** a place by the sea to which people go for swimming and other leisure activities

watermelon /ˈwɔːtəˌmelən/ *noun* FRUIT a large green fruit with red flesh and black seeds

water park /ˈwɔːtə pɑːk/ *noun* a leisure area or theme park with water-based facilities such as slides with flowing water

waterproof /ˈwɔːtəpruːf/ *adjective* not allowing water through ○ *You will need plenty of waterproof clothing if you are going sea fishing.* ■ *noun* a coat which will not let water through ○ *Only a light basic waterproof need be carried.*

waterskier /ˈwɔːtəskiːə/ *noun* SPORT somebody who goes waterskiing

waterskiing /ˈwɔːtəskiːɪŋ/ *noun* SPORT the sport of gliding along the surface of a lake or river on large skis, pulled by a fast boat

water skis /ˈwɔːtə skiːz/ *plural noun* SPORT wider shorter skis for gliding over water

water slide /ˈwɔːtə slaɪd/ *noun* a slide with water flowing down it at a swimming pool or an amusement park

water sports /ˈwɔːtə spɔːts/ *plural noun* SPORT activities which take place on or in water, e.g. swimming, water polo and scuba diving

water tank /ˈwɔːtə tæŋk/ *noun* a tank for holding water

water taxi /ˈwɔːtə ˌtæksi/ *noun* SHIPS AND BOATS a small boat which goes along a river or canal, or round a lake, taking passengers on a regular schedule

'…on the island there are taxis, water taxis, rental cars and mountain bikes, tours and charter boats to get you around' [*Food & Travel*]

waterwings /ˈwɔːtəwɪŋz/ *plural noun* inflatable rings attached to the arms of a child learning to swim

wave /weɪv/ *noun* a ridge of higher water on the surface of the sea ○ *Watch out for the big waves on the beach.* ○ *The sea was calm, with hardly any waves.* ■ *verb* to move your hand up and down □ **to wave to someone** to signal to someone with the hand □ **to wave someone on** to tell someone to go on by a movement of the hand

wax /wæks/ *noun* a solid substance made from fat or oil, used for making candles, polish, etc. ■ *verb* to cover floors, skis, etc. with wax

way /weɪ/ *noun* **1.** ROAD TRAVEL a road or path □ **on the way** during the journey ○ *We will stop at the carpet shop on the way to the restaurant.* **2.** the direction that leads to something ○ *Is this the way to the post office?* ○ *Can you show me the way to the ruins?*

WC, W.C. *abbreviation* water closet

W/C *noun* a desk where letters, documents or tickets can be picked up by guests. Full form **will call**

weather /ˈweðə/ *noun* conditions outside, e.g. if it is raining, hot, cold or sunny ○ *The weather can be very wet in spring.* ○ *I hope the weather will be fine for our climb.* ○ *What's the weather like in Italy in May?*

weather bureau /ˈweðə ˈbjuːrəʊ/, **weather centre** /ˌweðə ˈsentə/ *noun* an office which analyses weather reports and forecasts the weather ○ *The weather centre is forecasting a period of dry sunny weather.*

weather forecast /ˈweðə ˌfɔːkɑːst/ *noun* a description of what the weather will be for a period in the future ○ *The weather forecast is good.* ○ *Switch on the radio – I want to hear the weather forecast.*

weather report /ˈweðə rɪˌpɔːt/ *noun* a written or spoken statement describing what the weather has been like recently, what it is like at the moment or what it will be for a period in the future

website /ˈwebsaɪt/ *noun* MARKETING a collection of pages on the Internet which have been produced by one company and are linked together ○ *For more information visit our company website.*

wedding /ˈwedɪŋ/ *noun* a marriage ceremony

wedding breakfast /ˈwedɪŋ ˌbrekfəst/ *noun* CATERING a full meal served after a wedding which can take the form of a buffet, at the end of which speeches are made and the wedding cake is cut

wedding reception /ˈwedɪŋ rɪˌsepʃən/ *noun* CATERING the party held after a marriage ceremony, including the wedding breakfast, drinks, toasts, cake-cutting, etc.

wedding venue /ˈwedɪŋ ˌvenjuː/ *noun* a place where wedding receptions are often held ○ *The old house is a popular wedding venue.*

week /wiːk/ *noun* a period of seven days from Monday to Sunday ○ *a three-week cruise in the Caribbean* □ **to be paid by the week** to be paid a particular amount of money each week ○ *He earns £500 a week or per week.* ○ *She works thirty-five hours per week or She works a thirty-five-hour week.*

weekend /wiːkˈend/ *noun* Saturday and Sunday, or the period from Friday evening to Sunday evening

weekend break /ˌwiːkˈend breɪk/ *noun* TOURISM a short holiday of two or three nights over a weekend at a specially low tariff ○ *They are offering weekend breaks in Amsterdam from £100.*

weekend business /ˌwiːkend ˈbɪznɪs/ *noun* BUSINESS business done at the weekend, i.e. the number of customers on Saturdays and Sundays ○ *Weekend business is slow.*

weekend return /ˌwiːkend rɪˈtɜːn/ *noun* TRAVEL a ticket available at a reduced price if you go and come back between Friday and Monday

weekly /ˈwiːkli/ *adverb* done every week ○ *a weekly flight to the Shetland Isles* □ **a weekly newspaper**, **a weekly** newspaper which is published once a week

weekly room rate /ˌwiːkli ˈruːm ˌreɪt/ *noun* HOTELS the rate charged for a hotel room for seven nights

weigh /weɪ/ *verb* **1.** to measure how heavy something is ○ *She weighed the packet at the post office.* ○ *Please put all your luggage onto the scales to be weighed.* **2.** to have a particular weight ○ *The packet weighs twenty-five grams.*

weigh in /ˌweɪ ˈɪn/ *verb* AIR TRAVEL to have your baggage weighed before a flight

weighing machine /ˈweɪɪŋ məˌʃiːn/ *noun* a machine which measure how heavy something or someone is

weight /weɪt/ *noun* how heavy someone or something is □ **to sell fruit by weight** to sell fruit at a price calculated per pound or per kilo of the fruit □ **to give short weight** to sell something which is lighter than it should be

Weil's disease /ˈweɪlz dɪˌziːz/ *noun* MEDICAL an infectious disease caused transmitted to humans from rats' urine, causing jaundice and kidney damage (NOTE: Weil's disease can also be caught from windsurfing on stagnant water.)

welcome /ˈwelkəm/ *noun* a greeting or reception □ **they gave the visitors a very warm welcome** they greeted the visitors very warmly ■ *verb* to greet someone as they arrive ○ *The hotel manager welcomed the tourist group.* ■ *adjective* **1.** received with pleasure ○ *After the walk, we had a welcome hot bath* or *a hot bath was very welcome.* **2.** willingly permitted ○ *Visitors are welcome to use the hotel gardens.* **3.** □ **you're welcome** it was a pleasure to serve you (*informal: as a reply to 'thank you'*)

well- /wel/ *prefix* in a good way ○ *a well-equipped bedroom* ○ *a well-known spa town*

well-appointed /ˌwel əˈpɔɪntɪd/ *adjective* well furnished and equipped, which has luxurious furnishings and equipment

well done /ˌwel ˈdʌn/ *adjective* CATERING completely cooked

well-hung /ˌwel ˈhʌŋ/ *adjective* (*of meat*) hung up long enough to mature and be good to eat

Welsh rarebit /ˌwelʃ ˈreəbɪt/ *noun* FOOD cooked cheese on toast

west /west/ *noun* one of the points of the compass, the direction of the setting sun ○

The sun sets in the west and rises in the east. ■ *adjective* referring to the west ○ *the west coast* ■ *adverb* towards the west ○ *Drive west along the motorway for ten miles.*

westbound /'westbaʊnd/ *adjective* going towards the west ○ *The westbound carriageway of the motorway is closed.*

West End /ˌwest 'end/ *noun* ENTERTAIN-MENT **1.** the fashionable part of London, where the main shops can be found ○ *Crowds go shopping in the West End on Sunday afternoons.* Compare **East End 2.** the central London theatres, which put on major plays ○ *Her first play was a hit in the West End.* ○ *He wrote three West End musicals.* Compare **fringe** (NOTE: The US equivalent for main theatres is **Broadway.**)

westerly /'westəli/ *adjective* towards the west

western /'westən/ *adjective* referring to the west

westernmost /'westənməʊst/ *adjective* furthest west

Westminster /'westmɪnstə/ *noun* a borough in London where the Houses of Parliament are situated ○ *Tourists always go to Westminster as part of their visit to London.*

westward /'westwəd/ *adjective, adverb* towards the west

westwards /'westwədz/ *adverb* towards the west

west wind /ˌwest 'wɪnd/ *noun* a wind coming from the west

wet /wet/ *adjective* **1.** covered or soaked with water or other liquid □ **I'm wet through** *or* **soaking wet** all my clothes are very wet **2.** rainy ○ *If it is wet, the walk to the beach will be cancelled.* ○ *There's nothing I like better than a wet Sunday in London.*

wet sales /'wet seɪlz/ *plural noun* BUSI-NESS sales of beer and other drinks in a pub ○ *The trade split is: wet 20%, food 50%, accommodation 30%.*

'…the pub has been totally no-smoking for eight years and, apart from an initial negative impact on wet sales, it has traded successfully ever since' [*Caterer & Hotelkeeper*]

wetsuit /'wetsuːt/ *noun* SPORT a suit worn by divers, windsurfers, etc., which keeps the body warm with a layer of water between the body and the suit

whale /weɪl/ *noun* a huge mammal that lives in the sea ○ *You can take a boat into the mouth of the river to see the whales.*

whale watching /'weɪl ˌwɒtʃɪŋ/ *noun* TOURISM the tourist attraction of watching whales ○ *They run whale-watching tours into the bay.*

wharf /wɔːf/ *noun* SHIPS AND BOATS a place in a dock where a ship can tie up and load or unload (NOTE: The plural form is **wharfs** or **wharves.**)

wheat /wiːt/ *noun* FOOD a grain harvested in temperate regions from a widely cultivated cereal plant, used for making flour for bread, pasta, and other foods

wheat germ /'wiːt dʒɜːm/ *noun* FOOD the centre of the wheat grain that is milled finely and sometimes toasted, and is used for sprinkling over cereals or in cooking

wheel /wiːl/ *noun* **1.** a round object on which a vehicle such as a bicycle, a car or a train runs **2.** any similar round object which turns ■ *verb* to push along something that has wheels ○ *The waiter wheeled in a sweet trolley.*

wheelchair /'wiːltʃeə/ *noun* a chair on wheels used by people who cannot walk

wheelchair access /'wiːltʃeə ˌækses/ *noun* a slope for wheelchairs ○ *There is no wheelchair access into the restaurant.*

whelk /welk/ *noun* SEAFOOD a type of edible sea snail ○ *We bought some whelks at a stall on the pier.*

whey /weɪ/ *noun* DAIRY the watery liquid that separates from the solid part of milk when it turns sour or when enzymes are added in cheese making. Compare **curd**

whip /wɪp/ *verb* CATERING to make food such as batter or cream stiff and creamy by adding air to it with short quick movements, using a fork, whisk, or electric beater

whipped cream /ˌwɪpt 'kriːm/ *noun* DAIRY cream, beaten until it is stiff, flavoured with sugar and vanilla

whipping cream /'wɪpɪŋ kriːm/ *noun* a heavy cream containing a high proportion of butterfat, which causes it to stiffen when whipped

whirlpool /'wɜːlpuːl/ *noun* water which turns rapidly round and round ○ *Be careful, there are whirlpools in the river.*

whirlpool bath /'wɜːlpuːl bɑːθ/ *noun* a type of bath, often in a spa, where the water is made to turn round and round

whisk /wɪsk/ CATERING *noun* a kitchen tool made of curved or coiled wires attached to a handle, or of a bundle of twigs or stalks, used to whip soft or liquid foods ■ *verb* to whip a soft or liquid substance with a fork, whisk, or other utensil

whiskey /'wɪski/ *noun* BEVERAGES whisky, made in Ireland and the USA

whisky /'wɪski/ *noun* **1.** BEVERAGES a strong alcohol distilled from grain, usually made in Scotland □ **whisky sour** cocktail of whisky, lemon juice and sugar **2.** BEVERAGES a glass of this alcohol ○ *Two large whiskies, please.*

COMMENT: Whisky may be drunk on its own (neat), with ice cubes (on the rocks) or diluted with water, soda water or a ginger-flavoured fizzy drink.

whisky and soda /ˌwɪski ən ˈsəʊdə/ *noun* BEVERAGES a drink of whisky with soda water

whisky sour /ˌwɪski ˈsaʊə/ *noun* BEVERAGES a cocktail of whisky, lemon juice and sugar

white /waɪt/ *adjective, noun* the colour of snow or milk ■ *noun, adjective* FOOD same as **egg white**

whitebait /ˈwaɪtbeɪt/ *noun* SEAFOOD a small young fish fried and eaten whole (NOTE: The plural form is **whitebait**.)

whiteboard /ˈwaɪtbɔːd/ *noun* a board on a wall which can be written on using coloured pens

white bread /ˌwaɪt ˈbred/ *noun* BREAD, ETC. bread made from refined white flour

white coffee /ˌwaɪt ˈkɒfi/ *noun* BEVERAGES coffee with milk or cream

white meat /waɪt ˈmiːt/ *noun* FOOD light-coloured meat, like the breast meat on a chicken

whites /waɪts/ *plural noun* white clothes ○ *the traditional chef's whites*

white sale /ˌwaɪt ˈseɪl/ *noun* a sale of sheets, towels, etc.

white sauce /ˌwaɪt ˈsɔːs/ *noun* SAUCES, ETC. a basic sauce made from fat, flour and liquid usually milk or stock

white sugar /ˌwaɪt ˈʃʊgə/ *noun* FOOD same as **granulated sugar**

white tie /ˌwaɪt ˈtaɪ/ *adjective* referring to a formal evening banquet or reception at which men wear a white bow tie and black tail coat. ◊ **black tie**

whiteware /ˈwaɪtweə/ *noun* CATERING white plates, cups and saucers, etc., as opposed to decorated china

'…the recession has forced caterers to be price-conscious and whiteware can cost a third less than colourfully designed products. We have seen three- and four-star hotels moving to whiteware, but still striving for standards with elegant design or embossed lines' [*Caterer & Hotelkeeper*]

white-water canoeing /ˈrɑːftɪŋ/, **rafting** *noun* SPORT the sport of riding in a canoe or on a raft down rapidly flowing rivers

white wine /ˌwaɪt ˈwaɪn/ *noun* BEVERAGES wine made without leaving the grape skins in the fermenting mixture, making the wine pale yellow or green instead of deep red

COMMENT: Dry white wines are drunk with fish, and also as apéritifs. Sweet white wines are drunk as dessert wines. All white wines are drunk chilled.

whiting /ˈwaɪtɪŋ/ *noun* SEAFOOD a type of small sea fish (NOTE: The plural form is **whiting**.)

Whitsun /ˈwɪtsən/ *noun* a Christian festival on the seventh Sunday after Easter

Whit Sunday /ˌwɪt ˈsʌndeɪ/ *noun* the seventh Sunday after Easter

wholefood /ˈhəʊlfuːd/ *noun* FOOD food, grown naturally, which has not been given artificial fertilisers and has not been processed ○ *A wholefood diet is healthier than eating processed foods.*

wholegrain /ˈhəʊlgreɪn/ *noun* FOOD food such as rice of which the whole of the seed is eaten

wholemeal /ˈhəʊlmiːl/ *adjective* containing wheat germ and bran

wholemeal bread /ˈhəʊlˌmiːl bred/, **wholewheat bread** /ˈhəʊlˌwiːt bred/ *noun* BREAD, ETC. bread made from wholemeal flour

wholemeal flour /ˌhəʊlmiːl ˈflaʊə/ *noun* FOOD flour which has had nothing removed or added to it and contains a large proportion of the original wheat seed, including the bran

wholesale /ˈhəʊlseɪl/ *noun* the sale of goods in large quantities to retailers

wholesome /ˈhəʊls(ə)m/ *adjective* healthy, good for one's health

wholesome food /ˌhəʊls(ə)m ˈfuːd/ *noun* CATERING food that is good for your health

wholewheat /ˈhəʊlwiːt/ *noun mainly US* FOOD same as **wholemeal**

wide-bodied aircraft /ˌwaɪd ˌbɒdid ˈeəkrɑːft/ *noun* AIR TRAVEL an aircraft with a body wider than 5 metres, e.g. the Airbus or a Boeing 747

wiener /ˈwiːnə/ *noun US* FOOD same as **frankfurter** ○ *We cooked wieners on the barbecue.*

Wiener schnitzel /ˌwiːnə ˈʃnɪts(ə)l/ *noun* FOOD a slice of veal, covered in breadcrumbs and fried ○ *I've been in Germany for four days and all I've eaten are Wiener Schnitzels.*

wife /waɪf/ *noun* a woman to whom a man is married ○ *He and his wife are both vegetarians.* (NOTE: The plural form is **wives**.)

wild fowl /'waɪld faʊl/ *noun* SPORT game birds which are shot for sport

wildlife /'waɪldlaɪf/ *noun* birds, plants and animals in their natural conditions ○ *They spent the week studying the wildlife in the national park.* (NOTE: There is no plural form.)

wildlife park /'waɪld,laɪf pɑːk/ *noun* ENTERTAINMENT a park where wild animals are allowed to run free

wild mushroom /,waɪld 'mʌʃruːm/ *noun* VEGETABLES any of various types of edible mushroom found in the countryside and which are now also cultivated (NOTE: Ceps and chanterelles are the best-known wild mushrooms.)

wild rice /,waɪld 'raɪs/ *noun* FOOD a species of grass which is found naturally in North America and which is similar to rice

wind *verb* /waɪnd/ to roll up or to roll down ○ *You can wind down the window if it is too hot.* (NOTE: **winding – wound**) ■ *noun* /wɪnd/ air moving outdoors ○ *The wind is blowing from the sea.* □ **in high winds** in very strong winds

windbreak /'wɪndbreɪk/ *noun* a fence, hedge or screen which protects against the wind

wind chill factor /'wɪnd tʃɪl ,fæktə/ *noun* a way of calculating the risk of exposure in cold weather by adding the speed of the wind to the number of degrees of temperature below zero

window /'wɪndəʊ/ *noun* an opening in a wall or door or the side of a vehicle, filled with glass

window seat /'wɪndəʊ siːt/ *noun* TRAVEL a seat in a train, plane, etc., next to a window

windscreen /'wɪndskriːn/ *noun* ROAD TRAVEL a glass window in the front of a vehicle

windscreen washer /'wɪndskriːn ,wɒʃə/ *noun* ROAD TRAVEL an attachment on a car which squirts water on to the windscreen to clean the glass

windscreen wiper /'wɪndskriːn ,waɪpə/ *noun* ROAD TRAVEL a device on a vehicle which wipes rain away from the windscreen

windshield /'wɪndʃiːld/ *noun* **1.** ROAD TRAVEL a screen on a motorcycle **2.** *US* a windscreen

windsurfer /'wɪnsɜːfə/ *noun* SPORT somebody who does windsurfing ○ *Windsurfers were waiting for some wind to make really big waves.*

windsurfing /'wɪndsɜːfɪŋ/ *noun* SPORT the sport of riding on water on a special board with a sail attached ○ *This is a very popular beach for windsurfing.*

windward /'wɪndwəd/ *adjective, adverb* SHIPS AND BOATS on or to the side of a ship from which the wind is blowing. Compare **leeward**

windy /'wɪndi/ *adjective* when a strong wind is blowing ○ *We have a lot of windy weather in March.* ○ *Dress warmly, it's a cold windy day outside.*

wine /waɪn/ *noun* BEVERAGES **1.** an alcoholic drink made from the juice of grapes ○ *We'll have a bottle of the house wine.* ○ *Do you sell wine by the glass?* **2.** an alcoholic drink made from the juice of fruit or flowers ○ *elderberry wine* ■ *verb* □ **to wine and dine someone** to take someone out for an expensive dinner and drinks

wine bar /'waɪn bɑː/ *noun* BARS a bar which serves wine, and usually food

wine basket, wine cradle *noun* CATERING **1.** a wickerwork cradle with handles for holding a bottle of vintage red wine at an angle, so that the wine can be served without holding the bottle upright and the sediment is not disturbed **2.** a wickerwork container holding several bottles of wine upright, used for serving wine on an aircraft

wine bucket /'waɪn ,bʌkɪt/ *noun* BARS same as **ice bucket**

wine cellar /'waɪn ,selə/ *noun* BARS an underground room where wine is kept or served

wine cooler /'waɪn ,kuːlə/ *noun* **1.** BARS a bucket with ice and water, in which a bottle of wine is placed to keep cold **2.** MEDICAL a special plastic holder in which a bottle of chilled wine is placed to keep cold

wine glass /'waɪn glɑːs/ *noun* CATERING a glass for serving wine ○ *These wine glasses are very expensive.*

wine-growing /'waɪn ,grəʊɪŋ/ *adjective* in which vines are grown to produce wine

wine list /'waɪn lɪst/ *noun* CATERING a list of wines which are available at a restaurant

wine merchant /'waɪn ,mɜːtʃənt/ *noun* somebody who sells wines

wine route /'waɪn ruːt/ *noun* ROAD TRAVEL a road which goes through vineyards

winery /'waɪnəri/ *noun* US a vineyard, where wine is made

wine tasting /'waɪn ,teɪstɪŋ/ *noun* ENTERTAINMENT a visit to a vineyard or a wine merchant's to taste wine before buying it

wine waiter /'waɪn ˌweɪtə/ *noun* CATER-ING the person in charge of serving the wines in a restaurant. Also called **sommelier**

wing /wɪŋ/ *noun* **1.** part of a bird used for flying, eaten as food ○ *Which part of the chicken do you prefer, white meat or a wing?* **2.** AIR TRAVEL one of two large flat surface at the side of aircraft, which enable it to fly ○ *He had a seat over the wing, so could not see much out of the cabin window.*

winkle /'wɪŋkəl/ *noun* SEAFOOD a type of small edible sea-snail ○ *We bought winkles and jellied eels from the stall on the pier.*

winter /'wɪntə/ *noun* the last season of the year, following autumn and before spring, when the weather is coldest and the days are short

winter resort /ˌwɪntə rɪ'zɔːt/ *noun* TOURISM a town which is mainly visited in the winter because of skiing nearby

winter schedule /'taɪmteɪb(ə)l/, **winter timetable** *noun* TRAVEL a special timetable for planes or trains or ferries, which applies during the low season

winter sports /ˌwɪntə 'spɔːts/ *plural noun* SPORT sports which take place in the winter, e.g. skiing or skating

winter sports destination /ˌwɪntə 'spɔːts ˌdestɪneɪʃ(ə)n/ *noun* TOURISM a place where people go to for winter sports ○ *Flights to winter sports destinations are full around Easter.*

wiper /'waɪpə/ *noun* same as **windscreen wiper**

wire /'waɪə/ *noun* **1.** a thin metal line or thread ○ *Do not touch the electric wires.* **2.** a telegram ○ *to send someone a wire* ■ *verb* to send a telegram ○ *She wired the hotel to confirm her arrival on the 5th of May.*

wok /wɒk/ *noun* CATERING a Chinese round-bottomed frying pan ○ *A wok is used for stir-fry cooking.*

woman /'wʊmən/ *noun* a female adult human being (NOTE: The plural form is **women**.)

women's toilet /ˌwɪmɪnz 'tɔɪlət/ *noun* a public toilet for women

won ton /'wʌn tʌn/ *noun* FOOD in Chinese cookery, a small dumpling made from a square of noodle dough with a little filling in the middle, boiled in soup or deep-fried

wooden spoon /ˌwʊd(ə)n 'spuːn/ *noun* CATERING a spoon made of wood, used for cooking

wood pigeon /'wʊd ˌpɪdʒən/ *noun* MEAT a wild pigeon which is shot for food

Worcester sauce, Worcestershire sauce *noun* SAUCES, ETC. a trademark for a bottled sauce, made of vinegar, herbs and spices ○ *a tomato juice with a dash of Worcester sauce in it*

word processing /ˌwɜːd 'prəʊsesɪŋ/ *noun* the use of a computer to produce, check and change texts, reports and letters

work /wɜːk/ *noun* a job □ **in work** having a job □ **out of work** with no job ■ *verb* **1.** to have a job ○ *She works in a travel agent's.* ○ *He works at the Swan Hotel.* ○ *He is working as a commis in a London restaurant.* **2.** to make a machine operate ○ *Do you know how to work the cash register?* **3.** to have the desired effect or result ○ *The plan worked.*

worker /'wɜːkə/ *noun* somebody who is employed □ **hotel worker, shop worker** a person who works in a hotel or a shop

workforce /'wɜːkfɔːs/ *noun* BUSINESS all the employees in a hotel or a company

working /'wɜːkɪŋ/ *adjective* referring to work □ **the normal working week** the usual number of hours worked per week, generally about 35 hours ○ *Even though he is a casual worker, he works a normal working week.*

working capital /'wɜːkɪŋ ˌkæpɪt(ə)l/ *noun* BUSINESS capital in the form of cash, stocks and debtors, used by a company in its day-to-day operations

working conditions /'wɜːkɪŋ kən-ˌdɪʃ(ə)nz/ *plural noun* the general state of the place where people work, e.g. whether it is well lit, well ventilated, too hot, noisy, dark or dangerous

working holiday /ˌwɜːkɪŋ 'hɒlɪdeɪ/ *noun* a holiday during which volunteers work on a project of benefit to a community

work permit /'wɜːk ˌpɜːmɪt/ *noun* BUSI-NESS an official document which allows someone who is not a citizen to work in a country

work schedule /'wɜːk ˌʃedʒuːl/ *noun* a timetable of jobs to be done, with dates and times for finishing them

workstation /'wɜːkˌsteɪʃ(ə)n/ *noun* BUSINESS a desk with a terminal, monitor, keyboard and mouse, where a computer operator works ○ *The system has five work-stations linked in a network.*

workwear /'wɜːkweə/ *noun* clothing worn for work, especially a uniform

world /wɜːld/ *noun* **1.** the planet Earth **2.** the people in a particular business, or people with a special interest ○ *the world of big business* ○ *the world of lawyers* or *the legal world*

World Heritage site /ˌwɜːld ˈherɪtɪdʒ ˌsaɪt/ *noun* a place that is considered to be of outstanding value to humanity and is given special protection

world tour /ˌwɜːld ˈtʊə/ *noun* TOURISM a tour which visits various countries in different parts of the world and goes round the world

World Tourism Organisation /ˌwɜːld ˈtʊərɪz(ə)m ˌɔːgənaɪzeɪʃ(ə)n/ *noun* an agency of the United Nations that aims to promote tourism, especially responsible and sustainable tourism, throughout the world. Abbr **WTO**

worldwide /ˈwɜːldwaɪd/ *adjective, adverb* all over the world ○ *a worldwide network of couriers* ○ *Our hotels have a worldwide reputation for good service.* ○ *The airline operates worldwide.*

wrap /ræp/ *noun* FOOD a soft bread, like a tortilla, wrapped round a filling to make a snack ○ *chargrilled aubergines, courgettes and peppers, served in a warm tortilla wrap*

wrapping /ˈræpɪŋ/ *noun* the paper or plastic used to wrap something up

wrapping paper /ˈræpɪŋ ˌpeɪpə/ *noun* paper used to wrap presents

wrap up /ˌræp ˈʌp/ *verb* **1.** to wear warm clothes ○ *You need to wrap up warmly – it is very cold outside.* **2.** to cover up completely ○ *She wrapped the book up in coloured paper.*

wreck /rek/ SHIPS AND BOATS *noun* **1.** same as **shipwreck 2.** the act of wrecking a ship or of being wrecked ■ *verb* to cause severe damage to a ship ○ *The ship was wrecked on the coast of Ireland.*

write /raɪt/ *verb* to put down words on paper ○ *Please write your home address on the registration form.* ○ *He wrote a letter to the management to complain about the service.* (NOTE: **writing – wrote – written**)

writing table /ˈraɪtɪŋ ˌteɪb(ə)l/ *noun* a table where someone can write letters, etc.

written permission /ˌrɪt(ə)n pə ˈmɪʃ(ə)n/ *noun* a document which allows someone to do something ○ *You need the written permission of the owner to visit the castle.*

wrong /rɒŋ/ *adjective* **1.** not right, containing a mistake ○ *The bill was wrong, and we had to ask the waiter to check it.* ○ *Our meal was sent to the wrong table.* ○ *There is something wrong with the television in our room.* ○ *They took a wrong turning and ended up in an industrial estate.* **2.** morally bad

wrongful dismissal /ˌrɒŋf(ə)l dɪs ˈmɪs(ə)l/ *noun* BUSINESS removal of someone from a job for a reason which does not justify dismissal and which is in breach of the contract of employment

wrong number /ˌrɒŋ ˈnʌmbə/ *noun* a telephone number which is not the one you wanted to dial ○ *We tried dialling several times, but each time got a wrong number.*

WTB *abbreviation* Wales Tourist Board

WTO *abbreviation* World Tourism Organisation

WTTC *abbreviation* World Travel and Tourism Council

XYZ

XC skiing SPORT same as **cross-country skiing**

xenophobia /ˌzenəˈfəʊbiə/ *noun* a dislike of foreigners

Y *noun* a YMCA or YWCA hostel (*informal*)

yacht /jɒt/ *noun* SHIPS AND BOATS **1.** a sailing boat, or a boat used for pleasure and sport **2.** a large luxurious boat with a motor ○ *She spent her holiday on a yacht in the Mediterranean.*

yacht club /ˈjɒt klʌb/ *noun* SPORT a sailing club

yachting /ˈjɒtɪŋ/ *noun* SPORT the activity of sailing a yacht ○ *Yachting holidays in the Greek Islands are very popular.*

yachting harbour /ˈjɒtɪŋ ˌhɑːbə/ *noun* SPORT a harbour with special facilities for yachts such as mooring buoys

yachtsman /ˈjɒtsmən/, **yachtswoman** /ˈjɒtswʊmən/ *noun* SPORT somebody who sails a yacht

yam /jæm/ *noun* VEGETABLES **1.** the thick tuber of a tropical plant *Dioscorea* **2.** *US* same as **sweet potato**

year /jɪə/ *noun* a period of twelve months ○ *We are going back to the hotel where we stayed last year.* ○ *Next year they are going to Corsica.*

year end /ˌjɪə ˈend/ *noun* BUSINESS the end of the financial year, when a company's accounts are prepared ○ *The accounts department has started work on the year-end accounts.*

yeast /jiːst/ *noun* FOOD a living fungus used to make bread and beer

yeast extract /ˈjiːst ˌekstrækt/ *noun* FOOD a thick sticky brown food obtained from yeast and eaten as a spread or used in cooking

yellow fever /ˈjeləʊ ˌfiːvə/ *noun* MEDICAL an infectious disease, found especially in Africa and South America, caused by a virus carried by the mosquito *Aedes aegypti*

COMMENT: The fever affects the liver and causes jaundice. There is no known cure

for yellow fever and it can be fatal, but vaccination can prevent it. Yellow fever is endemic in Central Africa and the northern part of South America; travellers to these areas should carry a certificate of vaccination.

yen /jen/ *noun* FINANCE the currency used in Japan (NOTE: This is usually written as ¥ before a figure: *¥2,700* (say 'two thousand seven hundred yen').)

yield /jiːld/ BUSINESS *noun* money produced as a return on an investment, i.e. revenue from sales minus operating costs and cost of sales ■ *verb* to produce as interest or dividend ○ *shares which yield 10%* ○ *Government stocks which yield a small interest.*

COMMENT: To work out the yield on an investment, take the gross dividend per annum, multiply it by 100 and divide by the price you paid for it (in pence): an investment paying a dividend of 20p per share and costing £3.00, is yielding 6.66%.

YMCA *noun* a worldwide welfare organisation that runs hostels providing inexpensive accommodation for young people. Full form **Young Men's Christian Association**

yoghurt, yogurt /ˈjɒgət/ *noun* DAIRY fermented milk usually eaten as a dessert

Yorkshire pudding /ˌjɔːkʃə ˈpʊdɪŋ/ *noun* FOOD a mixture of eggs, flour and milk, cooked in the oven, the traditional accompaniment to roast beef

COMMENT: Yorkshire pudding may be cooked in the oven in one large dish or in several small ones. It used to be cooked in the oven in a pan under the roasting beef, so that the juices of the meat dripped onto the pudding. The pudding is usually served with the meat as part of the main course.

youth hostel /ˈjuːθ ˌhɒst(ə)l/ *noun* TOURISM a building where young travellers can stay the night cheaply ○ *If you can find places at youth hostels, that's the cheapest way of travelling.*

YWCA *noun* a worldwide welfare organisation that runs hostels providing inexpensive accommodation for young people. Full form **Young Women's Christian Association**

zabaglione /ˌzæbəlˈjəʊni/ *noun* a dessert made of egg yolks, sugar, and Marsala wine beaten over hot water until pale and foamy and served hot with sponge finger biscuits

zebra crossing /ˌzebrə ˈkrɒsɪŋ/ *noun* same as **pedestrian crossing**

zest /zest/ *noun* FOOD the thin outer rind of the peel of a citrus fruit that is cut, scraped, or grated to yield a sharp fruity flavouring for foods and drinks

ZIP code /ˈzɪp kəʊd/ *noun US* letters and numbers used to indicate a town or street in an address (NOTE: The British English is **postcode**.)

zone /zəʊn/ *noun* an area of a town or country, considered for administrative pur- poses ■ *verb* to divide a town into different areas for planning purposes

zoning regulations /ˌzəʊnɪŋ ˌregjʊ ˈleɪʃ(ə)nz/, **zoning ordinances** *plural noun* local bylaws which regulate the types of building and land use in a town

zoological gardens /ˌzuːəlɒdʒɪk(ə)l ˈgɑːd(ə)nz/, **zoo** /zuː/ *noun* ENTERTAIN- MENT a place where wild animals are kept for the public to see

zucchini /zʊˈkiːni/ *noun US* VEGETABLES same as **courgette**

zwieback /ˈzwiːbæk/ *noun US* BREAD, ETC. a type of biscuit made of bread baked hard

SUPPLEMENTS

Aircraft registration codes
Airline codes
Airport codes
Local times around the world
International dialling codes
International currencies
Public holidays
Accommodation ratings
HLTT (Hospitality, Leisure, Travel and Tourism) classifications
Websites

Aircraft registration codes

These codes are painted on all aircraft, showing their country of registration.

3A	Monaco	A2	Botswana
3B	Mauritius	A3	Tonga
3C	Equatorial Guinea	A40	Oman
3D	Swaziland	A5	Bhutan
3X	Guinea	A6	United Arab Emirates
4K	Azerbaijan	A7	Qatar
4R	Sri Lanka	A9C	Bahrain
4U	United Nations Organisation	AP	Pakistan
4X	Israel	B	China & Taiwan
5A	Libya	B-H	Hong Kong
5B	Cyprus	B-M	Macau
5H	Tanzania	C	Canada
5N	Nigeria	C2	Nauru
5R	Madagascar	C3	Andorra
5T	Mauritania	C5	Gambia
5U	Niger	C6	Bahamas
5V	Togo	C9	Mozambique
5W	Samoa	CC	Chile
5X	Uganda	CN	Morocco
5Y	Kenya	CP	Bolivia
6O	Somalia	CS	Portugal
6V	Senegal	CU	Cuba
6Y	Jamaica	CX	Uruguay
7O	Yemen	D	Germany
7P	Lesotho	D2	Angola
7Q	Malawi	D4	Cape Verde
7T	Algeria	D6	Comoros Islands
8P	Barbados	DQ	Fiji
8Q	Maldives	EC	Spain
8R	Guyana	EI	Ireland
9A	Croatia	EK	Armenia
9G	Ghana	EP	Iran
9H	Malta	ER	Moldova
9J	Zambia	ES	Estonia
9K	Kuwait	ET	Ethiopia
9L	Sierra Leone	EW	Belarus
9M	Malaysia	EY	Tajikistan
9N	Nepal	EZ	Turkmenistan
9Q	Democratic Republic of the Congo	F	France
		F	New Caledonia (France)
9U	Burundi	F	Guadeloupe (France)
9V	Singapore	F	Martinique (France)
9XR	Rwanda	F	Tahiti (French Polynesia)
9Y	Trinidad and Tobago	G	United Kingdom

Aircraft registration codes *continued*

H4	Solomon Islands	RA	Russian Federation
HA	Hungary	RP	Philippines
HB	Switzerland and Liechtenstein	S2	Bangladesh
		S5	Slovenia
HC	Ecuador	S7	Seychelles
HH	Haiti	S9	Sao Tome and Principe
HI	Dominican Republic	SE	Sweden
HK	Colombia	SP	Poland
HL	South Korea	ST	Sudan
HP	Panama	SU	Egypt
HR	Honduras	SX	Greece
HS	Thailand	T2	Tuvalu
HV	The Vatican	T3	Kiribati
HZ	Saudi Arabia	T7	San Marino
I	Italy	T8A	Palau
J2	Djibouti	T9	Bosnia-Herzegovina
J3	Grenada	TC	Turkey
J5	Guinea Bissau	TF	Iceland
J6	St Lucia	TG	Guatemala
J7	Dominica	TI	Costa Rica
J8	St Vincent and the Grenadines	TJ	Cameroon
		TL	Central African Republic
JA	Japan	TN	Congo-Brazzaville
JU	Mongolia	TR	Gabon
JY	Jordan	TS	Tunisia
LN	Norway	TT	Chad
LV	Argentina	TU	Cote d'Ivoire
LX	Luxembourg	TY	Benin
LY	Lithuania	TZ	Mali
LZ	Bulgaria	UK	Uzbekistan
N	USA	UR	Ukraine
OB	Peru	V2	Antigua and Barbuda
OD	Lebanon	V3	Belize
OE	Austria	V4	St Kitts and Nevis
OH	Finland	V5	Namibia
OK	Czech Republic	V6	Micronesia
OO	Belgium	V7	Marshall Islands
OY	Denmark	V8	Brunei
P	North Korea	VH	Australia
P2	Papua New Guinea	VN	Vietnam
P4	Aruba	VP, VQ	British Overseas Territories
PH	Netherlands		
PJ	Netherland Antilles	VP-A	Anguilla (UK)
PK	Indonesia	VP-B	Bermuda (UK)
PP	Brazil	VP-C	Cayman Islands (UK)
PZ	Surinam	VP-F	Falkland Islands

Aircraft registration codes *continued*

Code	Country	Code	Country
VP-G	Gibraltar (UK)	YA	Afghanistan
VP-L	British Virgin Islands	YI	Iraq
VP-M	Montserrat	YJ	Vanuatu
VQ-H	St Helena (UK)	YK	Syria
VQ-T	Turks and Caicos	YL	Latvia
	Islands (UK)	YN	Nicaragua
VR-B	Bermuda	YR	Romania
VR-C	Cayman Island	YS	El Salvador
VR-G	Gibraltar	YU	Serbia & Montenegro
VR-H	Hong Kong	YV	Venezuela
VT	India	Z	Zimbabwe
XA	Mexico	ZA	Albania
XT	Burkina Faso	ZK	New Zealand
XU	Cambodia	ZP	Paraguay
XY	Myanmar	ZS	South Africa

Airline codes

2J	Air Burkina
4U	GermanWings
9U	Air Moldova
AA	American Airlines
AB	Air Berlin
AC	Air Canada
AF	Air France
AH	Air Algerie
AI	Air India
AM	Aeromexico
AQ	Aloha Airlines
AR	Aerolineas Argentinas
AS	Alaska Airlines
AT	Royal Air Maroc
AY	Finnair
AZ	Alitalia
BA	British Airways
BB	Seaborne Airlines
BD	bmi British Midland
BG	Biman Bangladesh Airlines
BH	Transtate Airlines
BI	Royal Brunei Airlines
BL	Pacific Airlines
BM	Air Sicilia
BO	Bouraq Indonesia Airlines
BP	Air Botswana
BR	EVA Air
BU	Braathens ASA
BW	BWIA – West Indies Airways
CA	Air China International
CB	ScotAirways
CI	China Airlines
CJ	China Northern Airlines
CM	COPA (Compania Panamena de Aviación)
CO	Continental Airlines
CU	Cubana
CX	Cathay Pacific Airways
CY	Cyprus Airways
CZ	China Southern Airlines
DL	Delta Air Lines
DS	Easyjet Switzerland
DT	TAAG Angola Airlines
DU	Hemus Air
DY	Air Djibouti
EI	Aer Lingus
EK	Emirates
ET	Ethiopian Airlines
FC	Finncomm
FG	Ariana Afghan Airlines
FI	IcelandAir
FJ	Air Pacific
FO	Airlines of Tasmania
FR	Ryanair
GA	Garuda Indonesia
GC	Gambia International Airlines
GF	Gulf Air
GH	Ghana Airways
GL	Air Greenland
GN	Air Gabon
GR	Aurigny Air Services
GY	Guyana Airways
HA	Hawaiian Airlines
HM	Air Seychelles
HP	America West Airlines
HV	Transavia Airlines
HY	Uzbekistan Airways
IB	Iberia
IC	Indian Airlines
IE	Solomon Airlines
IR	Iran Air
IV	Wind Jet
IY	Yemenia – Yemen Airways
JL	Japan Airlines
JM	Air Jamaica
JP	Adria Airways
JU	JAT Airways
JY	Interisland Airways
KE	Korean Air Lines
KL	KLM Royal Dutch Airlines
KM	Air Malta
KP	Kiwi International Airlines
KQ	Kenya Airways
KU	Kuwait Airways
KV	Kavminvodyavia
KX	Cayman Airways
KY	Linhas Aereas de Air Sao Tome and Principe
LA	Lan-Chile
LG	Luxair
LH	Lufthansa
LN	Jamahiriya Libyan Arab Airlines
LO	LOT Polish Airlines
LY	El Al Israel Airlines
LX	Swiss
LZ	Balkan-Bulgarian Airlines

Airline codes *continued*

MA	MALEV Hungarian Airlines	RK	Royal Khymer Airlines
MD	Air Madagascar	RO	TAROM
MH	Malaysia Airlines	SA	South African Airways
MK	Air Mauritius	SD	Sudan Airways
MN	Commercial Airways	SK	SAS
MR	Air Mauritanie	SN	SN Brussels Airlines
MS	Egyptair	SQ	Singapore Airlines
NF	Air Vanuatu	SU	Aeroflot Russian Airlines
NG	Lauda Air	SV	Saudi Arabian Airlines
NH	All Nippon Airways	SW	Air Namibia
NO	Aus-Air	TC	Air Tanzania
NQ	Air Japan	TE	Lithuanian Airlines
NV	Nakanihon Airlines	TG	Thai Airways International
NW	Northwest Airlines	TK	Turkish Airlines
NZ	Air New Zealand	TM	LAM – Lineas Aereas de Moçambique
OA	Olympic Airlines	TN	Air Tahiti Nui
OB	Astrakhan Airlines	TP	TAP – Air Portugal
OK	Czech Airlines	TU	Tunisair
OM	MIAT – Mongolian Airlines	U2	Easyjet
ON	Air Nauru	UA	United Airlines
OO	SkyWest Airlines	UB	Myanmar Airways
OS	Austrian Airlines	UI	Eurocypria Airlines
OU	Croatia Airlines	UL	SriLankan Airlines
OV	Estonian Air	UM	Air Zimbabwe
PB	Provincial Airlines	US	US Airways
PC	Air Fiji	UY	Cameroon Airlines
PH	Polynesian	VE	AVENSA
PK	Pakistan International Airlines	VH	Aeropostal
PR	Philippine Airlines	VJ	Jatayu Airlines
PS	Ukraine International Airlines	VN	Vietnam Airlines
PU	Pluna Lineas Aereas Uruguayas	VO	Tyrolean Airlines
PX	Air Niugini	VR	TACV – Transportes Aereos de Cabo Verde
PY	Surinam Airways	VS	Virgin Atlantic
PZ	TAM – Transportes Aereos del Mercosur	VU	Air Ivoire
QF	Qantas Airways	VX	V Bird
QM	Air Malawi	W6	Wizz Air
QR	Qatar Airways	WG	Wasaya Airlines
QU	East African Airlines	WJ	Labrador Airways
QV	Lao Airlines	W6	Wizz Air
QX	Horizon Air	WG	Wasaya Airlines
RA	Royal Nepal Airlines	WJ	Labrador Airways
RB	Syrian Arab Airlines	WN	Southwest Airlines
RG	Varig	WR	Royal Tongan Airlines
RJ	Royal Jordanian	WY	Oman Aviation
		YK	Kibris Turk Hava Yollari
		YN	Air Creebec
		YU	Dominair
		ZB	Monarch Airlines

Airport codes

code	airport	country
ABJ	Abidjan	Côte d'Ivoire
ABZ	Aberdeen	UK
ACA	Acapulco	Mexico
ACC	Accra	Ghana
ADD	Addis Ababa	Ethiopia
ADL	Adelaide	Australia
AGP	Malaga	Spain
AKL	Auckland	New Zealand
ALC	Alicante	Spain
ALG	Algiers	Algeria
AMM	Amman	Jordan
AMS	Amsterdam	Netherlands
ANC	Anchorage	USA
ANK	Ankara	Turkey
ANR	Antwerp	Belgium
ANU	Antigua	Antigua
ARN	Stockholm Arlanda	Sweden
ASU	Asuncion	Paraguay
ATH	Athens	Greece
ATL	Atlanta	USA
AUH	Abu Dhabi	UAE
AXA	Wallblake	Anguilla
BAH	Bahrain	Bahrain
BCN	Barcelona	Spain
BDA	Bermuda	Bermuda
BER	Berlin	Germany
BEY	Beirut	Lebanon
BFS	Belfast	UK
BGI	Bridgetown	Barbados
BGO	Bergen	Norway
BHX	Birmingham	UK
BIO	Bilbao	Spain
BJL	Banjul	Gambia
BJM	Bujumbura	Burundi
BJS	Beijing	China
BKK	Bangkok	Thailand
BLQ	Bologna	Italy
BNE	Brisbane	Australia
BOD	Bordeaux	France
BOG	Bogota	Colombia
BOM	Mumbai	India
BOS	Boston	USA
BRE	Bremen	Germany
BRN	Berne	Switzerland
BRS	Bristol	UK

code	airport	country
BRU	Brussels	Belgium
BSL	Basle/Mulhouse	Switzerland
BTS	Bratislava	Slovakia
BUD	Budapest	Hungary
BUE	Buenos Aires	Argentina
BUH	Bucharest	Romania
BWI	Baltimore	USA
BZV	Brazzaville	Congo
CAI	Cairo	Egypt
CAS	Casablanca	Morocco
CBR	Canberra	Australia
CCS	Caracas	Venezuela
CCU	Calcutta	India
CDG	Paris Charles de Gaulle	France
CGK	Jakarta	Indonesia
CGN	Cologne	Germany
CHC	Christchurch	New Zealand
CHI	Chicago	USA
CLE	Cleveland	USA
CMB	Colombo	Sri Lanka
CMN	Casablanca Mohamed V	Morocco
CNS	Cairns	Australia
COO	Cotonou	Benin
CPH	Copenhagen	Denmark
CPT	Cape Town	South Africa
CUR	Curacao	Neth.Antilles
CVG	Cincinnati	USA
CWL	Cardiff	UK
DAC	Dhaka	Bangladesh
DAM	Damascus	Syria
DBV	Dubrovnik	Croatia
DCA	Washington National	USA
DCF	Dominica	Dominica
DEL	Delhi	India
DEN	Denver	USA
DFW	Dallas/Fort Worth	USA
DKR	Dakar	Senegal
DOM	Dominica	Oman
DRW	Darwin	Australia
DTT	Detroit	USA
DUB	Dublin	Ireland
DUR	Durban	South Africa
DUS	Dusseldorf	Germany
DXB	Dubai	UAE
EBB	Entebbe	Uganda

Airport codes *continued*

code	airport	country
EDI	Edinburgh	UK
EMA	East Midlands	UK
EWR	Newark	USA
FAO	Faro	Portugal
FCO	Rome Fiumicino	Italy
FIH	Kinshasa	Congo
FRA	Frankfurt	Germany
FUK	Fukuoka	Japan
GBE	Gabarone	Botswana
GCI	Guernsey	UK
GCM	Grand Cayman	Cayman Islands
GEO	Georgetown	Guyana
GIB	Gibraltar	Gibraltar
GIG	Rio de Janeiro	Brazil
GLA	Glasgow	UK
GND	Grenada	Grenada
GOA	Genoa	Italy
GOT	Gothenburg	Sweden
GRU	Sao Paulo	Brazil
GRZ	Graz	Austria
GUA	Guatemala City	Guatemala
GVA	Geneva	Switzerland
HAJ	Hanover	Germany
HAM	Hamburg	Germany
HAV	Havana	Cuba
HEL	Helsinki	Finland
HKG	Hong Kong	Hong Kong
HNL	Honolulu	USA
HOU	Houston	USA
HRE	Harare	Zimbabwe
IAD	Washington Dulles	USA
IAH	Houston Intl.	USA
INN	Innsbruck	Austria
ISB	Islamabad	Pakistan
IST	Istanbul	Turkey
JED	Jeddah	Saudi Arabia
JER	Jersey	UK
JFK	New York Kennedy Intl.	USA
JKT	Jakarta	Indonesia
JNB	Johannesburg	South Africa
KEF	Reykjavik	Iceland
KHI	Karachi	Pakistan
KIN	Kingston	Jamaica
KLU	Klagenfurt	Austria
KOJ	Kagoshima	Japan

Airport codes *continued*

code	*airport*	*country*
KRT	Khartoum	Sudan
KUL	Kuala Lumpur	Malaysia
KWI	Kuwait	Kuwait
LAD	Luanda	Angola
LAS	Las Vegas	USA
LAX	Los Angeles	USA
LBA	Leeds/Bradford	UK
LCA	Larnaca	Cyprus
LCY	London City	UK
LED	St Petersburg	Russia
LEJ	Leipzig	Germany
LGA	New York La Guardia	USA
LGW	London Gatwick	UK
LHR	London Heathrow	UK
LIL	Lille	France
LIM	Lima	Peru
LIN	Milan	Italy
LIS	Lisbon	Portugal
LJU	Ljubljana	Slovenia
LLW	Lilongwe	Malawi
LNZ	Linz	Austria
LOS	Lagos	Nigeria
LPA	Gran Canaria	Spain
LPB	La Paz	Bolivia
LPL	Liverpool	UK
LTN	London Luton	UK
LUN	Lusaka	Zambia
LUX	Luxembourg	Luxembourg
LYS	Lyons	France
MAA	Chennai	India
MAD	Madrid	Spain
MAN	Manchester	UK
MBA	Mombasa	Kenya
MCI	Kansas City Intl.	USA
MCO	Orlando	USA
MCT	Muscat	Oman
MEL	Melbourne	Australia
MEX	Mexico City	Mexico
MIA	Miami	USA
MIL	Milan	Italy
MKC	Kansas City	USA
MLA	Malta	Malta
MLW	Monrovia	Liberia
MME	Teeside	UK
MNL	Manila	Philippines

Airport codes *continued*

code	airport	country
MOW	Moscow	Russia
MPM	Maputo	Mozambique
MQS	Mustique	Grenadines
MRS	Marseilles	France
MRU	Mauritius	Mauritius
MSP	Minneapolis St Paul	USA
MSY	New Orleans	USA
MUC	Munich	Germany
MVD	Montevideo	Uruguay
MXP	Milan	Italy
NAP	Naples	Italy
NAS	Nassau	Bahamas
NBO	Nairobi	Kenya
NCE	Nice	France
NCL	Newcastle	UK
NGO	Nagoya	Japan
NOU	Nourrea	New Caledonia
NRT	Tokyo Narita	Japan
NUE	Nuremburg	Germany
NYC	New York	USA
ORD	Chicago O'Hare	USA
ORK	Cork	Ireland
ORL	Orlando	USA
ORY	Paris Orly	France
OSA	Osaka	Japan
OSL	Oslo	Norway
OTP	Bucharest Otopeni	Romania
PAR	Paris	France
PBM	Paramaribo	Surinam
PDX	Portland	USA
PEK	Beijing	China
PER	Perth	Australia
PHL	Philadelphia	USA
PHX	Phoenix	USA
PIT	Pittsburgh	USA
PLH	Plymouth	UK
PMI	Palma de Mallorca	Spain
POM	Port Moresby	Papua New Guinea
POS	Port of Spain	Trinidad and Tobago
PPT	Papeete	French Polynesia
PRG	Prague	Czech Republic
PSA	Florence Pisa	Italy
PTY	Panama City	Panama
RAR	Rarotonga	Cook Islands
REK	Reykjavik	Iceland

Airport codes *continued*

code	airport	country
RIO	Rio de Janeiro	Brazil
RIX	Riga	Latvia
ROM	Rome	Italy
RTM	Rotterdam	Netherlands
RUH	Riyadh	Saudi Arabia
SAH	Sana'a	Yemen
SAN	San Diego	USA
SAO	Sao Paulo	Brazil
SCL	Santiago	Chile
SEA	Seattle	USA
SEL	Seoul	South Korea
SFO	San Francisco	USA
SHA	Shanghai	China
SHJ	Sharjah	UAE
SIN	Singapore	Singapore
SKG	Thessaloniki	Greece
SLC	Salt Lake City	USA
SLU	Saint Lucia	Saint Lucia
SNN	Shannon	Ireland
SOF	Sofia	Bulgaria
SOU	Southampton	UK
STL	Saint Louis	USA
STN	London Stansted	UK
STO	Stockholm	Sweden
STR	Stuttgart	Germany
SVG	Stavanger	Norway
SVO	Moscow Sheremetyevo	Russia
SVQ	Seville	Spain
SXB	Strasbourg	France
SXF	Berlin Schoenefeld	Germany
SYD	Sydney	Australia
SZG	Salzburg	Austria
TCI	Tenerife	Spain
TGU	Tegucigalpa	Honduras
THF	Berlin Tempelhof	Germany
THR	Tehran	Iran
TLL	Tallinn	Estonia
TLS	Toulouse	France
TLV	Tel Aviv	Israel
TPA	Tampa	USA
TPE	Taipei	Taiwan
TRN	Turin	Italy
TUN	Tunis	Tunisia
TYO	Tokyo	Japan
UIO	Quito	Ecuador

Airport codes *continued*

code	*airport*	*country*
VCE	Venice	Italy
VIE	Vienna	Austria
VLC	Valencia	Spain
VNO	Vilnius	Lithuania
WAS	Washington DC	USA
WAW	Warsaw	Poland
WDH	Windhoek	Namibia
WLG	Wellington	New Zealand
YEA	Edmonton	Canada
YEG	Edmonton Intl.	Canada
YMQ	Montreal Mirabel	Canada
YOW	Ottawa	Canada
YTO	Toronto	Canada
YUL	Montreal Pierre Elliot Trudeau Intl.	Canada
YVR	Vancouver	Canada
YWG	Winnipeg	Canada
YYC	Calgary	Canada
YYZ	Toronto Lester Pearson	Canada
ZAG	Zagreb	Croatia
ZRH	Zurich	Switzerland

Local times around the world

Universal Time (UT)	**1200**	London	1200
Abu Dhabi	1600	Luanda	1300
Adelaide	2130	Luxembourg	1300
Algiers	1300	Madagascar	1500
Amsterdam	1300	Madrid	1300
Ankara	1400	Malé	1700
Astana	1800	Malta	1300
Athens	1400	Manila	2000
Baghdad	1500	Mexico	0600
Bangkok	1900	Minsk	1400
Beijing	2000	Montevideo	0900
Beirut	1400	Montreal	0700
Berlin	1300	Moscow	1500
Bern(e)	1300	Mumbai	1730
Bogota	0700	Nairobi	1500
Brasilia	0900	Nassau	0700
Brazzaville	1300	New York	0700
Brussels	1300	Oslo	1300
Bucharest	1400	Ottawa	0700
Budapest	1300	Panama	0700
Buenos Aires	0900	Paris	1300
Cairo	1400	Perth	2000
Calcutta (Kolkata)	1730	Phnom Penh	1900
Canberra	2200	Prague	1300
Cape Town	1400	Pretoria	1400
Caracas	0800	Pyongyang	2100
Chicago	0600	Quebec	0700
Colombo	1730	Rangoon	1830
Copenhagen	1300	Reykjavik	1200
Costa Rica	0600	Rio de Janeiro	0900
Damascus	1400	Riyadh	1500
Delhi	1730	Rome	1300
Dhaka	1800	San Francisco	0400
Dublin	1200	Santiago	0800
Gibraltar	1300	Seoul	2100
Hanoi	1900	Seychelles	1600
Harare	1400	Singapore	2000
Helsinki	1400	Stockholm	1300
Hong Kong	2000	Sydney	2200
Honolulu	0200	Taipei	2000
Istanbul	1400	Tallinn	1400
Jakarta	1900	Tbilisi	1600
Jerusalem	1400	Tehran	1530
Kabul	1630	Tirana	1300
Karachi	1700	Tokyo	2100
Khartoum	1400	Toronto	0700
Kiev	1400	Tripoli	1300
Kinshasa	1400	Tunis	1300
Kuala Lumpur	2000	Ulan Bator	2000
Kuwait	1500	Vienna	1300
Lagos	1300	Warsaw	1300
La Paz	0800	Washington DC	0700
Lima	0700	Wellington	0000 (+1 day)
Lisbon	1200	Yaoundé	1300

International dialling codes

Afghanistan	93	Egypt	20
Albania	355	El Salvador	503
Algeria	213	Equatorial Guinea	240
Andorra	376	Estonia	372
Angola	244	Ethiopia	251
Anguilla	1264	Falkland Islands	500
Antigua	1268	Fiji	679
Argentina	54	Finland	358
Armenia	374	France	33
Australia	61	French Guiana	594
Austria	43	Gabon	241
Bahamas	1242	Gambia	220
Bahrain	973	Georgia	679
Bangladesh	880	Germany	49
Barbados	1246	Ghana	233
Belarus	375	Gibraltar	350
Belgium	32	Great Britain	44
Belize	501	Greece	30
Benin	229	Grenada	1473
Bermuda	1441	Guatemala	502
Bhutan	975	Guinea	224
Bolivia	591	Guinea-Bissau	245
Bosnia	387	Guyana	592
Botswana	267	Haiti	509
Brazil	55	Honduras	504
Brunei	673	Hong Kong	852
Bulgaria	359	Hungary	36
Burkina Faso	226	Iceland	354
Burma (*see* Myanmar)		India	91
Burundi	257	Indonesia	62
Cambodia	855	Iran	98
Cameroon	237	Iraq	964
Canada	1	Irish Republic	353
Cape Verde Islands	238	Israel	972
Cayman Islands	1345	Italy	39
Central African Republic	236	Ivory Coast	225
Chad	235	Jamaica	1876
Chile	56	Japan	81
China	86	Jordan	962
Colombia	57	Kazakhstan	7
Comoros	269	Kenya	254
Congo (Republic of the)	242	Kuwait	965
Congo	243	Kyrgyzstan	996
(Democratic Republic of the)		Laos	856
Costa Rica	506	Latvia	371
Croatia	385	Lebanon	961
Cuba	53	Lesotho	266
Cyprus	357	Liberia	231
Czech Republic	420	Libya	218
Denmark	45	Liechtenstein	423
Djibouti	253	Lithuania	370
Dominica	1767	Luxembourg	352
Dominican Republic	1809	Macao	853
Ecuador	593		

International dialling codes *continued*

Macedonia	389	St Vincent	1784
(Former Yugoslav Republic of)		Samoa	378
Madagascar	261	Saudi Arabia	966
Madeira	351	Senegal	221
Malawi	265	Serbia & Montenegro	381
Malaysia	60	Seychelles	248
Maldives	960	Sierra Leone	232
Mali	223	Singapore	65
Malta	356	Slovakia	42
Mauritania	222	Slovenia	386
Mauritius	230	Somalia	252
Mexico	52	South Africa	27
Moldova	373	South Korea	82
Monaco	377	Spain	34
Mongolia	976	Sri Lanka	94
Montserrat	1664	Sudan	249
Morocco	212	Suriname	597
Mozambique	258	Swaziland	268
Myanmar	95	Sweden	46
Namibia	264	Switzerland	41
Nauru	674	Syria	963
Nepal	977	Taiwan	886
Netherlands	31	Tanzania	255
New Zealand	64	Thailand	66
Nicaragua	505	Togo	228
Niger	227	Tonga	676
Nigeria	234	Trinidad & Tobago	1868
North Korea	850	Tunisia	216
Norway	47	Turkey	90
Oman	968	Turkmenistan	993
Pakistan	92	Tuvalu	688
Panama	507	Uganda	256
Papua New Guinea	675	Ukraine	380
Paraguay	595	United Arab Emirates	971
Peru	51	United Kingdom	44
Philippines	63	USA	1
Poland	48	Uruguay	598
Portugal	351	Uzbekistan	998
Puerto Rico	1787	Vanuatu	678
Qatar	974	Venezuela	58
Réunion	262	Vietnam	84
Romania	40	Yemen	967
Russia	7	Zambia	260
Rwanda	250	Zimbabwe	263
St Lucia	1758		

International currencies

In the following list, units of currency marked (*) usually have no plural: e.g. 1 kyat (one kyat), 200 kyat (two hundred kyat), etc.

Country	Currency	Divided into	Abbreviation
Afghanistan	Afghani*	puli	Af *or* Afs
Albania	Lek*	qindars	Lk
Algeria	Algerian dinar	centimes	DA
Andorra	Euro	cents	€
Angola	Kwanza*	lwei	Kzrl
Antigua	East Caribbean dollar	cents	Ecar$ *or* EC$
Argentina	Argentinian peso	australes	
Australia	Australian dollar	cents	A$
Austria	Euro	cents	€
Bahamas	Bahamian dollar	cents	B$
Bahrain	Bahraini dinar	fils	BD
Bangladesh	Taka*	poisha	Tk
Barbados	Barbados dollar	cents	Bd$ *or* BD$
Belarus	Rouble	kopeks	
Belgium	Euro	cents	€
Belize	Belize dollar	cents	BZ$
Benin	CFA franc	centimes	CFA Fr
Bermuda	Bermuda dollar	cents	Bda$
Bhutan	Ngultrum*	chetrum	N
Bolivia	Boliviano *or* Bolivian peso	centavos	$b
Bosnia	Marka	para	
Botswana	Pula	thebe	P
Brazil	Real	centavos	R$
Brunei	Brunei dollar	sen	B$
Bulgaria	Lev*	stotinki	Lv
Burkina Faso	CFA franc	centimes	CFA Fr
Burma (*see* Myanmar)			
Burundi	Burundi franc	centimes	Bur Fr *or* FrBr
Cambodia	Riel*	sen	RI
Cameroon	CFA franc	centimes	CFA Fr
Canada	Canadian dollar	cents	Can$ *or* C$
Cape Verde Islands	Escudo Caboverdiano	centavos	CV esc
Cayman Islands	Cayman Island dollar	cents	CayI$
Central African Republic	CFA franc	centimes	CFA Fr
Chad	CFA franc	centimes	CFA Fr
Chile	Chilean peso	centavos	Ch$
China	Yuan* *or* renminbi*	fen	Y
Colombia	Colombian peso	centavos	Col$
Comoros	CFA franc	centimes	CFA Fr
Congo (Republic of)	CFA franc	centimes	CFA Fr

International currencies *continued*

Country	Currency	Divided into	Abbreviation
Congo (Democratic Republic of)	Congolese franc	centimes	
Costa Rica	Colón*	centimos	₡
Croatia	Kuna	lipas	
Cuba	Cuban peso	centavos	Cub$
Cyprus	Cyprus pound	cents	£C *or* C£
Czech Republic	Koruna	haleru	K¢
Dahomey (*see* Benin)			
Denmark	Krone	öre	DKr *or* DKK
Djibouti	Djibouti franc	centimes	Dj Fr
Dominica	East Caribbean dollar	cents	EC$
Dominican Republic	Dominican peso	centavos	DR$
Ecuador	Sucre*	centavos	Su
Egypt	Egyptian pound	piastres	£E *or* E£
Eire (*see* Irish Republic)			
El Salvador	Colón*	centavos	ES¢
Equatorial Guinea	CFA franc	centimes	CFA Fr
Estonia	Kroon	sents	
Ethiopia	Birr* *or* Ethiopian dollar	cents	EB
Fiji	Fiji dollar	cents	$F *or* F$
Finland	Euro	cents	€
France	Euro	cents	€
French Guiana	Euro	cents	€
Gabon	CFA franc	centimes	CFA Fr
Gambia, The	Dalasi*	butut	Di
Germany	Euro	cents	€
Ghana	Cedi*	pesewas	¢
Georgia	Lari	tetri	
Great Britain (*see* United Kingdom)			
Greece	Euro	cents	€
Grenada	East Caribbean dollar	cents	Ecar$ *or* EC$
Guatemala	Quetzal	centavos	Q
Guinea	Guinea franc	centimes	
Guinea-Bissau	CFA franc	centimes	CFA Fr
Guyana	Guyana dollar	cents	G$ *or* Guy$
Haiti	Gourde*	centimes	Gde
Holland (*see* Netherlands)			
Honduras	Lempira*	centavos	La
Hong Kong	Hong Kong dollar	cents	HK$
Hungary	Forint	filler	Ft
Iceland	Króna	aurar	Ikr
India	Rupee	paisa	R *or* Re *or* R$ representative
Indonesia	Rupiah*	sen	

International currencies *continued*

Country	Currency	Divided into	Abbreviation
Iran	Rial*	dinars	RI
Iraq	Iraqi dinar	fils	ID
Irish Republic	Euro	cents	€
Israel	Shekel	agora	IS
Italy	Euro	cents	€
Ivory Coast	CFA franc	centimes	CFA Fr
Jamaica	Jamaican dollar	cents	J$
Japan	Yen*	sen	Y *or* ¥
Jordan	Jordanian Dinar	fils	JD
Kazakhstan	Tenge		
Kenya	Kenya shilling	cents	KSh *or* Sh
Korea (North)	North Korean won*	chon	NK W
Korea (South)	South Korean won*	jeon	SK W
Kuwait	Kuwaiti dinar	fils	KD
Kyrgystan	Som	tyin	
Laos	Kip*	at	K *or* Kp
Latvia	Lat	santims	
Lebanon	Lebanese pound	piastres	£Leb *or* L£
Lesotho	Loti*	lisente	L
Liberia	Liberian dollar	cents	L$
Libya	Libyan dinar	dirhams	LD
Liechtenstein	Swiss franc	centimes	SFr *or* FS
Lithuania	Lita		
Luxembourg	Euro	cents	€
Macedonia	Dinar	paras	
Macau	Pataca*	avos	P *or* $
Madeira	Euro	cents	€
Malagasy Republic	Malagasy franc	centimes	FMG *or* Mal Fr
Malawi	Kwacha*	tambala	K *or* MK
Malaysia	Ringgit *or* Malaysian Dollar	sen	M$
Maldives	Rufiyaa	laaris	MvRe
Mali	CFA franc	cents	CFA Fr
Malta	Maltese pound *or* lira	cents	£M *or* M£
Mauritania	Ouguiya*	khoums	U
Mauritius	Mauritius rupee	cents	Mau Rs *or* R
Mexico	Peso	centavos	Mex$
Moldova	Leu		
Monaco	Euro	cents	€
Mongolian Republic	Tugrik*	möngös	Tug
Montserrat	East Caribbean dollar	cents	Ecar$ *or* EC$
Morocco	Dirham	centimes	DH
Mozambique	Metical*	centavos	M

International currencies *continued*

Country	Currency	Divided into	Abbreviation
Myanmar	Kyat*	pyas	Kt
Namibia	Namibian dollar	cents	
Nauru	Australian dollar	cents	A$
Nepal	Nepalese rupee	paise	NR or Nre
Netherlands	Euro	cents	€
New Hebrides (*see* Vanuatu)			
New Zealand	New Zealand dollar	cents	NZ$
Nicaragua	Córdoba	centavos	C$ or C
Niger	CFA franc	centimes	CFA Fr
Nigeria	Naira*	kobo	N or ₦
Norway	Krone	ore	NKr
Oman	Rial Omani	baizas	RO
Pakistan	Pakistan rupee	paise	R or Pak Re
Panama	Balboa	centesimos	Ba
Papua New Guinea	Kina*	toea	Ka or K
Paraguay	Guarani*	centimos	G
Peru	Sol	cents	S
Philippines	Philippine peso	centavos	P or PP
Poland	Zloty	groszy	Zl
Portugal	Euro	cents	€
Puerto Rico	US dollar	cents	$ or US$
Qatar	Qatar Riyal	dirhams	QR
Reunion	CFA franc	centimes	CFA Fr
Romania	Leu*	bani	L or l
Russia	Rouble	kopeks	Rub
Rwanda	Rwanda franc	centimes	Rw Fr
St Lucia	East Caribbean dollar	cents	Ecar$ or EC$
St Vincent	East Caribbean dollar	cents	Ecar$ or EC$
Samoa	Tala	sene	
Saudi Arabia	Saudi riyal *or* rial	halala	SA R
Senegal	CFA franc	centimes	CFA Fr
Serbia & Montenegro	Dinar	paras	DN
Seychelles	Seychelles rupee	cents	Sre or R
Sierra Leone	Leone	cents	Le
Singapore	Singapore dollar	cents	S$ or Sing$
Slovakia	Koruna	haliers	Sk
Slovenia	Tolar	stotin	SIT
Solomon Islands	Solomon Island dollar	cents	SI$
Somalia	Somali shilling	cents	Som Sh or So Sh
South Africa	Rand*	cents	R
Spain	Euro	cents	€
Sri Lanka	Sri Lankan rupee	cents	SC Re

International currencies *continued*

Country	Currency	Divided into	Abbreviation
Sudan	Sudanese dinar	pounds	SD
Suriname	Suriname guilder	cents	S Gld
Swaziland	Lilangeni*	cents	Li *or* E
Sweden	Krona	örer	SKr
Syria	Syrian pound	piastres	S£
Taiwan	New Taiwan dollar	cents	T$ *or* NT$
Tanzania	Tanzanian shilling	cents	TSh
Thailand	Baht*	satang	Bt
Togo	CFA franc	centimes	CFA Fr
Tonga	Pa'anga	seniti	
Trinidad & Tobago	Trinidad & Tobago dollar	cents	TT$
Tunisia	Tunisian dinar	millimes	TD
Turkey	Turkish lira	kurus	TL
Turkmenistan	Manat	tenesi	
Tuvalu	Australian dollar	cents	$A
Uganda	Uganda Shilling	cents	Ush
Ukraine	Hryvna	kopiykas	
United Arab Emirates	UAE dirham	fils	UAE Dh *or* UD
United Kingdom	Pound sterling	pence	£ *or* £Stg
USA	Dollar	cents	$ *or* US$
Uruguay	Uruguayan peso	centesimos	N$
Uzbekistan	Sum	tiyin	
Vanuatu	Vatu	centimes	
Venezuela	Bolívar	centimos	BS
Vietnam	Dong*	xu	D
Virgin Islands	US dollar	cents	US$
Yemen	Riyal	fils	YR
Zambia	Kwacha*	ngwee	K
Zimbabwe	Zimbabwe dollar	cents	Z$

Public holidays

Most countries have many public holidays: some are observed worldwide, while some are particular to each country. Many countries celebrate the birthday of their ruler, or past rulers. Many countries also celebrate their independence.

International Public Holidays

1st January
New Year's Day: Observed almost universally as a public holiday.

1st May
May Day or *Labour Day*: Observed in many socialist and western countries.

12th October
Columbus Day or *Discovery of America Day:* Observed in many countries in South and Central America.

24th October
United Nations Day: Observed in some (but not all) member countries of the United Nations.

International Religious Holidays

These are observed in many countries, depending on their religion. Many religious festivals are not celebrated on a single fixed date, but vary from year to year depending on the calendar.

end of January or February
Chinese New Year: Observed in China, and many other countries with large Chinese populations.

October or November
Diwali: Observed in India and many other countries with Hindu populations.

March or April
Easter: Observed in most Christian countries or countries with large Christian populations; the date of Easter is not the same in the Western or Catholic Church, and the Eastern or orthodox Church.

May
Wesak or *Buddha Day*: Celebrated in Thailand and other Buddhist countries.

15th August
Assumption: Observed in most Catholic countries.

25th December
Christmas Day: Observed in most countries; the orthodox Christmas varies in date.

Muslim Festivals

Ramadan: The most important Muslim festival is Ramadan (the ninth month in the Muslim calendar) which varies in date from year to year. The *Eid al-Fitr* holiday is the last three days of Ramadan.

Hajj: The Hajj (or pilgrimage to Mecca) takes place during the last month of the Muslim calendar; the last day of the pilgrimage is the holiday of *Eid al-Adha*.

30th August
Observed in most Muslim countries.

Public holidays *continued*

National Holidays

1st January
Haiti (Independence Day)
Sudan (Independence Day)

4th January
Myanmar (Independence Day)

26th January
Australia Day
India (Republic Day)

4th February
Sri Lanka (Independence Day)

11th February
Iran (Republic Day)

16th February
Lithuania (Independence Day)

18th February
Gambia (Independence Day)

23rd February
Guyana (Republic Day)

24th February
Estonia (Independence Day)

25th February
Kuwait (National Day)

27th February
Dominican Republic
   (Independence Day)

17th March
Ireland (St Patrick's Day)

20th March
Tunisia (Independence Day)

21st March
Namibia (Independence Day)

23rd March
Pakistan (Republic Day)

25th March
Greece (Independence Day)
Gabon (National Day)

17th April
Syria (Independence Day)

18th April
Zimbabwe (Independence Day)

26th April
Tanzania (Union Day)
Israel (Independence Day)
NOTE: Although Israel declared
independence on 14 May 1948, as the

Jewish calendar is lunar the holiday
may occur in April or May.

27th April
Sierra Leone (Independence Day)
South Africa (Freedom Day)

3rd May
Japan (Constitution Day)
Poland (Constitution Day)

14th May
Paraguay (Independence Day)

17th May
Norway (Constitution Day)

20th May
Cameroon (Republic Day)

22nd May
Yemen (Unification Day)

24th May
Bermuda Day

25th May
Jordan (Independence Day)
Argentina (Revolution Day)

2nd June
Italy (Republic Day)

5th June
Denmark (Constitution Day)

10th June
Portugal Day

12th June
Philippines (Independence Day)

17th June
Iceland (Independence Day)

25th June
Mozambique (Independence Day)
Slovenia (Statehood Day)

26th June
Madagascar (Independence Day)

30th June
Democratic Republic of the Congo
   (Independence Day)

1st July
Burundi (Independence Day)
Canada Day
Rwanda (Independence Day)

4th July
USA (Independence Day)

Public holidays *continued*

6th July
  Malawi (Independence Day)

11th July
  Mongolia (Independence Day)

14th July
  France (Bastille Day)

17th July
  Iraq (Revolution Day)

20th July
  Colombia (Independence Day)

21st July
  Belgium (National Day)

26th July
  Liberia (Independence Day)
  Cuba (Rebellion Day)

28th July
  Peru (Independence Day)

30th July
  Morocco (Throne Day)

1st August
  Switzerland (National Day)
  Benin (National Day)

1st Monday in August
  Jamaica (Independence Day)

6th August
  Bolivia (Independence Day)

7th August
  Cote d'Ivoire (Independence Day)

9th August
  Singapore (Independence Day)

10th August
  Ecuador (Independence Day)

11th August
  Chad (Independence Day)

15th August
  Republic of the Congo
   (Independence Day)
  South Korea (Liberation Day)

17th August
  Indonesia (Independence Day)

20th August
  Hungary (St Stephen's Day)

25th August
  Uruguay (Independence Day)

31st August
  Malaysia (Independence Day)

31st August
  Trinidad & Tobago (Independence Day)

1st September
  Libya (Revolution Day)

6th September
  Swaziland (Independence Day)

7th September
  Brazil (Independence Day)

9th September
  North Korea (Founding of DPR Korea)

15th September
  Costa Rica (Independence Day)
  El Salvador (Independence Day)
  Guatemala (Independence Day)
  Honduras (Independence Day)
  Nicaragua (Independence Day)

16th September
  Mexico (Independence Day)

18th September
  Chile (Independence Day)

22nd September
  Mali (Independence Day)

1st October
  Botswana Day
  China (Anniversary of the Founding of
   the People's Republic of China)
  Nigeria (Independence Day)
  Cyprus (Independence Day)
  NOTE: the Turkish Cypriot area
  celebrates Independence Day on 15
  November

2nd October
  Guinea (Independence Day)

3rd October
  Germany (Unity Day)

4th October
  Lesotho (Independence Day)

9th October
  Uganda (Independence Day)

12th October
  Spain (National Day)
  Equatorial Guinea (Independence Day)

2nd Monday in October
  Fiji (Independence Day)

24th October
  Zambia (Independence Day)

Public holidays *continued*

26th October
Austria (National Day)

29th October
Turkey (Independence Day)

1st November
Algeria (Revolution Day)

2nd November
Antigua & Barbuda (Independence Day)

3rd November
Dominica (Independence Day)

11th November
Angola (Independence Day)

18th November
Latvia (Independence Day)

22nd November
Lebanon (Independence Day)

25th November
Suriname (Independence Day)

28th November
Mauritania (Independence Day)

30th November
Barbados (Independence Day)

1st December
Central African Republic (Republic Day)
Romania (Unification Day)

2nd December
Laos (Republic Day)
United Arab Emirates
 (Independence Day)

6th December
Finland (Independence Day)

10th December
Cuba (Independence Day)

11th December
Burkina Faso (Republic Day)

12th December
Kenya (Independence Day)

16th December
Bahrain (National Day)
Bangladesh (Victory Day)

17th December
Bhutan (National Day)

18th December
Niger (Republic Day)

Accommodation ratings

In response to consumer demand, VisitBritain, the Automobile Association and RAC created one overall rating scheme for serviced accommodation, using stars to represent hotels and diamonds for guest accommodation (guesthouses, inns, farmhouses, bed & breakfasts).

Serviced Accommodation: Star ratings

Star ratings symbolise the level of service, range of facilities and quality of guest care that you can expect. Hotels are required to meet progressively higher standards as they move up the scale from one to five stars.

The gradings are:

☆   Practical accommodation with a limited range of facilities and services, but a high standard of cleanliness throughout. Restaurant/eating area. 75% of bedrooms with ensuite or private facilities.

☆☆   Better-equipped bedrooms, all with ensuite/private bathroom and a colour TV. A lift is normally available. Dinner available.

☆☆☆   Higher standard of services and facilities including larger public areas and bedrooms, a receptionist, room service, laundry.

☆☆☆☆   Accommodation offering superior comfort and quality; all bedrooms with ensuite bath, fitted overhead shower and WC. Spacious and well-appointed public areas. More emphasis on food and drink. Room service for all meals and 24 hour drinks, refreshments and snacks. Dry cleaning service. Excellent customer service.

☆☆☆☆☆   A spacious, luxurious establishment offering the highest quality of accommodation, facilities, services and cuisine, with a range of extra facilities. Professional, attentive staff should provide flawless guest services.

Serviced Accommodation: Diamond ratings

Diamond ratings for guest accommodation reflect visitor expectations, where quality is seen as more important than facilities and services. Guest accommodation is required to meet progressively higher standards of quality and guest care as they move up the scale from one to five diamonds.

◊   Clean, comfortable accommodation, providing breakfast.

◊◊   Good overall level of quality and comfort, more emphasis on guest care.

◊◊◊   Well-maintained, a good choice of breakfast dishes, a very good level of customer care.

◊◊◊◊   An even higher level of quality and comfort. Very good levels of customer care.

◊◊◊◊◊   Exceptional overall quality in furnishing, rooms and customer care, anticipating guests' needs.

Accommodation ratings *continued*

Self-catering Accommodation

All properties have to meet an extensive list of minimum requirements before they can be considered for a star rating. Serviced apartments provide self-catering accommodation with additional elements of service, such as a 24-hour concierge service, or a 5 out of 7 day cleaning service.

☆	Acceptable overall level of quality. Adequate provision of furniture, furnishings and fittings.
☆☆	Good overall level of quality. All units self-contained; 2 bathrooms where there are eight or more guests.
☆☆☆	Good to very good level of quality. Good standard of maintenance and decoration. Ample space and good quality furniture. All double beds with access from both sides. Microwaves.
☆☆☆☆	Excellent overall level of quality. Very good care and attention to detail. Either access to washing machine and drier, or a 24-hour laundry service.
☆☆☆☆☆	Exceptional overall level of quality. High levels of décor, fixtures and fittings, together with excellent standards guest services. Excellent range of accessories and personal touches.

Holiday, Touring and Camping Parks

Every year the National Tourist Boards inspect more than 1,000 parks. They assess over 50 separate aspects of the parks, from landscaping and layout to maintenance, customer care, and most importantly cleanliness.

☆	Acceptable – to achieve this grade, the park must be clean with good standards of maintenance and customer care.
☆☆	Good – all the above points plus an improved level of landscaping, lighting, refuse disposal and maintenance.
☆☆☆	Very good – most parks fall within this category; three stars represent the industry standard. The range of facilities provided may vary from park to park, but they will be of a very good standard and will be well maintained.
☆☆☆☆	Excellent quality – careful attention to detail in the provision of all services and facilities.
☆☆☆☆☆	Exceptional standards can be expected from these parks, with the highest levels of customer care and attractive surroundings. All facilities will be maintained in pristine condition.

As well as the star rating, all parks have a designator to explain the type of accommodation.

Holiday Parks offer caravan holiday homes for hire or for sale.

Touring Parks are for people who want to take their own touring caravan, motorhome or tent.

Camping Parks have pitches available for tents only.

Many parks offer combinations of these, for example 'Holiday and Touring Park' or 'Touring and Camping Park'.

Accommodation ratings *continued*

Hostels: Star ratings

Hostels are rated from one to five stars. They must meet a minimum entry requirement for both the provision and quality of facilities and services, including fixtures, fittings, furnishings, décor and any other extra facilities. The more stars, the higher the overall level of quality.

Group Hostels provide hostel style accommodation that caters for groups only.

Bunkhouses offer a similar style of accommodation to hostels, but usually with more limited service and facilities, usually on a self-catering basis. Bunkhouses are not star rated but meet the same minimum requirements as hostels, where applicable.

Camping Barns provide very simple self-catering accommodation. Often referred to as 'stone tents', they have the advantage of being roomy and dry. Camping Barns are not Star rated and will be assessed as being fit for the purpose, meeting a specific minimum entry requirement.

Campus Accommodation: Star ratings

Campus accommodation includes educational establishments such as universities and colleges with sleeping accommodation in halls of residence. It is rated from one to five stars.

Holiday Villages: Star ratings

Holiday villages are rated from one to five stars. A holiday village usually offers a variety of types of accommodation, with the majority provided in custom-built rooms (e.g. chalets, hotel rooms). A range of facilities and activities are also available which may, or may not, be included in the tariff.

HLTT classifications

Business Activity

UK SIC	Description	Sector
55.1	Hotels	Hospitality
55.2	Camping sites and other provision of short stay accommodation	Hospitality
55.3	Restaurants	Hospitality
55.4	Bars	Hospitality
55.5	Canteens and catering	Hospitality
60.22	Taxi operation	Travel
60.23	Renting of buses and coaches	Travel
60.3	Activities of travel agents and tour operators	Tourism/Travel
74.873	Activities of exhibition and fair organisers	Tourism
74.874	Activities of conference organisers	Tourism
92.13	Motion picture projection	Leisure
92.311	Live theatrical presentations	Leisure
92.32	Operation of arts facilities	Leisure
92.33	Fair and amusement park activities	Leisure
92.34	Dance halls, discos & dance instructors; other entertainment activities	Leisure
92.52	Museum activities and preservation of historical sites/buildings	Leisure
92.53	Botanical and zoological gardens and nature reserves activities	Leisure
92.61	Operation of sports arenas and stadiums	Leisure
92.62	Other sporting activities	Leisure
92.7	Other recreational activities	Leisure

HLTT classifications *continued*

Occupation

SOC	Description
1221	Hotel and accommodation managers
1222	Conference and exhibition managers
1223	Restaurant and catering managers
1224	Publicans and managers of licensed premises
1225	Leisure and sports managers
1226	Travel agency managers
5434	Chefs, cooks
6211	Sports and leisure assistants
6212	Travel agents
6213	Travel and tour guides
6214	Air travel assistants
6215	Rail travel assistants
6219	Leisure and travel service occupations
6231	Housekeepers and related occupations
8213	Bus and coach drivers
9222	Hotel porters
9223	Kitchen and catering assistants
9224	Waiters, waitresses
9225	Bar staff
9226	Leisure and theme park attendants
Marginal	
2452	Archivists and curators
8214	Taxi drivers and chauffeurs

Websites

Academy of Food and Wine Service   www.acfws.org

The Academy of Food and Wine Service is the industry's professional training body, dedicated to improving the basic knowledge of all restaurant staff, incorporating bar skills, wine service and food service.

British Hospitality Organisation   www.bha-online.org.uk

The British Hospitality Association has been representing the hotel, restaurant and catering industry for 90 years. The Association exists to ensure that the views of the British hospitality industry are represented to government and policy makers in the UK and internationally, in order that its members' businesses can flourish.

British Institute of Innkeeping   www.bii.org

With over 16,000 members, this is the professional body for the licensed retail sector. It promotes high standards of professionalism throughout the licensed retail sector; aims to encourage new entrants into the industry, and to help them develop their long-term careers.

Caterer   www.caterer.com

Online recruitment resource for hotel, restaurant and bar jobs.

Hospitality Training Foundation   www.htf.org.uk

The Restaurant Association   www.bha-online.org.uk/restaurantassociation.asp

Part of the British Hospitality Organisation, representing the interests of restaurateurs for over 40 years

Springboard UK Limited   www.springboarduk.org.uk

Springboard UK is a young dynamic organisation which promotes careers in hospitality, leisure, tourism and travel to a range of potential recruits and influencers through a network of centres across the UK.

VisitBritain   www.visitbritain.org

VisitBritain was created on 1 April 2004, to market Britain to the rest of the world and to the British.